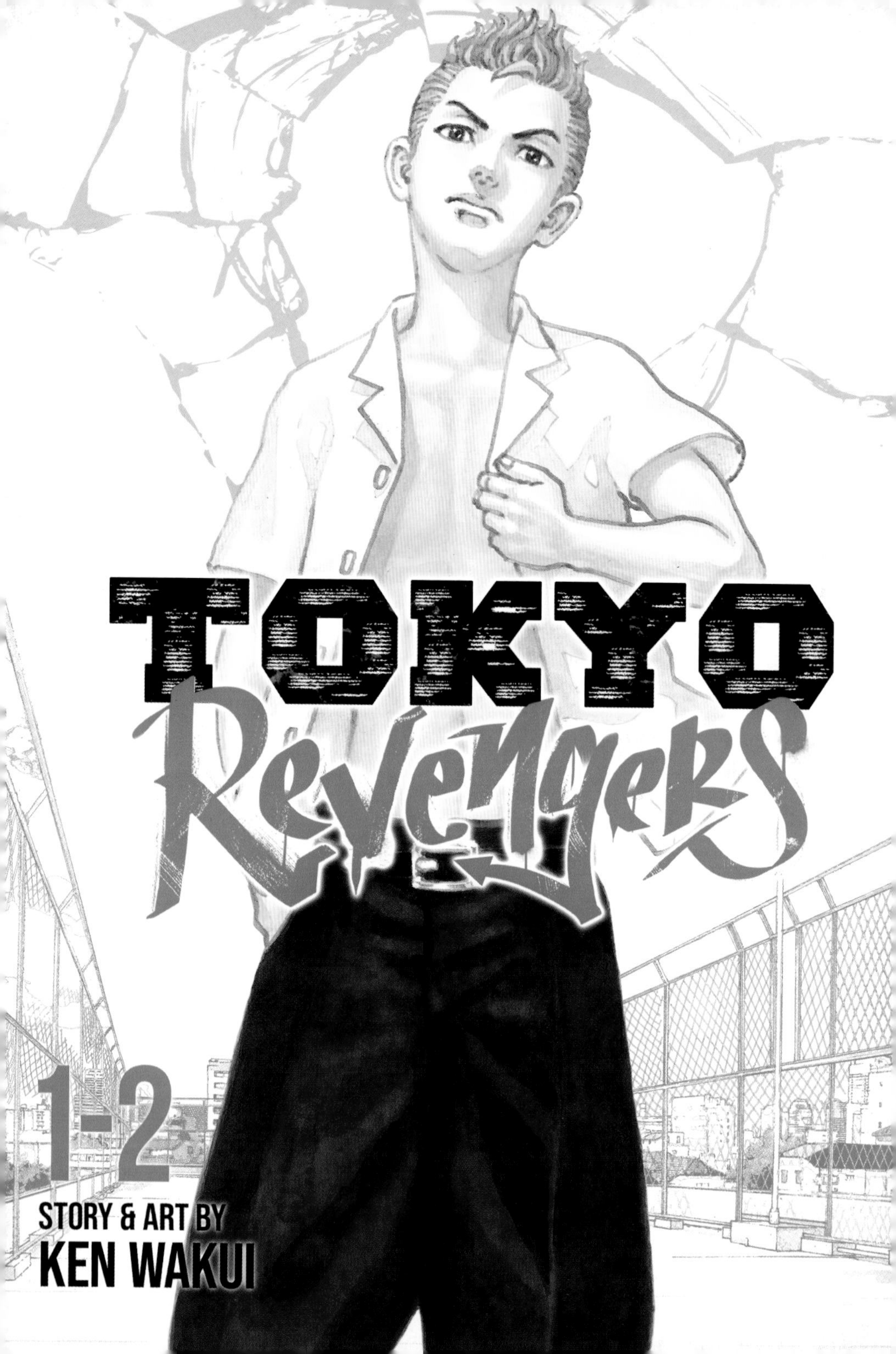
TOKYO
Revengers
1-2
STORY & ART BY
KEN WAKUI

MANJI

In East Asia, the **manji** (卍) is an ancient religious symbol of power and good fortune for many different countries and religions around the world, including Buddhism, Hinduism, Jainism, and a number of Indo-European and Native American religions as well. The specific meaning of the symbol varies by nation and religion, and also by the position of the "arms" of the cross—whether they face to the right or left, or whether the cross is tilted or straight. In the 1930s, the *swastika* symbol—a clockwise, tilted cross— was adopted by the Nazi political party in Germany, and gained a negative reputation as a symbol of hatred in the modern world.

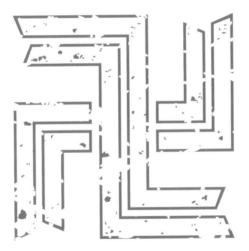

The manji used by the Tokyo Manji Gang as their emblem is intended to be the ancient Buddhist symbol, as evidenced by the appearance of its counterclockwise, straight arms. Both the manji and the gang's name are probably a reference to their leader, Sano Manjiro (though the symbol itself does not appear in his name), and the fact that the gang often meets at temples, which are marked on maps with the manji symbol.

The manji in this book are unedited, and presented as they appear in the original Japanese edition of *Tokyo Revengers*.

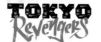

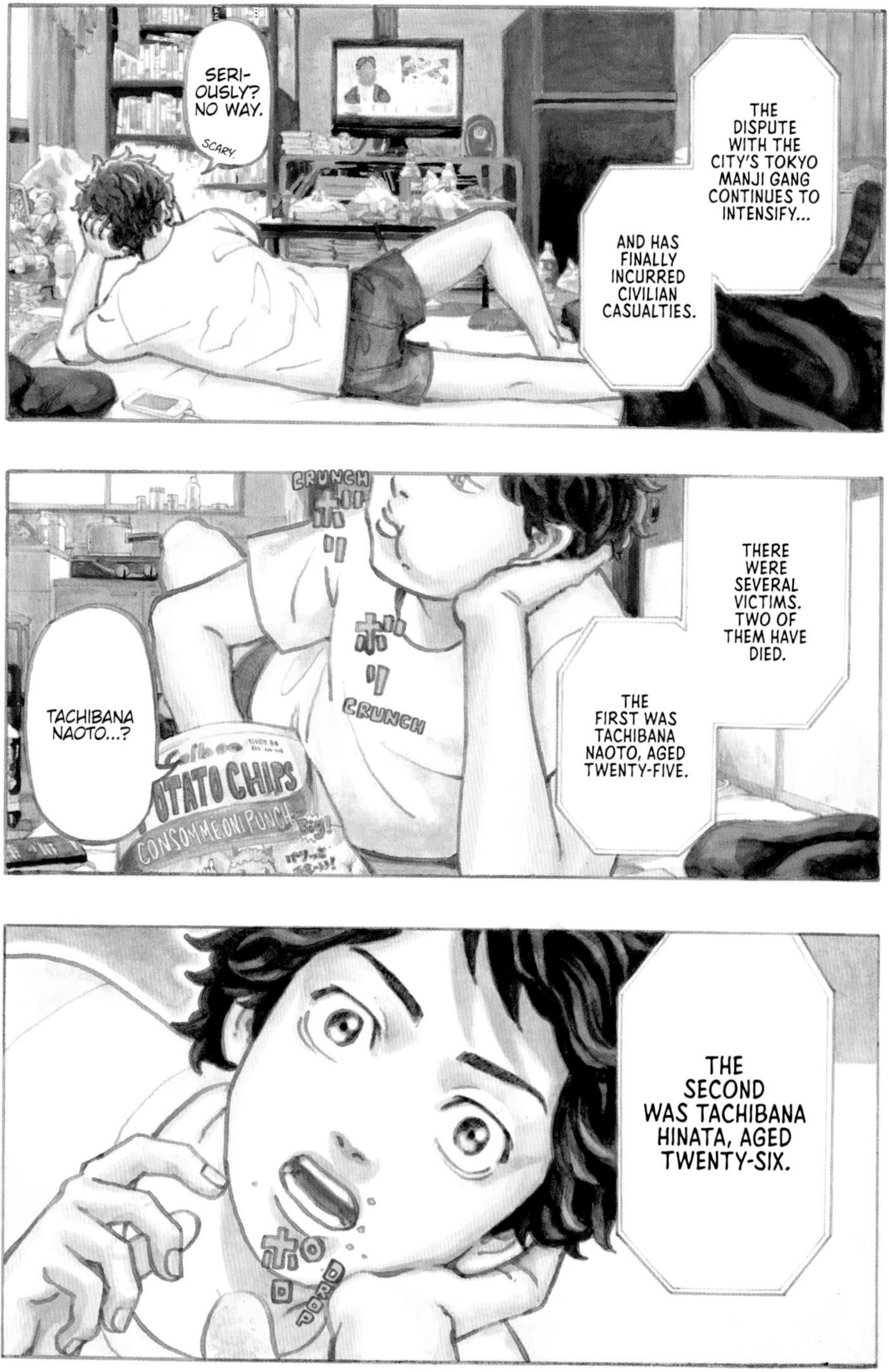
THE DISPUTE WITH THE CITY'S TOKYO MANJI GANG CONTINUES TO INTENSIFY...
AND HAS FINALLY INCURRED CIVILIAN CASUALTIES.
SERI-OUSLY? NO WAY.
SCARY.
THERE WERE SEVERAL VICTIMS. TWO OF THEM HAVE DIED.
THE FIRST WAS TACHIBANA NAOTO, AGED TWENTY-FIVE.
CRUNCH
CRUNCH
TACHIBANA NAOTO...?
THE SECOND WAS TACHIBANA HINATA, AGED TWENTY-SIX.
PORO

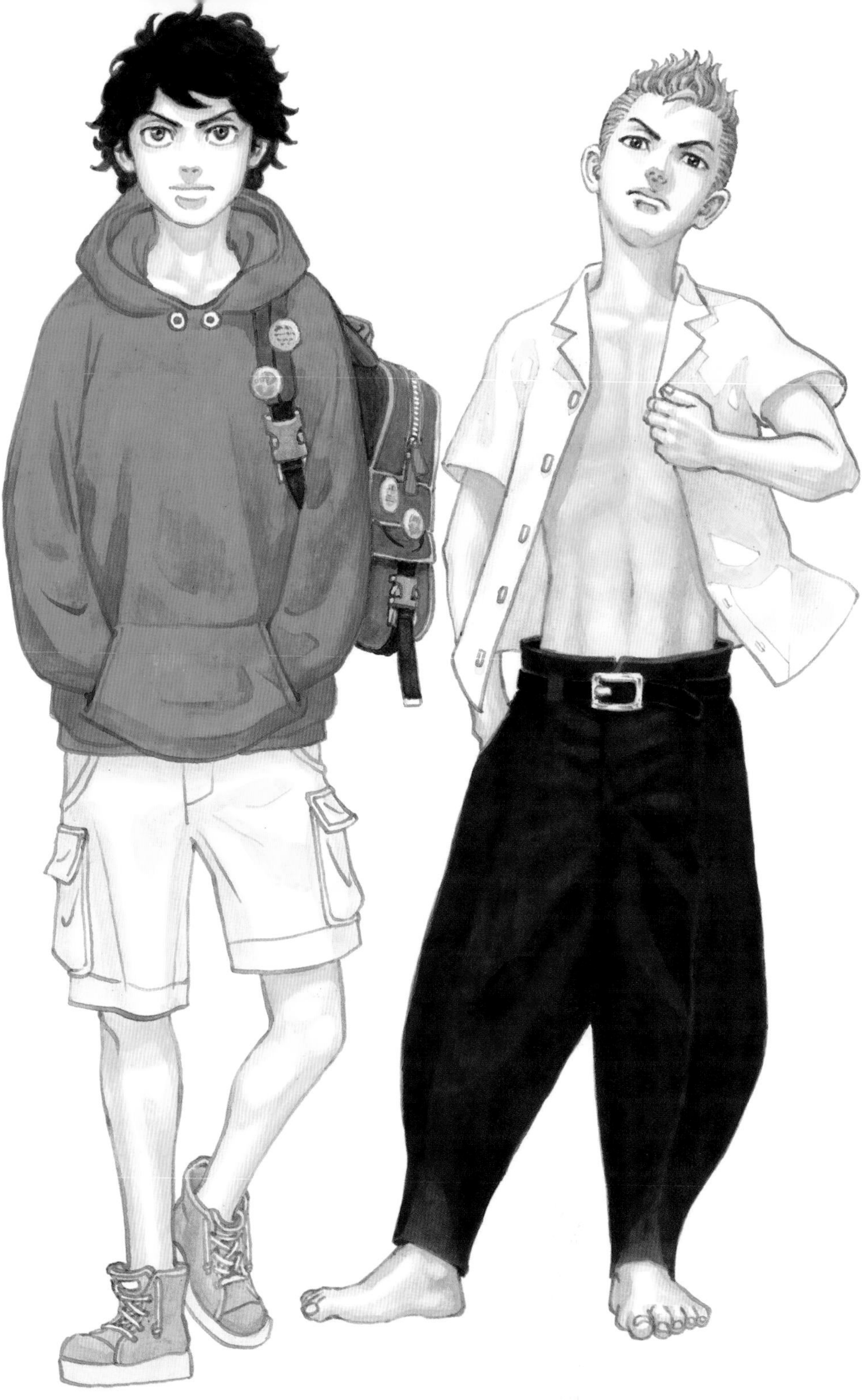

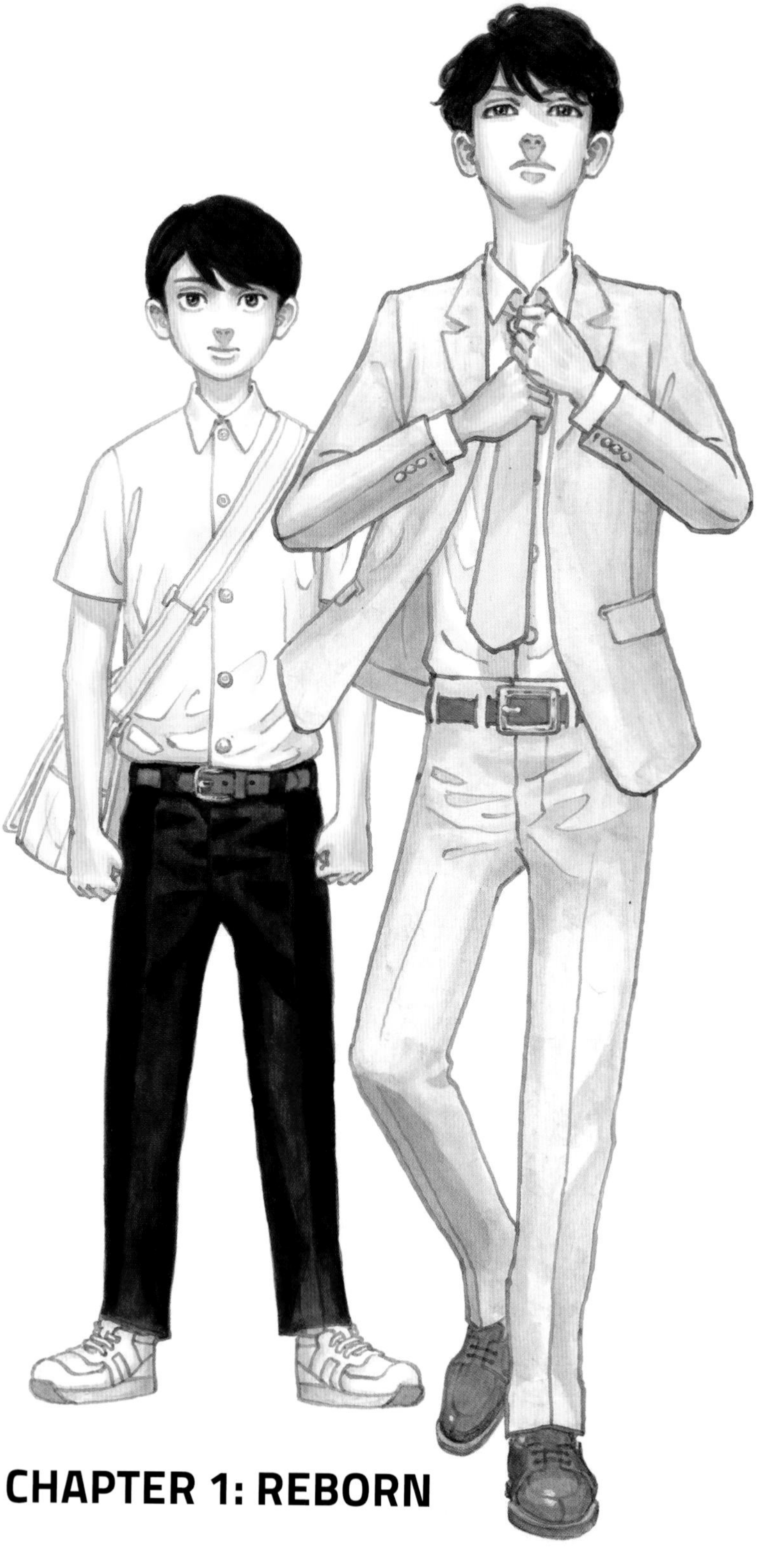

CHAPTER 1: REBORN

CONTENTS

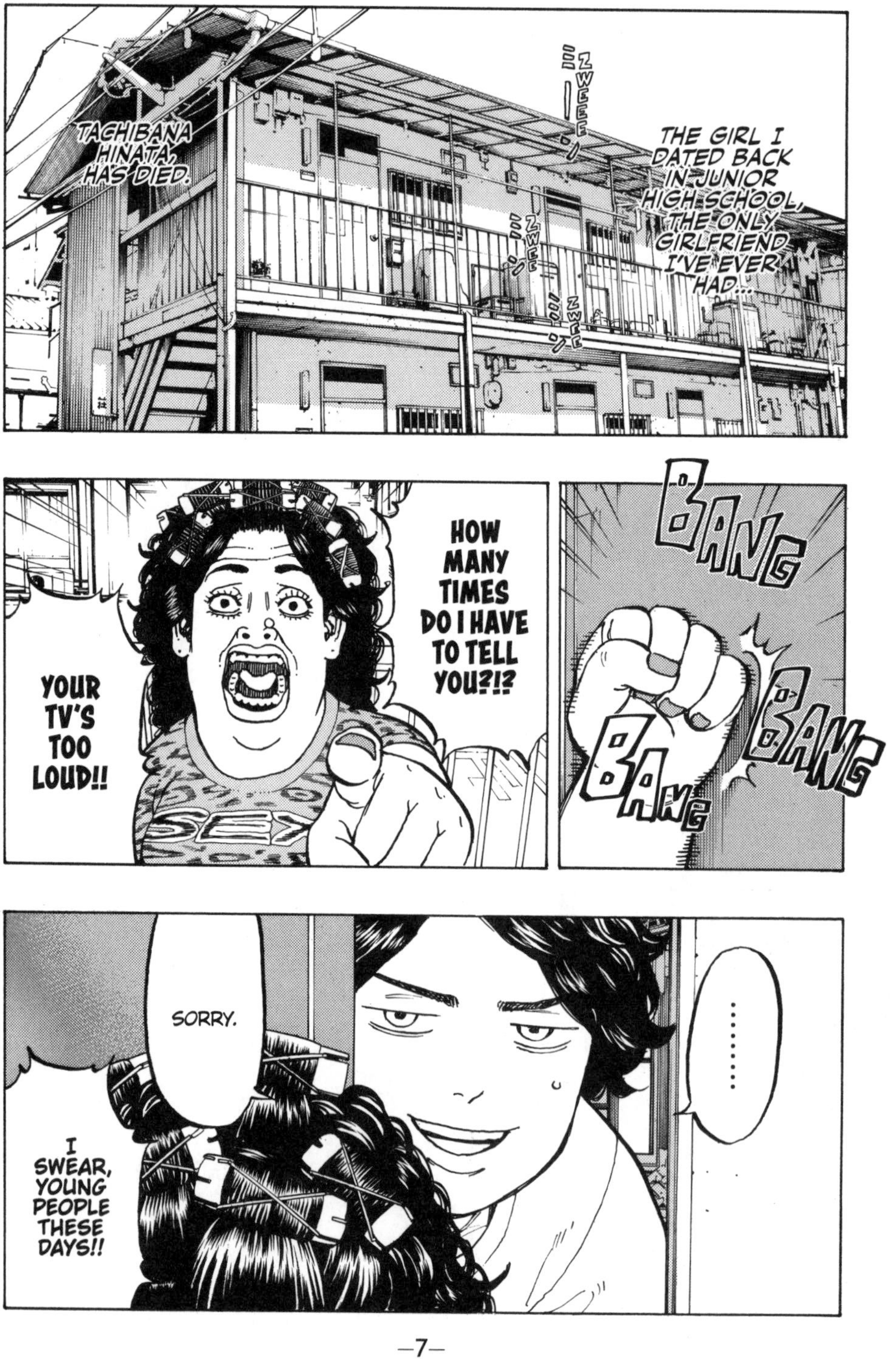
THE GIRL I DATED BACK IN JUNIOR HIGH SCHOOL, THE ONLY GIRLFRIEND I'VE EVER HAD...
ZWEEE!!
ZWEE!!
ZWEE!!
TACHIBANA HINATA, HAS DIED.
BANG
BANG
BANG
HOW MANY TIMES DO I HAVE TO TELL YOU?!?
YOUR TV'S TOO LOUD!!
......
SORRY.
I SWEAR, YOUNG PEOPLE THESE DAYS!!

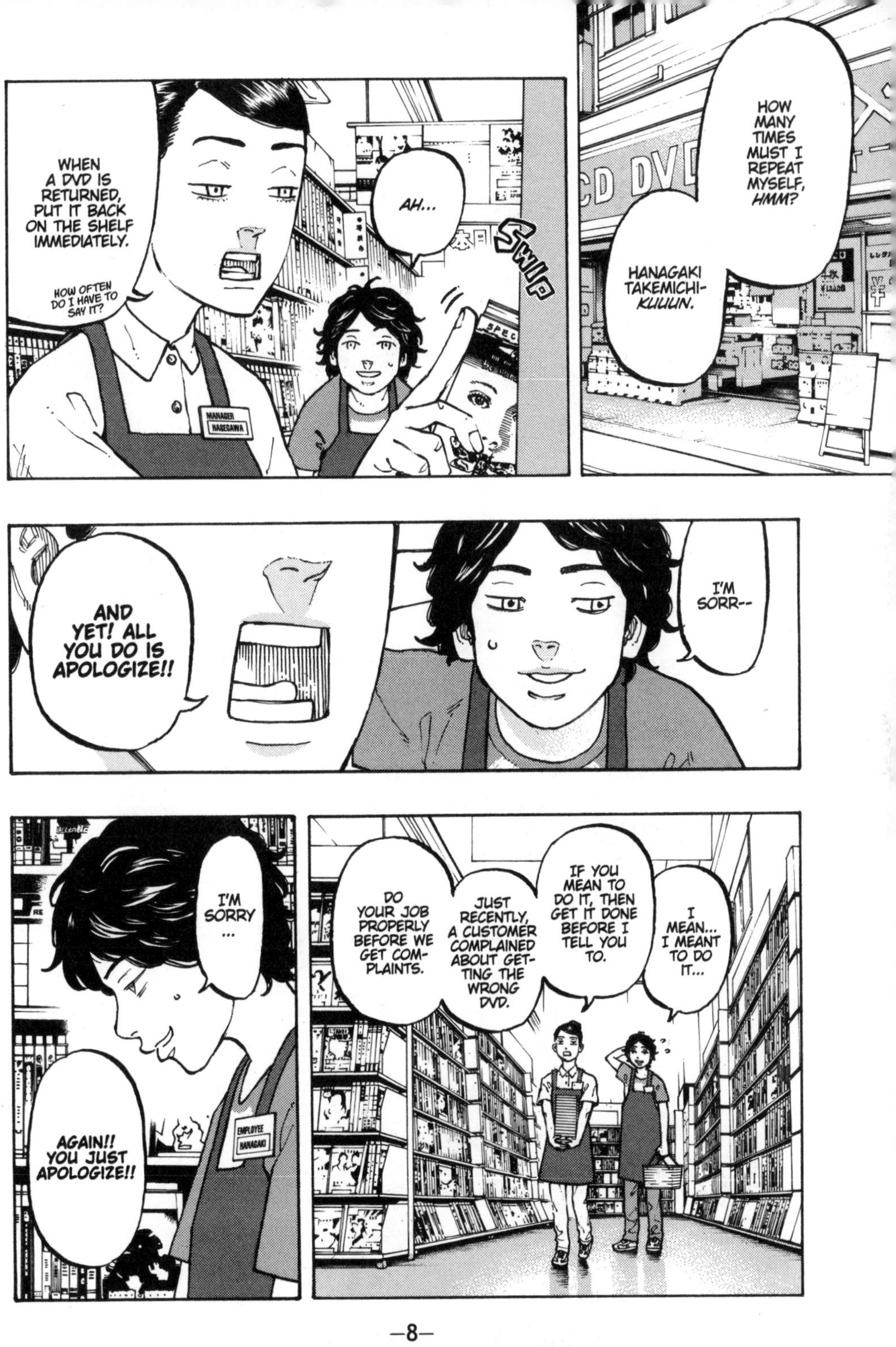
CD DVD
HOW MANY TIMES MUST I REPEAT MYSELF, *HMM?*
HANAGAKI TAKEMICHI-*KUUUN.*
WHEN A DVD IS RETURNED, PUT IT BACK ON THE SHELF IMMEDIATELY.
HOW OFTEN DO I HAVE TO SAY IT?
MANAGER HASEGAWA
AH...
SWIP
I'M SORR--
AND YET! ALL YOU DO IS APOLOGIZE!!
I MEAN... I MEANT TO DO IT...
IF YOU MEAN TO DO IT, THEN GET IT DONE BEFORE I TELL YOU TO.
JUST RECENTLY, A CUSTOMER COMPLAINED ABOUT GETTING THE WRONG DVD.
DO YOUR JOB PROPERLY BEFORE WE GET COMPLAINTS.
I'M SORRY ...
EMPLOYEE HANAGAKI
AGAIN!! YOU JUST APOLOGIZE!!

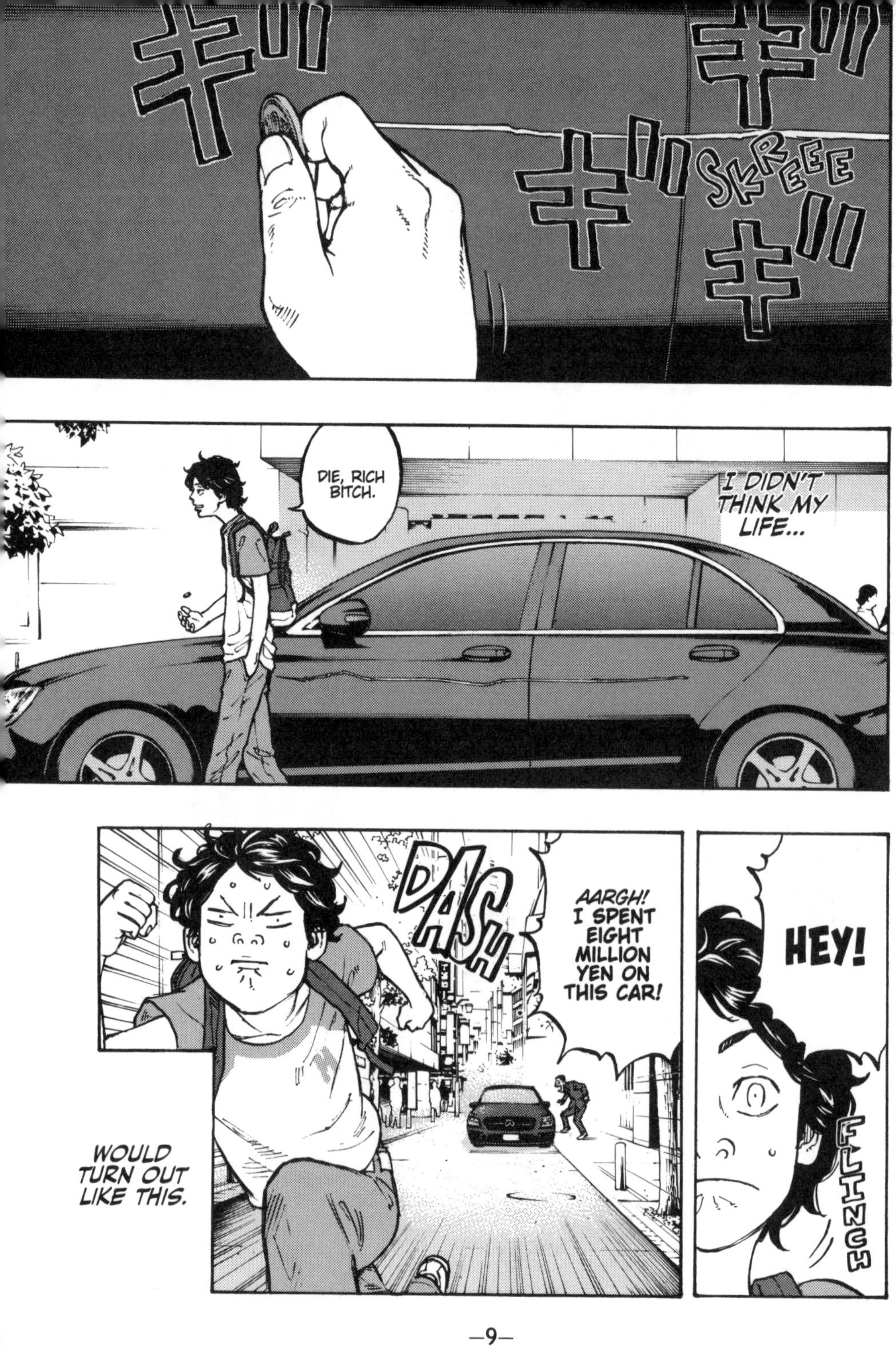
SKREEE
I DIDN'T THINK MY LIFE...
DIE, RICH BITCH.
HEY!
FLINCH
AARGH! I SPENT EIGHT MILLION YEN ON THIS CAR!
DASH
WOULD TURN OUT LIKE THIS.

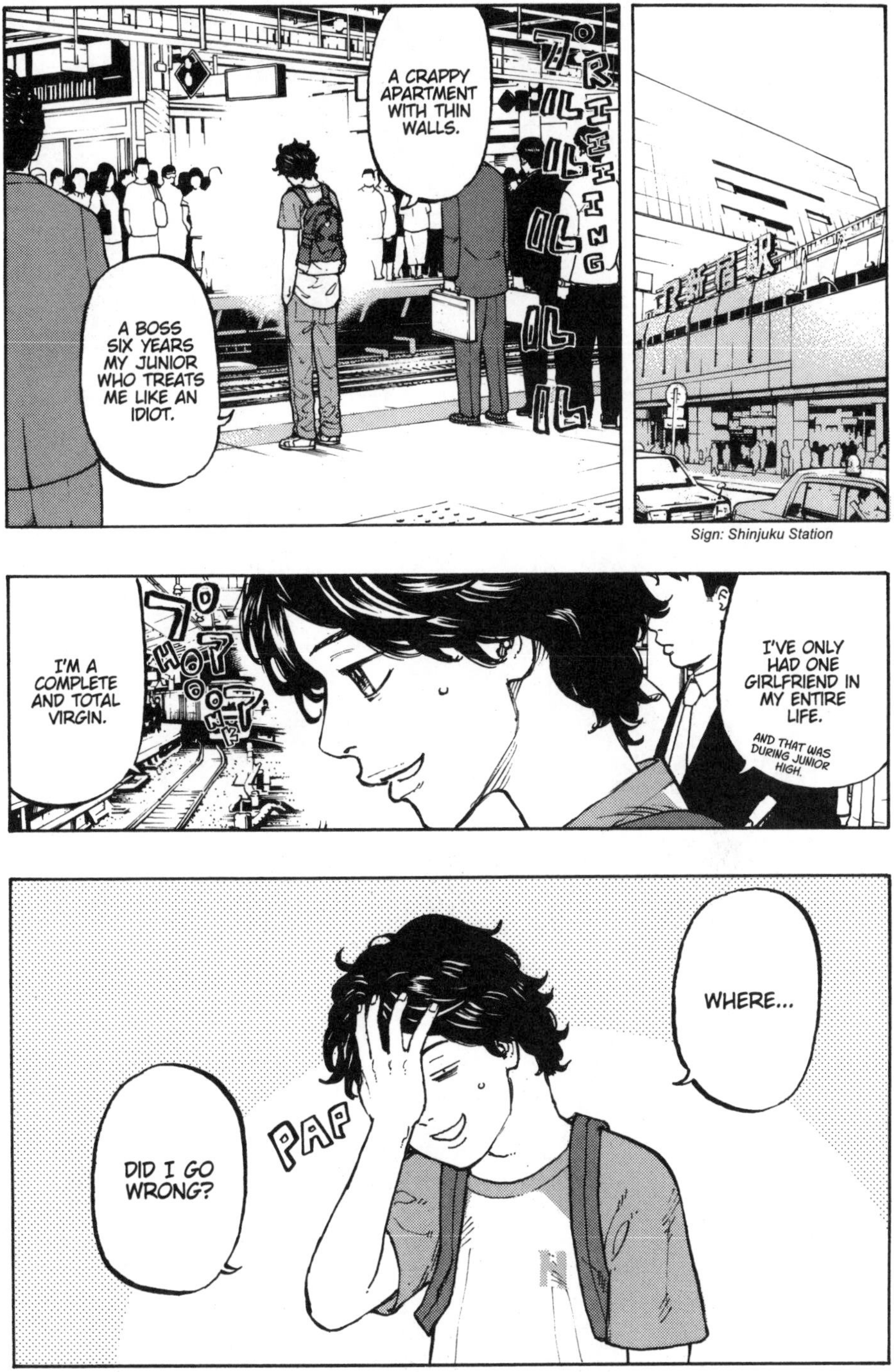
A CRAPPY APARTMENT WITH THIN WALLS.
RIIIING
A BOSS SIX YEARS MY JUNIOR WHO TREATS ME LIKE AN IDIOT.
I'VE ONLY HAD ONE GIRLFRIEND IN MY ENTIRE LIFE.
AND THAT WAS DURING JUNIOR HIGH.
HOOONK
I'M A COMPLETE AND TOTAL VIRGIN.
WHERE...
PAP
DID I GO WRONG?

Sign: Shinjuku Station

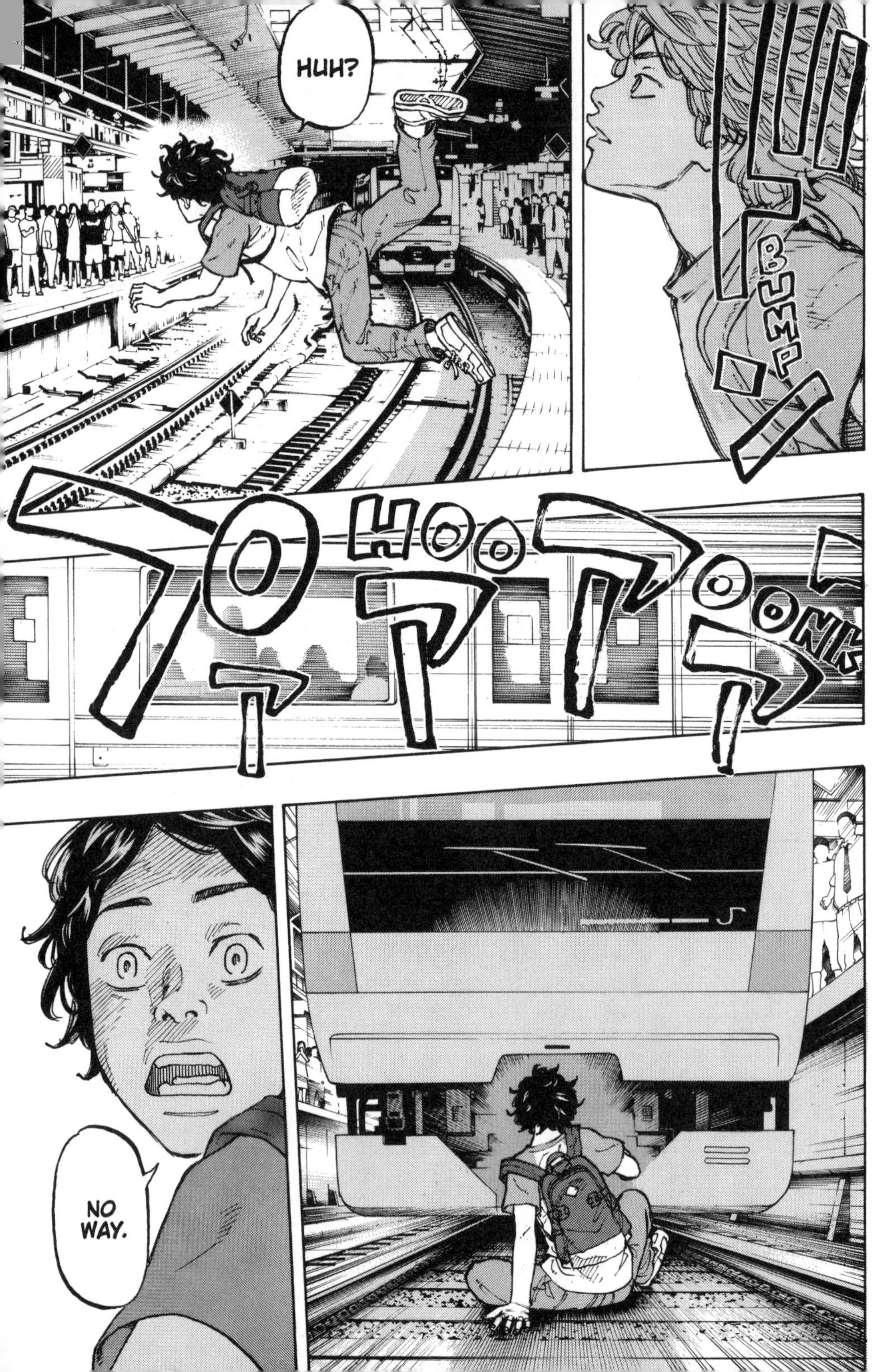
BUMP
HUH?
HOO-OONK
NO WAY.

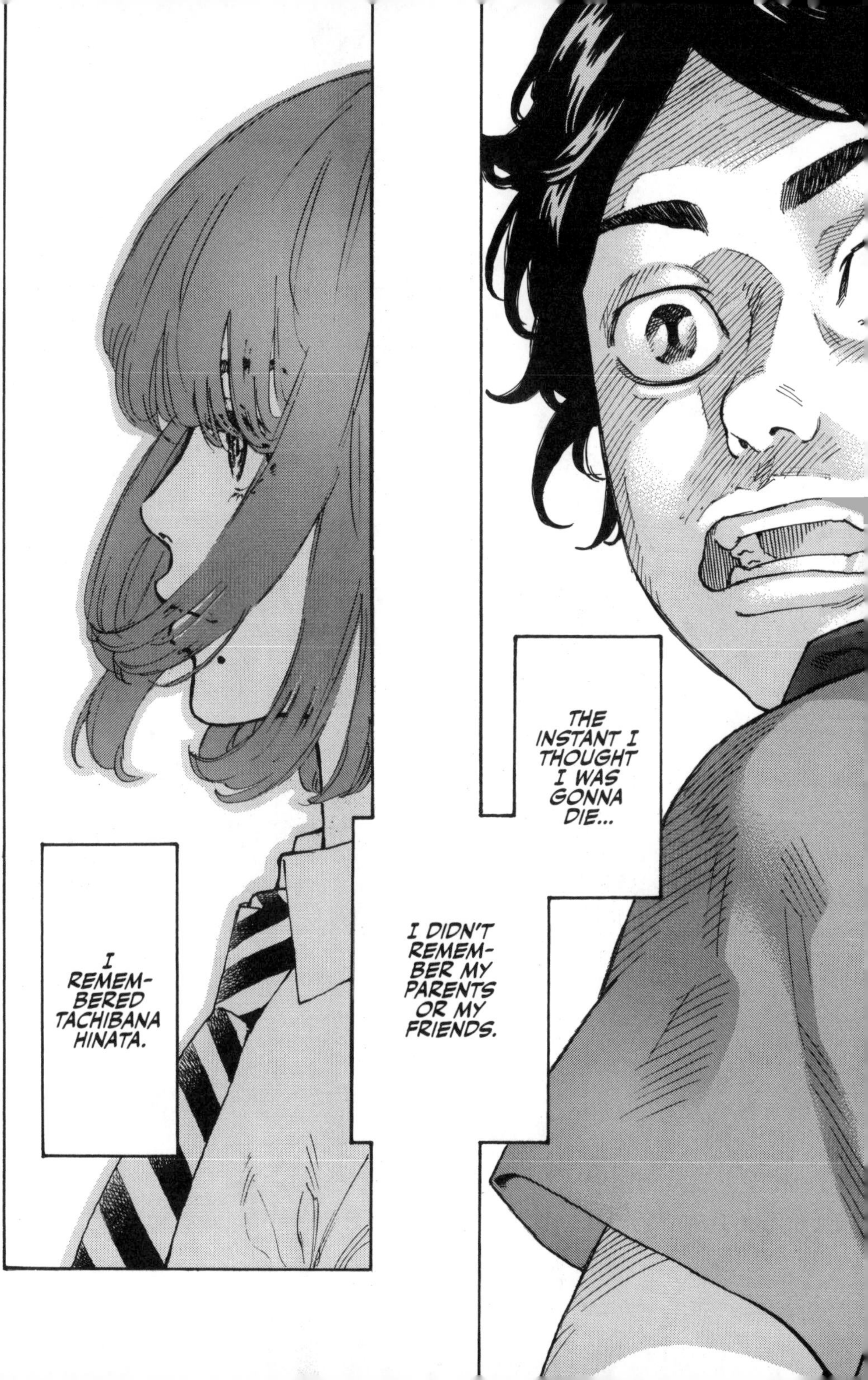
THE INSTANT I THOUGHT I WAS GONNA DIE...
I DIDN'T REMEMBER MY PARENTS OR MY FRIENDS.
I REMEMBERED TACHIBANA HINATA.

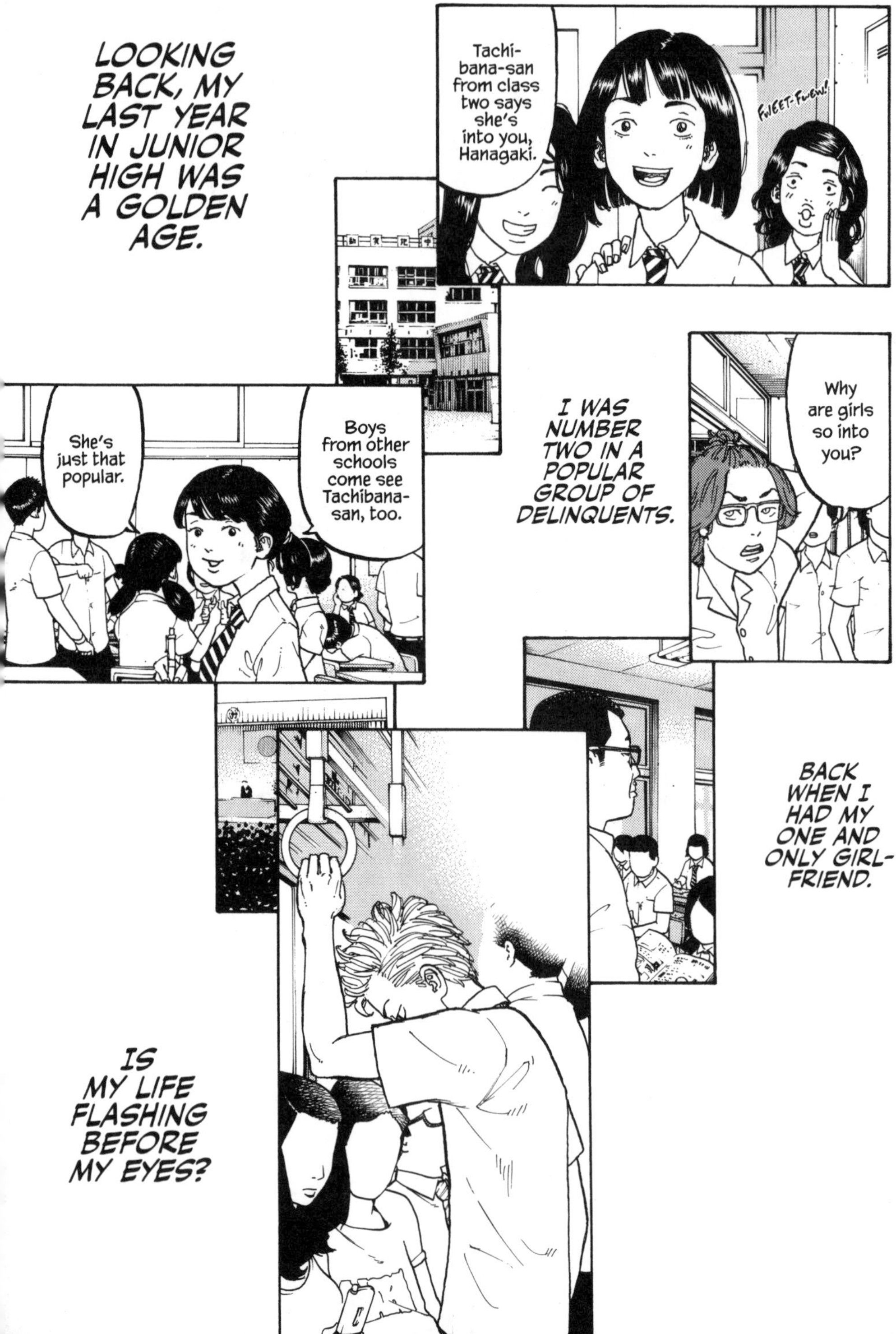
Tachi-bana-san from class two says she's into you, Hanagaki.
FWEET-FWEW!
LOOKING BACK, MY LAST YEAR IN JUNIOR HIGH WAS A GOLDEN AGE.
Why are girls so into you?
I WAS NUMBER TWO IN A POPULAR GROUP OF DELINQUENTS.
Boys from other schools come see Tachibana-san, too.
She's just that popular.
BACK WHEN I HAD MY ONE AND ONLY GIRL-FRIEND.
IS MY LIFE FLASHING BEFORE MY EYES?

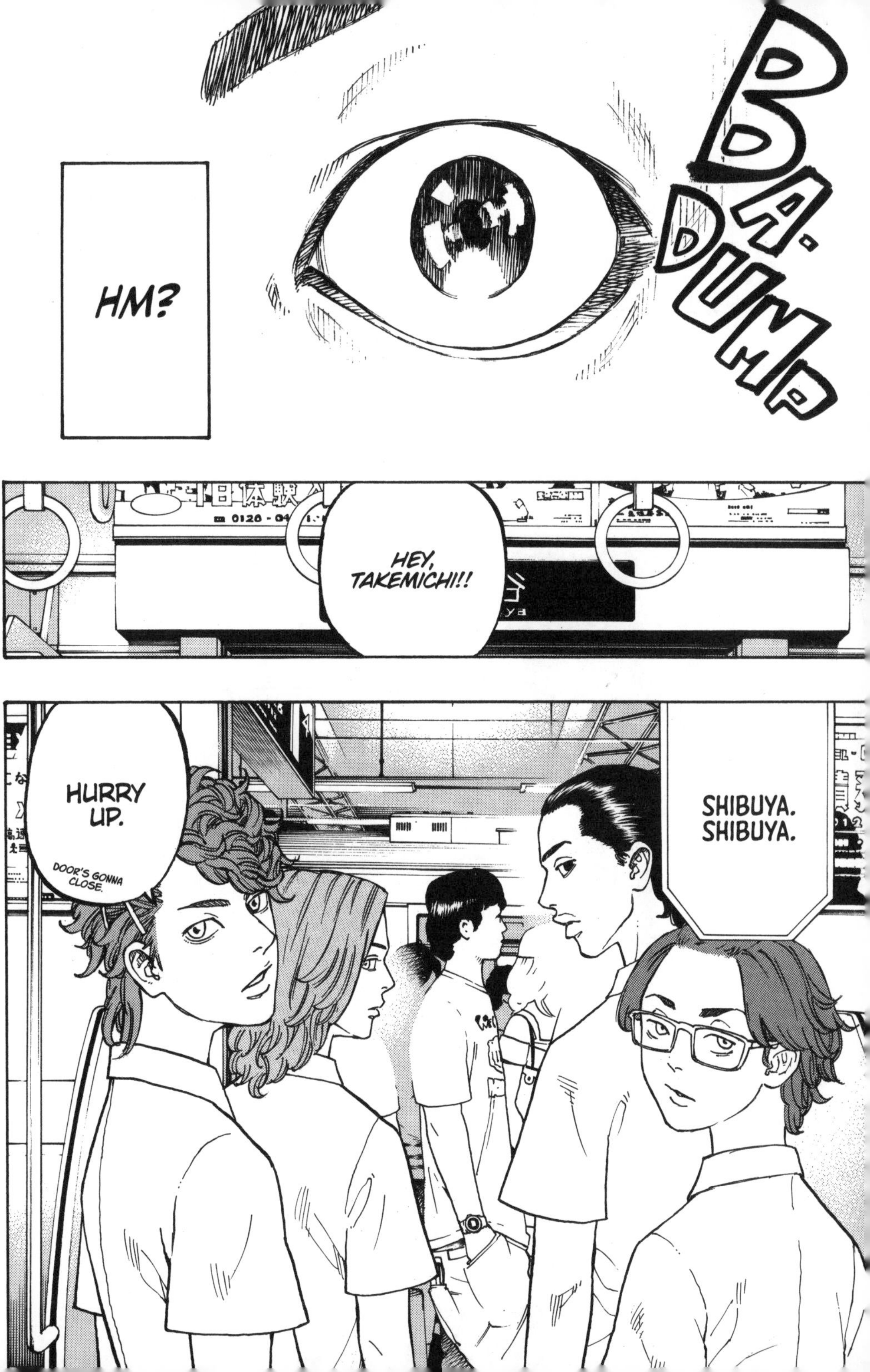
BA-DUMP
HM?
HEY, TAKEMICHI!!
SHIBUYA. SHIBUYA.
HURRY UP.
DOOR'S GONNA CLOSE.

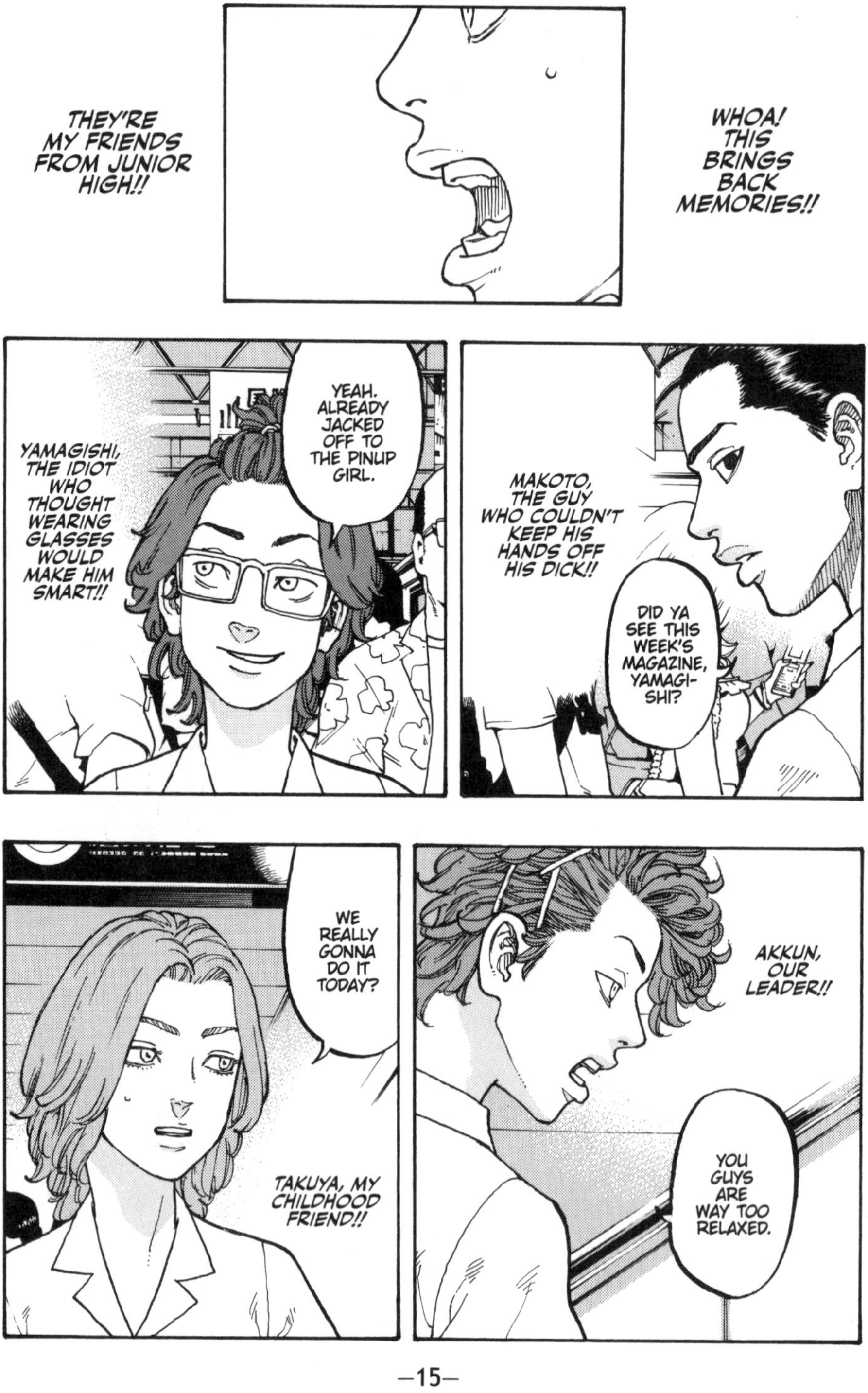
WHOA! THIS BRINGS BACK MEMORIES!!
THEY'RE MY FRIENDS FROM JUNIOR HIGH!!
MAKOTO, THE GUY WHO COULDN'T KEEP HIS HANDS OFF HIS DICK!!
DID YA SEE THIS WEEK'S MAGAZINE, YAMAGI-SHI?
YEAH. ALREADY JACKED OFF TO THE PINUP GIRL.
YAMAGISHI, THE IDIOT WHO THOUGHT WEARING GLASSES WOULD MAKE HIM SMART!!
AKKUN, OUR LEADER!!
YOU GUYS ARE WAY TOO RELAXED.
WE REALLY GONNA DO IT TODAY?
TAKUYA, MY CHILDHOOD FRIEND!!

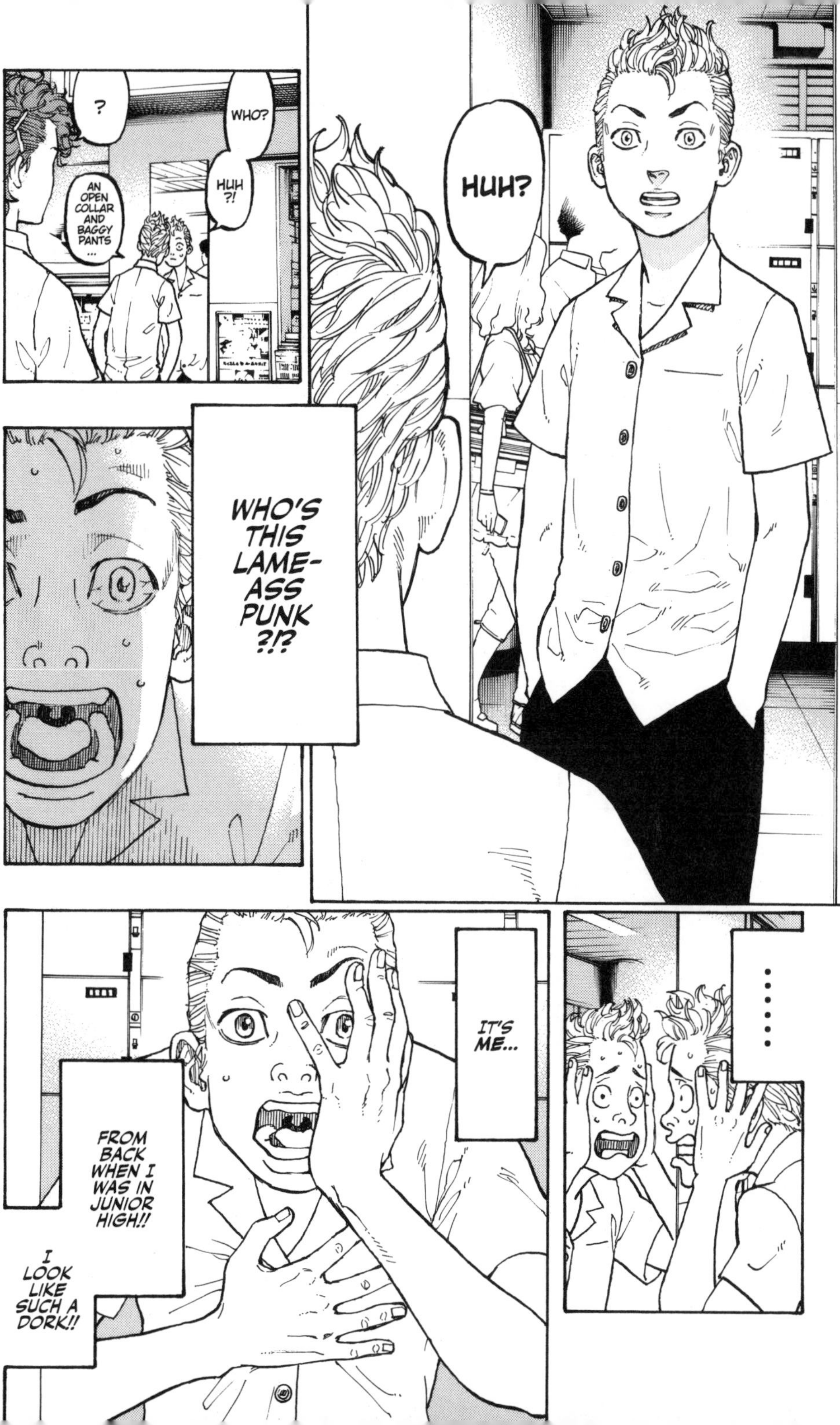
HUH?
WHO?
?
HUH?!
AN OPEN COLLAR AND BAGGY PANTS...
WHO'S THIS LAME-ASS PUNK?!?
......
IT'S ME...
FROM BACK WHEN I WAS IN JUNIOR HIGH!!
I LOOK LIKE SUCH A DORK!!

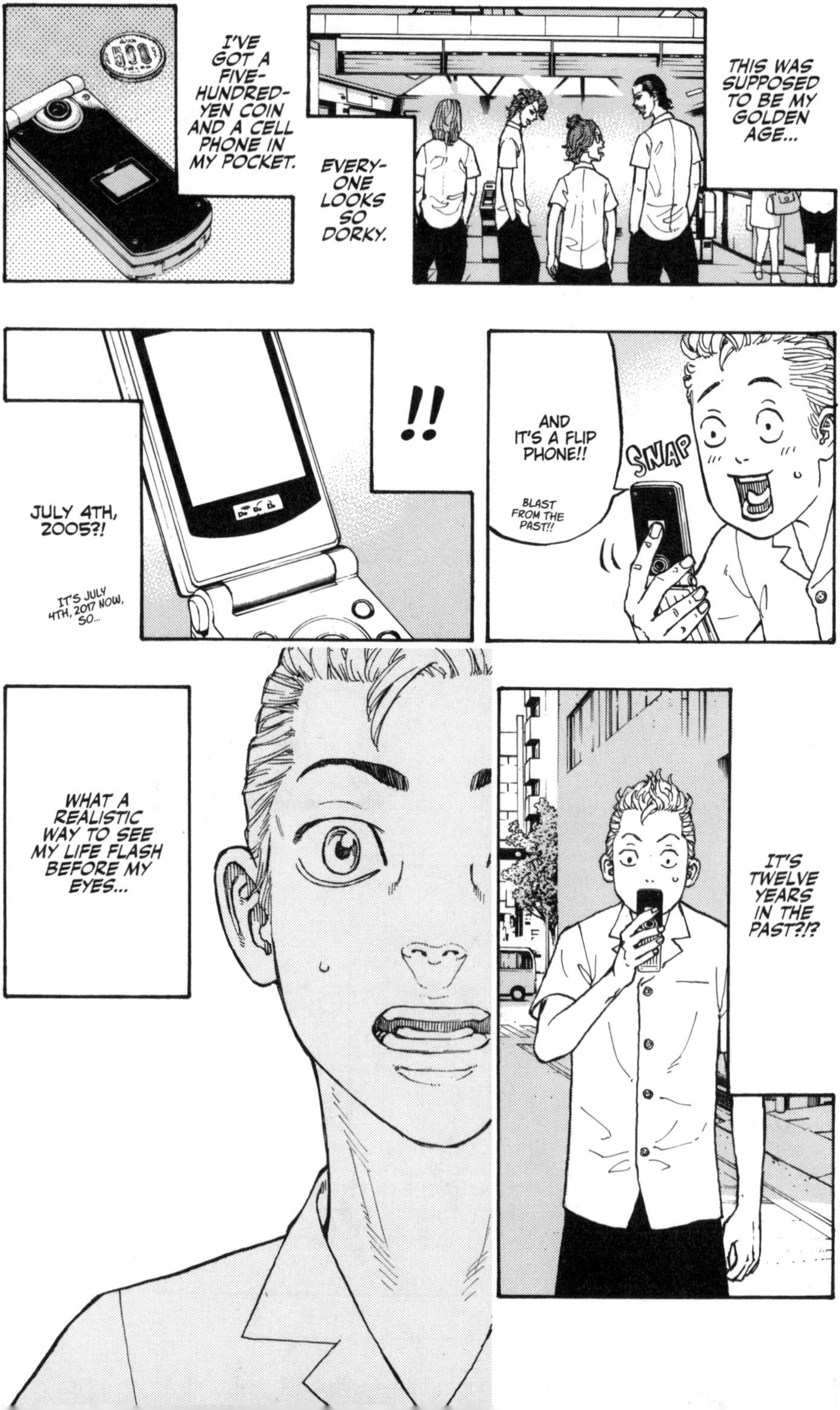
THIS WAS SUPPOSED TO BE MY GOLDEN AGE...
EVERY-ONE LOOKS SO DORKY.
I'VE GOT A FIVE-HUNDRED-YEN COIN AND A CELL PHONE IN MY POCKET.
AND IT'S A FLIP PHONE!!
SNAP
BLAST FROM THE PAST!!
!!
JULY 4TH, 2005?!
IT'S JULY 4TH, 2017 NOW, SO...
IT'S TWELVE YEARS IN THE PAST?!?
WHAT A REALISTIC WAY TO SEE MY LIFE FLASH BEFORE MY EYES...

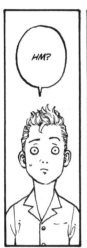

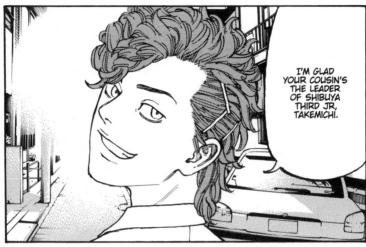

I'M GLAD YOUR COUSIN'S THE LEADER OF SHIBUYA THIRD JR, TAKEMICHI.
HM?
IF ANY THIRD-YEARS SHOW UP, WE'LL JUST NAME-DROP MASARU-KUN!
OH?
WAIT A SEC. I WANNA PROCESS THIS INFO.
?
Masaru... Masaru...
Uh...
GASP
I'M READY TO THROW DOWN.
OH YEAH! MY COUSIN, MASARU-KUN!!
A THIRD-YEAR FROM SHIBUYA THIRD JR!! HE SAID HE WAS THE BOSS!!
FWIP

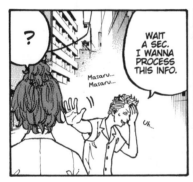

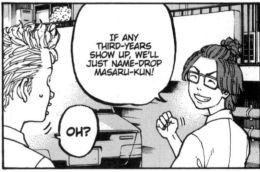

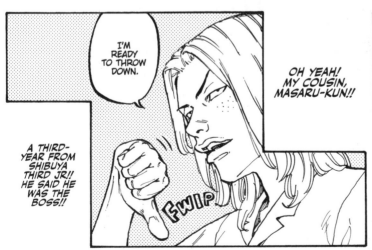

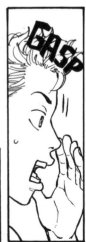

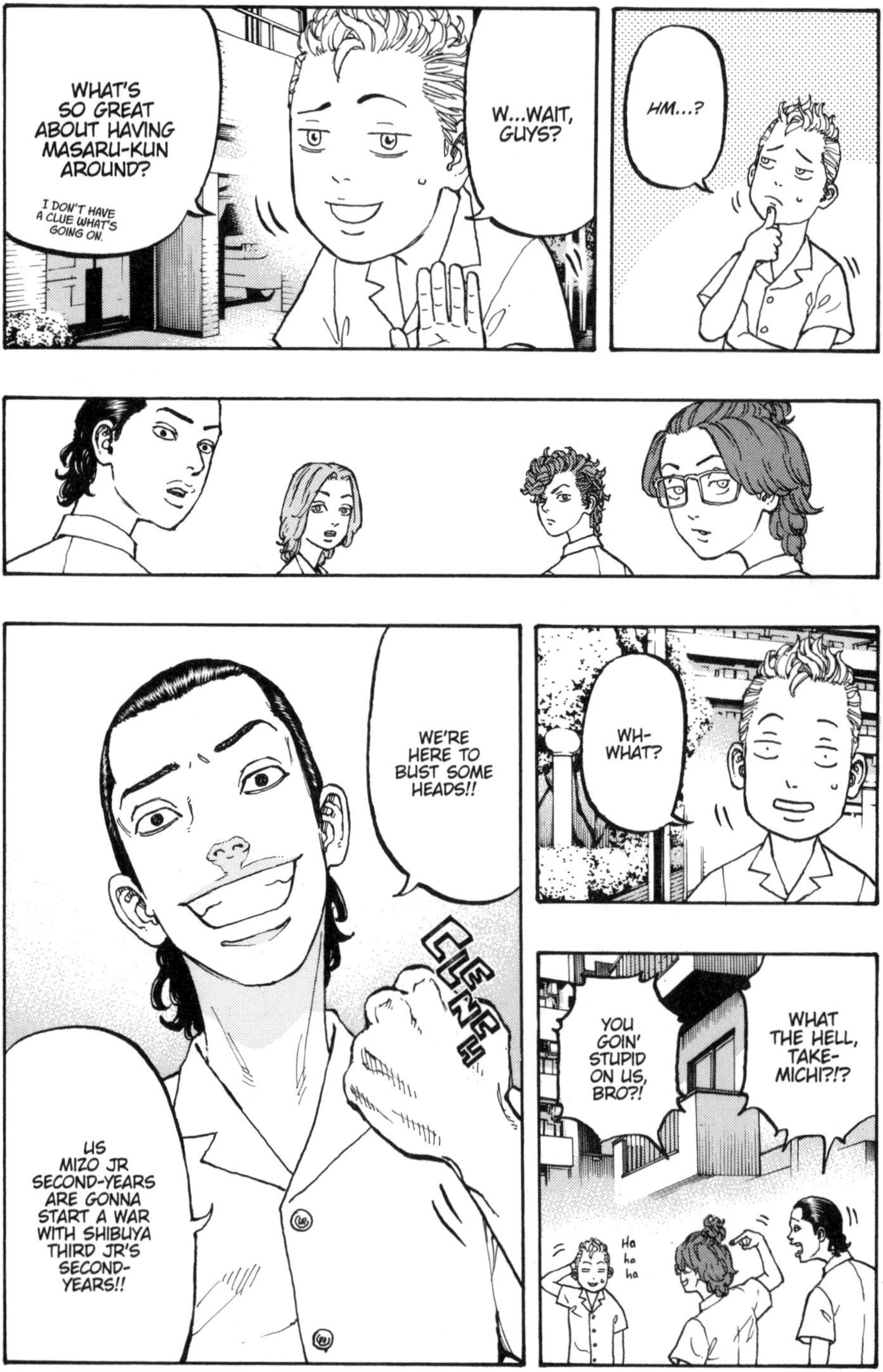
HM...?
W...WAIT, GUYS?
WHAT'S SO GREAT ABOUT HAVING MASARU-KUN AROUND?
I DON'T HAVE A CLUE WHAT'S GOING ON.
WH-WHAT?
WHAT THE HELL, TAKE-MICHI?!?
YOU GOIN' STUPID ON US, BRO?!
Ha ha ha
WE'RE HERE TO BUST SOME HEADS!!
CLENCH
US MIZO JR SECOND-YEARS ARE GONNA START A WAR WITH SHIBUYA THIRD JR'S SECOND-YEARS!!

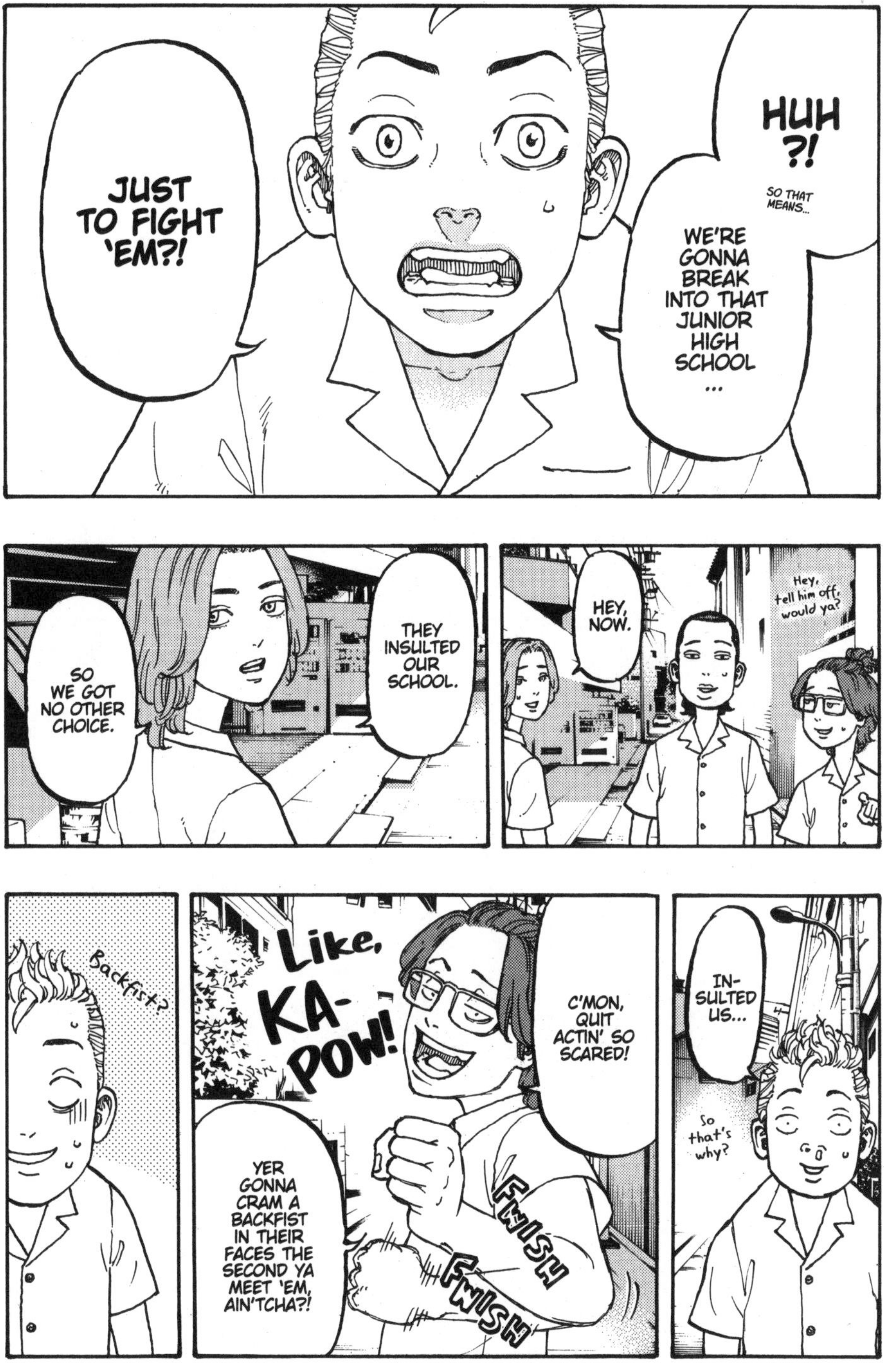
HUH ?!
SO THAT MEANS...
WE'RE GONNA BREAK INTO THAT JUNIOR HIGH SCHOOL ...
JUST TO FIGHT 'EM?!
Hey, tell him off, would ya?
HEY, NOW.
THEY INSULTED OUR SCHOOL.
SO WE GOT NO OTHER CHOICE.
IN-SULTED US...
So that's why?
C'MON, QUIT ACTIN' SO SCARED!
Like, KA-POW!
YER GONNA CRAM A BACKFIST IN THEIR FACES THE SECOND YA MEET 'EM, AIN'TCHA?!
FWISH
FWISH
Backfist?

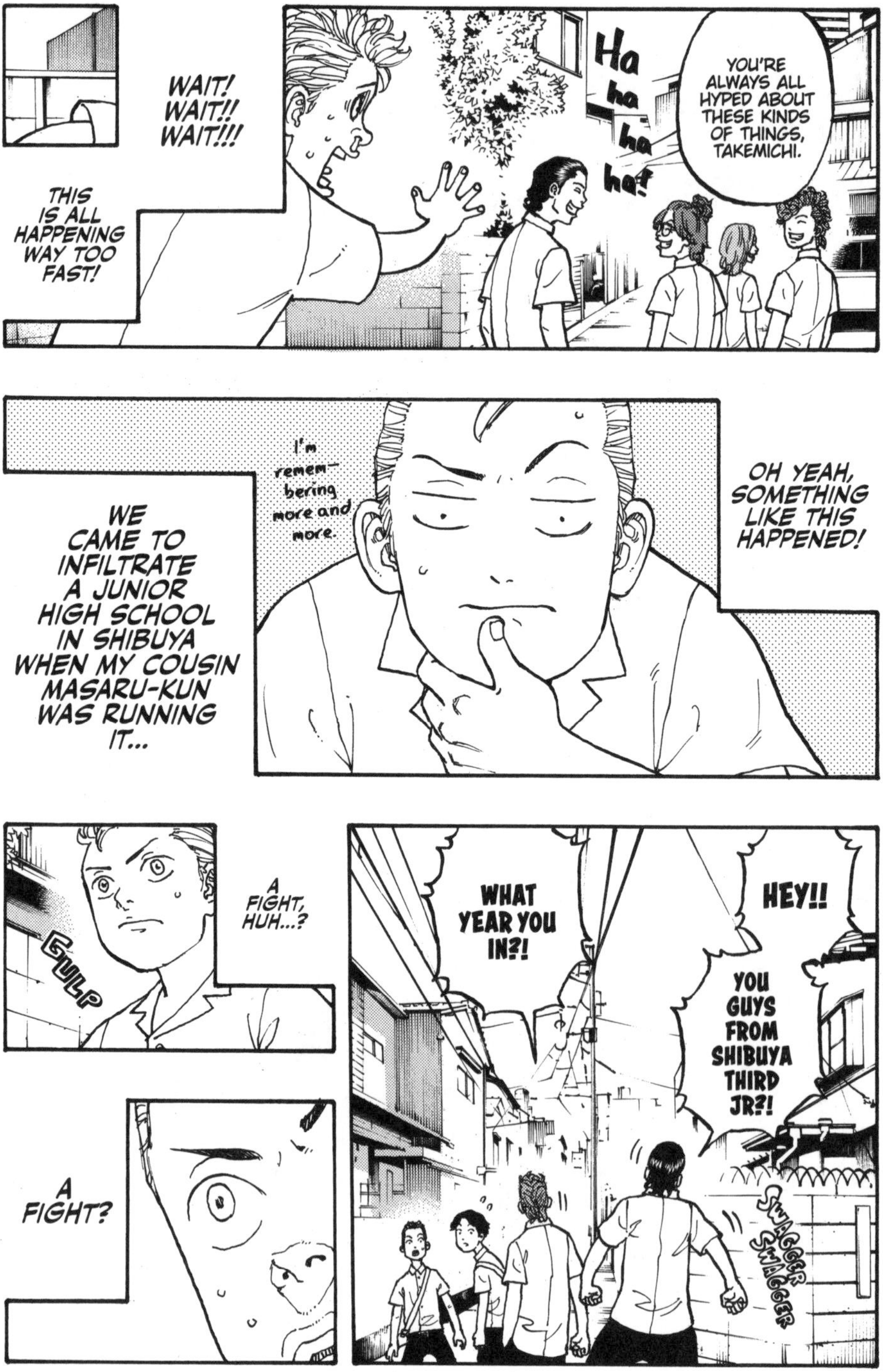
YOU'RE ALWAYS ALL HYPED ABOUT THESE KINDS OF THINGS, TAKEMICHI.
Ha ha ha ha!
WAIT! WAIT!! WAIT!!!
THIS IS ALL HAPPENING WAY TOO FAST!
OH YEAH, SOMETHING LIKE THIS HAPPENED!
I'm remembering more and more.
WE CAME TO INFILTRATE A JUNIOR HIGH SCHOOL IN SHIBUYA WHEN MY COUSIN MASARU-KUN WAS RUNNING IT...
HEY!!
YOU GUYS FROM SHIBUYA THIRD JR?!
WHAT YEAR YOU IN?!
SWAGGER SWAGGER
A FIGHT, HUH...?
GULP
A FIGHT?

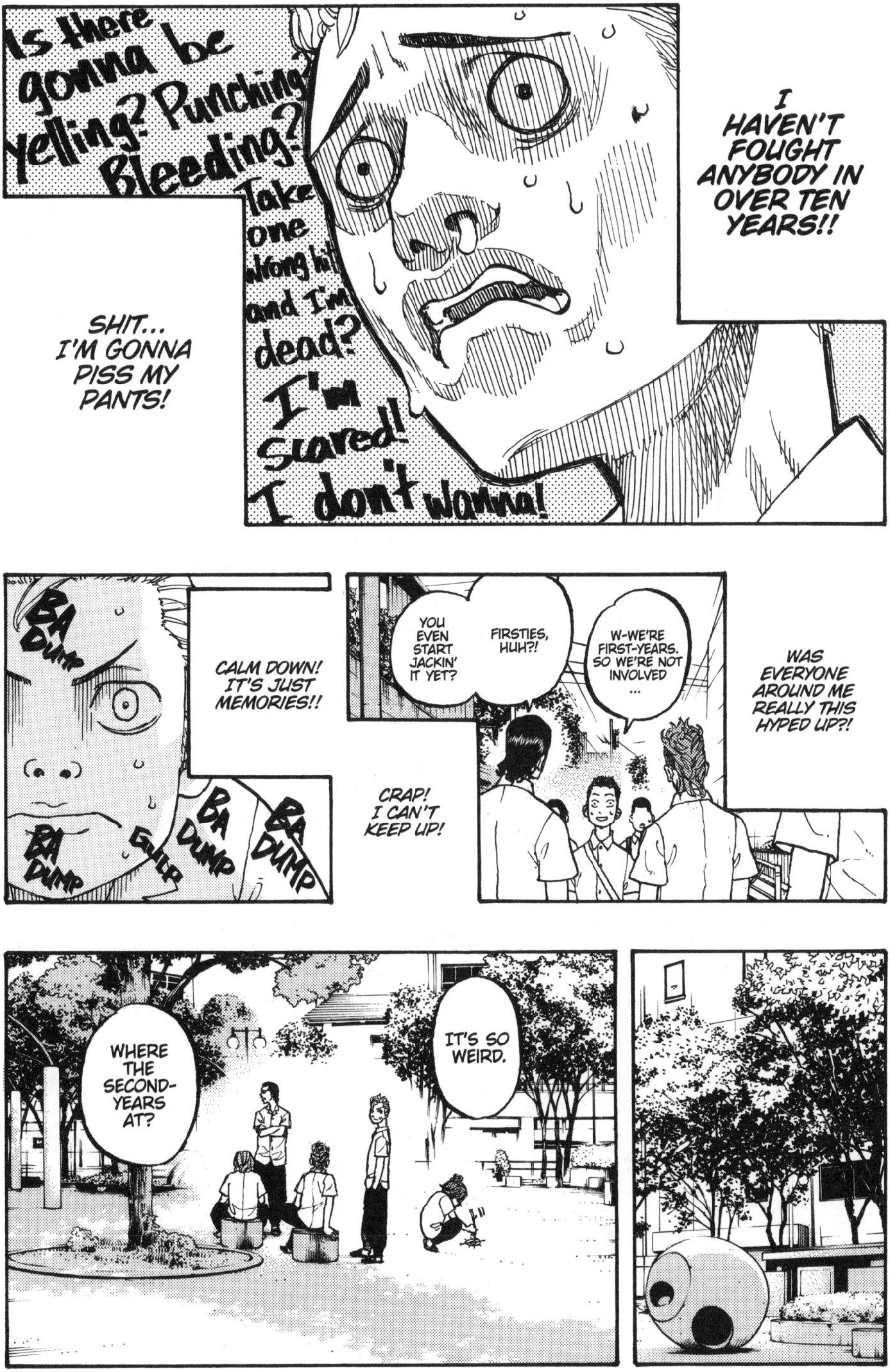
I HAVEN'T FOUGHT ANYBODY IN OVER TEN YEARS!!
Is there gonna be yelling? Punching? Bleeding?
Take one wrong hit and I'm dead?
I'm scared! I don't wanna!
SHIT... I'M GONNA PISS MY PANTS!
WAS EVERYONE AROUND ME REALLY THIS HYPED UP?!
W-WE'RE FIRST-YEARS. SO WE'RE NOT INVOLVED ...
FIRSTIES, HUH?!
YOU EVEN START JACKIN' IT YET?
CRAP! I CAN'T KEEP UP!
CALM DOWN! IT'S JUST MEMORIES!!
BA DUMP
BA DUMP
GULP
BA DUMP
BA DUMP
IT'S SO WEIRD.
WHERE THE SECOND-YEARS AT?

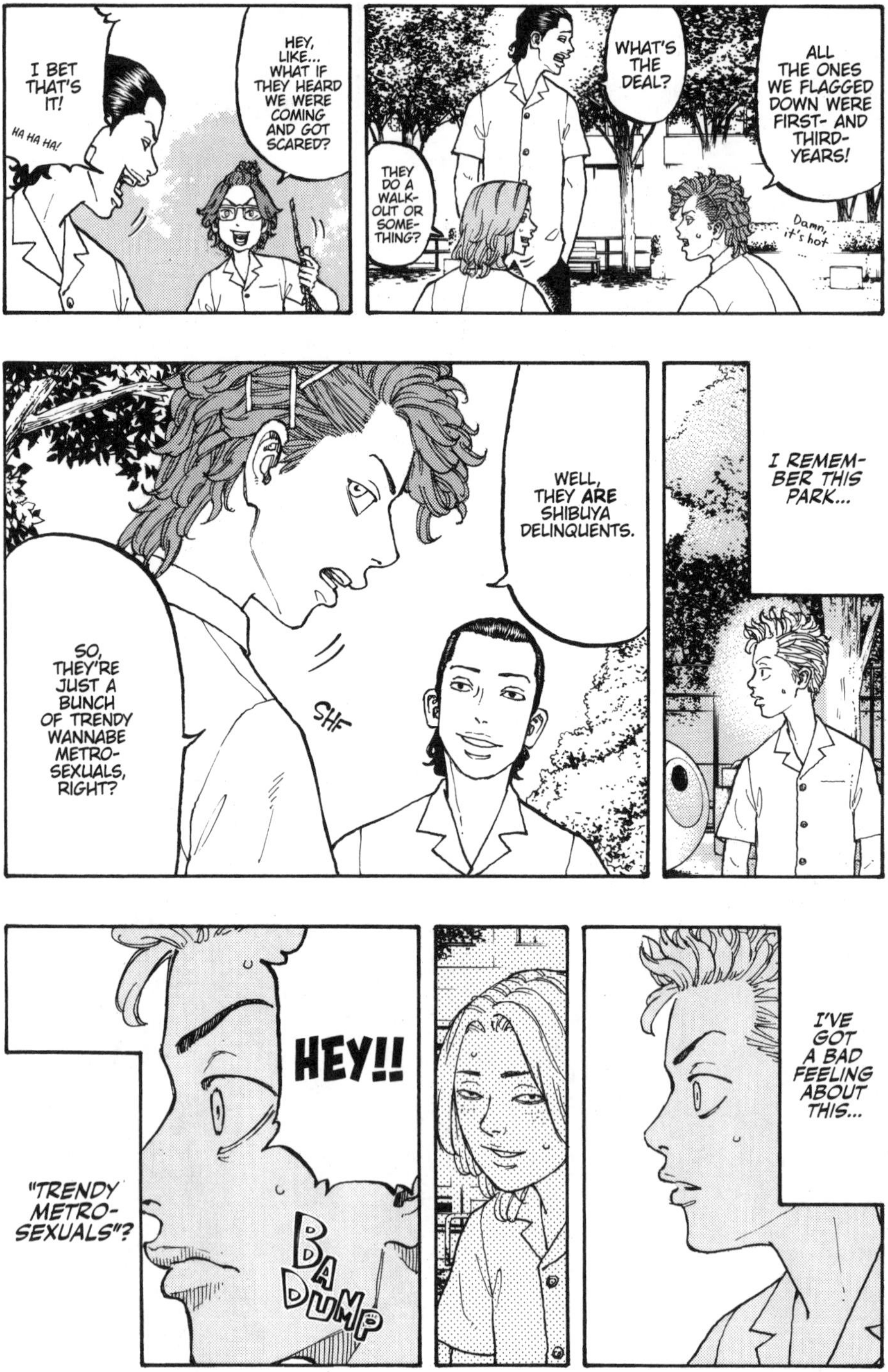
ALL THE ONES WE FLAGGED DOWN WERE FIRST- AND THIRD-YEARS!
WHAT'S THE DEAL?
Damn, it's hot ...
THEY DO A WALK-OUT OR SOMETHING?
HEY, LIKE... WHAT IF THEY HEARD WE WERE COMING AND GOT SCARED?
I BET THAT'S IT!
HA HA HA!
I REMEMBER THIS PARK...
WELL, THEY **ARE** SHIBUYA DELINQUENTS.
SO, THEY'RE JUST A BUNCH OF TRENDY WANNABE METROSEXUALS, RIGHT?
SHF
I'VE GOT A BAD FEELING ABOUT THIS...
HEY!!
BA DUMP
"TRENDY METROSEXUALS"?

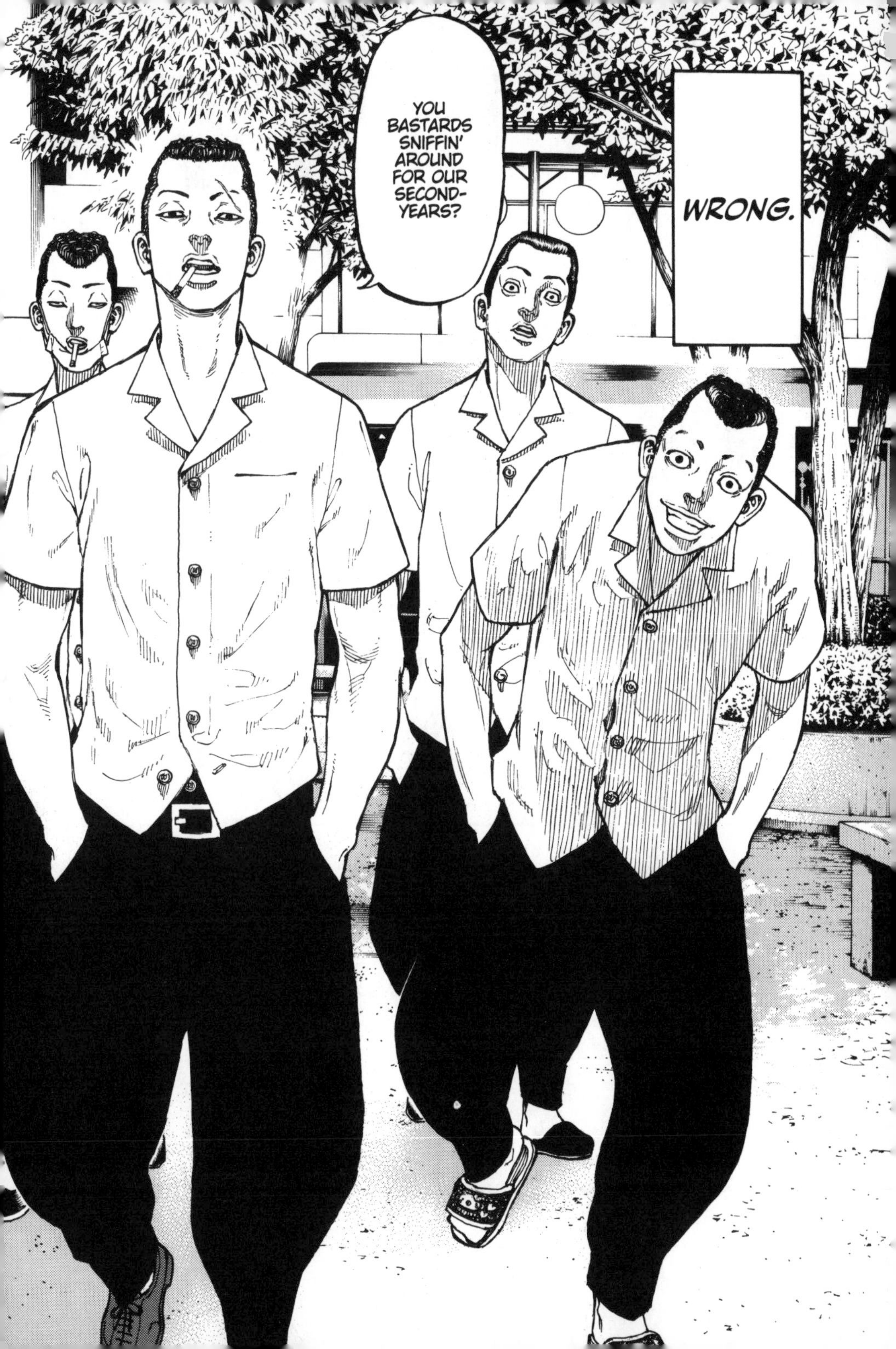
WRONG.
YOU BASTARDS SNIFFIN' AROUND FOR OUR SECOND-YEARS?

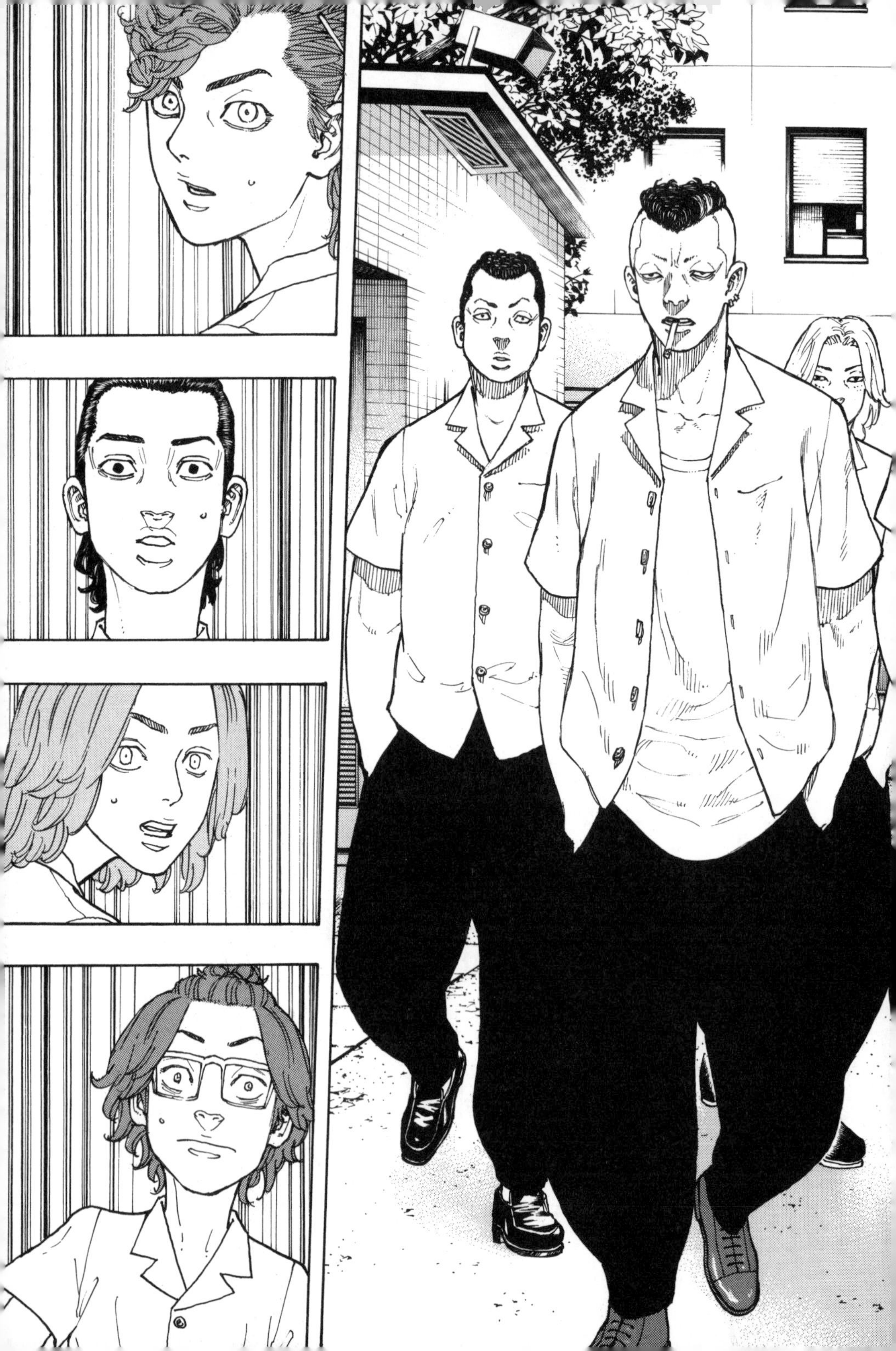

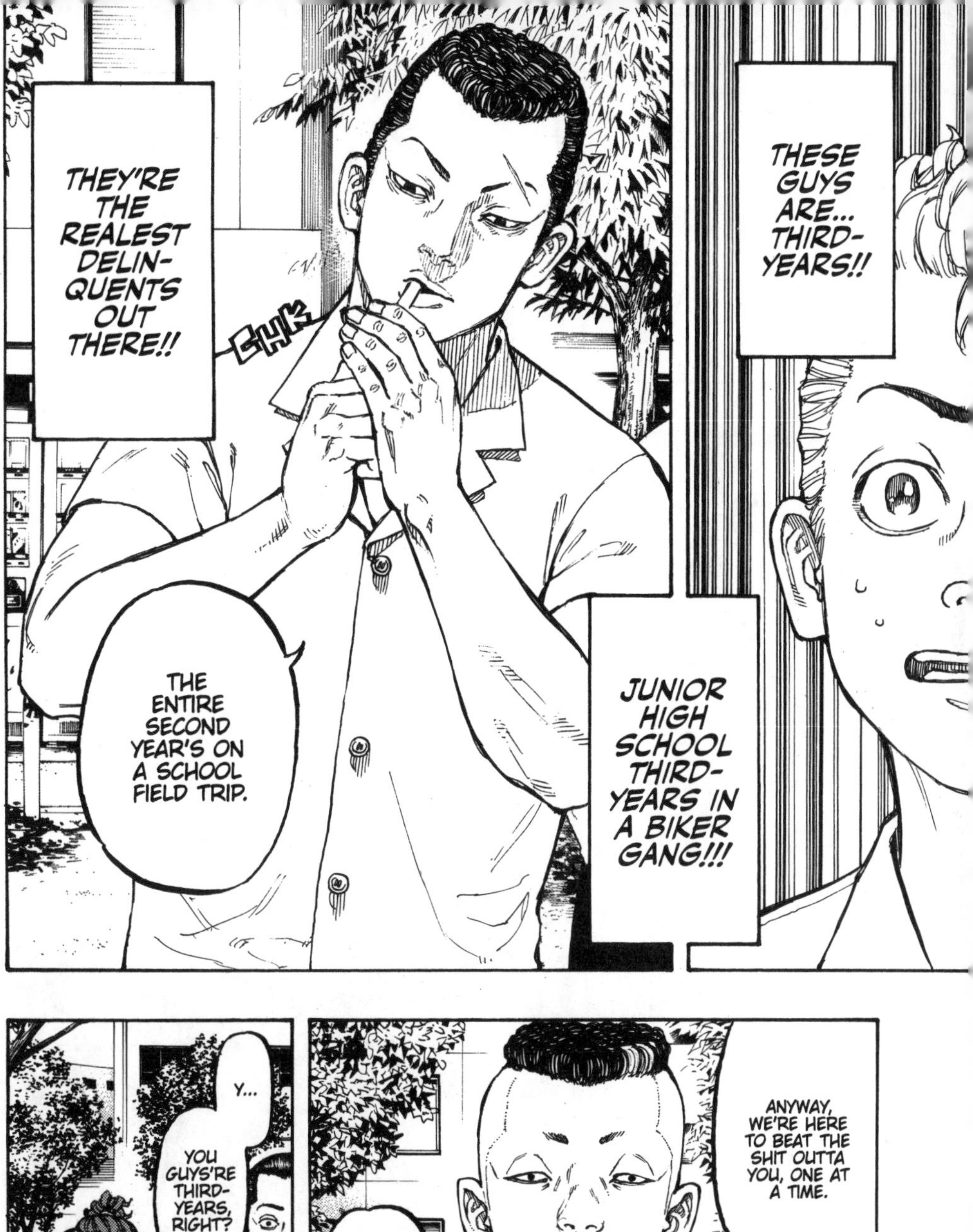
THESE GUYS ARE... THIRD-YEARS!!
JUNIOR HIGH SCHOOL THIRD-YEARS IN A BIKER GANG!!!
THEY'RE THE REALEST DELIN-QUENTS OUT THERE!!
CHK
THE ENTIRE SECOND YEAR'S ON A SCHOOL FIELD TRIP.
ANYWAY, WE'RE HERE TO BEAT THE SHIT OUTTA YOU, ONE AT A TIME.
LINE UP.
Y...
YOU GUYS'RE THIRD-YEARS, RIGHT?

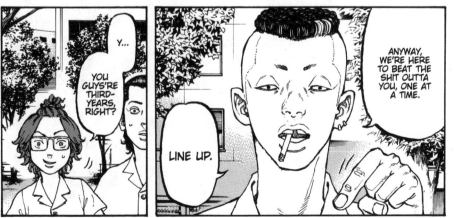

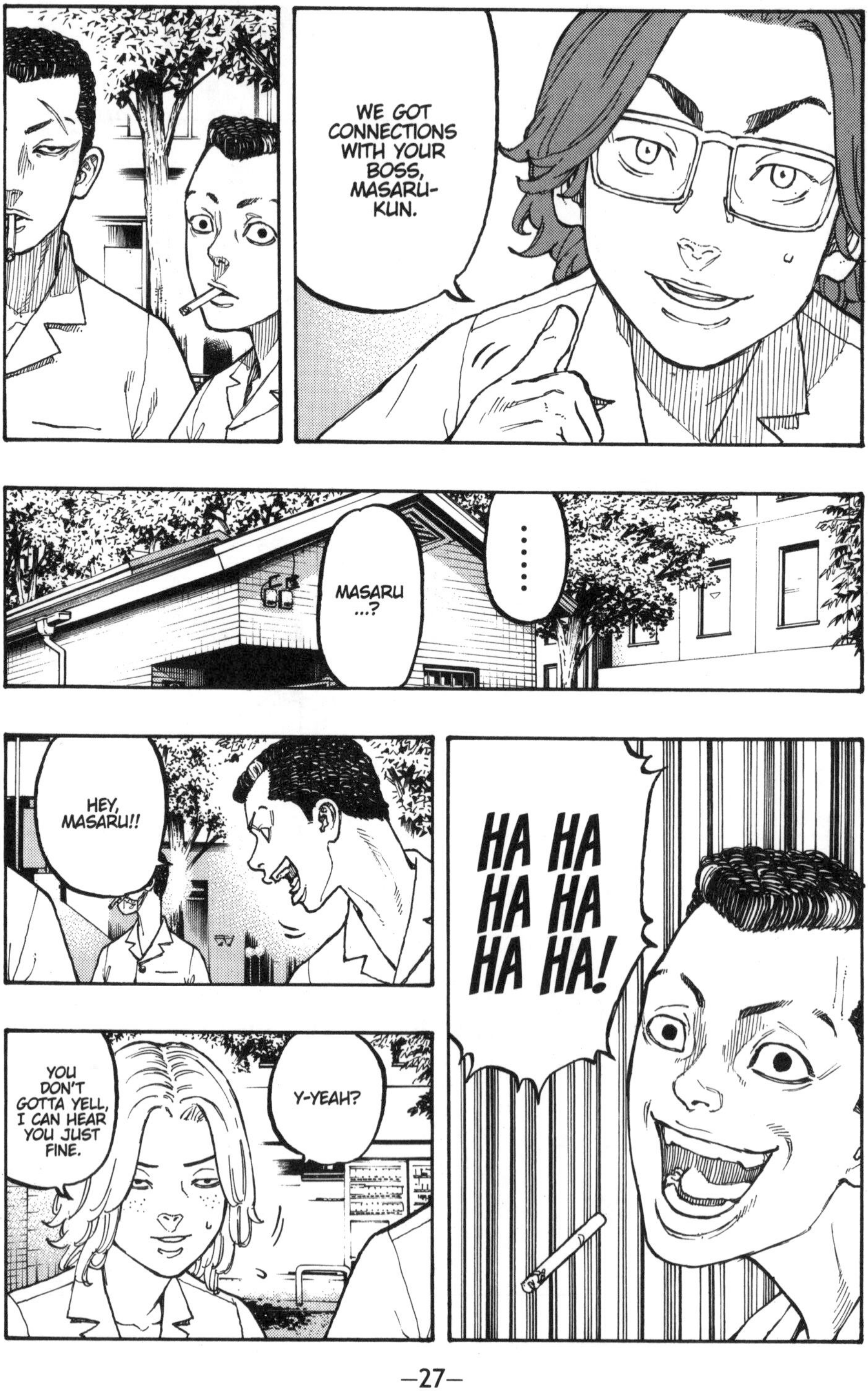
WE GOT CONNECTIONS WITH YOUR BOSS, MASARU-KUN.
......
MASARU ...?
HA HA HA HA HA HA!
HEY, MASARU!!
Y-YEAH?
YOU DON'T GOTTA YELL, I CAN HEAR YOU JUST FINE.

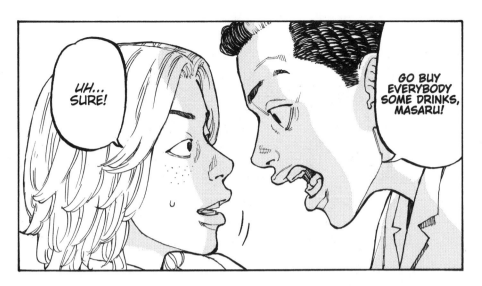

GO BUY EVERYBODY SOME DRINKS, MASARU!
UH... SURE!
GOT SOME MONEY?
HUH?
I'LL GIVE YOU A HUNDRED YEN PER PUNCH! HOW 'BOUT IT?!
HOW'S TEN OF THOSE SOUND?
CLENCH
UH.
I'LL PAY FOR 'EM.
OH YEAH...
HE ACTED LIKE HOT SHIT BECAUSE HE WAS OLDER AND WANTED TO IMPRESS ME.
GLANCE
MASARU-KUN WAS JUST A GOFER TO THEM.

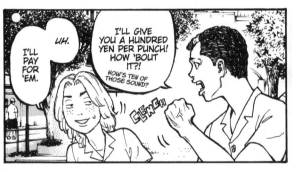

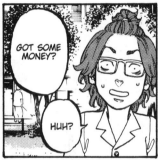

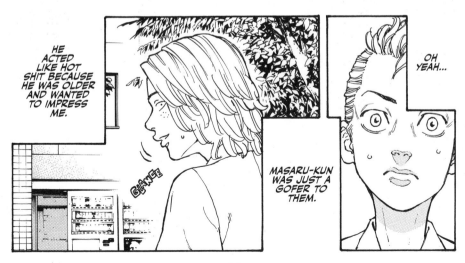

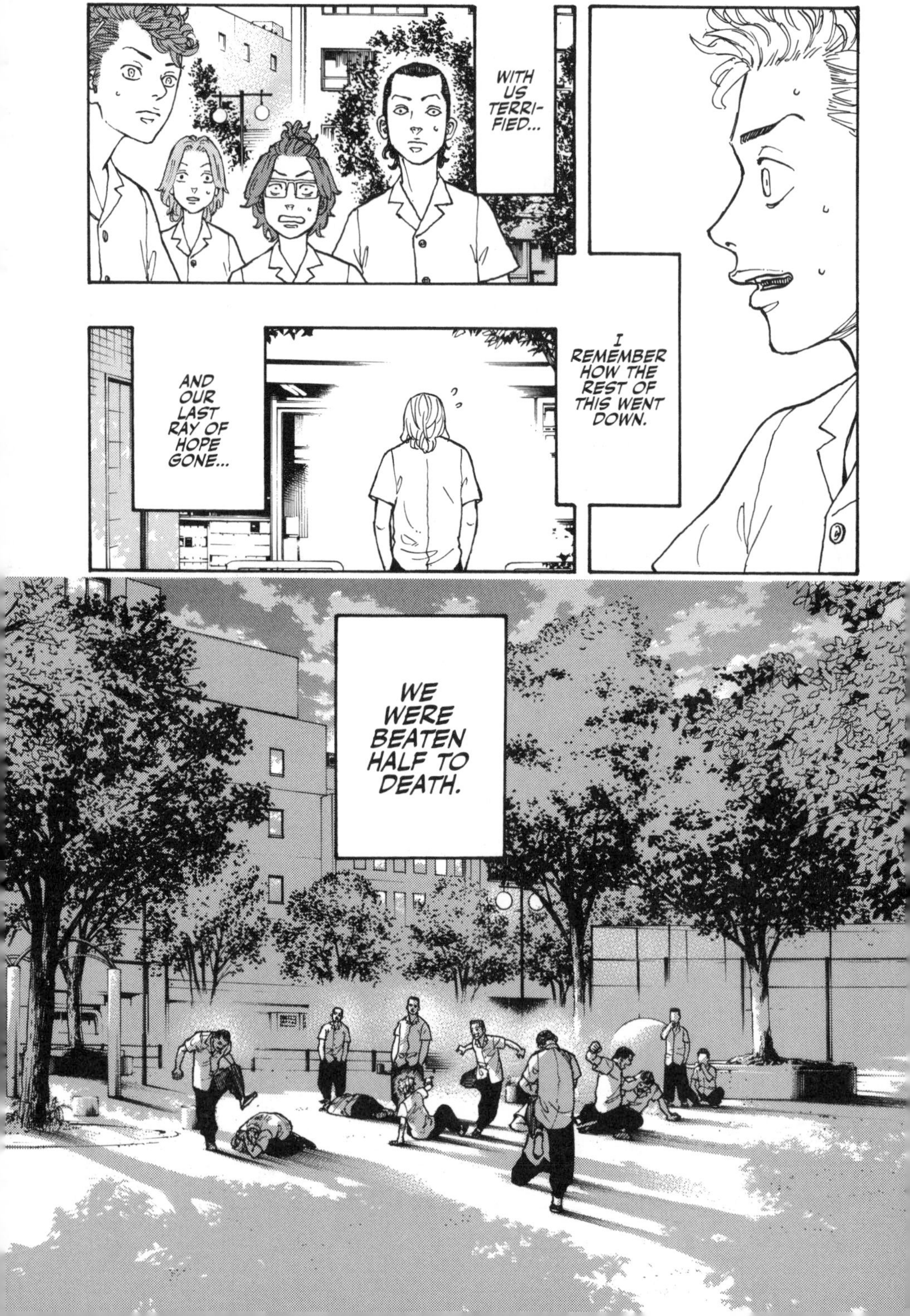
WITH US TERRIFIED...
AND OUR LAST RAY OF HOPE GONE...
I REMEMBER HOW THE REST OF THIS WENT DOWN.
WE WERE BEATEN HALF TO DEATH.

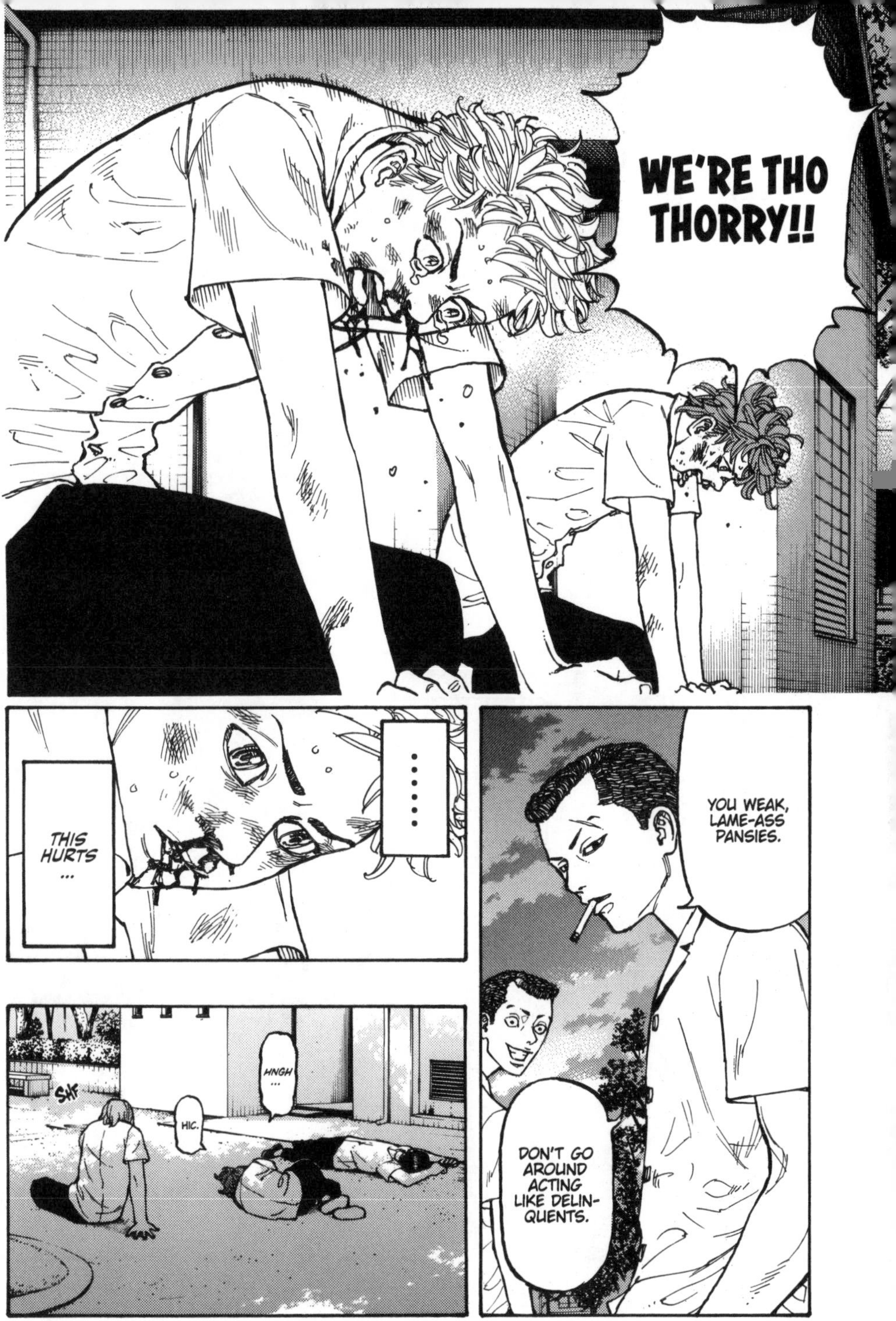
WE'RE THO THORRY!!
YOU WEAK, LAME-ASS PANSIES.
DON'T GO AROUND ACTING LIKE DELINQUENTS.
......
THIS HURTS ...
HNGH ...
HIC.
SHF

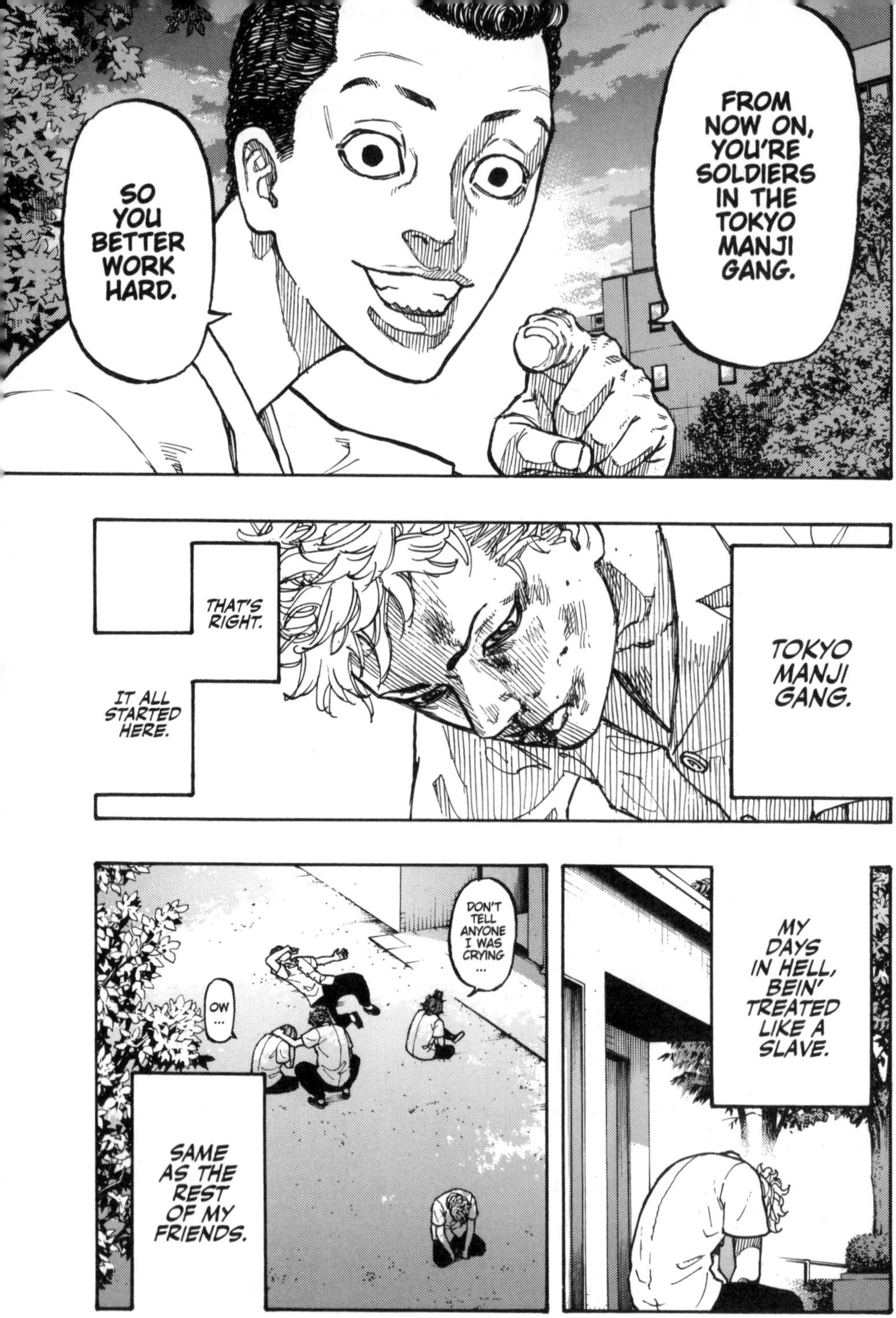
FROM NOW ON, YOU'RE SOLDIERS IN THE TOKYO MANJI GANG.
SO YOU BETTER WORK HARD.
TOKYO MANJI GANG.
THAT'S RIGHT.
IT ALL STARTED HERE.
MY DAYS IN HELL, BEIN' TREATED LIKE A SLAVE.
DON'T TELL ANYONE I WAS CRYING ...
OW ...
SAME AS THE REST OF MY FRIENDS.

Sign: Graduation Ceremony

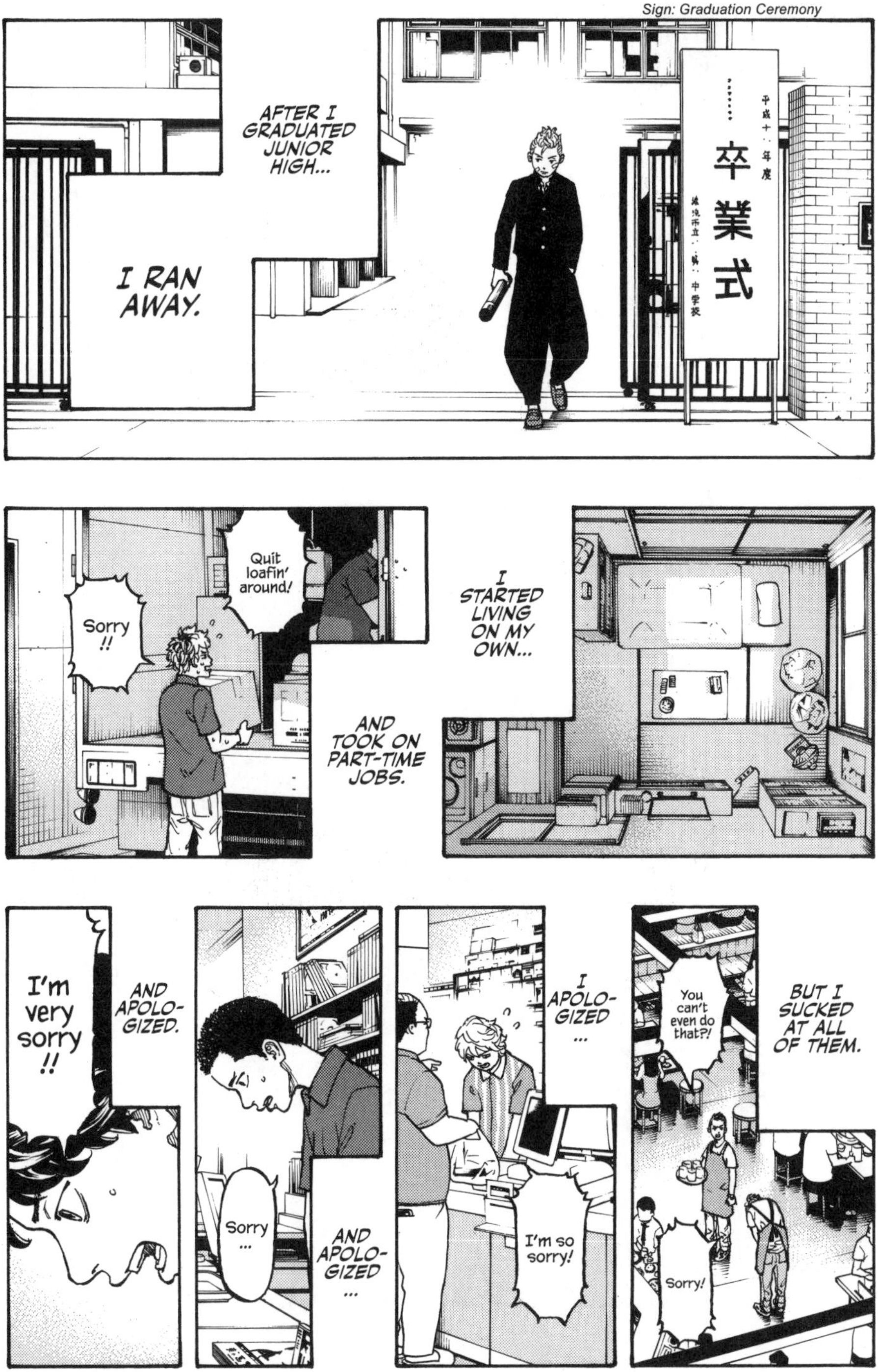
AFTER I GRADUATED JUNIOR HIGH...
I RAN AWAY.
卒業式
I STARTED LIVING ON MY OWN...
AND TOOK ON PART-TIME JOBS.
Quit loafin' around!
Sorry!!
BUT I SUCKED AT ALL OF THEM.
You can't even do that?!
Sorry!
I APOLOGIZED...
I'm so sorry!
AND APOLOGIZED...
Sorry...
AND APOLOGIZED.
I'm very sorry!!

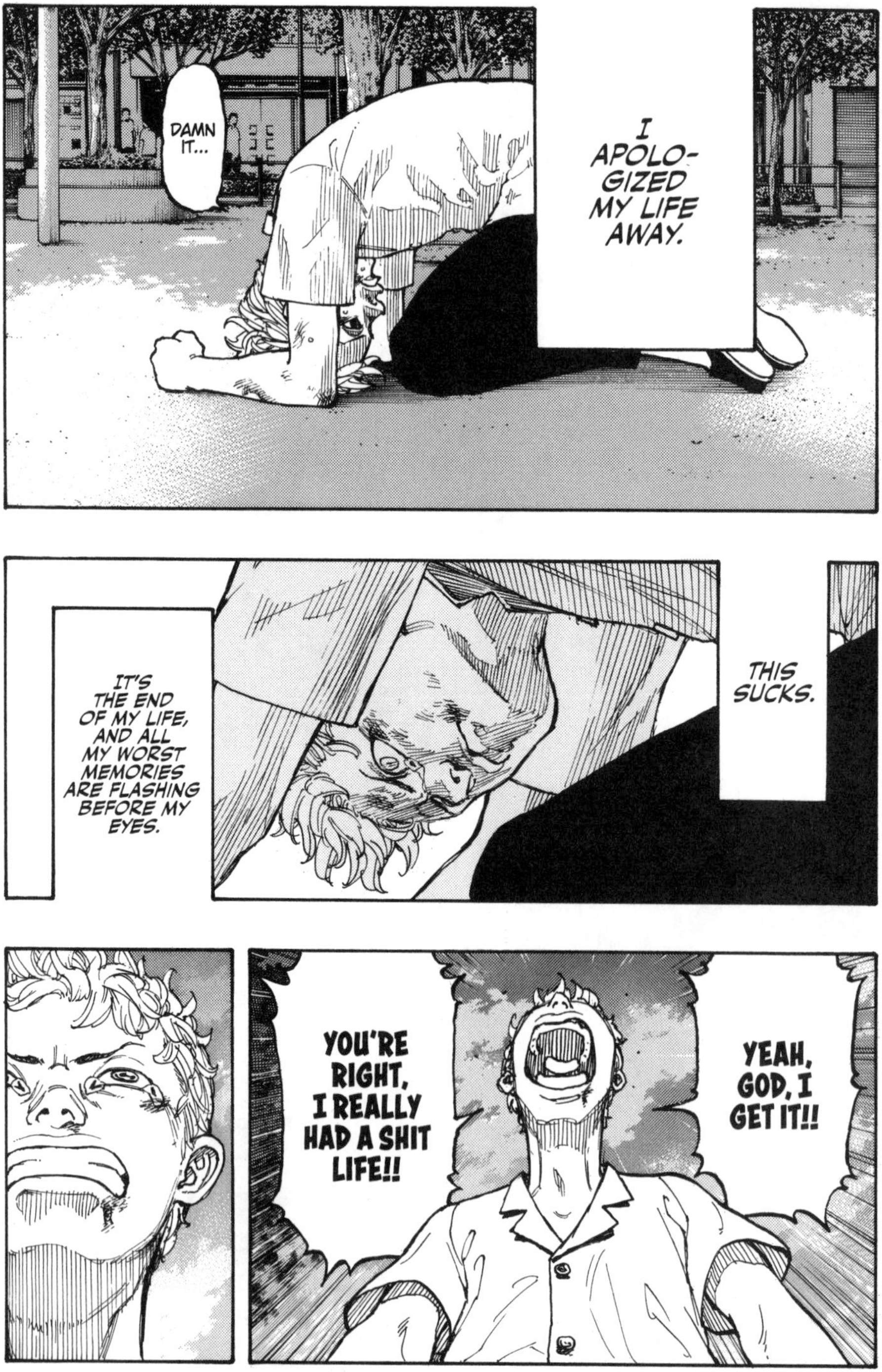
I APOLOGIZED MY LIFE AWAY.
DAMN IT...
THIS SUCKS.
IT'S THE END OF MY LIFE, AND ALL MY WORST MEMORIES ARE FLASHING BEFORE MY EYES.
YEAH, GOD, I GET IT!!
YOU'RE RIGHT, I REALLY HAD A SHIT LIFE!!

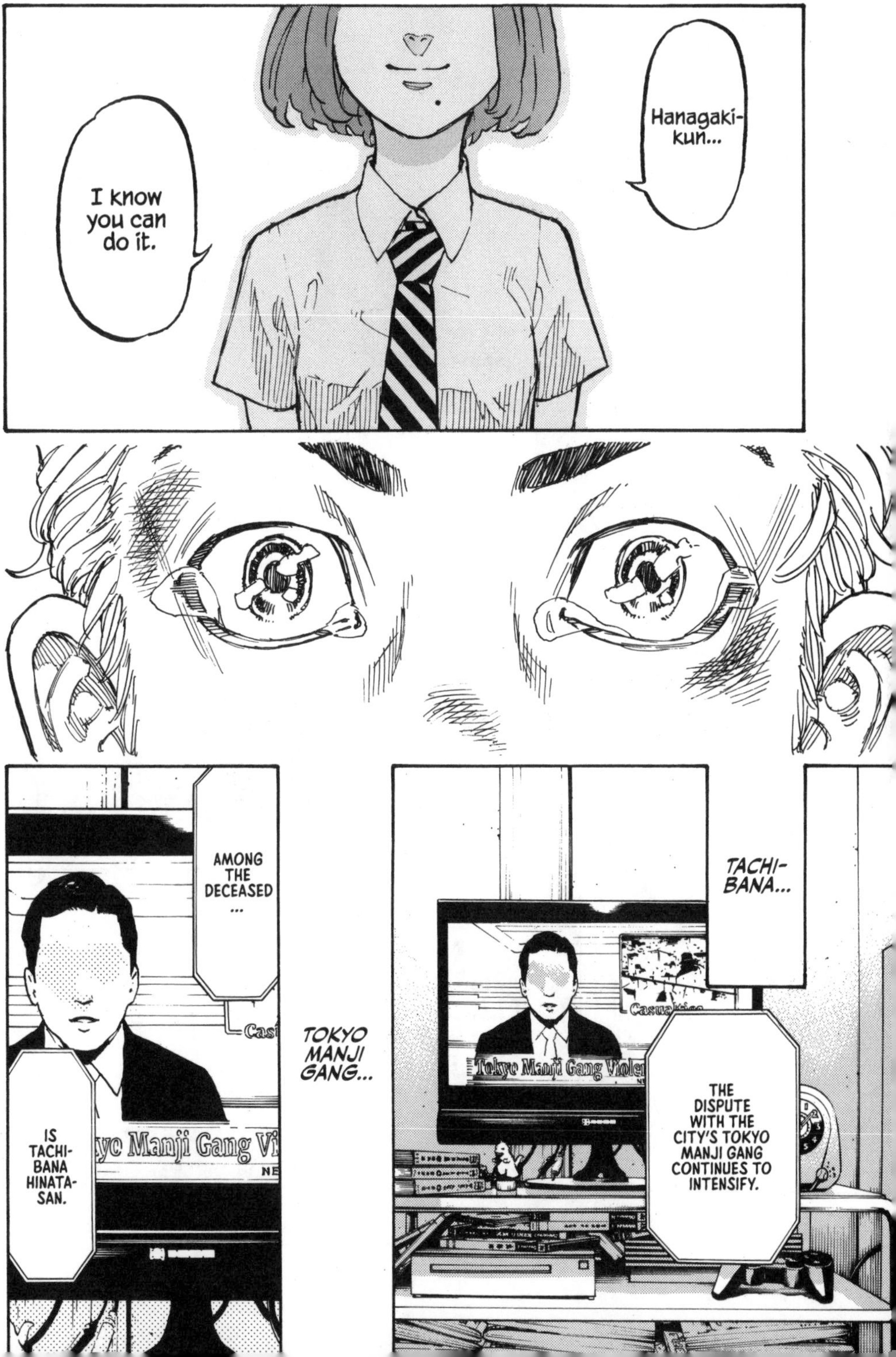
Hanagaki-kun...
I know you can do it.
TACHI-BANA...
THE DISPUTE WITH THE CITY'S TOKYO MANJI GANG CONTINUES TO INTENSIFY.
TOKYO MANJI GANG...
AMONG THE DECEASED...
IS TACHI-BANA HINATA-SAN.

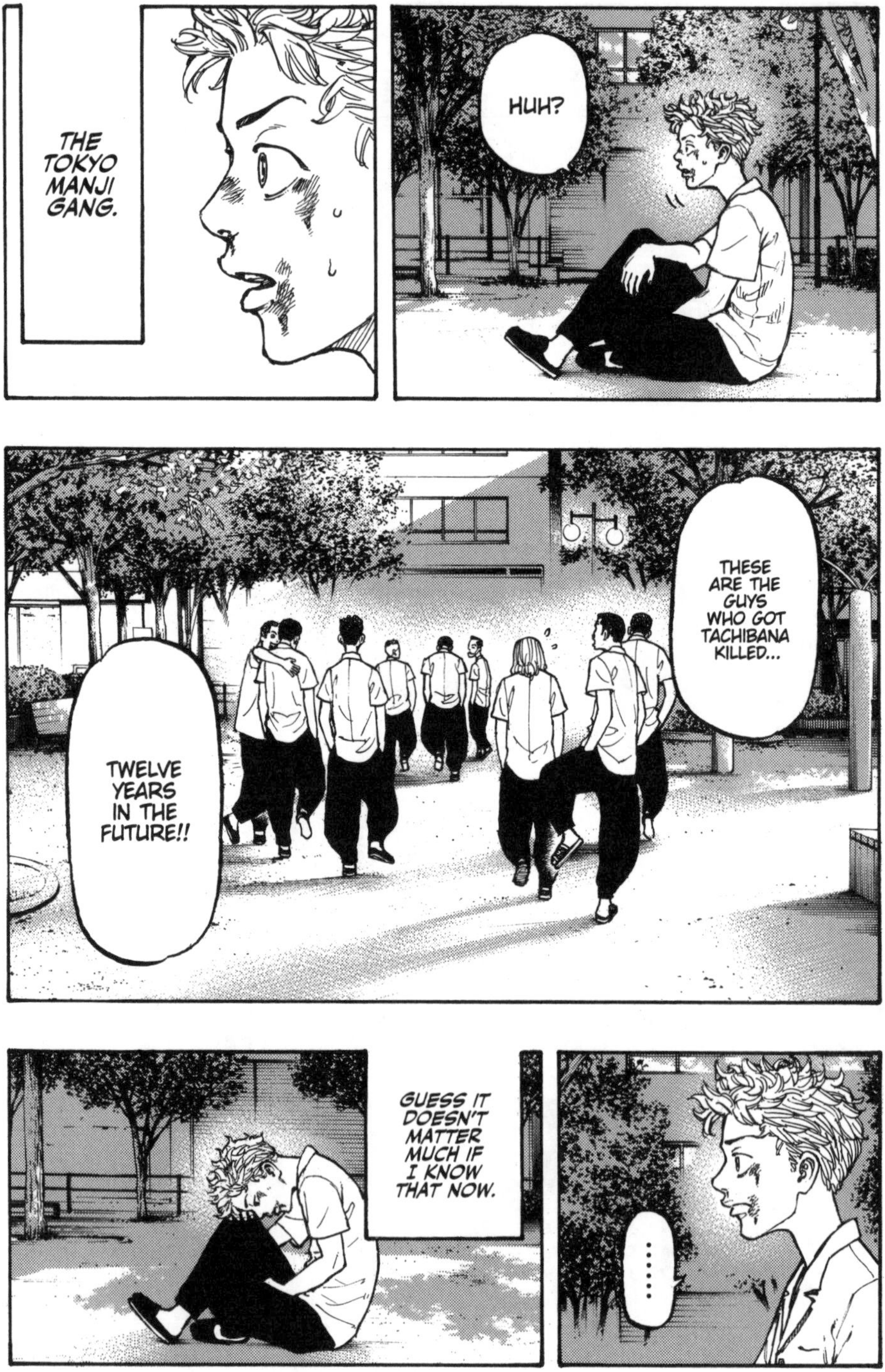
HUH?
THE TOKYO MANJI GANG.
THESE ARE THE GUYS WHO GOT TACHIBANA KILLED...
TWELVE YEARS IN THE FUTURE!!
......
GUESS IT DOESN'T MATTER MUCH IF I KNOW THAT NOW.

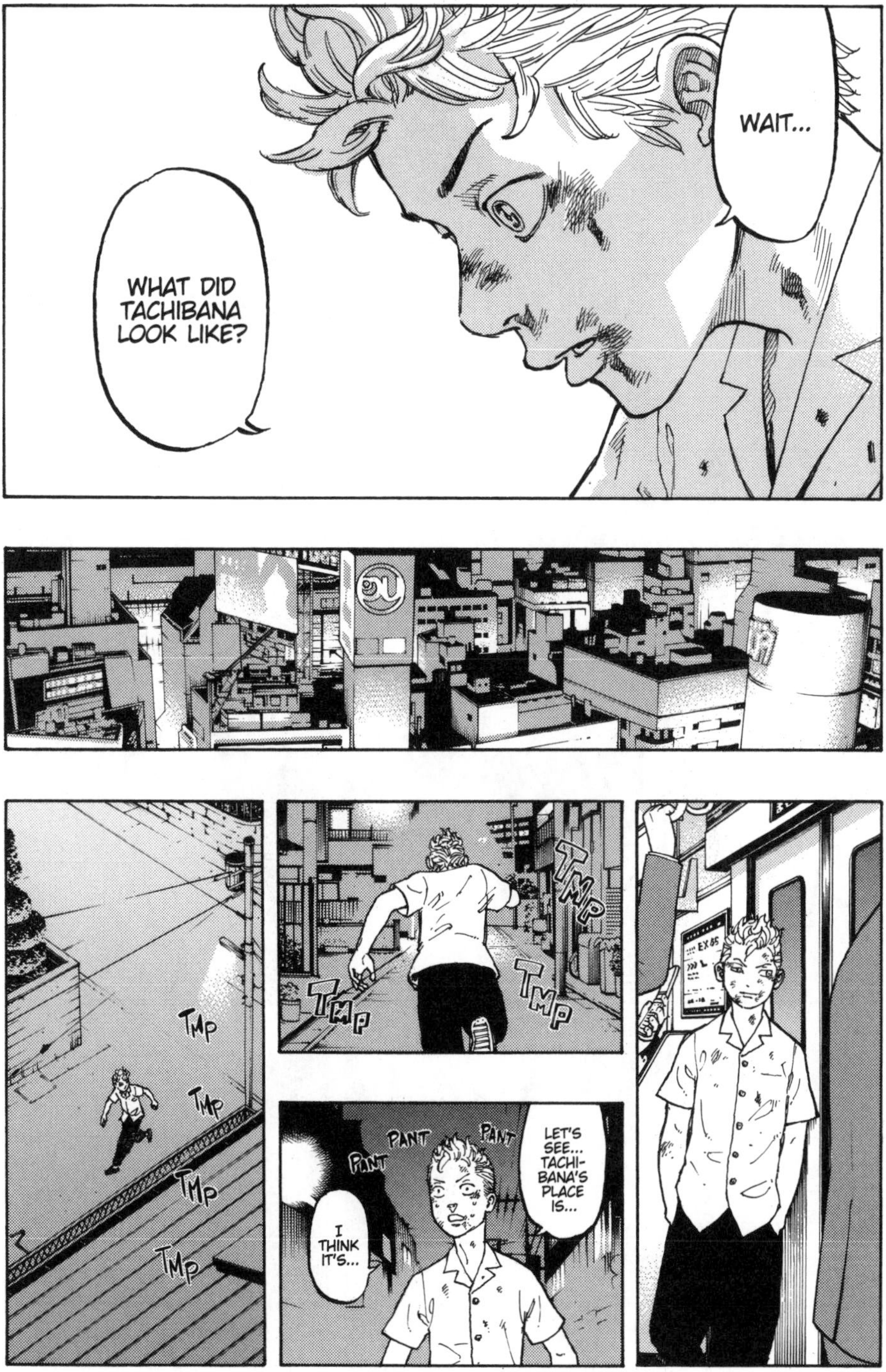
WAIT...
WHAT DID TACHIBANA LOOK LIKE?
TMP
TMP
TMP
PANT
PANT
PANT
LET'S SEE... TACHI-BANA'S PLACE IS...
I THINK IT'S...
TMP
TMP
TMP
TMP

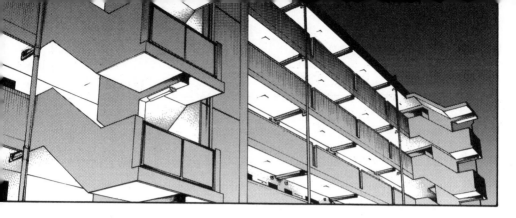

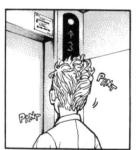

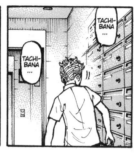

TACHI-
BANA
...

TACHI-
BANA
...

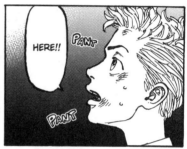

HERE!!

PANT

PANT

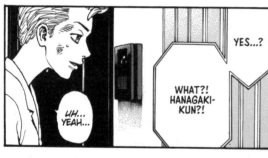

UH...
YEAH...

YES...?

WHAT?!
HANAGAKI-
KUN?!

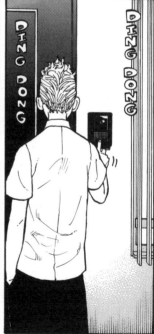

DING DONG

DING DONG

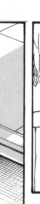

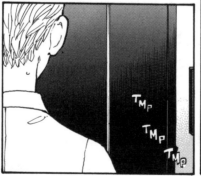

TMP

TMP

TMP

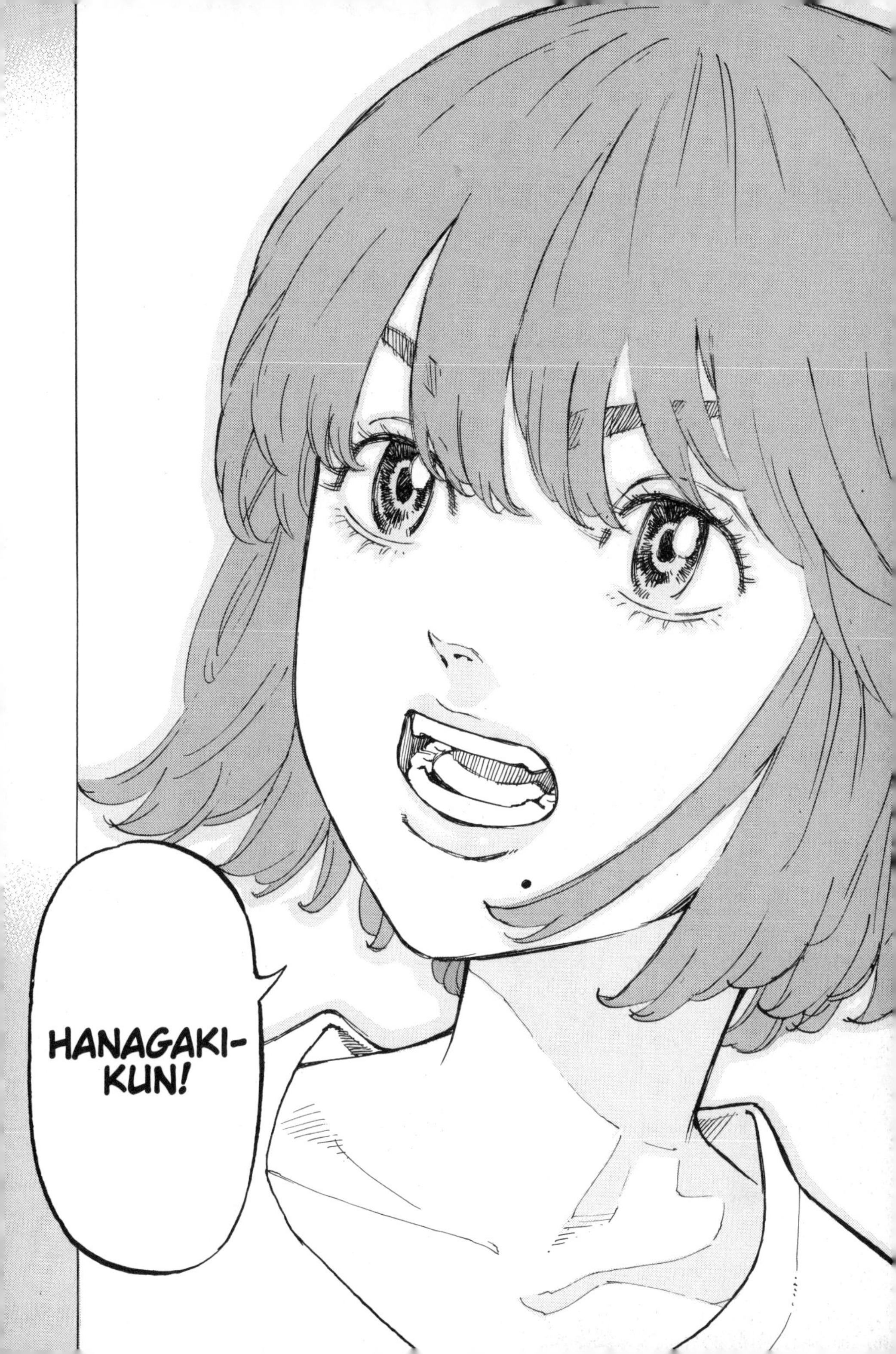
HANAGAKI-KUN!

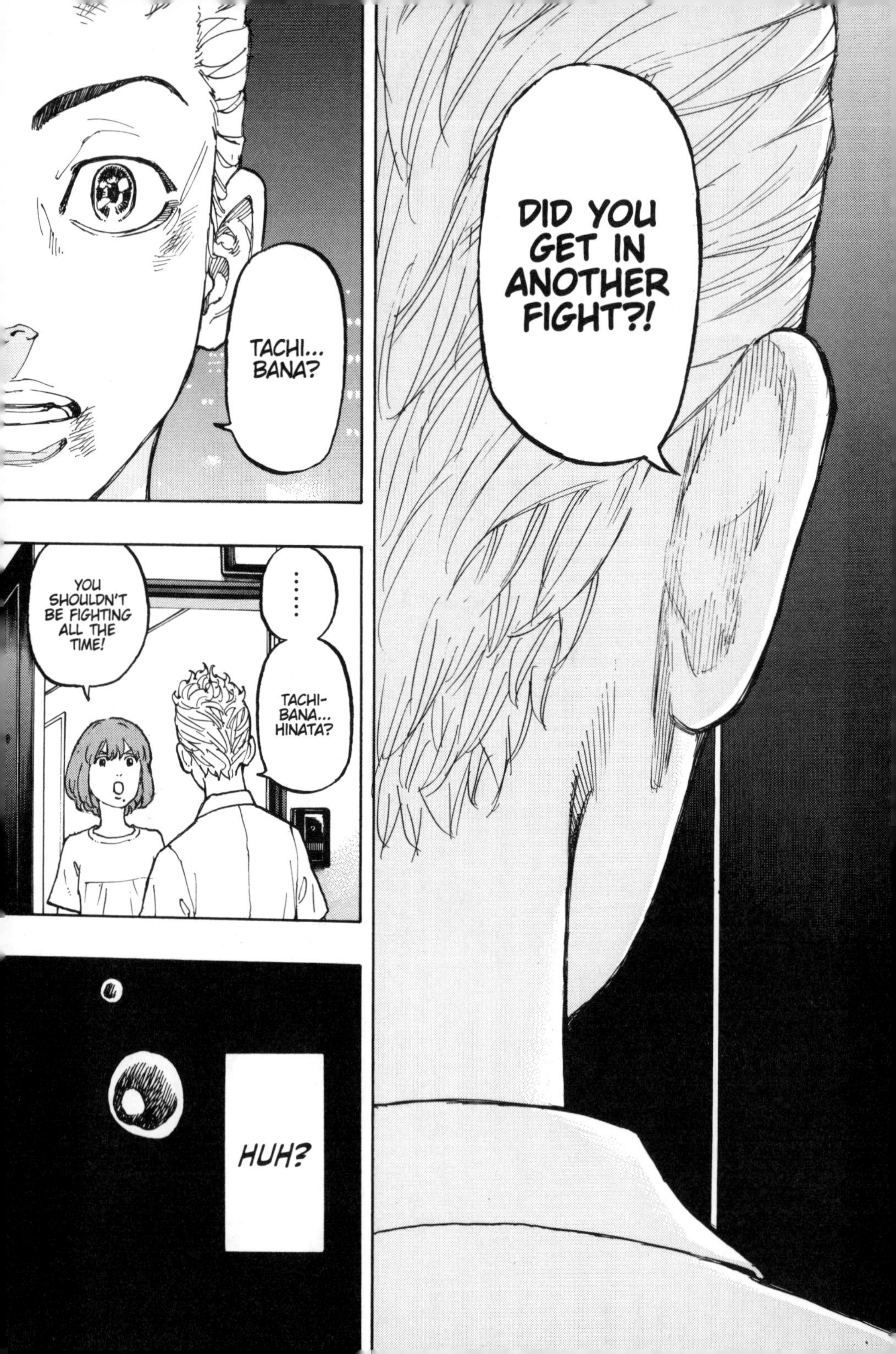
DID YOU GET IN ANOTHER FIGHT?!
TACHI... BANA?
......
TACHI-BANA... HINATA?
YOU SHOULDN'T BE FIGHTING ALL THE TIME!
HUH?

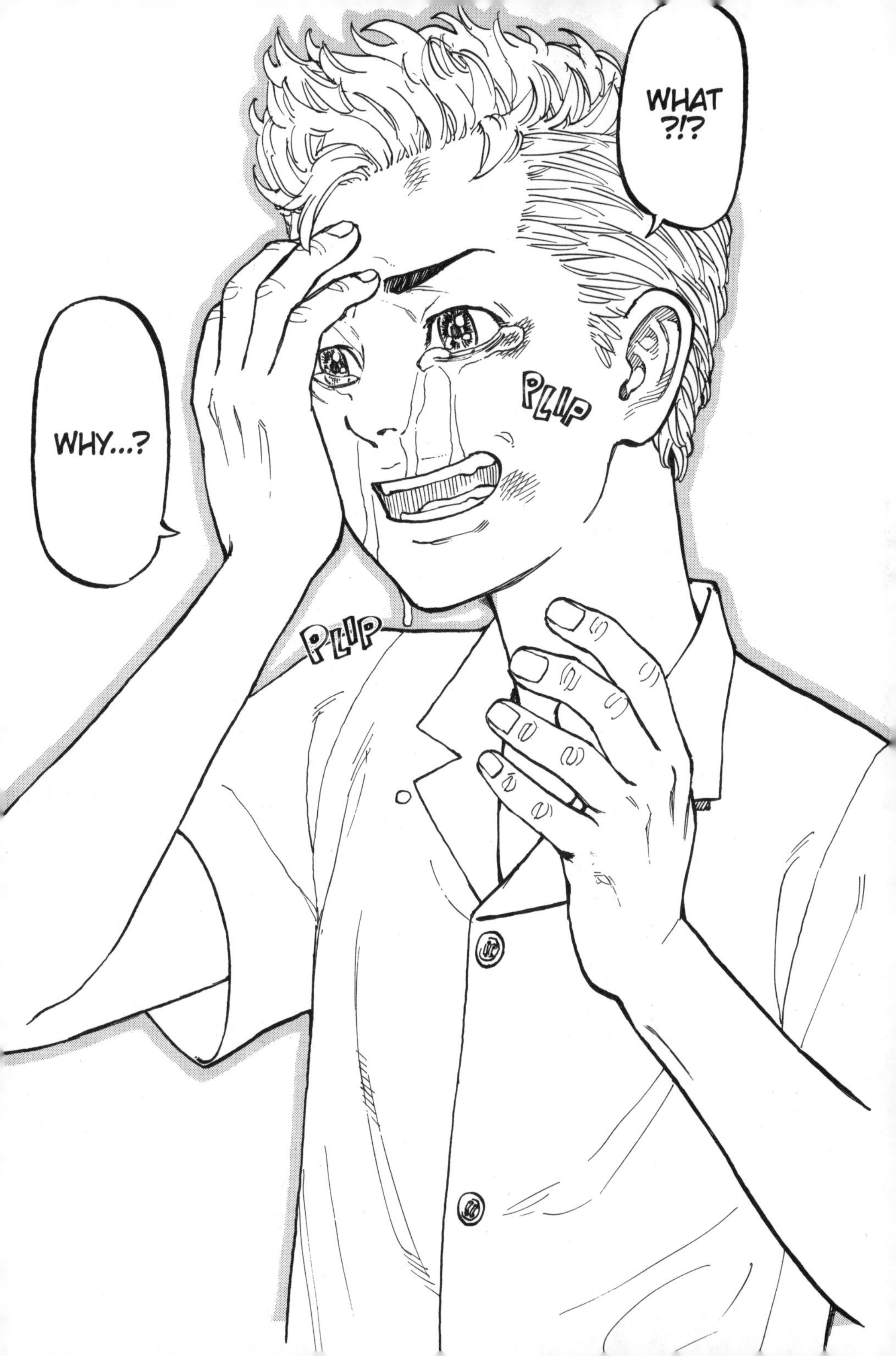
WHAT
?!?
PLIP
PLIP
WHY...?

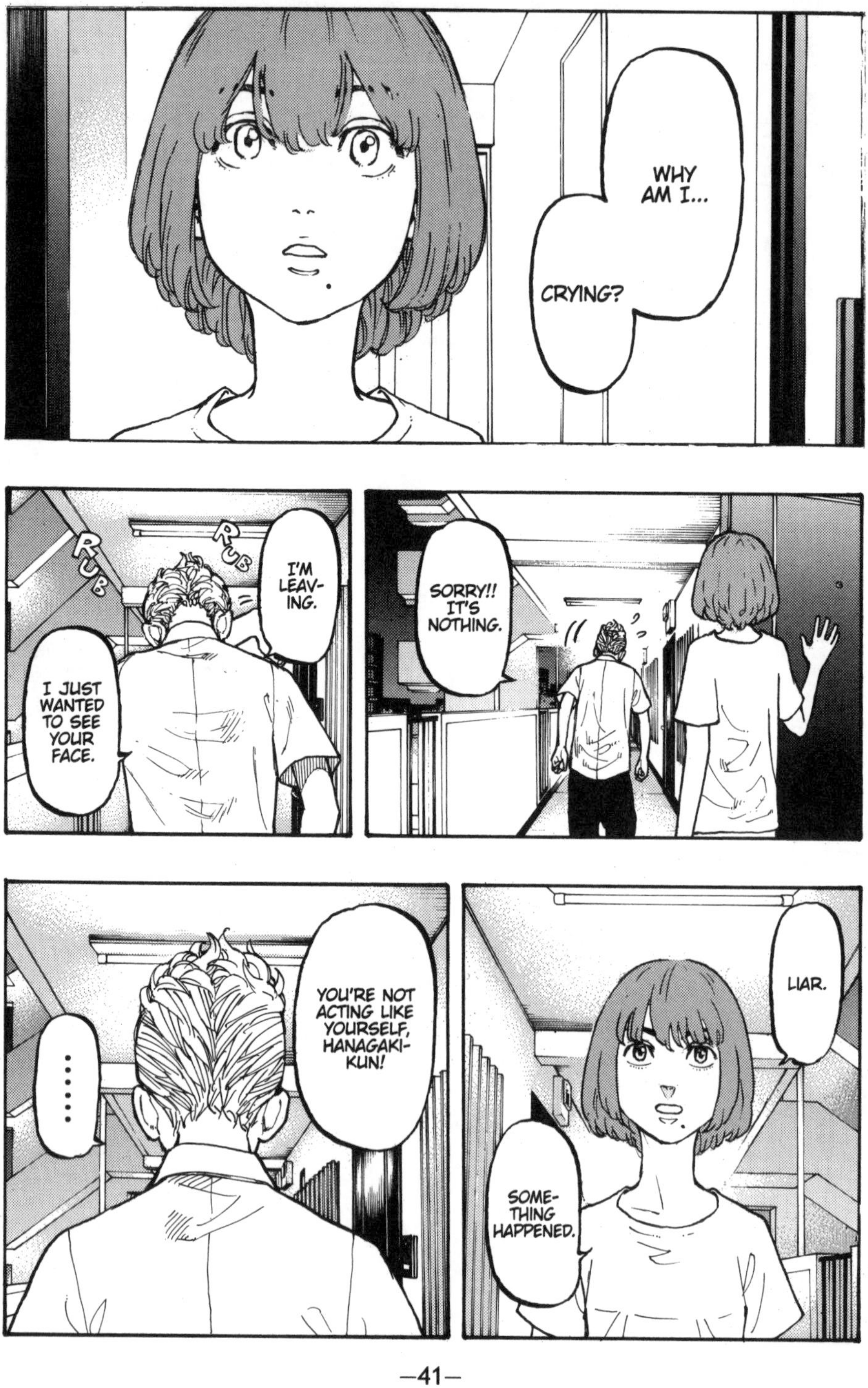
WHY AM I...
CRYING?
SORRY!! IT'S NOTHING.
I'M LEAV-ING.
RUB
RUB
I JUST WANTED TO SEE YOUR FACE.
LIAR.
SOME-THING HAPPENED.
YOU'RE NOT ACTING LIKE YOURSELF, HANAGAKI-KUN!
......

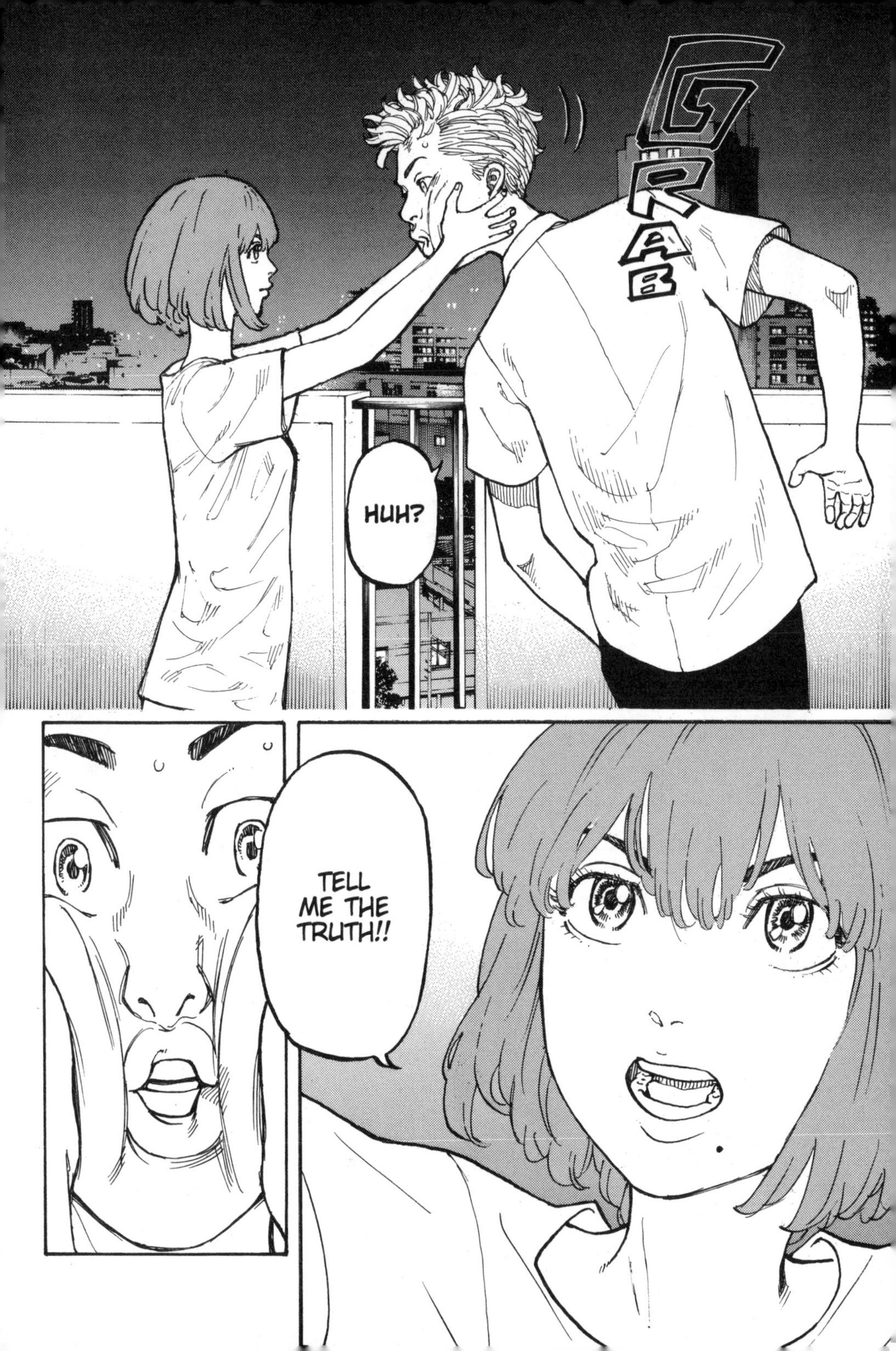
GRAB
HUH?
TELL ME THE TRUTH!!

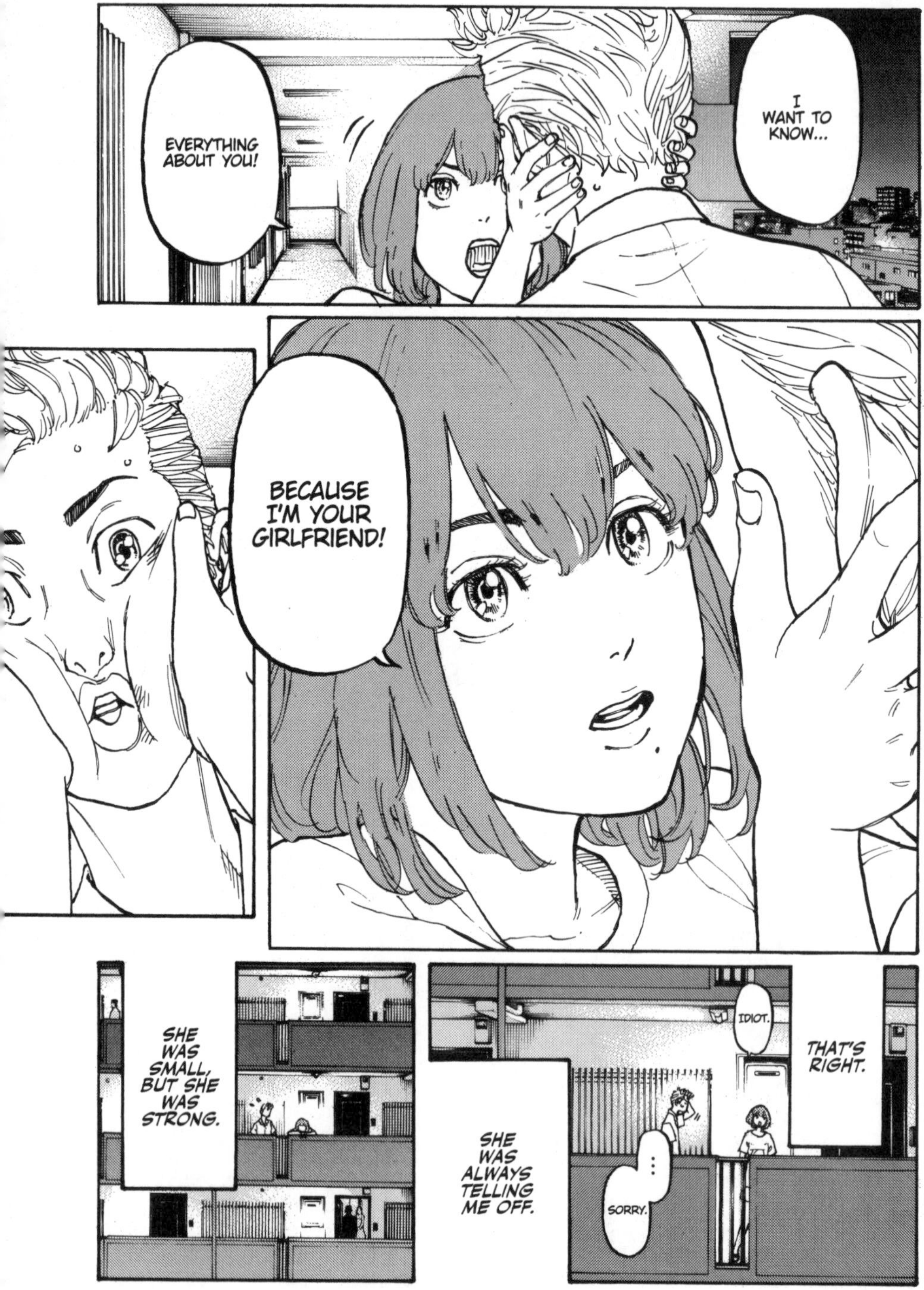
I WANT TO KNOW...
EVERYTHING ABOUT YOU!
BECAUSE I'M YOUR GIRLFRIEND!
THAT'S RIGHT.
IDIOT.
SHE WAS ALWAYS TELLING ME OFF.
...
SORRY.
SHE WAS SMALL, BUT SHE WAS STRONG.

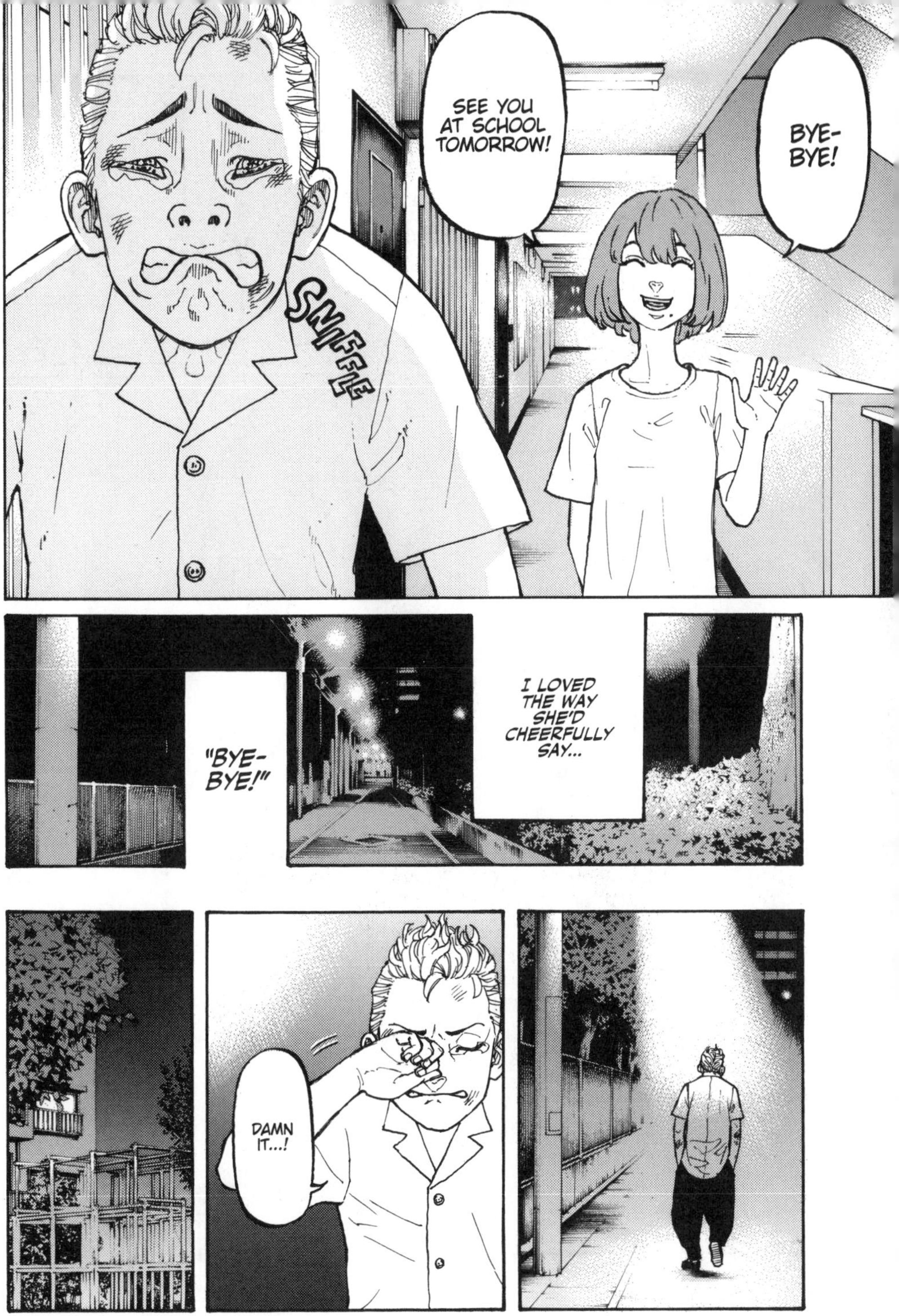
BYE-BYE!
SEE YOU AT SCHOOL TOMORROW!
SNIFFLE
I LOVED THE WAY SHE'D CHEERFULLY SAY...
"BYE-BYE!"
DAMN IT...!

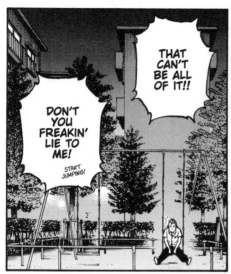

CREAK
CREAK
THAT CAN'T BE ALL OF IT!!
DON'T YOU FREAKIN' LIE TO ME!
START JUMPING!
YOU STILL GOT SOME IN YOUR POCKET!
HOP
HOP
JINGLE
COUGH IT ALL UP!
RIGHT NOW!
SHUT UP, ALREADY.
TRYIN' TO BASK IN MY MISERY OVER HERE.
QUIT DICKIN' AROUND!
HEY.
WHAT?

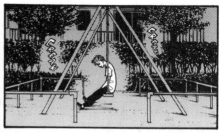

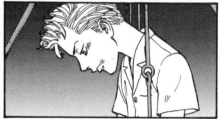

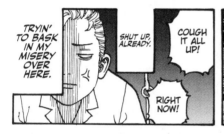

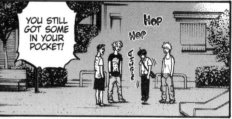

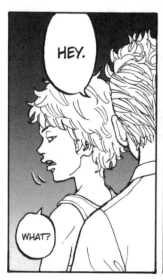

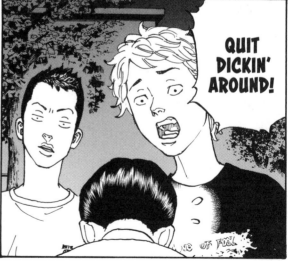

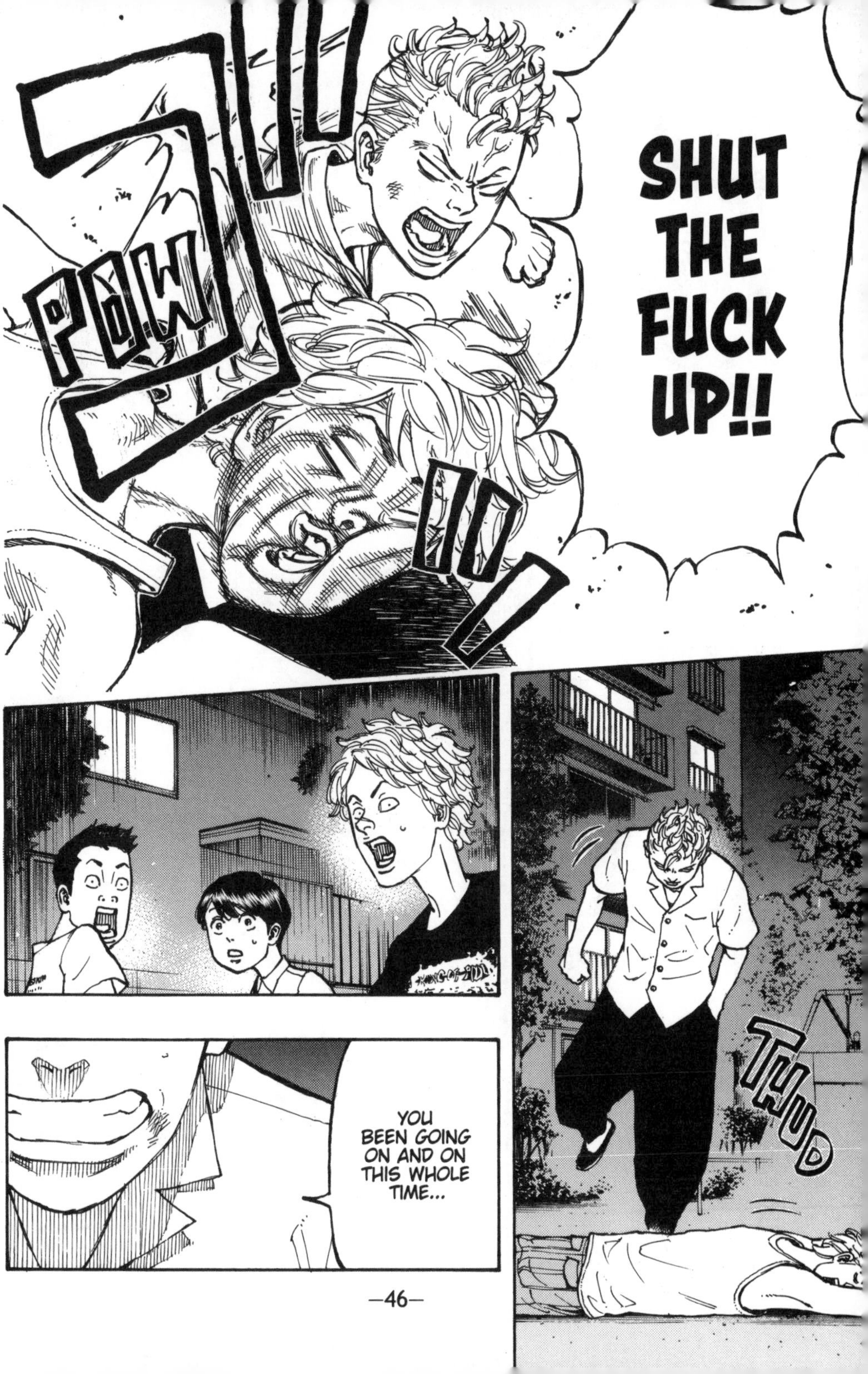
SHUT THE FUCK UP!!
POW
THUD
YOU BEEN GOING ON AND ON THIS WHOLE TIME...

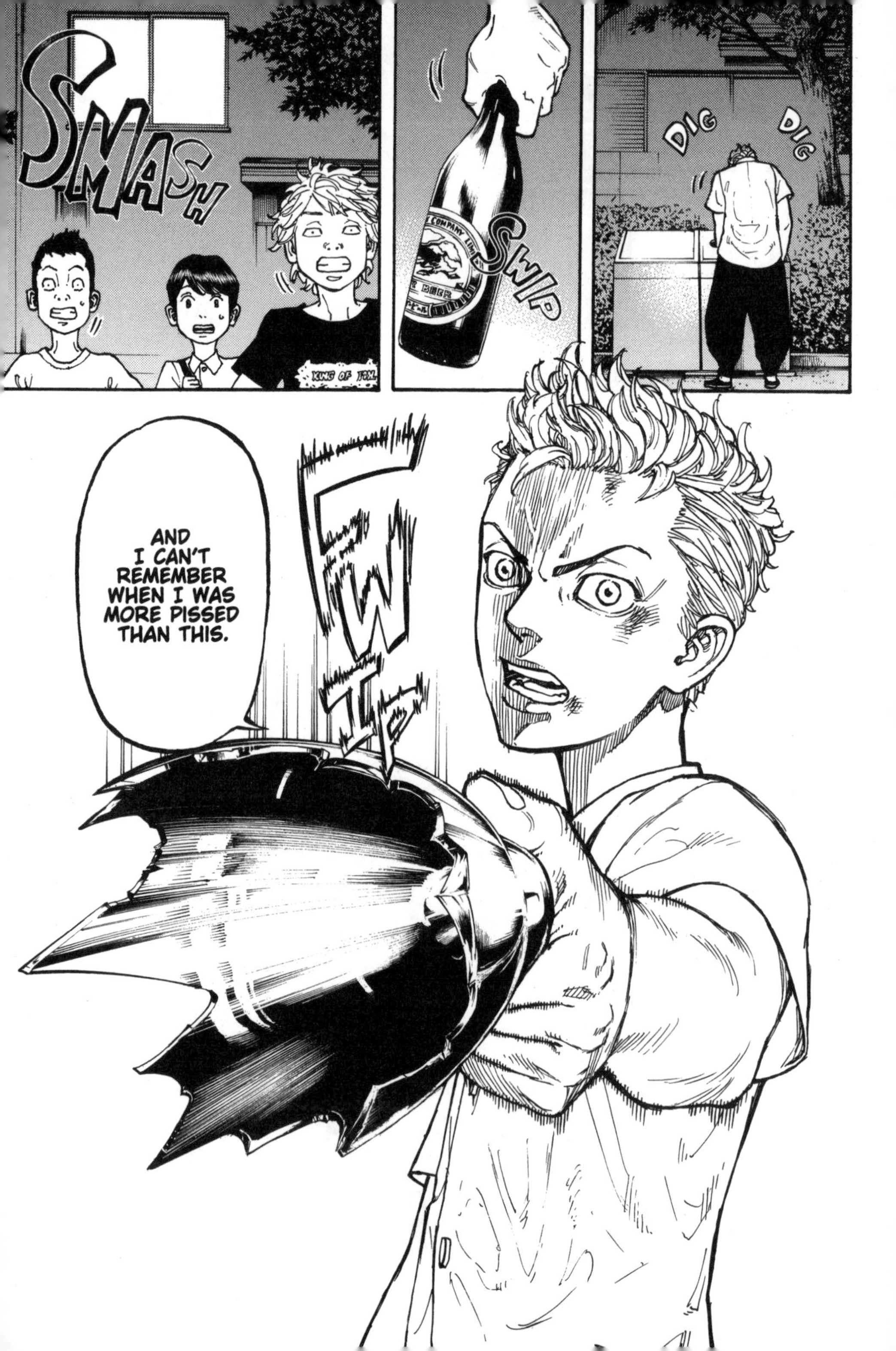
DIG DIG
SWIP
SMASH
FWIP
AND I CAN'T REMEMBER WHEN I WAS MORE PISSED THAN THIS.

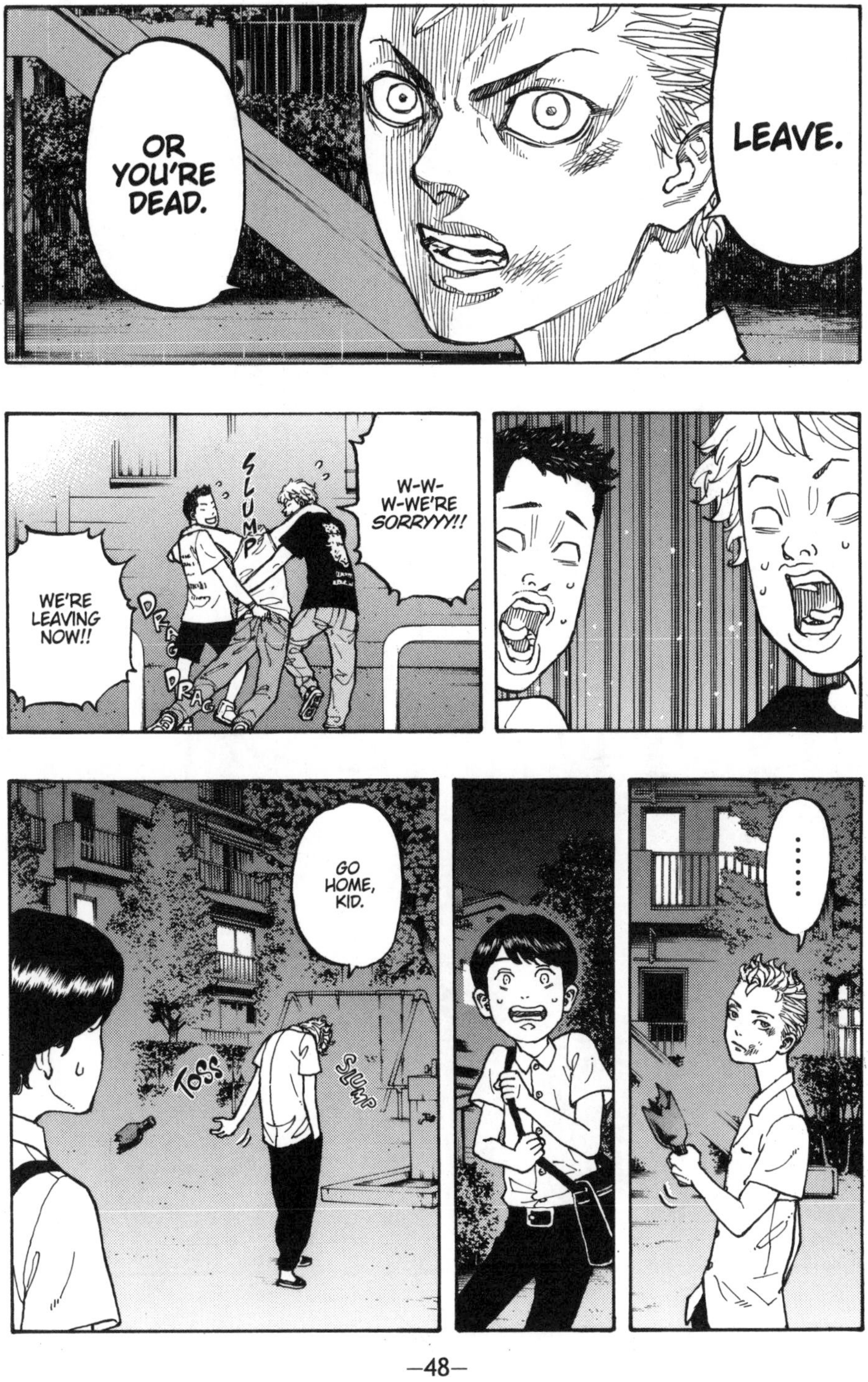
LEAVE.
OR YOU'RE DEAD.
W-W-W-WE'RE SORRYYY!!
SLUMP
WE'RE LEAVING NOW!!
DRAG
DRAG
......
GO HOME, KID.
SLUMP
TOSS

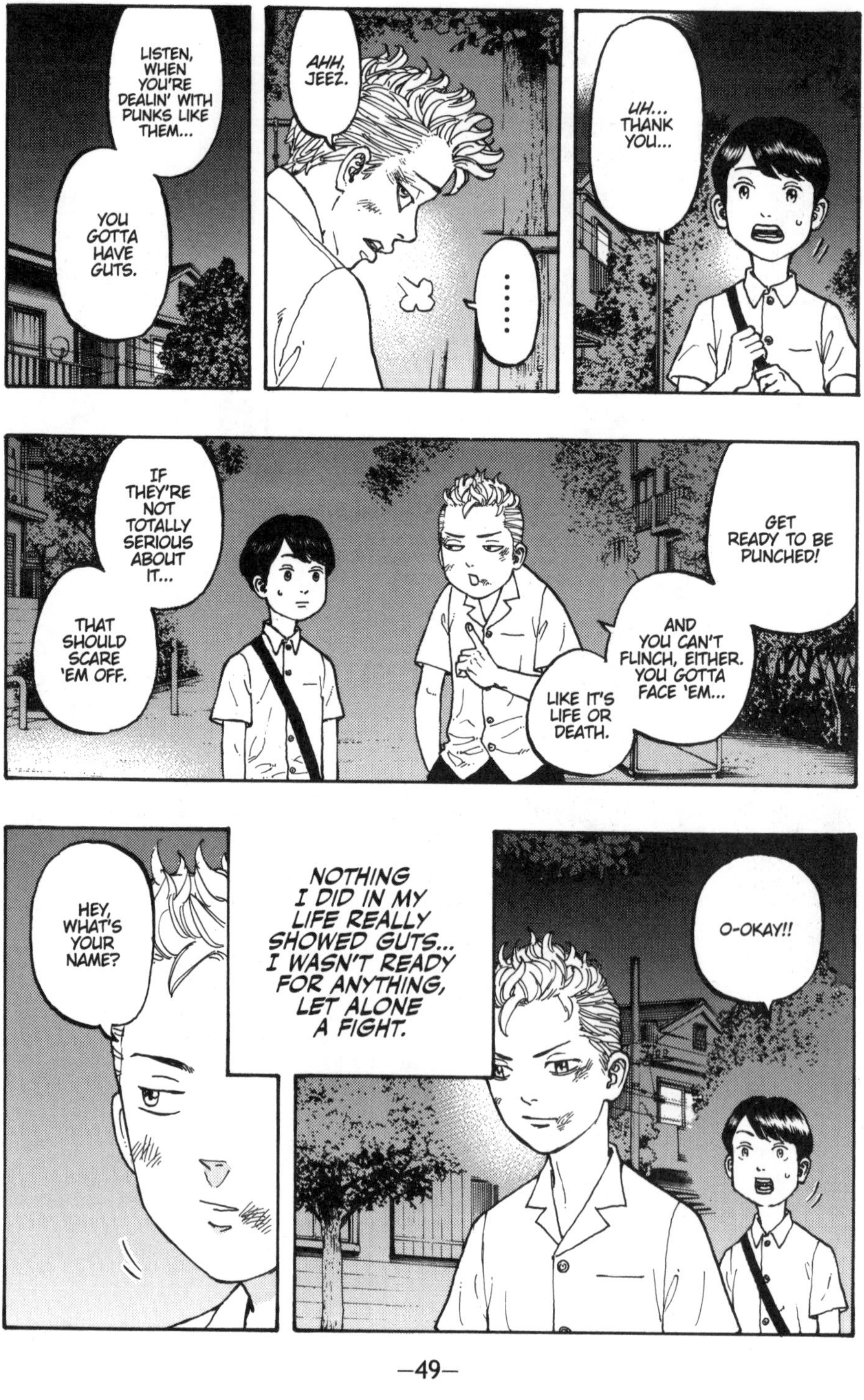
UH... THANK YOU...
AHH, JEEZ.
......
LISTEN, WHEN YOU'RE DEALIN' WITH PUNKS LIKE THEM...
YOU GOTTA HAVE GUTS.
GET READY TO BE PUNCHED!
AND YOU CAN'T FLINCH, EITHER. YOU GOTTA FACE 'EM...
LIKE IT'S LIFE OR DEATH.
IF THEY'RE NOT TOTALLY SERIOUS ABOUT IT...
THAT SHOULD SCARE 'EM OFF.
O-OKAY!!
NOTHING I DID IN MY LIFE REALLY SHOWED GUTS... I WASN'T READY FOR ANYTHING, LET ALONE A FIGHT.
HEY, WHAT'S YOUR NAME?

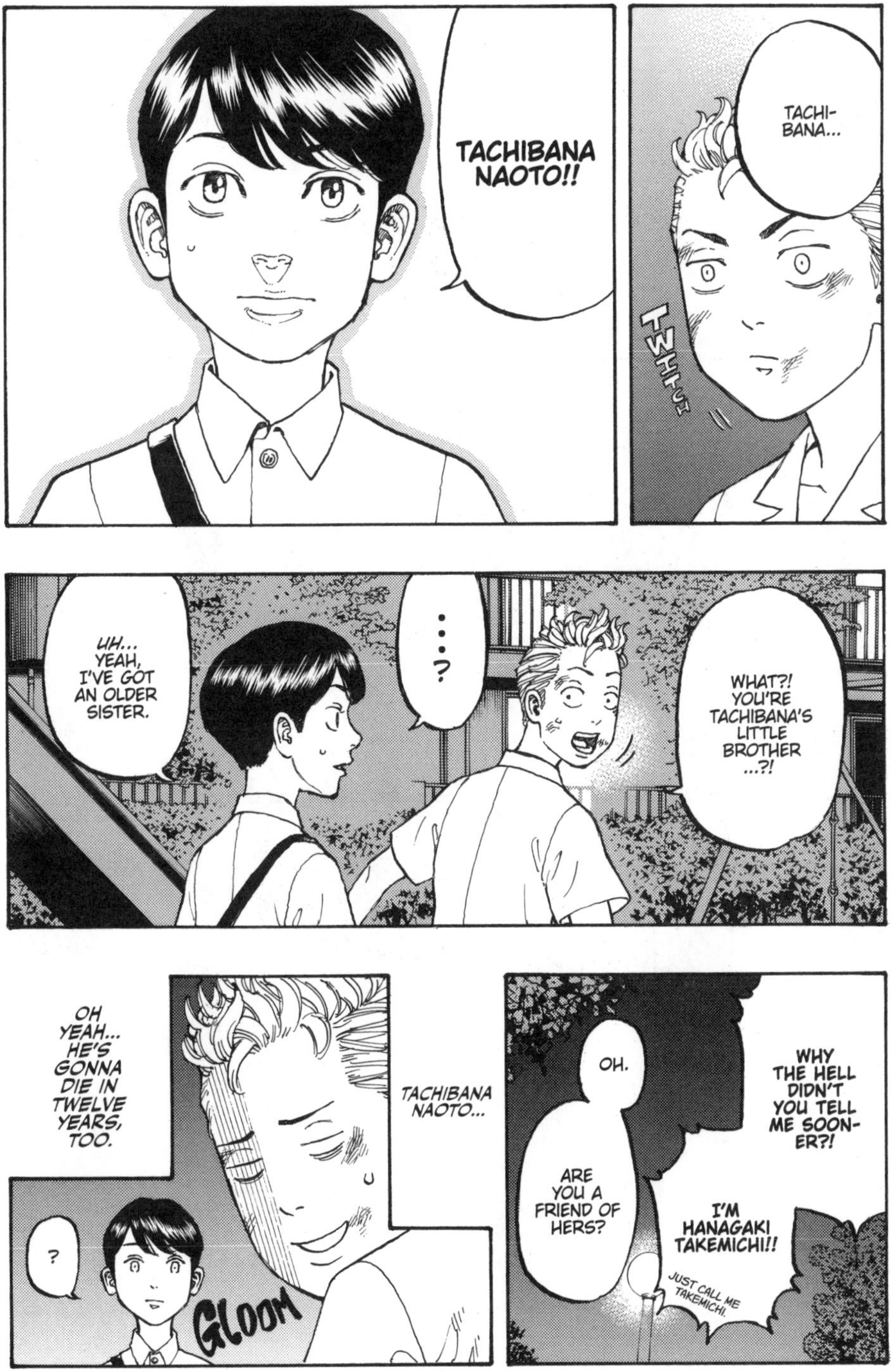
TACHI-BANA...
TWITCH
TACHIBANA NAOTO!!
WHAT?! YOU'RE TACHIBANA'S LITTLE BROTHER ...?!
...?
UH... YEAH, I'VE GOT AN OLDER SISTER.
WHY THE HELL DIDN'T YOU TELL ME SOON-ER?!
I'M HANAGAKI TAKEMICHI!!
JUST CALL ME TAKEMICHI.
OH.
ARE YOU A FRIEND OF HERS?
TACHIBANA NAOTO...
OH YEAH... HE'S GONNA DIE IN TWELVE YEARS, TOO.
?
GLOOM

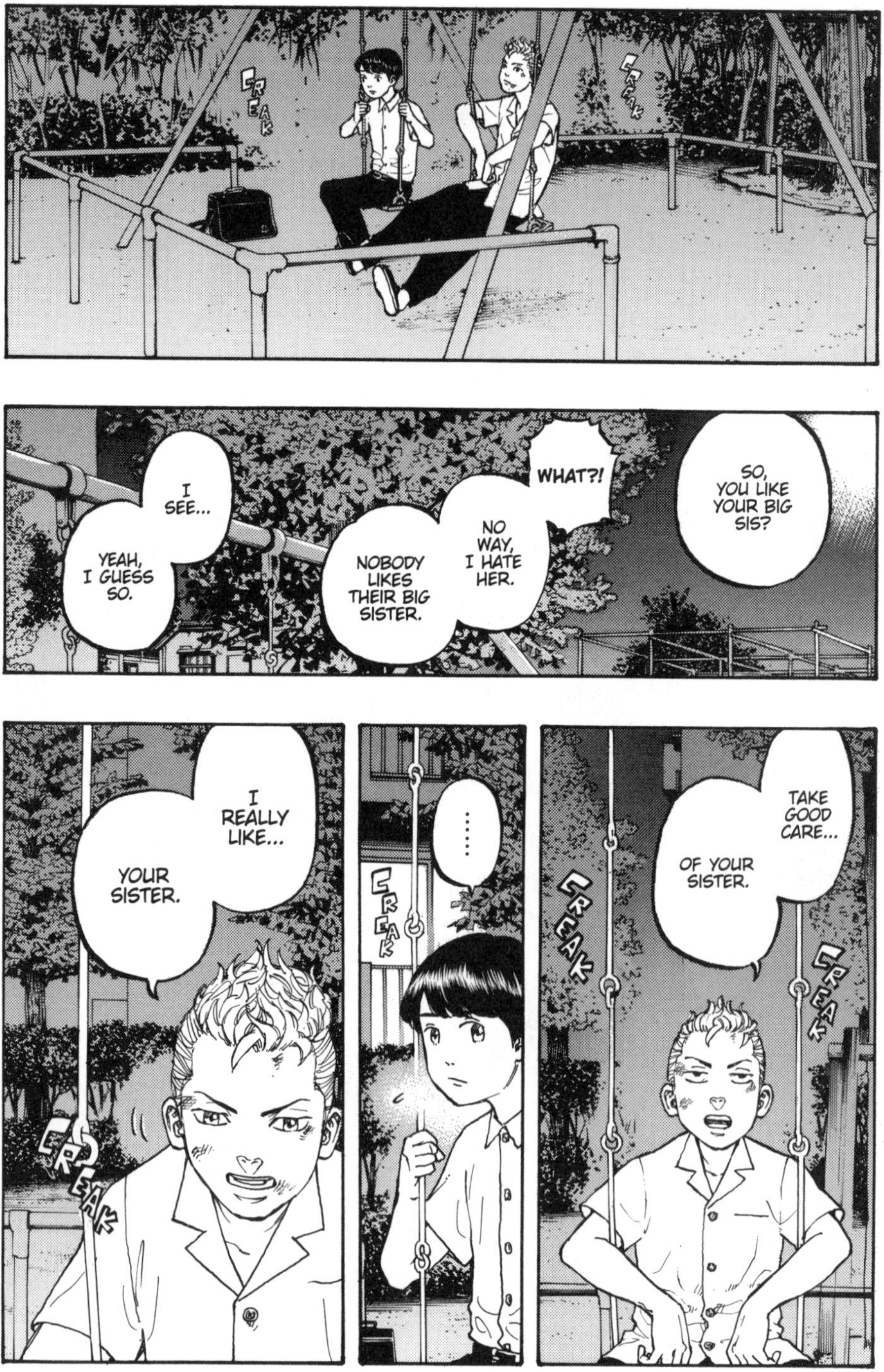
CREAK
CREAK
SO, YOU LIKE YOUR BIG SIS?
WHAT?!
NO WAY, I HATE HER.
NOBODY LIKES THEIR BIG SISTER.
I SEE...
YEAH, I GUESS SO.
TAKE GOOD CARE...
OF YOUR SISTER.
CREAK
CREAK
......
CREAK
I REALLY LIKE...
YOUR SISTER.
CREAK

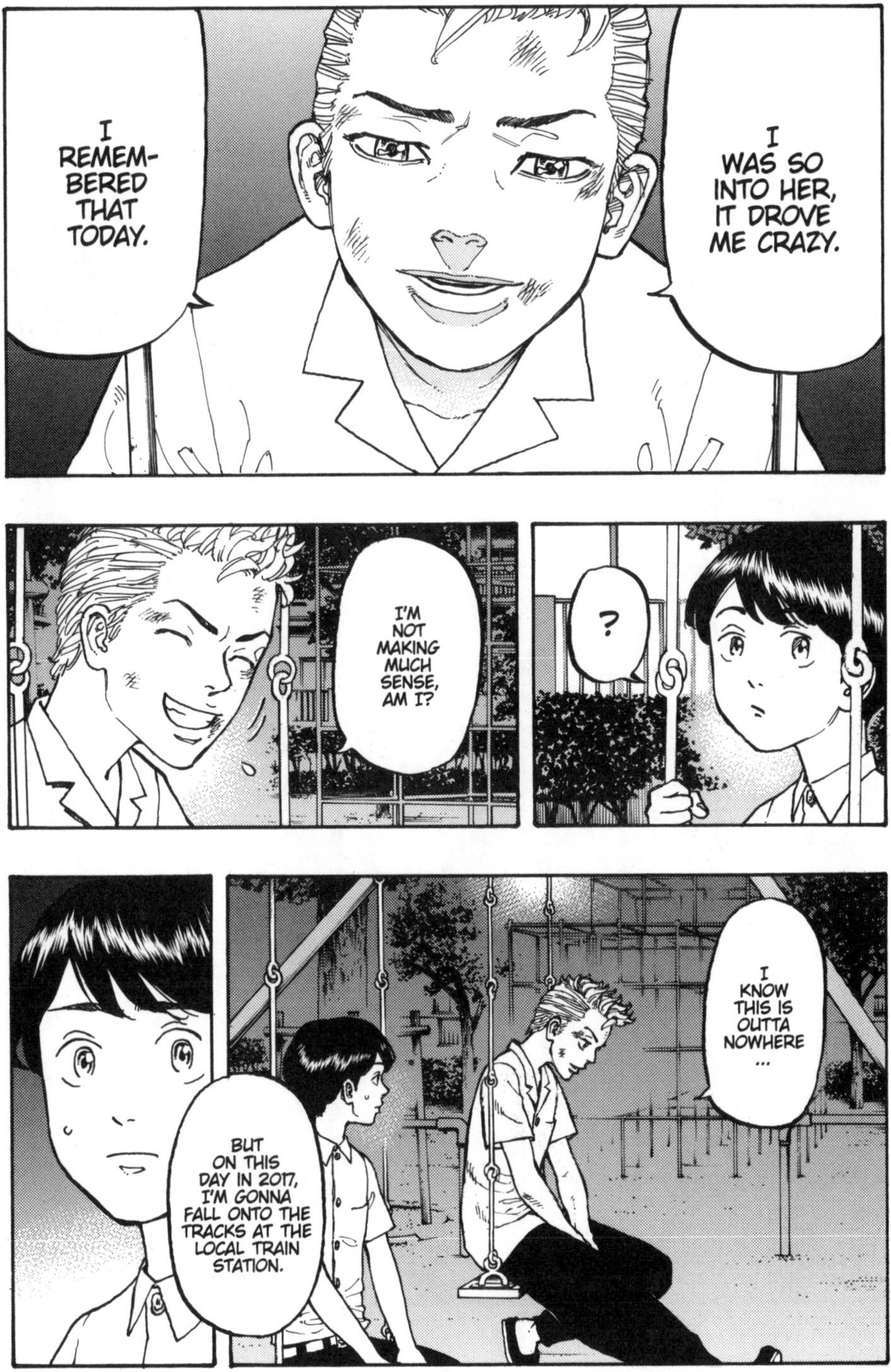
I WAS SO INTO HER, IT DROVE ME CRAZY.
I REMEMBERED THAT TODAY.
?
I'M NOT MAKING MUCH SENSE, AM I?
I KNOW THIS IS OUTTA NOWHERE...
BUT ON THIS DAY IN 2017, I'M GONNA FALL ONTO THE TRACKS AT THE LOCAL TRAIN STATION.

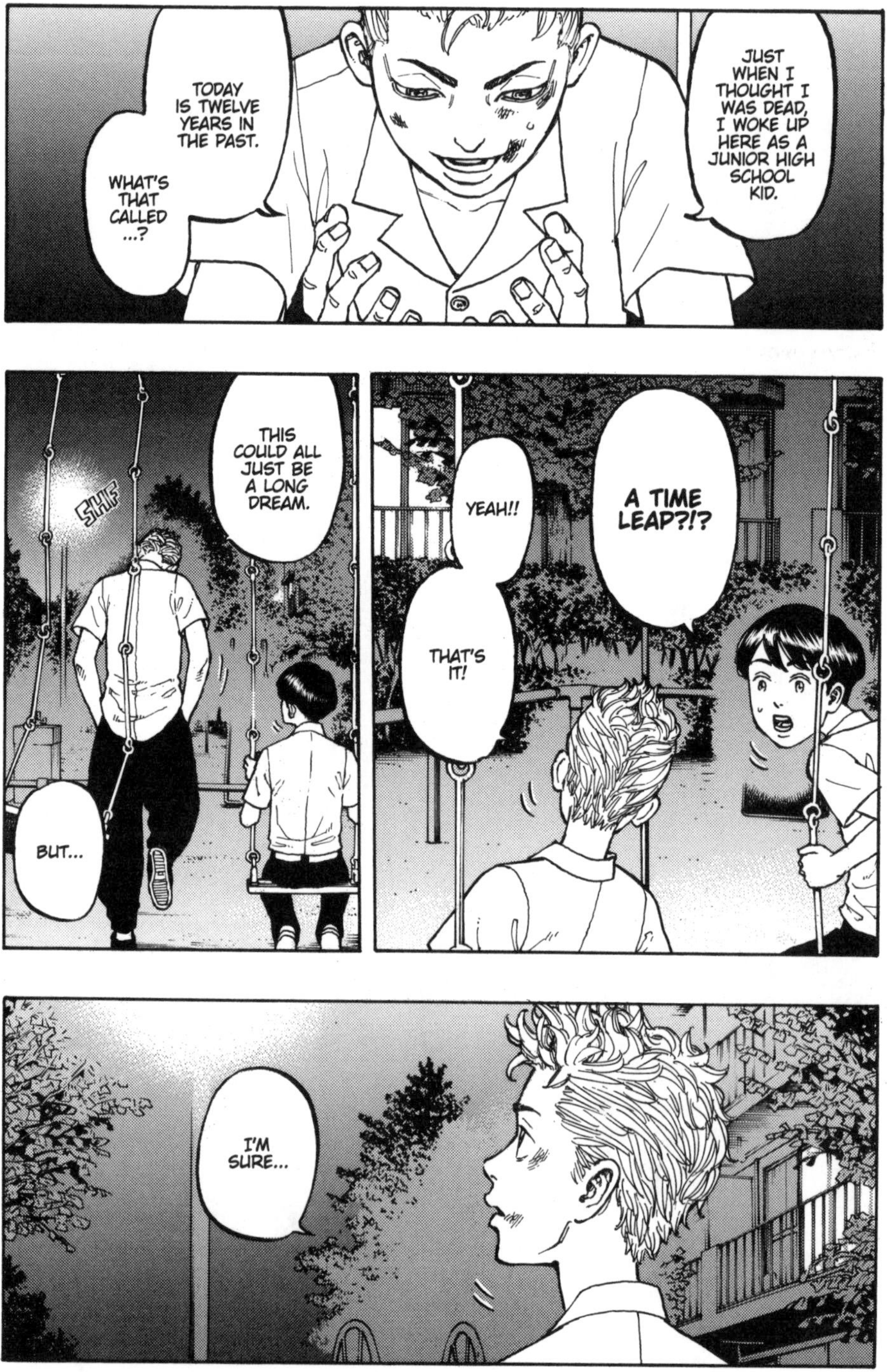
JUST WHEN I THOUGHT I WAS DEAD, I WOKE UP HERE AS A JUNIOR HIGH SCHOOL KID.
TODAY IS TWELVE YEARS IN THE PAST.
WHAT'S THAT CALLED ...?
A TIME LEAP?!?
YEAH!!
THAT'S IT!
THIS COULD ALL JUST BE A LONG DREAM.
SHF
BUT...
I'M SURE...

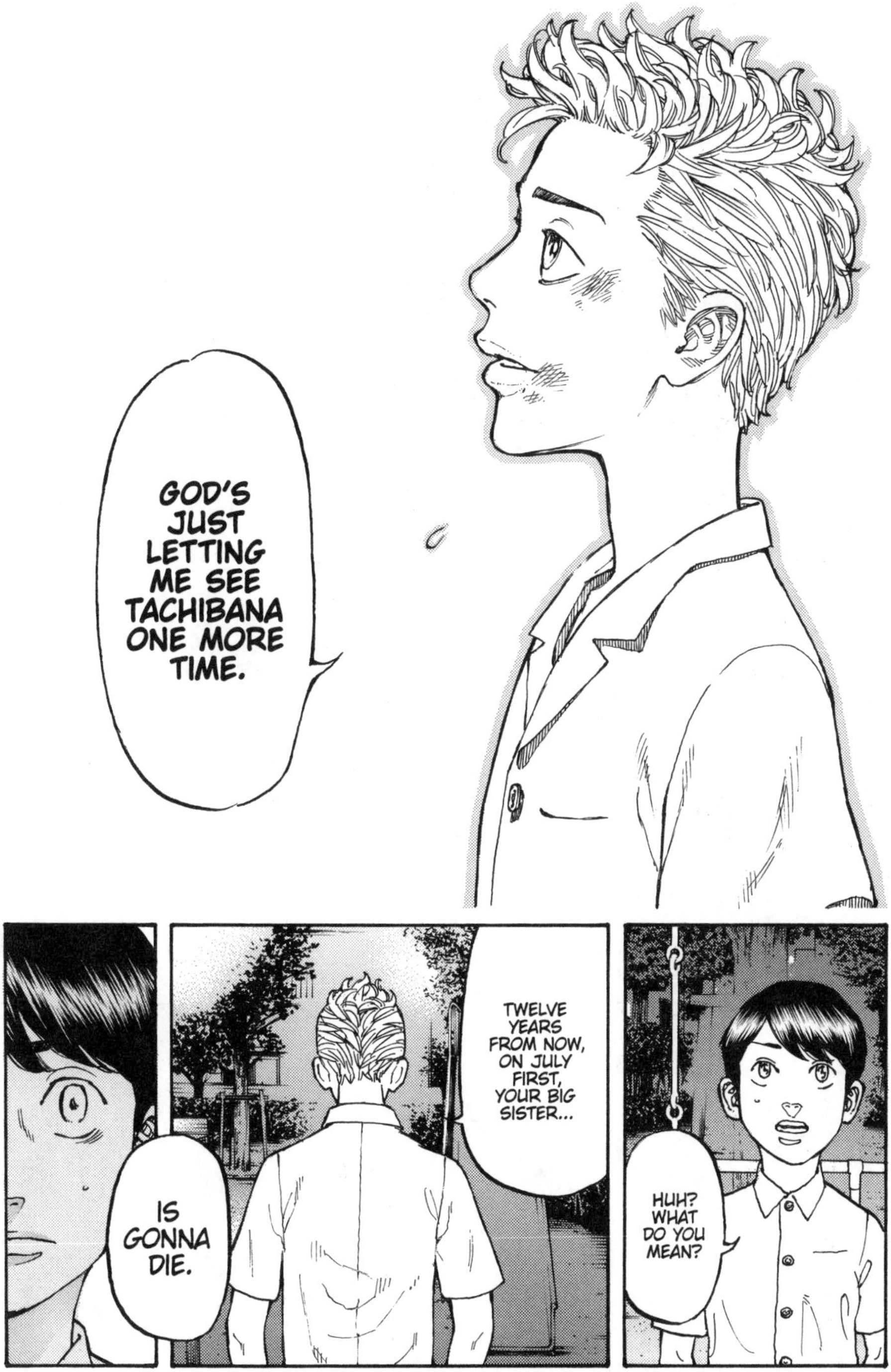
GOD'S JUST LETTING ME SEE TACHIBANA ONE MORE TIME.
HUH? WHAT DO YOU MEAN?
TWELVE YEARS FROM NOW, ON JULY FIRST, YOUR BIG SISTER...
IS GONNA DIE.

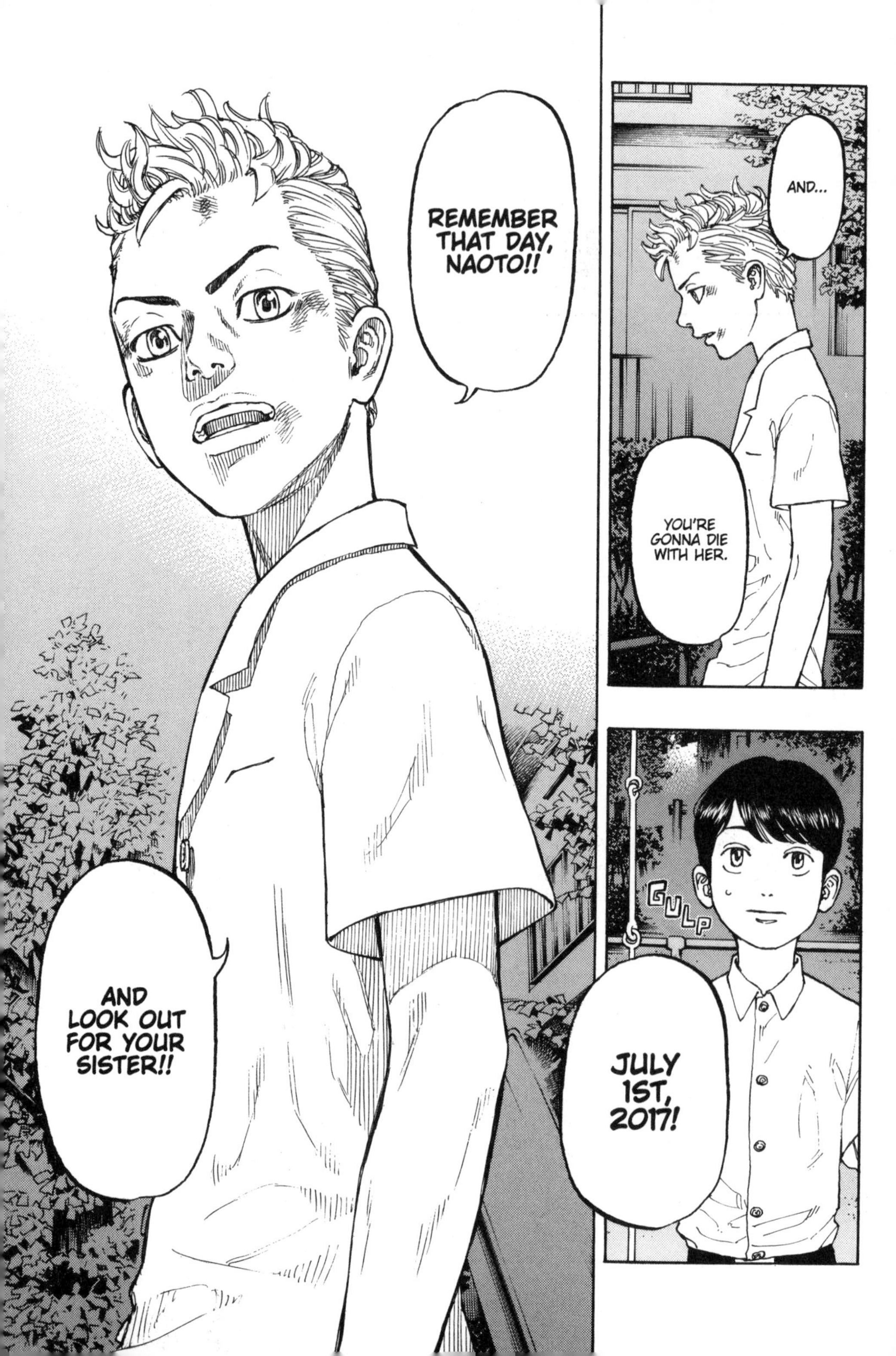
AND...
YOU'RE GONNA DIE WITH HER.
GULP
JULY 1ST, 2017!
REMEMBER THAT DAY, NAOTO!!
AND LOOK OUT FOR YOUR SISTER!!

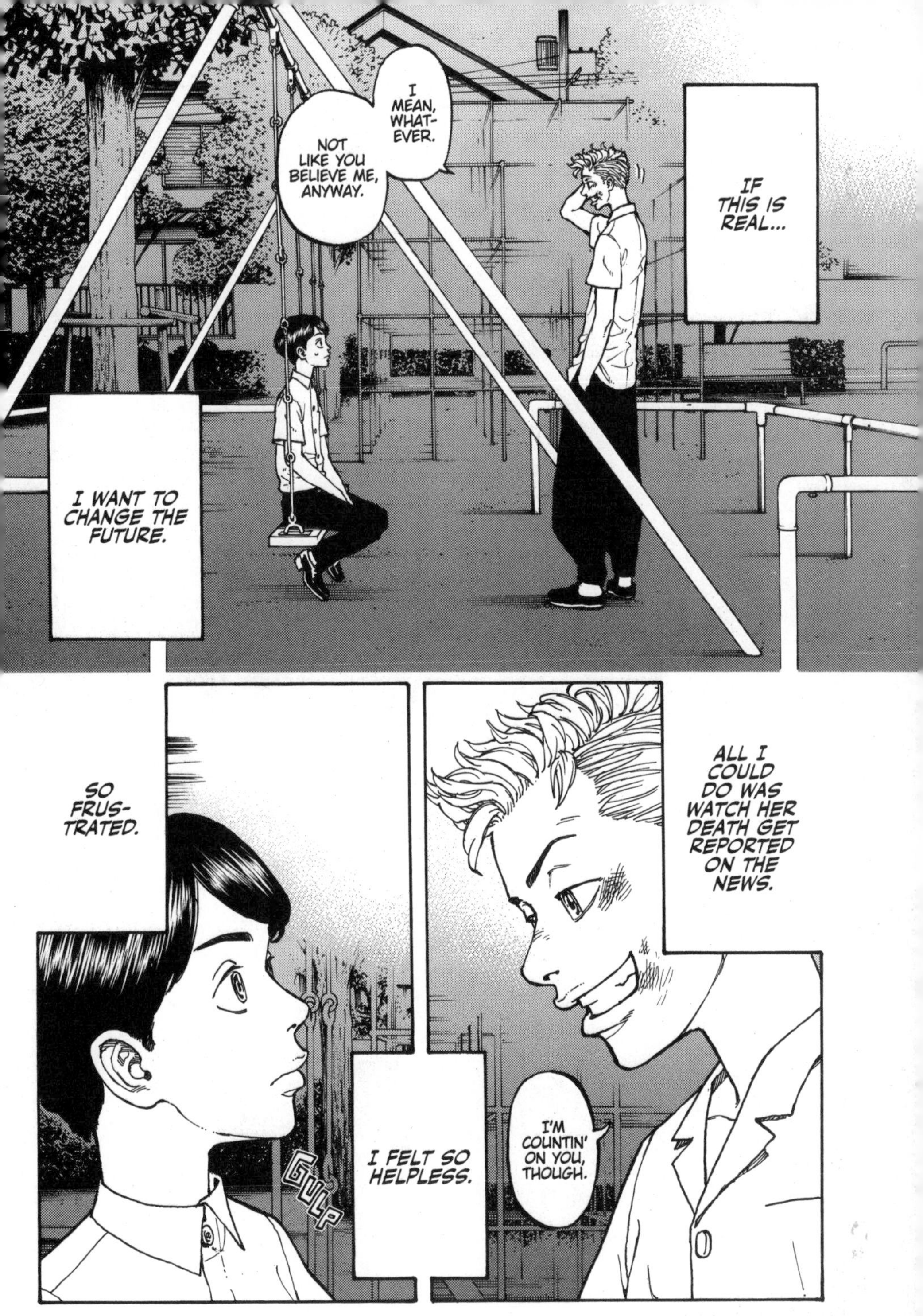
IF THIS IS REAL...
I MEAN, WHAT-EVER.
NOT LIKE YOU BELIEVE ME, ANYWAY.
I WANT TO CHANGE THE FUTURE.
ALL I COULD DO WAS WATCH HER DEATH GET REPORTED ON THE NEWS.
I'M COUNTIN' ON YOU, THOUGH.
I FELT SO HELPLESS.
SO FRUS-TRATED.
GULP

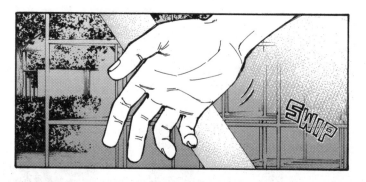

I WANT TO DO IT OVER.

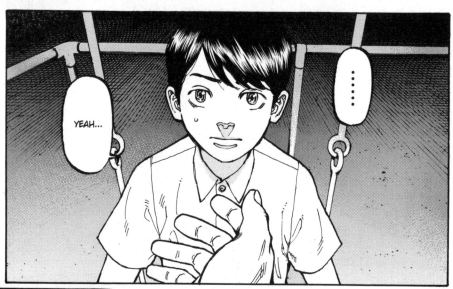

YEAH...

. . . . .

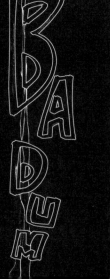

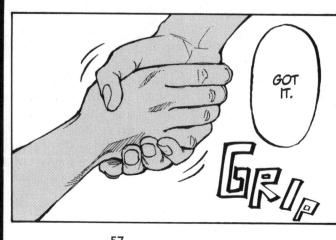

GOT IT.

GRIP

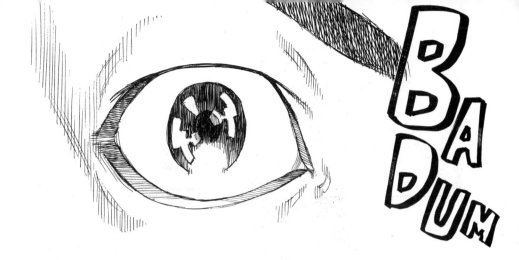

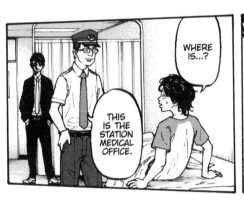

WHERE IS...?

THIS IS THE STATION MEDICAL OFFICE.

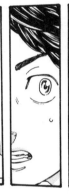

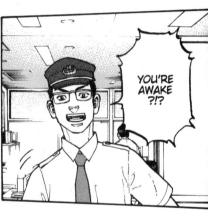

YOU'RE AWAKE?!?

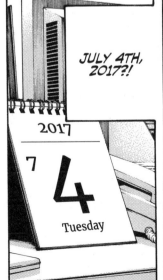

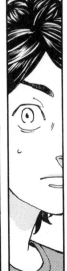

JULY 4TH, 2017?!

2017

7 4

Tuesday

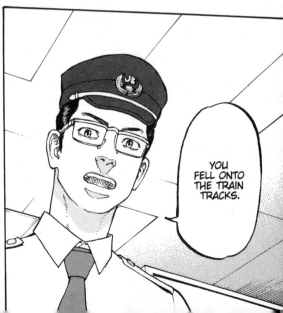

YOU FELL ONTO THE TRAIN TRACKS.

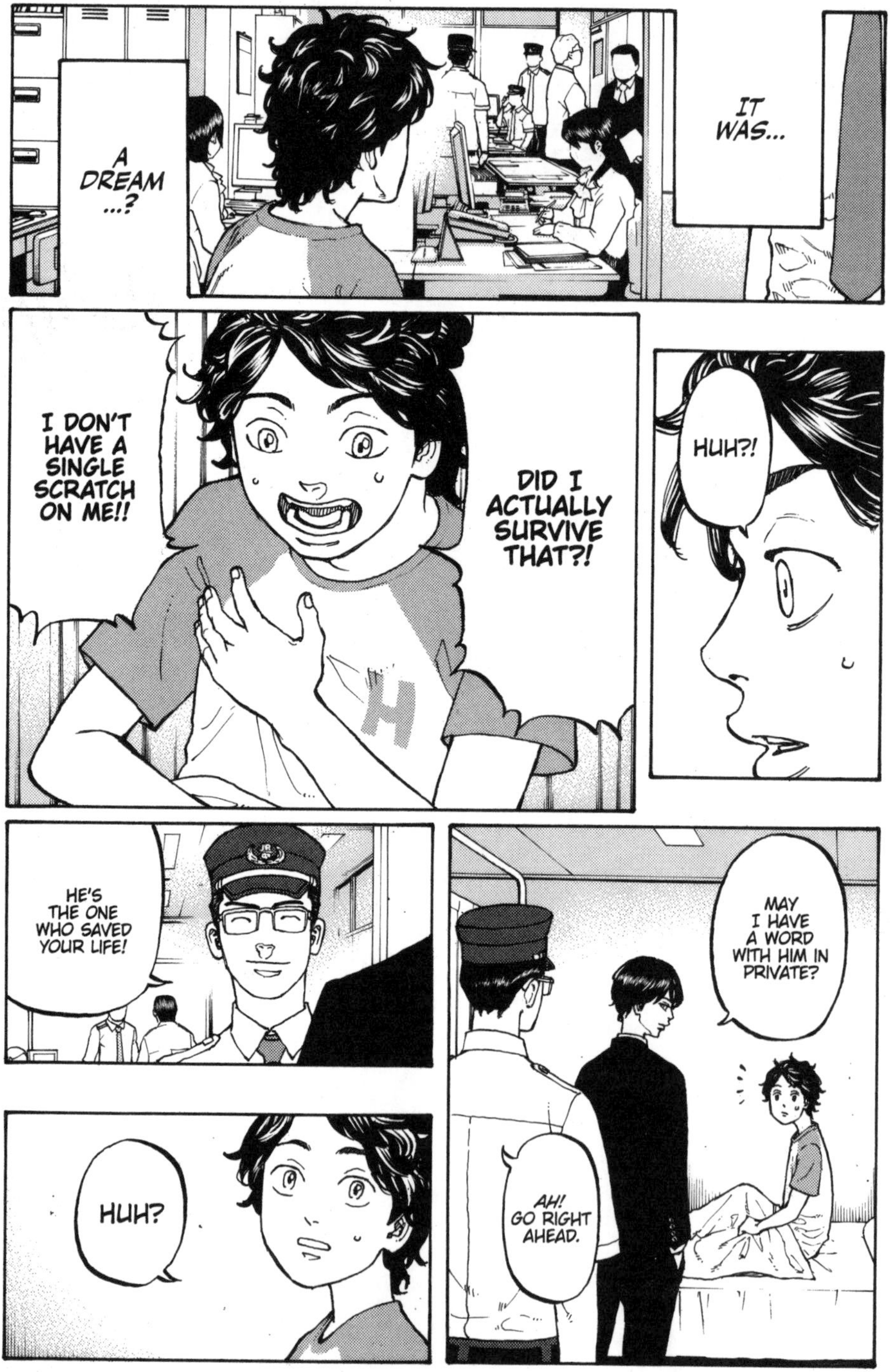
IT WAS...
A DREAM ...?
HUH?!
DID I ACTUALLY SURVIVE THAT?!
I DON'T HAVE A SINGLE SCRATCH ON ME!!
MAY I HAVE A WORD WITH HIM IN PRIVATE?
AH! GO RIGHT AHEAD.
HE'S THE ONE WHO SAVED YOUR LIFE!
HUH?

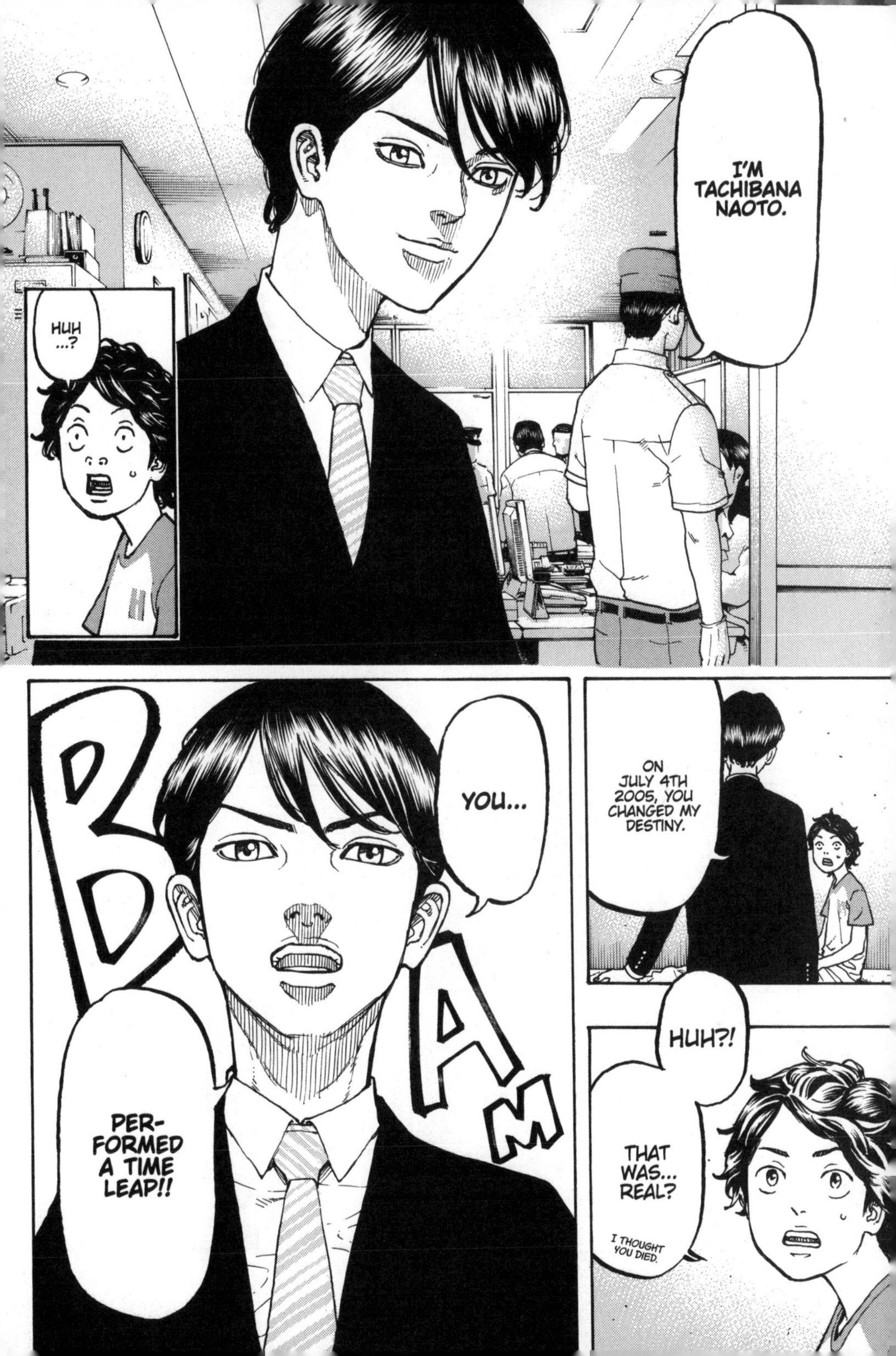
I'M TACHIBANA NAOTO.
HUH ...?
ON JULY 4TH 2005, YOU CHANGED MY DESTINY.
HUH?!
THAT WAS... REAL?
I THOUGHT YOU DIED.
YOU...
BDAM
PER-FORMED A TIME LEAP!!

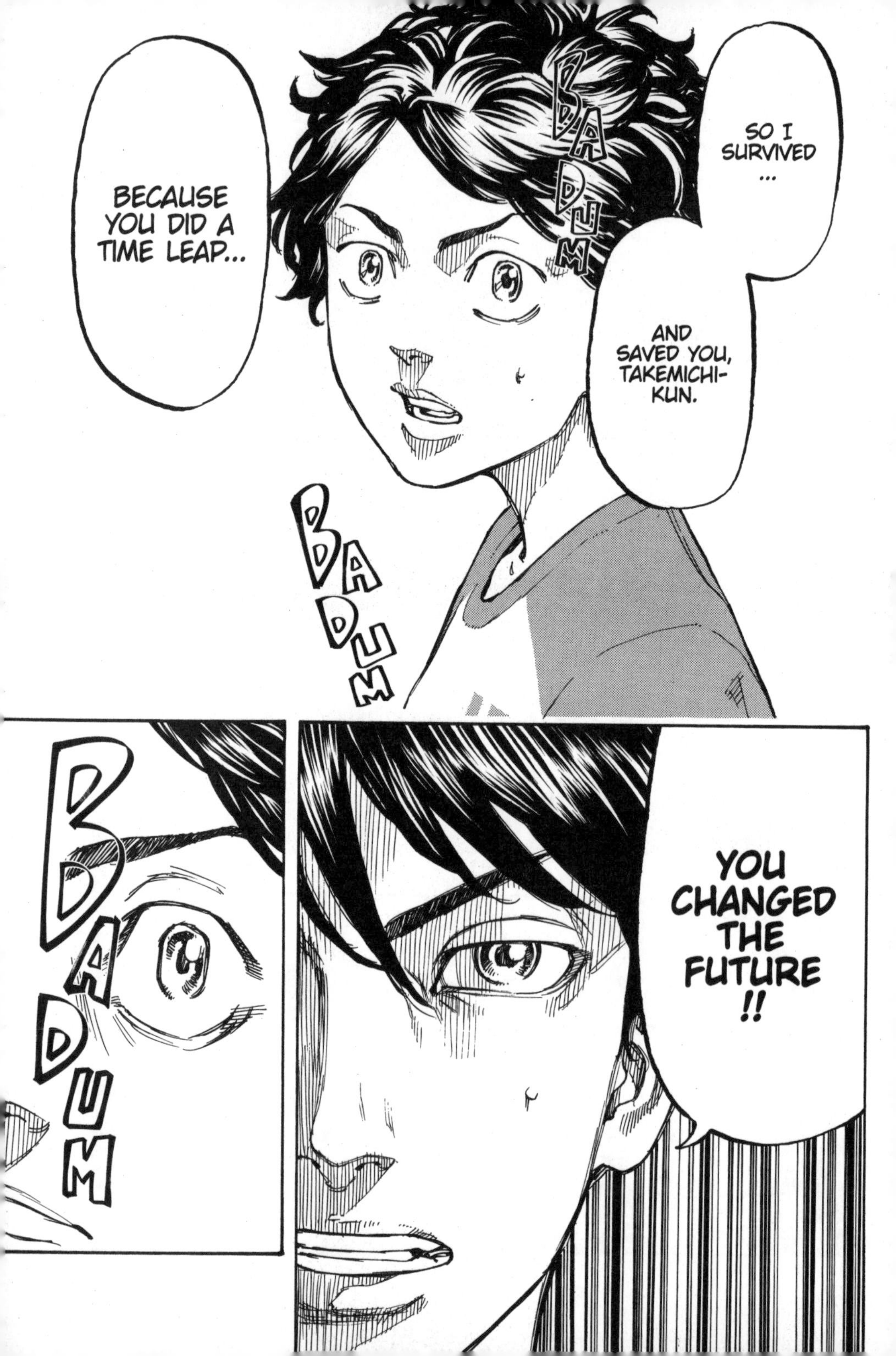
SO I SURVIVED ...
AND SAVED YOU, TAKEMICHI-KUN.
BADUM
BECAUSE YOU DID A TIME LEAP...
BADUM
YOU CHANGED THE FUTURE !!
BADUM

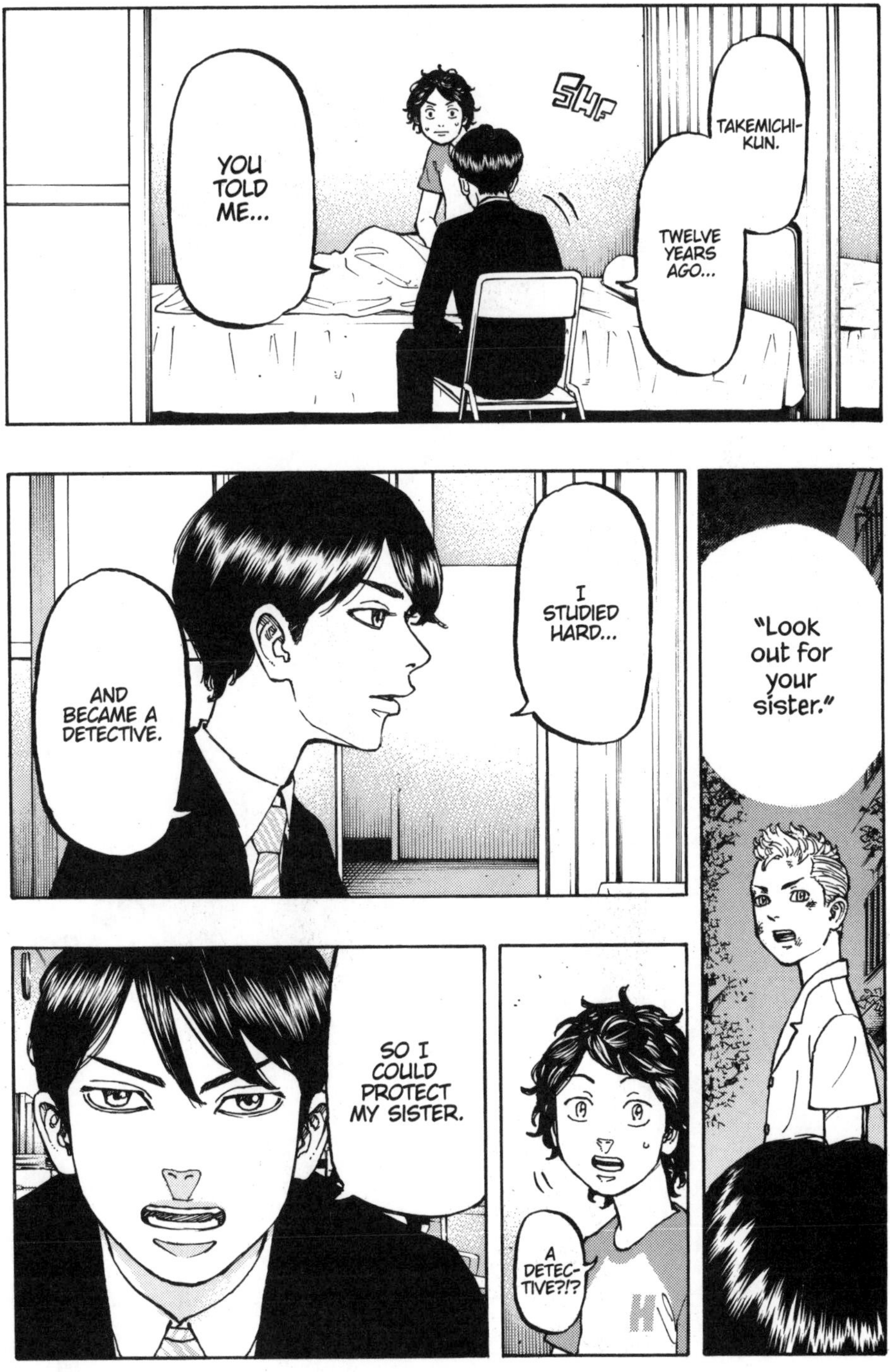
TAKEMICHI-KUN.
TWELVE YEARS AGO...
SHF
YOU TOLD ME...
"Look out for your sister."
I STUDIED HARD...
AND BECAME A DETECTIVE.
A DETEC-TIVE?!?
SO I COULD PROTECT MY SISTER.

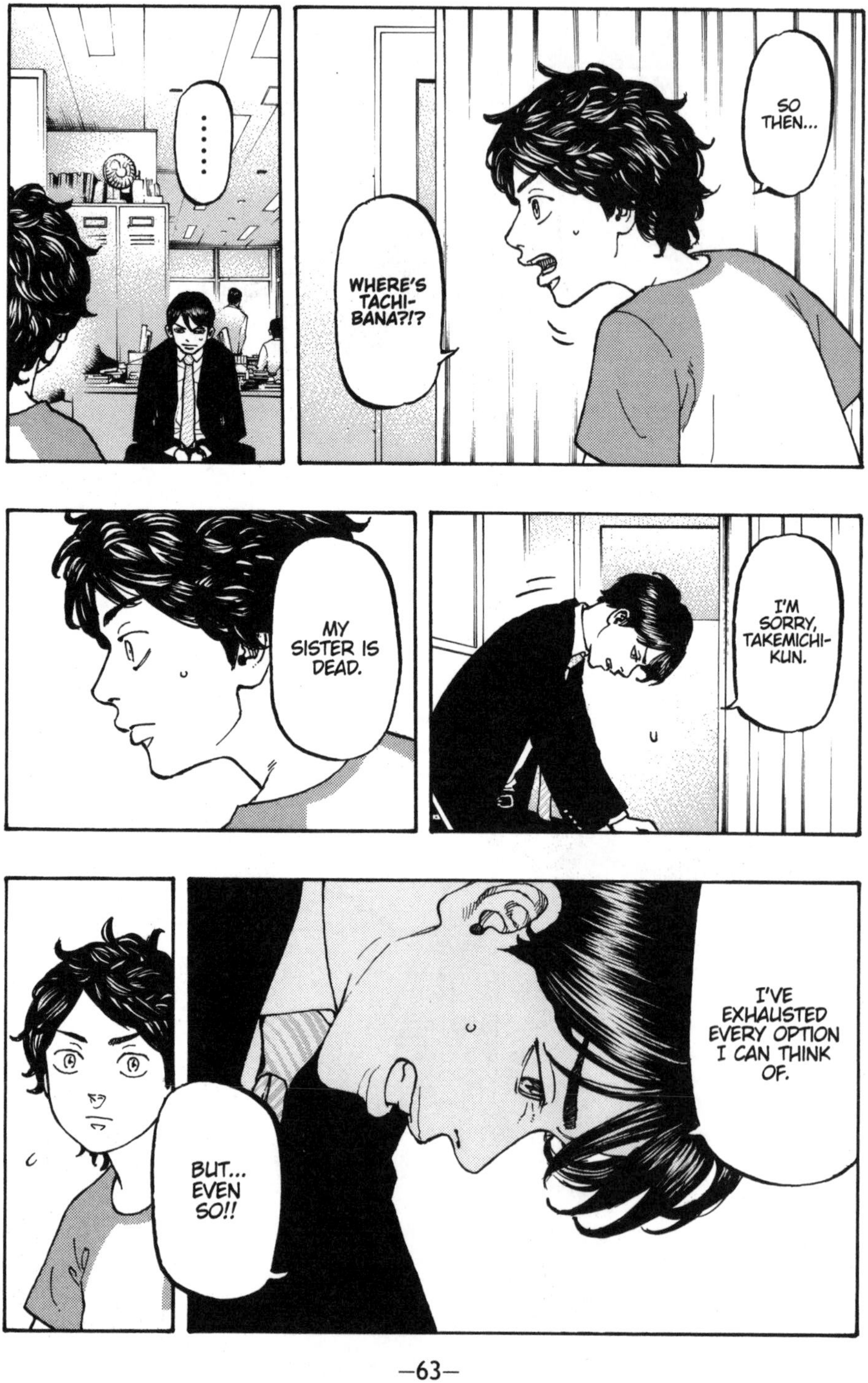
SO THEN...
WHERE'S TACHIBANA?!?
......
I'M SORRY, TAKEMICHI-KUN.
MY SISTER IS DEAD.
I'VE EXHAUSTED EVERY OPTION I CAN THINK OF.
BUT... EVEN SO!!

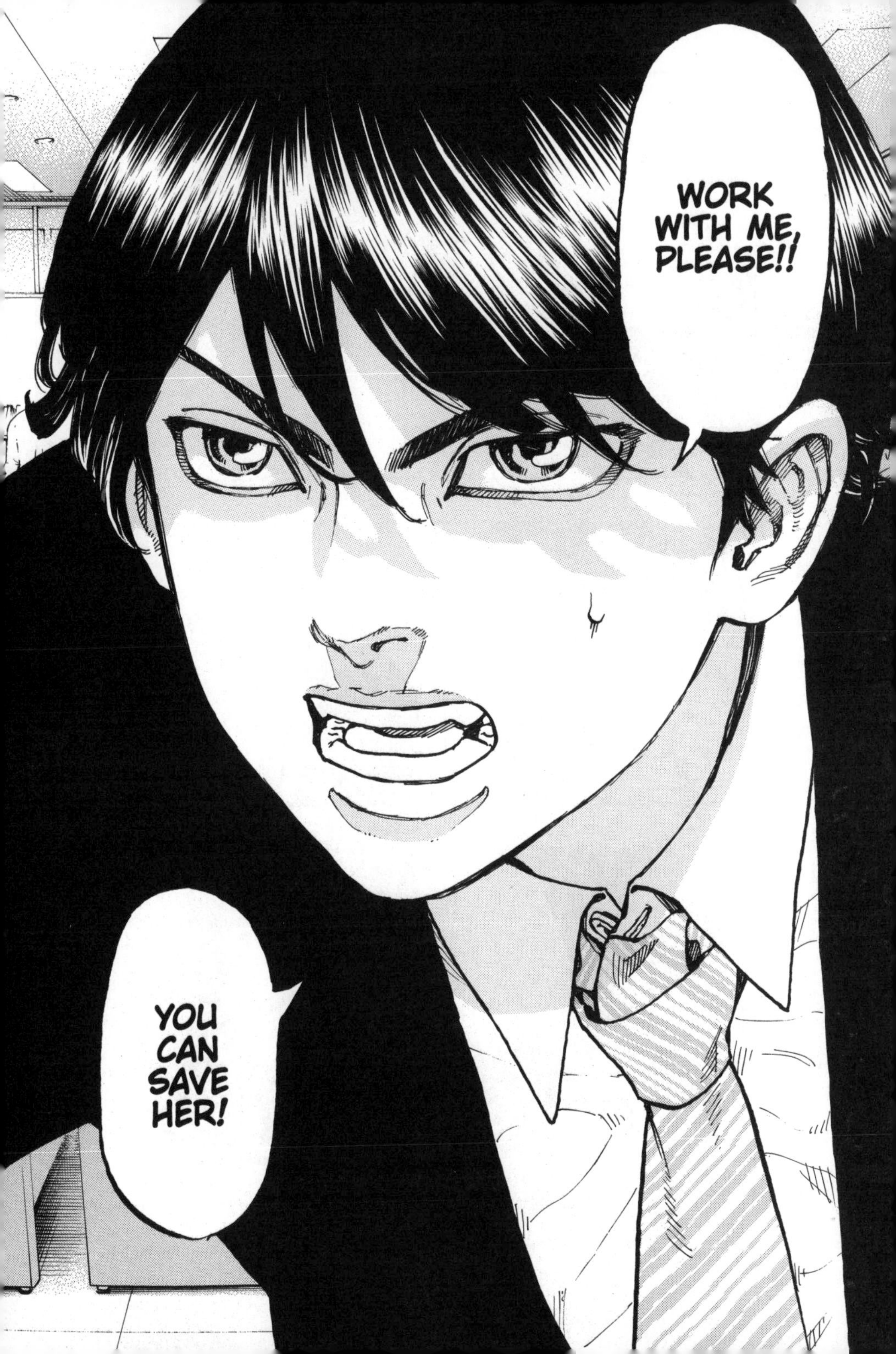
WORK WITH ME, PLEASE!!
YOU CAN SAVE HER!

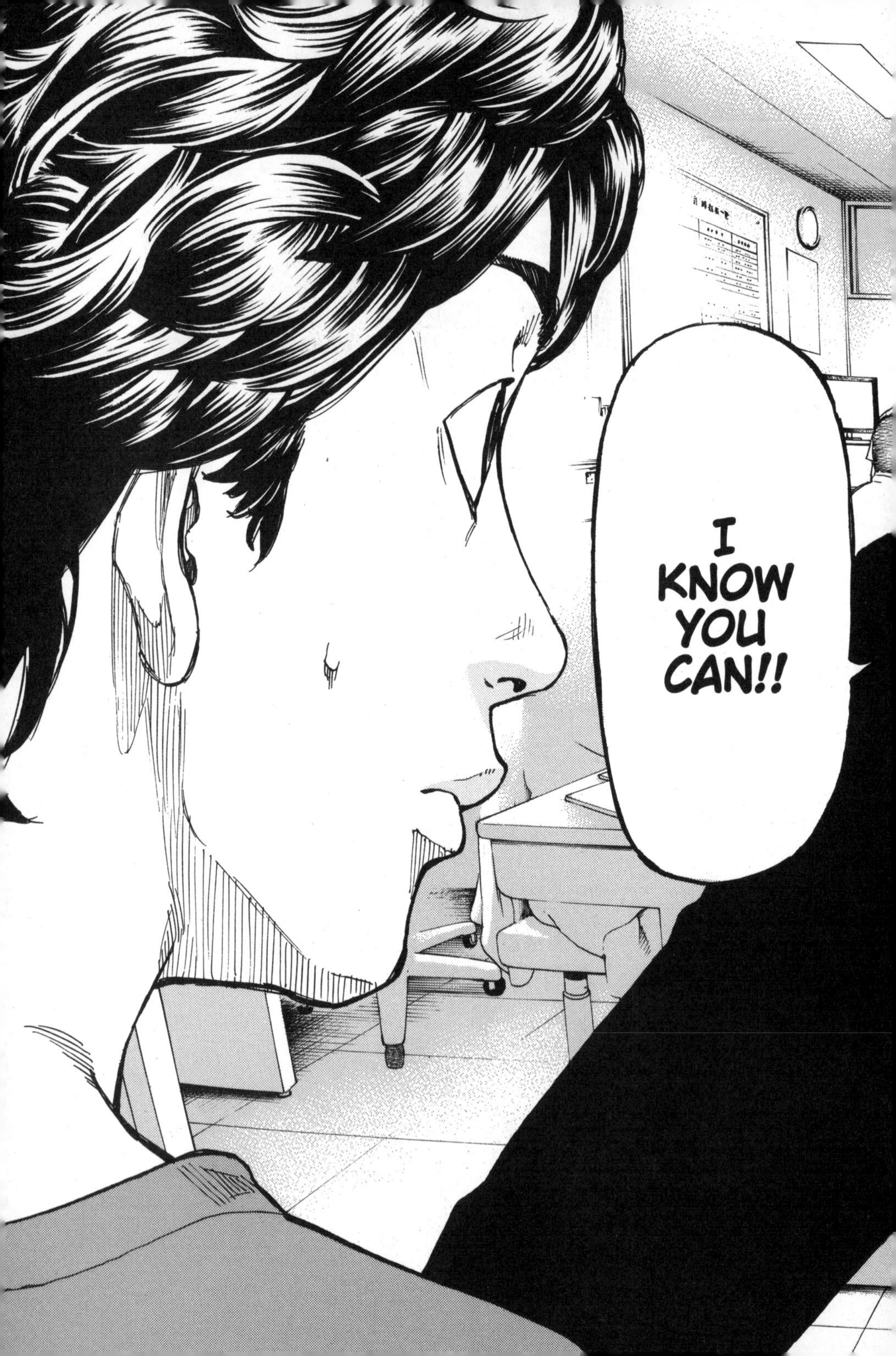
I KNOW YOU CAN!!

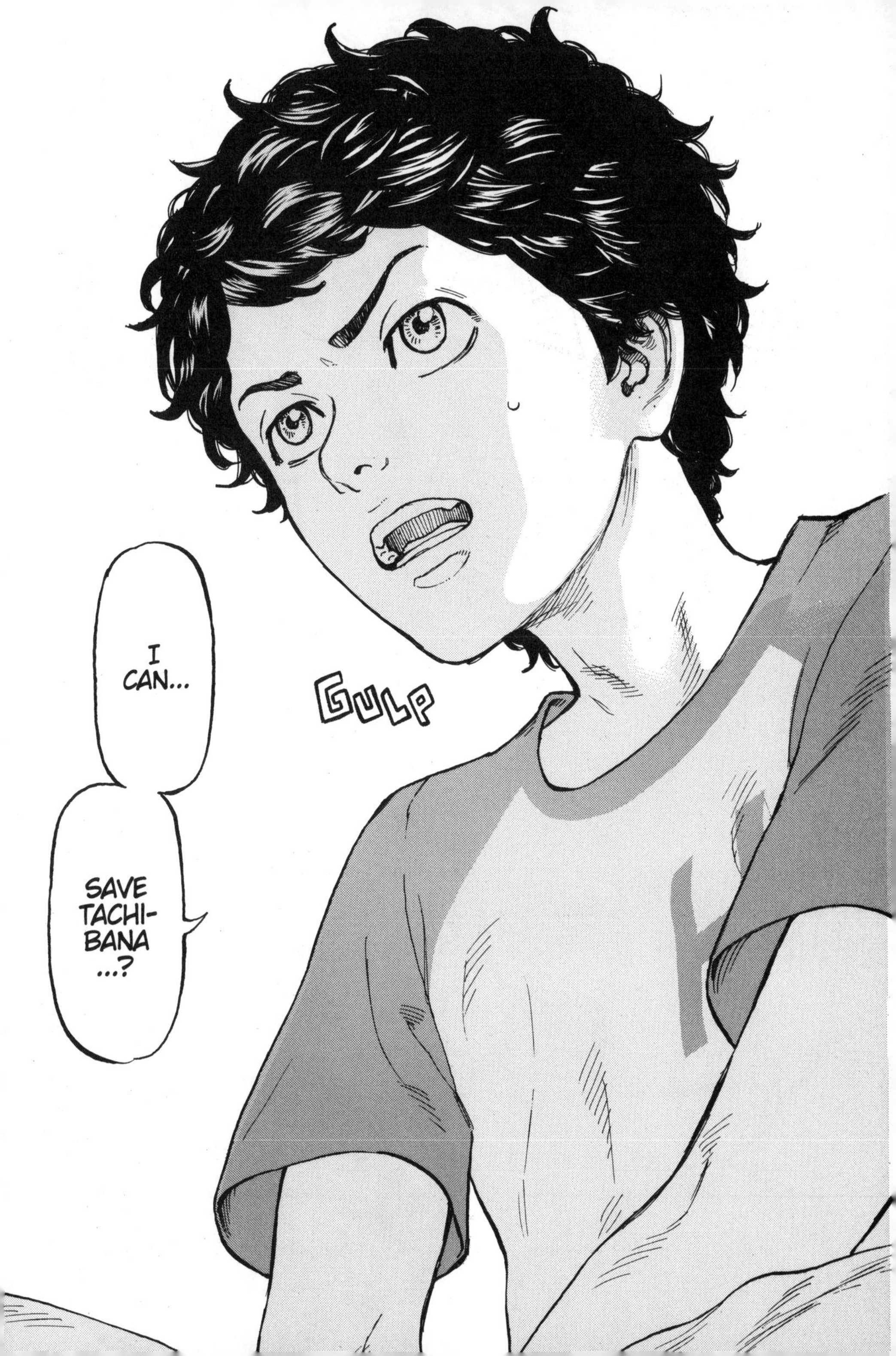
GULP
I CAN...
SAVE TACHIBANA...?

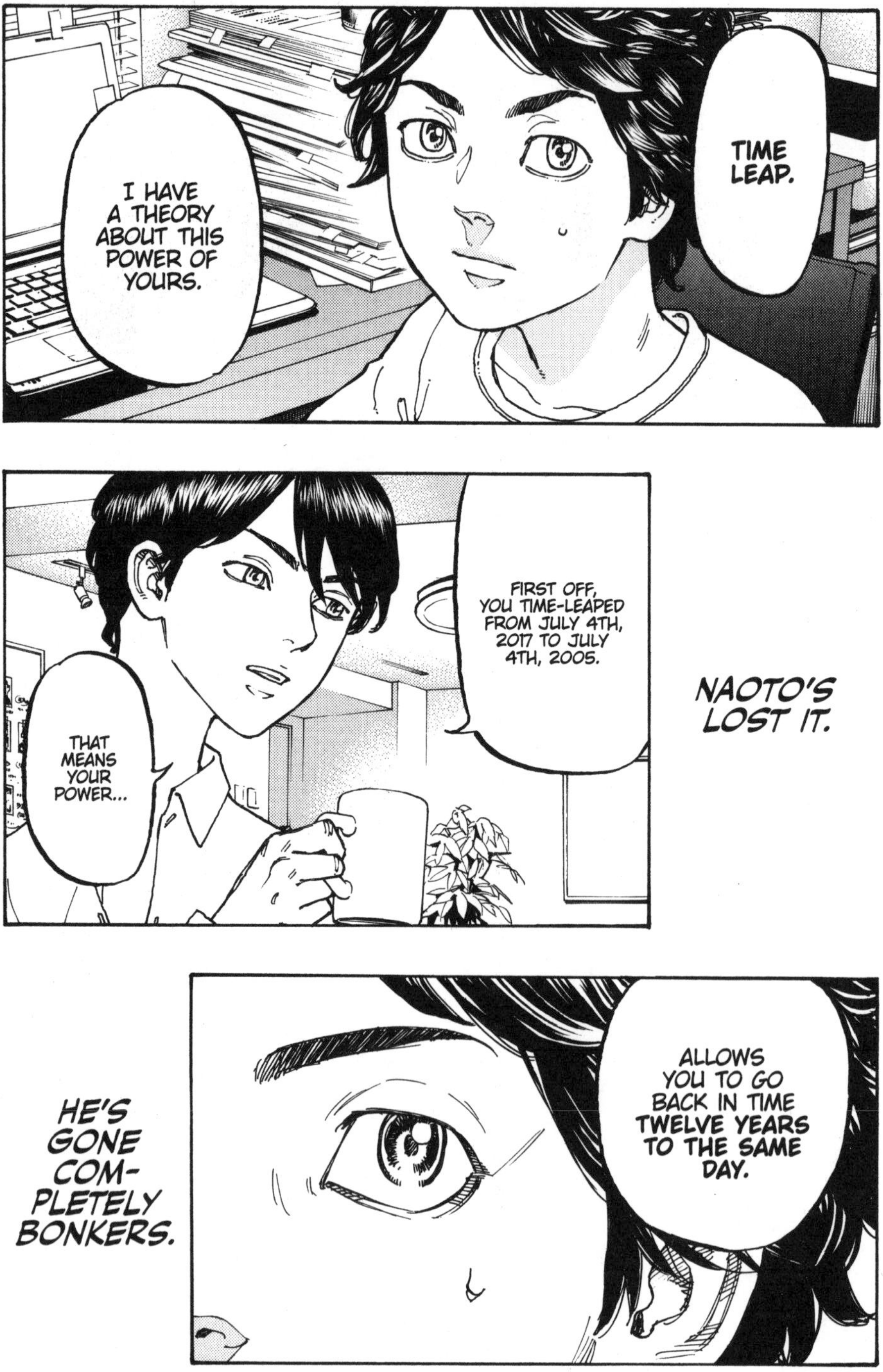
TIME LEAP.
I HAVE A THEORY ABOUT THIS POWER OF YOURS.
NAOTO'S LOST IT.
FIRST OFF, YOU TIME-LEAPED FROM JULY 4TH, 2017 TO JULY 4TH, 2005.
THAT MEANS YOUR POWER...
ALLOWS YOU TO GO BACK IN TIME **TWELVE YEARS TO THE SAME** DAY.
HE'S GONE COM-PLETELY BONKERS.

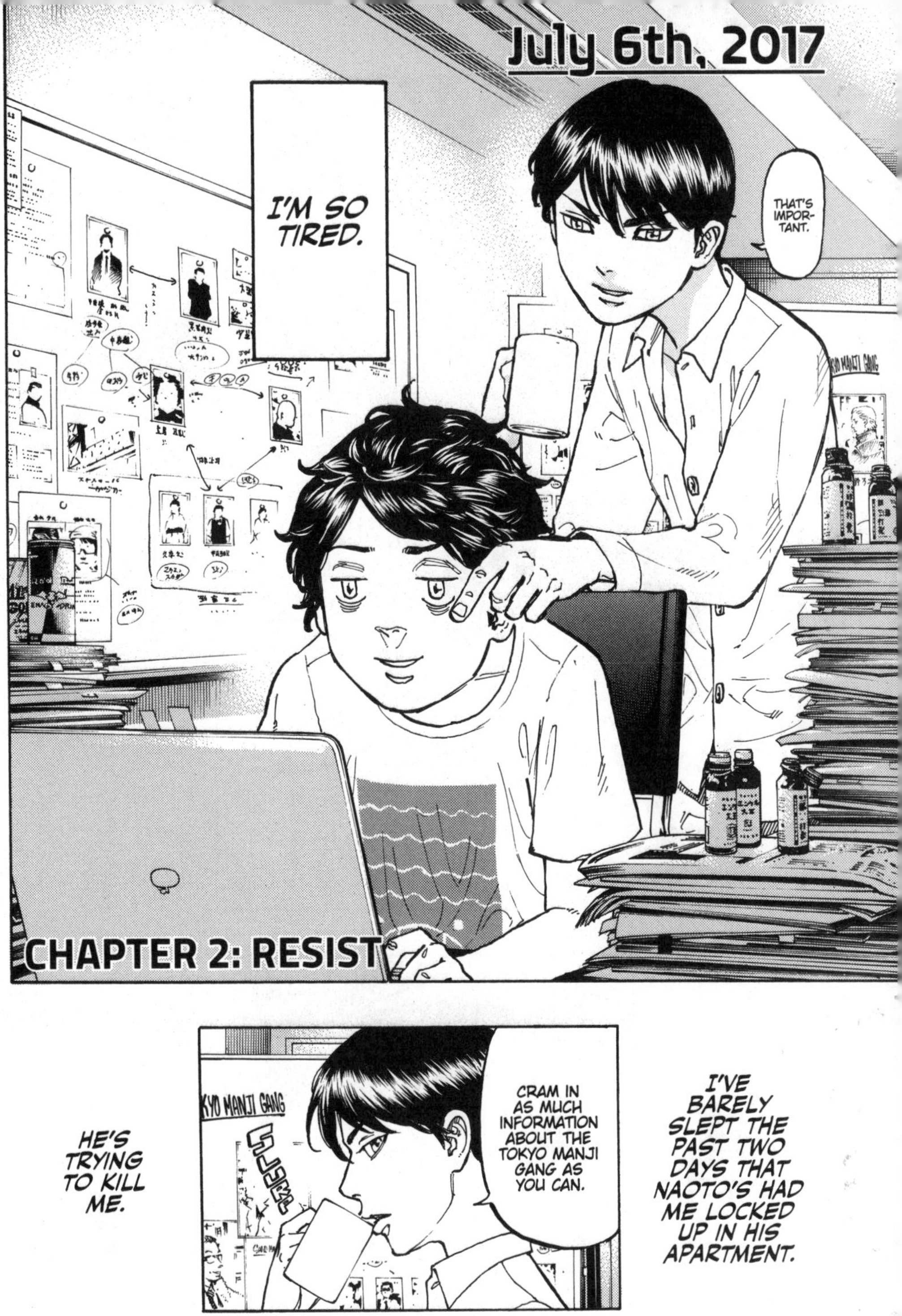
July 6th, 2017
THAT'S IMPORTANT.
I'M SO TIRED.
CHAPTER 2: RESIST
I'VE BARELY SLEPT THE PAST TWO DAYS THAT NAOTO'S HAD ME LOCKED UP IN HIS APARTMENT.
CRAM IN AS MUCH INFORMATION ABOUT THE TOKYO MANJI GANG AS YOU CAN.
HE'S TRYING TO KILL ME.

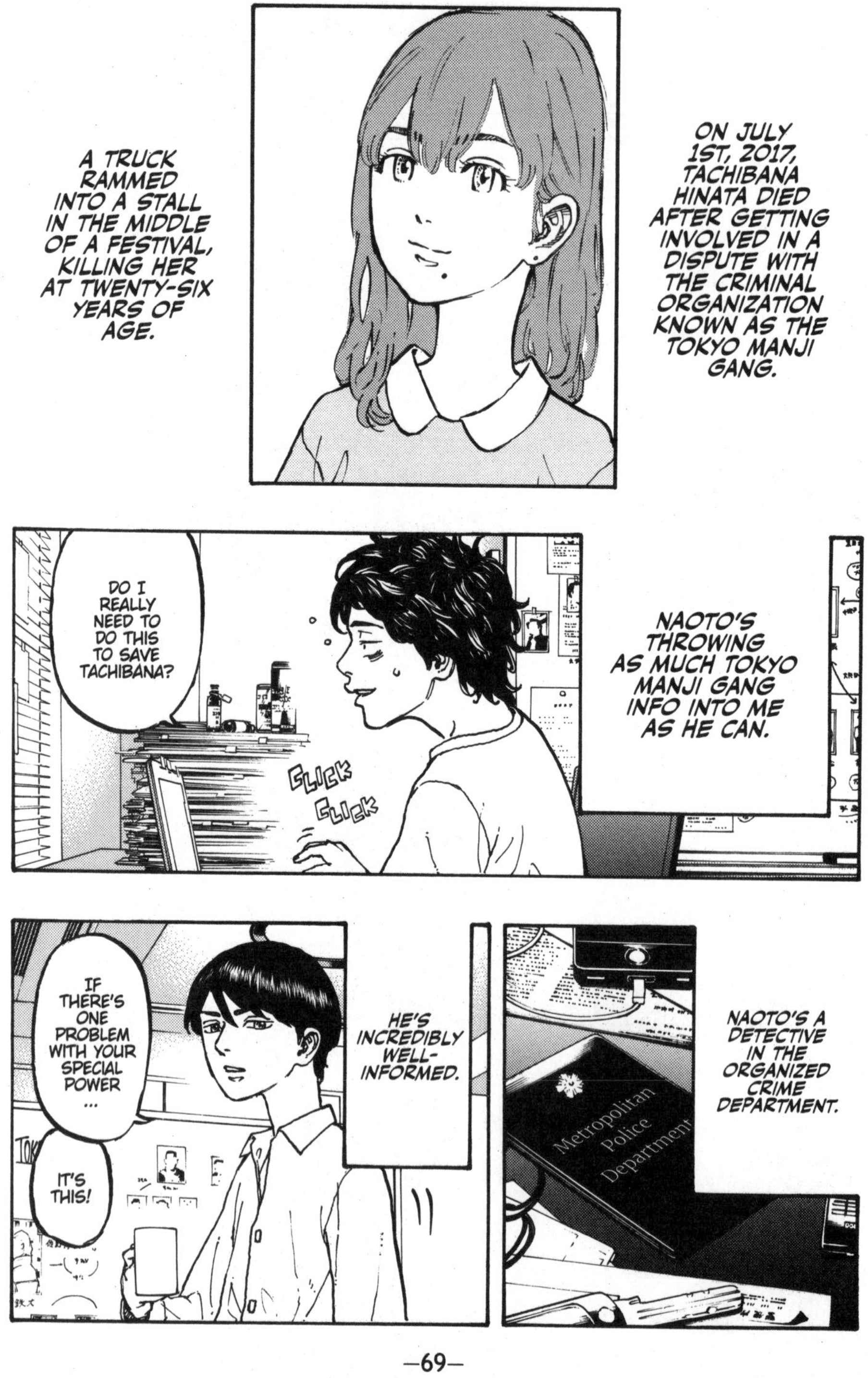
ON JULY 1ST, 2017, TACHIBANA HINATA DIED AFTER GETTING INVOLVED IN A DISPUTE WITH THE CRIMINAL ORGANIZATION KNOWN AS THE TOKYO MANJI GANG.
A TRUCK RAMMED INTO A STALL IN THE MIDDLE OF A FESTIVAL, KILLING HER AT TWENTY-SIX YEARS OF AGE.
NAOTO'S THROWING AS MUCH TOKYO MANJI GANG INFO INTO ME AS HE CAN.
DO I REALLY NEED TO DO THIS TO SAVE TACHIBANA?
CLICK
CLICK
NAOTO'S A DETECTIVE IN THE ORGANIZED CRIME DEPARTMENT.
Metropolitan Police Department
HE'S INCREDIBLY WELL-INFORMED.
IF THERE'S ONE PROBLEM WITH YOUR SPECIAL POWER...
IT'S THIS!

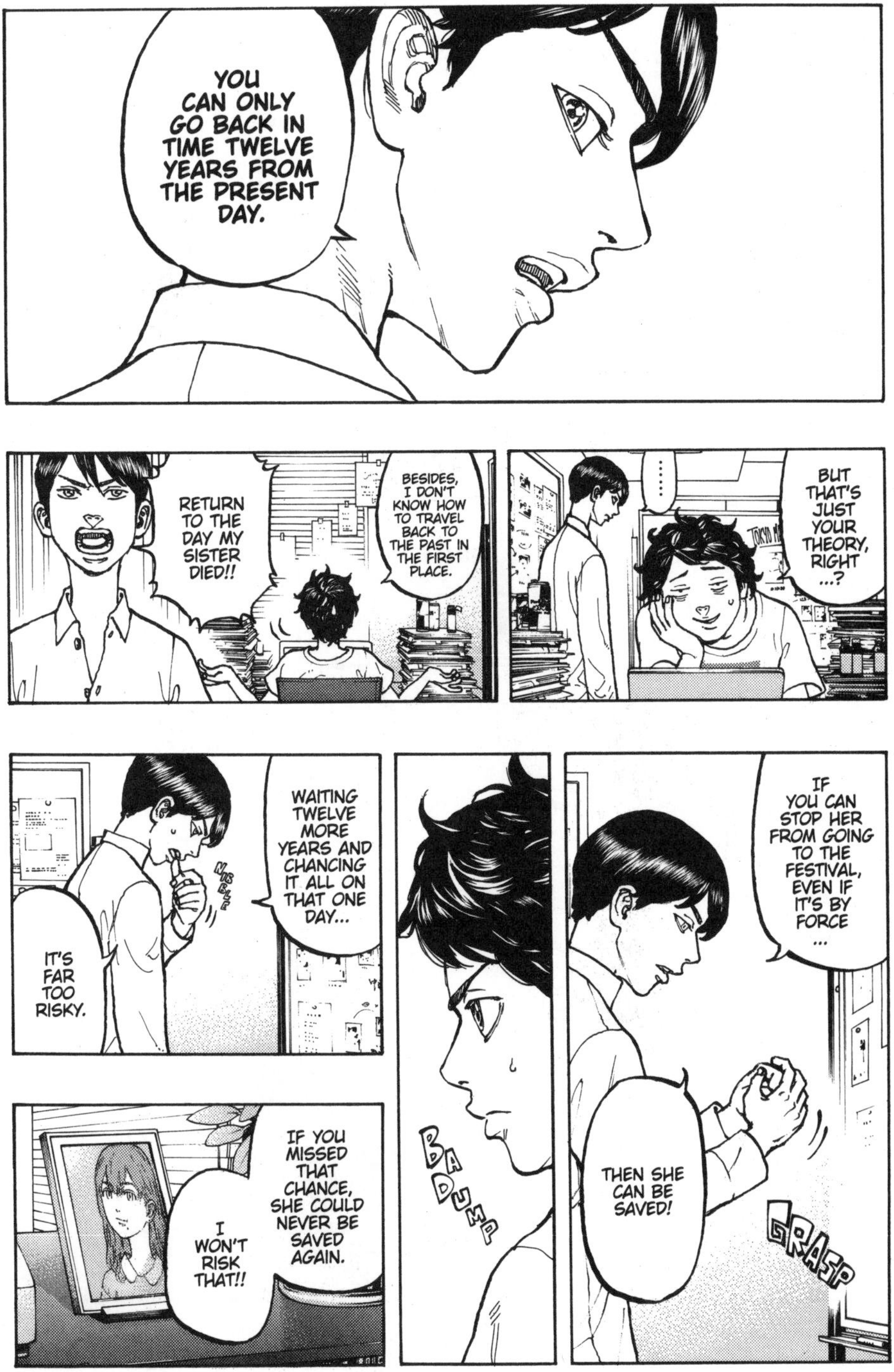
YOU CAN ONLY GO BACK IN TIME TWELVE YEARS FROM THE PRESENT DAY.
BUT THAT'S JUST YOUR THEORY, RIGHT ...?
......
BESIDES, I DON'T KNOW HOW TO TRAVEL BACK TO THE PAST IN THE FIRST PLACE.
RETURN TO THE DAY MY SISTER DIED!!
IF YOU CAN STOP HER FROM GOING TO THE FESTIVAL, EVEN IF IT'S BY FORCE ...
THEN SHE CAN BE SAVED!
GRASP
BADUMP
WAITING TWELVE MORE YEARS AND CHANCING IT ALL ON THAT ONE DAY...
NIBBLE
IT'S FAR TOO RISKY.
IF YOU MISSED THAT CHANCE, SHE COULD NEVER BE SAVED AGAIN.
I WON'T RISK THAT!!

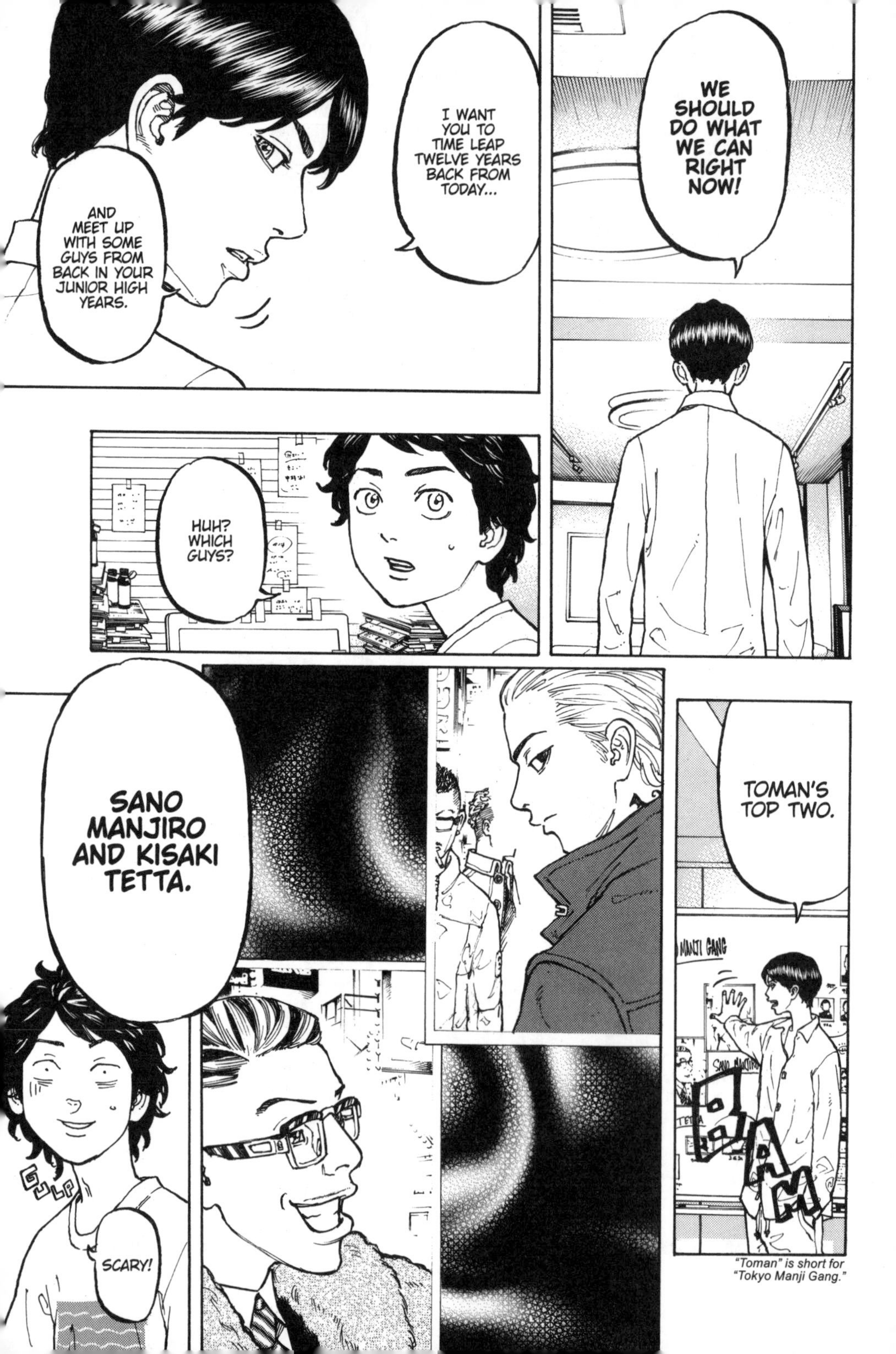
WE SHOULD DO WHAT WE CAN RIGHT NOW!
I WANT YOU TO TIME LEAP TWELVE YEARS BACK FROM TODAY...
AND MEET UP WITH SOME GUYS FROM BACK IN YOUR JUNIOR HIGH YEARS.
HUH? WHICH GUYS?
TOMAN'S TOP TWO.
MANJI GANG
SANO MANJIRO
TETTA
BAM
SANO MANJIRO AND KISAKI TETTA.
GULP
SCARY!

"Toman" is short for "Tokyo Manji Gang."

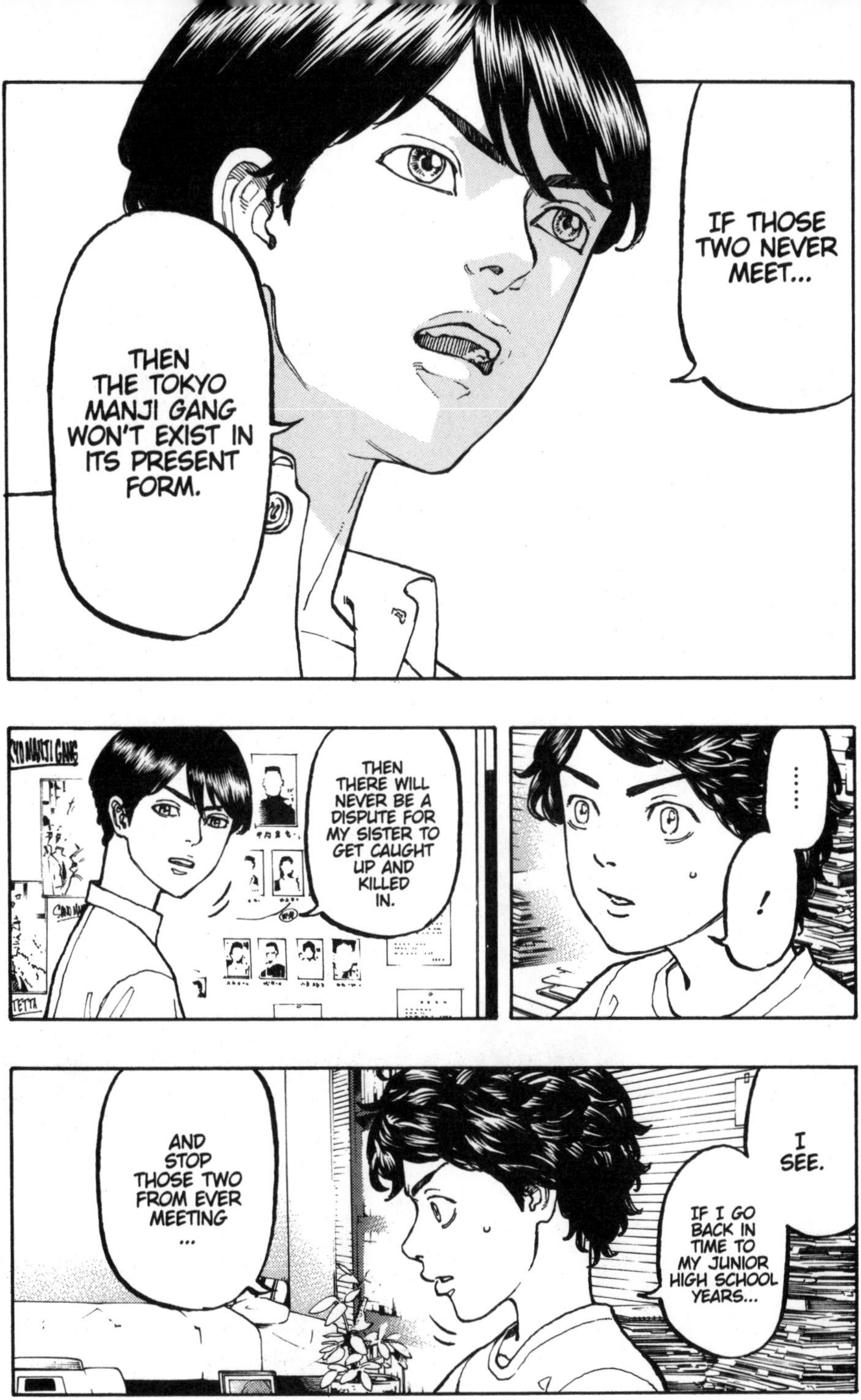
IF THOSE TWO NEVER MEET...
THEN THE TOKYO MANJI GANG WON'T EXIST IN ITS PRESENT FORM.
......
!
THEN THERE WILL NEVER BE A DISPUTE FOR MY SISTER TO GET CAUGHT UP AND KILLED IN.
I SEE.
IF I GO BACK IN TIME TO MY JUNIOR HIGH SCHOOL YEARS...
AND STOP THOSE TWO FROM EVER MEETING ...

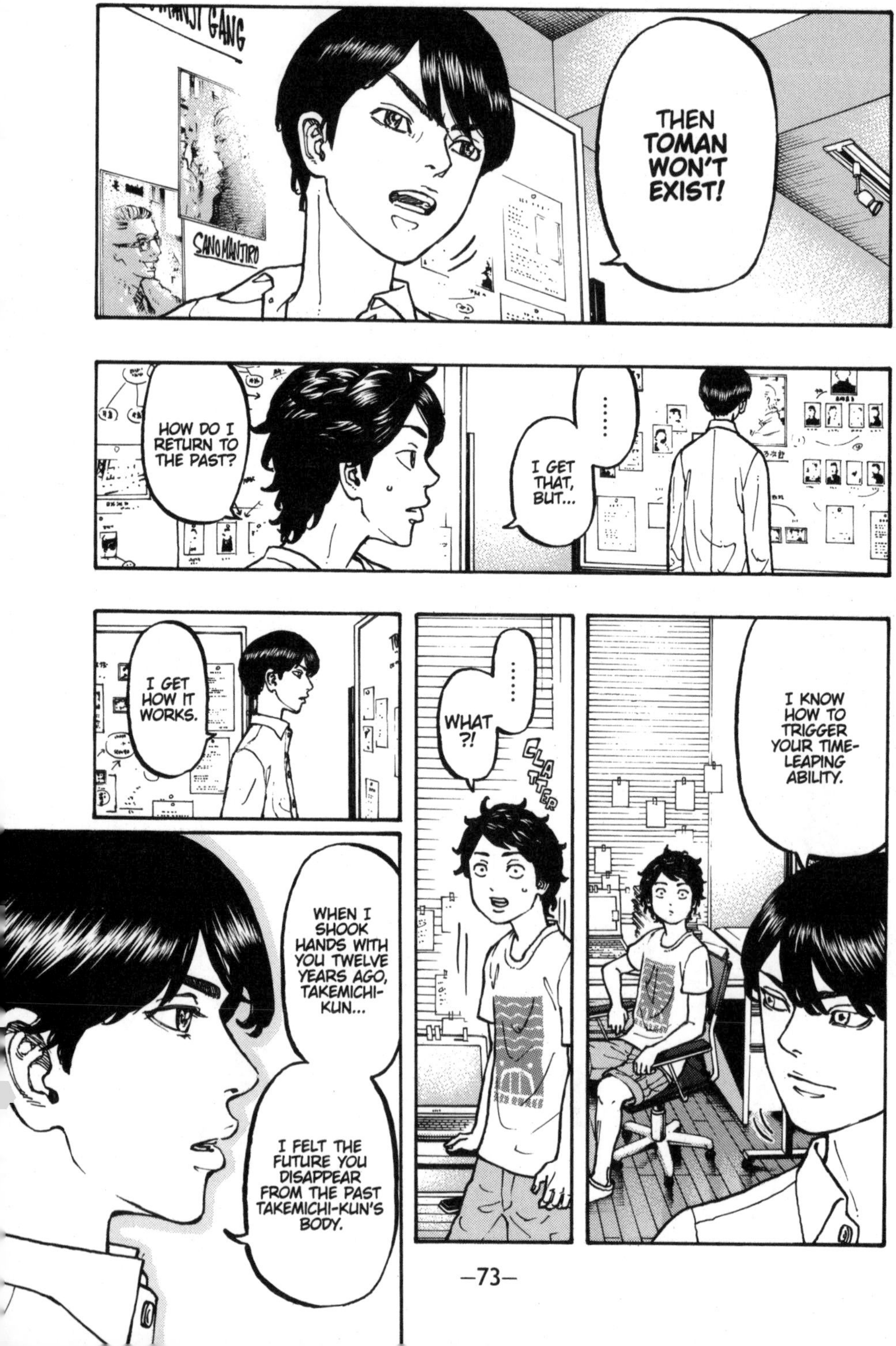
SANO MANJIRO
THEN TOMAN WON'T EXIST!
......
I GET THAT, BUT...
HOW DO I RETURN TO THE PAST?
I KNOW HOW TO TRIGGER YOUR TIME-LEAPING ABILITY.
......
WHAT?!
CLATTER
I GET HOW IT WORKS.
WHEN I SHOOK HANDS WITH YOU TWELVE YEARS AGO, TAKEMICHI-KUN...
I FELT THE FUTURE YOU DISAPPEAR FROM THE PAST TAKEMICHI-KUN'S BODY.

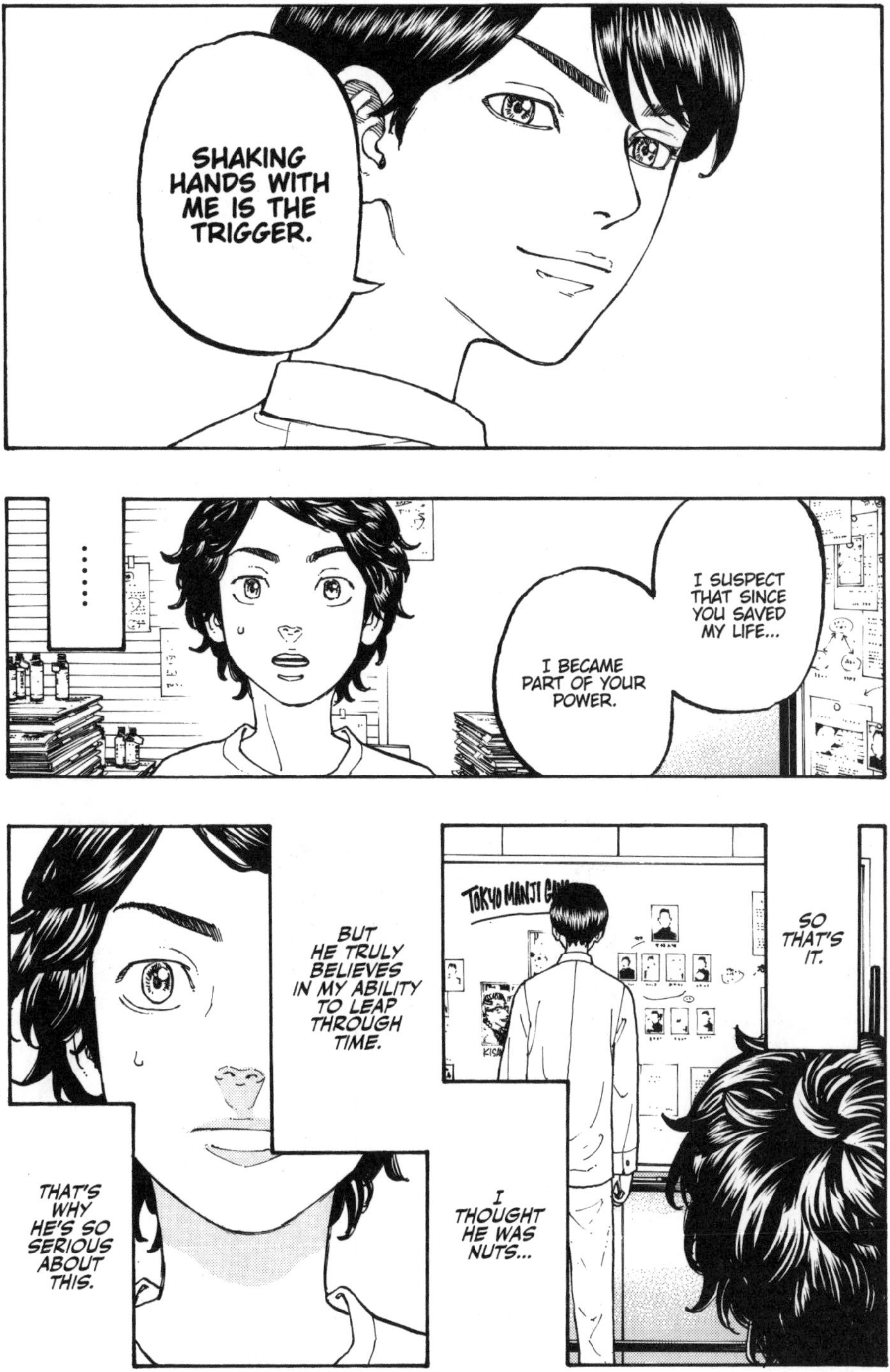
SHAKING HANDS WITH ME IS THE TRIGGER.
I SUSPECT THAT SINCE YOU SAVED MY LIFE...
I BECAME PART OF YOUR POWER.
......
SO THAT'S IT.
I THOUGHT HE WAS NUTS...
BUT HE TRULY BELIEVES IN MY ABILITY TO LEAP THROUGH TIME.
THAT'S WHY HE'S SO SERIOUS ABOUT THIS.

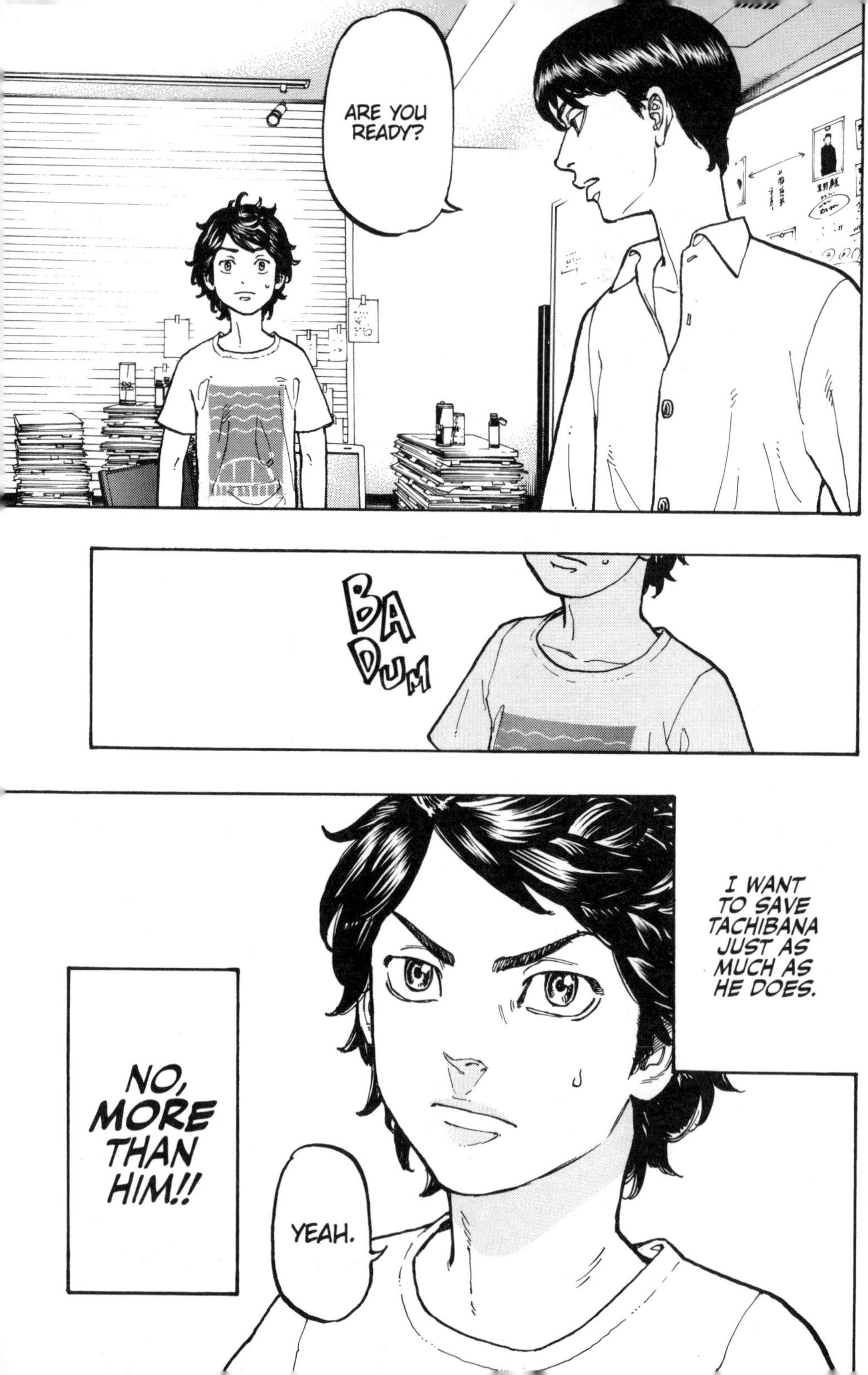
ARE YOU READY?
BA DUM
I WANT TO SAVE TACHIBANA JUST AS MUCH AS HE DOES.
NO, MORE THAN HIM!!
YEAH.

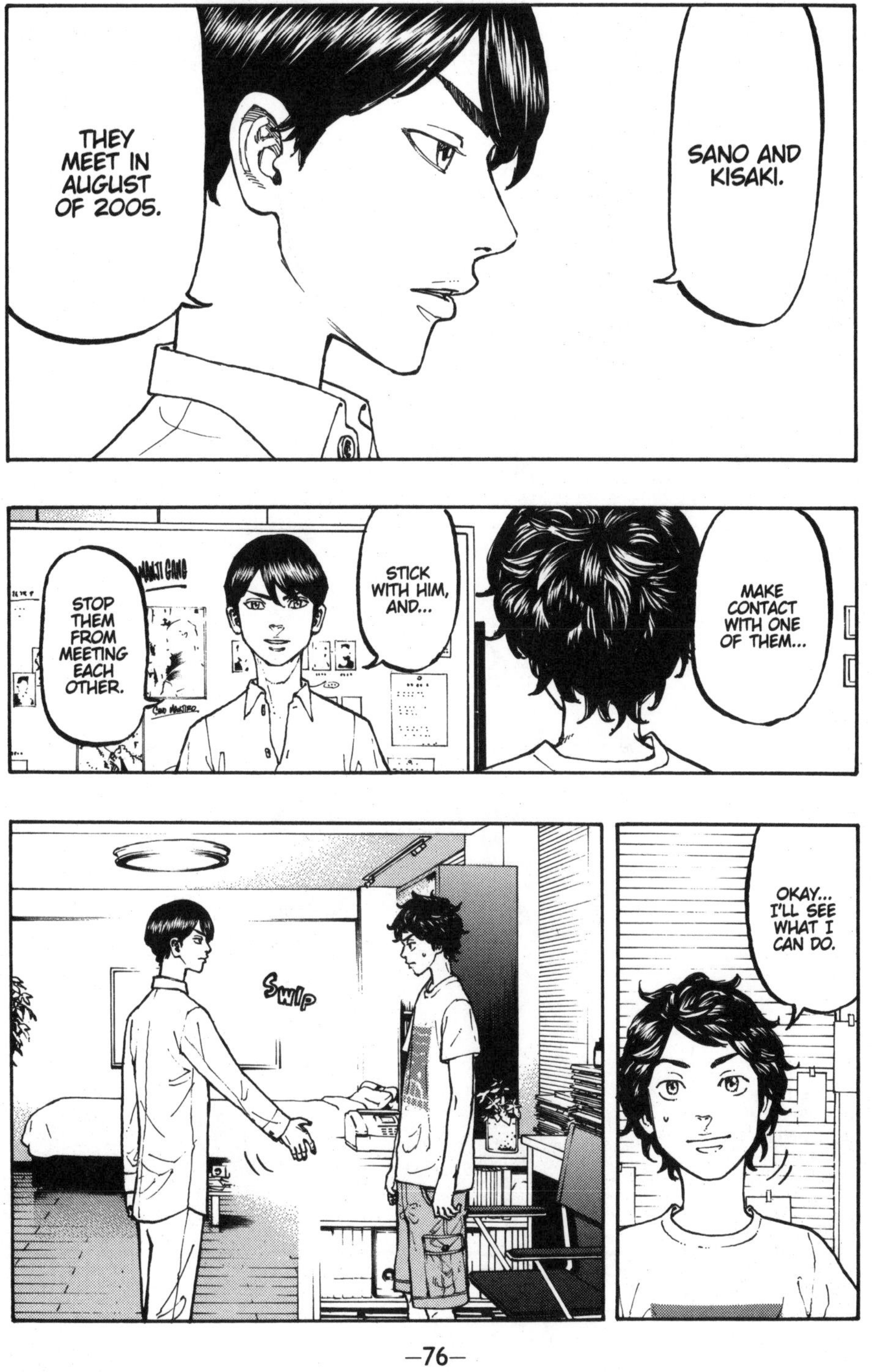
SANO AND KISAKI.
THEY MEET IN AUGUST OF 2005.
MAKE CONTACT WITH ONE OF THEM...
STICK WITH HIM, AND...
STOP THEM FROM MEETING EACH OTHER.
OKAY... I'LL SEE WHAT I CAN DO.
SWIP

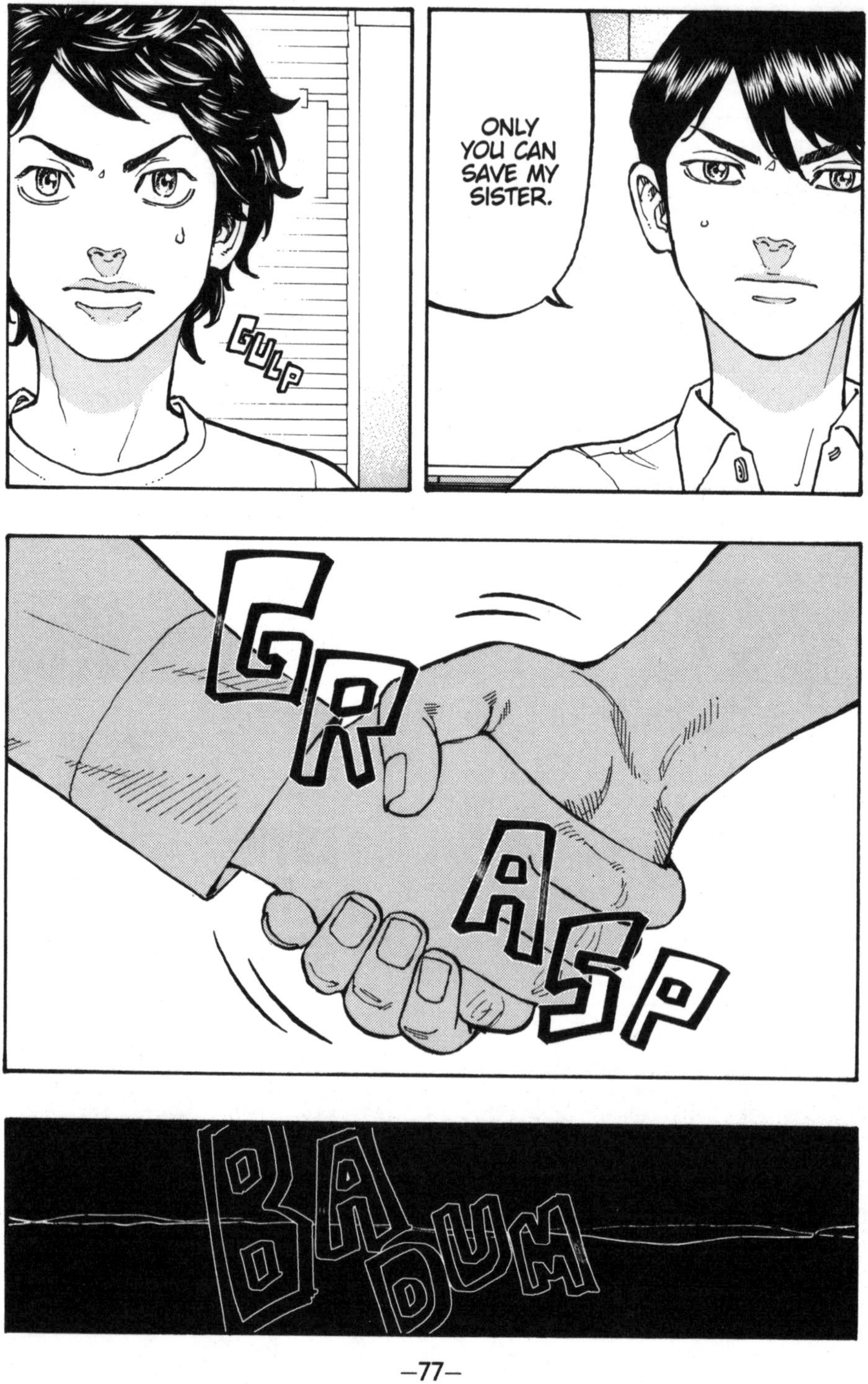
ONLY YOU CAN SAVE MY SISTER.
GULP
GRASP
BA DUM

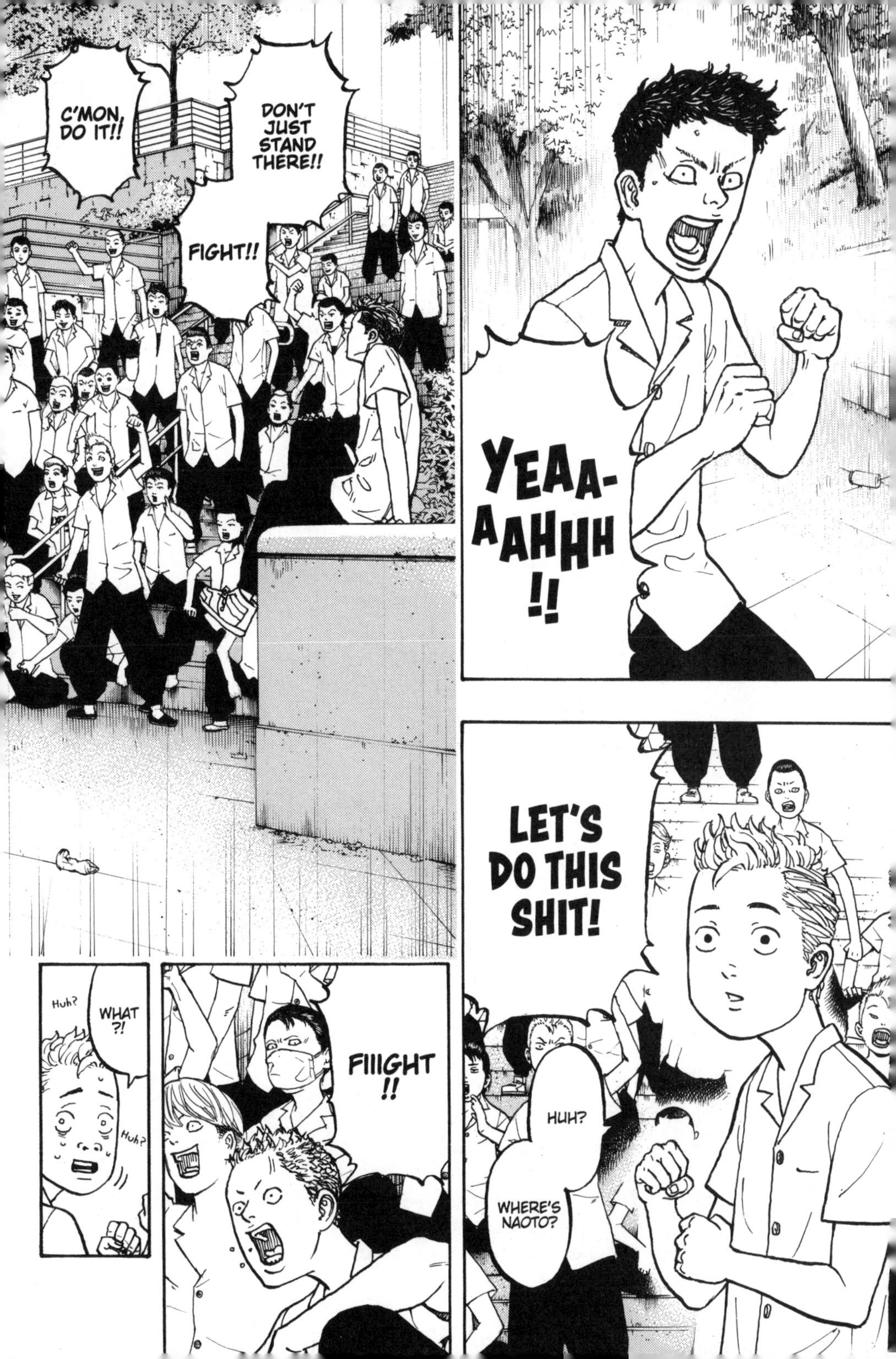

YEAAA-AAHHH!!
LET'S DO THIS SHIT!
HUH?
WHERE'S NAOTO?
DON'T JUST STAND THERE!!
C'MON, DO IT!!
FIGHT!!
FIIIGHT!!
WHAT?!
Huh?
Huh?

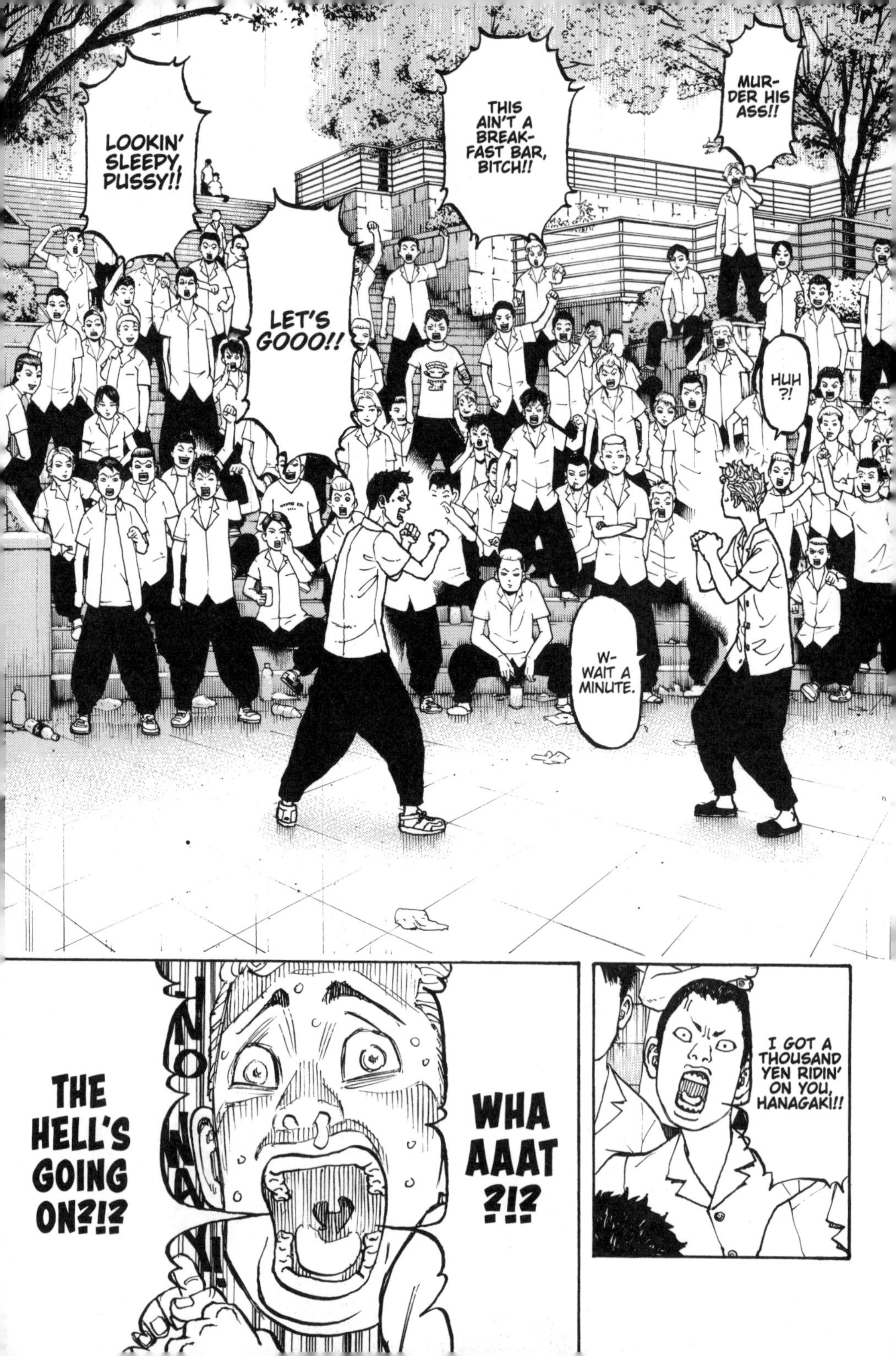
MUR-DER HIS ASS!!
HUH ?!
THIS AIN'T A BREAK-FAST BAR, BITCH!!
W-WAIT A MINUTE.
LET'S GOOO!!
LOOKIN' SLEEPY, PUSSY!!
I GOT A THOUSAND YEN RIDIN' ON YOU, HANAGAKI!!
WHA AAAT ?!?
THE HELL'S GOING ON?!?

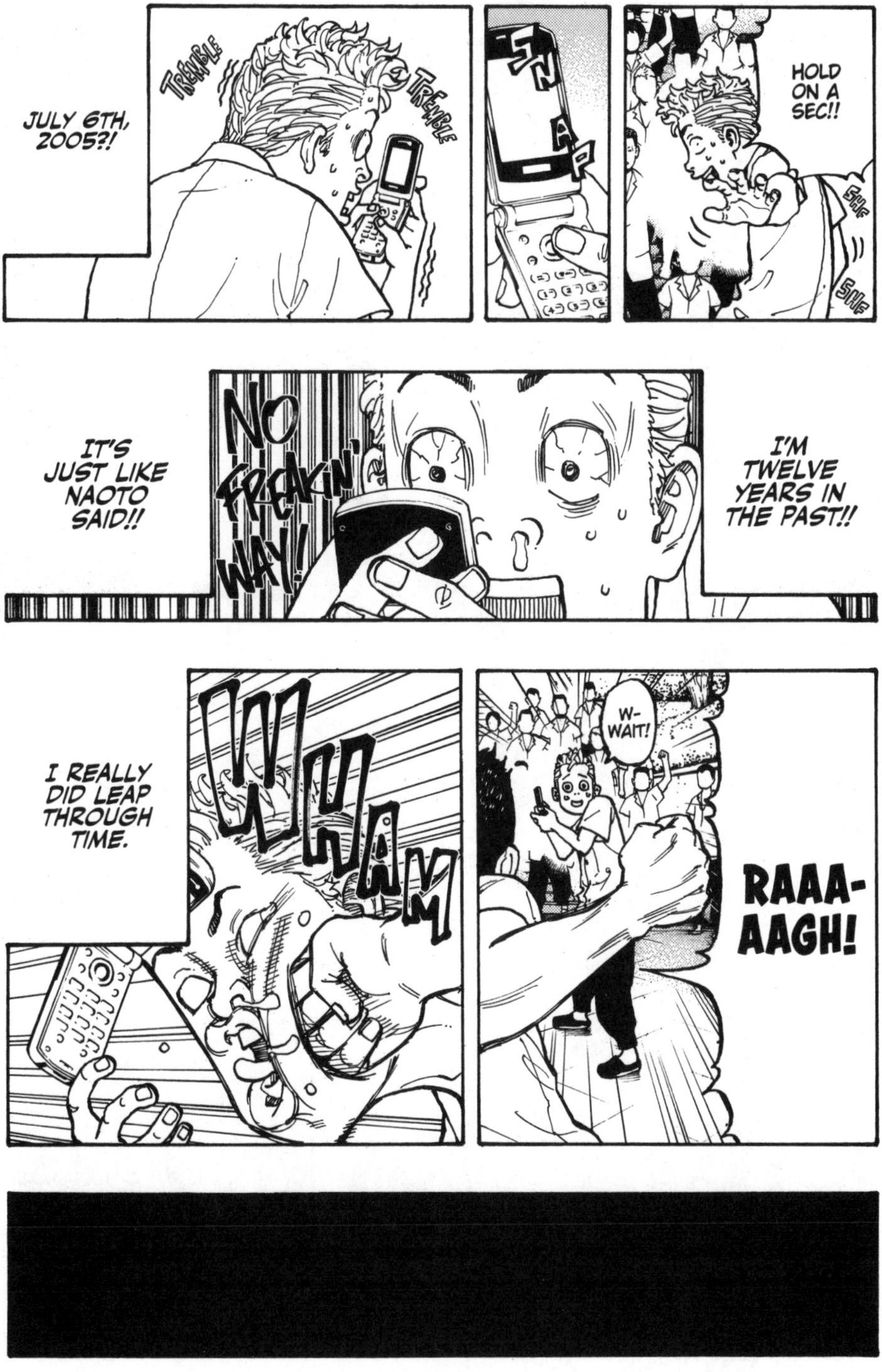
HOLD ON A SEC!!
SHF
SHF
SNAP
TREMBLE
TREMBLE
JULY 6TH, 2005?!
I'M TWELVE YEARS IN THE PAST!!
NO FREAKIN' WAY!
IT'S JUST LIKE NAOTO SAID!!
W-WAIT!
RAAAA-AAGH!
WHAM
I REALLY DID LEAP THROUGH TIME.

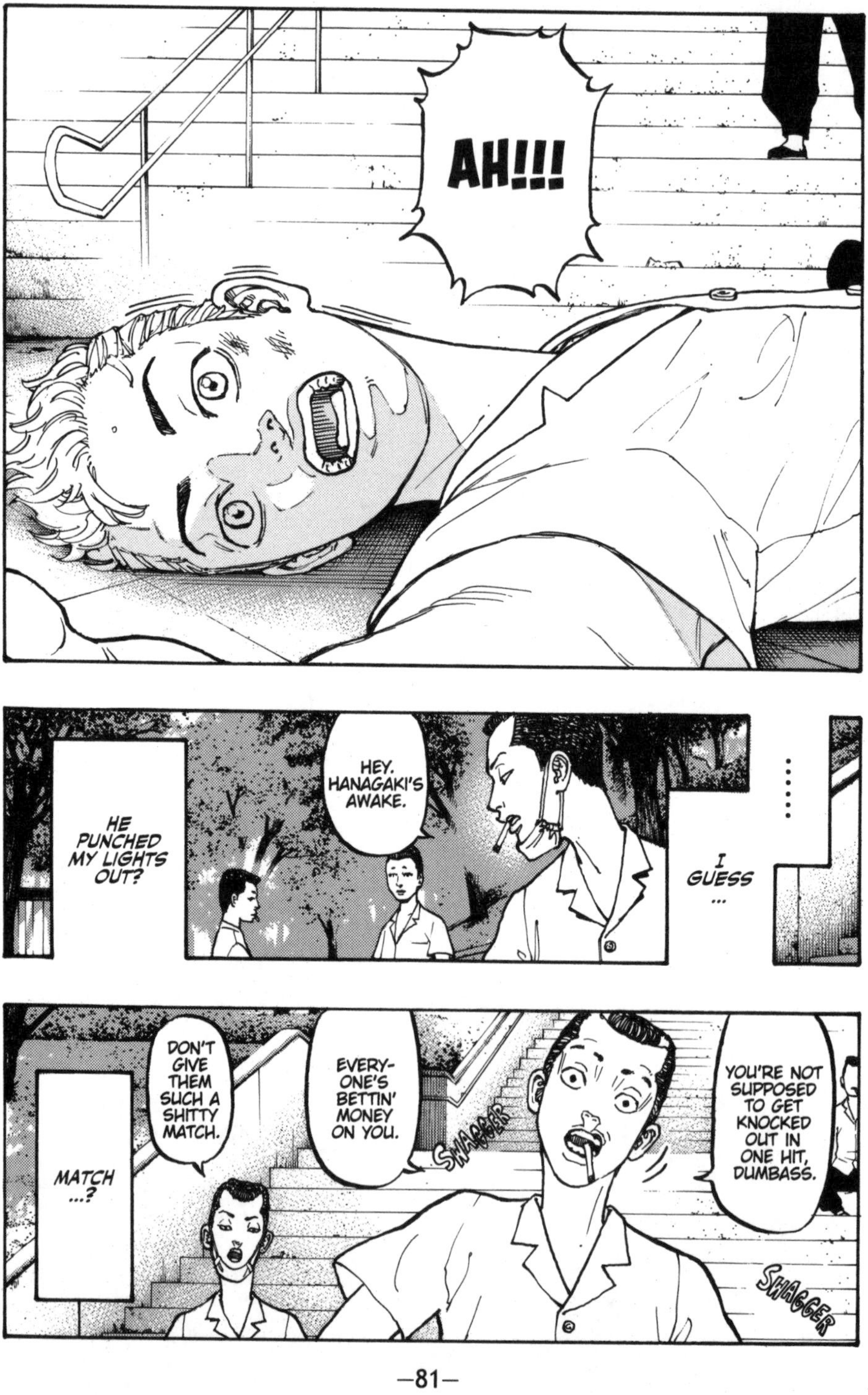
AH!!!
......
I GUESS ...
HEY. HANAGAKI'S AWAKE.
HE PUNCHED MY LIGHTS OUT?
YOU'RE NOT SUPPOSED TO GET KNOCKED OUT IN ONE HIT, DUMBASS.
SWAGGER
SWAGGER
EVERY-ONE'S BETTIN' MONEY ON YOU.
DON'T GIVE THEM SUCH A SHITTY MATCH.
MATCH ...?

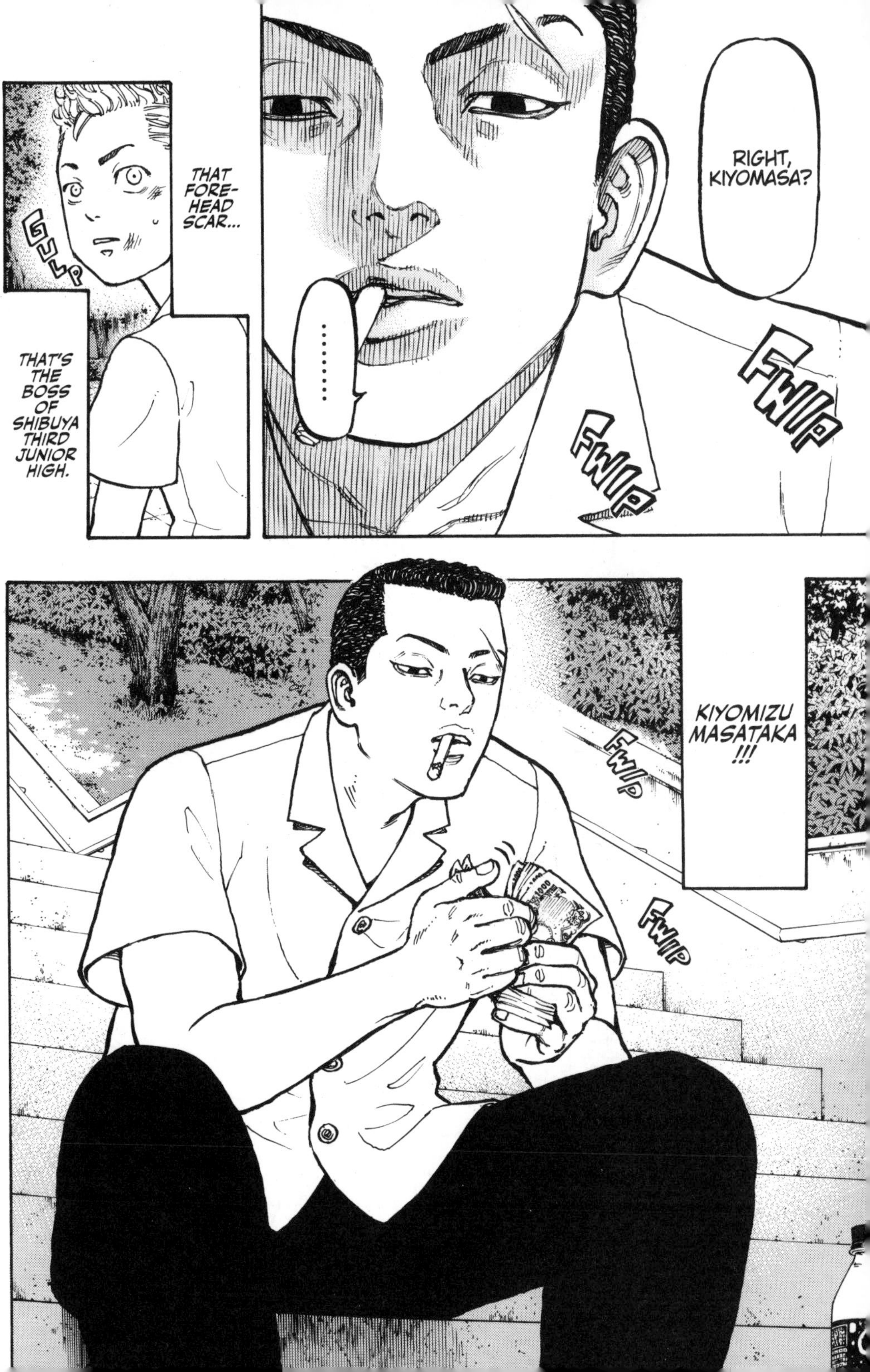
RIGHT, KIYOMASA?
......
FWIP
FWIP
THAT FORE-HEAD SCAR...
GULP
THAT'S THE BOSS OF SHIBUYA THIRD JUNIOR HIGH.
KIYOMIZU MASATAKA !!!
FWIP
FWIP

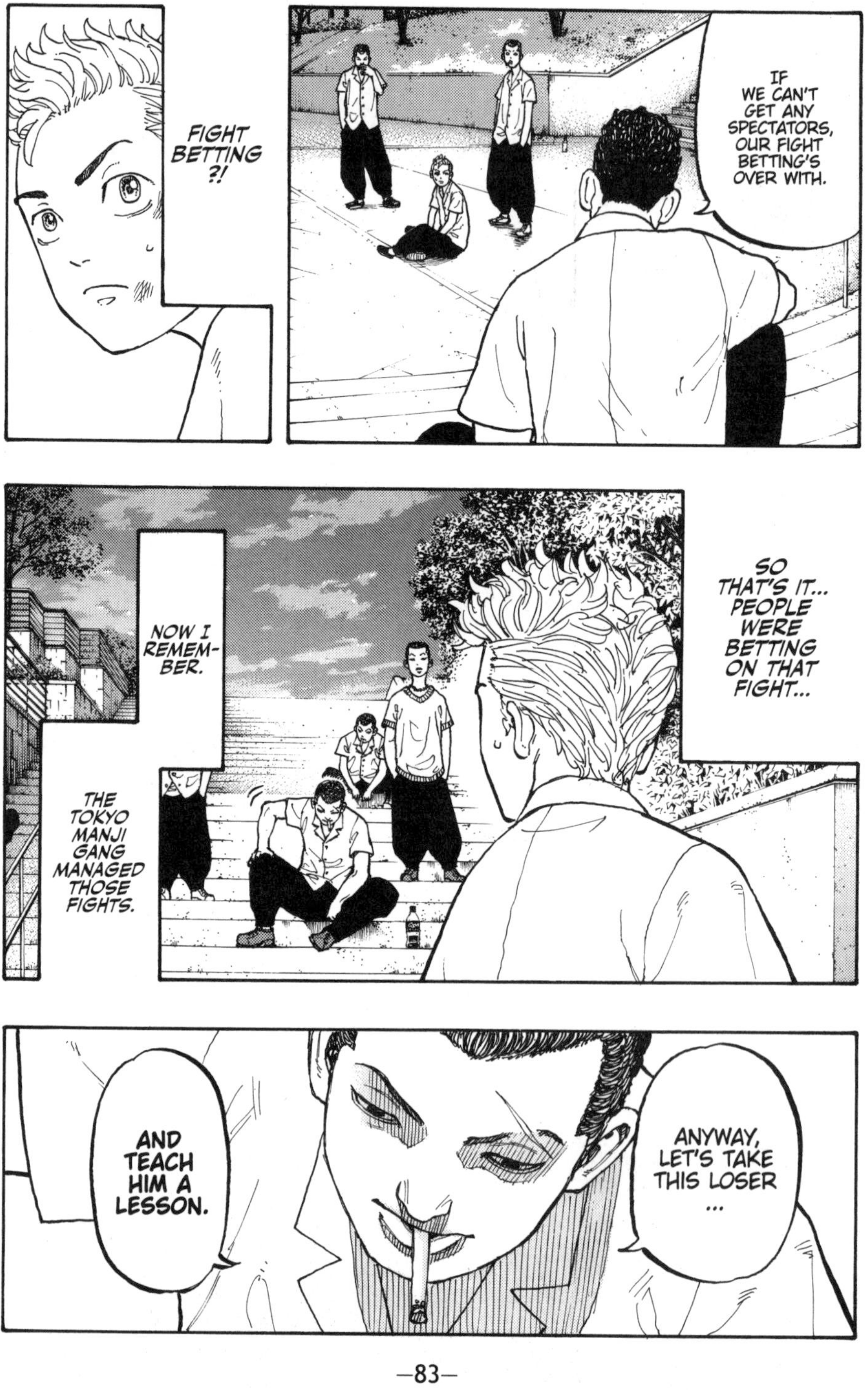
IF WE CAN'T GET ANY SPECTATORS, OUR FIGHT BETTING'S OVER WITH.
FIGHT BETTING ?!
SO THAT'S IT... PEOPLE WERE BETTING ON THAT FIGHT...
NOW I REMEMBER.
THE TOKYO MANJI GANG MANAGED THOSE FIGHTS.
ANYWAY, LET'S TAKE THIS LOSER ...
AND TEACH HIM A LESSON.

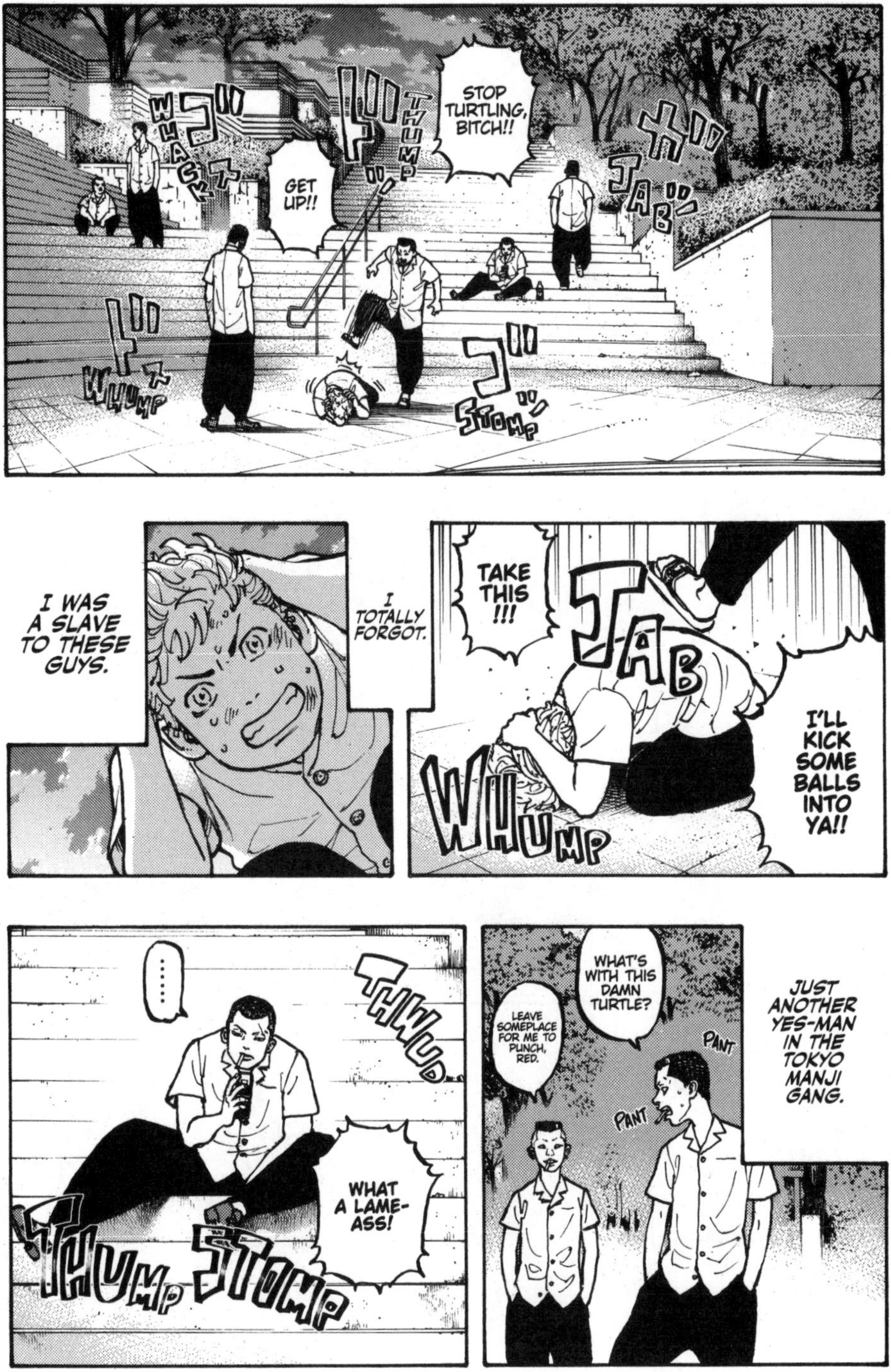
STOP TURTLING, BITCH!!
JAB
THUMP
GET UP!!
WHACK
WHUMP
STOMP
TAKE THIS!!!
JAB
I'LL KICK SOME BALLS INTO YA!!
WHUMP
I TOTALLY FORGOT.
I WAS A SLAVE TO THESE GUYS.
JUST ANOTHER YES-MAN IN THE TOKYO MANJI GANG.
WHAT'S WITH THIS DAMN TURTLE?
PANT
LEAVE SOMEPLACE FOR ME TO PUNCH, RED.
PANT
THWUD
......
WHAT A LAME-ASS!
STOMP
THUMP

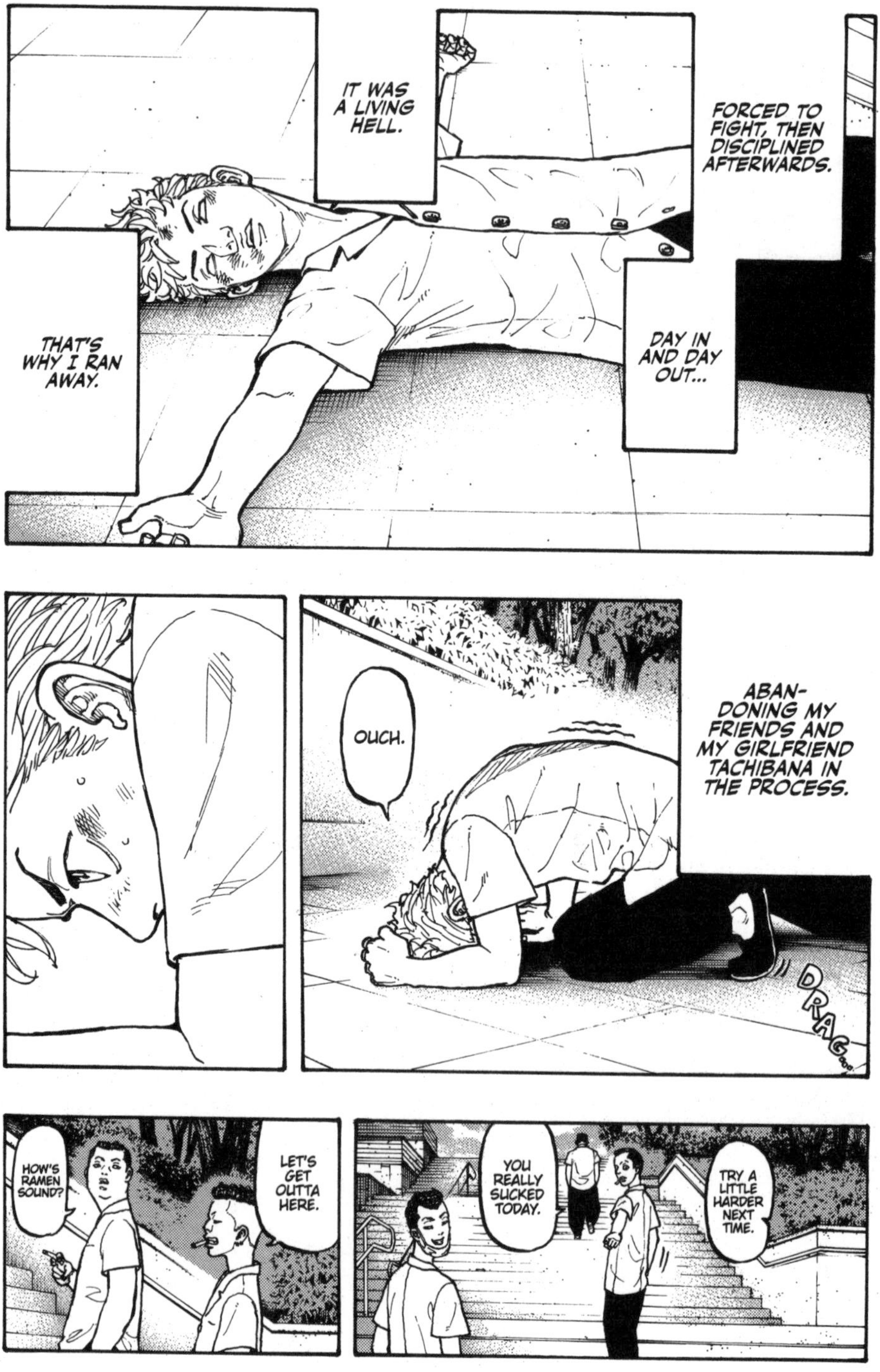
FORCED TO FIGHT, THEN DISCIPLINED AFTERWARDS.
DAY IN AND DAY OUT...
IT WAS A LIVING HELL.
THAT'S WHY I RAN AWAY.
ABAN-DONING MY FRIENDS AND MY GIRLFRIEND TACHIBANA IN THE PROCESS.
OUCH.
DRAG...
TRY A LITTLE HARDER NEXT TIME.
YOU REALLY SUCKED TODAY.
LET'S GET OUTTA HERE.
HOW'S RAMEN SOUND?

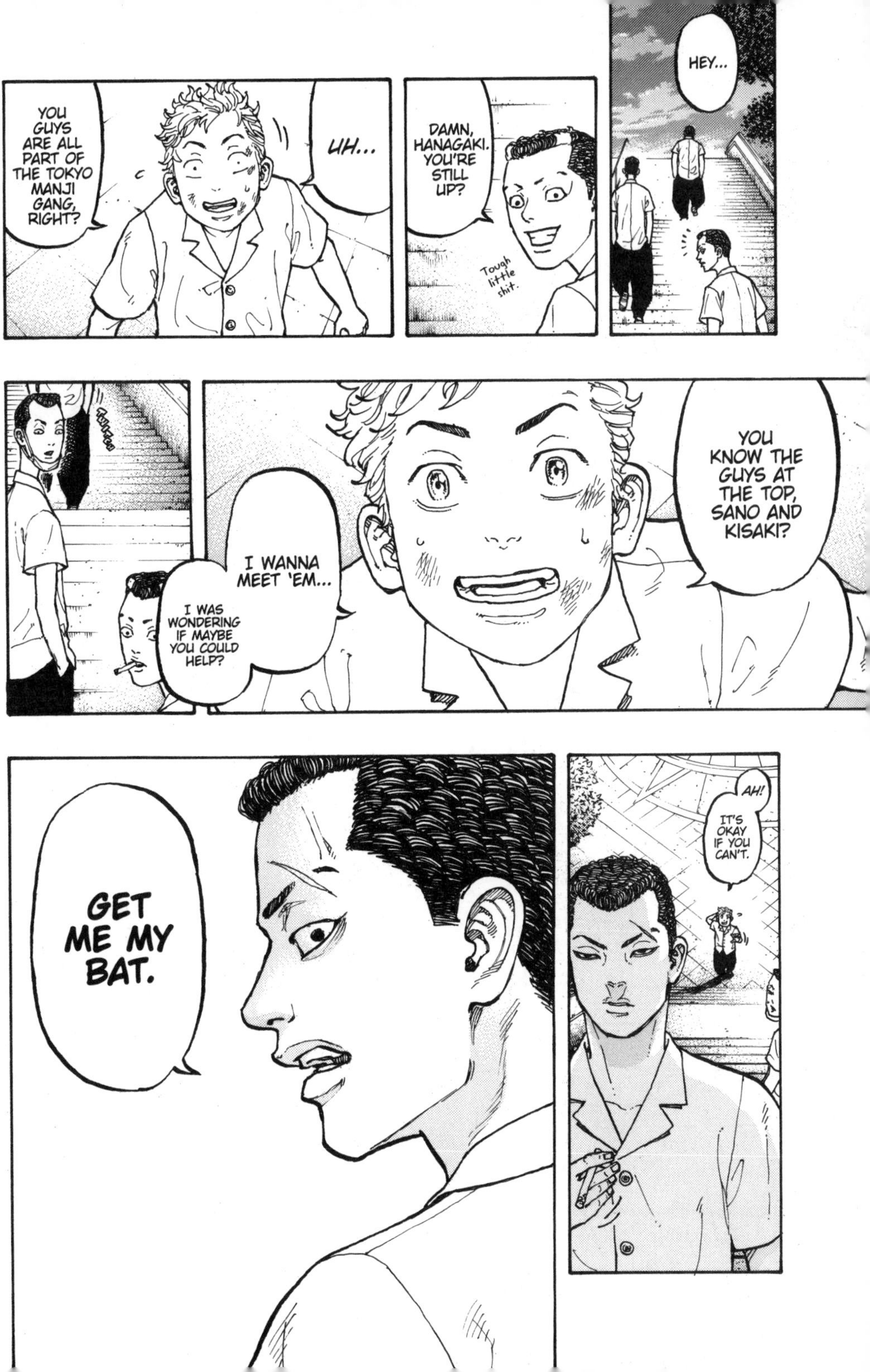
HEY...
DAMN, HANAGAKI. YOU'RE STILL UP?
Tough little shit.
UH...
YOU GUYS ARE ALL PART OF THE TOKYO MANJI GANG, RIGHT?
YOU KNOW THE GUYS AT THE TOP, SANO AND KISAKI?
I WANNA MEET 'EM...
I WAS WONDERING IF MAYBE YOU COULD HELP?
AH!
IT'S OKAY IF YOU CAN'T.
GET ME MY BAT.

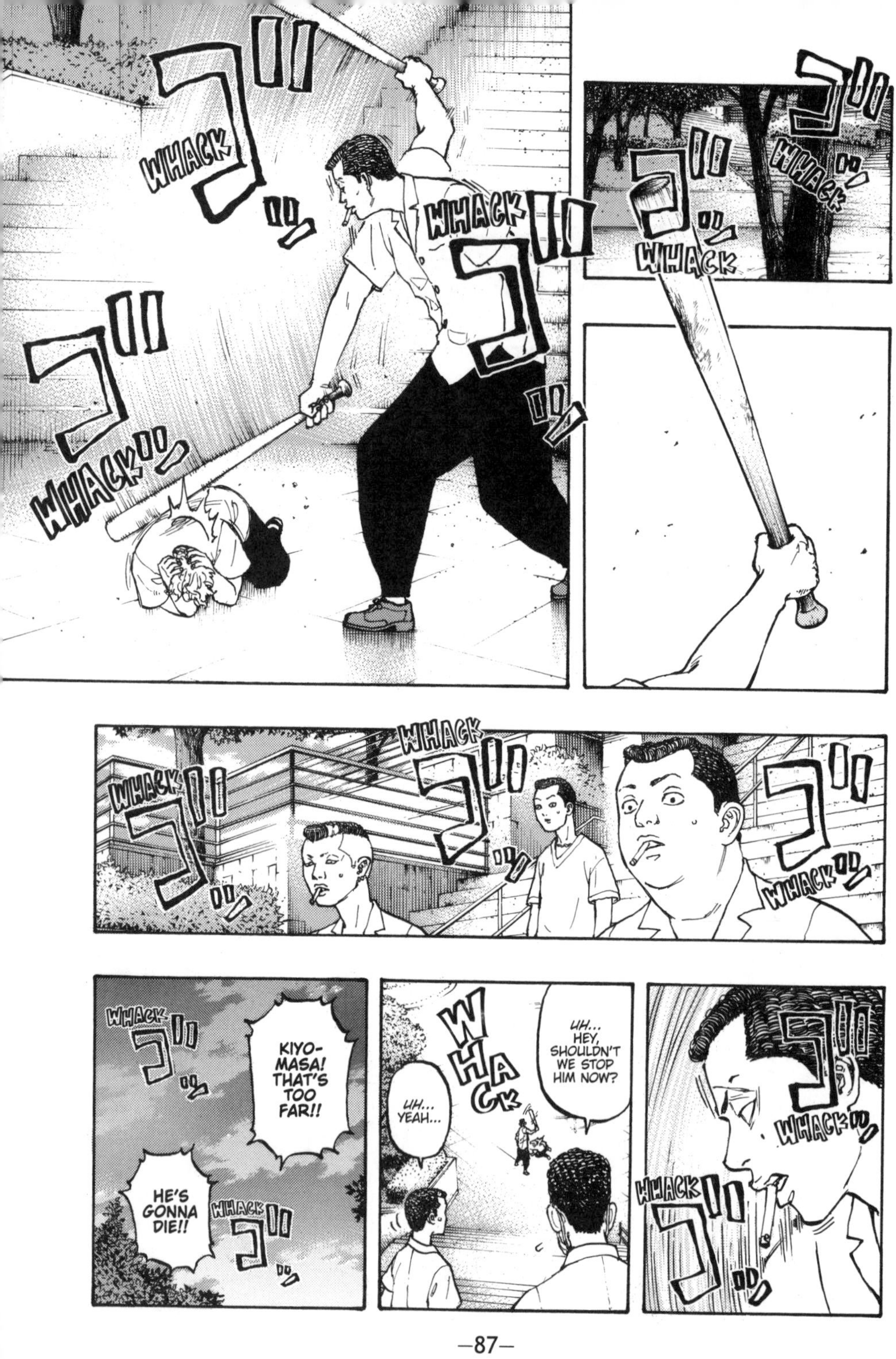
WHACK
WHACK
WHACK
WHACK
WHACK
WHACK
WHACK
WHACK
WHACK
WHACK
WHACK
UH... HEY, SHOULDN'T WE STOP HIM NOW?
WHACK
UH... YEAH...
KIYO-MASA! THAT'S TOO FAR!!
WHACK
HE'S GONNA DIE!!
WHACK

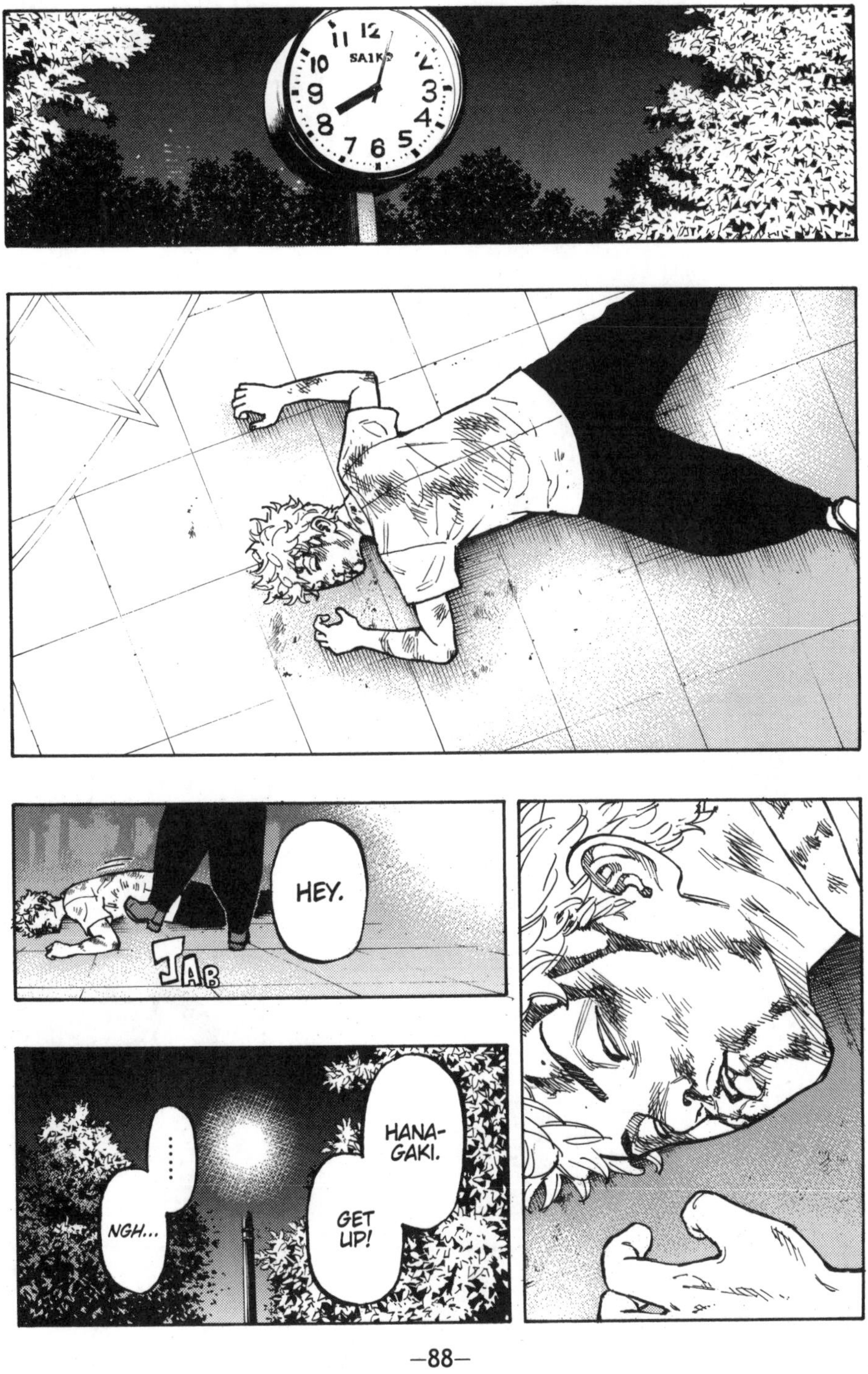
HEY.
JAB
HANA-GAKI.
GET UP!
......
NGH...

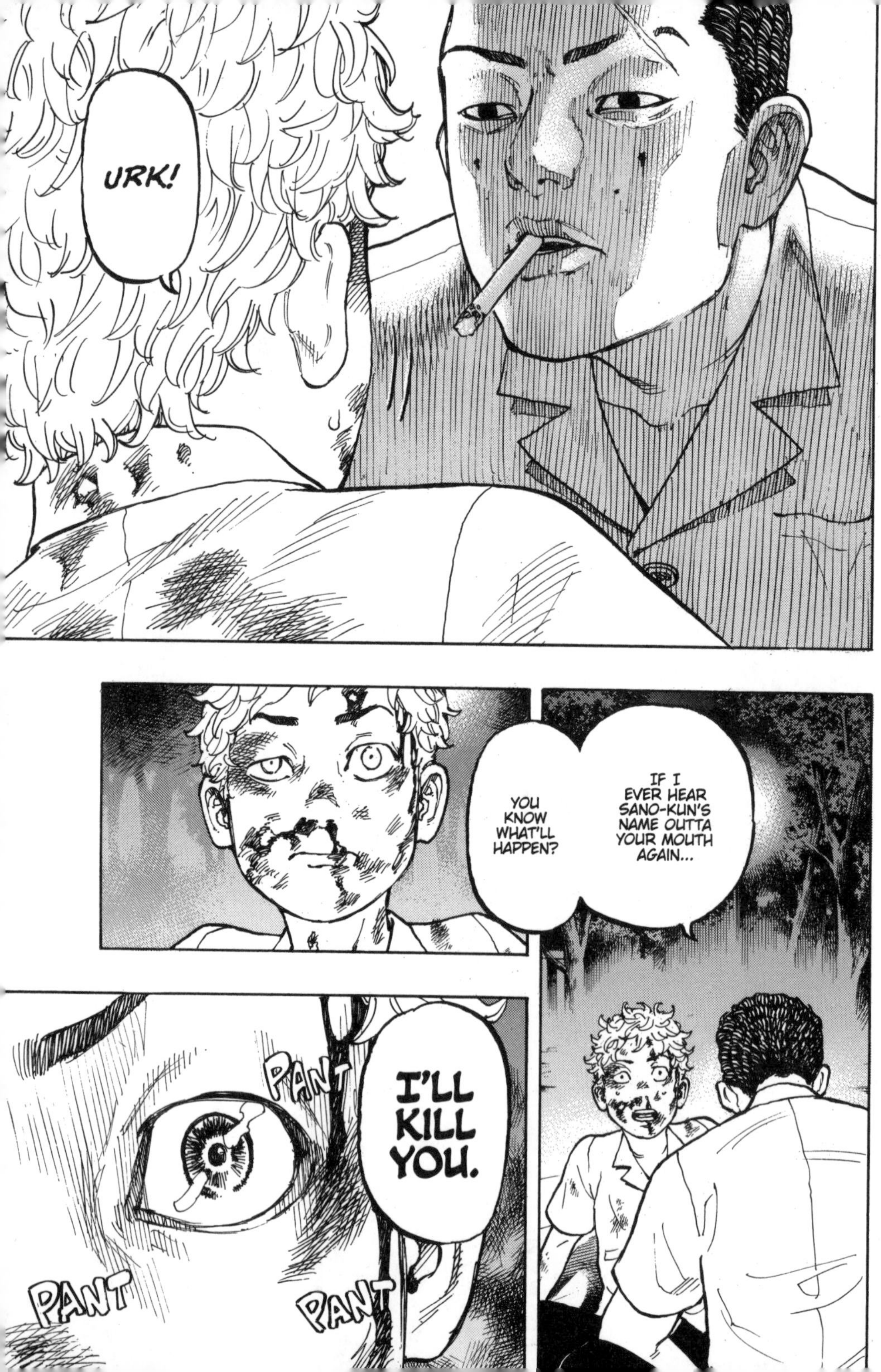
URK!
IF I EVER HEAR SANO-KUN'S NAME OUTTA YOUR MOUTH AGAIN...
YOU KNOW WHAT'LL HAPPEN?
I'LL KILL YOU.
PANT
PANT
PANT

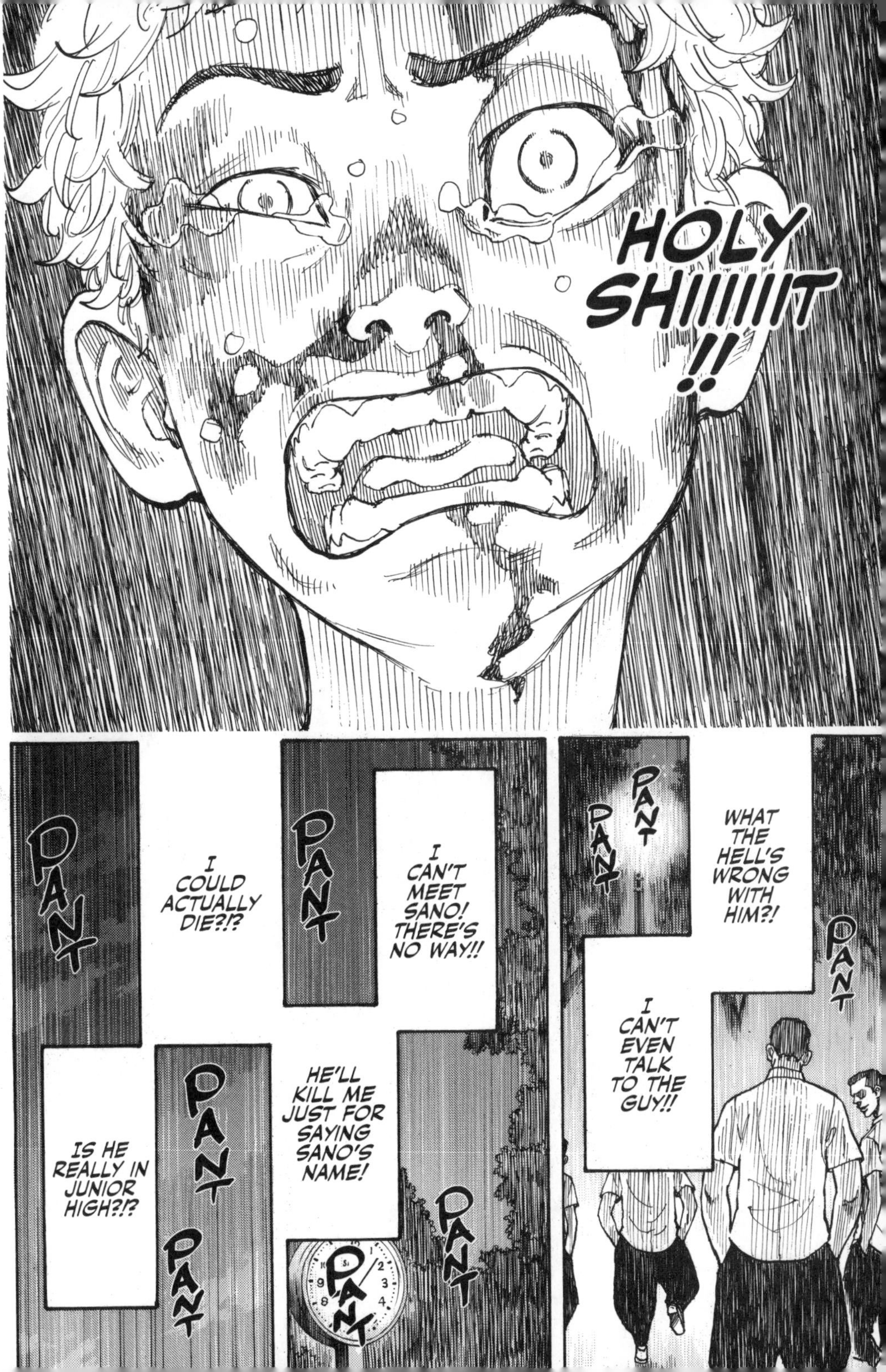
HOLY SHIIIIIIT!!
WHAT THE HELL'S WRONG WITH HIM?!
PANT
PANT
PANT
I CAN'T EVEN TALK TO THE GUY!!
I CAN'T MEET SANO! THERE'S NO WAY!!
PANT
HE'LL KILL ME JUST FOR SAYING SANO'S NAME!
PANT
PANT
I COULD ACTUALLY DIE?!?
PANT
PANT
IS HE REALLY IN JUNIOR HIGH?!?
PANT

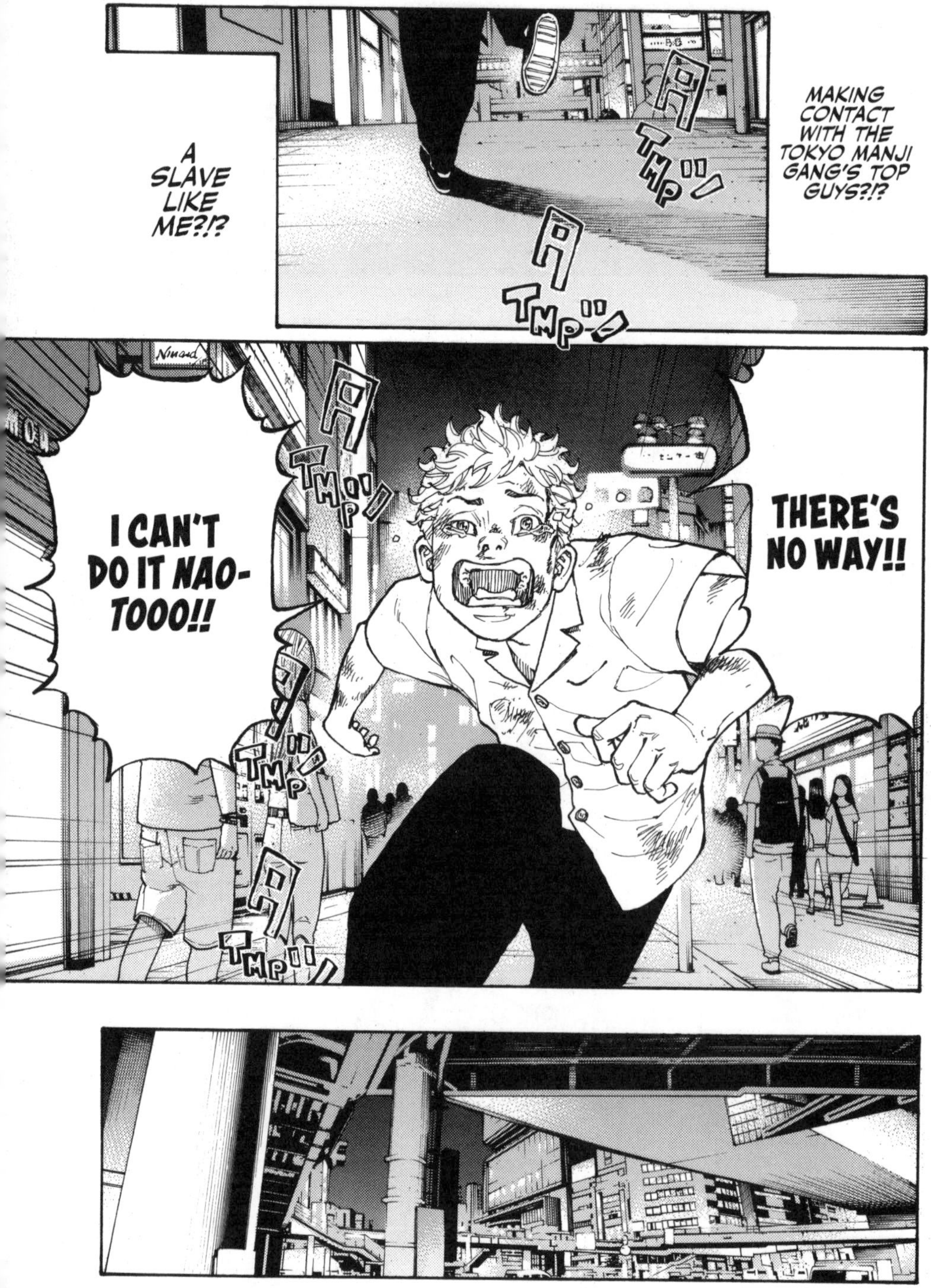
MAKING CONTACT WITH THE TOKYO MANJI GANG'S TOP GUYS?!?
A SLAVE LIKE ME?!?
TMP!!
TMP!!
THERE'S NO WAY!!
TMP!!
I CAN'T DO IT NAO-TOOO!!
TMP!!
TMP!!

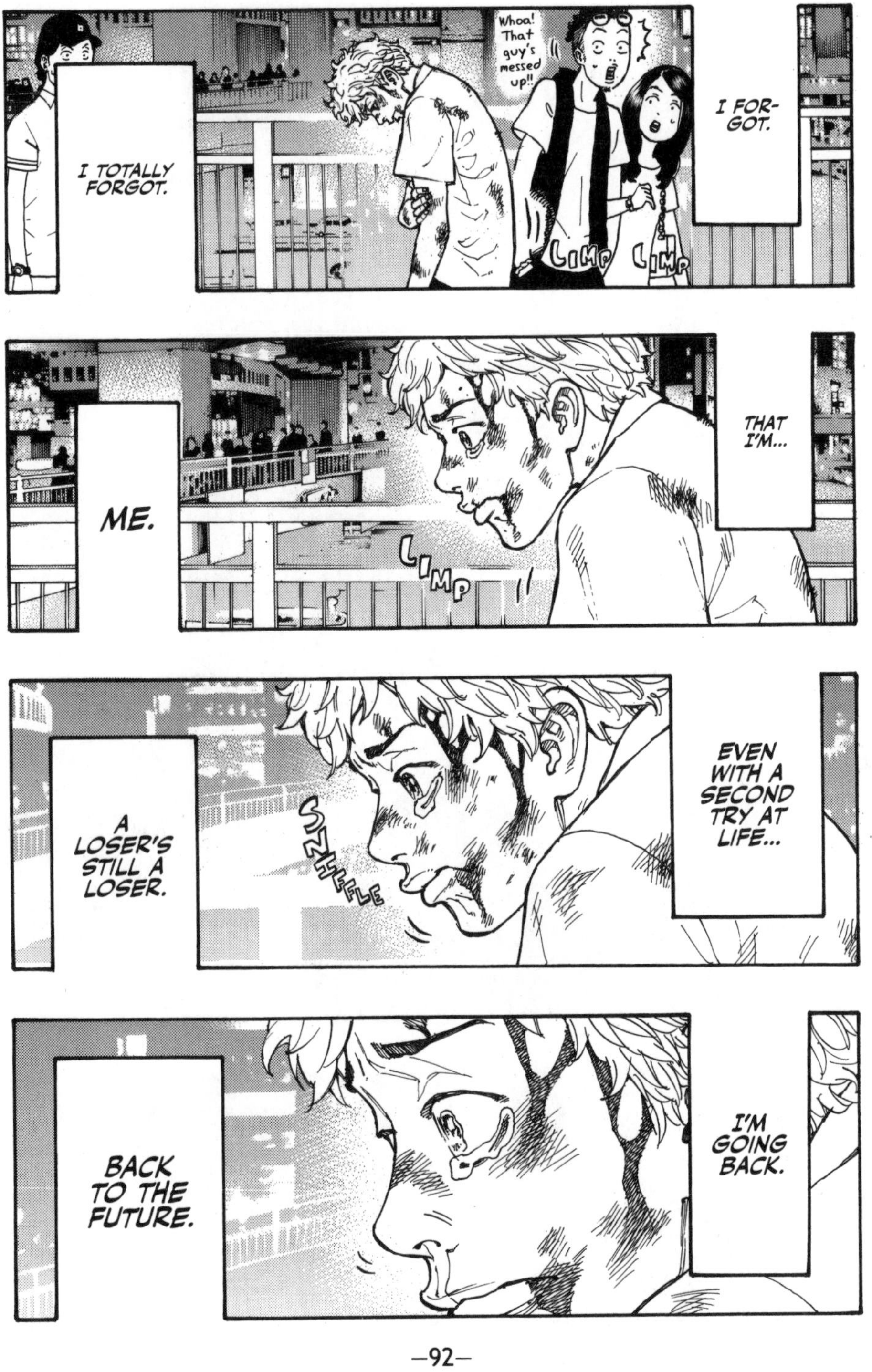
I FOR-GOT.
Whoa! That guy's messed up!!
LIMP LIMP
I TOTALLY FORGOT.
THAT I'M...
LIMP
ME.
EVEN WITH A SECOND TRY AT LIFE...
SNIFFLE
A LOSER'S STILL A LOSER.
I'M GOING BACK.
BACK TO THE FUTURE.

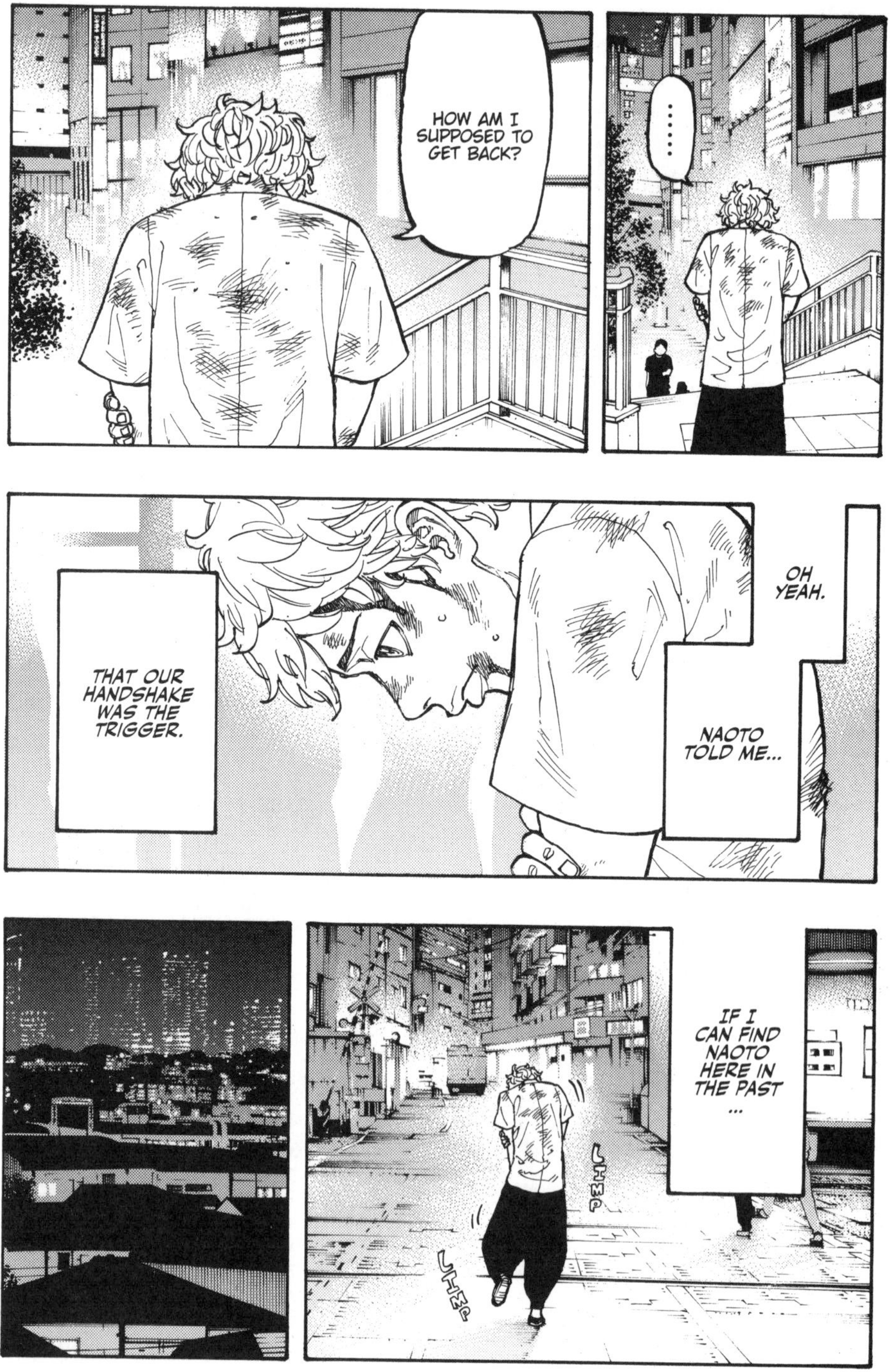
......
HOW AM I SUPPOSED TO GET BACK?
OH YEAH.
NAOTO TOLD ME...
THAT OUR HANDSHAKE WAS THE TRIGGER.
IF I CAN FIND NAOTO HERE IN THE PAST ...
LIMP
LIMP

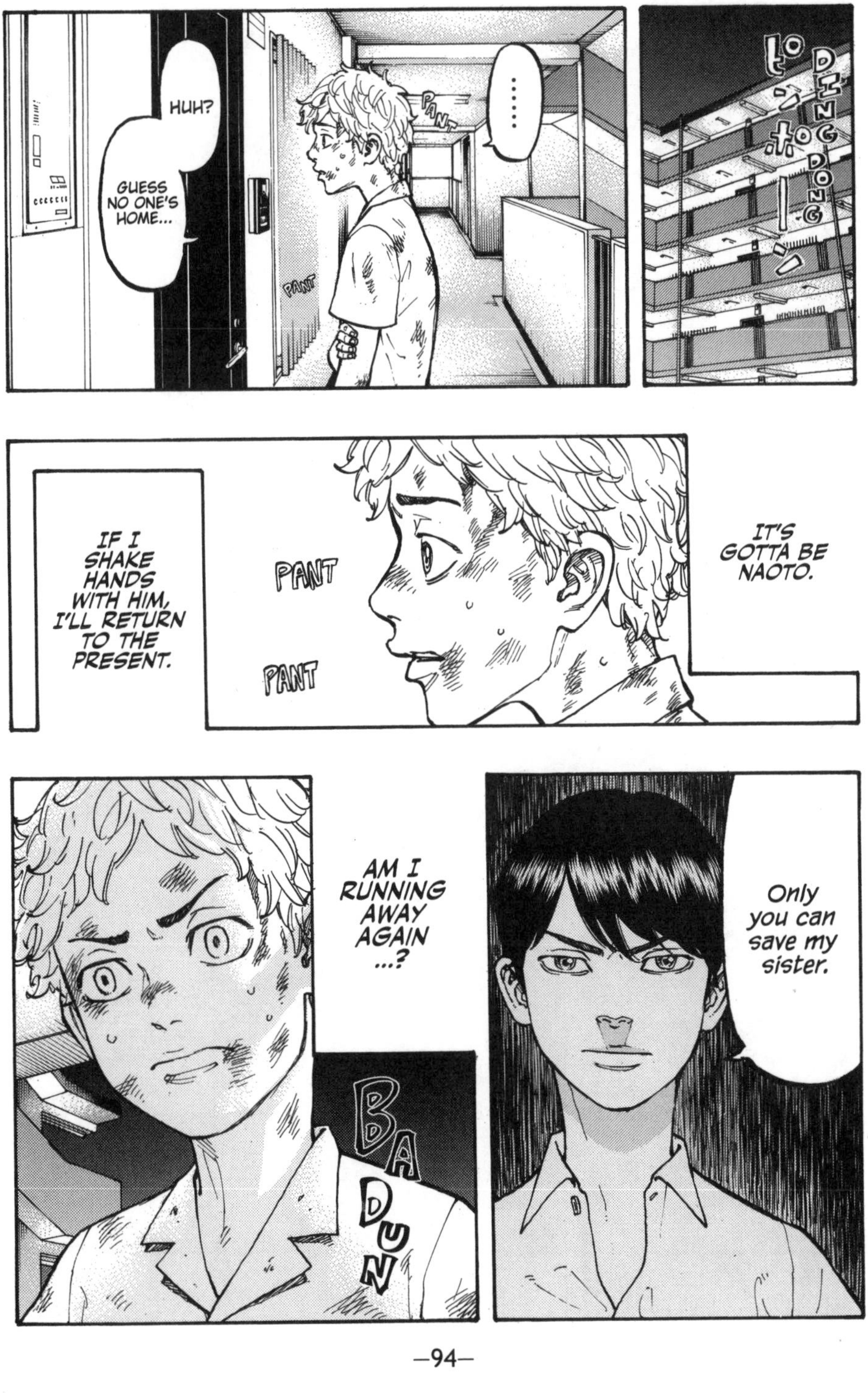
DING DONG
......
PANT
HUH?
GUESS NO ONE'S HOME...
PANT
IT'S GOTTA BE NAOTO.
PANT
PANT
IF I SHAKE HANDS WITH HIM, I'LL RETURN TO THE PRESENT.
Only you can save my sister.
AM I RUNNING AWAY AGAIN ...?
BADUN

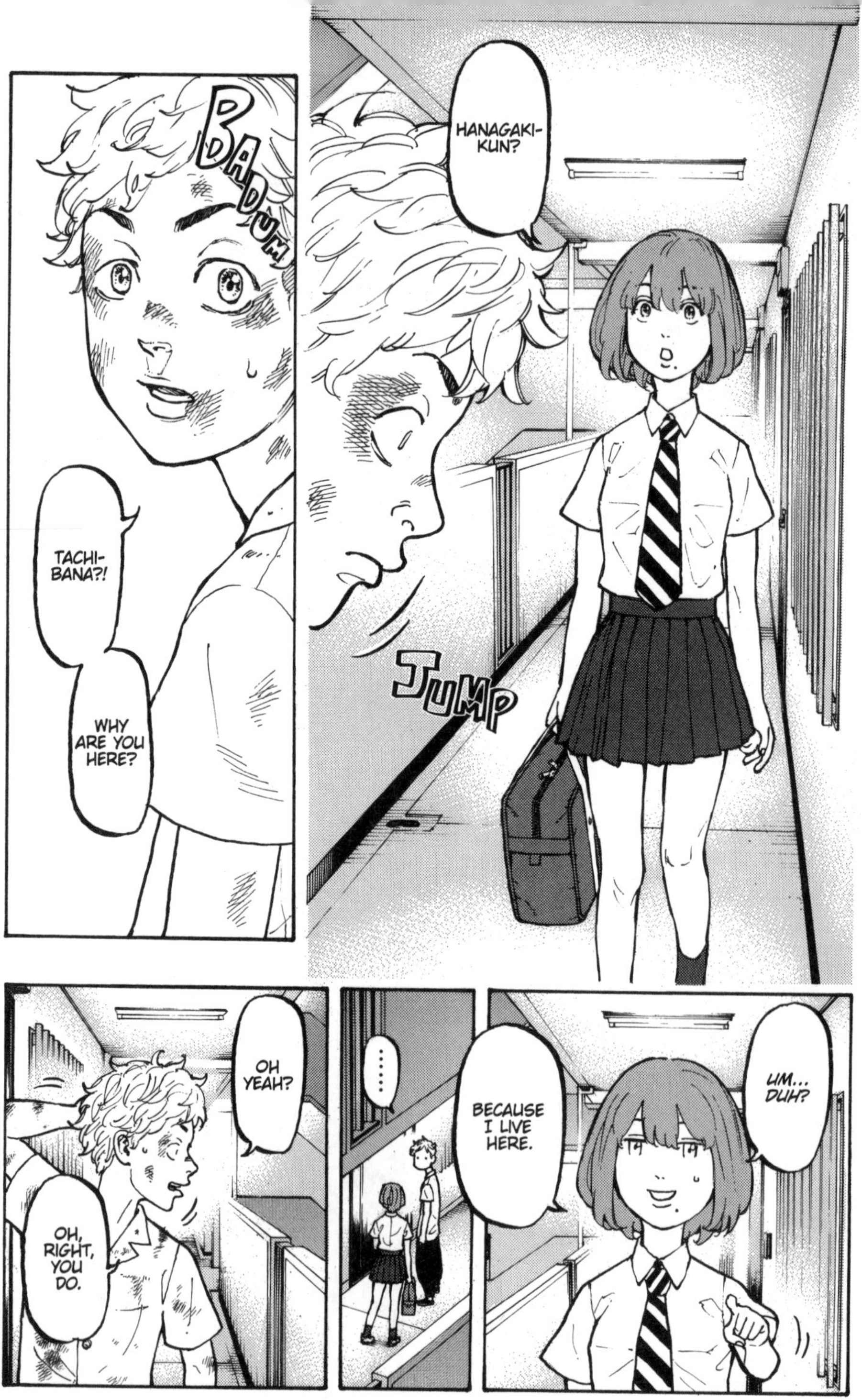
HANAGAKI-KUN?
JUMP
BADUM
TACHI-BANA?!
WHY ARE YOU HERE?
UM... DUH?
BECAUSE I LIVE HERE.
......
OH YEAH?
OH, RIGHT, YOU DO.

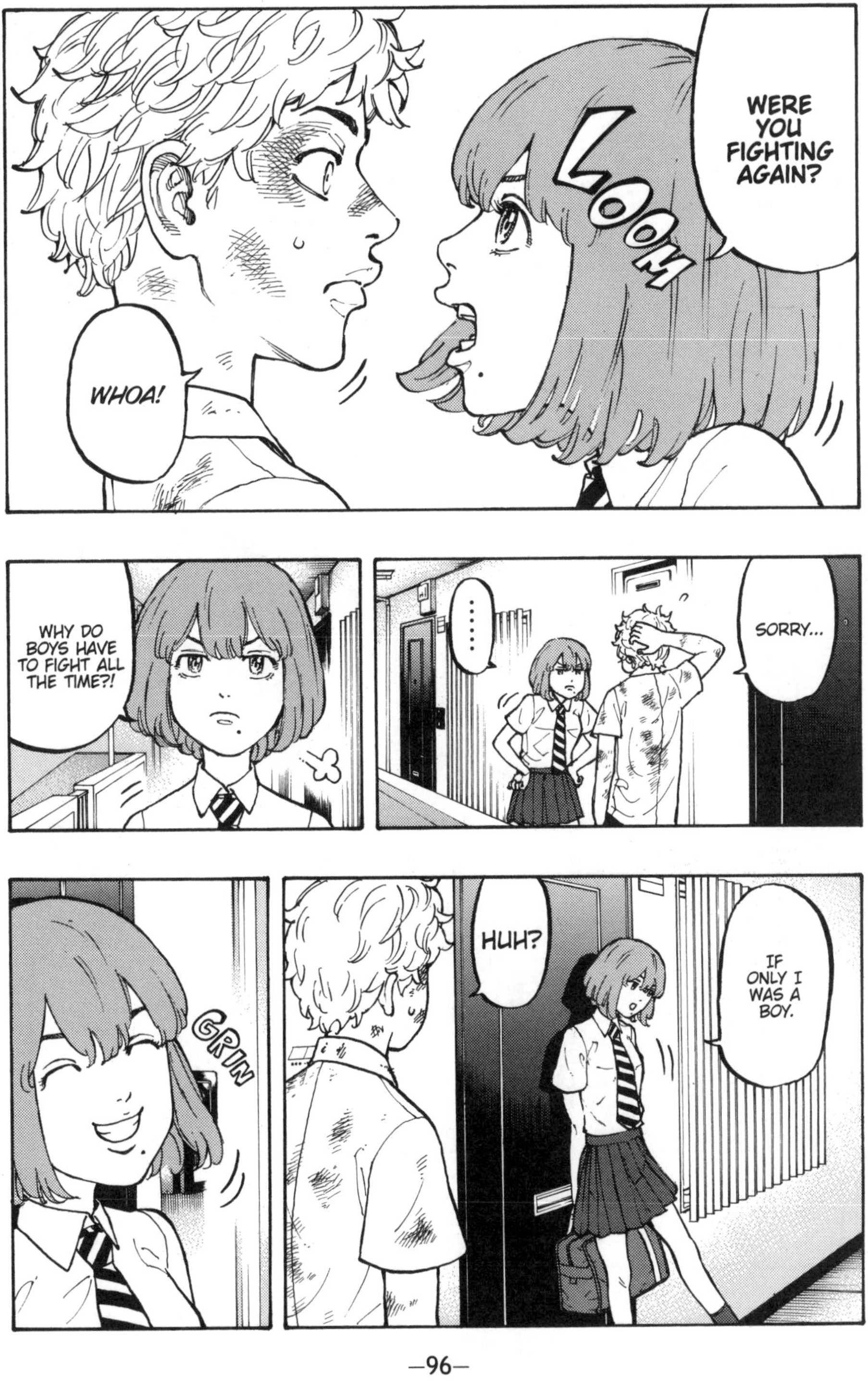
WERE YOU FIGHTING AGAIN?
LOOM
WHOA!
SORRY...
......
WHY DO BOYS HAVE TO FIGHT ALL THE TIME?!
IF ONLY I WAS A BOY.
HUH?
GRIN

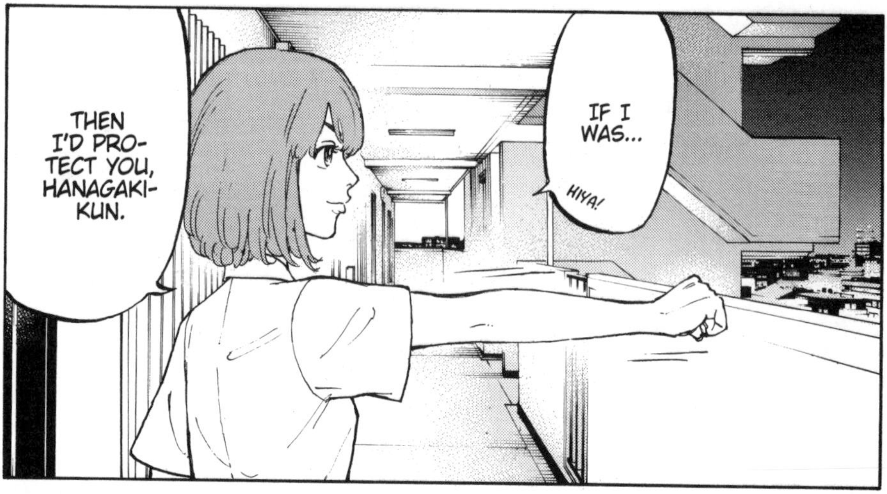
IF I WAS...
HIYA!
THEN I'D PROTECT YOU, HANAGAKI-KUN.
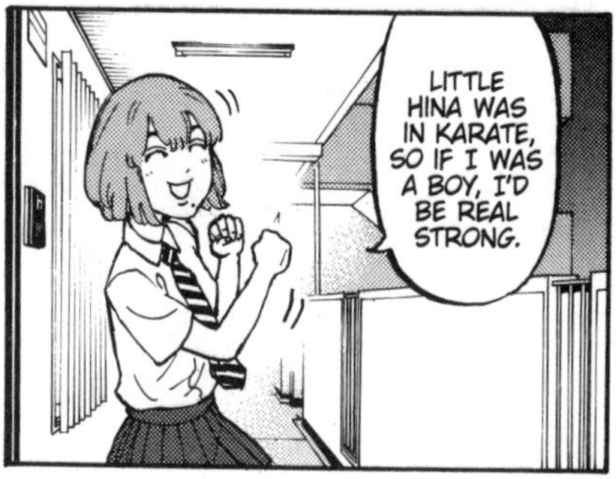
LITTLE HINA WAS IN KARATE, SO IF I WAS A BOY, I'D BE REAL STRONG.
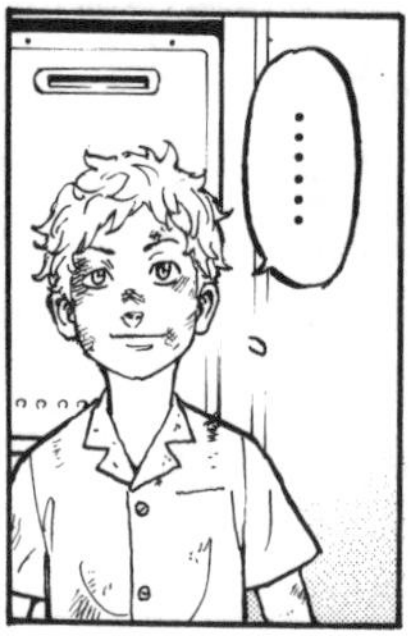
......
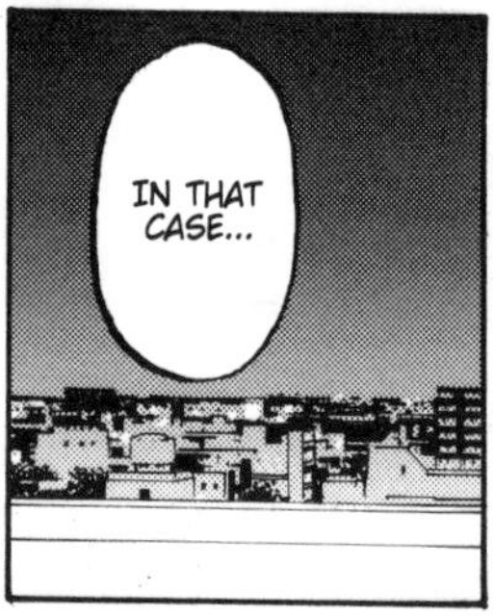
IN THAT CASE...
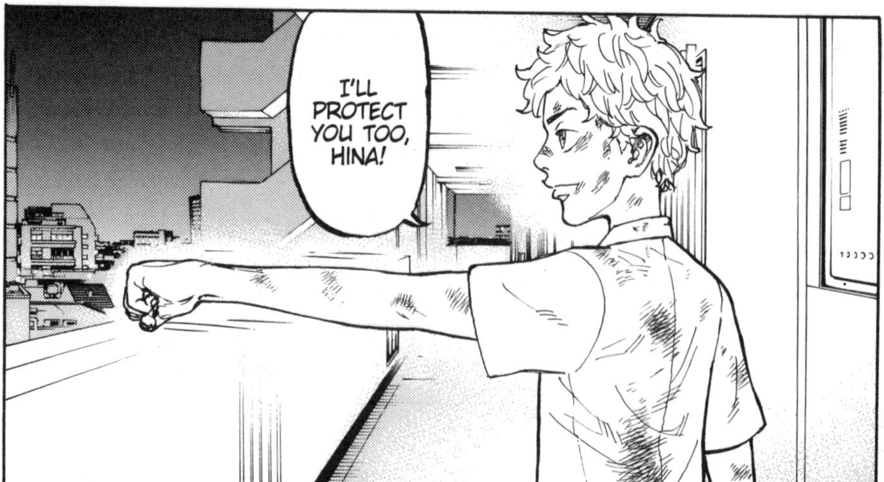
I'LL PROTECT YOU TOO, HINA!

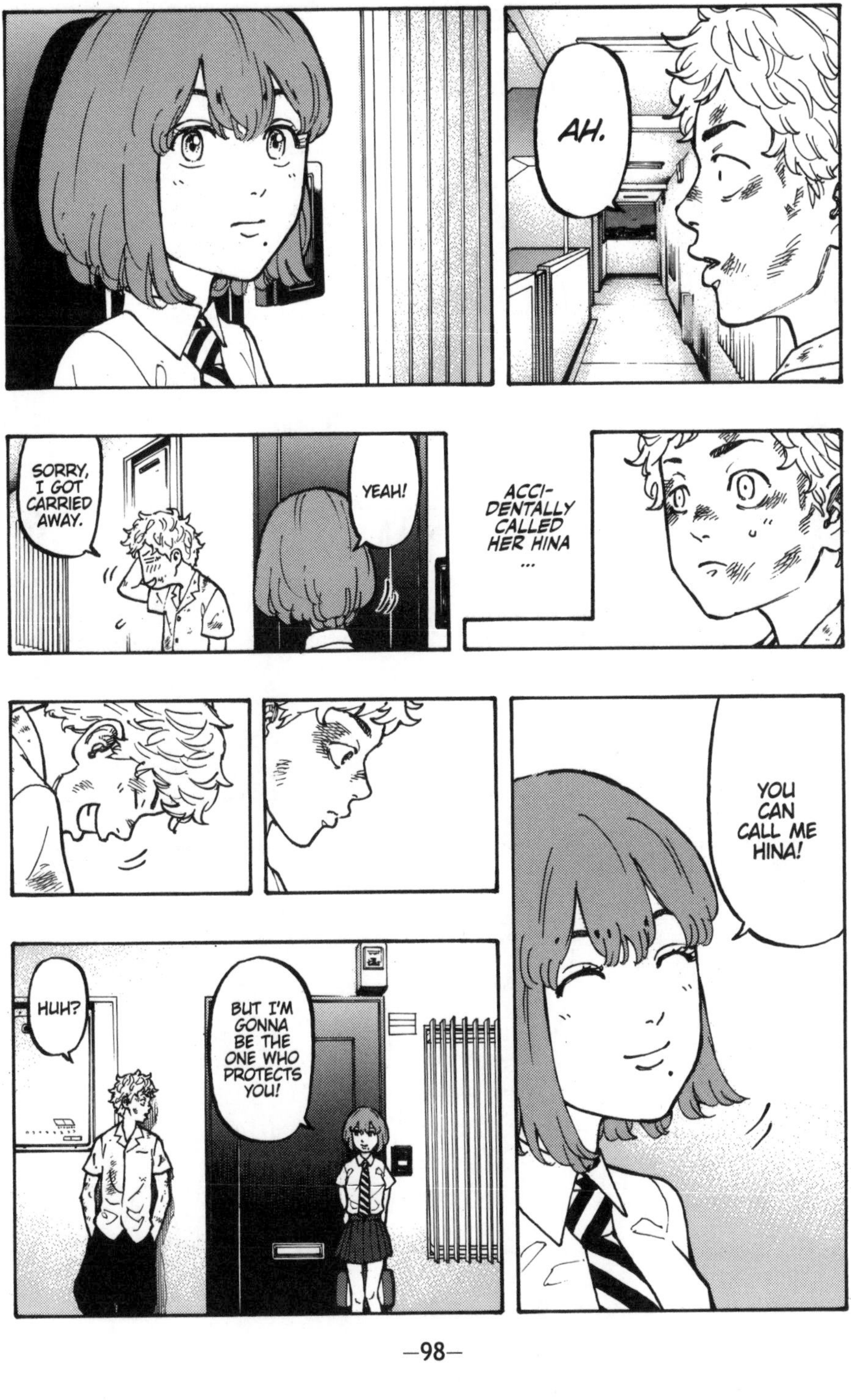
AH.
ACCI-DENTALLY CALLED HER HINA ...
YEAH!
SORRY, I GOT CARRIED AWAY.
YOU CAN CALL ME HINA!
BUT I'M GONNA BE THE ONE WHO PROTECTS YOU!
HUH?

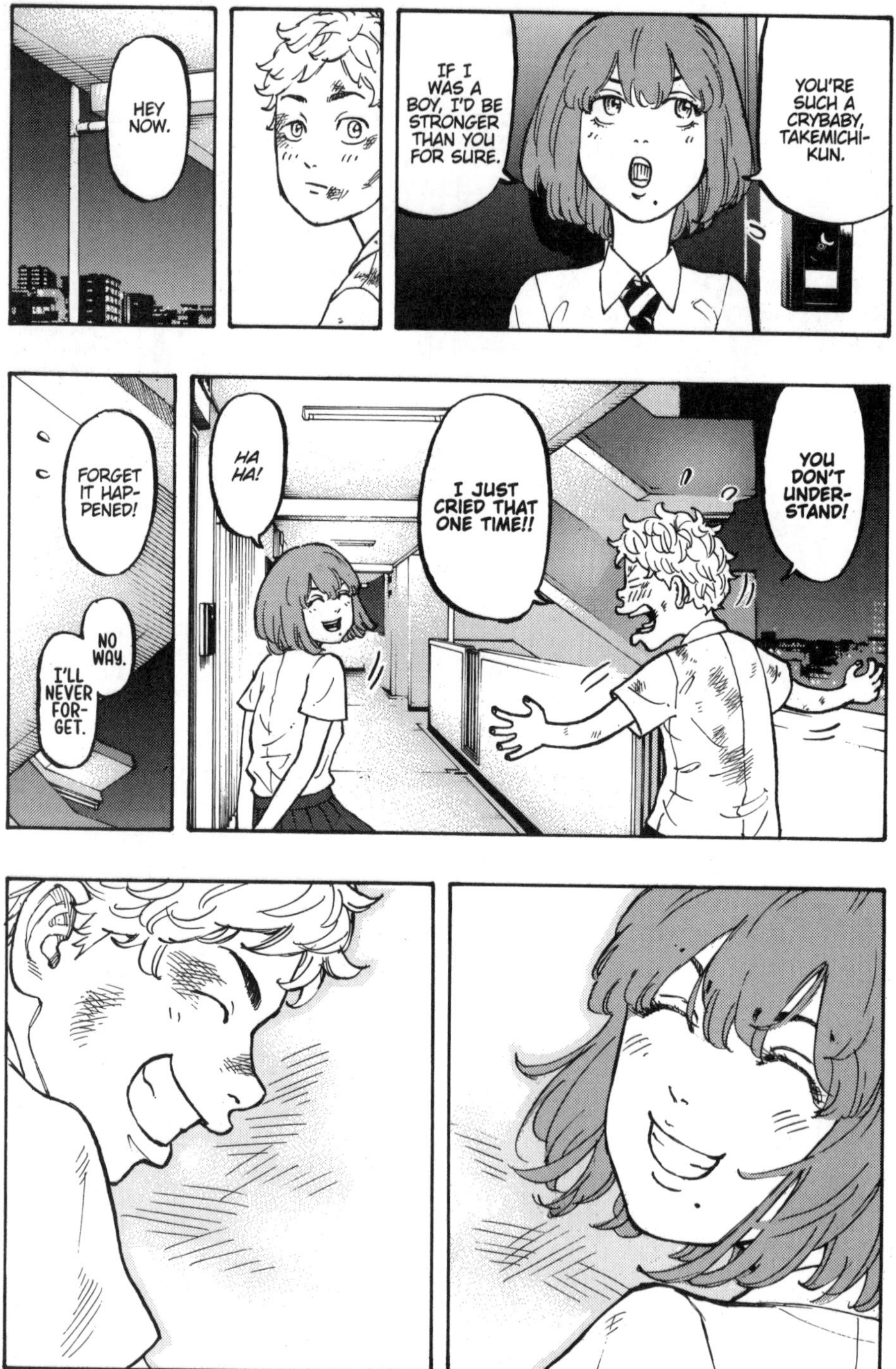
YOU'RE SUCH A CRYBABY, TAKEMICHI-KUN.
IF I WAS A BOY, I'D BE STRONGER THAN YOU FOR SURE.
HEY NOW.
YOU DON'T UNDER-STAND!
I JUST CRIED THAT ONE TIME!!
HA HA!
FORGET IT HAP-PENED!
NO WAY.
I'LL NEVER FOR-GET.

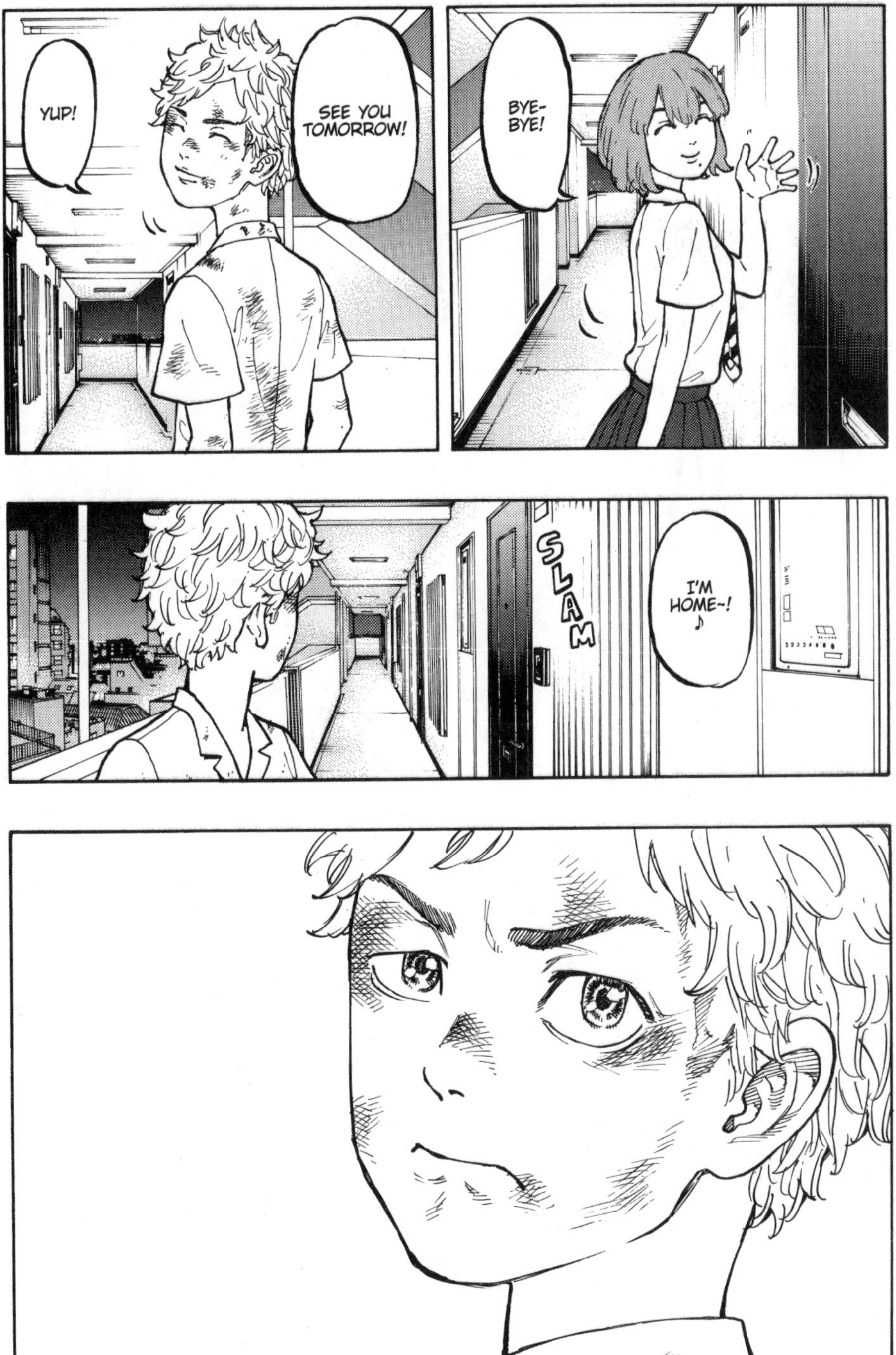
BYE-BYE!
SEE YOU TOMORROW!
YUP!
I'M HOME~! ♪
SLAM

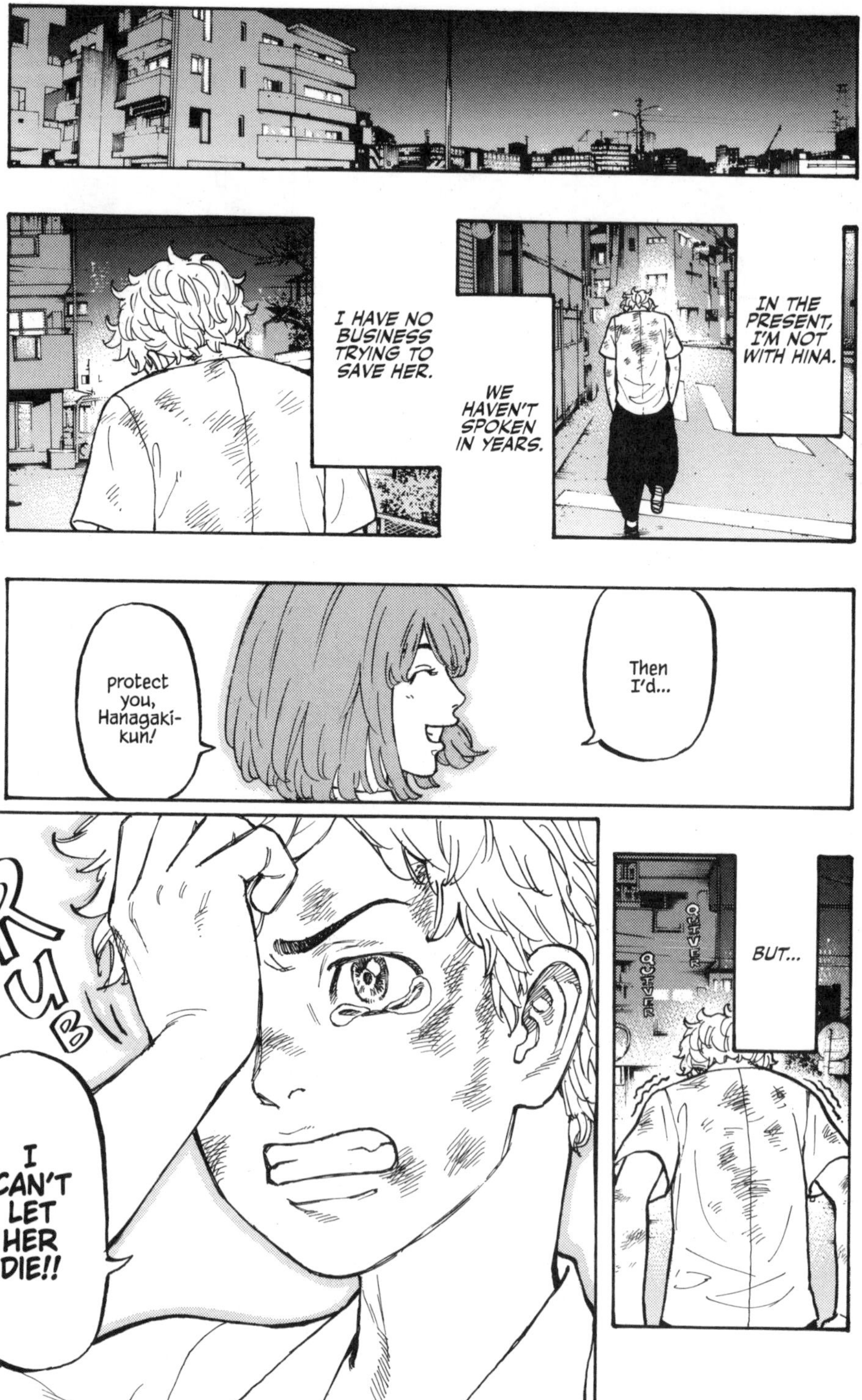
IN THE PRESENT, I'M NOT WITH HINA.
WE HAVEN'T SPOKEN IN YEARS.
I HAVE NO BUSINESS TRYING TO SAVE HER.
Then I'd...
protect you, Hanagaki-kun!
QUIVER
QUIVER
BUT...
RUB
I CAN'T LET HER DIE!!

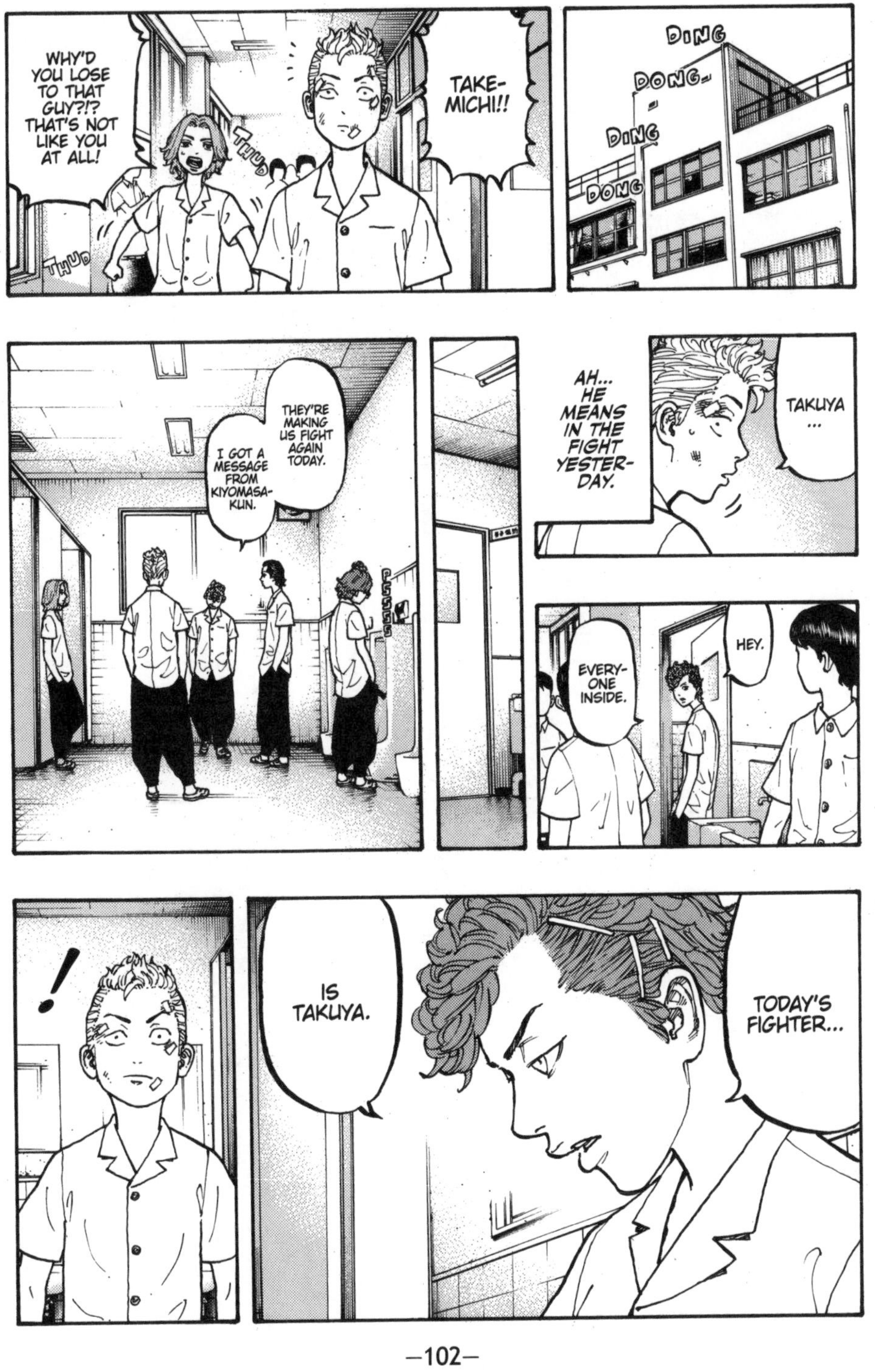
DING
DONG
DING
DONG
TAKE-MICHI!!
WHY'D YOU LOSE TO THAT GUY?!? THAT'S NOT LIKE YOU AT ALL!
THUD
THUD
TAKUYA ...
AH... HE MEANS IN THE FIGHT YESTER-DAY.
HEY.
EVERY-ONE INSIDE.
THEY'RE MAKING US FIGHT AGAIN TODAY.
I GOT A MESSAGE FROM KIYOMASA-KUN.
PSSSS
TODAY'S FIGHTER...
IS TAKUYA.
!

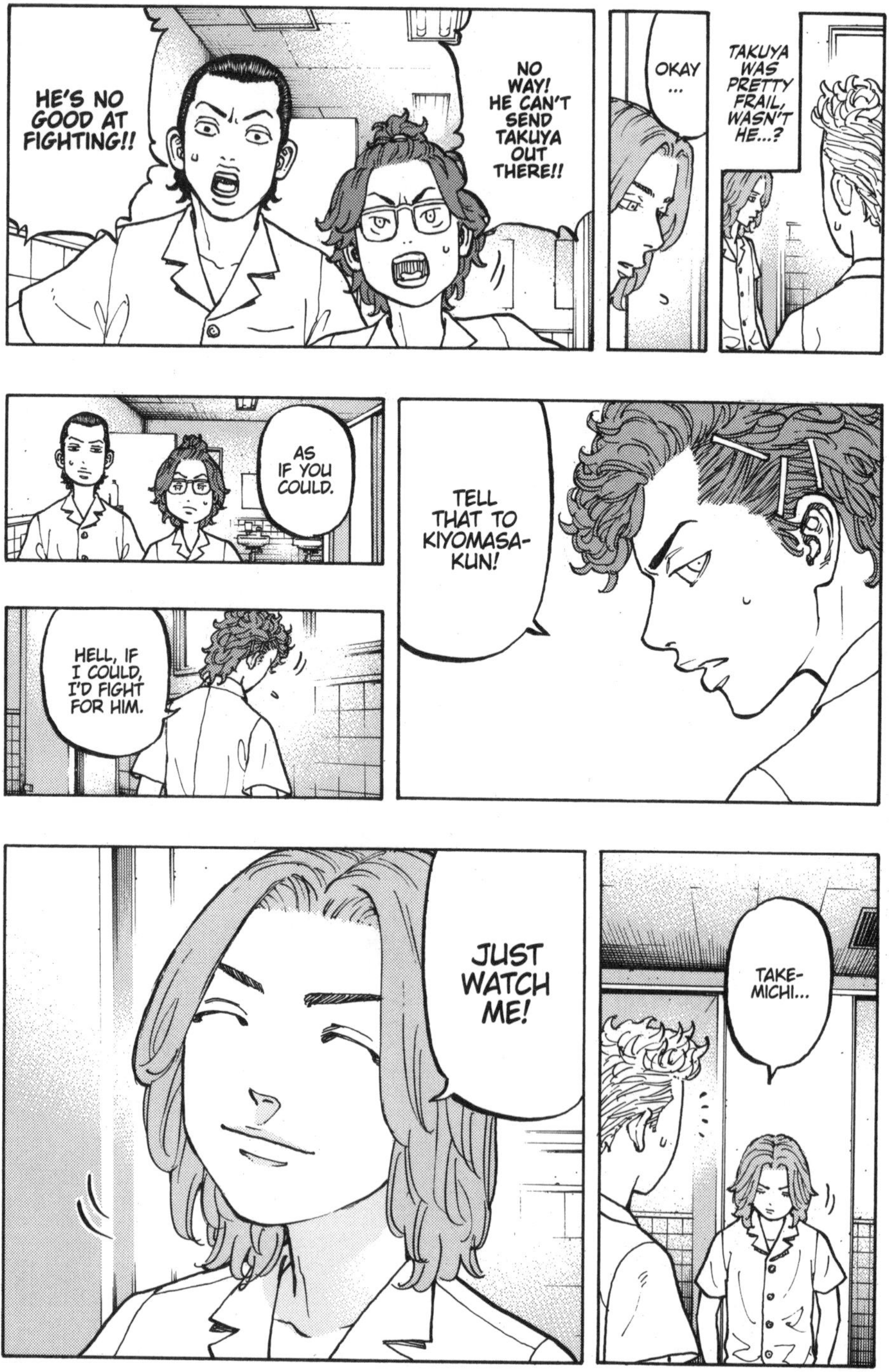
TAKUYA WAS PRETTY FRAIL, WASN'T HE...?
OKAY...
NO WAY! HE CAN'T SEND TAKUYA OUT THERE!!
HE'S NO GOOD AT FIGHTING!!
TELL THAT TO KIYOMASA-KUN!
AS IF YOU COULD.
HELL, IF I COULD, I'D FIGHT FOR HIM.
TAKE-MICHI...
JUST WATCH ME!

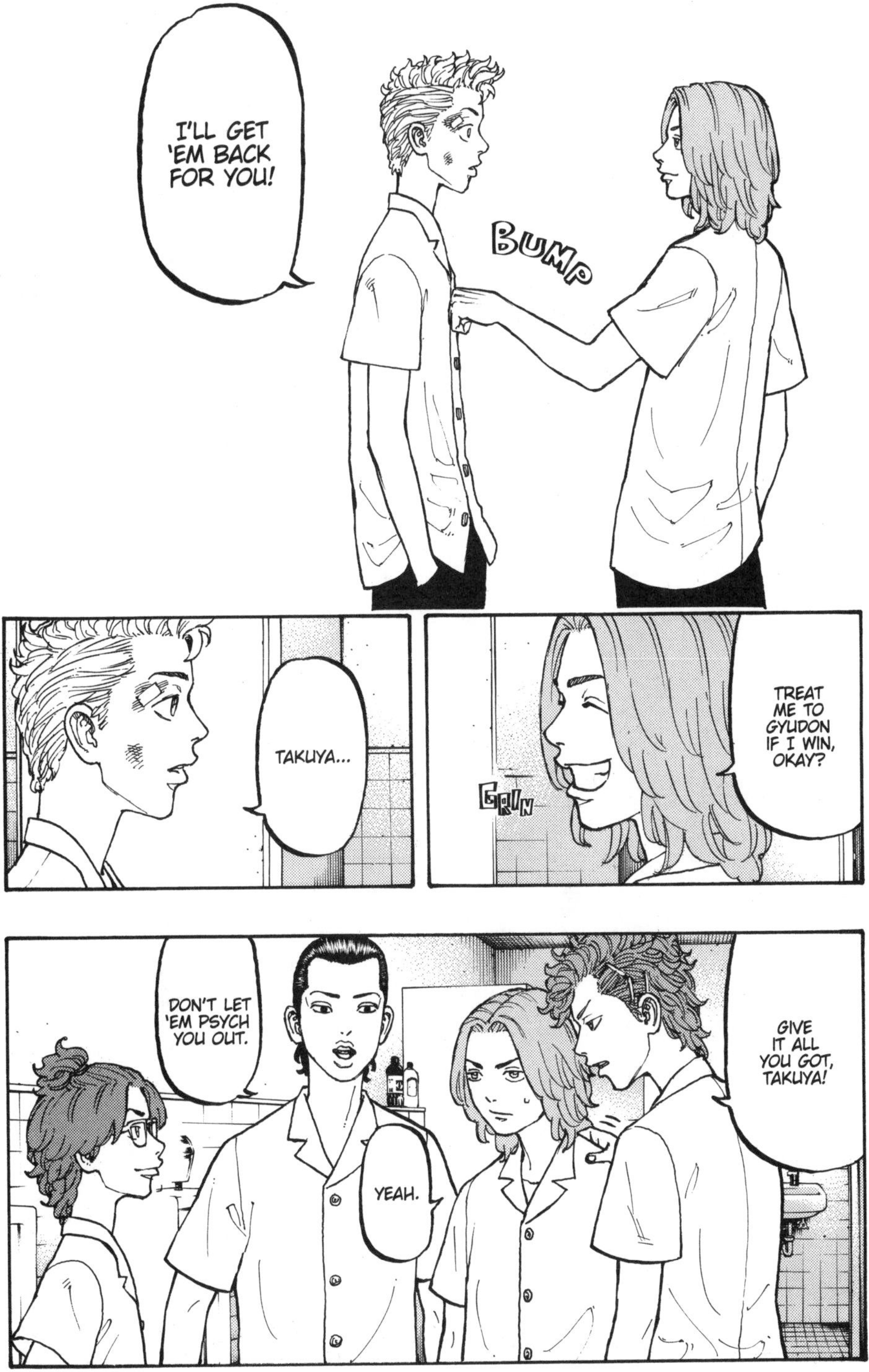
I'LL GET 'EM BACK FOR YOU!
BUMP
TREAT ME TO GYUDON IF I WIN, OKAY?
GRIN
TAKUYA...
GIVE IT ALL YOU GOT, TAKUYA!
DON'T LET 'EM PSYCH YOU OUT.
YEAH.

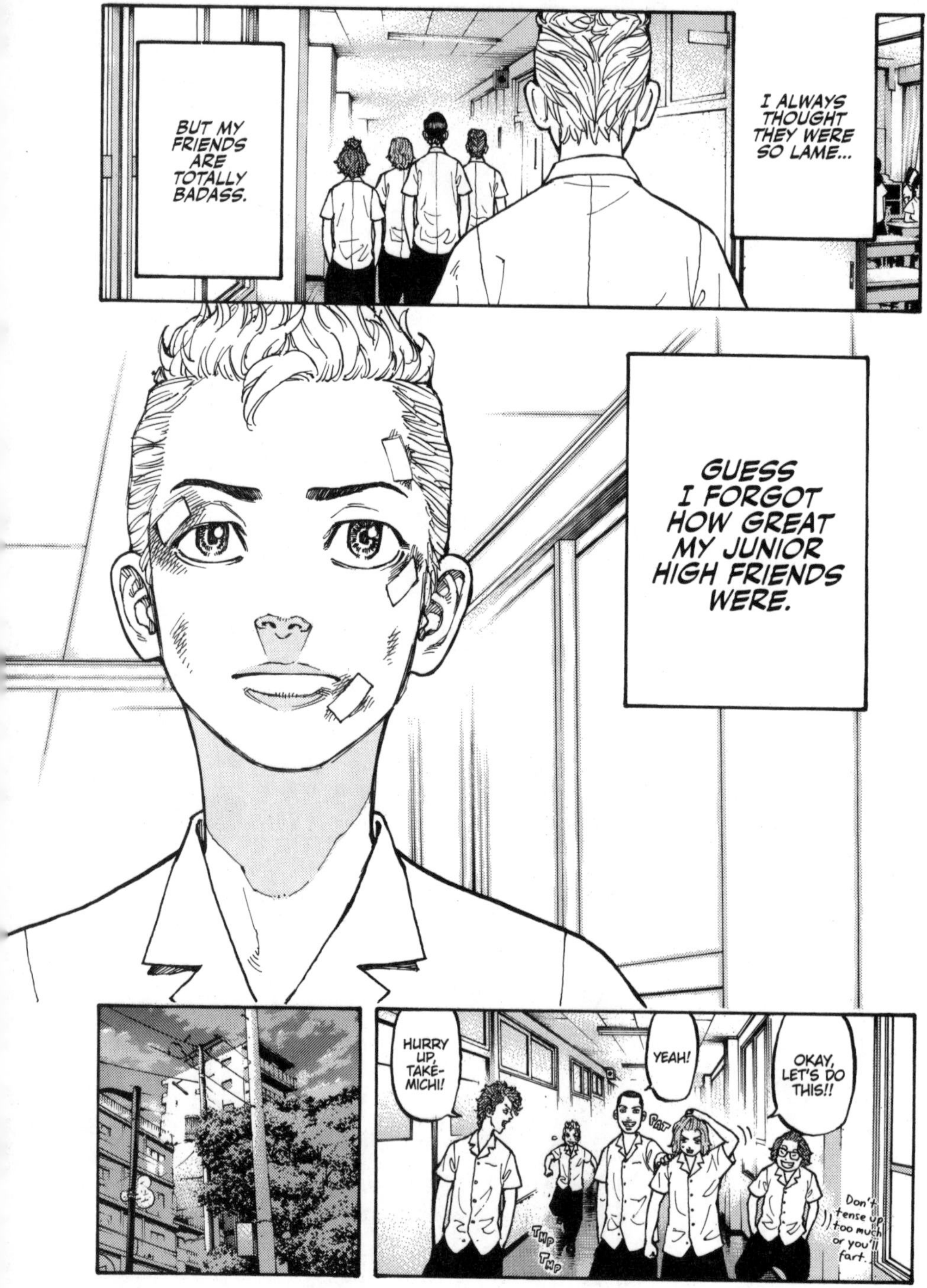
I ALWAYS THOUGHT THEY WERE SO LAME...
BUT MY FRIENDS ARE TOTALLY BADASS.
GUESS I FORGOT HOW GREAT MY JUNIOR HIGH FRIENDS WERE.
OKAY, LET'S DO THIS!!
Don't tense up too much or you'll fart.
YEAH!
PAT
HURRY UP, TAKE-MICHI!
THP THP

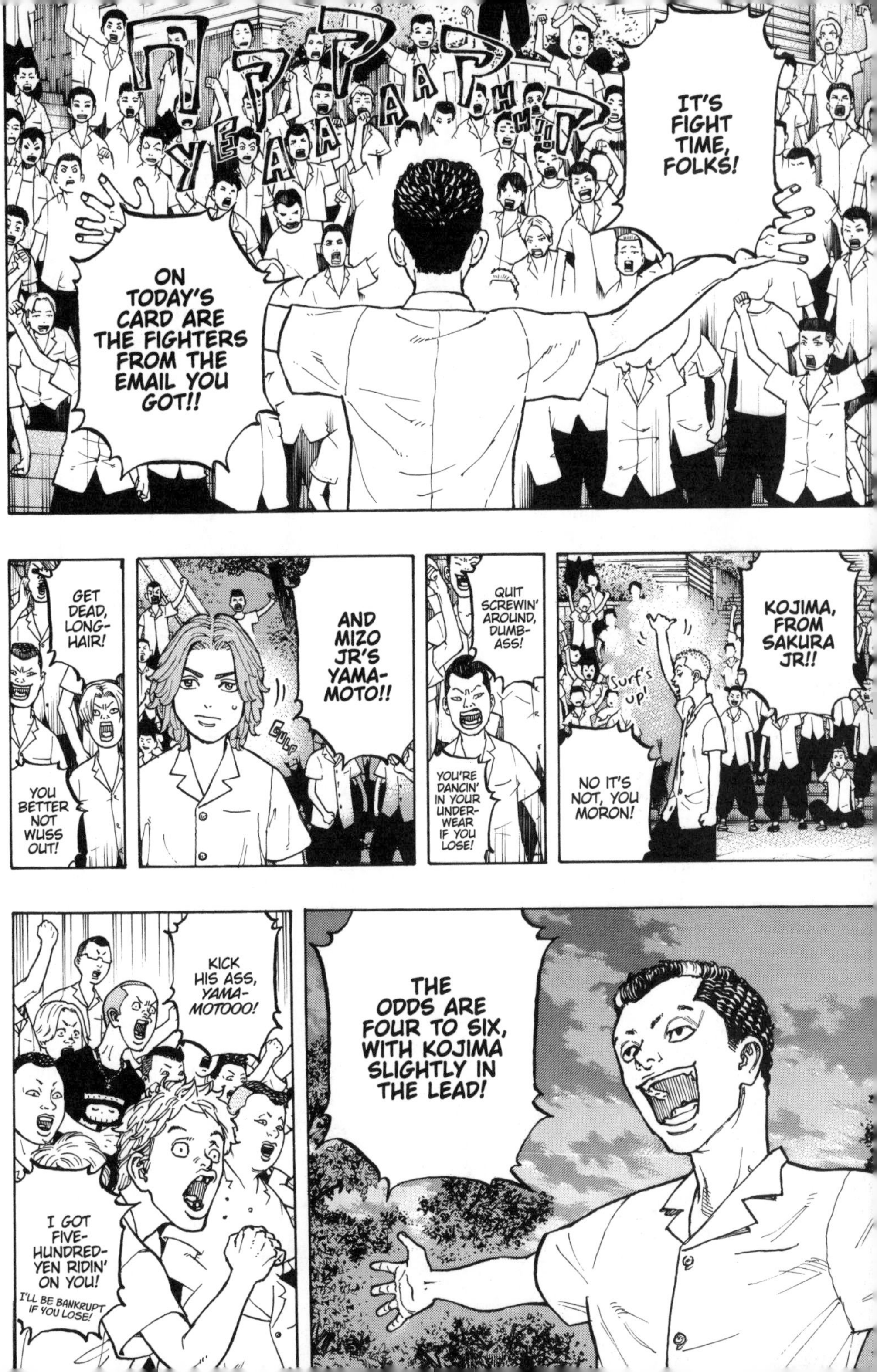
IT'S FIGHT TIME, FOLKS!
YEAAAAH!!
ON TODAY'S CARD ARE THE FIGHTERS FROM THE EMAIL YOU GOT!!
KOJIMA, FROM SAKURA JR!!
Surf's up!
NO IT'S NOT, YOU MORON!
QUIT SCREWIN' AROUND, DUMB-ASS!
YOU'RE DANCIN' IN YOUR UNDER-WEAR IF YOU LOSE!
AND MIZO JR'S YAMA-MOTO!!
GULP
GET DEAD, LONG-HAIR!
YOU BETTER NOT WUSS OUT!
THE ODDS ARE FOUR TO SIX, WITH KOJIMA SLIGHTLY IN THE LEAD!
KICK HIS ASS, YAMA-MOTOOO!
I GOT FIVE-HUNDRED-YEN RIDIN' ON YOU!
I'LL BE BANKRUPT IF YOU LOSE!

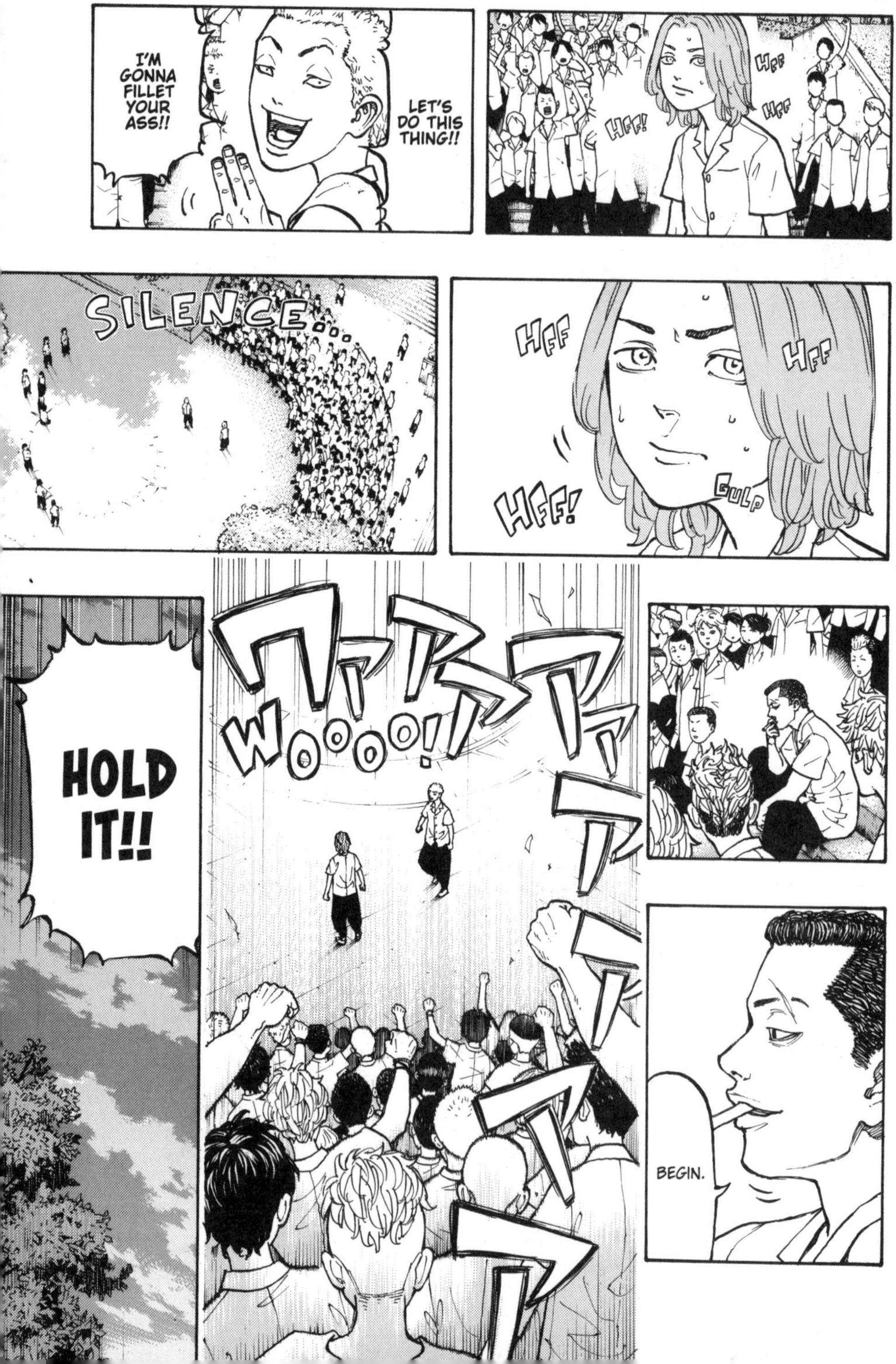
HFF
HFF
HFF!
LET'S DO THIS THING!!
I'M GONNA FILLET YOUR ASS!!
HFF
HFF
HFF!
GULP
SILENCE...
BEGIN.
ワァアァァアアァァ
WOOOO!!
HOLD IT!!

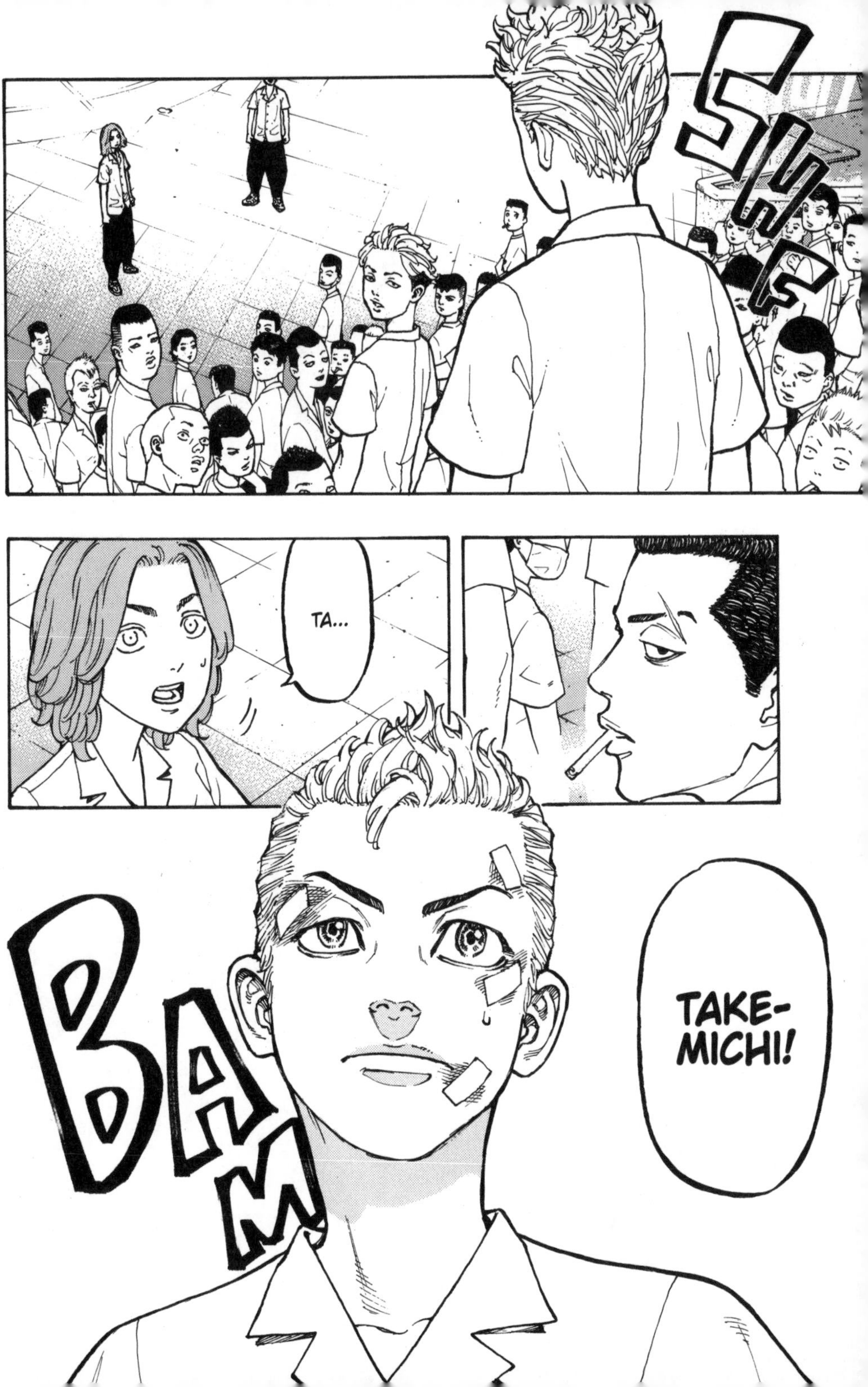
TA...
TAKE-
MICHI!
BAM

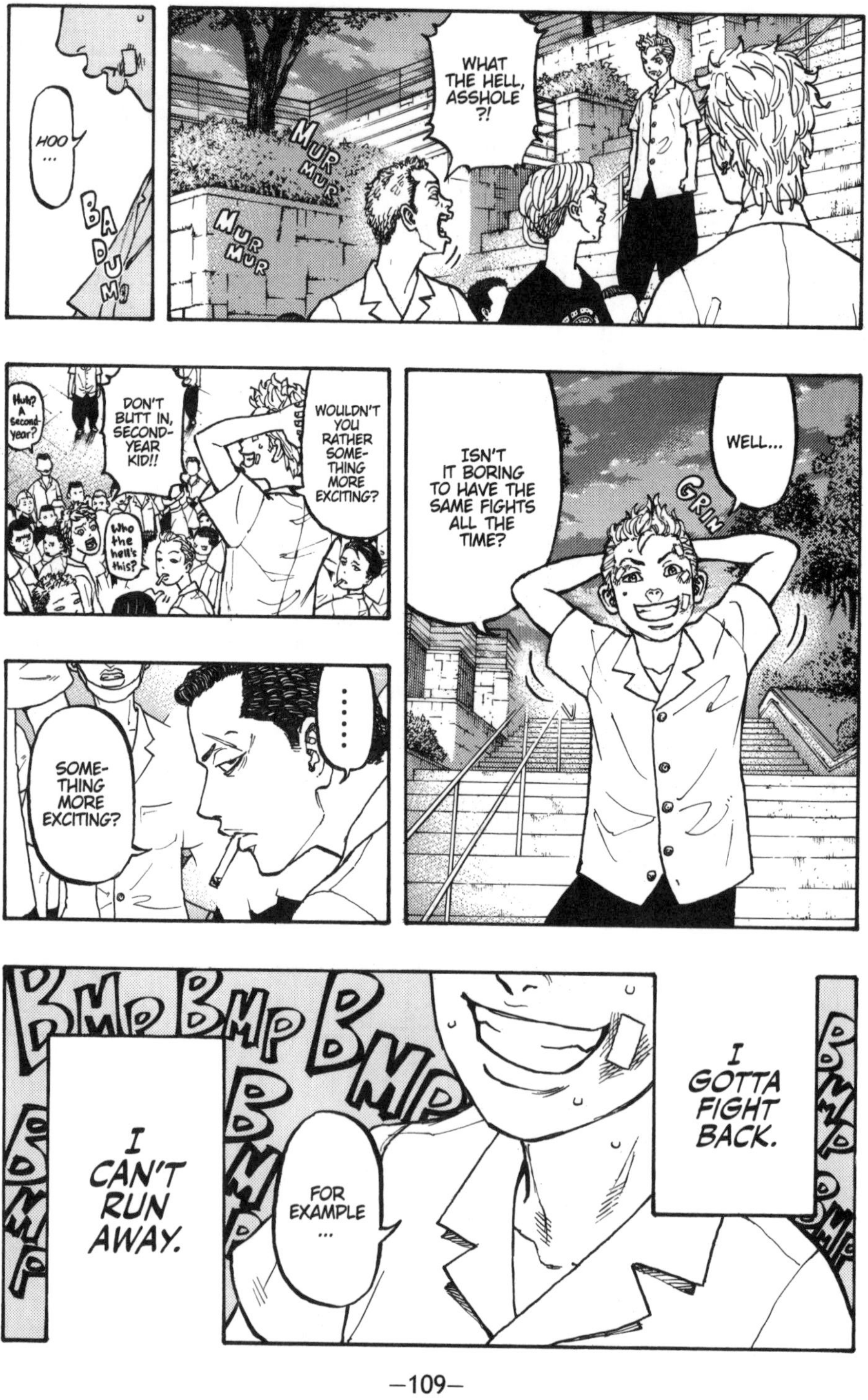
WHAT THE HELL, ASSHOLE?!
MUR MUR
MUR MUR
HOO...
BADUM
WELL...
GRIN
ISN'T IT BORING TO HAVE THE SAME FIGHTS ALL THE TIME?
WOULDN'T YOU RATHER SOMETHING MORE EXCITING?
DON'T BUTT IN, SECOND-YEAR KID!!
Huh? A second-year?
Who the hell's this?
......
SOMETHING MORE EXCITING?
BMP BMP BMP
I GOTTA FIGHT BACK.
FOR EXAMPLE...
I CAN'T RUN AWAY.

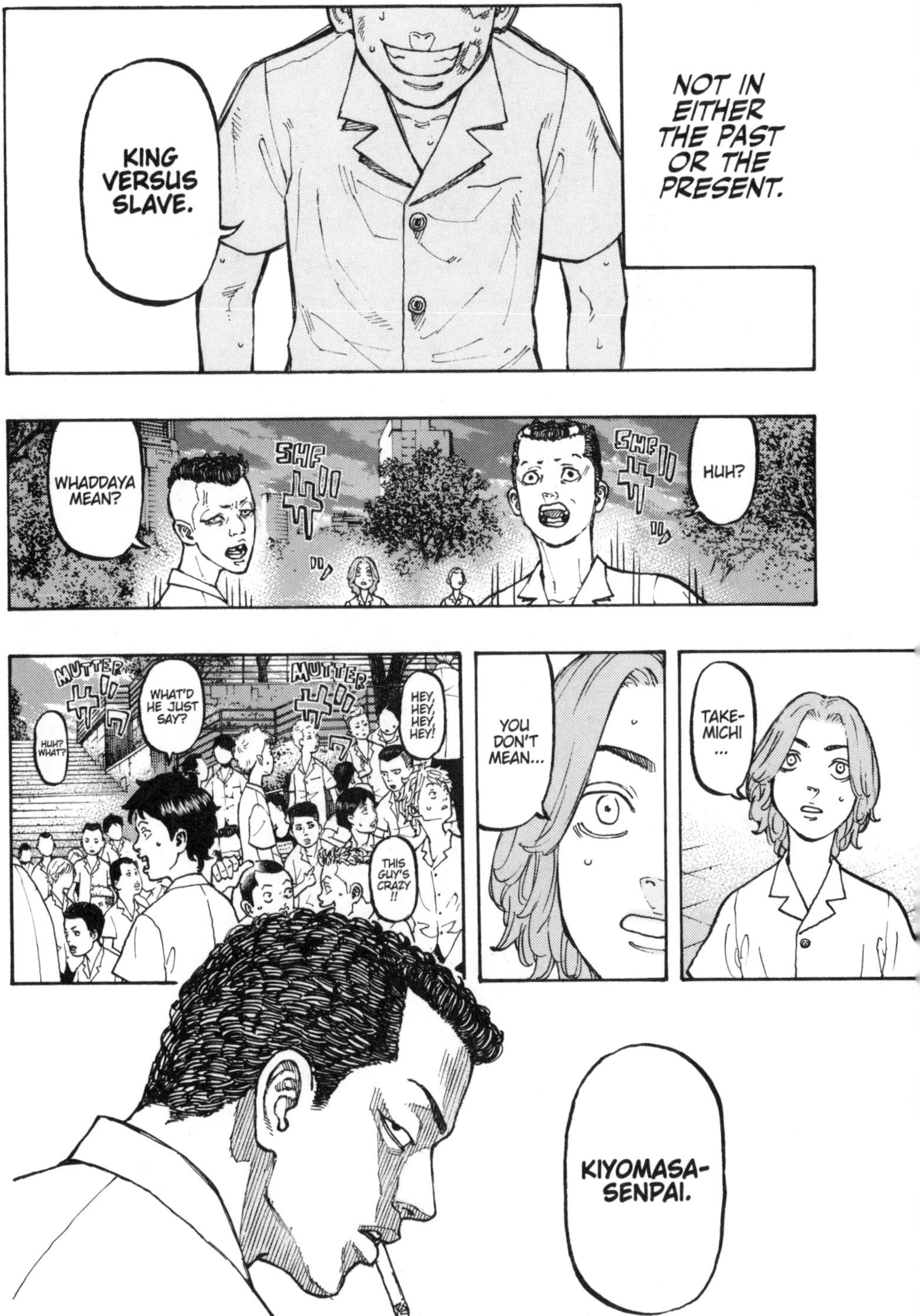
NOT IN EITHER THE PAST OR THE PRESENT.
KING VERSUS SLAVE.
HUH?
SHF
SHF
WHADDAYA MEAN?
TAKE-MICHI...
YOU DON'T MEAN...
HEY, HEY, HEY, HEY!
MUTTER
WHAT'D HE JUST SAY?
MUTTER
HUH? WHAT?
THIS GUY'S CRAZY!!
KIYOMASA-SENPAI.

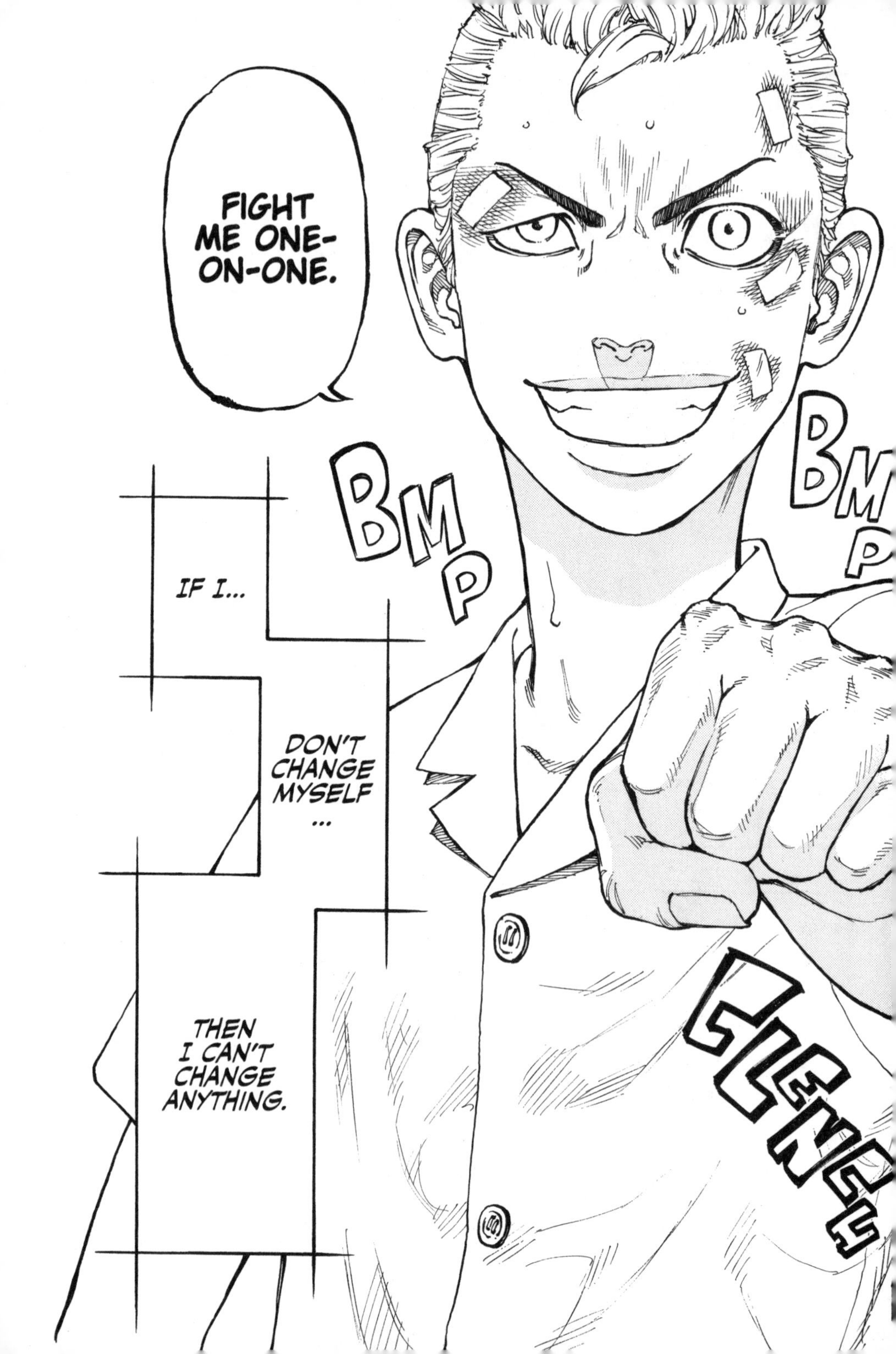
FIGHT ME ONE-ON-ONE.
BMP
BMP
CLENCH
IF I...
DON'T CHANGE MYSELF ...
THEN I CAN'T CHANGE ANYTHING.

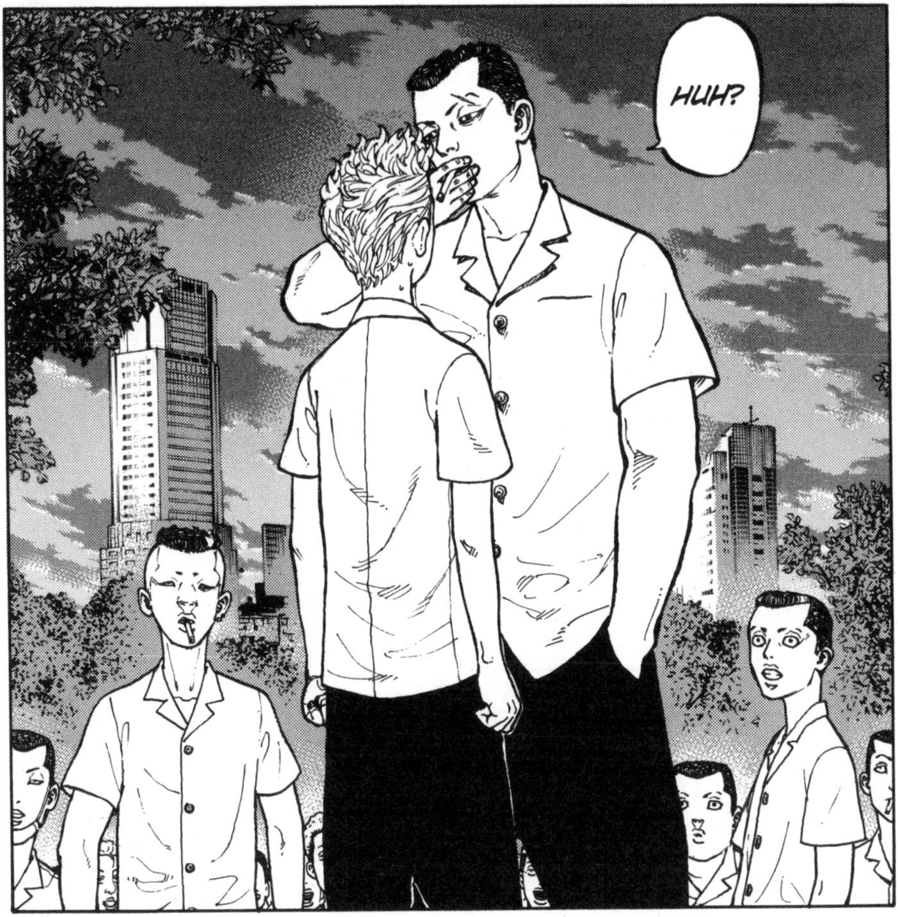
HUH?

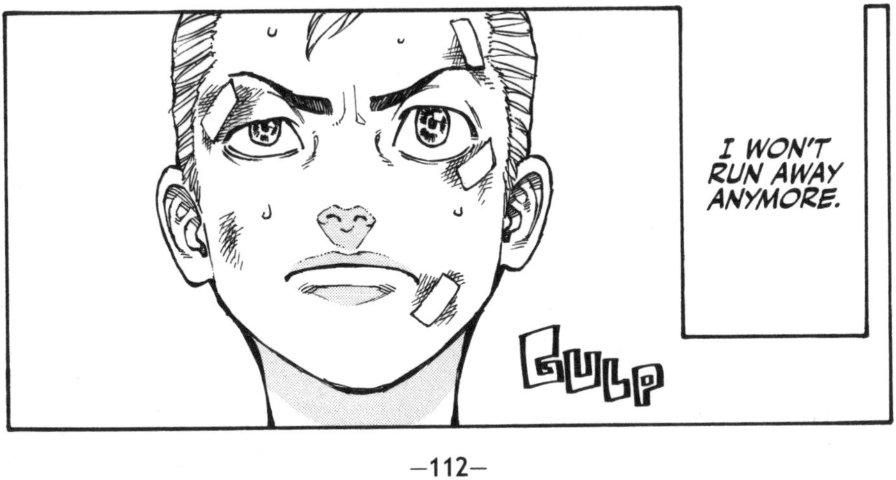
I WON'T RUN AWAY ANYMORE.
GULP

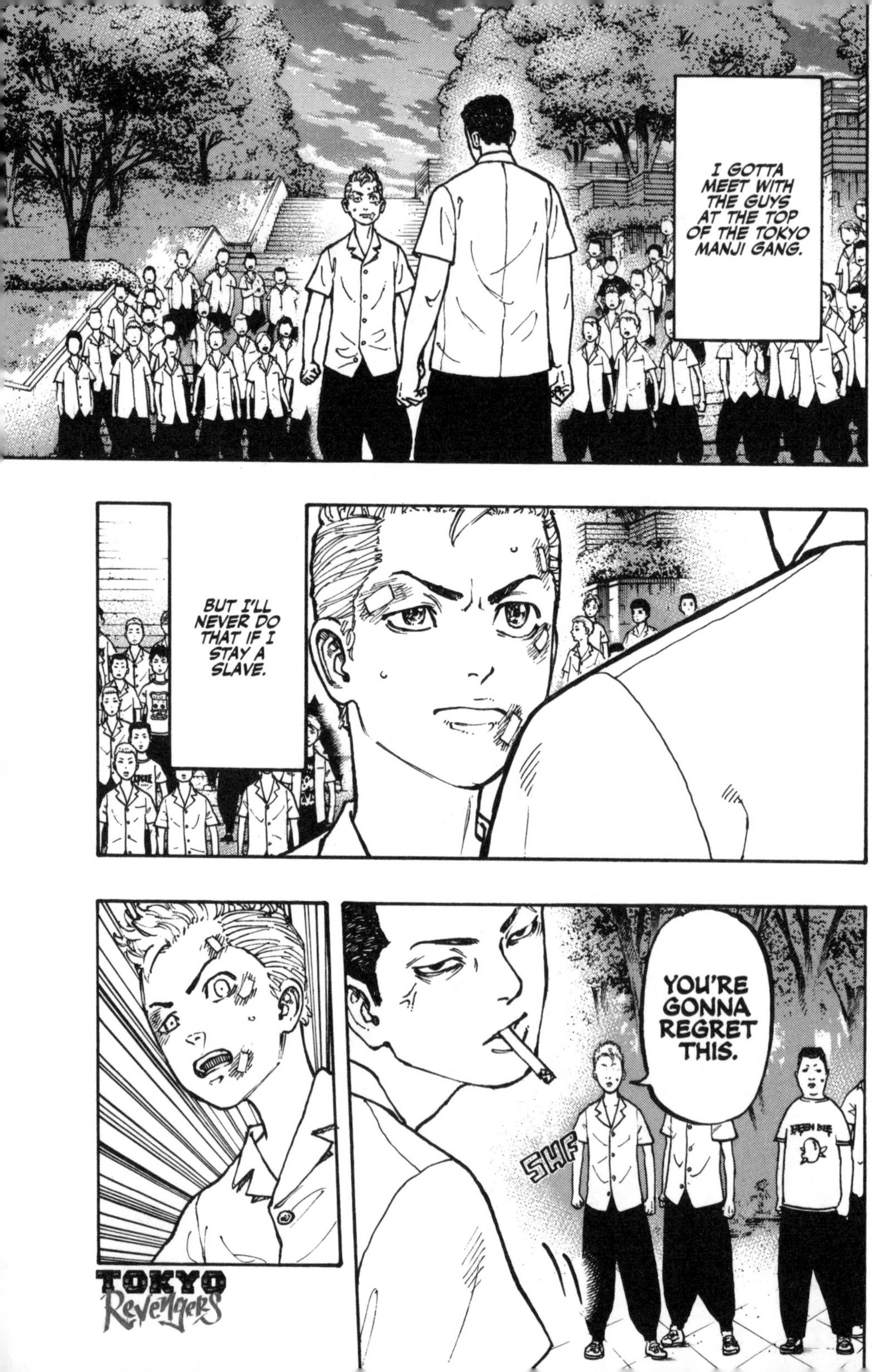
I GOTTA MEET WITH THE GUYS AT THE TOP OF THE TOKYO MANJI GANG.
BUT I'LL NEVER DO THAT IF I STAY A SLAVE.
YOU'RE GONNA REGRET THIS.
SHF
TOKYO Revengers

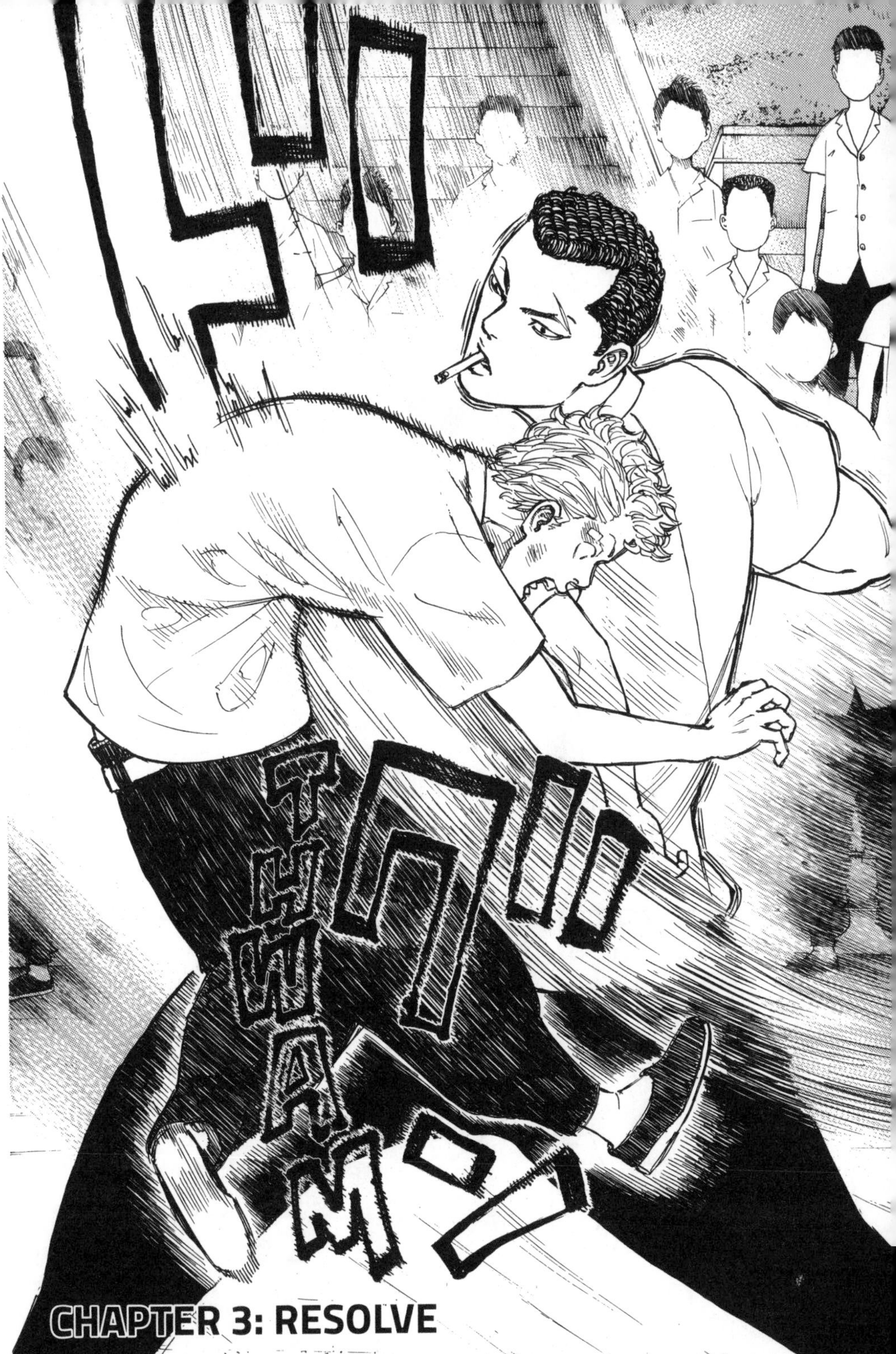
THWAM!

CHAPTER 3: RESOLVE

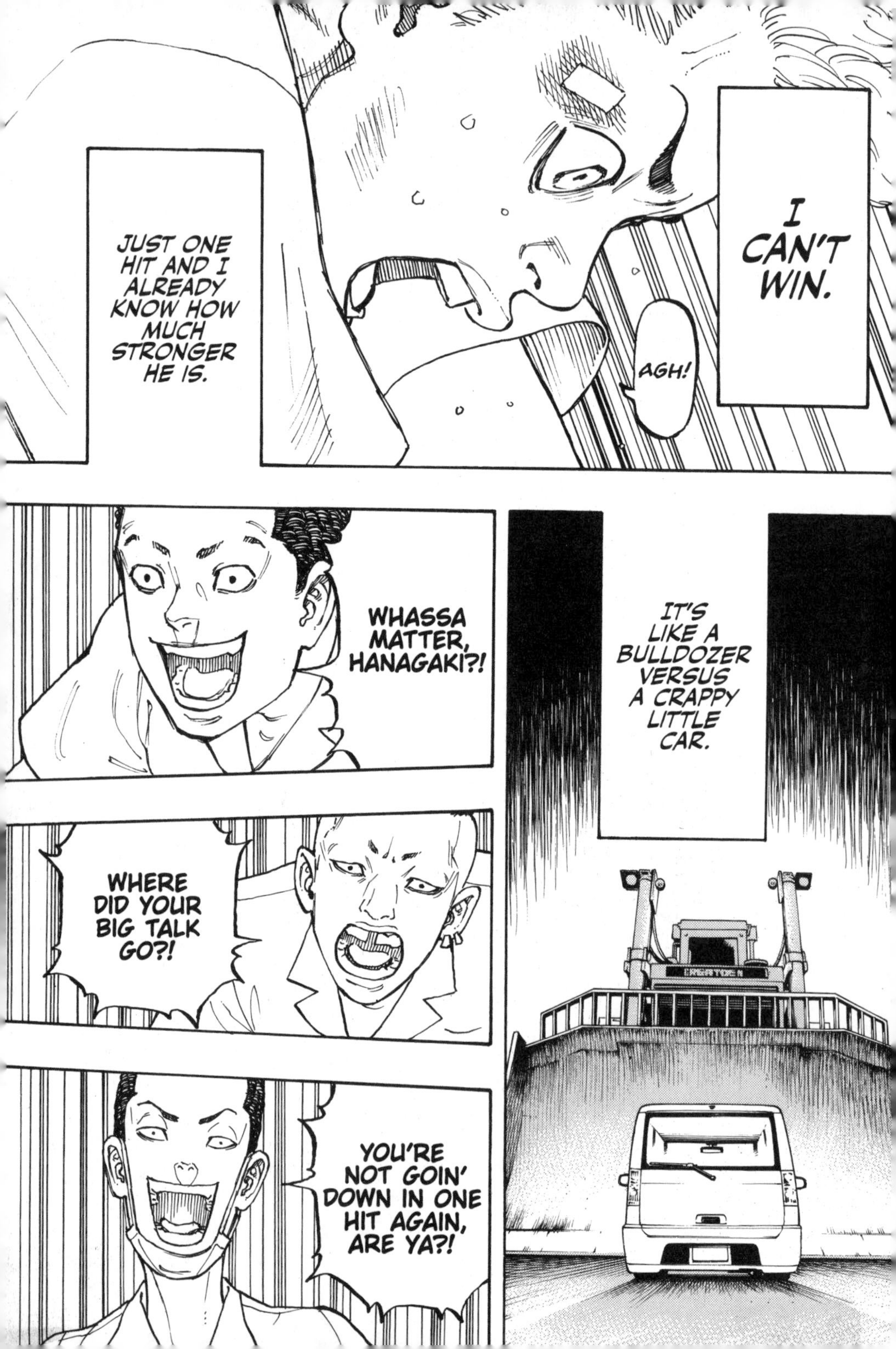
I CAN'T WIN.
AGH!
JUST ONE HIT AND I ALREADY KNOW HOW MUCH STRONGER HE IS.
IT'S LIKE A BULLDOZER VERSUS A CRAPPY LITTLE CAR.
WHASSA MATTER, HANAGAKI?!
WHERE DID YOUR BIG TALK GO?!
YOU'RE NOT GOIN' DOWN IN ONE HIT AGAIN, ARE YA?!

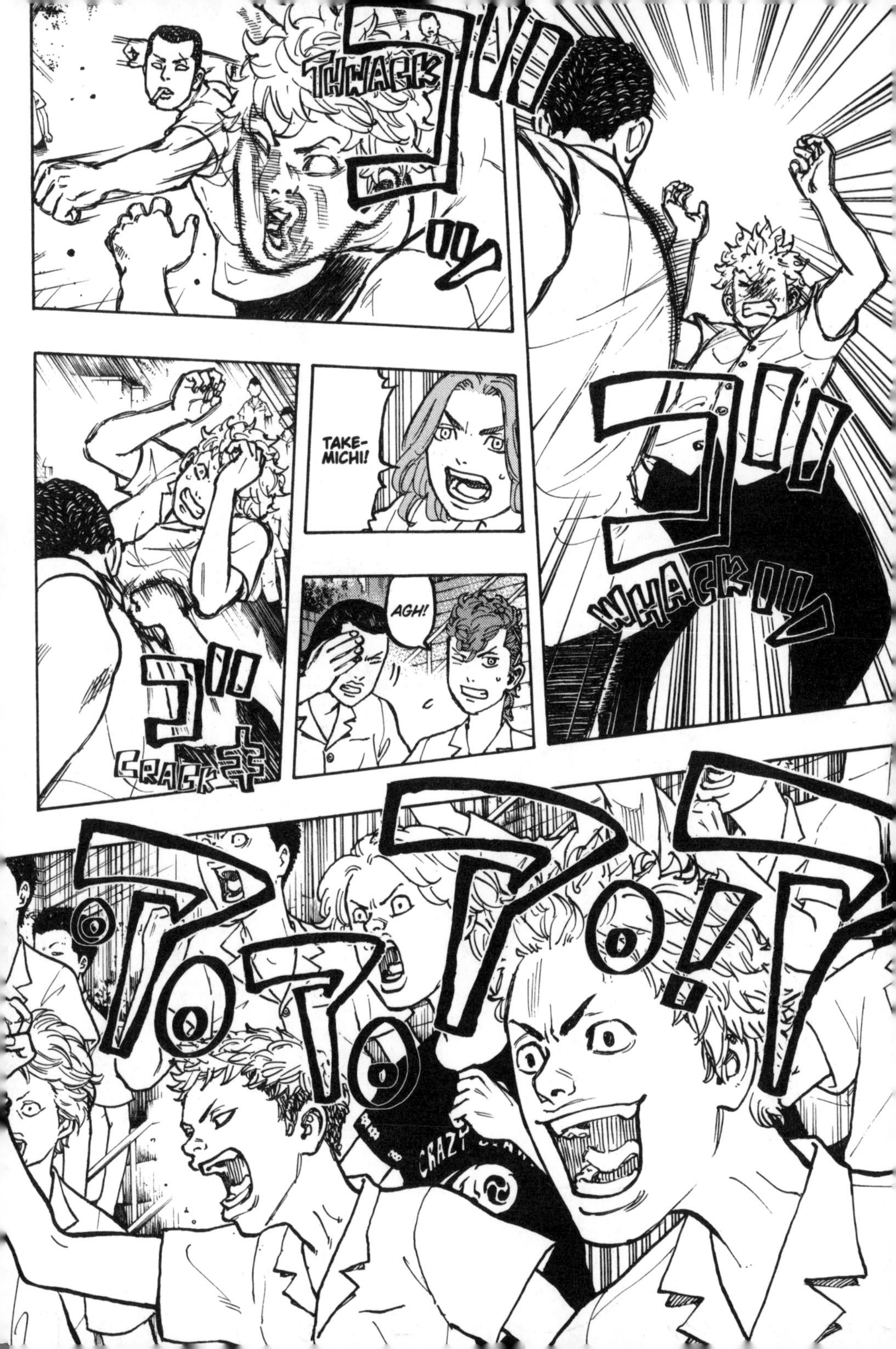
WHACK
THWACK
TAKE-MICHI!
AGH!
CRACK

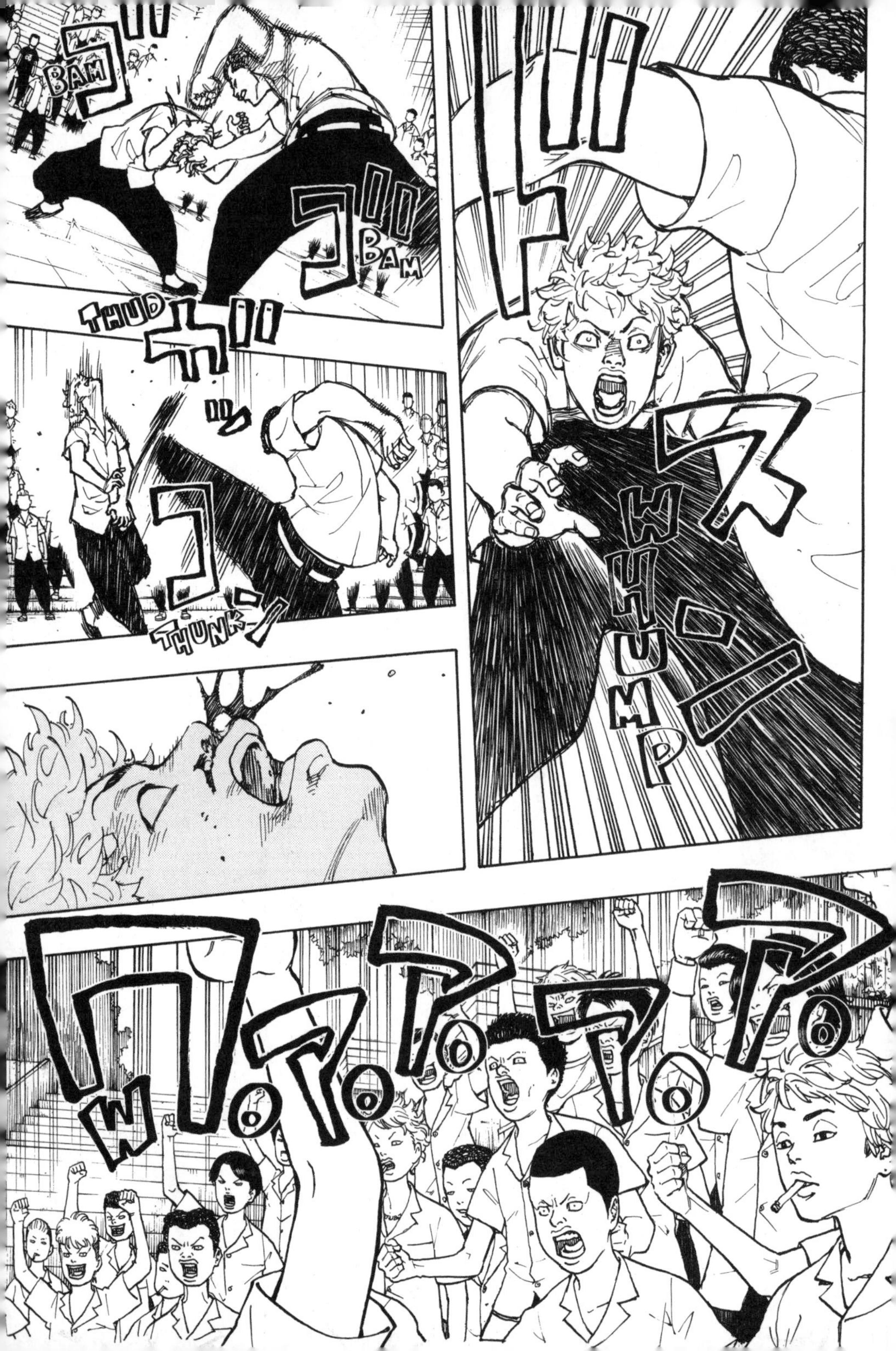
WHUMP
BAM
BAM
THUD
THUNK
WOOOOO

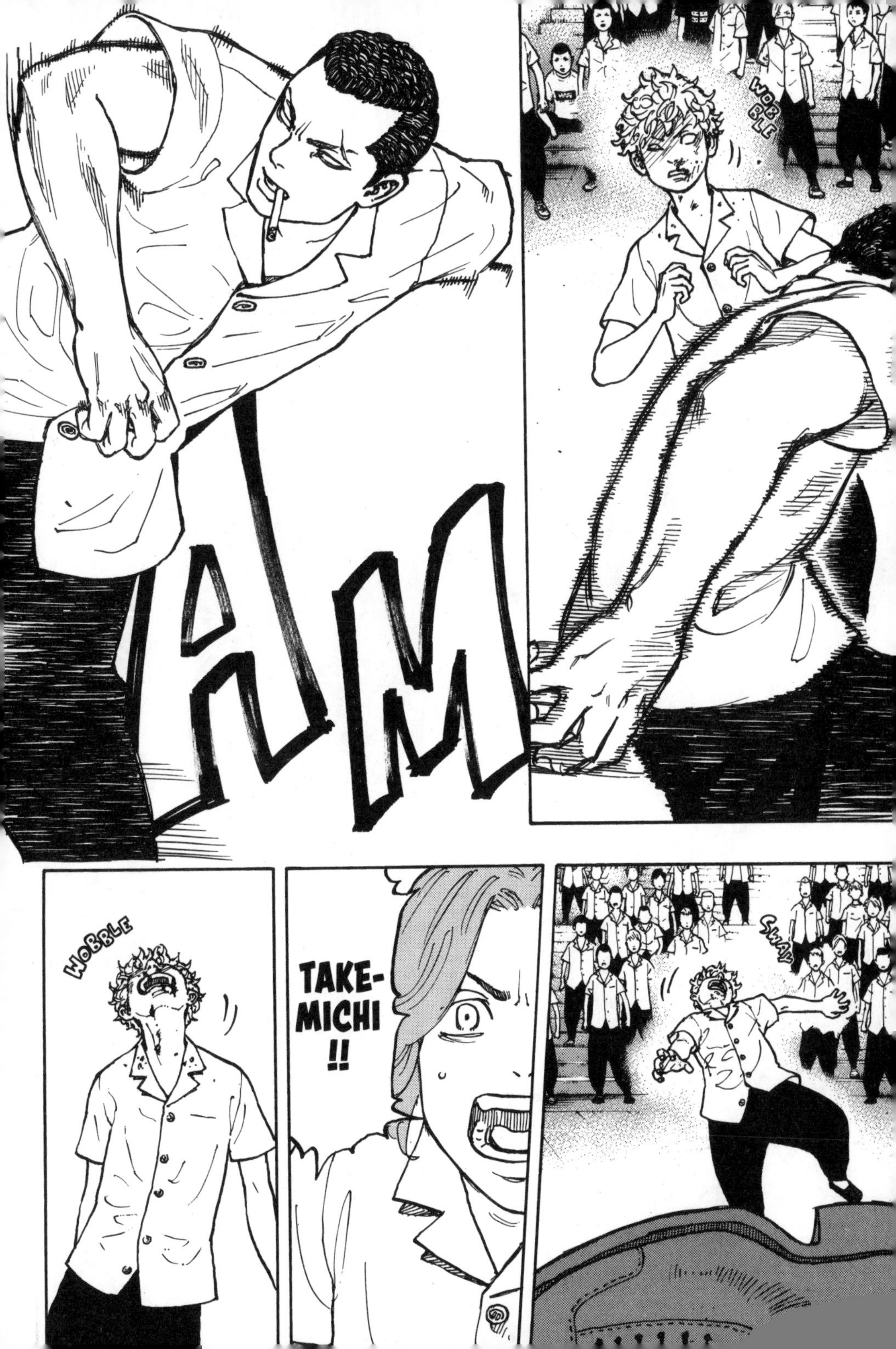
WOBBLE
AM
SWAY
TAKE-MICHI!!
WOBBLE

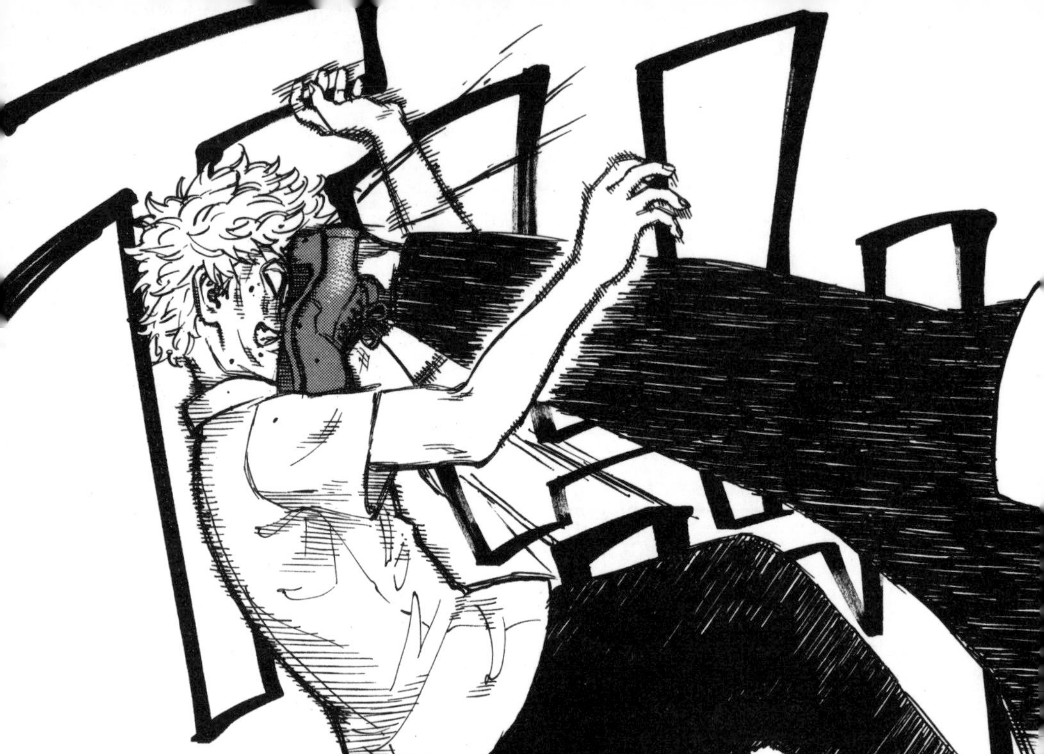

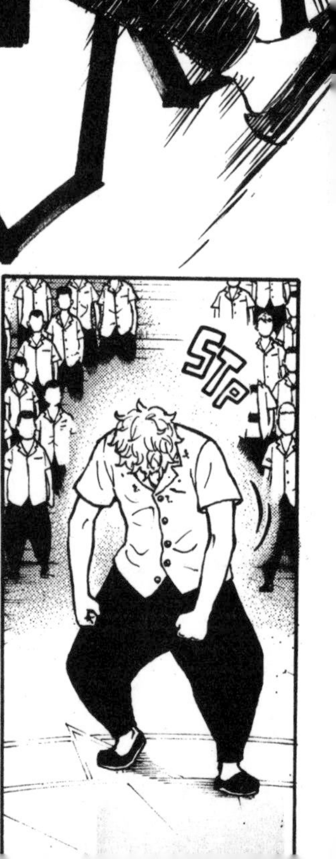
STP

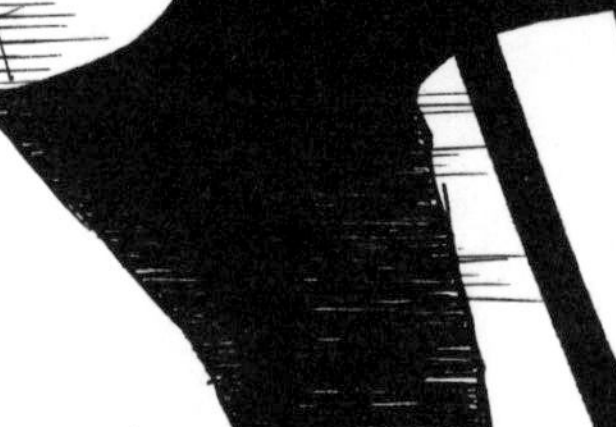

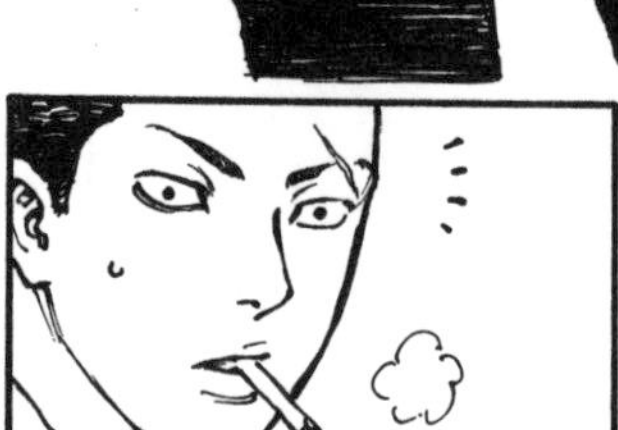

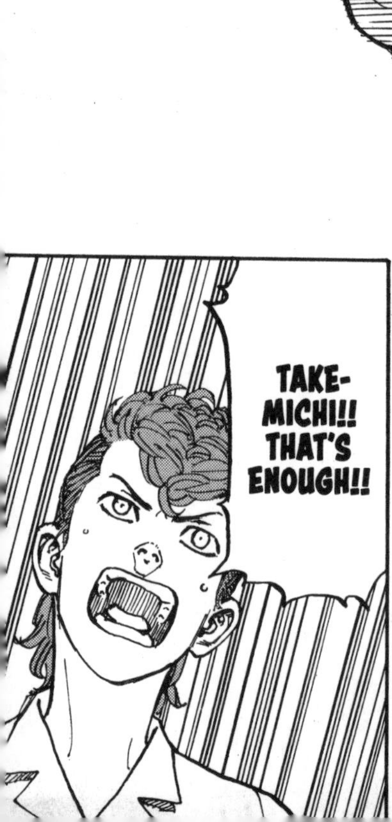
TAKE-MICHI!! THAT'S ENOUGH!!

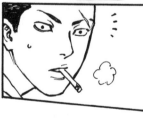

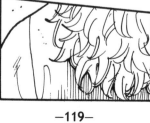

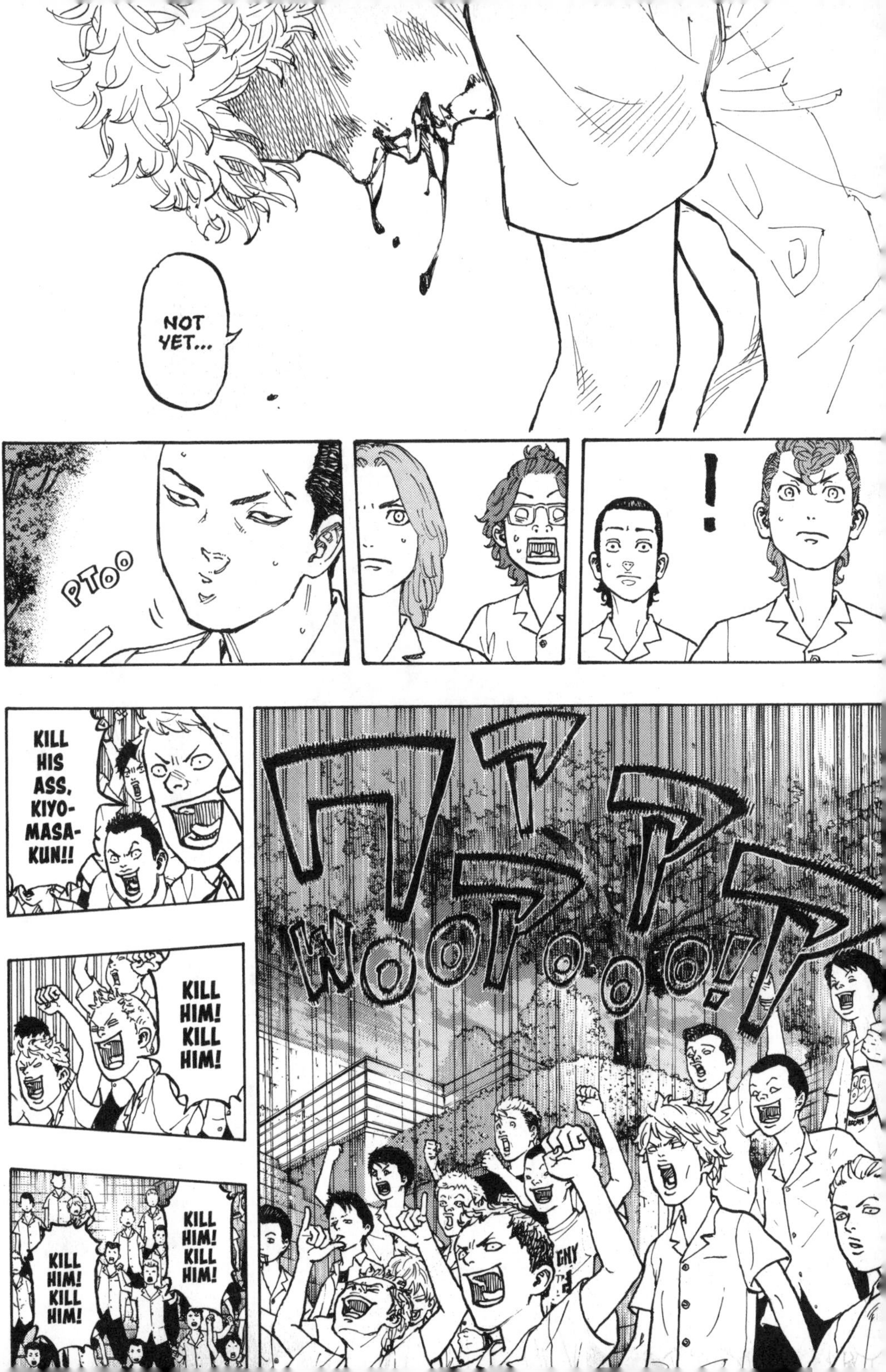
NOT YET...
!
PTOO
ワアアア
WOOOOOO!
KILL HIS ASS, KIYO-MASA-KUN!!
KILL HIM! KILL HIM!
KILL HIM! KILL HIM!
KILL HIM! KILL HIM!

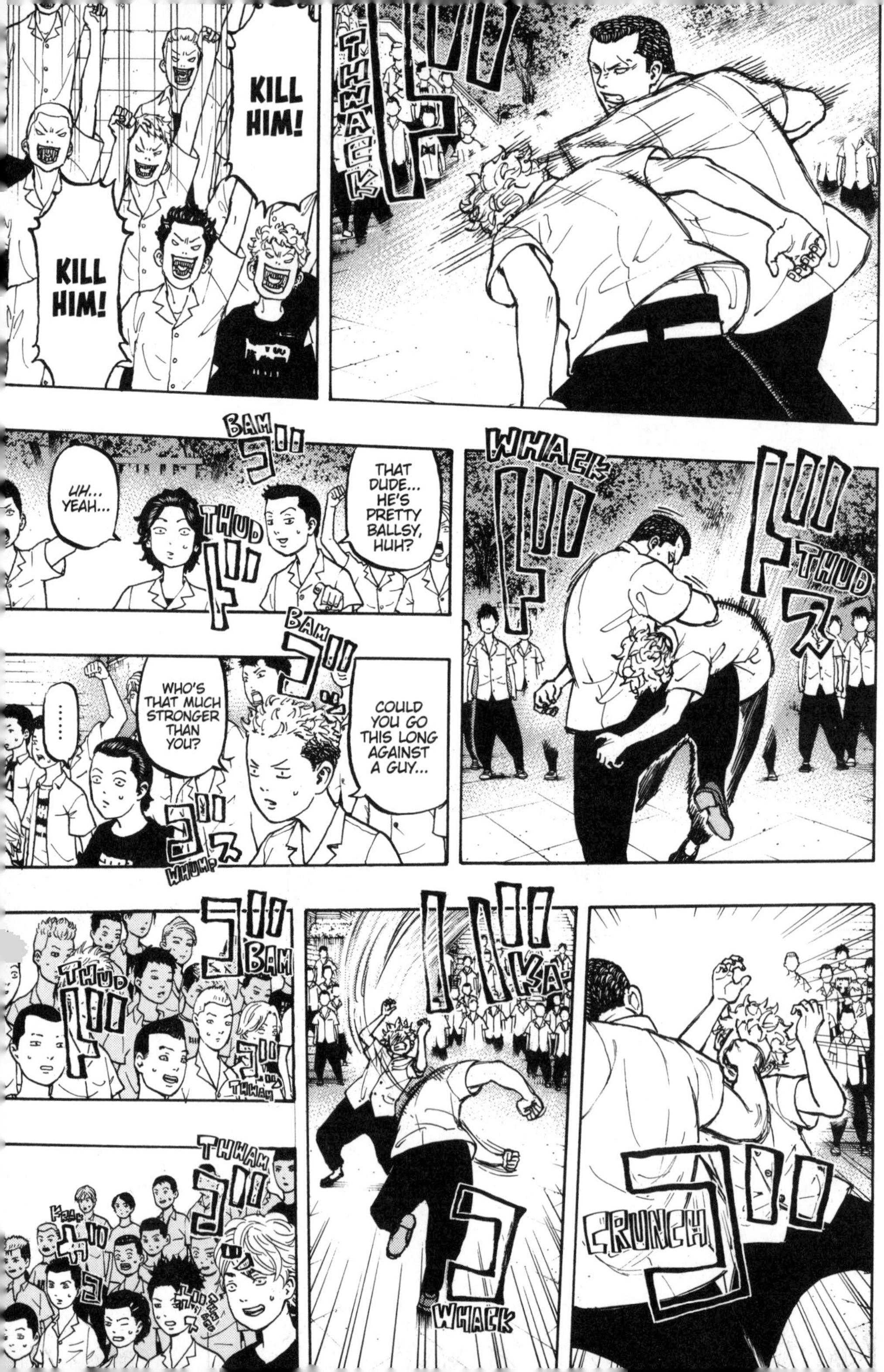
THWACK
KILL HIM!
KILL HIM!
WHACK
THUD
BAM
THAT DUDE... HE'S PRETTY BALLSY, HUH?
THUD
UH... YEAH...
BAM
COULD YOU GO THIS LONG AGAINST A GUY...
WHO'S THAT MUCH STRONGER THAN YOU?
......
WHUMP
CRUNCH
KA-
WHACK
BAM
THUD
THWAM
THWAM

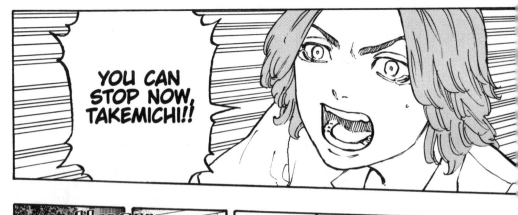

YOU CAN STOP NOW, TAKEMICHI!!

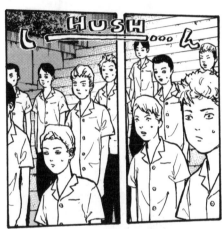

HUSH...

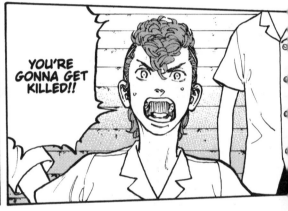

YOU'RE GONNA GET KILLED!!

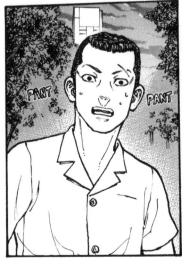

PANT PANT

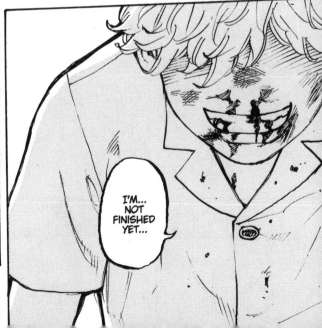

I'M... NOT FINISHED YET...

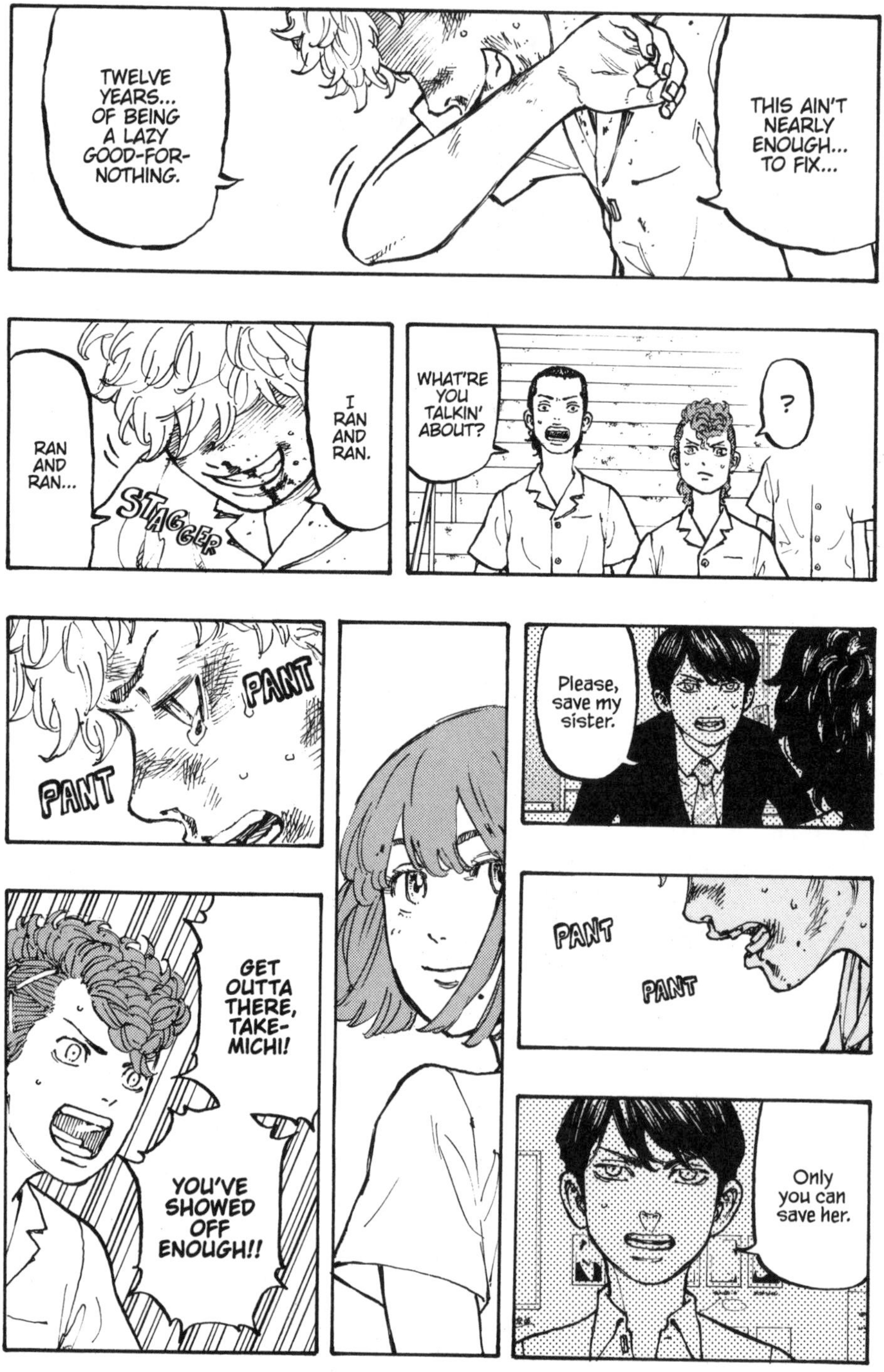
THIS AIN'T NEARLY ENOUGH... TO FIX...
TWELVE YEARS... OF BEING A LAZY GOOD-FOR-NOTHING.
?
WHAT'RE YOU TALKIN' ABOUT?
I RAN AND RAN.
RAN AND RAN...
STAGGER
Please, save my sister.
PANT
PANT
Only you can save her.
PANT
PANT
GET OUTTA THERE, TAKE-MICHI!
YOU'VE SHOWED OFF ENOUGH!!

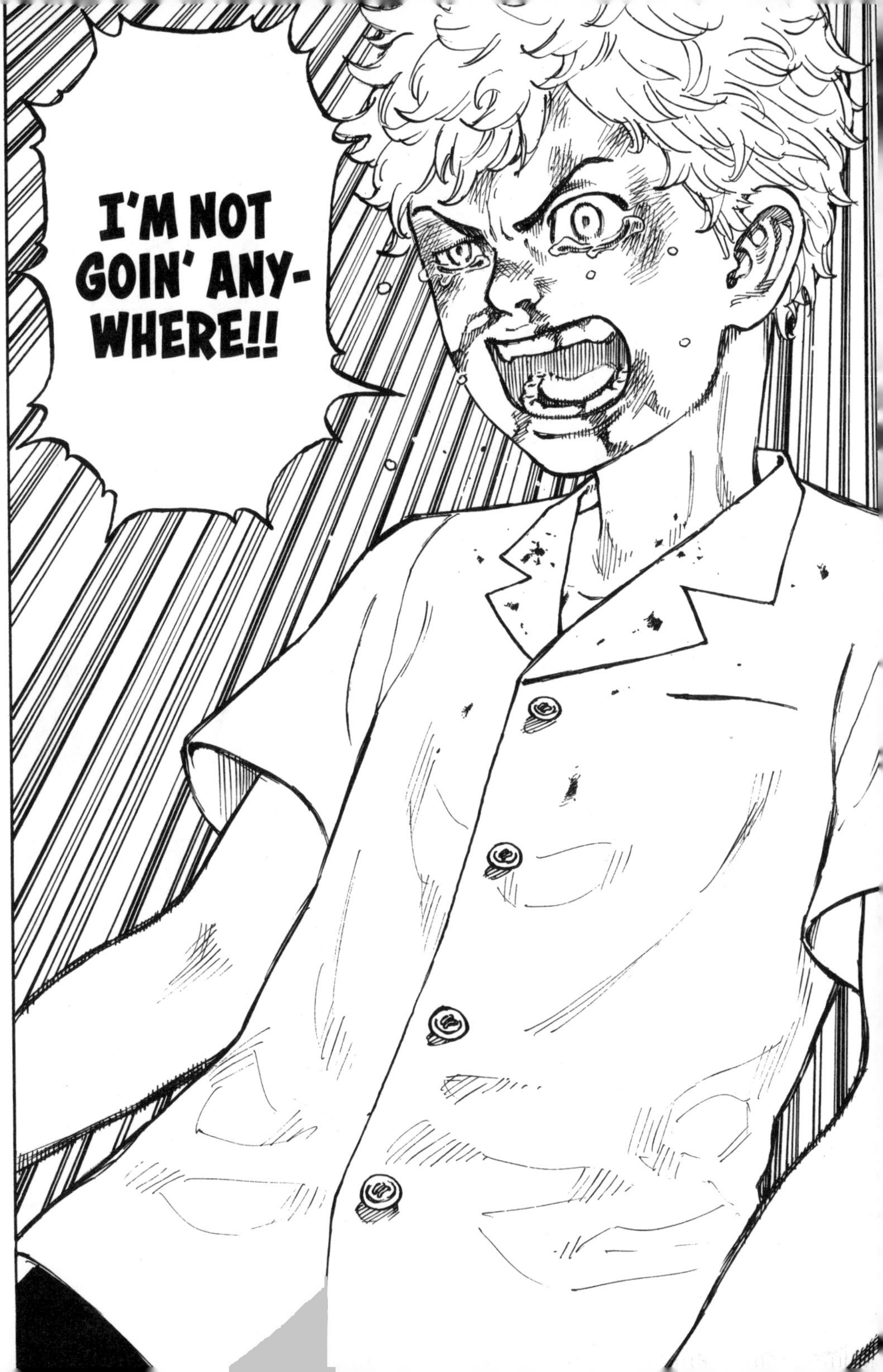
I'M NOT GOIN' ANY-WHERE!!

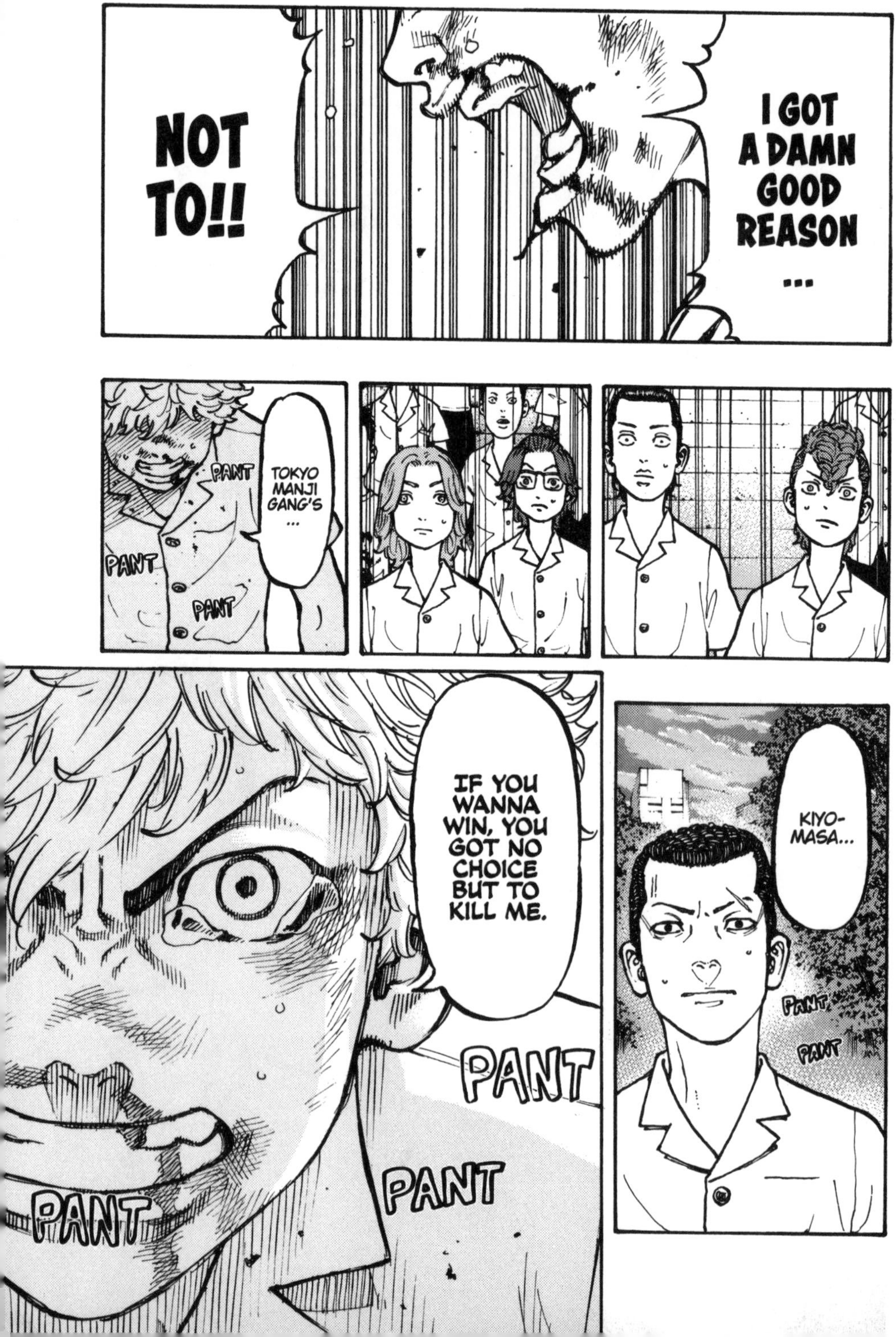
I GOT A DAMN GOOD REASON...
NOT TO!!
PANT
TOKYO MANJI GANG'S...
PANT
PANT
KIYO-MASA...
PANT
PANT
IF YOU WANNA WIN, YOU GOT NO CHOICE BUT TO KILL ME.
PANT
PANT
PANT

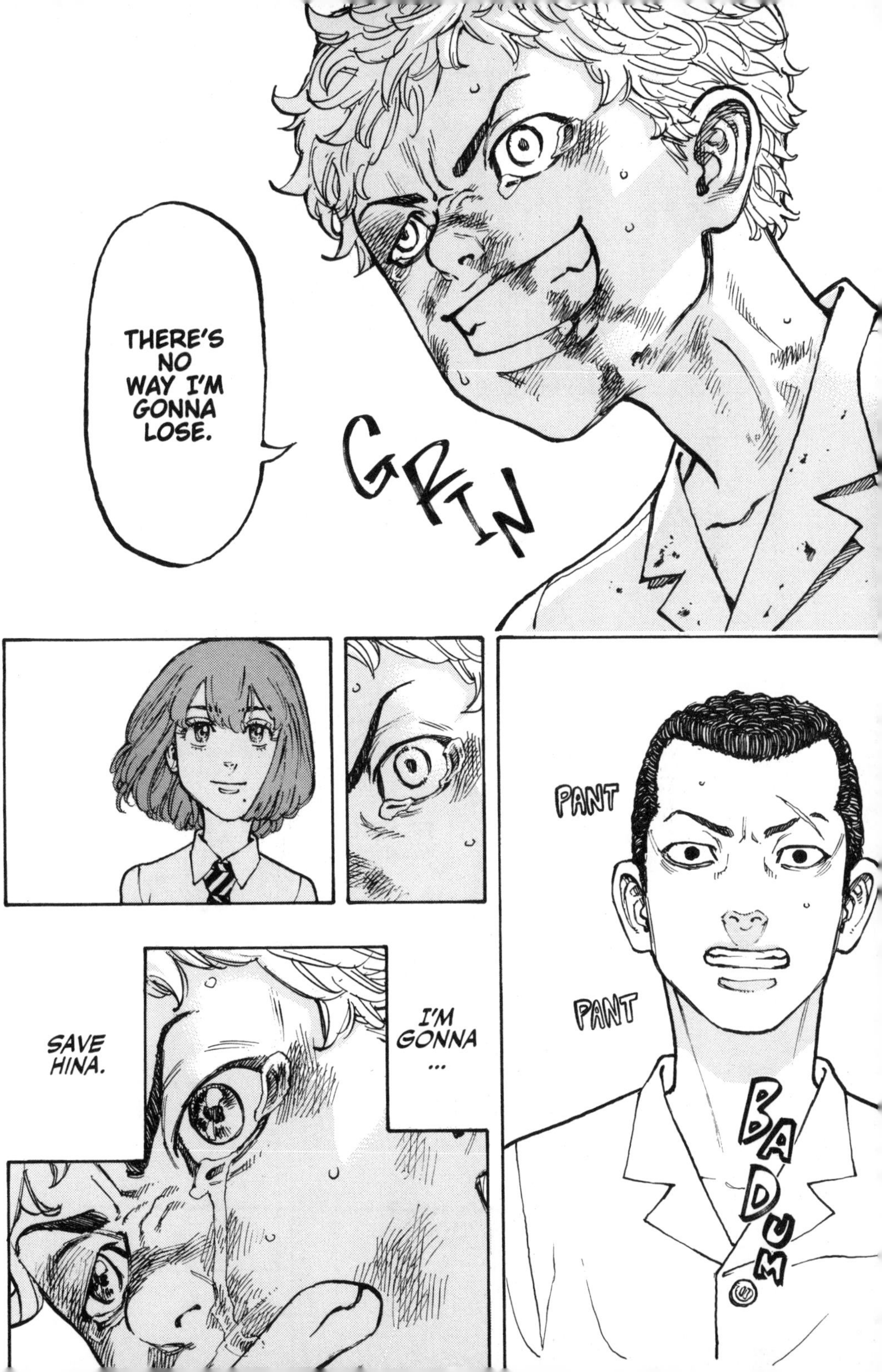
THERE'S NO WAY I'M GONNA LOSE.
GRIN
PANT
PANT
BADUM
I'M GONNA ...
SAVE HINA.

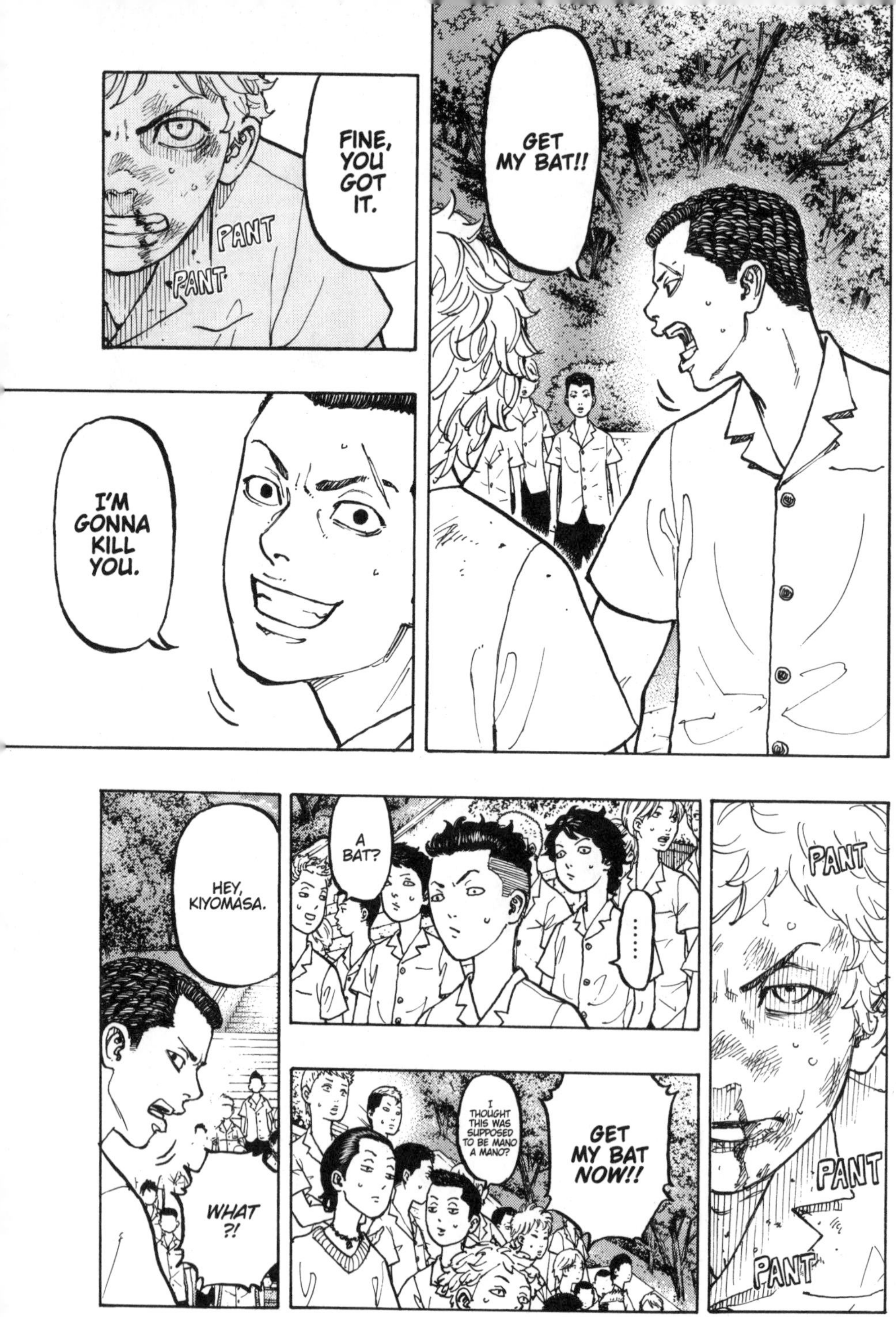
GET MY BAT!!
FINE, YOU GOT IT.
PANT
PANT
I'M GONNA KILL YOU.
PANT
PANT
PANT
A BAT?
......
GET MY BAT NOW!!
I THOUGHT THIS WAS SUPPOSED TO BE MANO A MANO?
HEY, KIYOMASA.
WHAT?!

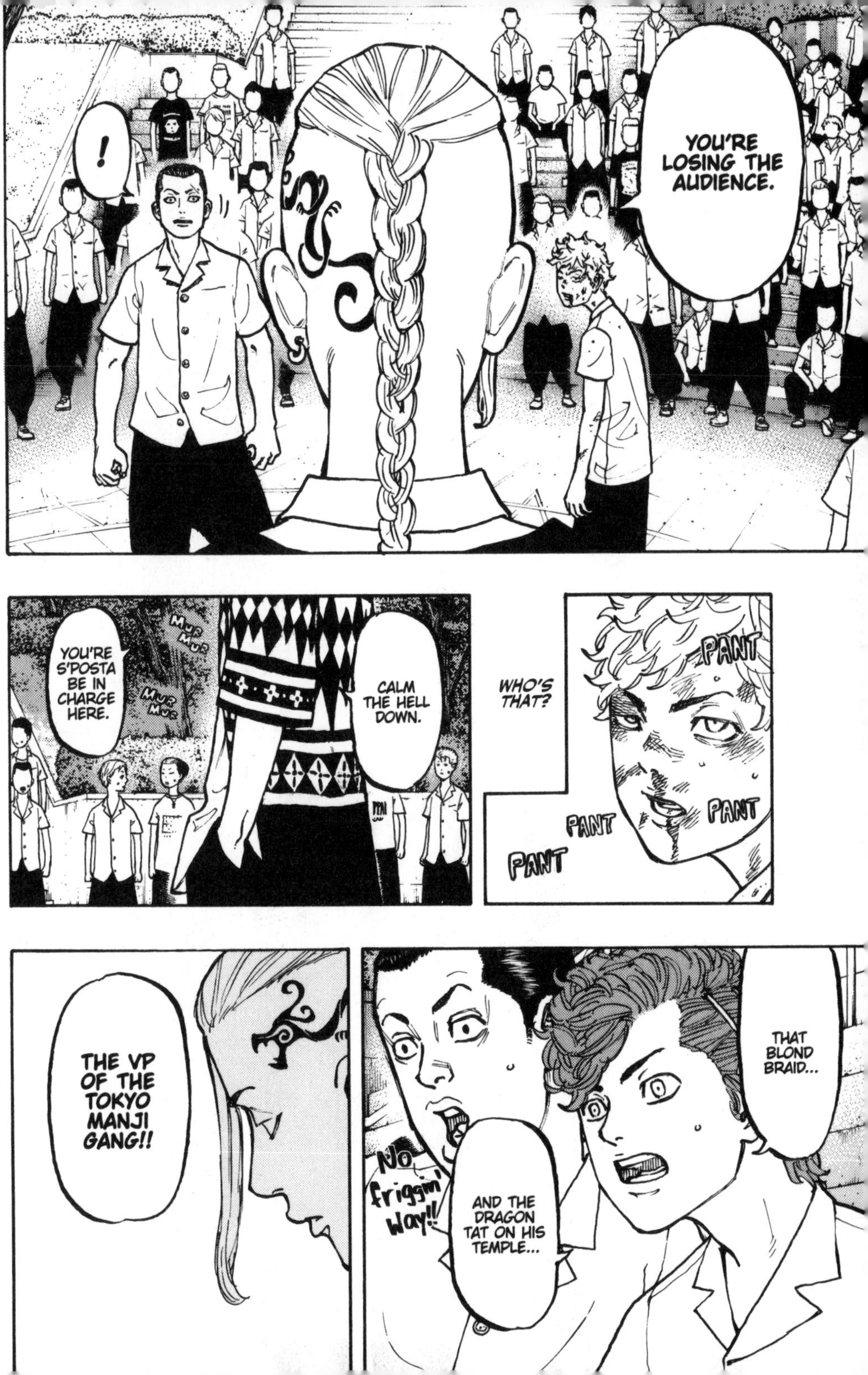
YOU'RE LOSING THE AUDIENCE.
!
WHO'S THAT?
PANT
PANT
PANT
PANT
CALM THE HELL DOWN.
MUR MUR
MUR MUR
YOU'RE S'POSTA BE IN CHARGE HERE.
THAT BLOND BRAID...
AND THE DRAGON TAT ON HIS TEMPLE...
No friggin' way!!
THE VP OF THE TOKYO MANJI GANG!!

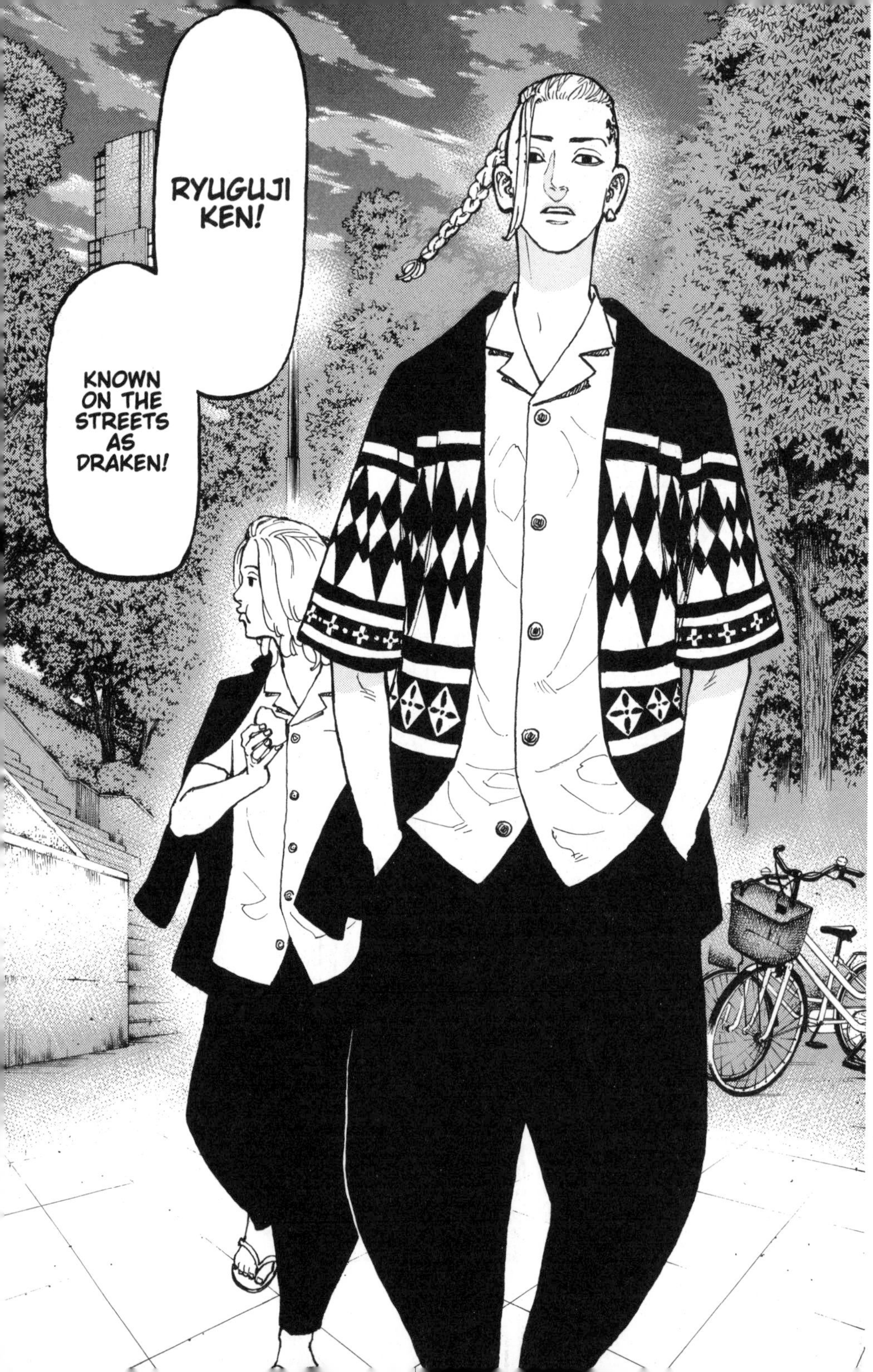
RYUGUJI KEN!
KNOWN ON THE STREETS AS DRAKEN!

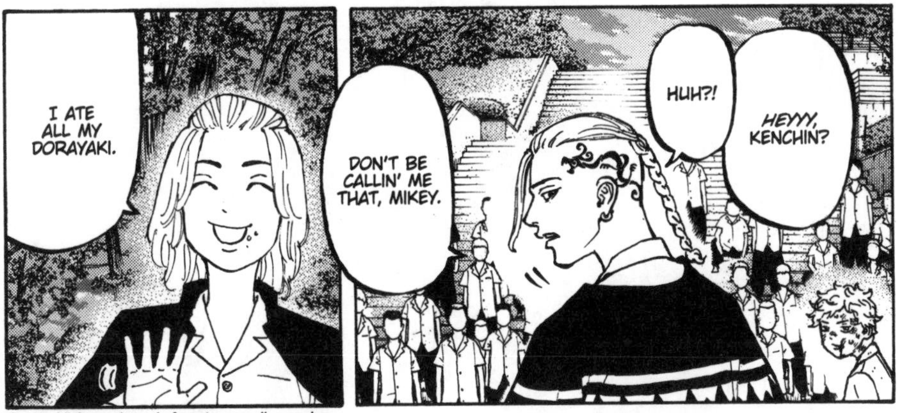
HEYYY, KENCHIN?
HUH?!
DON'T BE CALLIN' ME THAT, MIKEY.
I ATE ALL MY DORAYAKI.

Dorayaki: A snack made from two small pancakes with sweet red bean paste inside.

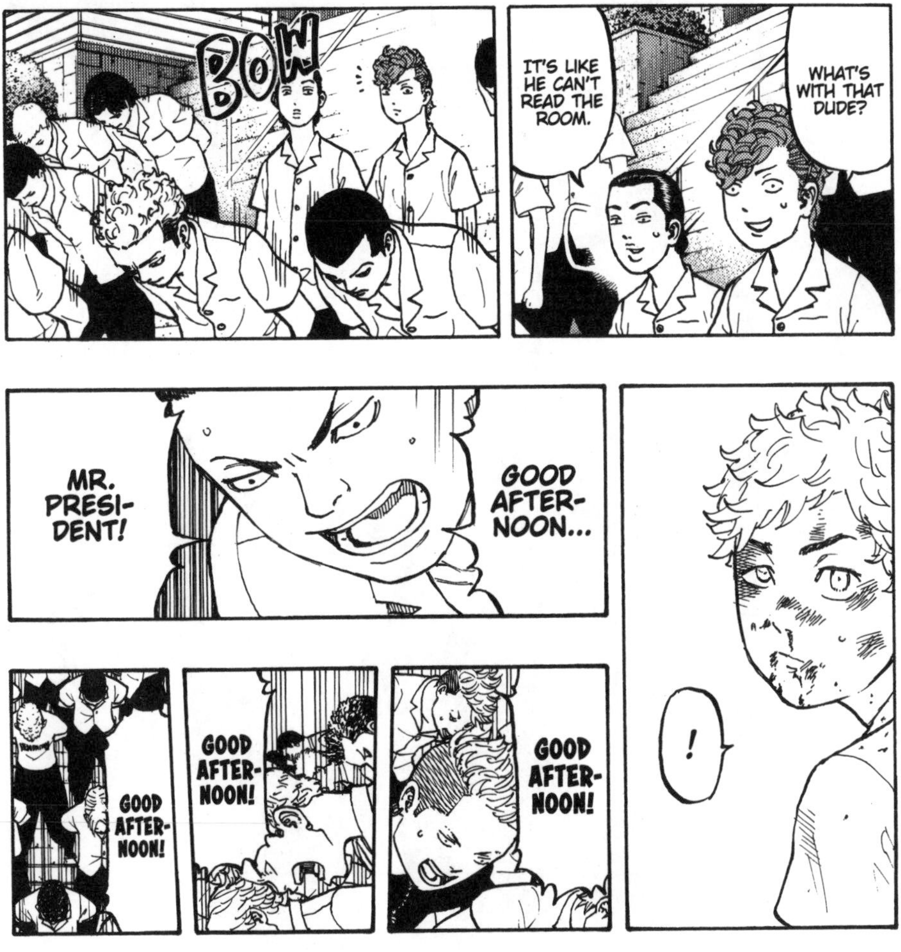
WHAT'S WITH THAT DUDE?
IT'S LIKE HE CAN'T READ THE ROOM.
BOW
!
GOOD AFTERNOON...
MR. PRESIDENT!
GOOD AFTERNOON!
GOOD AFTERNOON!
GOOD AFTERNOON!

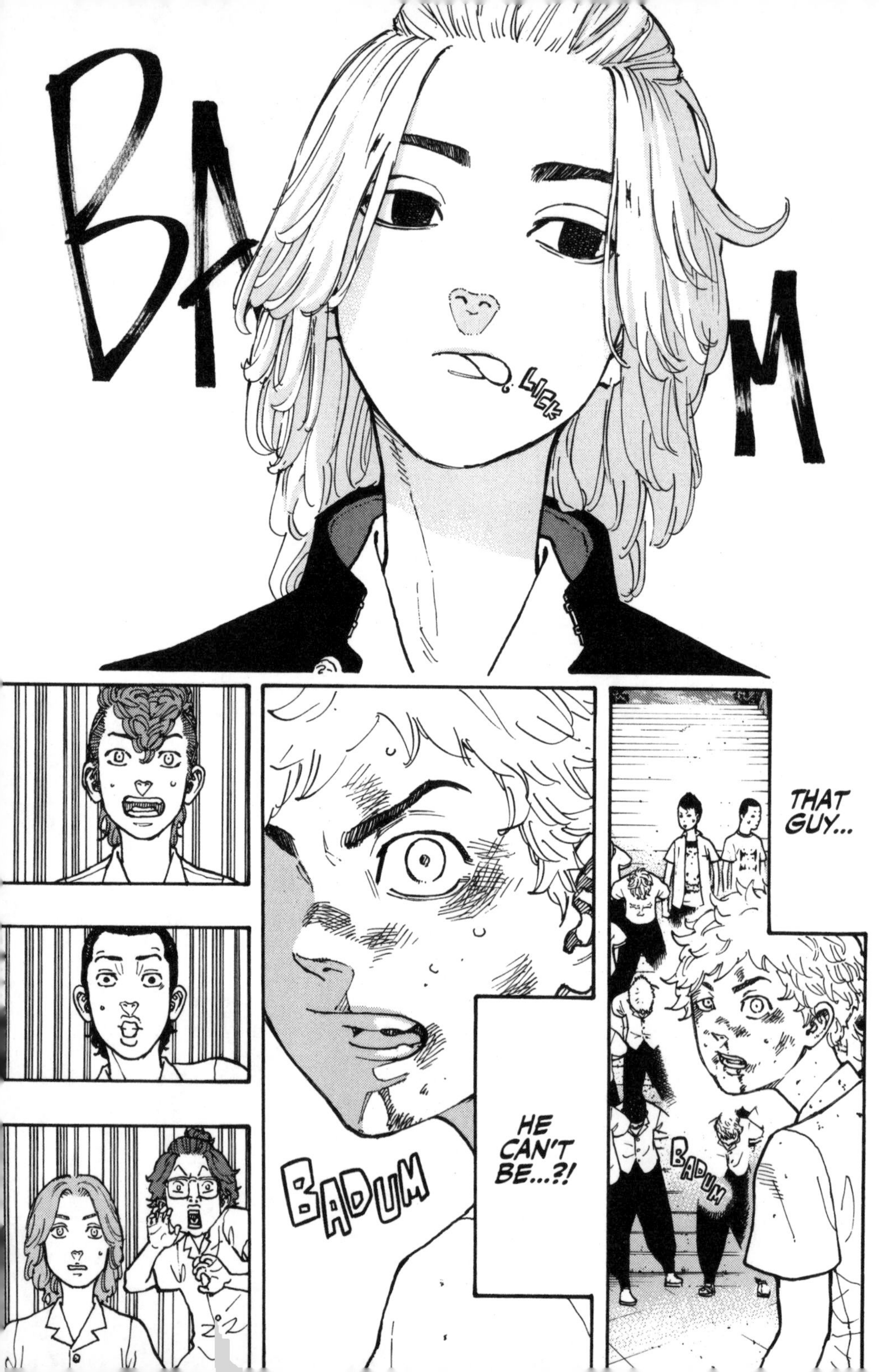
BAM
LICK
THAT GUY...
BADUM
HE CAN'T BE...?!
BADUM

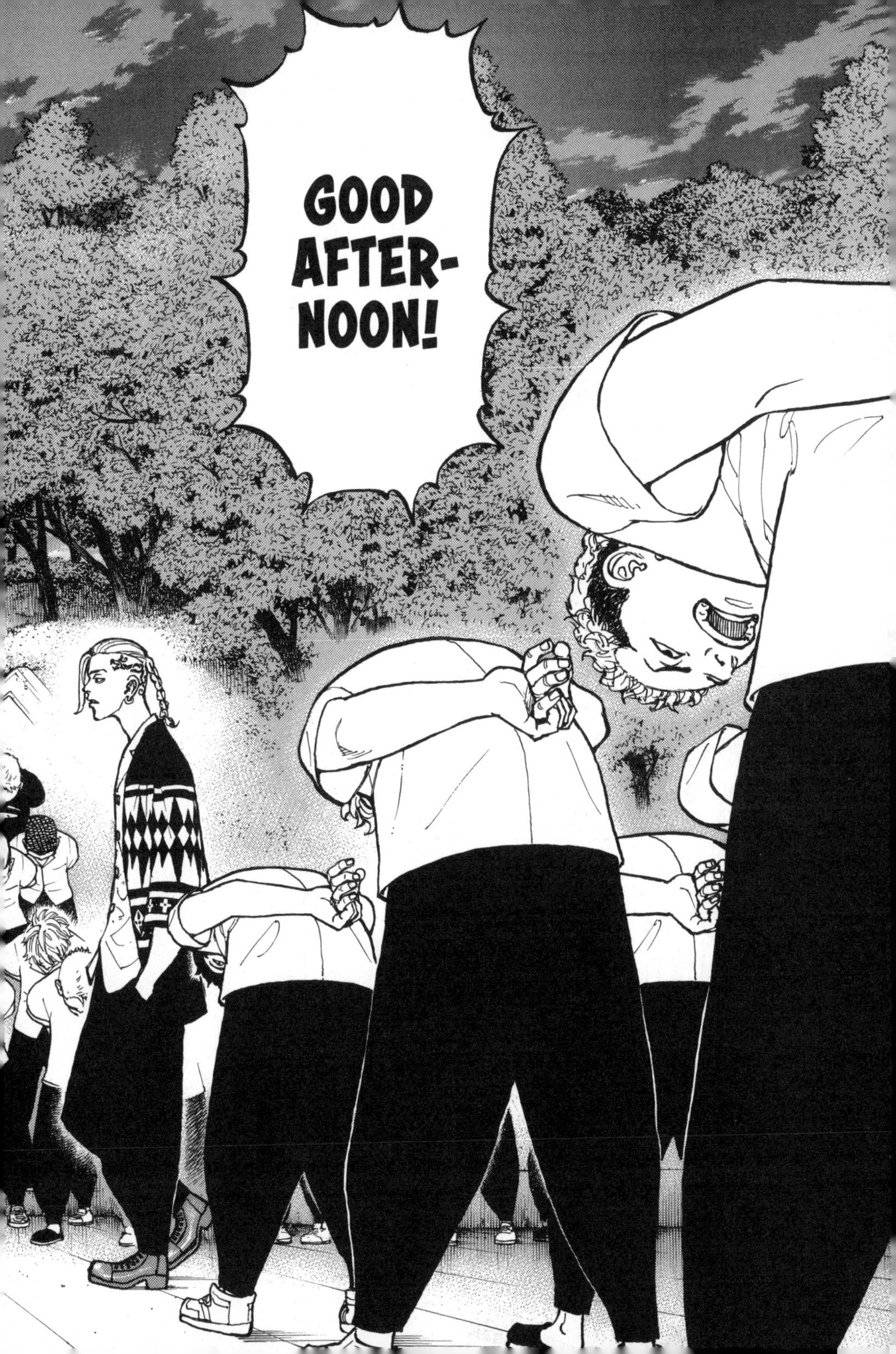
GOOD AFTER-NOON!

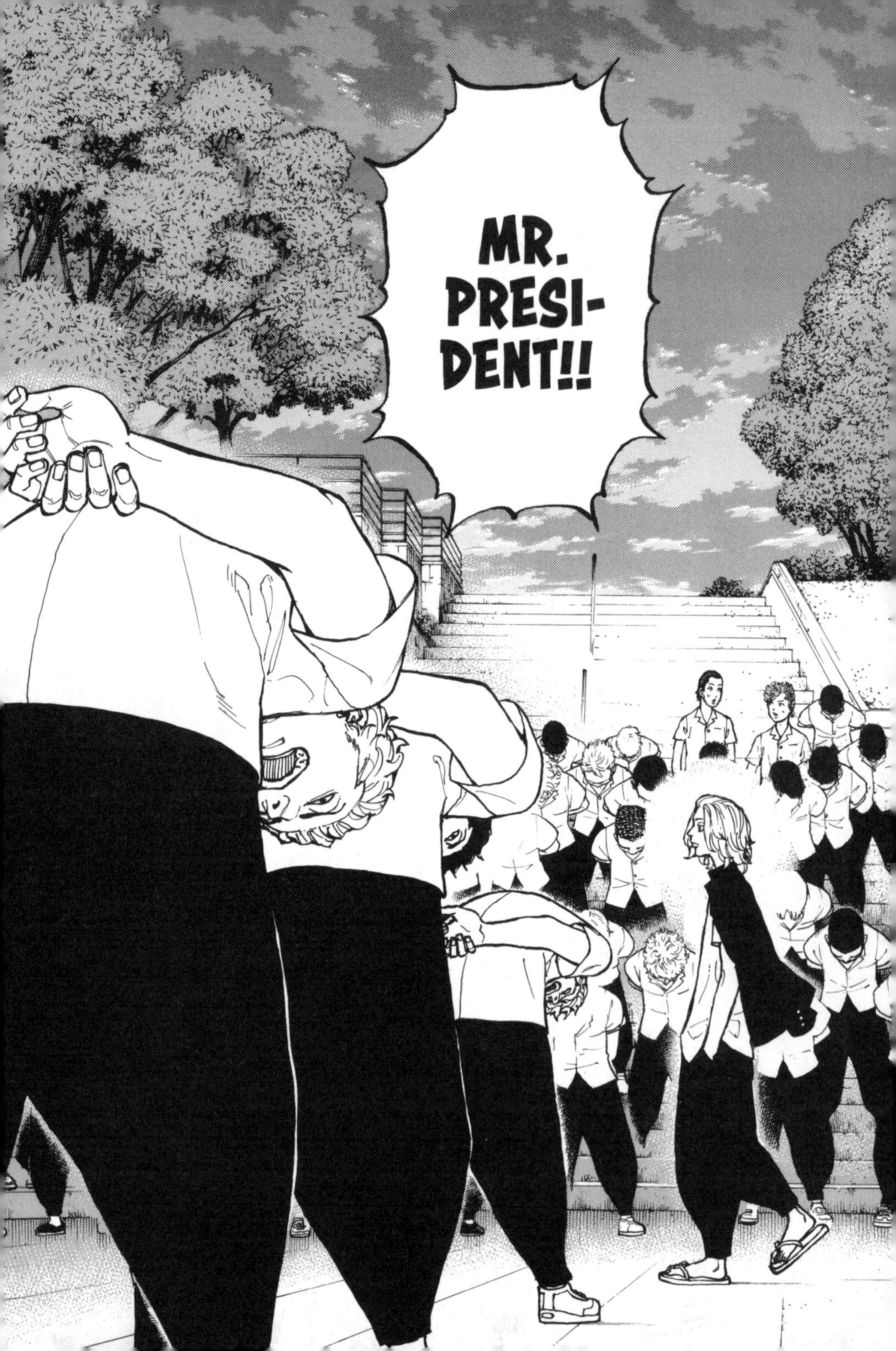
MR. PRESI-DENT!!

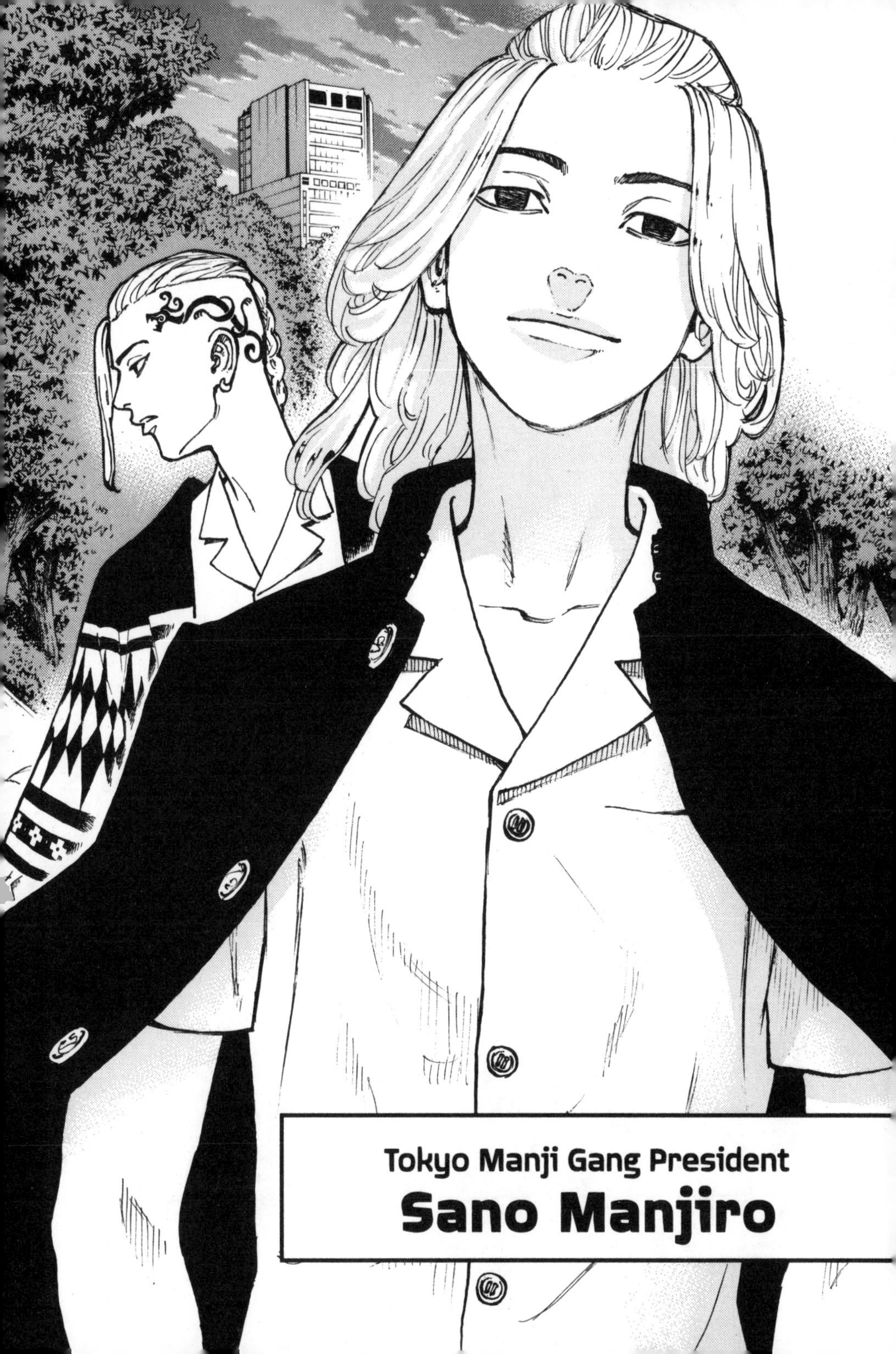
Tokyo Manji Gang President
Sano Manjiro

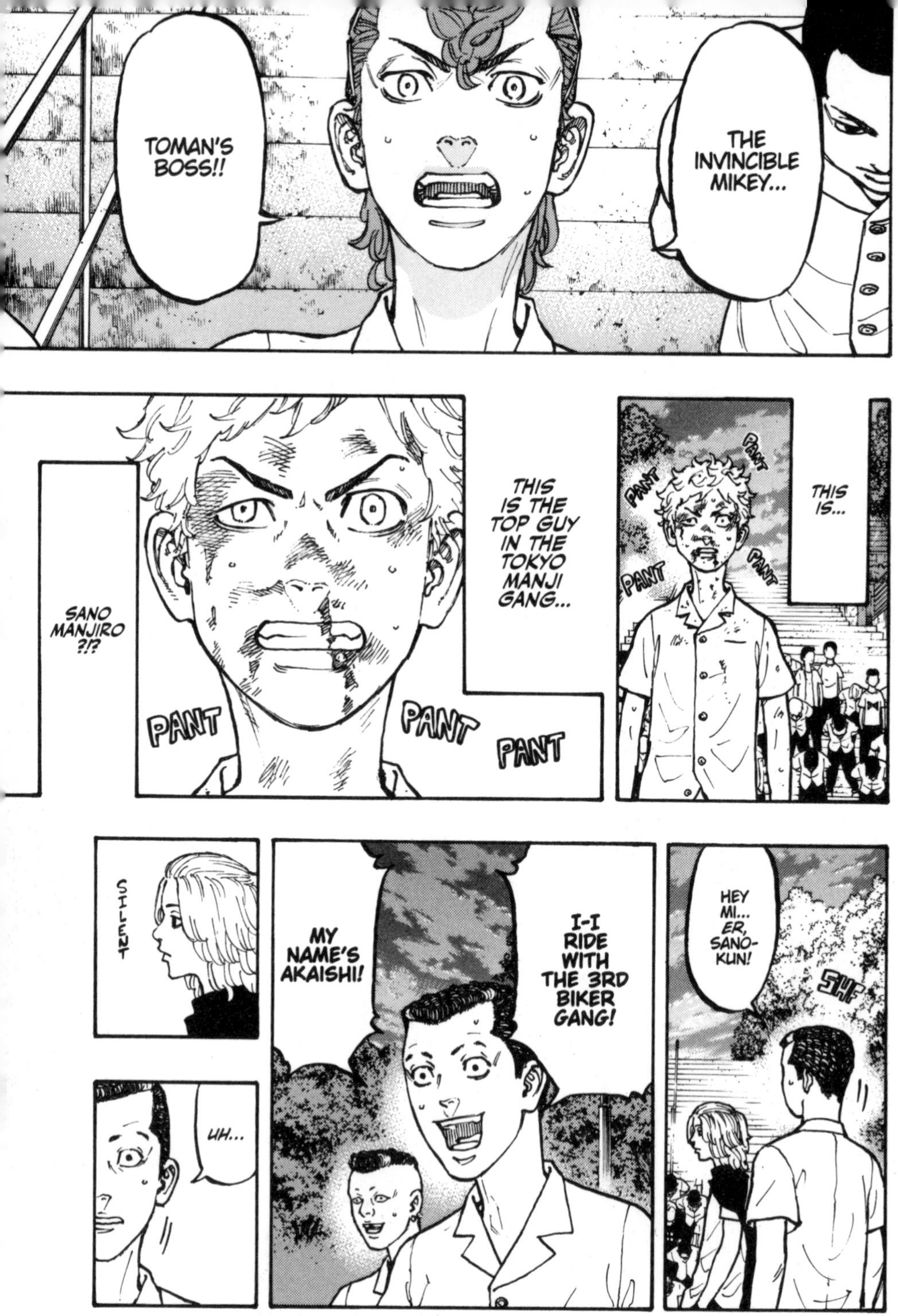
THE INVINCIBLE MIKEY...
TOMAN'S BOSS!!
THIS IS...
PANT
PANT
PANT
PANT
THIS IS THE TOP GUY IN THE TOKYO MANJI GANG...
PANT
PANT
PANT
SANO MANJIRO ?!?
HEY MI... ER, SANO-KUN!
SHF
I-I RIDE WITH THE 3RD BIKER GANG!
MY NAME'S AKAISHI!
SILENT
UH...

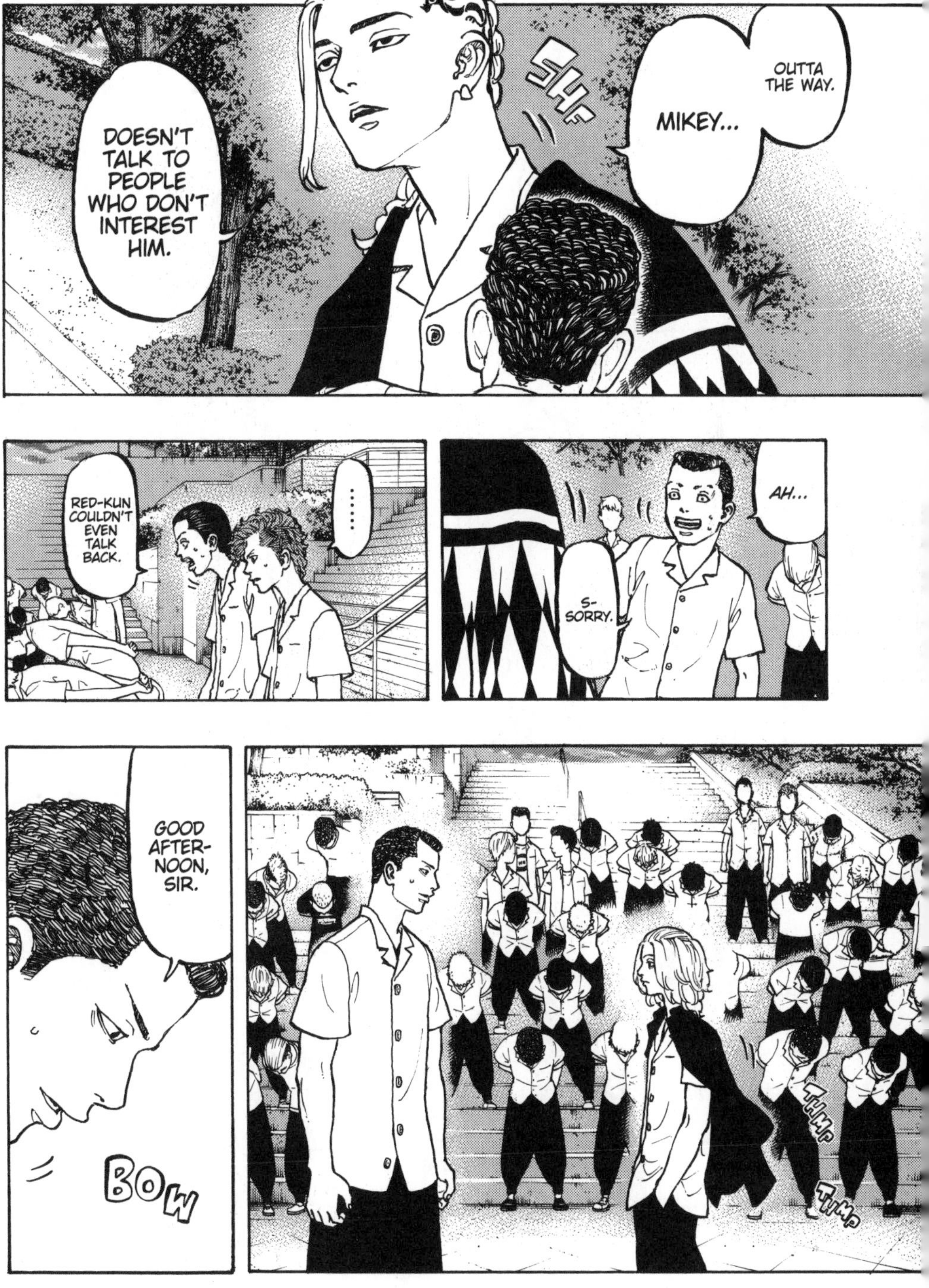
OUTTA THE WAY.
SHF
MIKEY...
DOESN'T TALK TO PEOPLE WHO DON'T INTEREST HIM.
AH...
S-SORRY.
......
RED-KUN COULDN'T EVEN TALK BACK.
THMP
THMP
GOOD AFTERNOON, SIR.
BOW

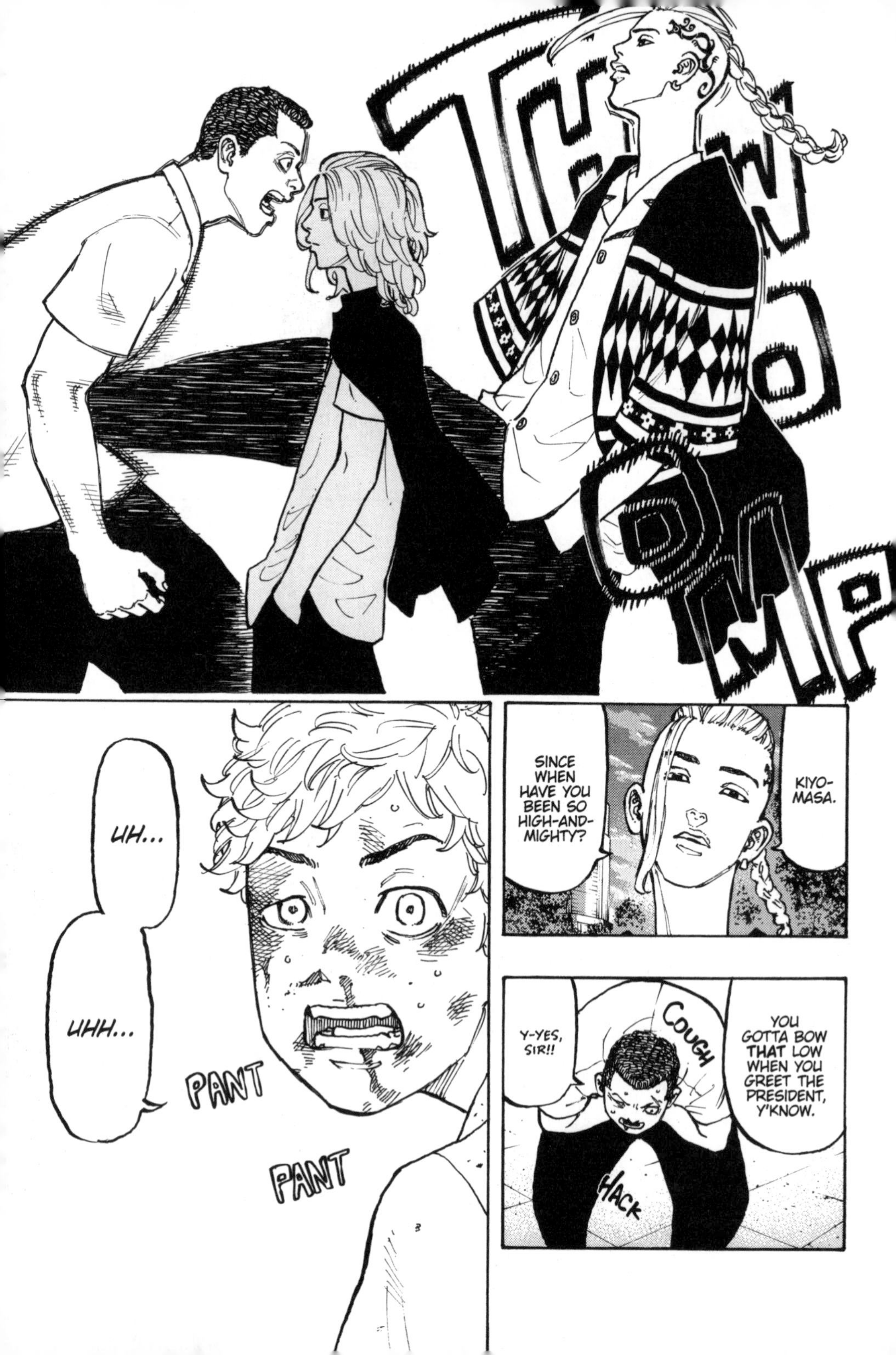
THWOMP
KIYO-MASA.
SINCE WHEN HAVE YOU BEEN SO HIGH-AND-MIGHTY?
YOU GOTTA BOW THAT LOW WHEN YOU GREET THE PRESIDENT, Y'KNOW.
COUGH
Y-YES, SIR!!
HACK
UH...
UHH...
PANT
PANT

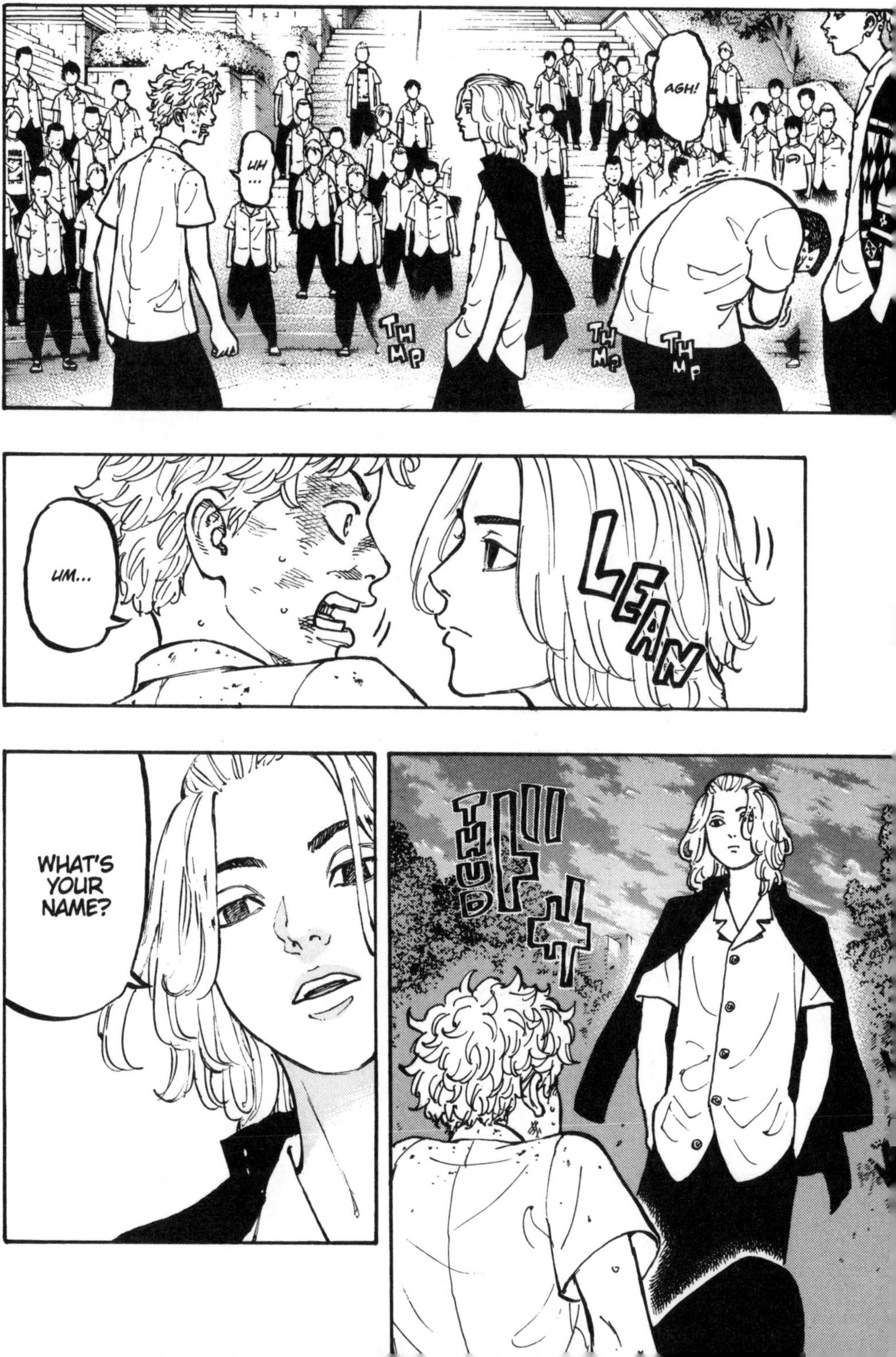
AGH!
THMP
THMP
THMP
UH ...
LEAN
UM...
THUD
WHAT'S YOUR NAME?

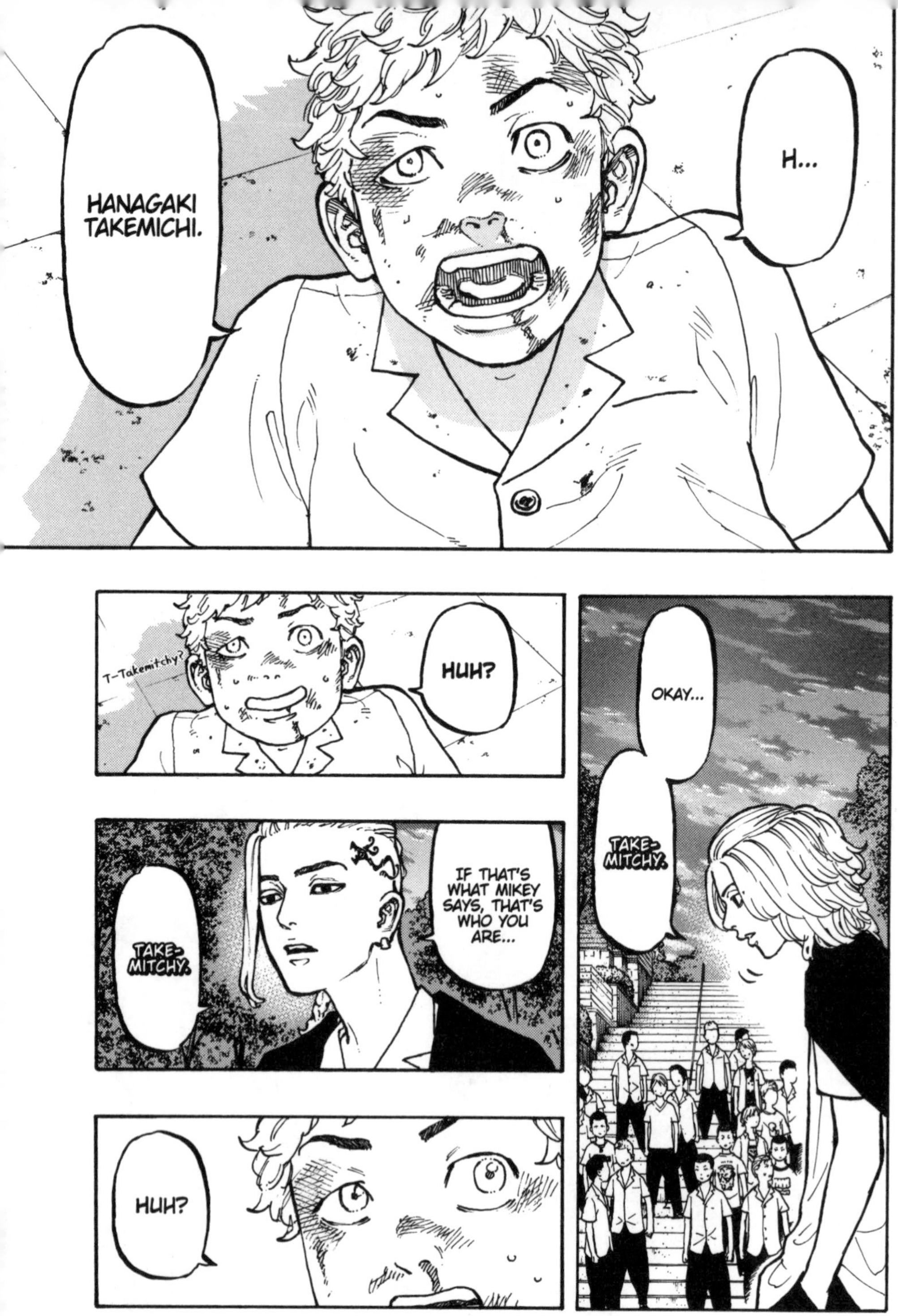
H...
HANAGAKI TAKEMICHI.
OKAY...
TAKE-MITCHY.
HUH?
T-Takemitchy?
IF THAT'S WHAT MIKEY SAYS, THAT'S WHO YOU ARE...
TAKE-MITCHY.
HUH?

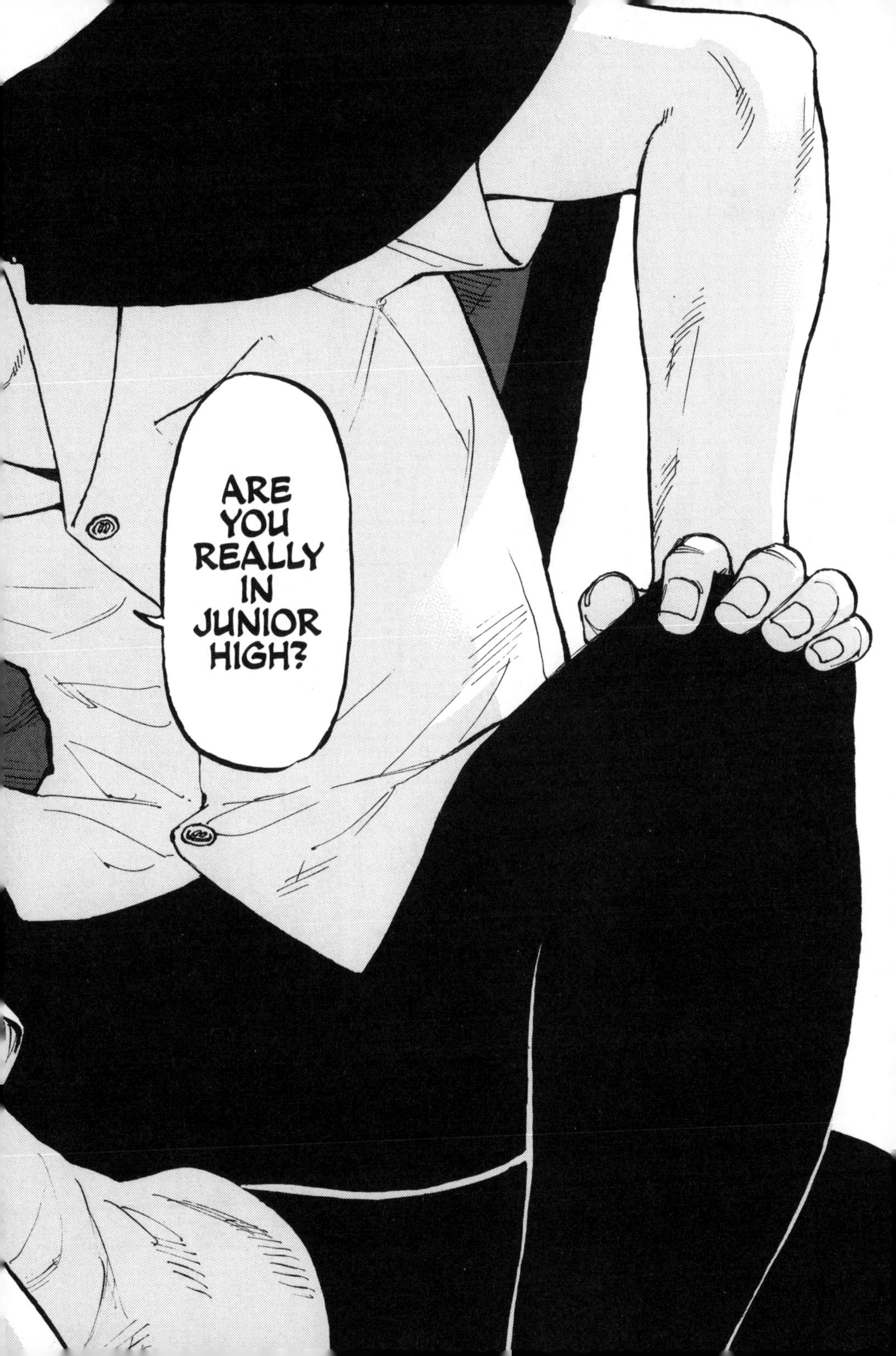
ARE YOU REALLY IN JUNIOR HIGH?

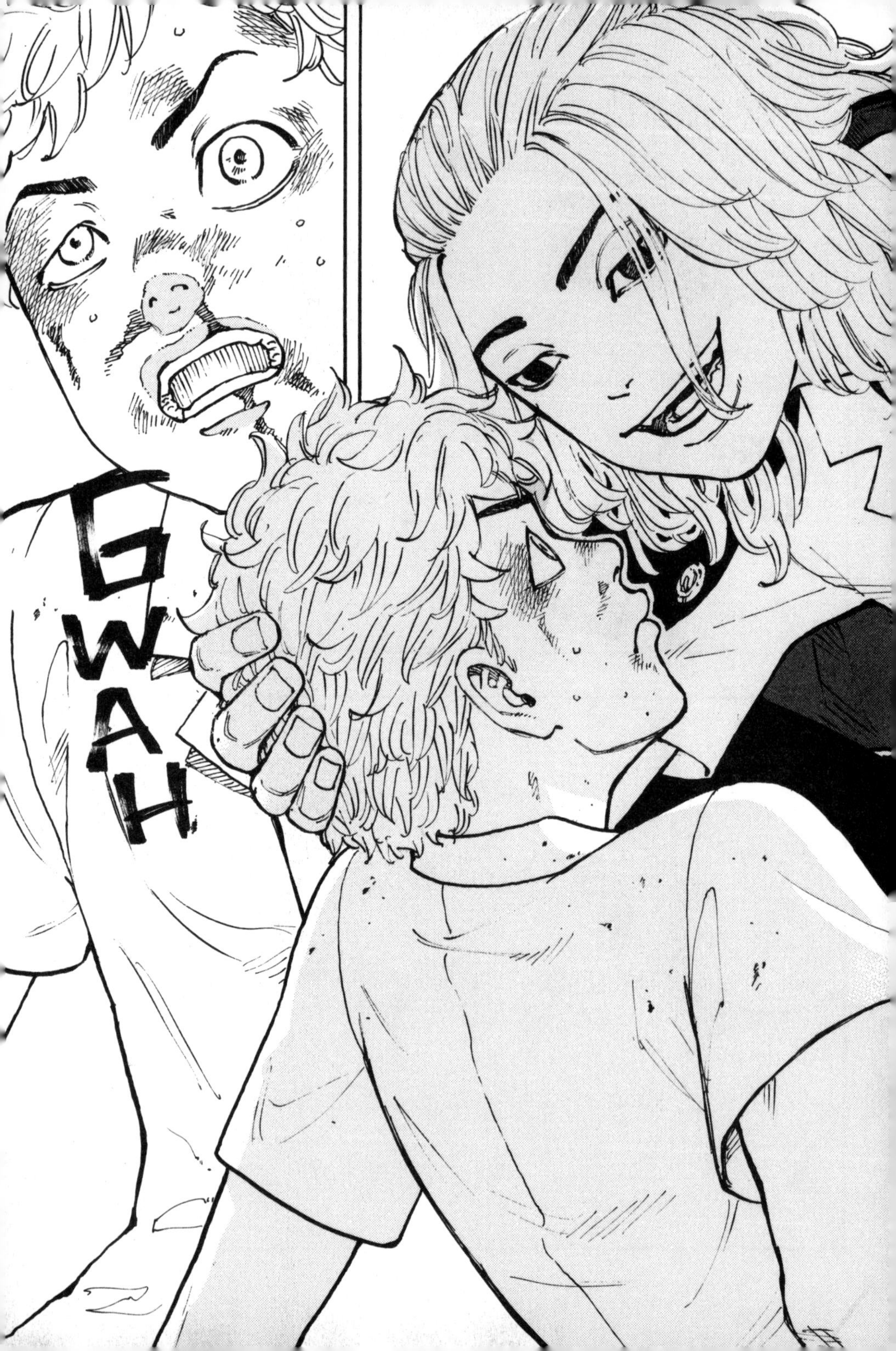
GWAH

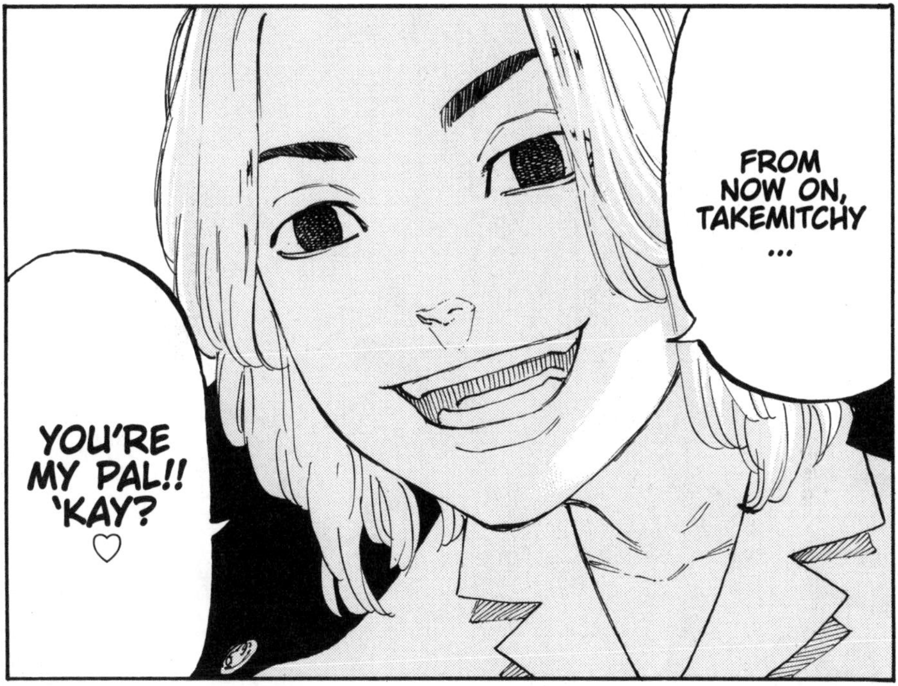
FROM NOW ON, TAKEMITCHY ...
YOU'RE MY PAL!! 'KAY? ♡

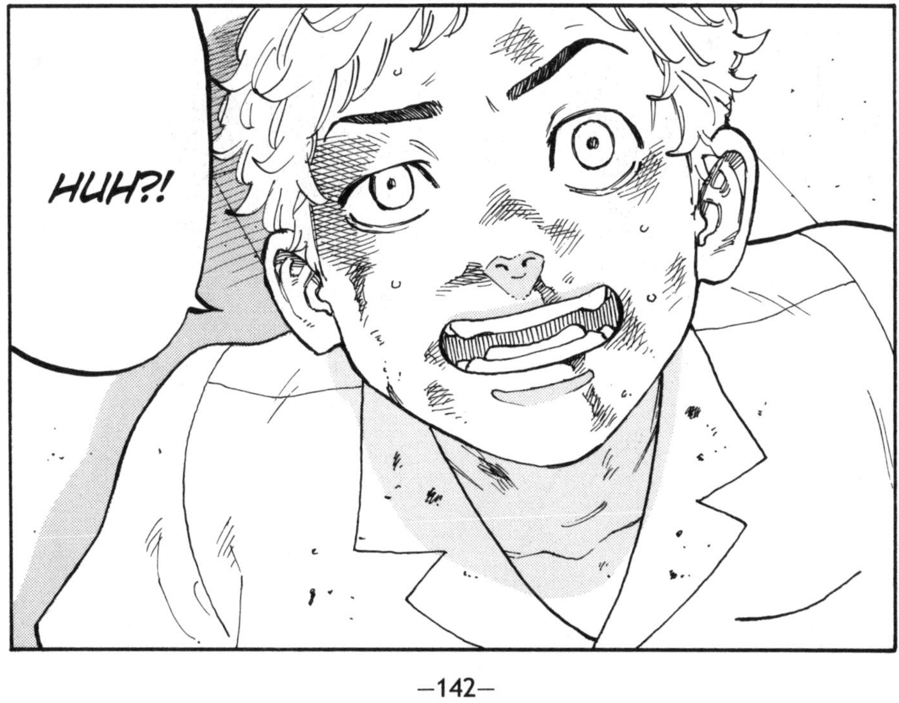
HUH?!

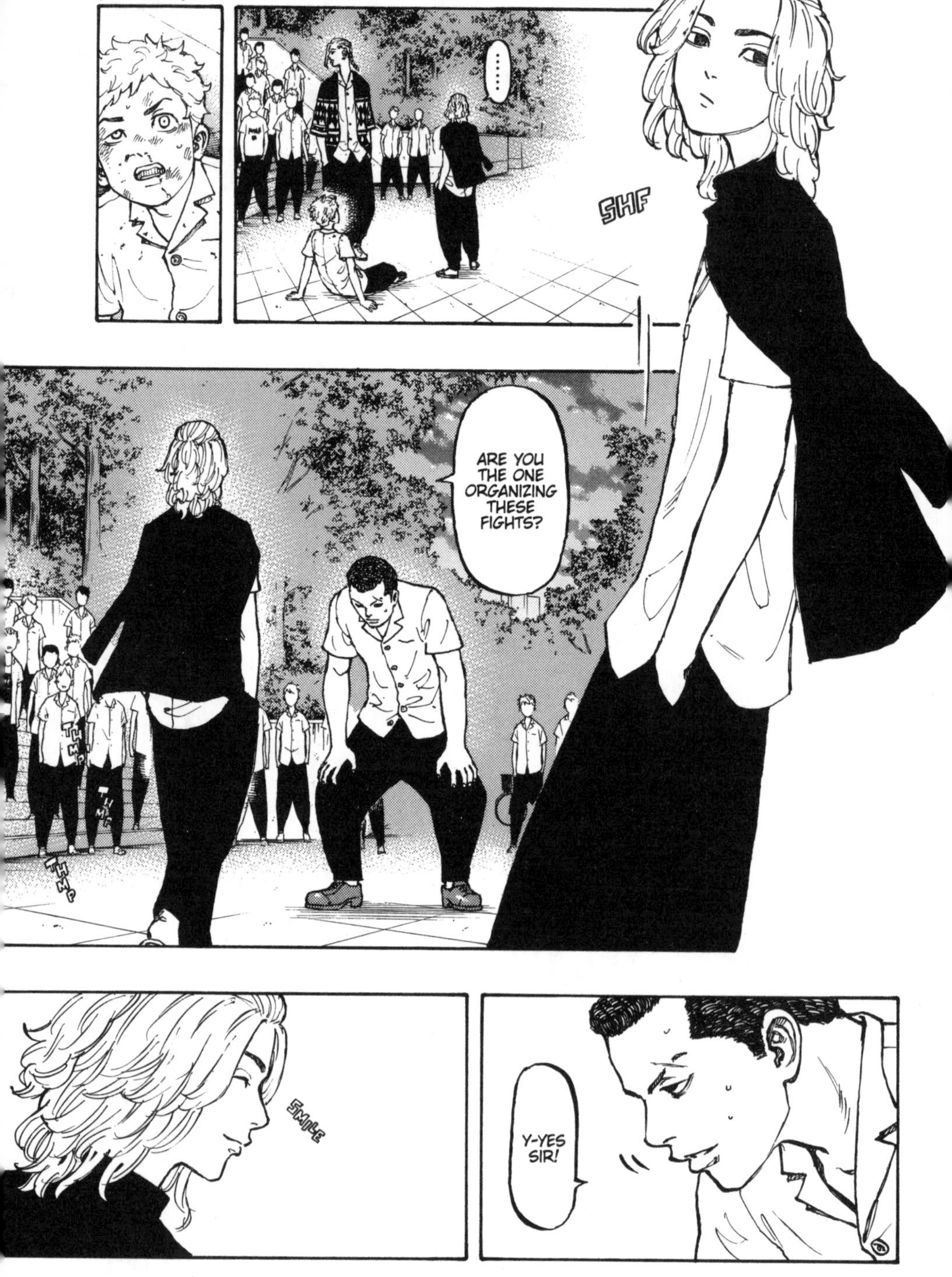
SHF
......
ARE YOU THE ONE ORGANIZING THESE FIGHTS?
THMP
THMP
THMP
Y-YES SIR!
SMILE

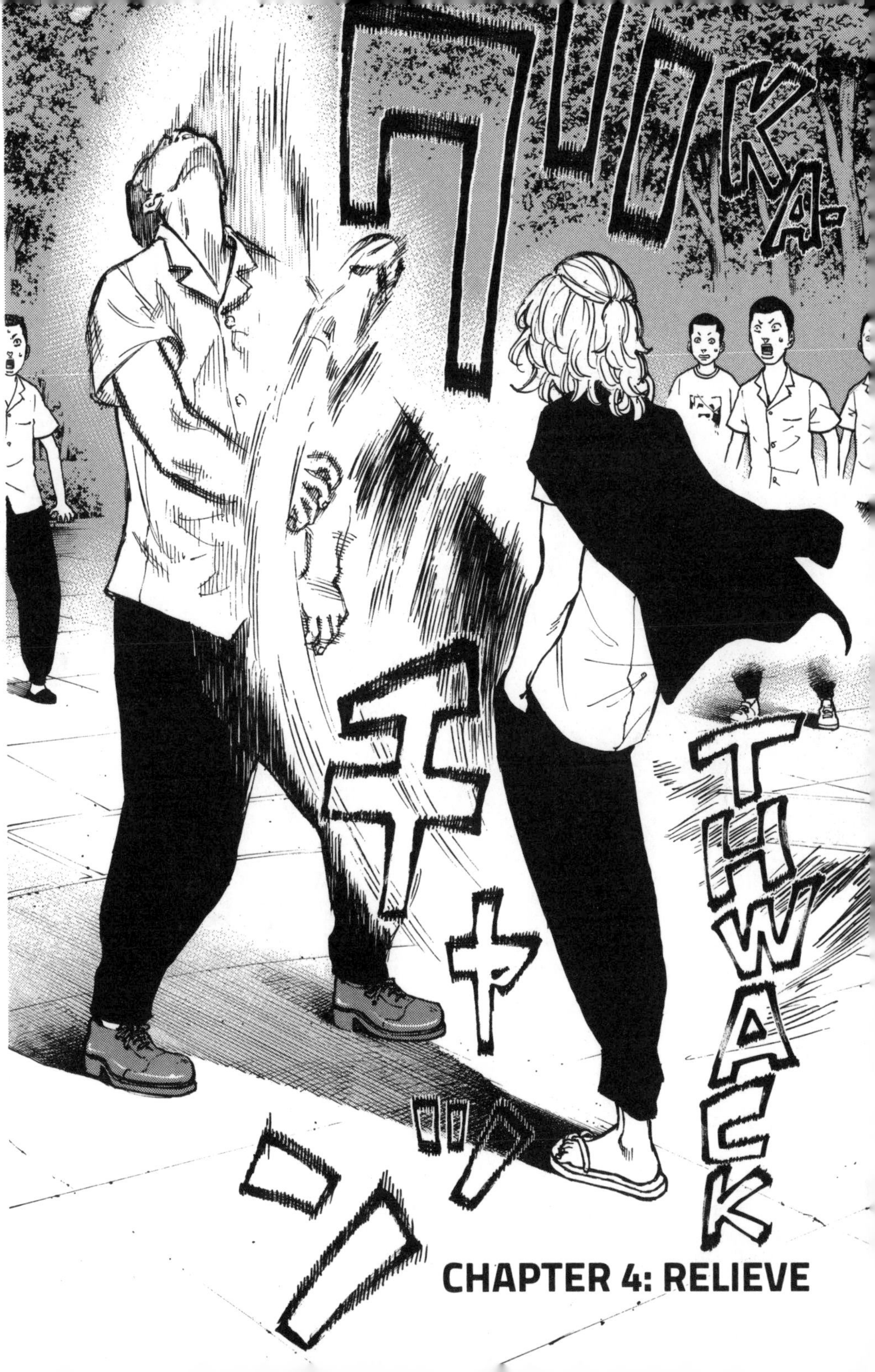
KA
THWACK

CHAPTER 4: RELIEVE

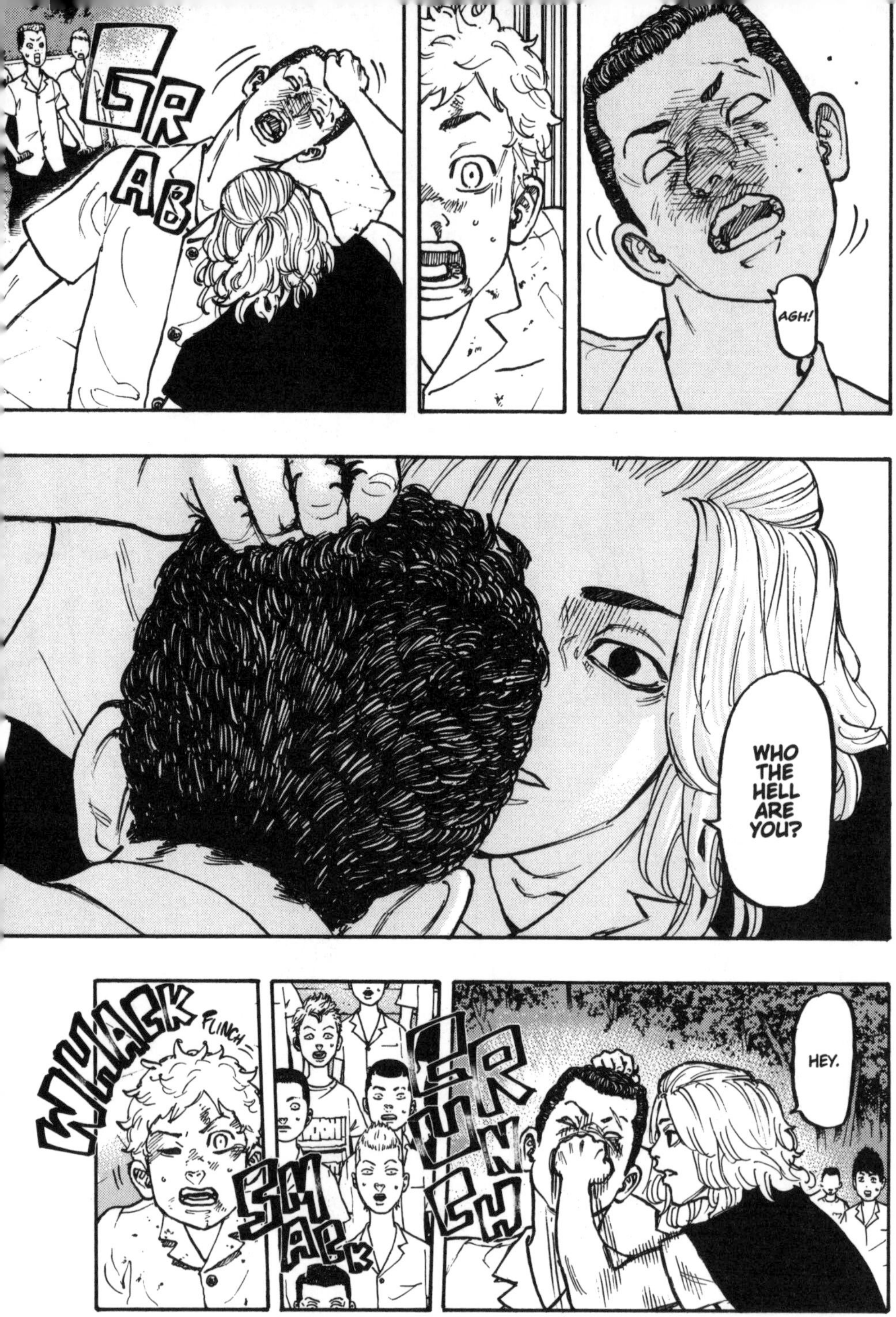
AGH!
GRAB
WHO THE HELL ARE YOU?
HEY.
CRUNCH
SMACK
WHACK
FLINCH

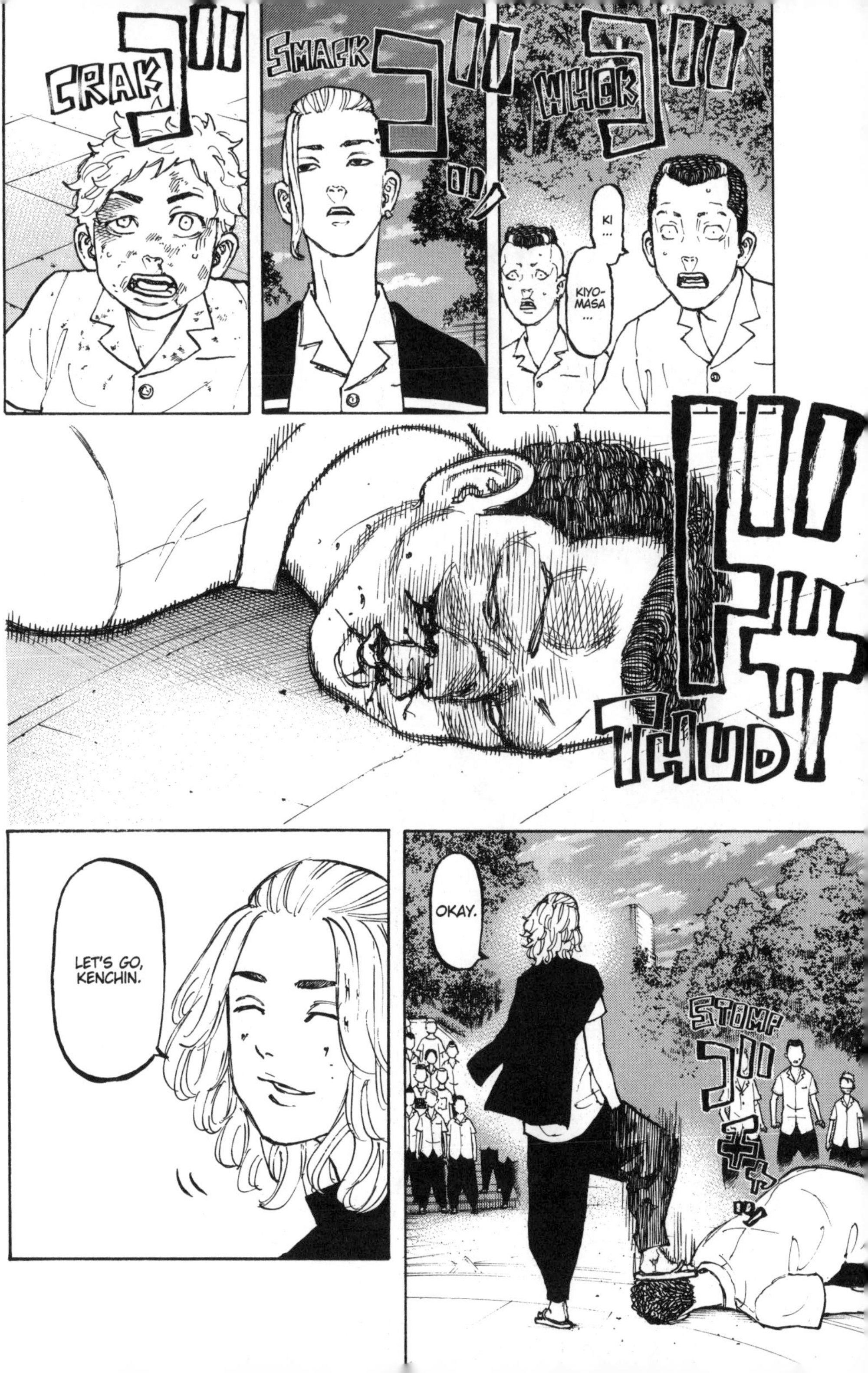
WHOR
KI...
KIYOMASA...
SMACK
CRAK
THUD
OKAY.
STOMP
LET'S GO, KENCHIN.

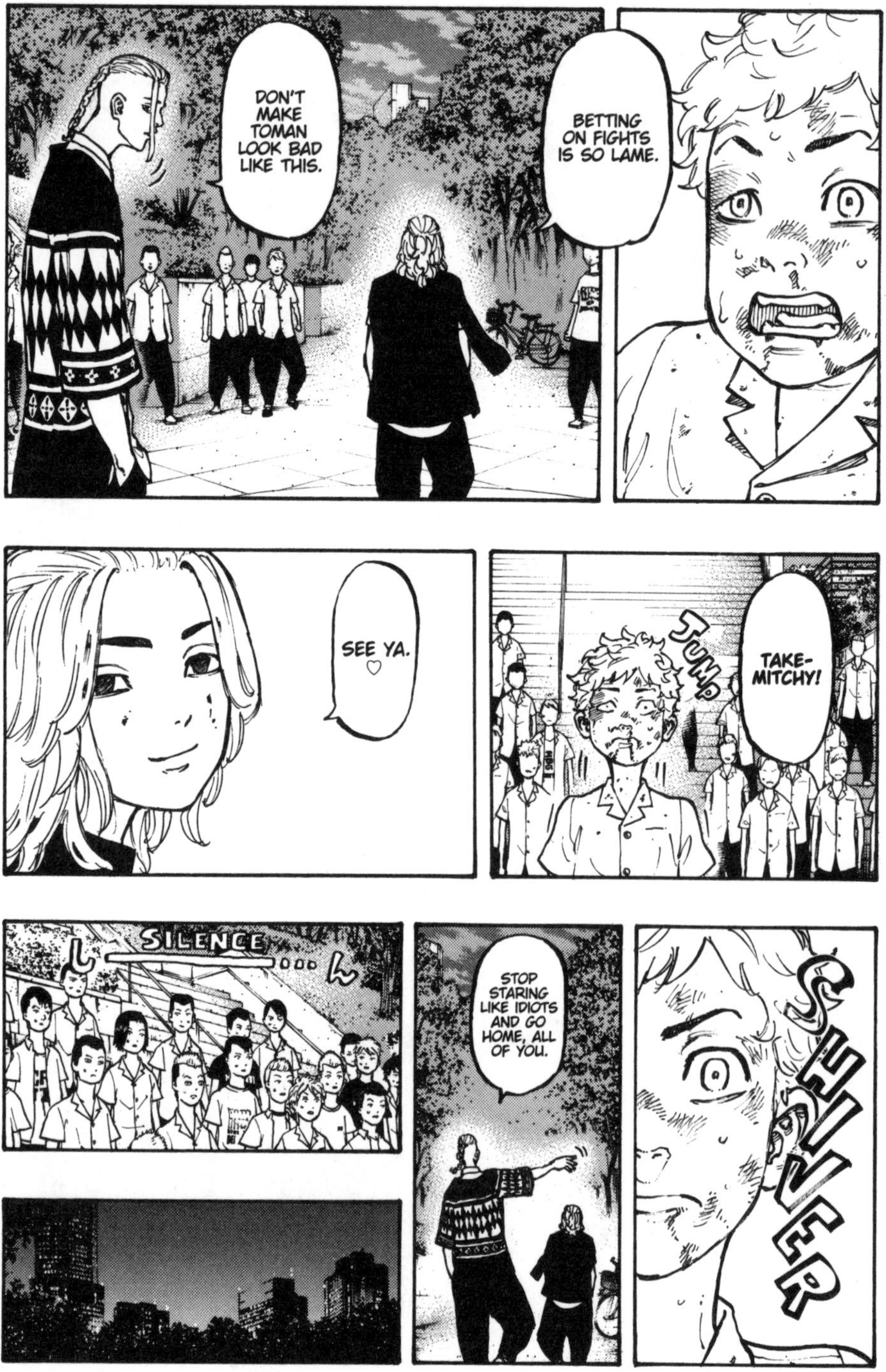
BETTING ON FIGHTS IS SO LAME.
DON'T MAKE TOMAN LOOK BAD LIKE THIS.
TAKE-MITCHY!
JUMP
SEE YA. ♡
SHIVER
STOP STARING LIKE IDIOTS AND GO HOME, ALL OF YOU.
SILENCE

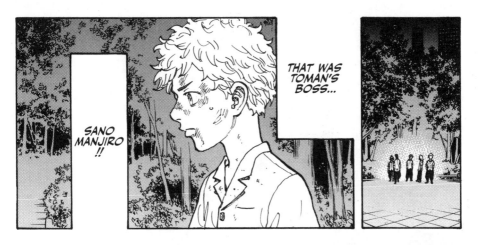

THAT WAS TOMAN'S BOSS...
SANO MANJIRO !!
STAARE
HM?
TAKE-MICHI! THAT WAS SO COOL!!
I WAS TOTALLY MOVED!!
HUH?
AND YOU GOT THE INVINCIBLE MIKEY TO LIKE YOU!!
LEAN
THAT'S SO RAD, TAKE-MICHI!!
THEY SAW IT TOO?

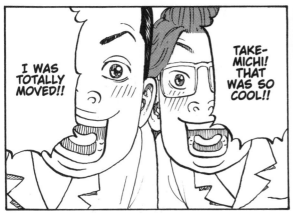

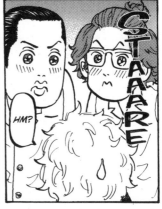

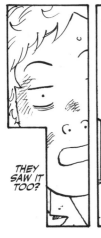

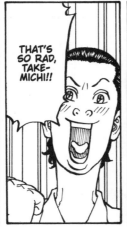

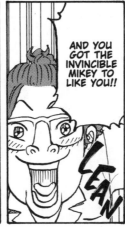

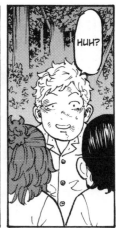

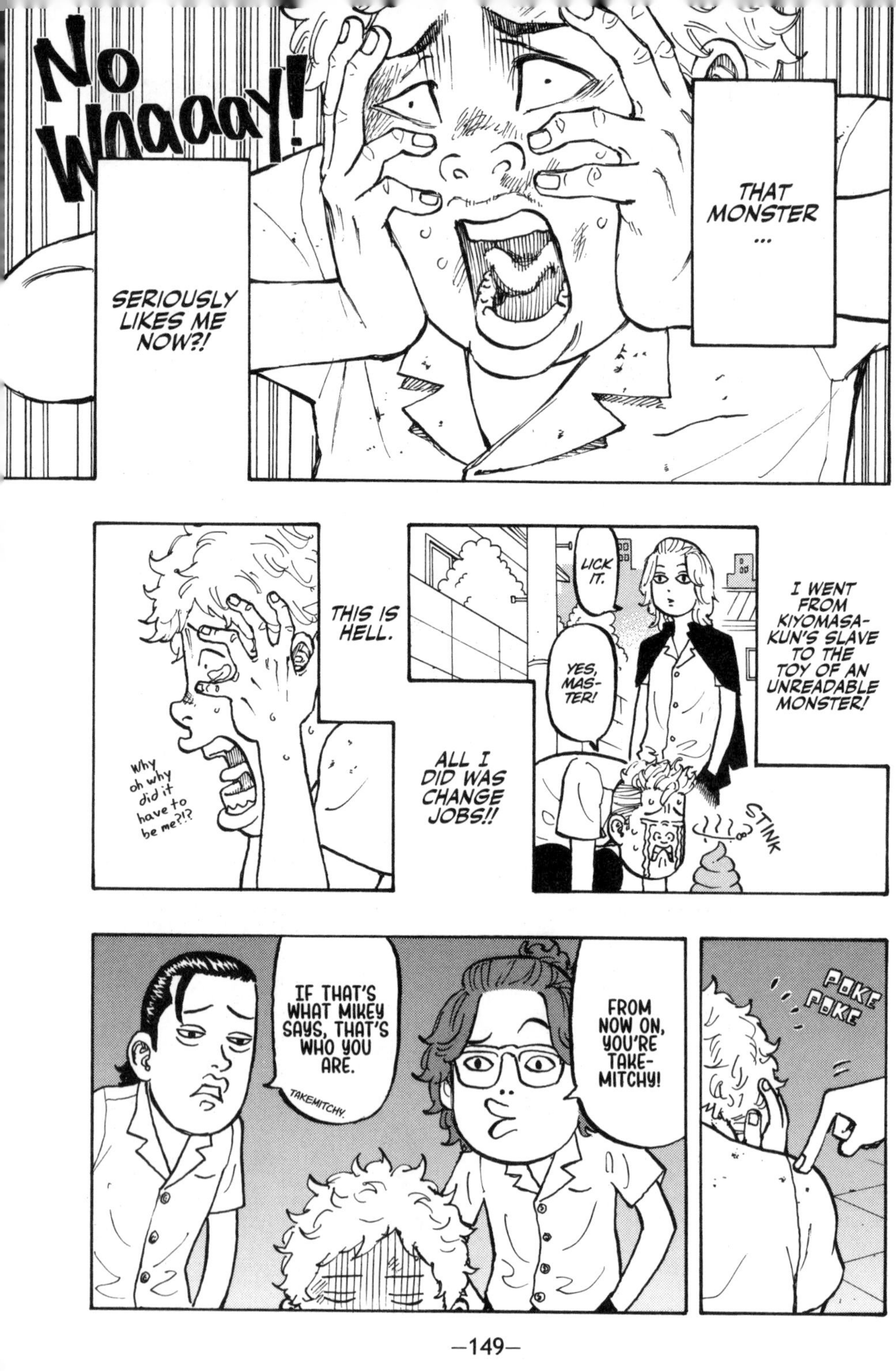
THAT MONSTER ...
No Waaaay!
SERIOUSLY LIKES ME NOW?!
I WENT FROM KIYOMASA-KUN'S SLAVE TO THE TOY OF AN UNREADABLE MONSTER!
LICK IT.
YES, MASTER!
STINK
THIS IS HELL.
ALL I DID WAS CHANGE JOBS!!
Why oh why did it have to be me?!?
POKE POKE
FROM NOW ON, YOU'RE TAKE-MITCHY!
IF THAT'S WHAT MIKEY SAYS, THAT'S WHO YOU ARE.
TAKEMITCHY.

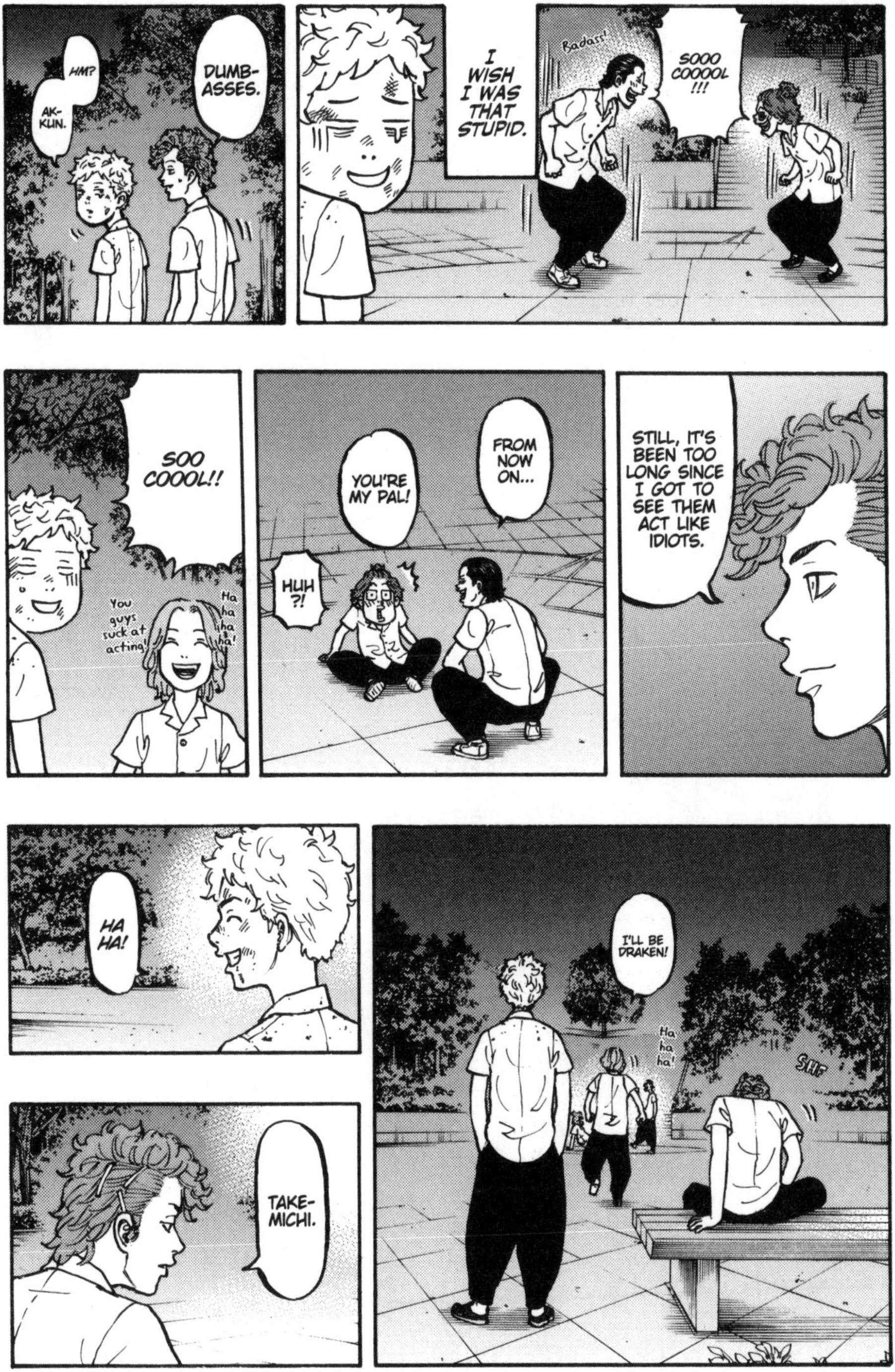
Badass!
SOOO COOOL!!!
I WISH I WAS THAT STUPID.
DUMB-ASSES.
HM?
AK-KUN.
STILL, IT'S BEEN TOO LONG SINCE I GOT TO SEE THEM ACT LIKE IDIOTS.
FROM NOW ON...
YOU'RE MY PAL!
HUH ?!
SOO COOOL!!
Ha ha ha ha!
You guys suck at acting!
I'LL BE DRAKEN!
Ha ha ha!
SHF
HA HA!
TAKE-MICHI.

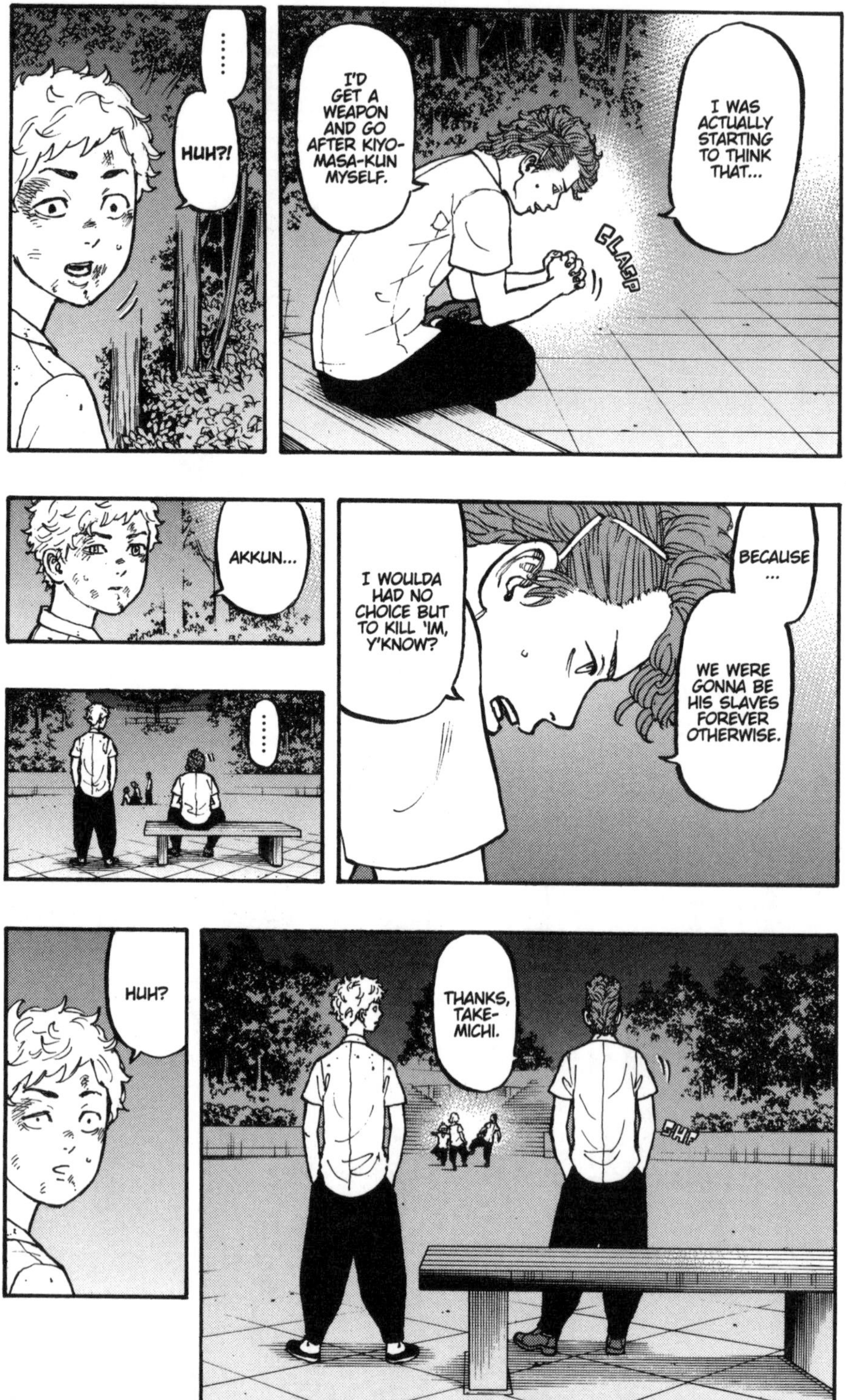
I WAS ACTUALLY STARTING TO THINK THAT...
I'D GET A WEAPON AND GO AFTER KIYO-MASA-KUN MYSELF.
CLASP
......
HUH?!
BECAUSE...
WE WERE GONNA BE HIS SLAVES FOREVER OTHERWISE.
I WOULDA HAD NO CHOICE BUT TO KILL 'IM, Y'KNOW?
AKKUN...
......
THANKS, TAKE-MICHI.
HUH?

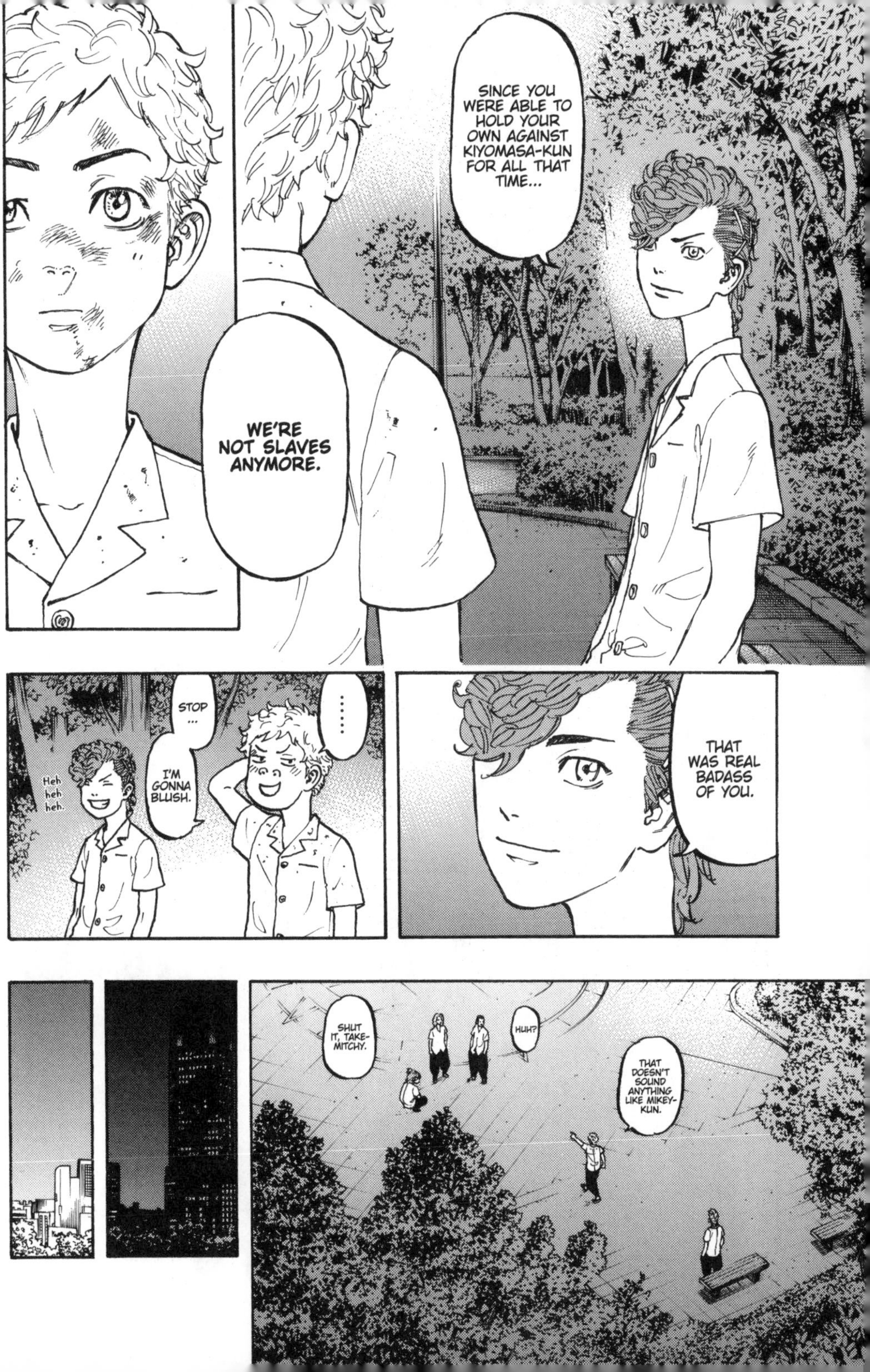
SINCE YOU WERE ABLE TO HOLD YOUR OWN AGAINST KIYOMASA-KUN FOR ALL THAT TIME...
WE'RE NOT SLAVES ANYMORE.
THAT WAS REAL BADASS OF YOU.
......
STOP ...
I'M GONNA BLUSH.
Heh heh heh.
SHUT IT, TAKE-MITCHY.
HUH?
THAT DOESN'T SOUND ANYTHING LIKE MIKEY-KUN.

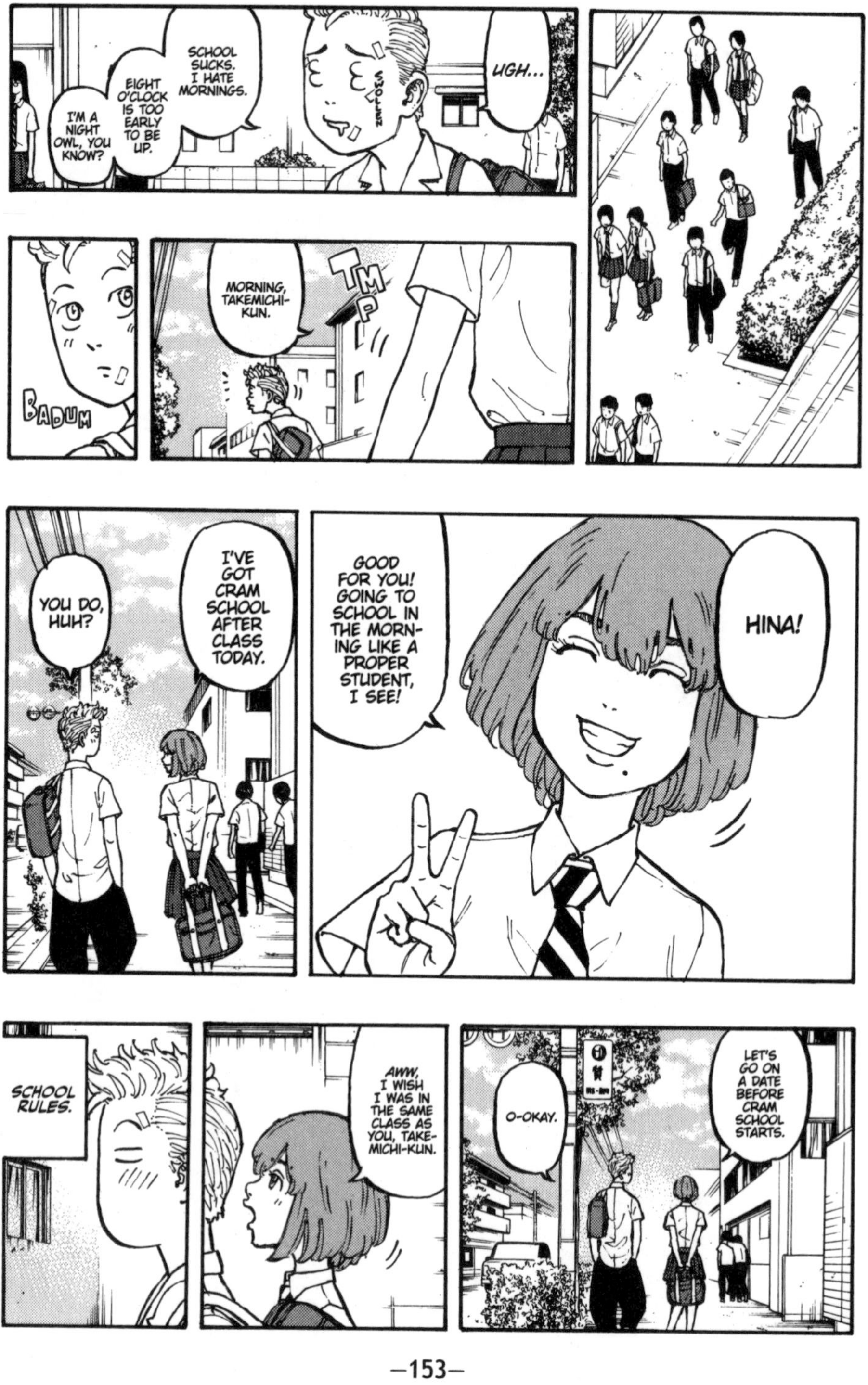
UGH...
SWOLLEN
SCHOOL SUCKS. I HATE MORNINGS.
EIGHT O'CLOCK IS TOO EARLY TO BE UP.
I'M A NIGHT OWL, YOU KNOW?
TMP
MORNING, TAKEMICHI-KUN.
BADUM
HINA!
GOOD FOR YOU! GOING TO SCHOOL IN THE MORNING LIKE A PROPER STUDENT, I SEE!
I'VE GOT CRAM SCHOOL AFTER CLASS TODAY.
YOU DO, HUH?
LET'S GO ON A DATE BEFORE CRAM SCHOOL STARTS.
O-OKAY.
AWW, I WISH I WAS IN THE SAME CLASS AS YOU, TAKE-MICHI-KUN.
SCHOOL RULES.

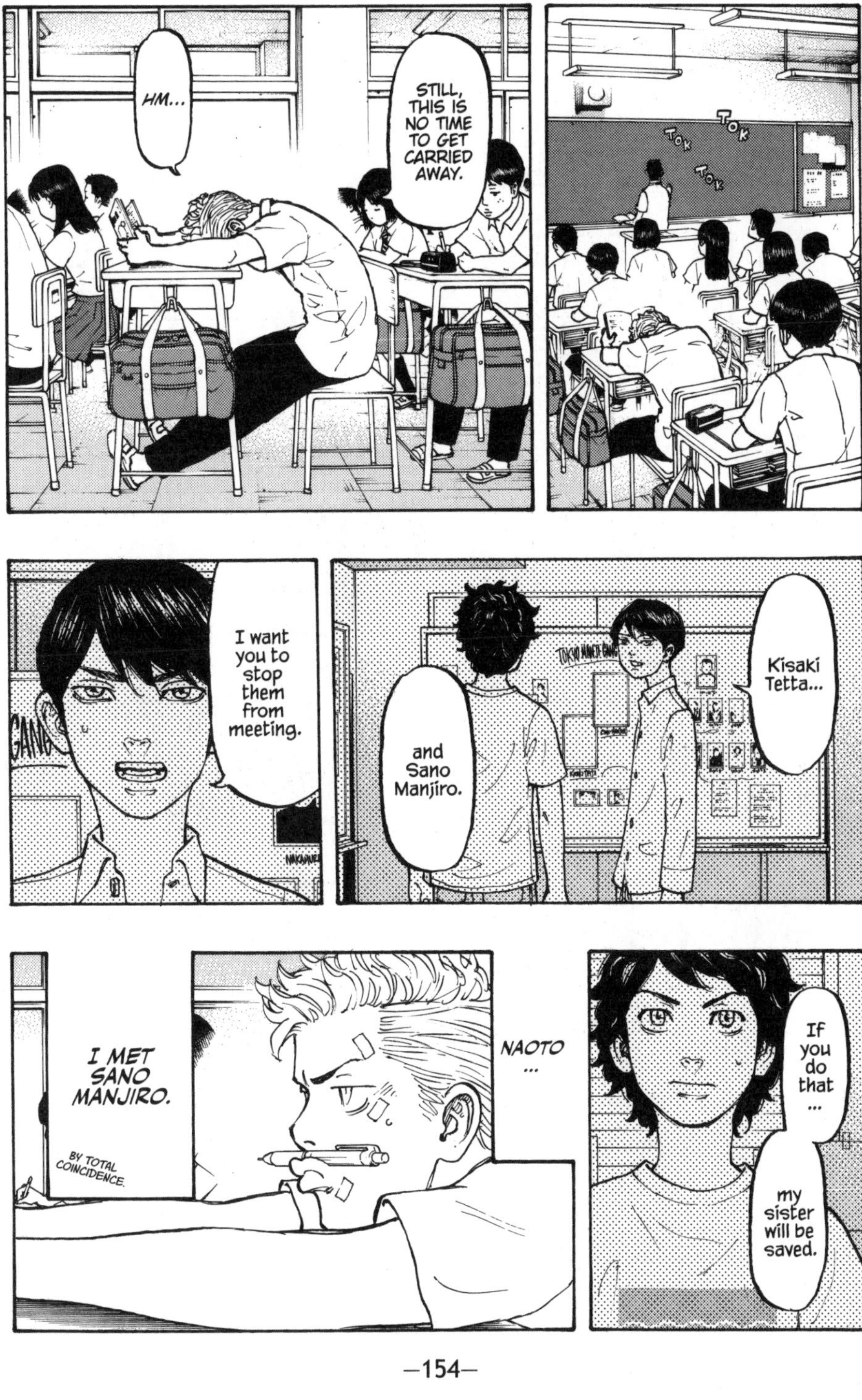
TOK
TOK
TOK
STILL, THIS IS NO TIME TO GET CARRIED AWAY.
HM...
Kisaki Tetta...
and Sano Manjiro.
I want you to stop them from meeting.
If you do that...
my sister will be saved.
NAOTO...
I MET SANO MANJIRO.
BY TOTAL COINCIDENCE.

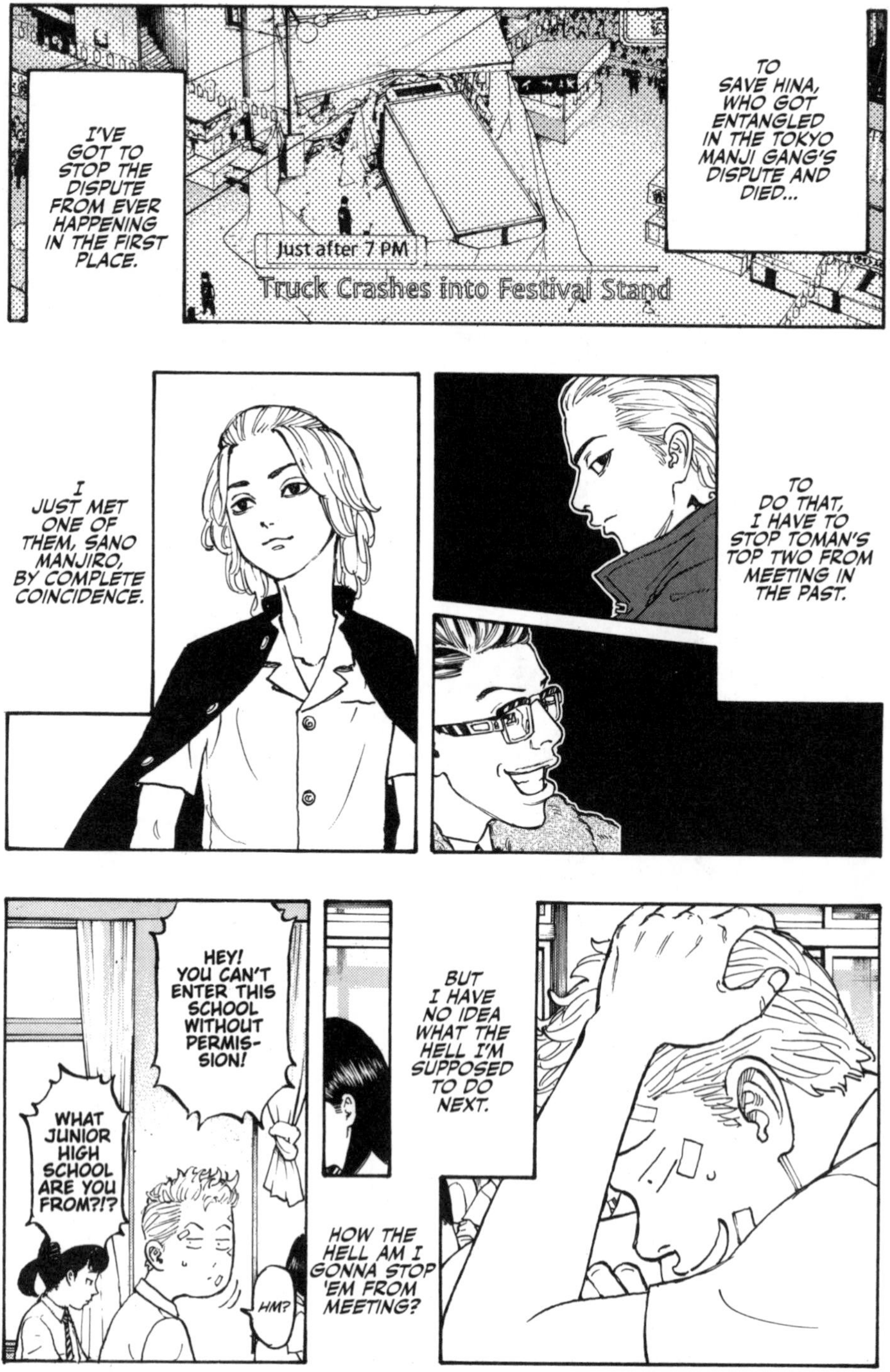
TO SAVE HINA, WHO GOT ENTANGLED IN THE TOKYO MANJI GANG'S DISPUTE AND DIED...
I'VE GOT TO STOP THE DISPUTE FROM EVER HAPPENING IN THE FIRST PLACE.
Just after 7 PM
Truck Crashes into Festival Stand
TO DO THAT, I HAVE TO STOP TOMAN'S TOP TWO FROM MEETING IN THE PAST.
I JUST MET ONE OF THEM, SANO MANJIRO, BY COMPLETE COINCIDENCE.
BUT I HAVE NO IDEA WHAT THE HELL I'M SUPPOSED TO DO NEXT.
HOW THE HELL AM I GONNA STOP 'EM FROM MEETING?
HEY! YOU CAN'T ENTER THIS SCHOOL WITHOUT PERMISSION!
WHAT JUNIOR HIGH SCHOOL ARE YOU FROM?!?
HM?

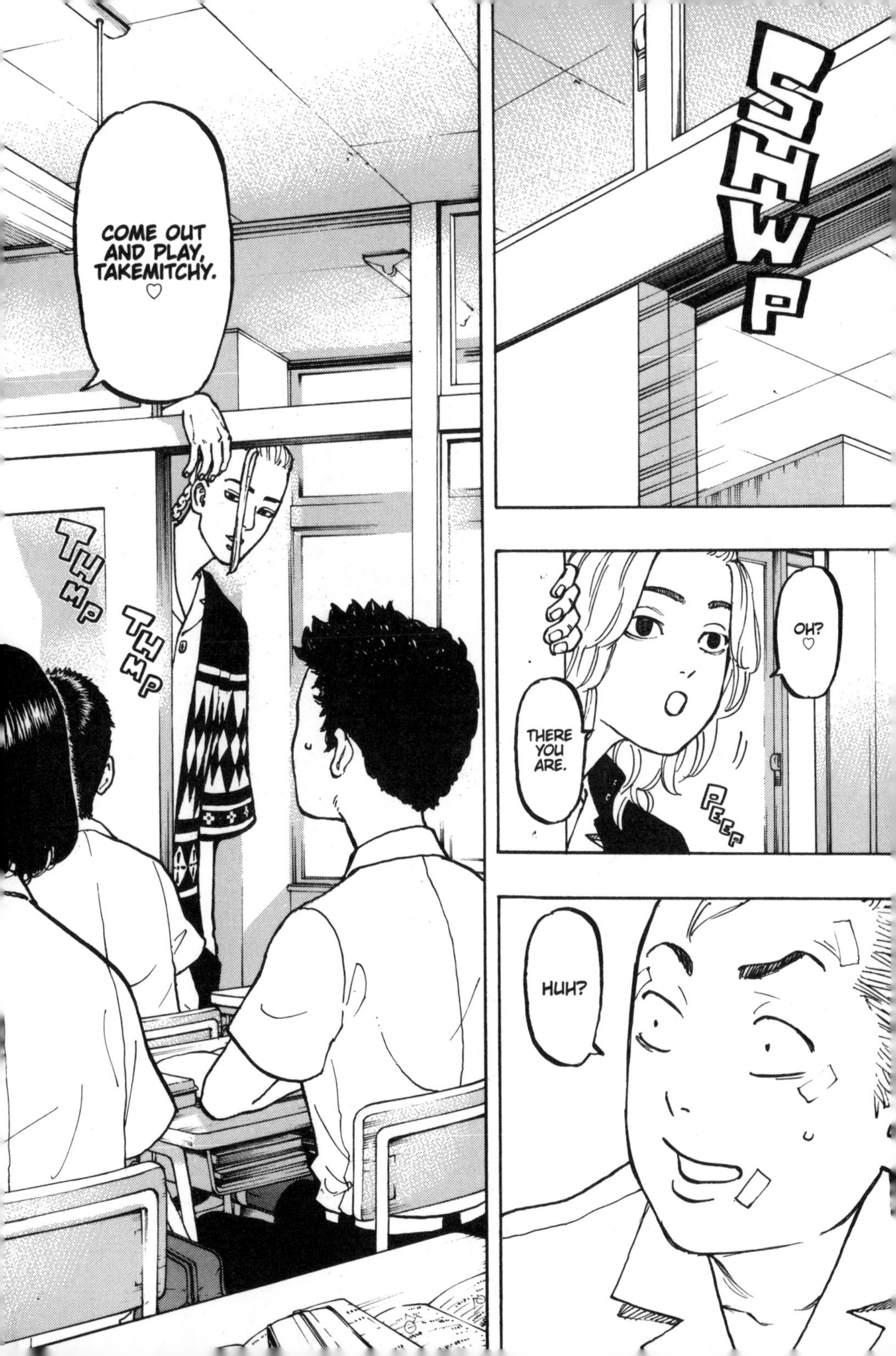
SHWP
OH? ♡
THERE YOU ARE.
PEEP
HUH?
COME OUT AND PLAY, TAKEMITCHY. ♡
THUMP
THUMP

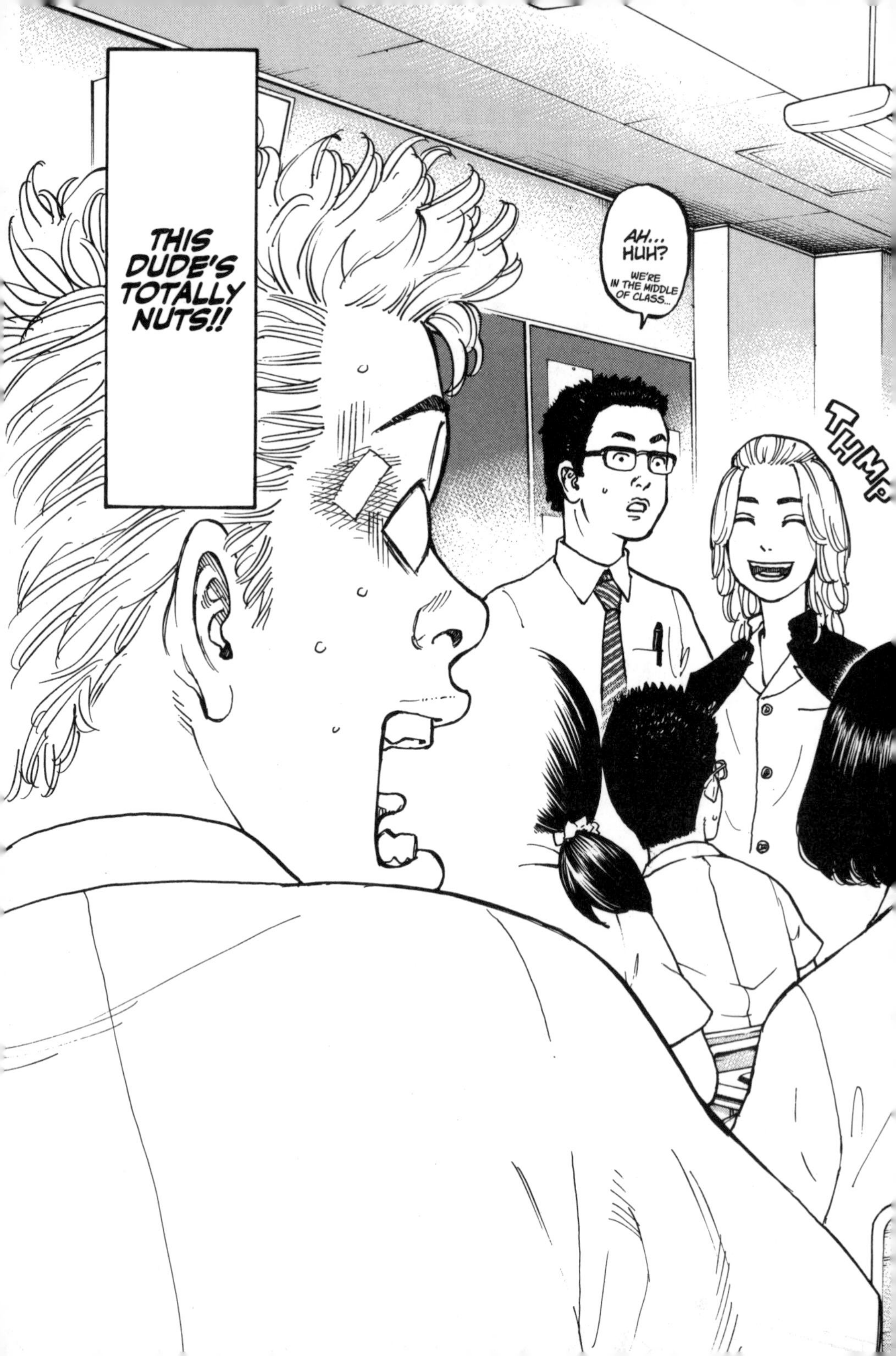
AH... HUH?
WE'RE IN THE MIDDLE OF CLASS...
THUMP
THIS DUDE'S TOTALLY NUTS!!

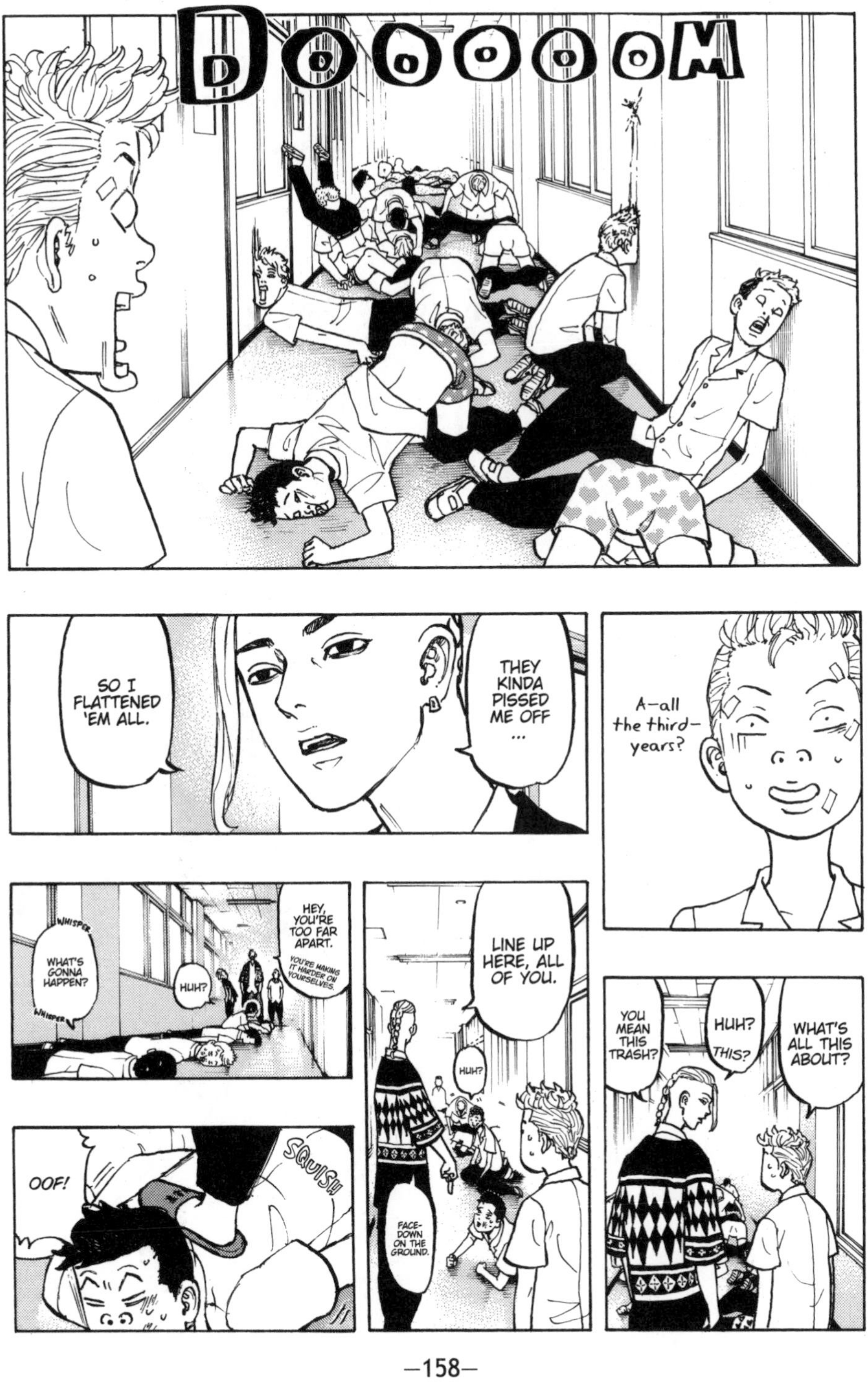
DOOOOOM
A-all the third-years?
THEY KINDA PISSED ME OFF ...
SO I FLATTENED 'EM ALL.
WHAT'S ALL THIS ABOUT?
HUH? THIS?
YOU MEAN THIS TRASH?
LINE UP HERE, ALL OF YOU.
HUH?
FACE-DOWN ON THE GROUND.
HEY, YOU'RE TOO FAR APART.
YOU'RE MAKING IT HARDER ON YOURSELVES.
HUH?
WHISPER
WHAT'S GONNA HAPPEN?
WHISPER
SQUISH
OOF!

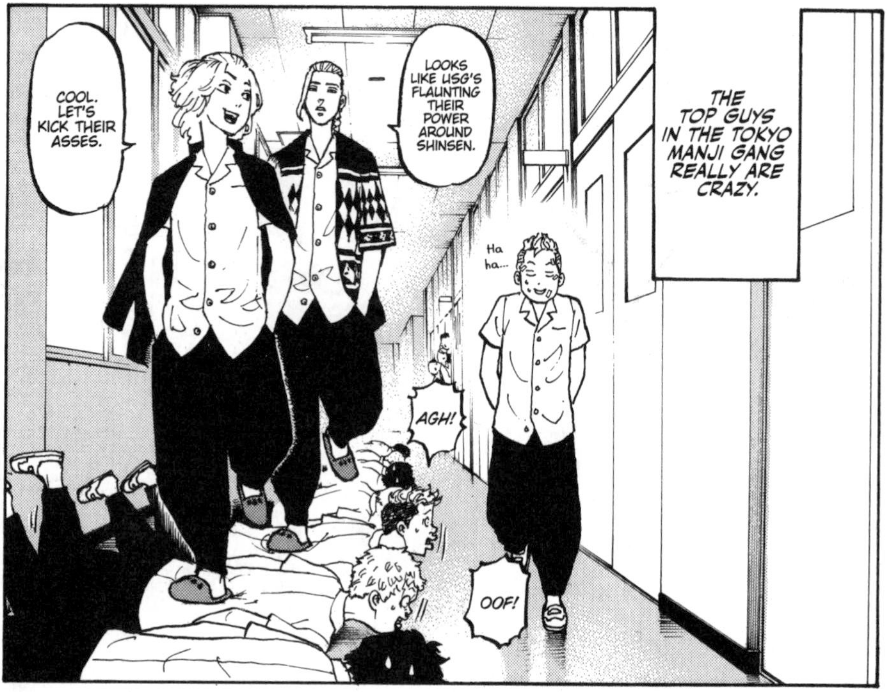
THE TOP GUYS IN THE TOKYO MANJI GANG REALLY ARE CRAZY.
Ha ha...
LOOKS LIKE USG'S FLAUNTING THEIR POWER AROUND SHINSEN.
COOL. LET'S KICK THEIR ASSES.
AGH!
OOF!

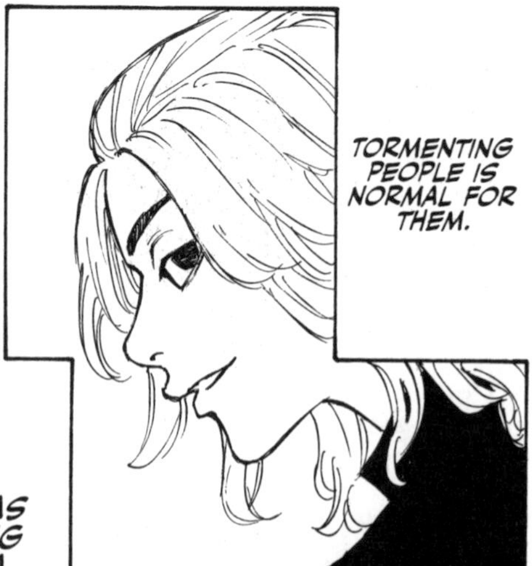
TORMENTING PEOPLE IS NORMAL FOR THEM.

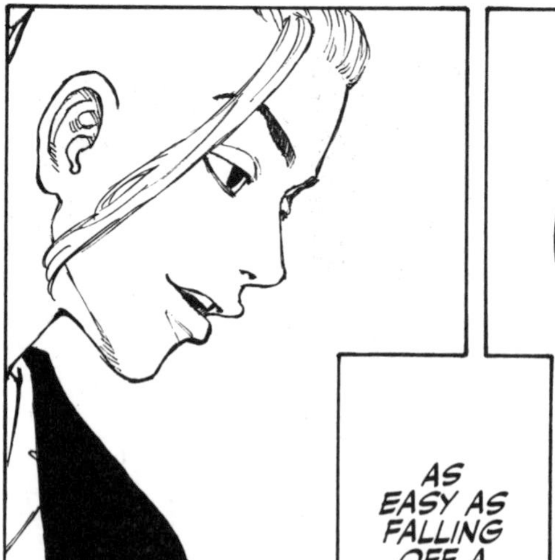
AS EASY AS FALLING OFF A LOG.

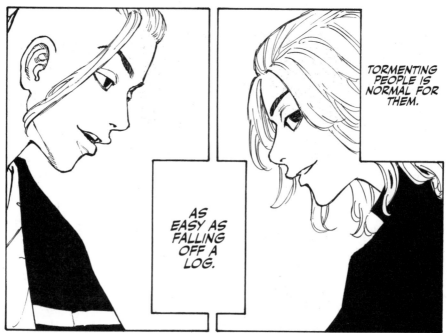

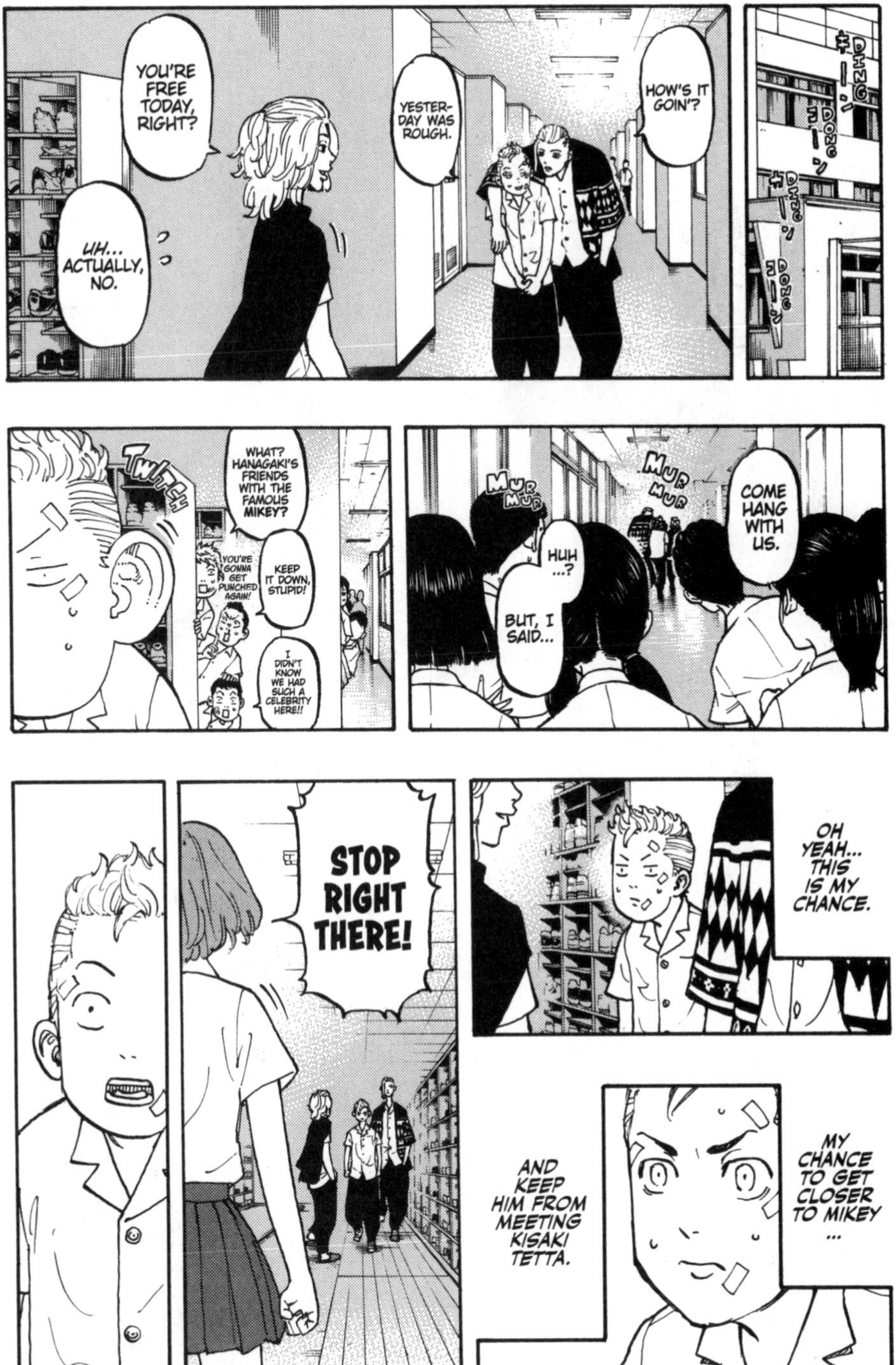
DING DONG
DING DONG
HOW'S IT GOIN'?
YESTER-DAY WAS ROUGH.
YOU'RE FREE TODAY, RIGHT?
UH... ACTUALLY, NO.
COME HANG WITH US.
MUR MUR
MUR MUR
HUH ...?
BUT, I SAID...
WHAT? HANAGAKI'S FRIENDS WITH THE FAMOUS MIKEY?
KEEP IT DOWN, STUPID!
I DIDN'T KNOW WE HAD SUCH A CELEBRITY HERE!!
YOU'RE GONNA GET PUNCHED AGAIN!
TWITCH
OH YEAH... THIS IS MY CHANCE.
MY CHANCE TO GET CLOSER TO MIKEY ...
AND KEEP HIM FROM MEETING KISAKI TETTA.
STOP RIGHT THERE!

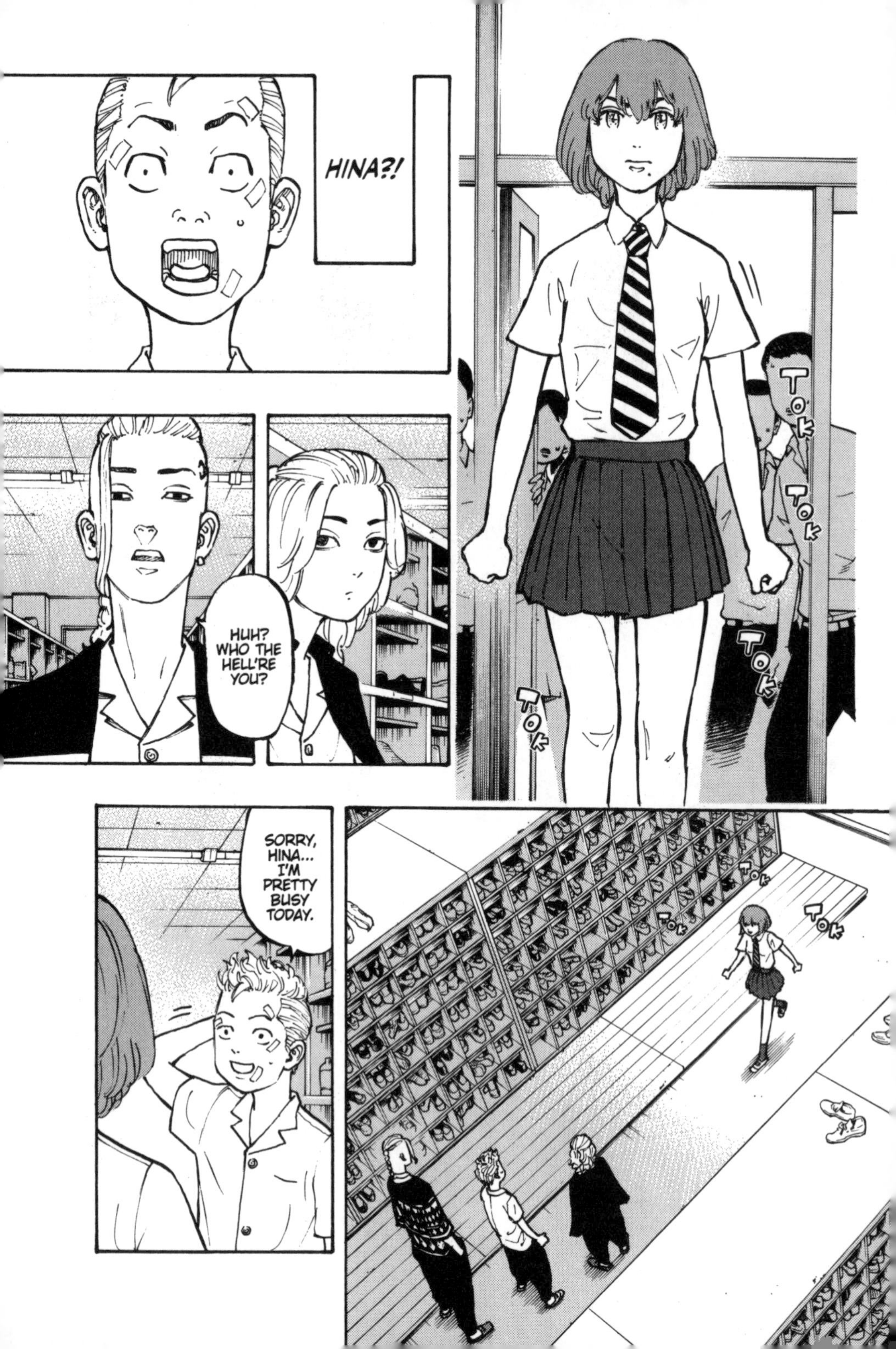
TOK
TOK
TOK
TOK
HINA?!
HUH? WHO THE HELL'RE YOU?
TOK
TOK
TOK
SORRY, HINA... I'M PRETTY BUSY TODAY.

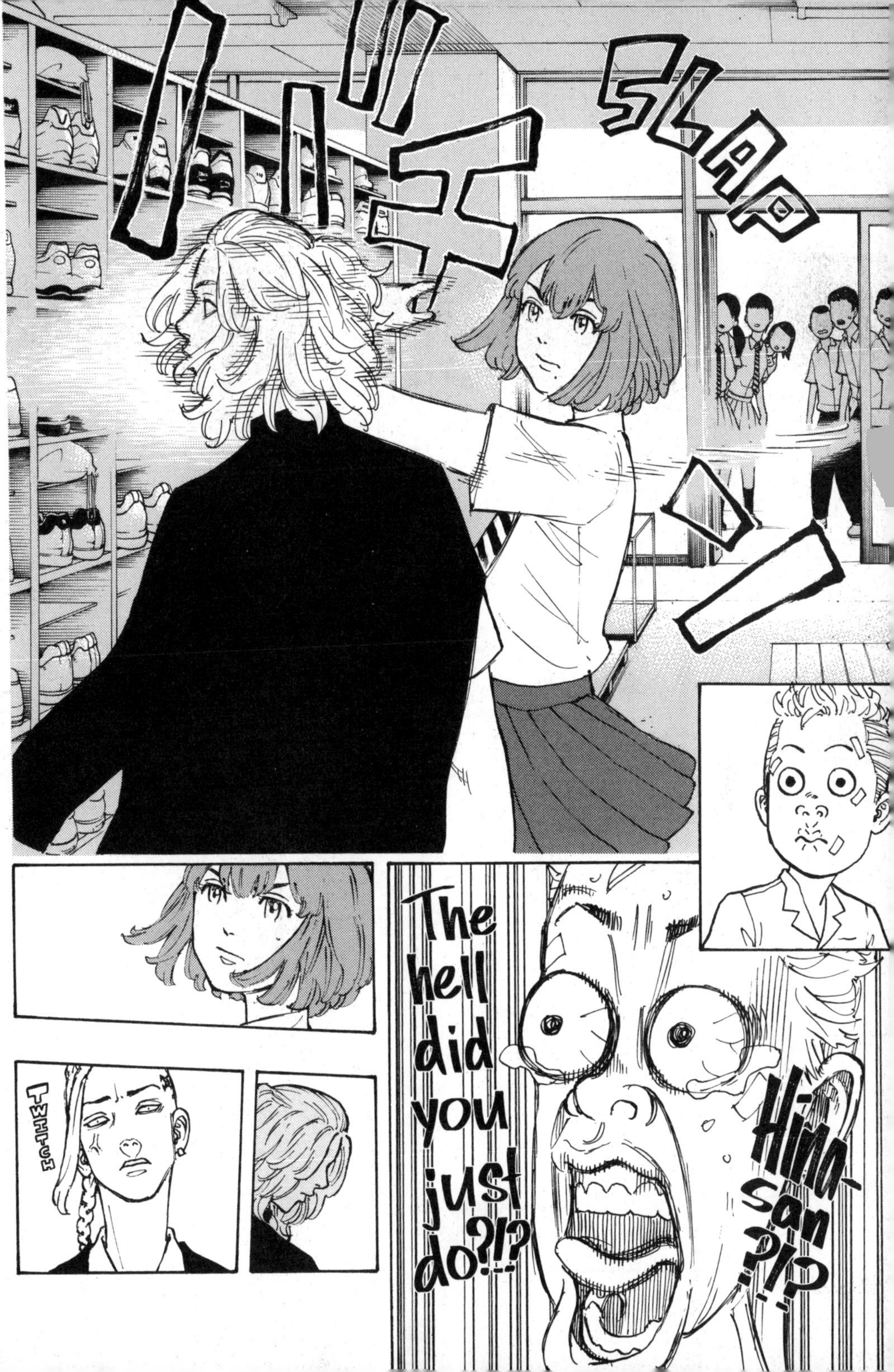
SLAP
H-Hina-san?!?
The hell did you just do?!?
TWITCH

TOKYO
Revengers

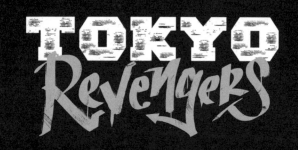

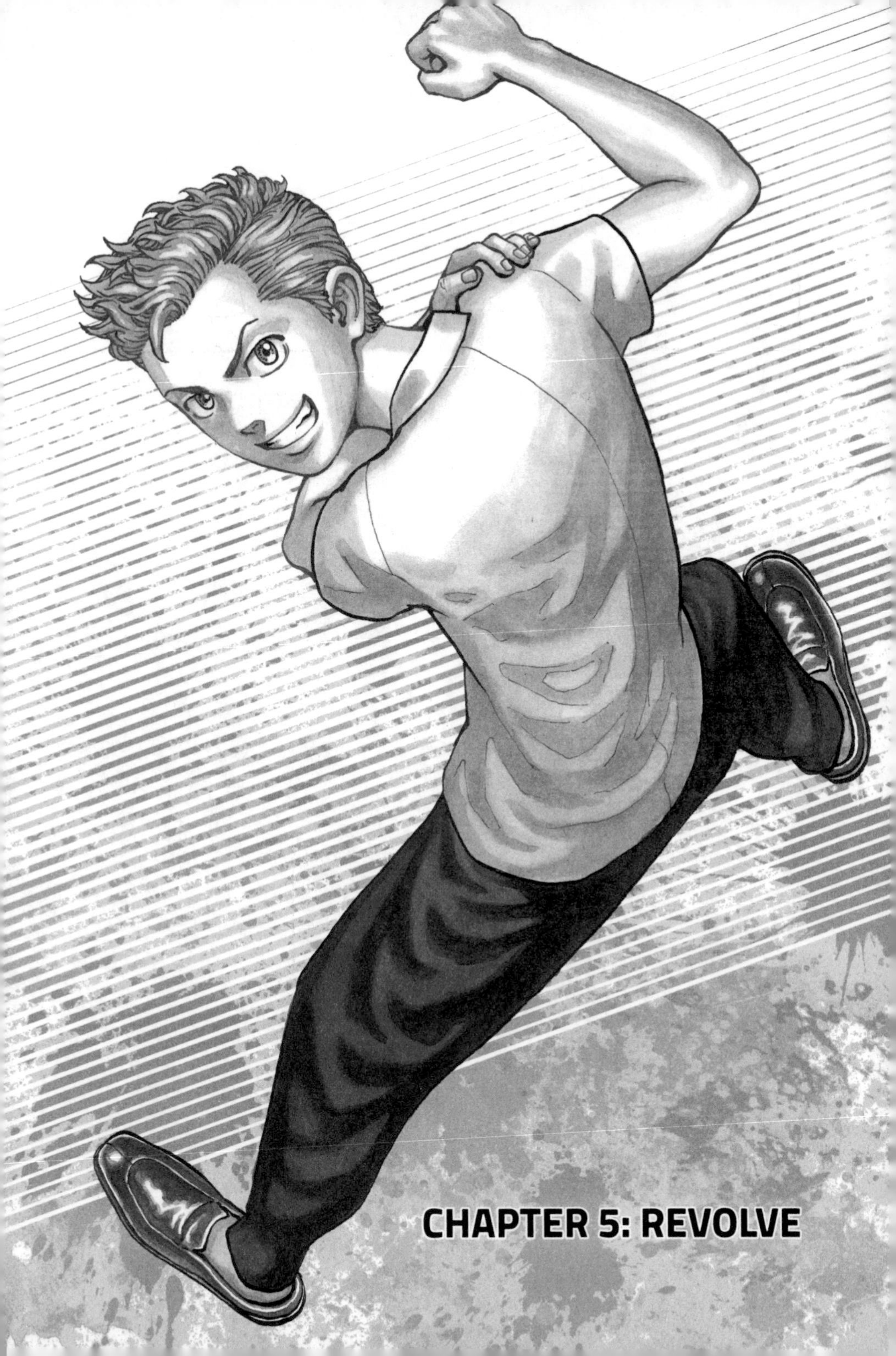

CHAPTER 5: REVOLVE

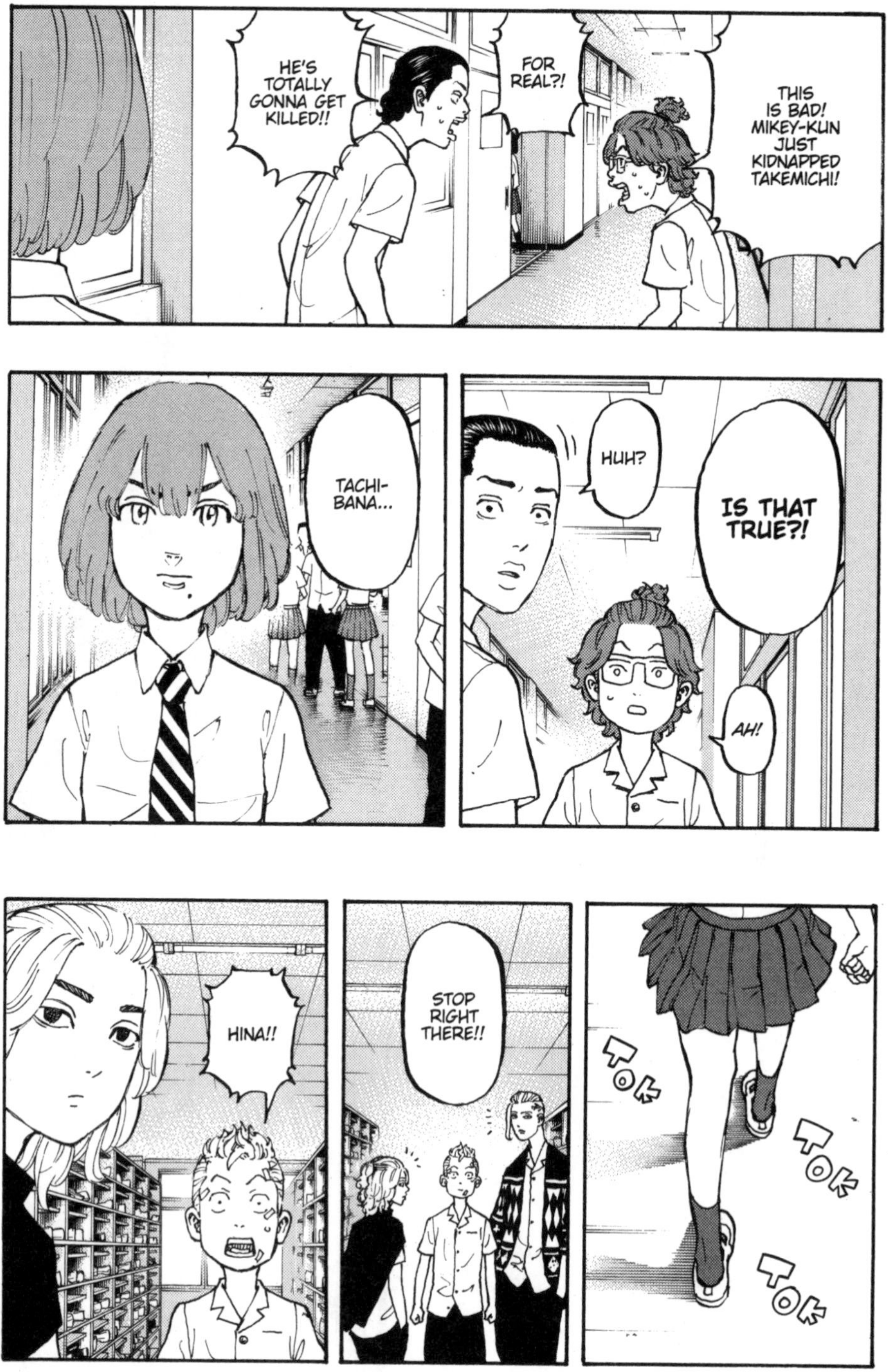
THIS IS BAD! MIKEY-KUN JUST KIDNAPPED TAKEMICHI!
FOR REAL?!
HE'S TOTALLY GONNA GET KILLED!!
HUH?
IS THAT TRUE?!
AH!
TACHI-BANA...
TOK
TOK
TOK
STOP RIGHT THERE!!
HINA!!

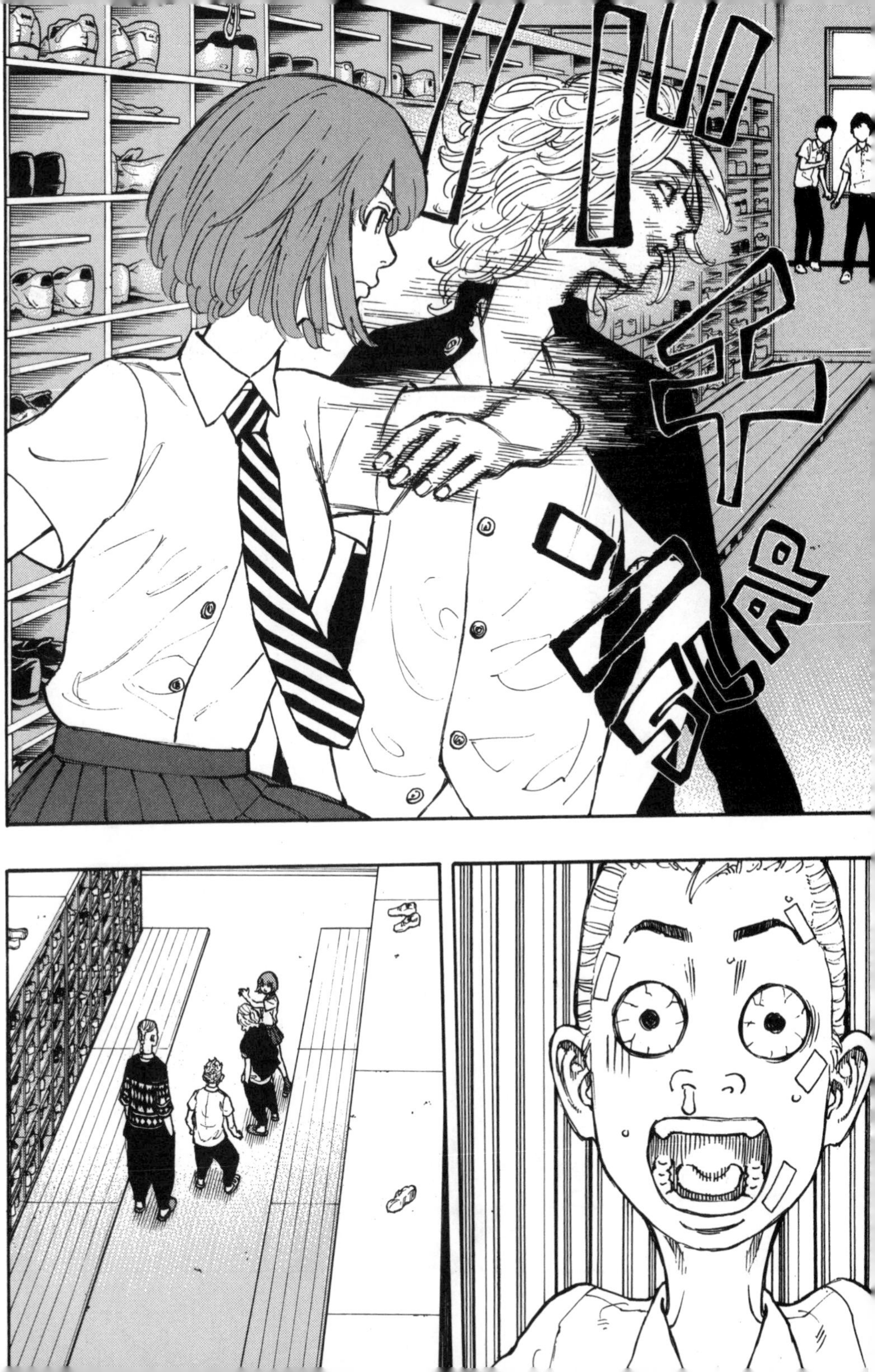
SLAP

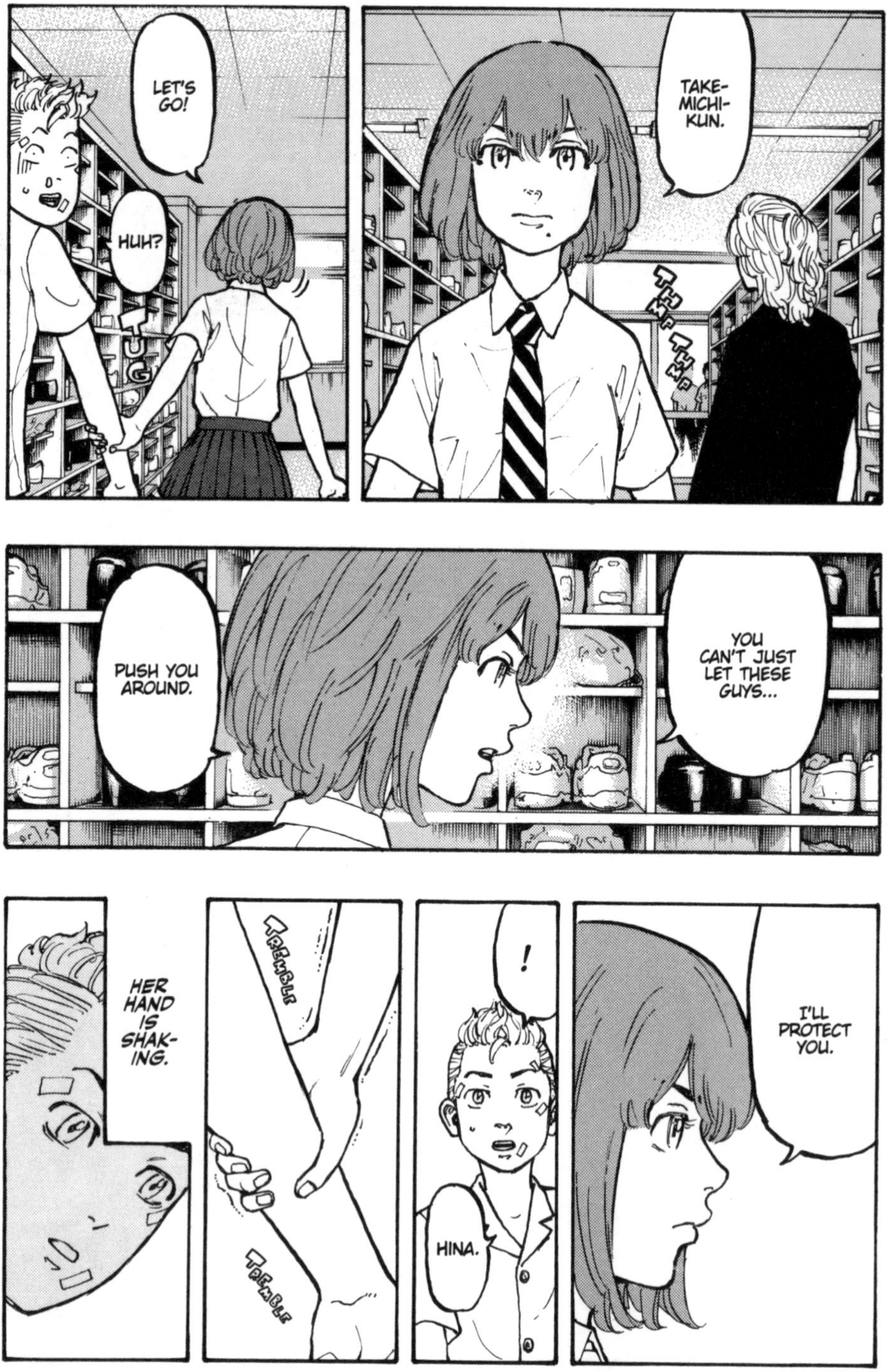
TAKE-MICHI-KUN.
THMP THMP
LET'S GO!
HUH?
TUG
YOU CAN'T JUST LET THESE GUYS...
PUSH YOU AROUND.
I'LL PROTECT YOU.
!
HINA.
TREMBLE
TREMBLE
HER HAND IS SHAK-ING.

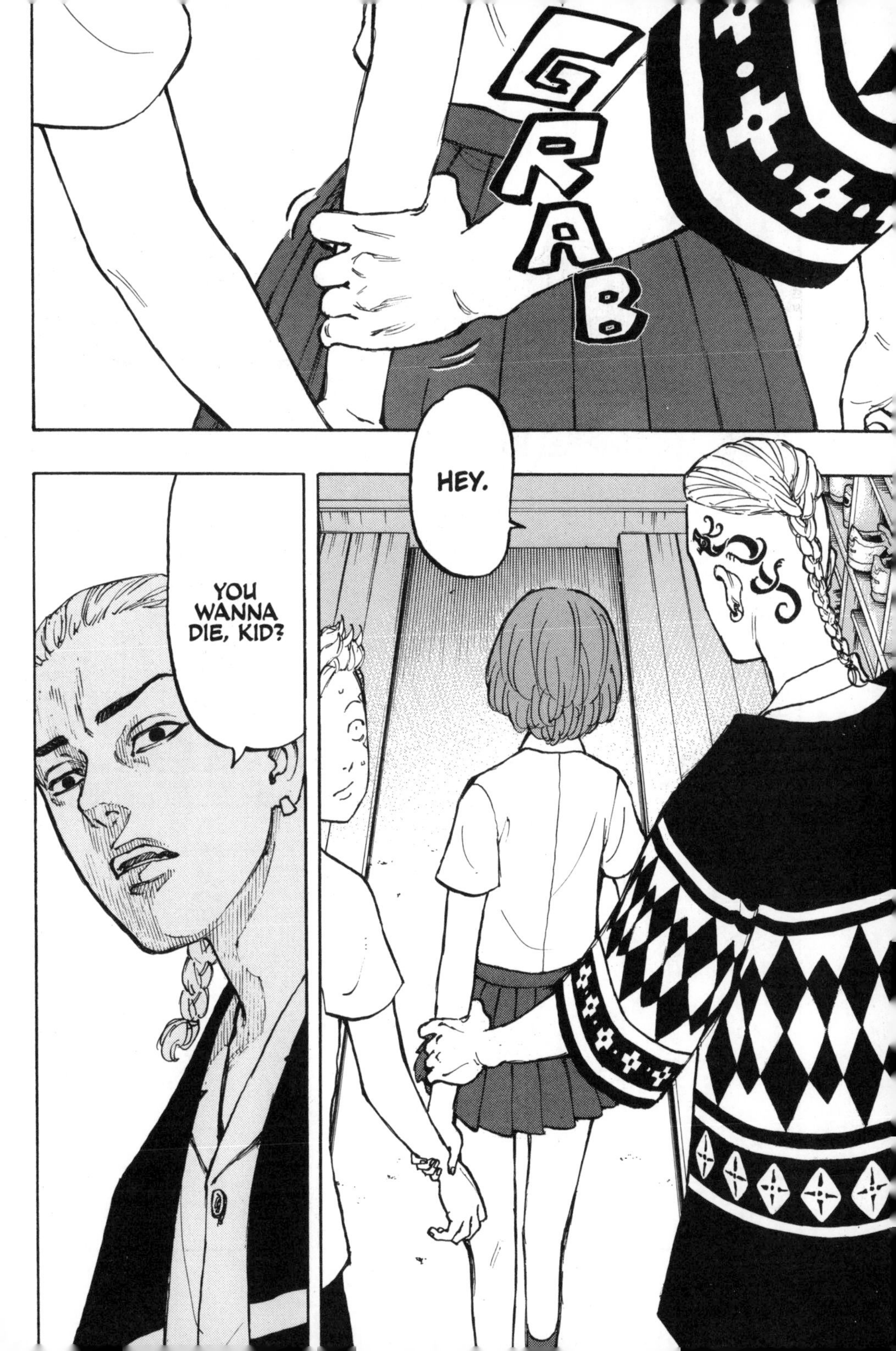
GRAB
HEY.
YOU WANNA DIE, KID?

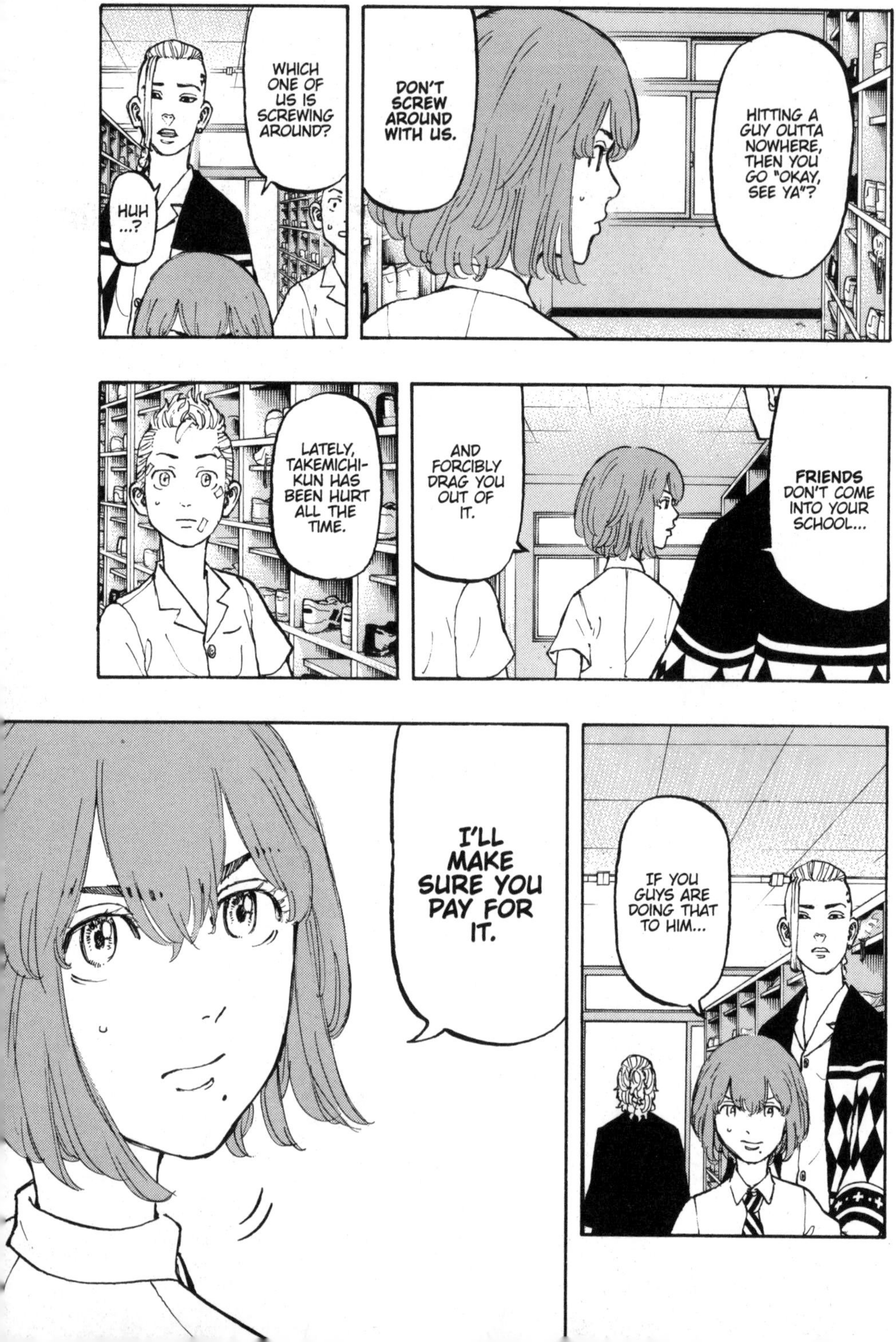
HITTING A GUY OUTTA NOWHERE, THEN YOU GO "OKAY, SEE YA"?
DON'T SCREW AROUND WITH US.
WHICH ONE OF US IS SCREWING AROUND?
HUH ...?
FRIENDS DON'T COME INTO YOUR SCHOOL...
AND FORCIBLY DRAG YOU OUT OF IT.
LATELY, TAKEMICHI-KUN HAS BEEN HURT ALL THE TIME.
IF YOU GUYS ARE DOING THAT TO HIM...
I'LL MAKE SURE YOU PAY FOR IT.

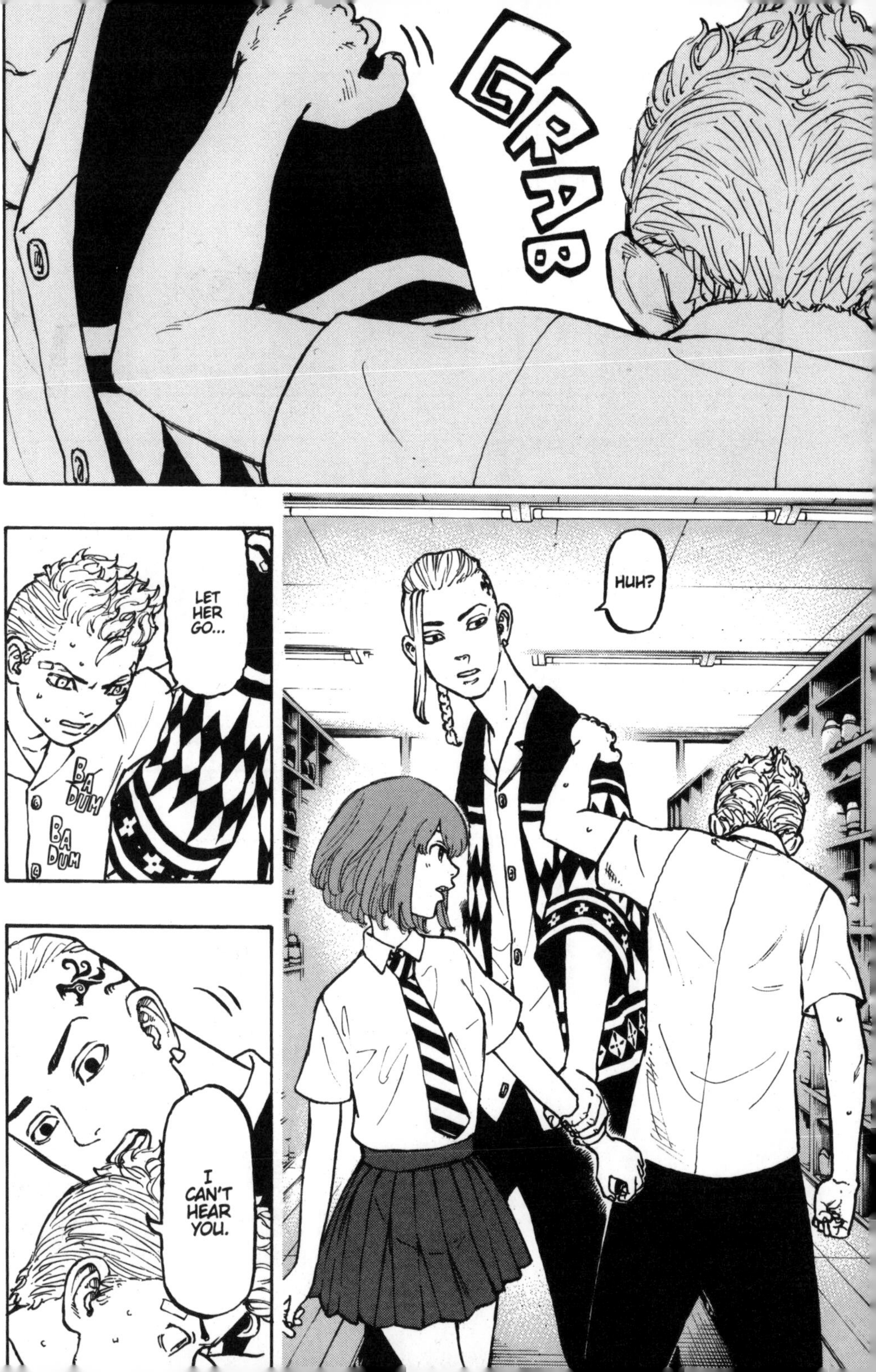
GRAB
HUH?
LET HER GO...
BA DUM
BA DUM
I CAN'T HEAR YOU.

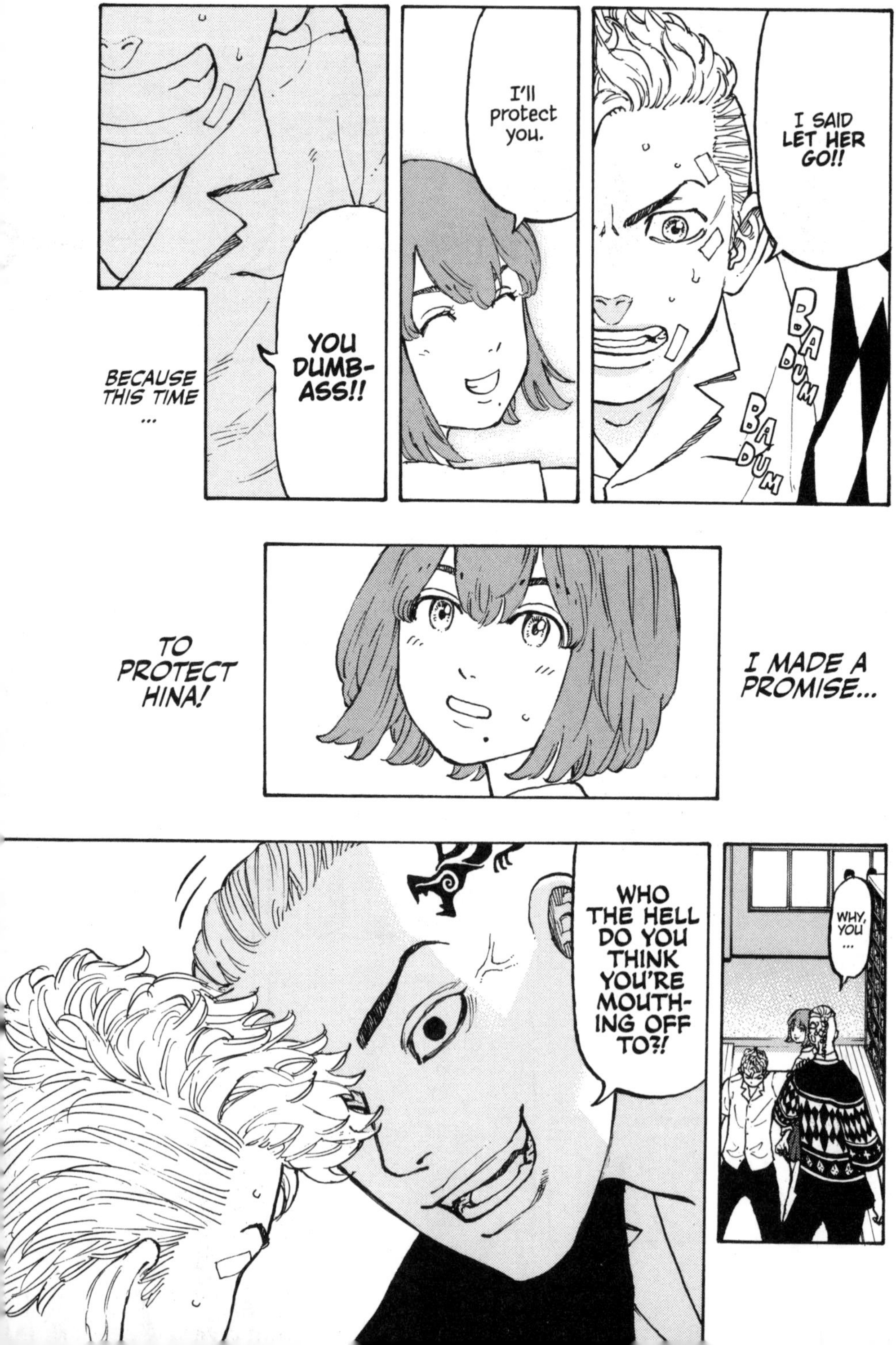
I SAID LET HER GO!!
BA DUM
BA DUM
I'll protect you.
YOU DUMB-ASS!!
BECAUSE THIS TIME ...
I MADE A PROMISE...
TO PROTECT HINA!
WHY, YOU ...
WHO THE HELL DO YOU THINK YOU'RE MOUTH-ING OFF TO?!

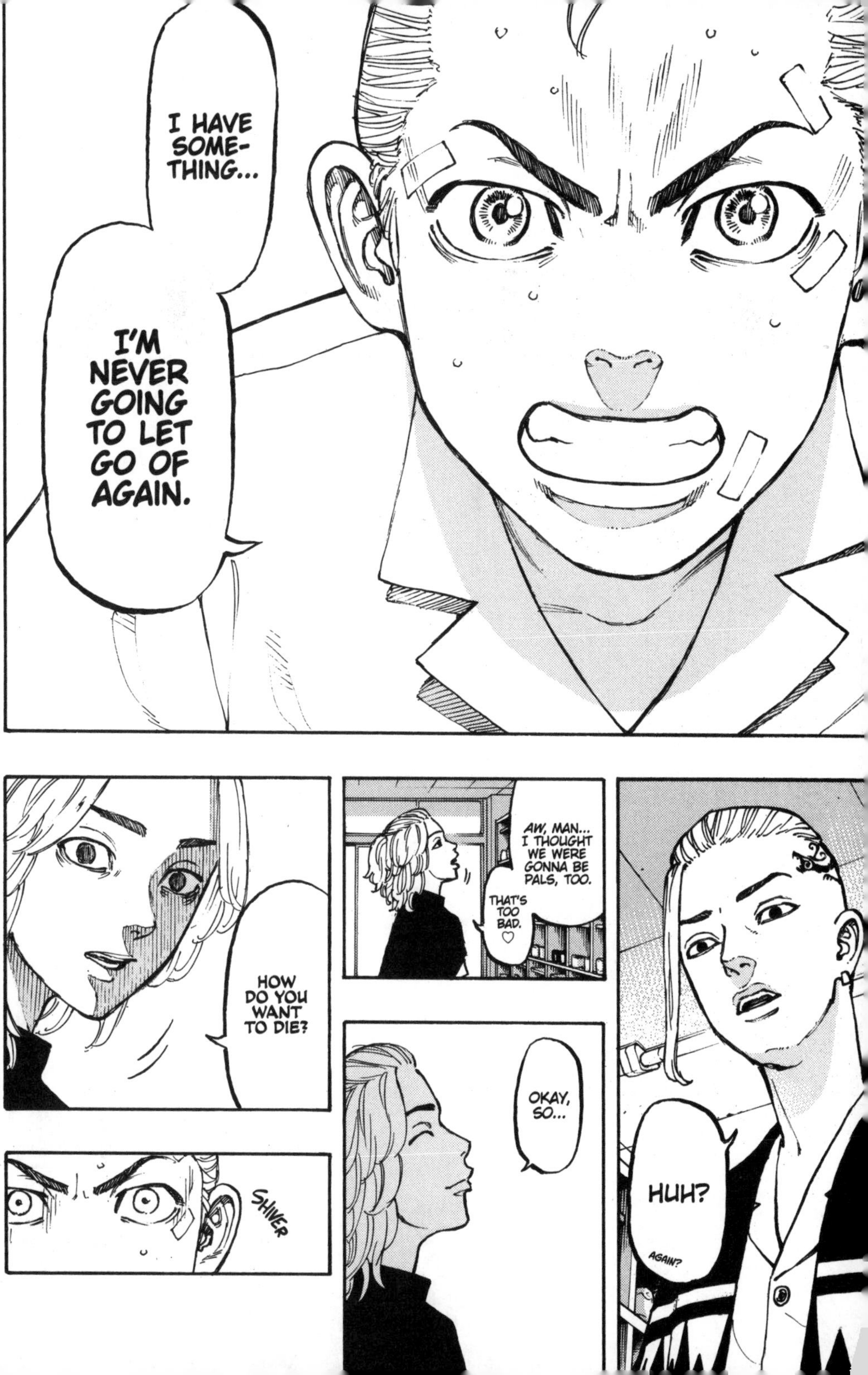
I HAVE SOMETHING...
I'M NEVER GOING TO LET GO OF AGAIN.
HUH?
AGAIN?
AW, MAN... I THOUGHT WE WERE GONNA BE PALS, TOO.
THAT'S TOO BAD. ♡
OKAY, SO...
HOW DO YOU WANT TO DIE?
SHIVER

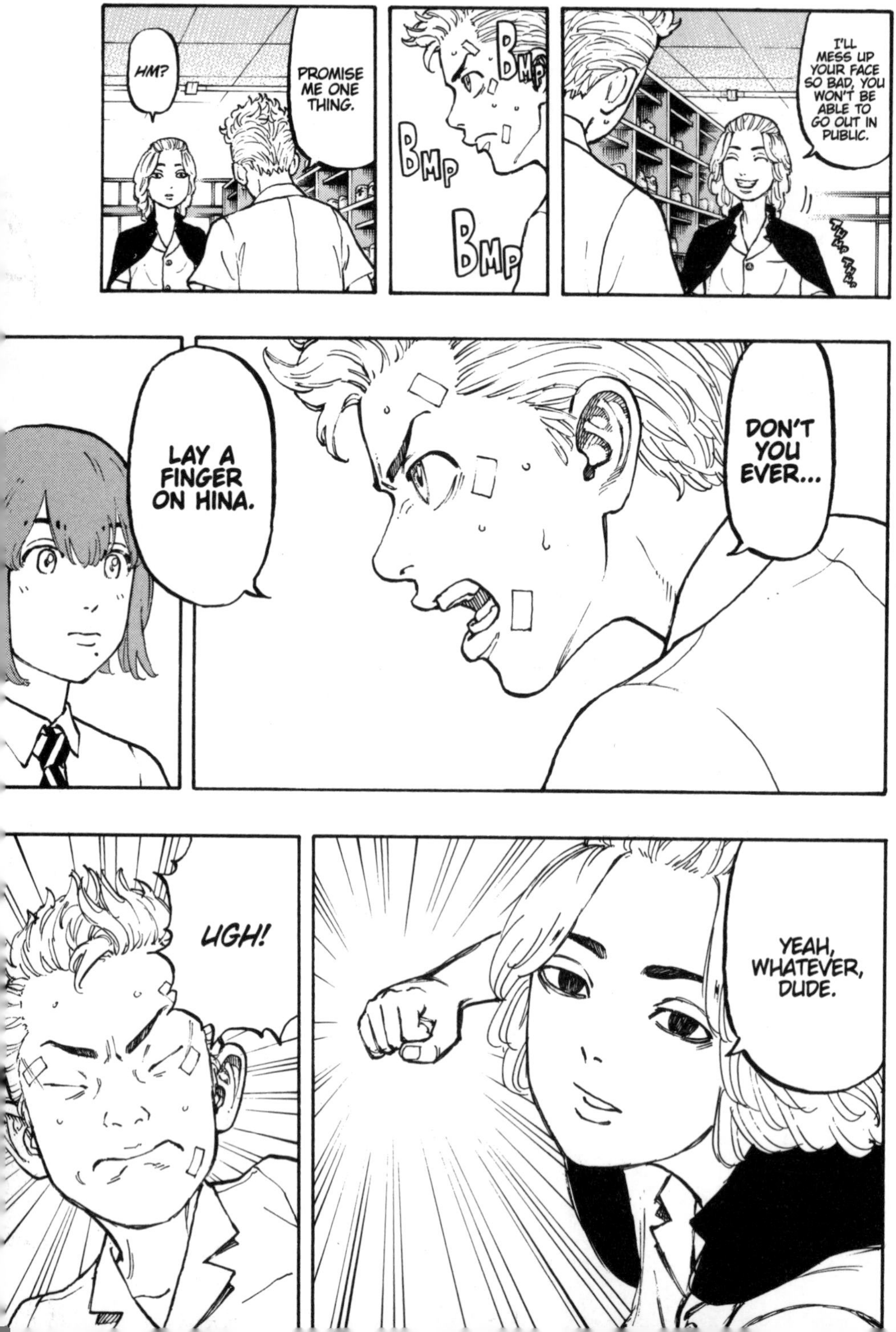
I'LL MESS UP YOUR FACE SO BAD, YOU WON'T BE ABLE TO GO OUT IN PUBLIC.
THMP THMP
BMP
BMP
BMP
PROMISE ME ONE THING.
HM?
DON'T YOU EVER...
LAY A FINGER ON HINA.
YEAH, WHATEVER, DUDE.
UGH!

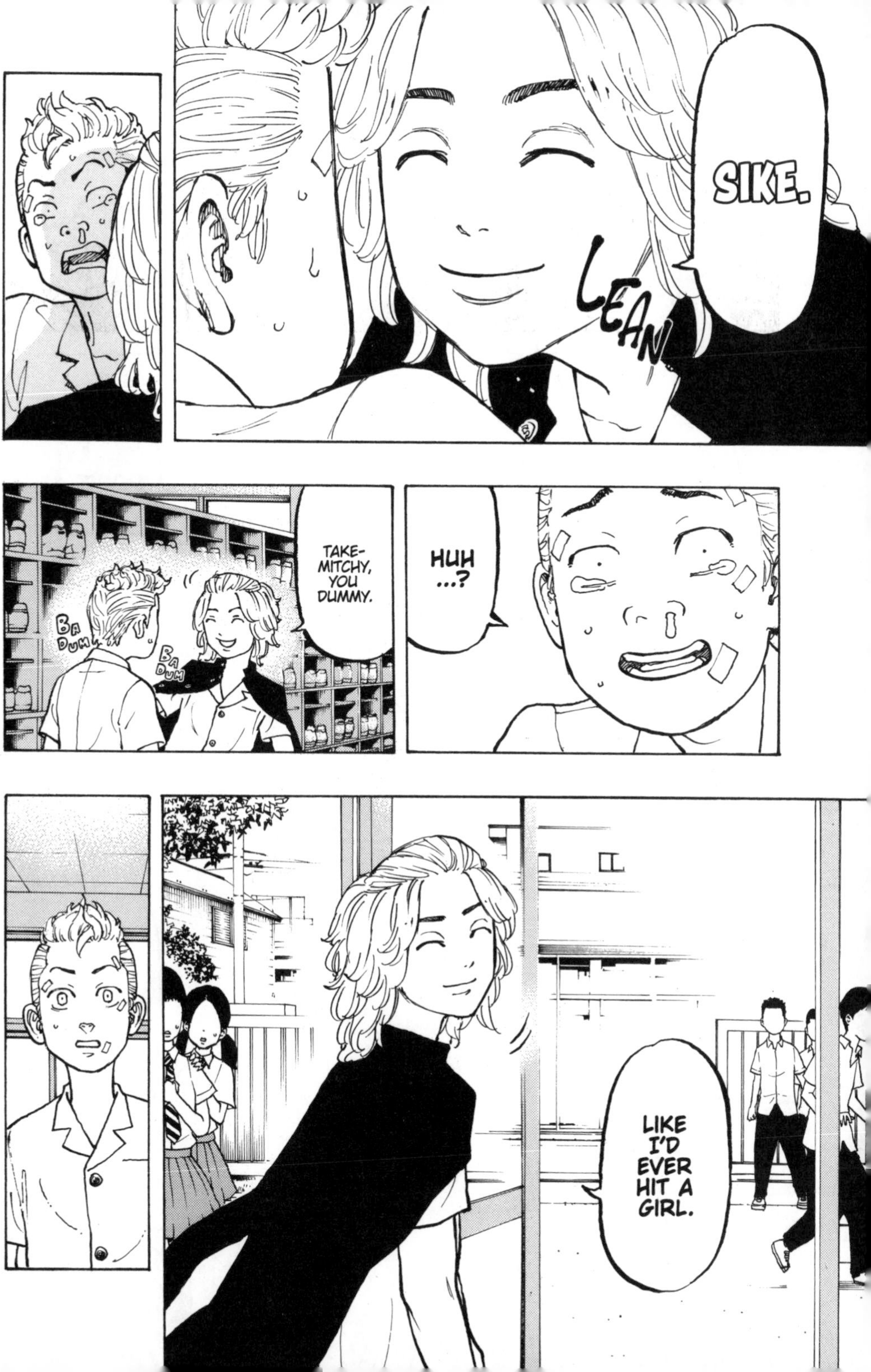
SIKE.
LEAN
HUH ...?
TAKE-MITCHY, YOU DUMMY.
BA DUM
BA DUM
LIKE I'D EVER HIT A GIRL.

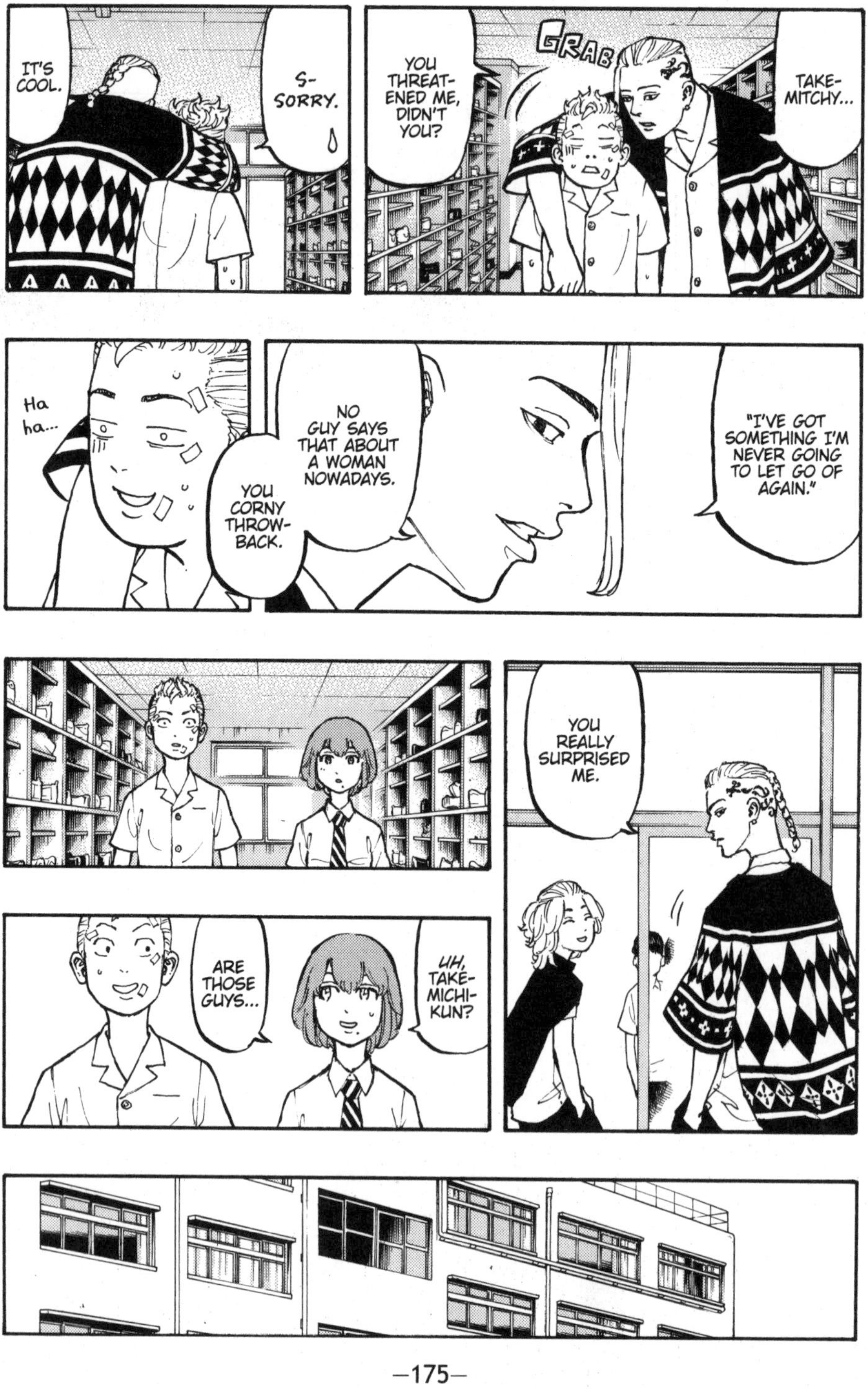
TAKE-MITCHY...
GRAB
YOU THREAT-ENED ME, DIDN'T YOU?
S-SORRY.
IT'S COOL.
"I'VE GOT SOMETHING I'M NEVER GOING TO LET GO OF AGAIN."
NO GUY SAYS THAT ABOUT A WOMAN NOWADAYS.
YOU CORNY THROW-BACK.
Ha ha...
YOU REALLY SURPRISED ME.
UH, TAKE-MICHI-KUN?
ARE THOSE GUYS...

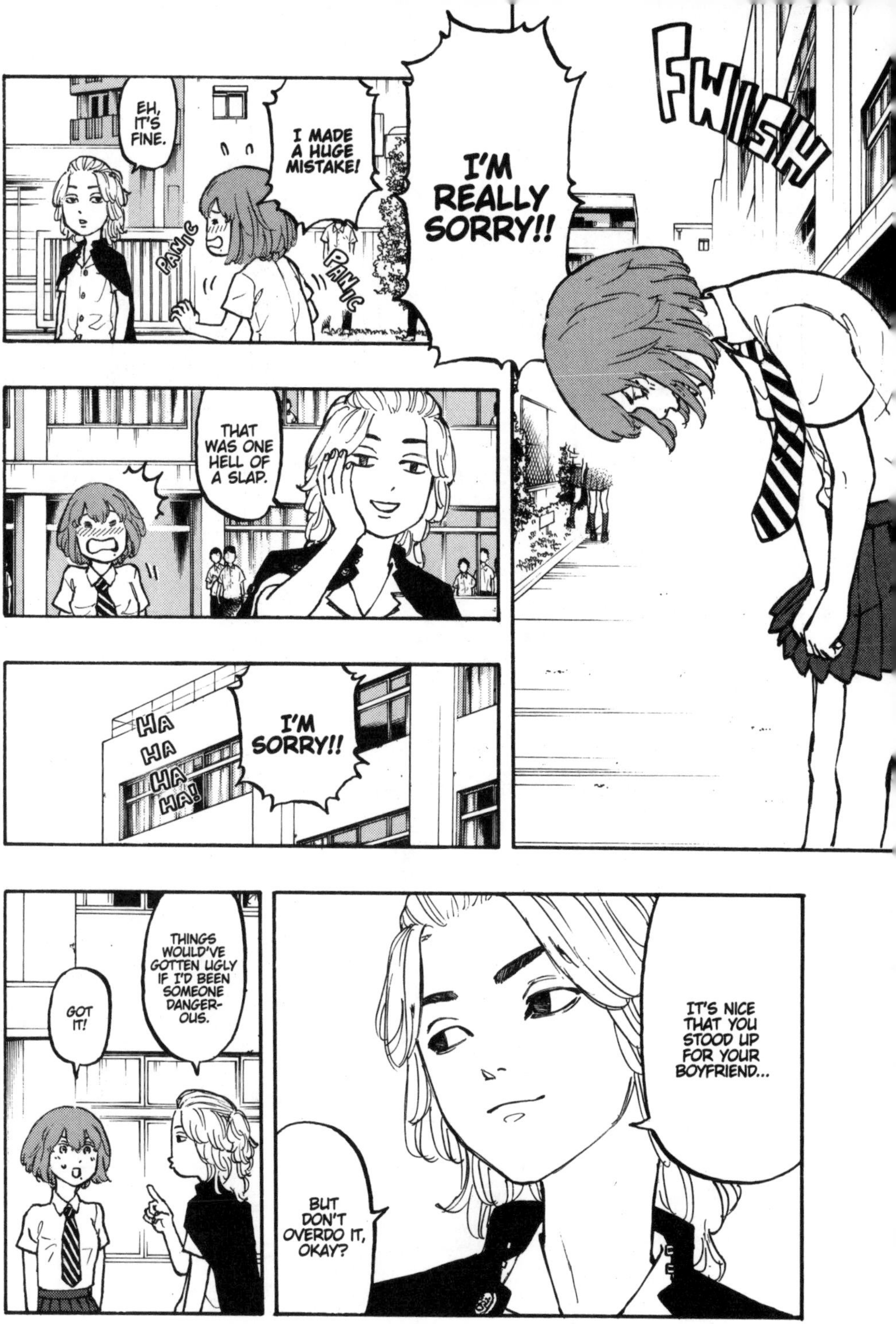
FWISH
I'M REALLY SORRY!!
I MADE A HUGE MISTAKE!
PANIC
PANIC
EH, IT'S FINE.
THAT WAS ONE HELL OF A SLAP.
I'M SORRY!!
HA HA HA HA!
IT'S NICE THAT YOU STOOD UP FOR YOUR BOYFRIEND...
BUT DON'T OVERDO IT, OKAY?
THINGS WOULD'VE GOTTEN UGLY IF I'D BEEN SOMEONE DANGER-OUS.
GOT IT!

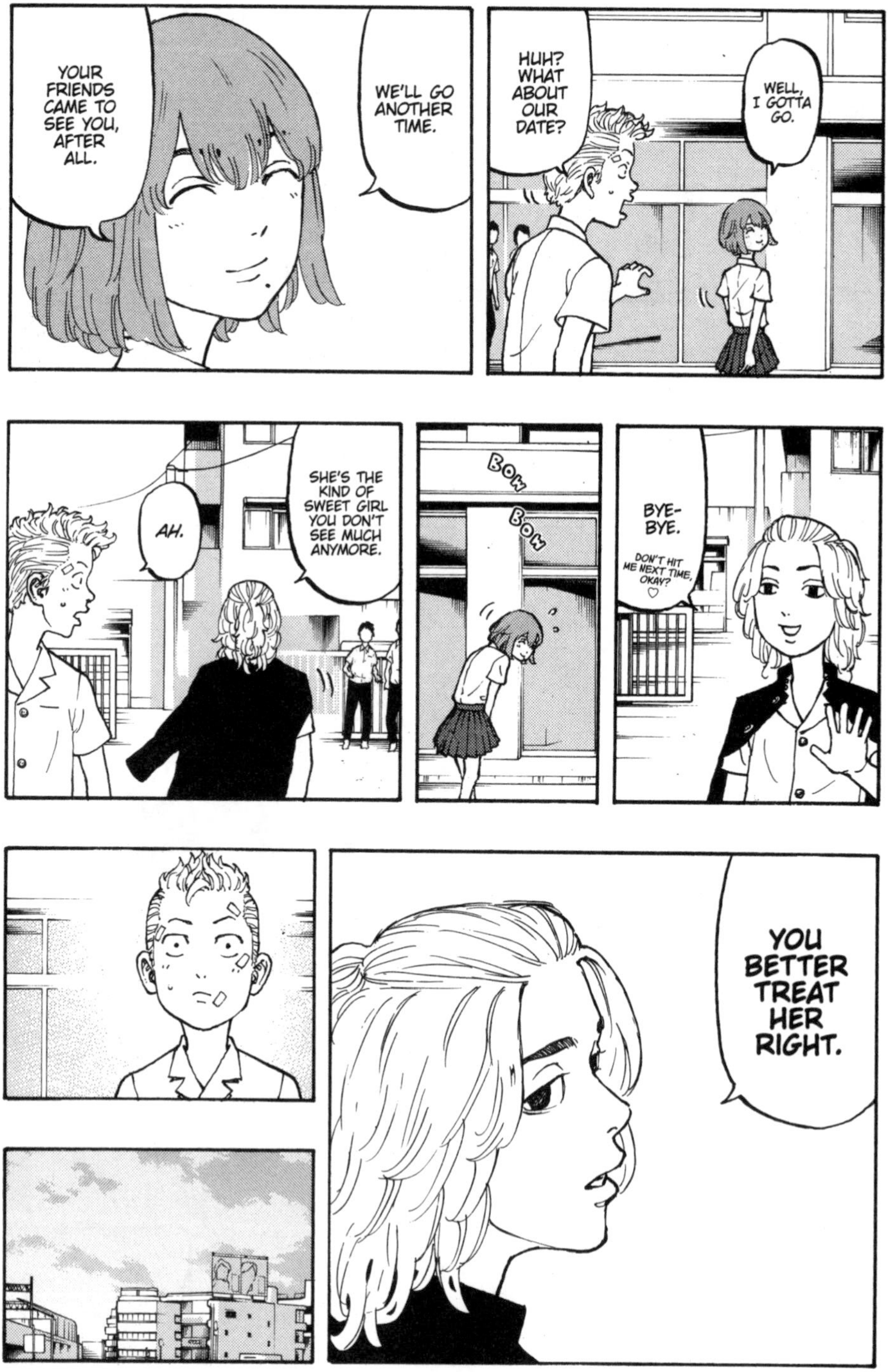
WELL, I GOTTA GO.
HUH? WHAT ABOUT OUR DATE?
WE'LL GO ANOTHER TIME.
YOUR FRIENDS CAME TO SEE YOU, AFTER ALL.
BYE-BYE.
DON'T HIT ME NEXT TIME, OKAY? ♡
BOW
BOW
SHE'S THE KIND OF SWEET GIRL YOU DON'T SEE MUCH ANYMORE.
AH.
YOU BETTER TREAT HER RIGHT.

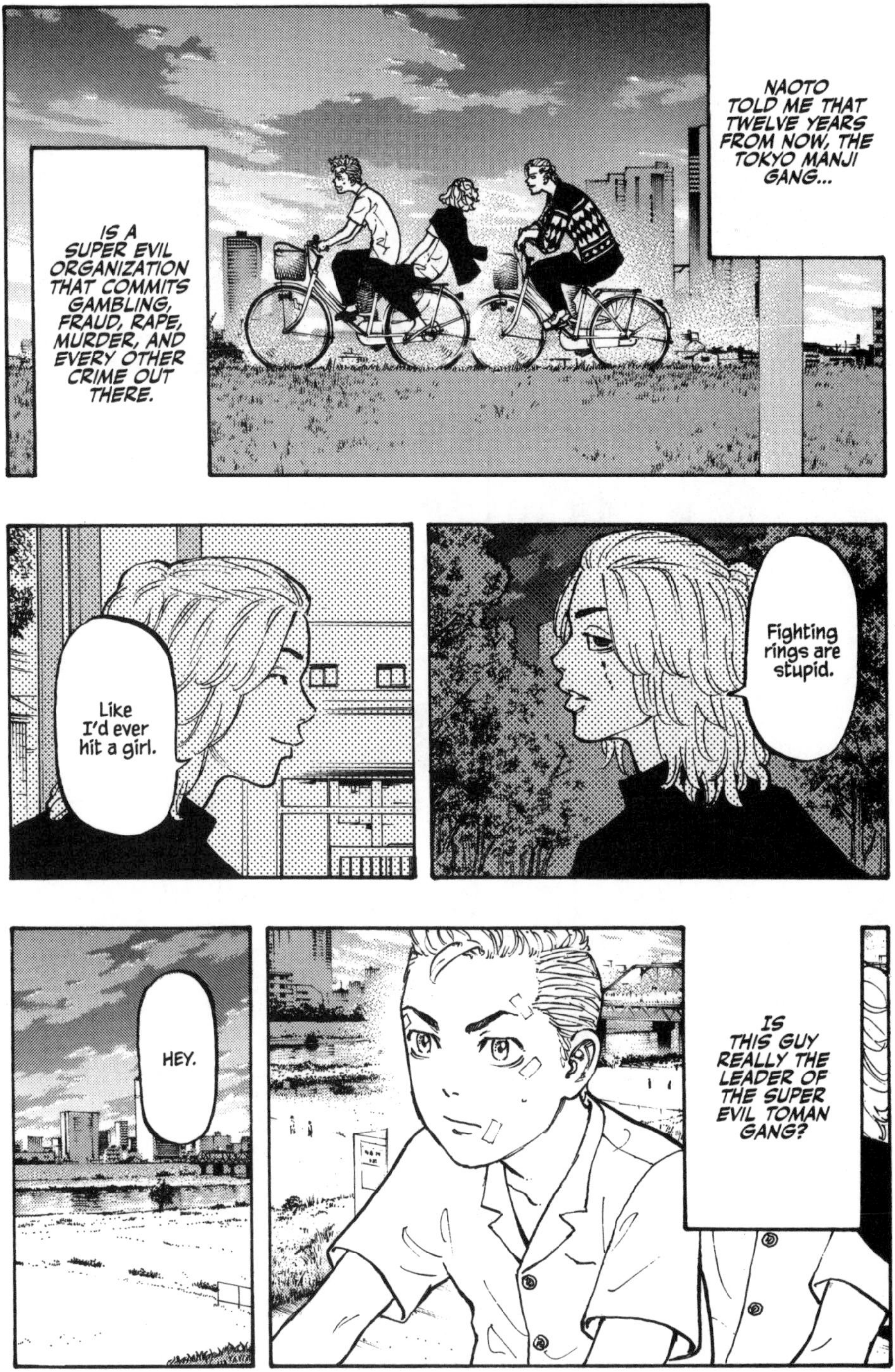
NAOTO TOLD ME THAT TWELVE YEARS FROM NOW, THE TOKYO MANJI GANG...
IS A SUPER EVIL ORGANIZATION THAT COMMITS GAMBLING, FRAUD, RAPE, MURDER, AND EVERY OTHER CRIME OUT THERE.
Fighting rings are stupid.
Like I'd ever hit a girl.
IS THIS GUY REALLY THE LEADER OF THE SUPER EVIL TOMAN GANG?
HEY.

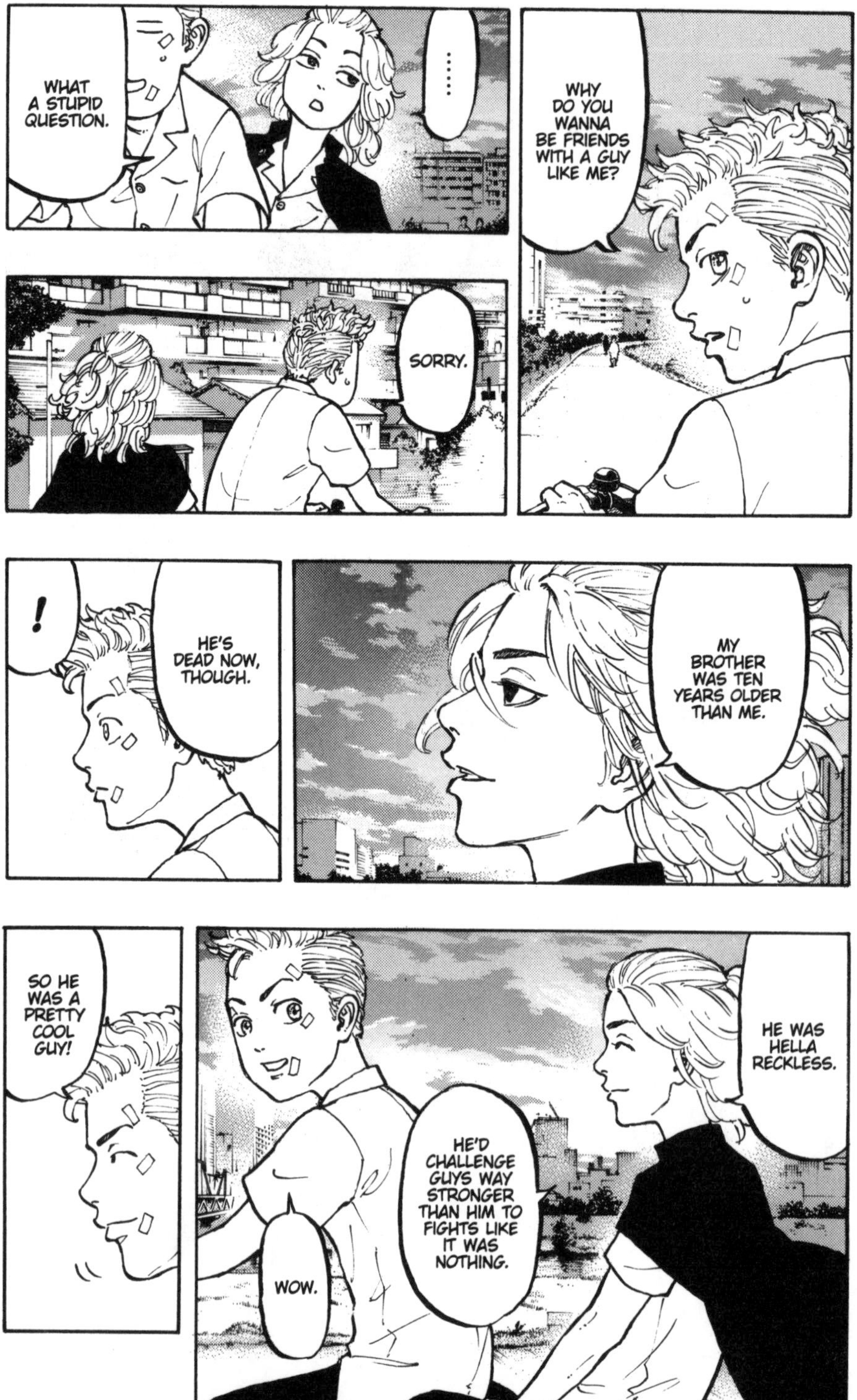
WHY DO YOU WANNA BE FRIENDS WITH A GUY LIKE ME?
......
WHAT A STUPID QUESTION.
SORRY.
MY BROTHER WAS TEN YEARS OLDER THAN ME.
HE'S DEAD NOW, THOUGH.
!
HE WAS HELLA RECKLESS.
HE'D CHALLENGE GUYS WAY STRONGER THAN HIM TO FIGHTS LIKE IT WAS NOTHING.
WOW.
SO HE WAS A PRETTY COOL GUY!

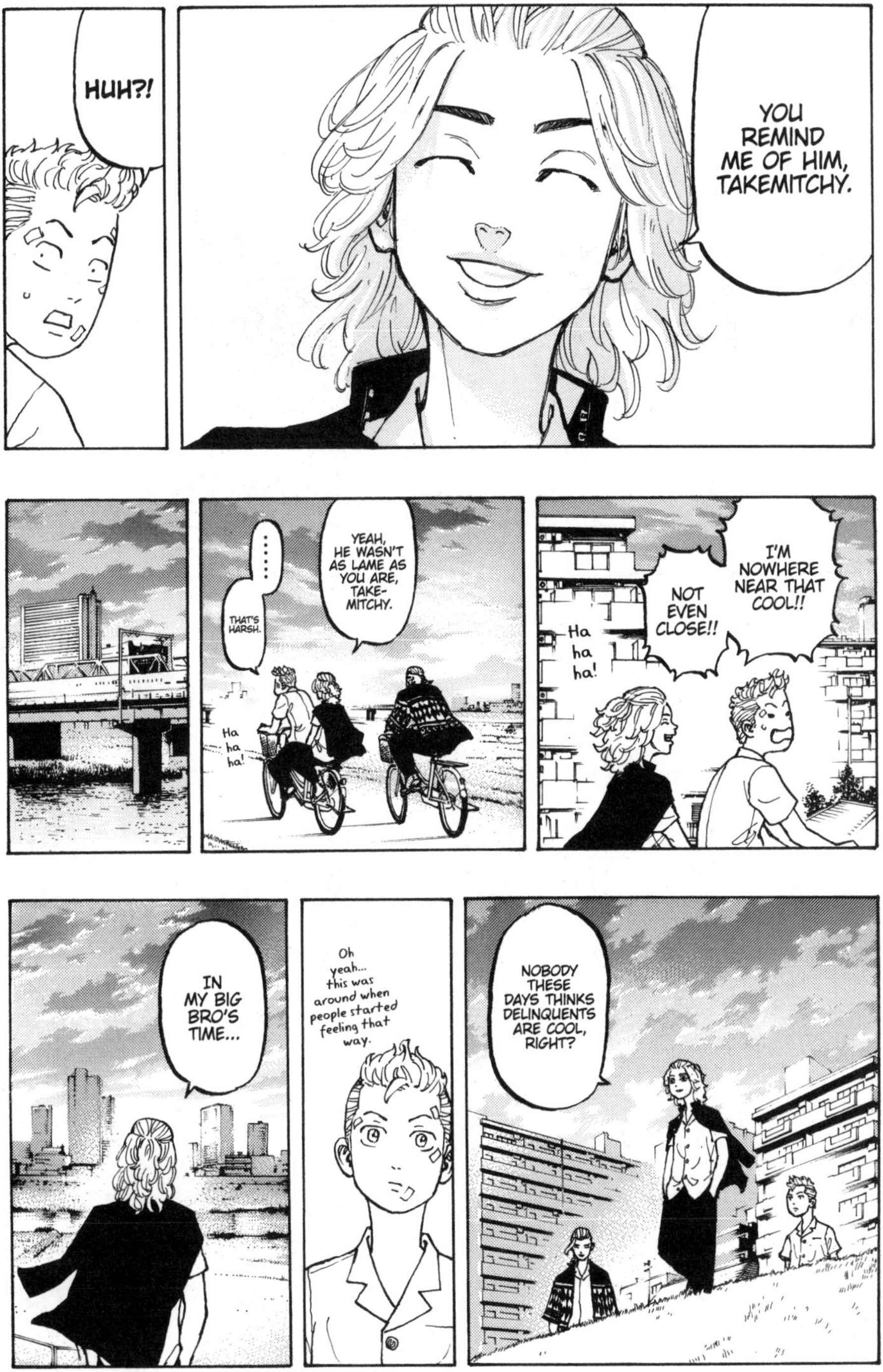
YOU REMIND ME OF HIM, TAKEMITCHY.
HUH?!
I'M NOWHERE NEAR THAT COOL!!
NOT EVEN CLOSE!!
Ha ha ha!
YEAH, HE WASN'T AS LAME AS YOU ARE, TAKE-MITCHY.
......
THAT'S HARSH.
Ha ha ha!
NOBODY THESE DAYS THINKS DELINQUENTS ARE COOL, RIGHT?
Oh yeah... this was around when people started feeling that way.
IN MY BIG BRO'S TIME...

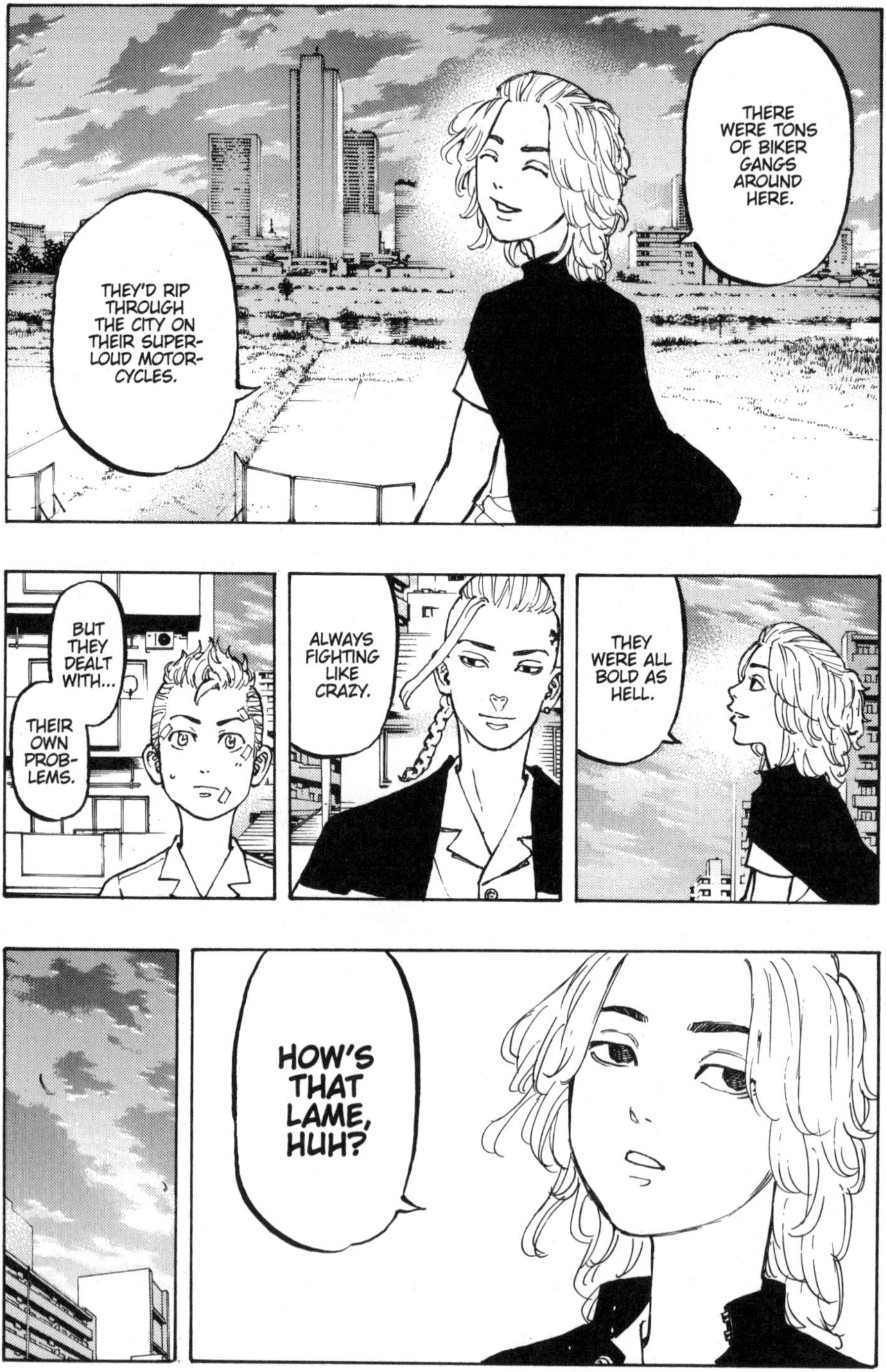
THERE WERE TONS OF BIKER GANGS AROUND HERE.
THEY'D RIP THROUGH THE CITY ON THEIR SUPER-LOUD MOTOR-CYCLES.
THEY WERE ALL BOLD AS HELL.
ALWAYS FIGHTING LIKE CRAZY.
BUT THEY DEALT WITH...
THEIR OWN PROB-LEMS.
HOW'S THAT LAME, HUH?

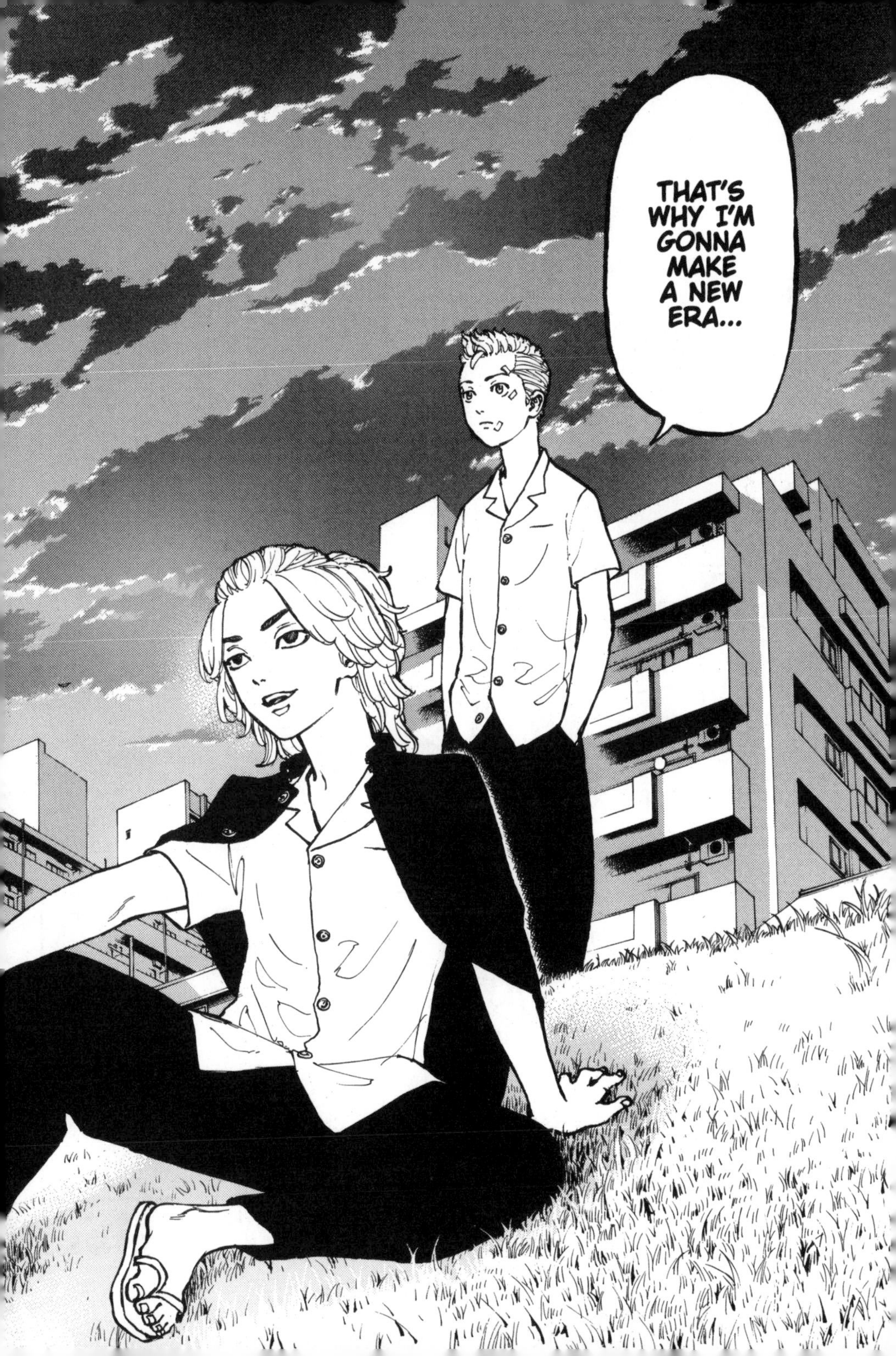
THAT'S WHY I'M GONNA MAKE A NEW ERA...

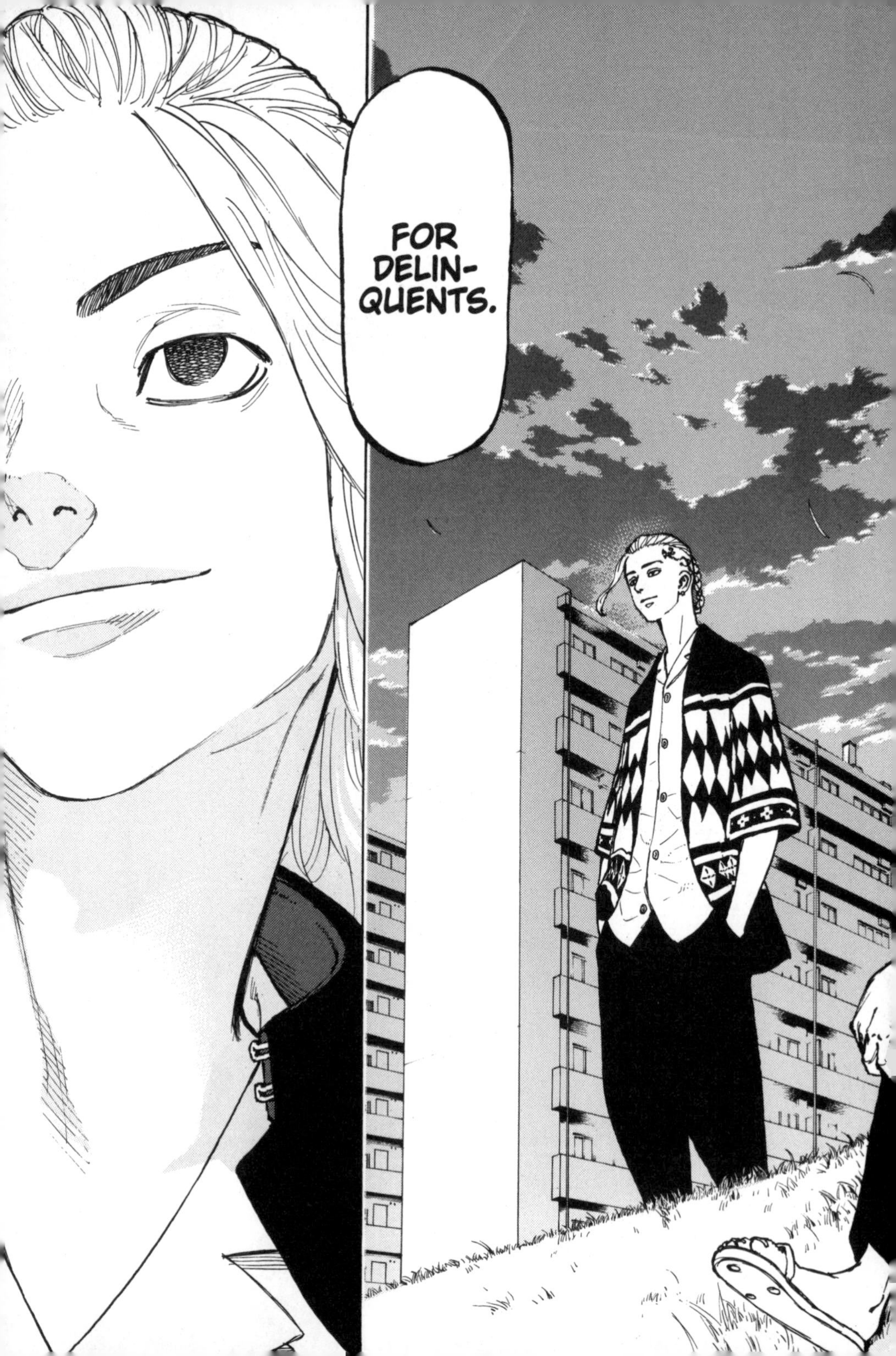
FOR DELIN-QUENTS.

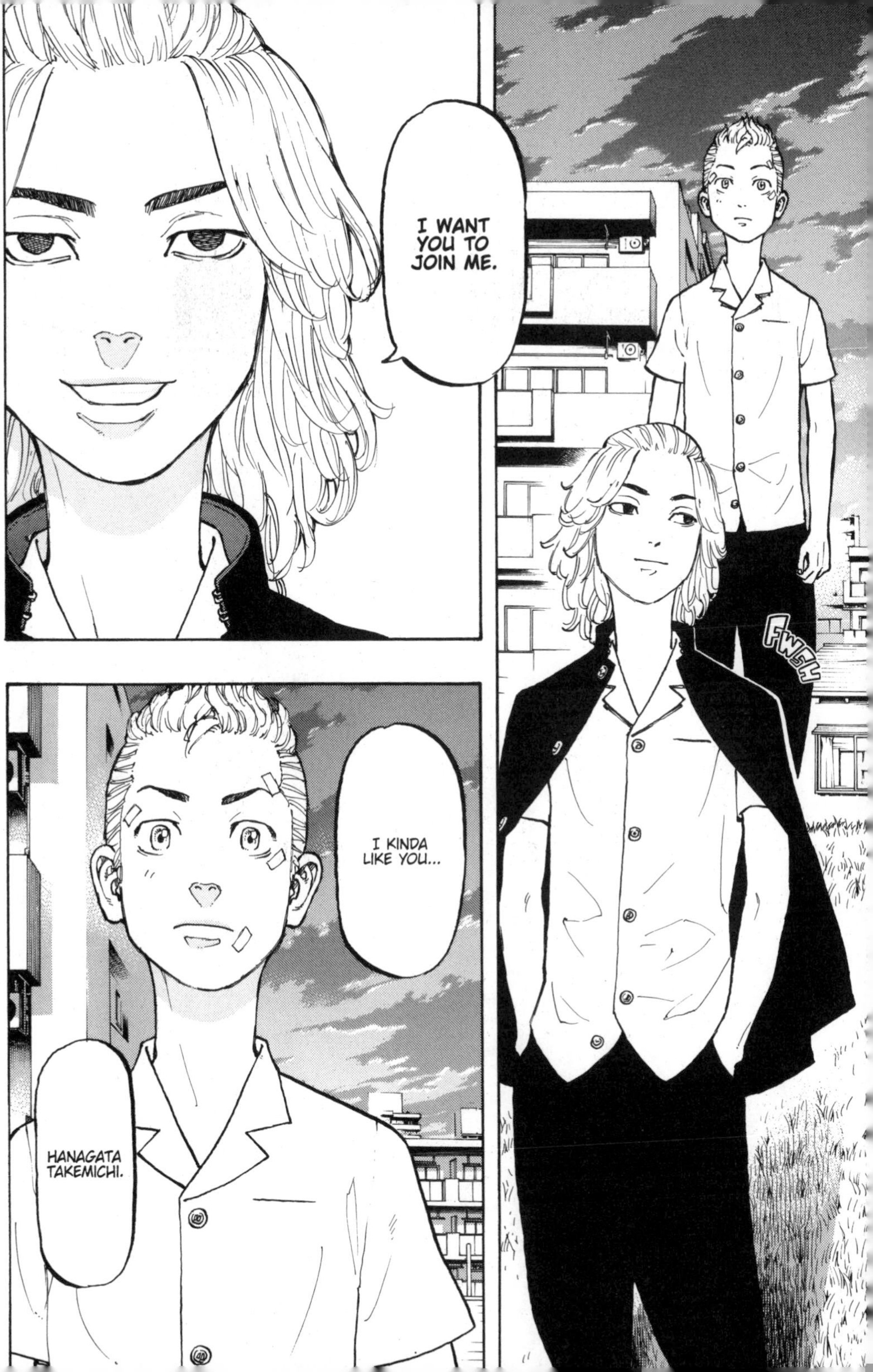
FWSH
I WANT YOU TO JOIN ME.
I KINDA LIKE YOU...
HANAGATA TAKEMICHI.

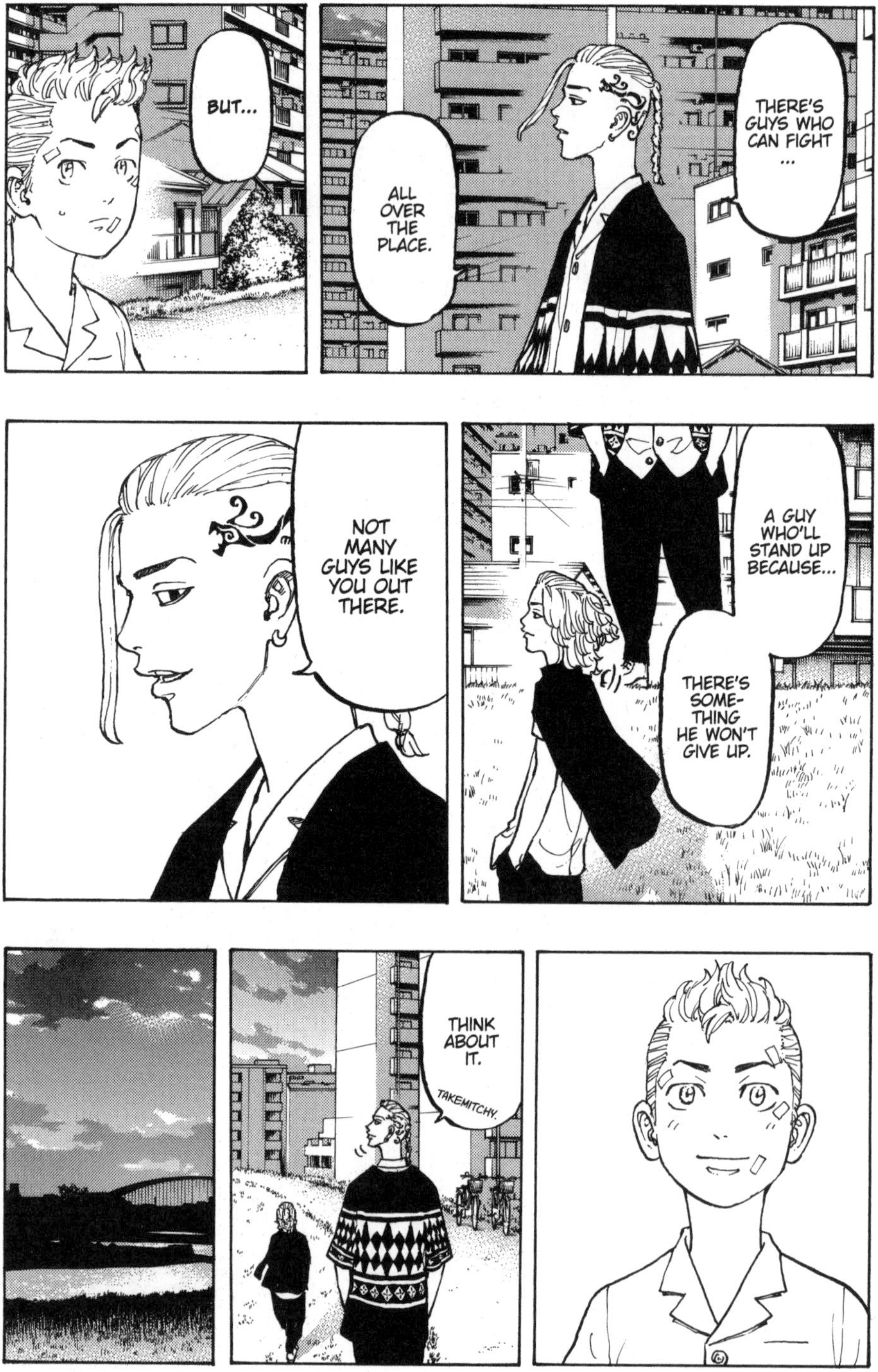
THERE'S GUYS WHO CAN FIGHT ...
ALL OVER THE PLACE.
BUT...
A GUY WHO'LL STAND UP BECAUSE...
THERE'S SOME-THING HE WON'T GIVE UP.
NOT MANY GUYS LIKE YOU OUT THERE.
THINK ABOUT IT.
TAKEMITCHY.

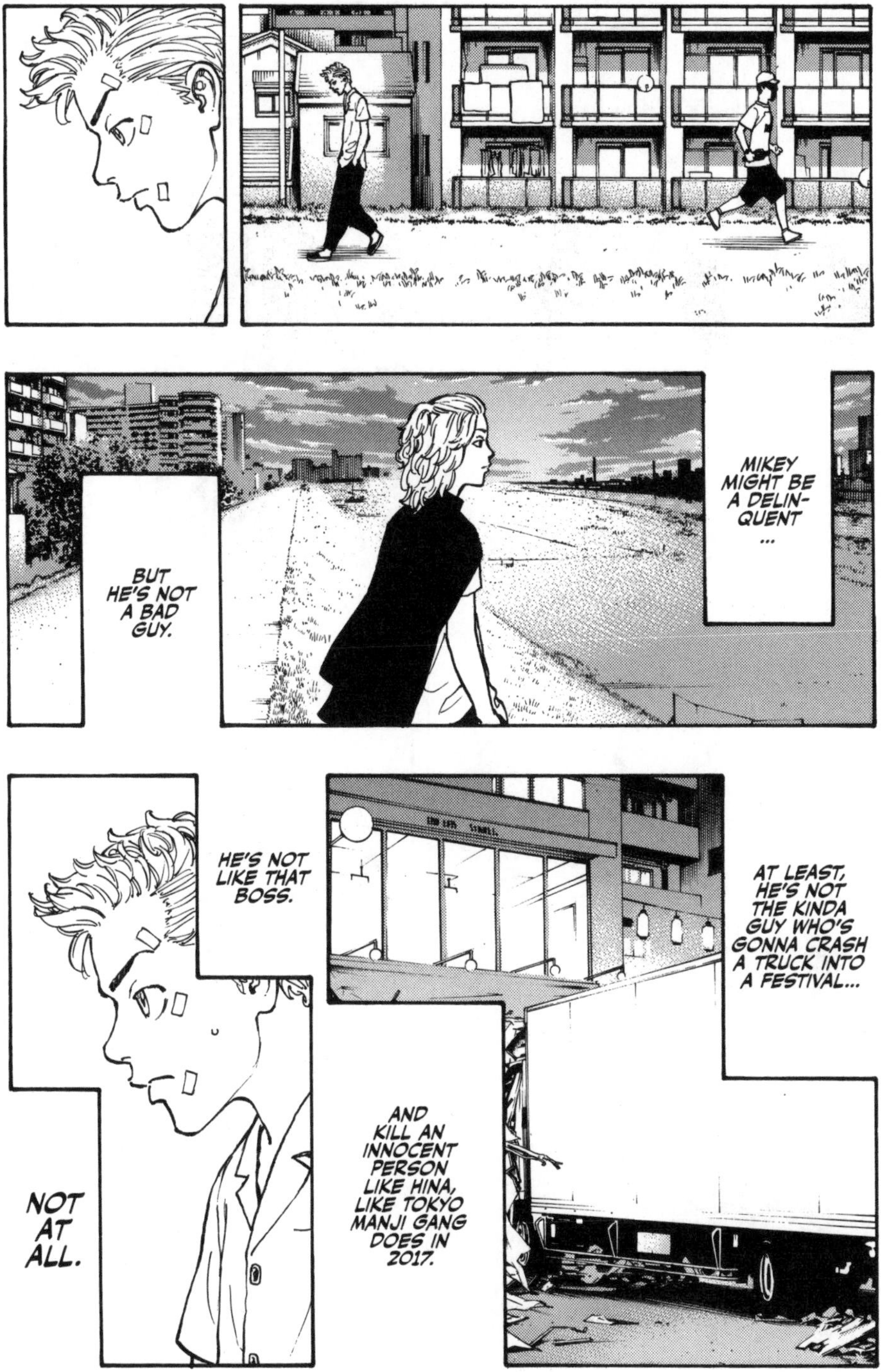
MIKEY MIGHT BE A DELIN-QUENT ...
BUT HE'S NOT A BAD GUY.
AT LEAST, HE'S NOT THE KINDA GUY WHO'S GONNA CRASH A TRUCK INTO A FESTIVAL...
AND KILL AN INNOCENT PERSON LIKE HINA, LIKE TOKYO MANJI GANG DOES IN 2017.
HE'S NOT LIKE THAT BOSS.
NOT AT ALL.

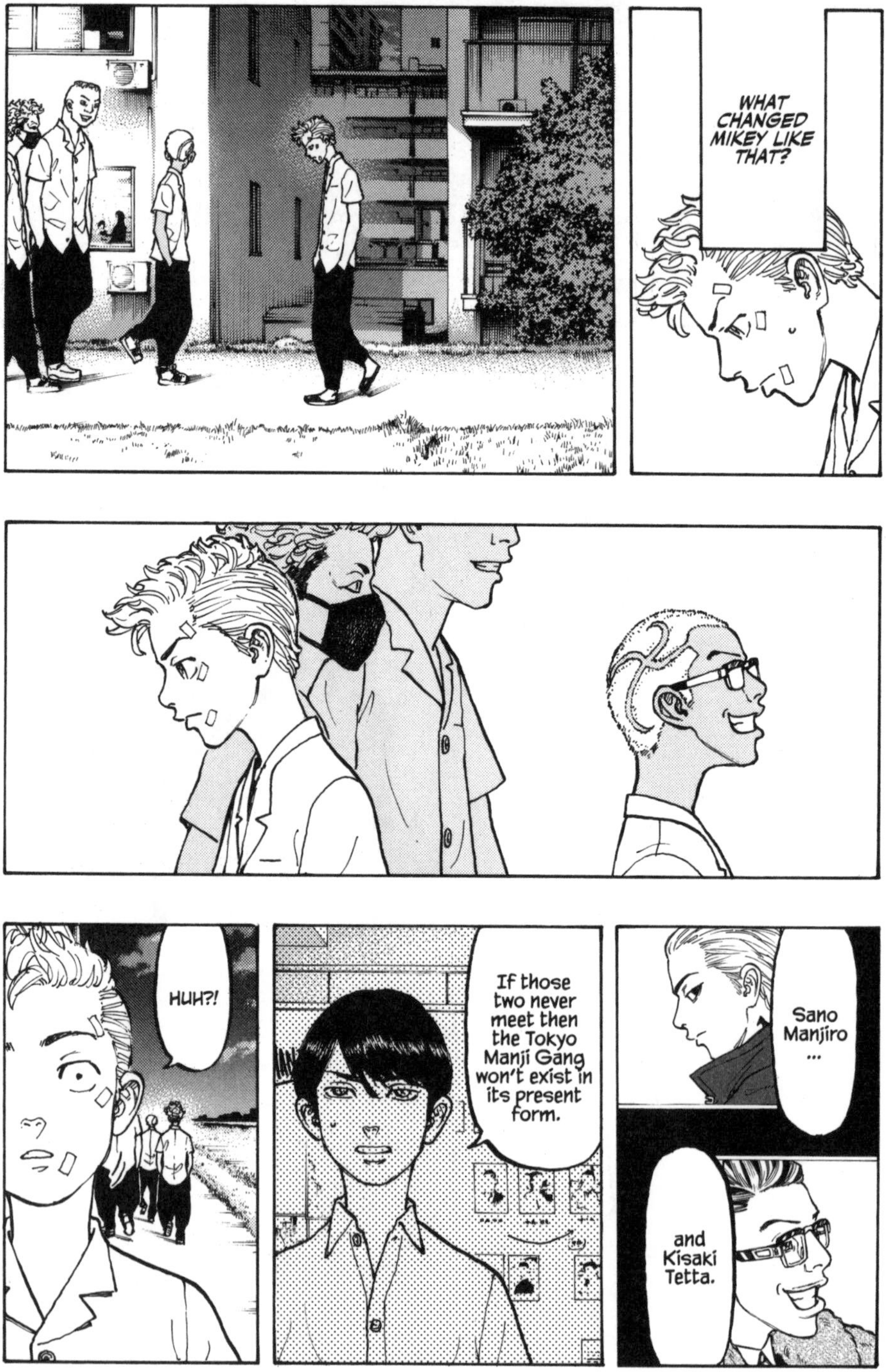
WHAT CHANGED MIKEY LIKE THAT?
Sano Manjiro ...
and Kisaki Tetta.
If those two never meet then the Tokyo Manji Gang won't exist in its present form.
HUH?!

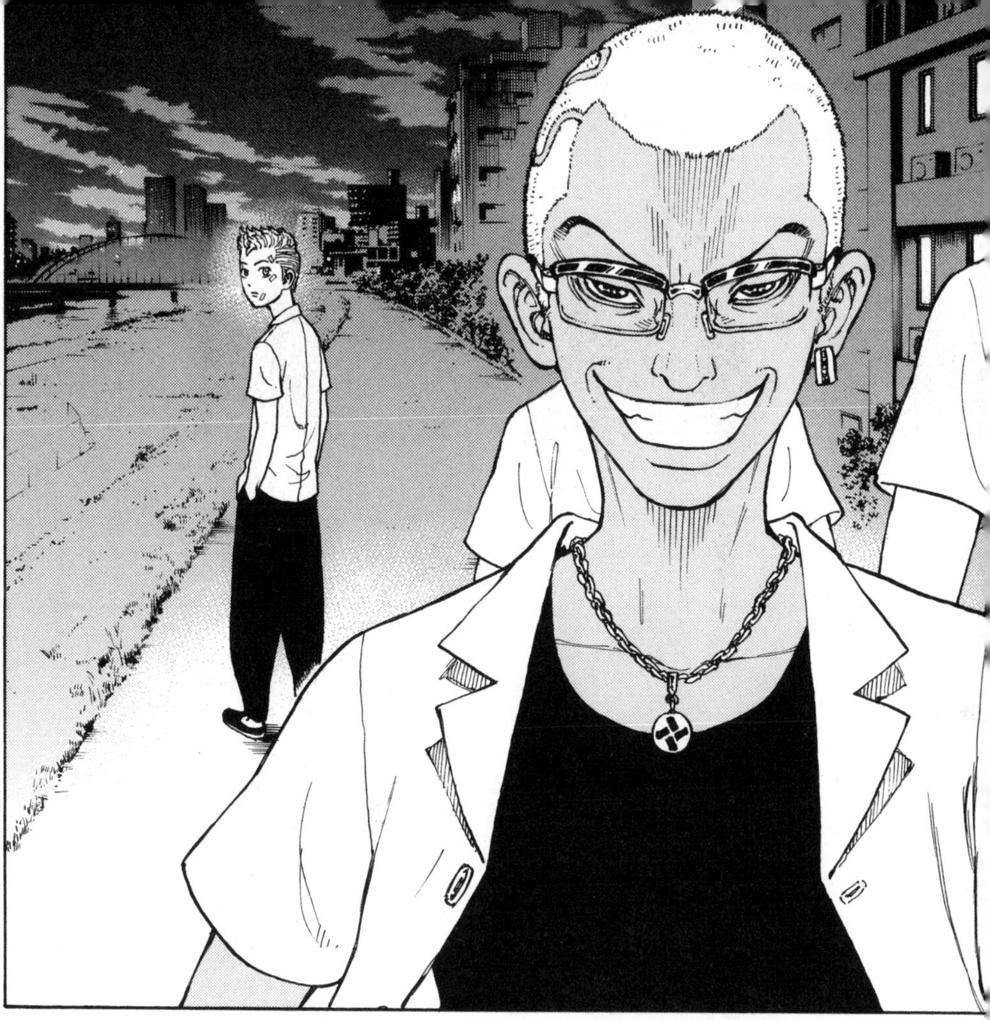

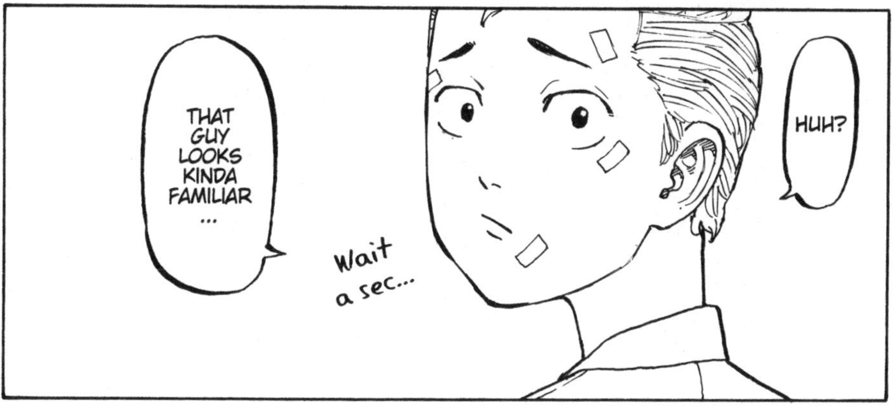
HUH?
Wait a sec...
THAT GUY LOOKS KINDA FAMILIAR ...

TOKYO
Revengers

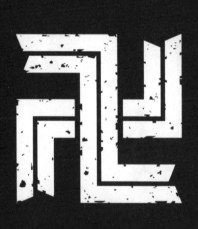

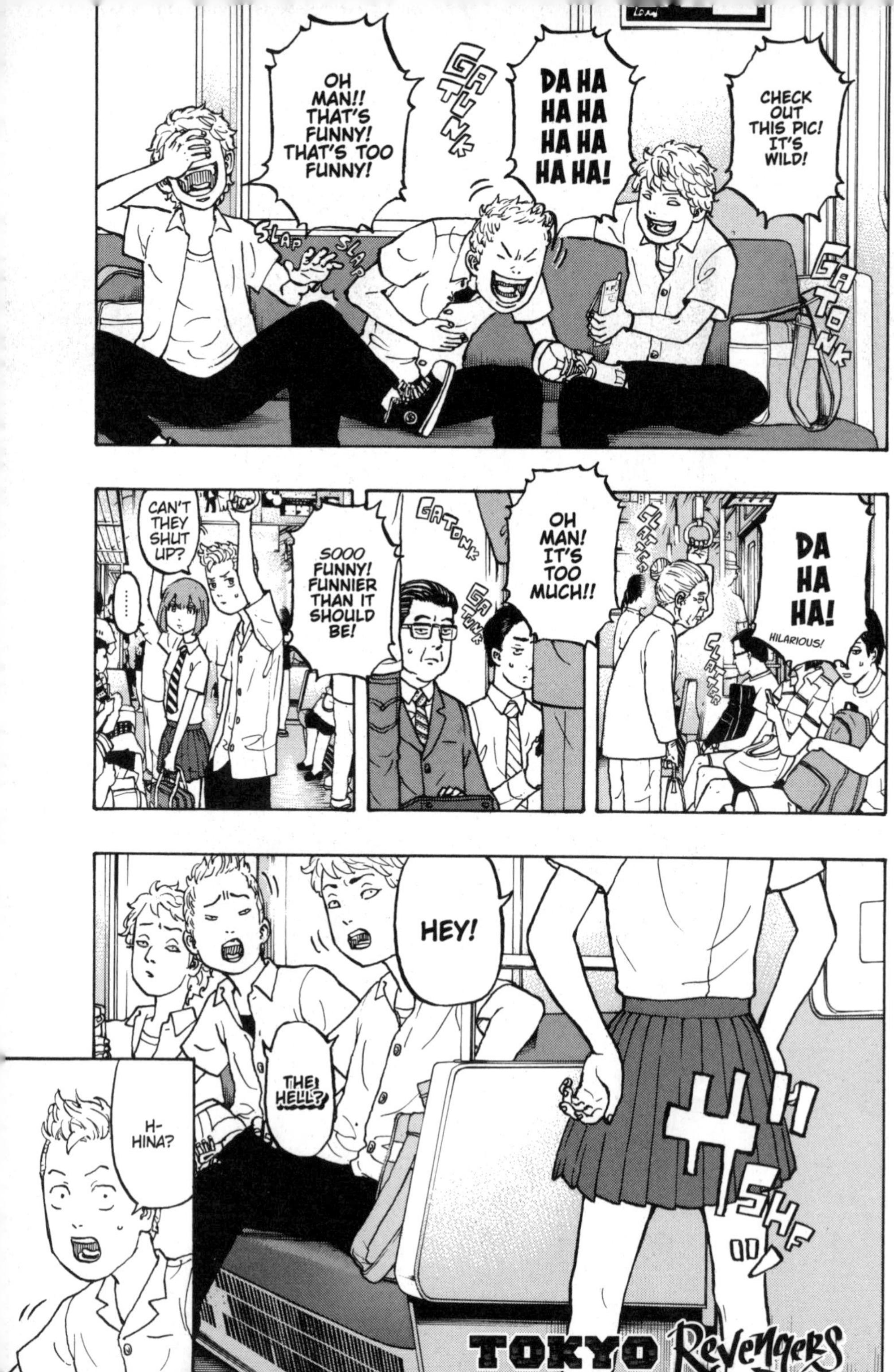

CHECK OUT THIS PIC! IT'S WILD!
GATONK
DA HA HA HA HA HA HA HA!
GATUNK
OH MAN!! THAT'S FUNNY! THAT'S TOO FUNNY!
SLAP SLAP
DA HA HA HA!
HILARIOUS!
CLATTER
CLATTER
OH MAN! IT'S TOO MUCH!!
GATONK
GATONK
SOOO FUNNY! FUNNIER THAN IT SHOULD BE!
CAN'T THEY SHUT UP?
......
HEY!
SHF SHF
THE HELL?
H-HINA?
TOKYO Revengers

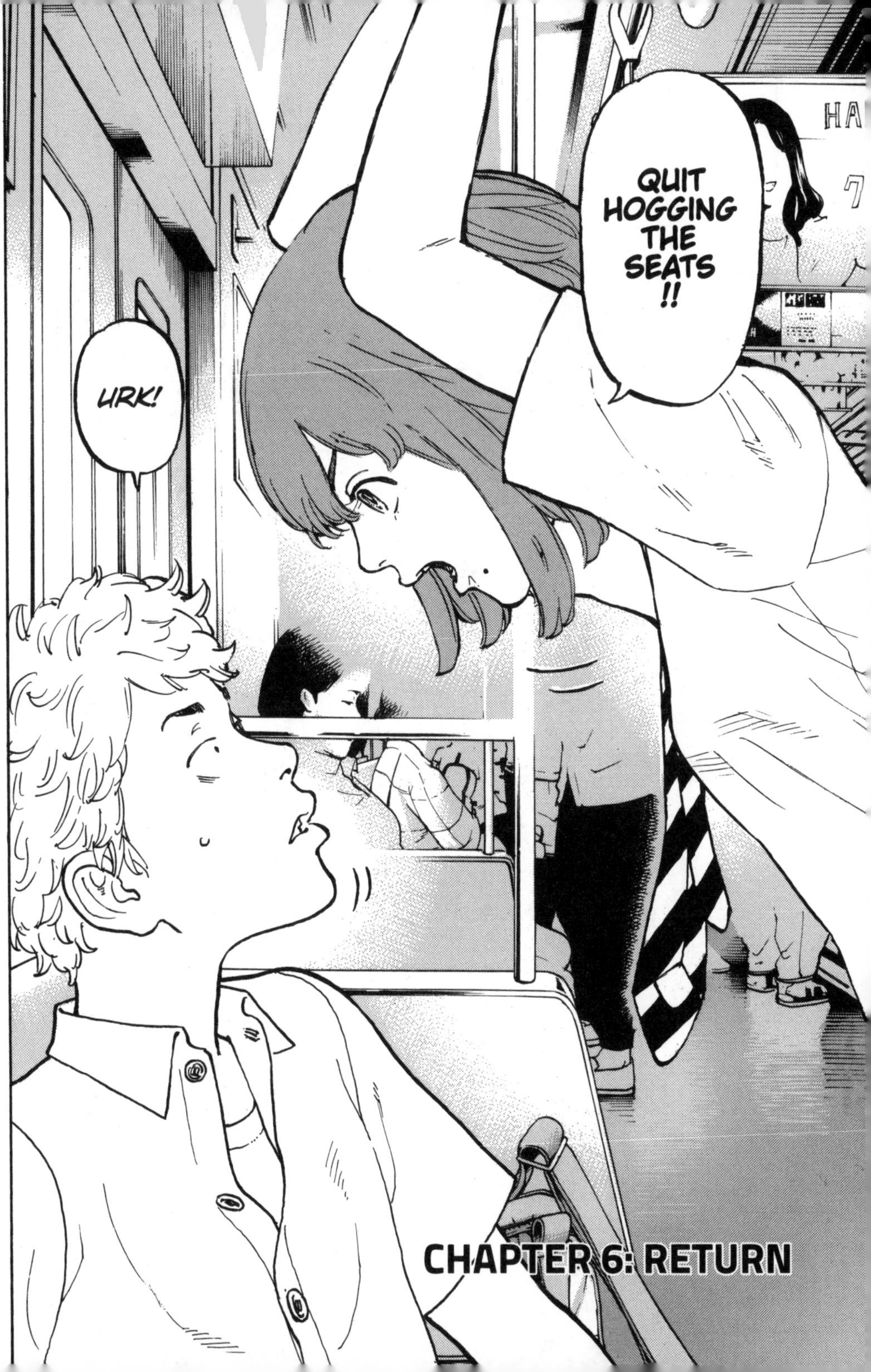
QUIT HOGGING THE SEATS!!
URK!
CHAPTER 6: RETURN

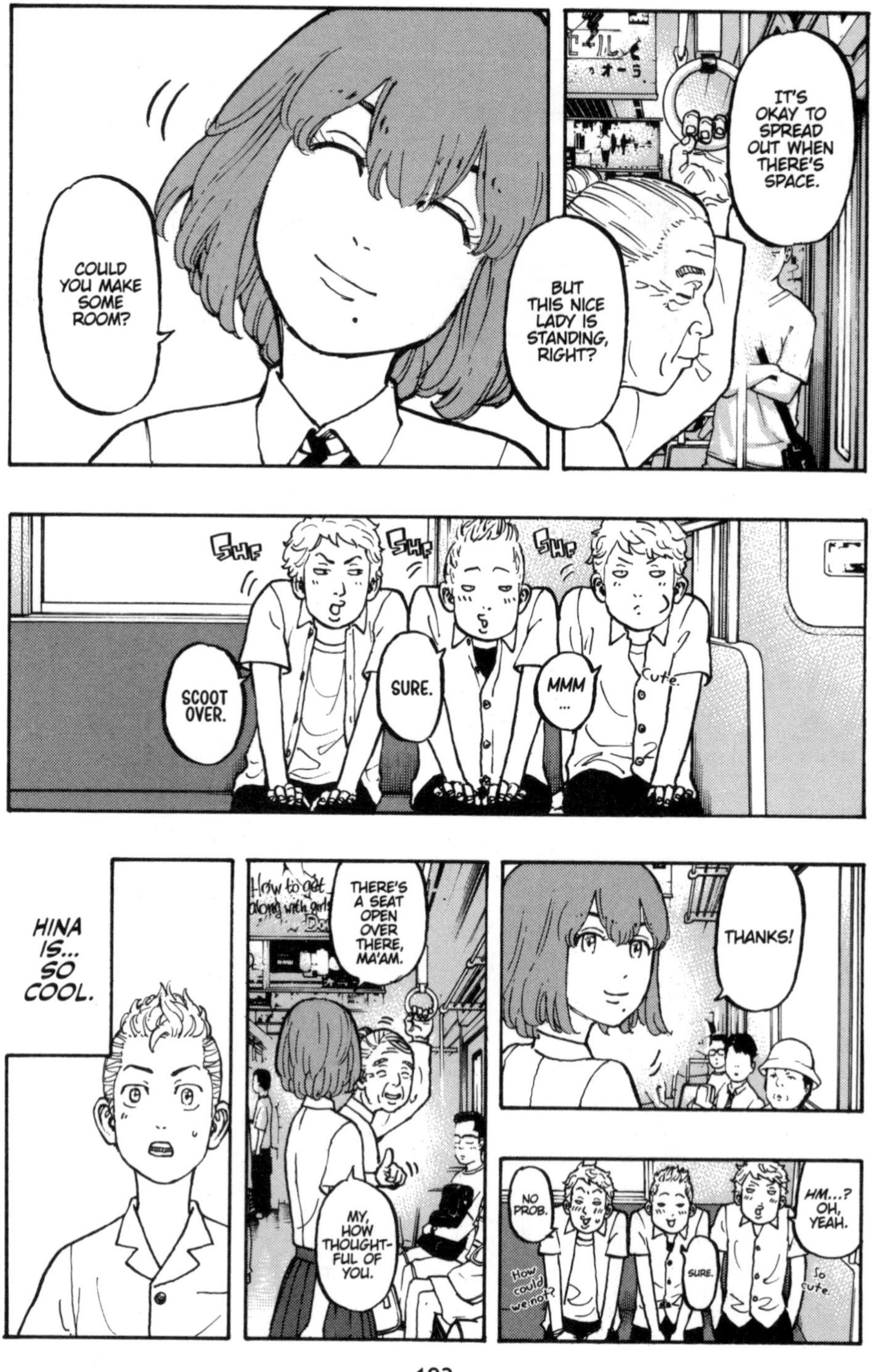
IT'S OKAY TO SPREAD OUT WHEN THERE'S SPACE.
BUT THIS NICE LADY IS STANDING, RIGHT?
COULD YOU MAKE SOME ROOM?
SHF
SHF
SHF
Cute.
MMM...
SURE.
SCOOT OVER.
THANKS!
HM...? OH, YEAH.
So cute.
SURE.
NO PROB.
How could we not?
How to get along with girls
THERE'S A SEAT OPEN OVER THERE, MA'AM.
MY, HOW THOUGHTFUL OF YOU.
HINA IS... SO COOL.

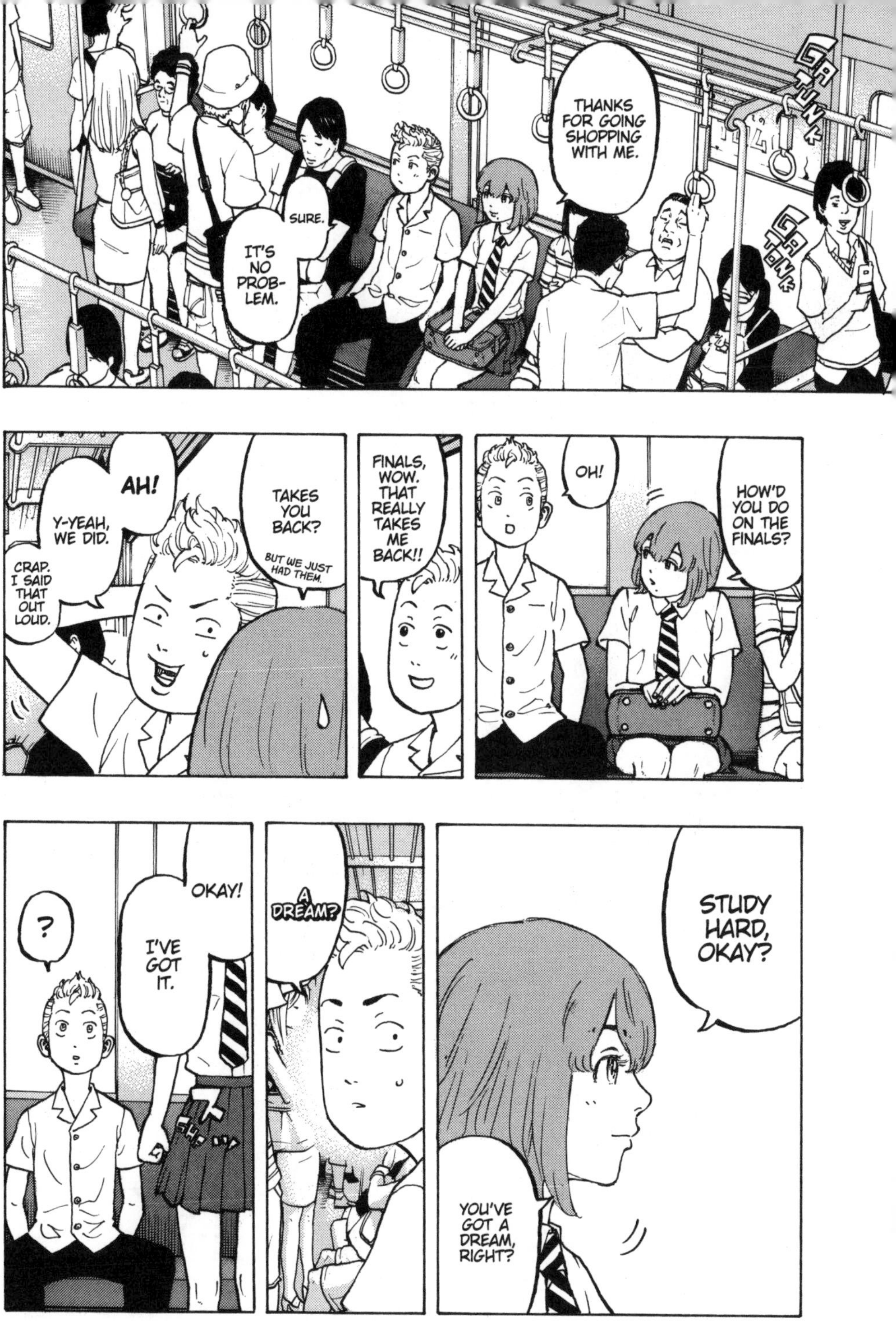
THANKS FOR GOING SHOPPING WITH ME.
SURE.
IT'S NO PROB-LEM.
HOW'D YOU DO ON THE FINALS?
OH!
FINALS, WOW. THAT REALLY TAKES ME BACK!!
TAKES YOU BACK?
BUT WE JUST HAD THEM.
AH!
Y-YEAH, WE DID.
CRAP. I SAID THAT OUT LOUD.
STUDY HARD, OKAY?
YOU'VE GOT A DREAM, RIGHT?
A DREAM?
OKAY!
I'VE GOT IT.
?

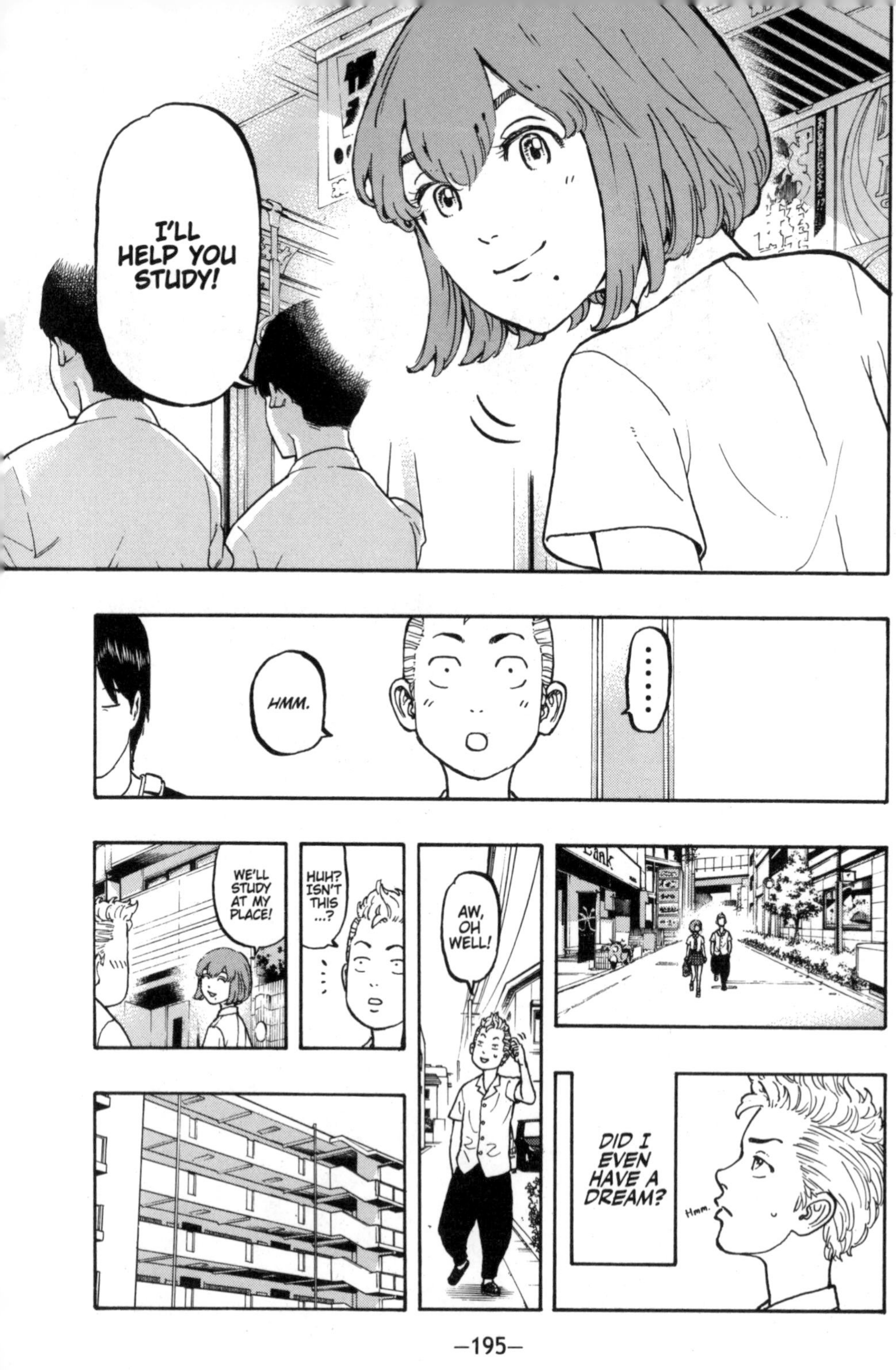
I'LL HELP YOU STUDY!
......
HMM.
DID I EVEN HAVE A DREAM?
Hmm.
AW, OH WELL!
HUH? ISN'T THIS ...?
WE'LL STUDY AT MY PLACE!

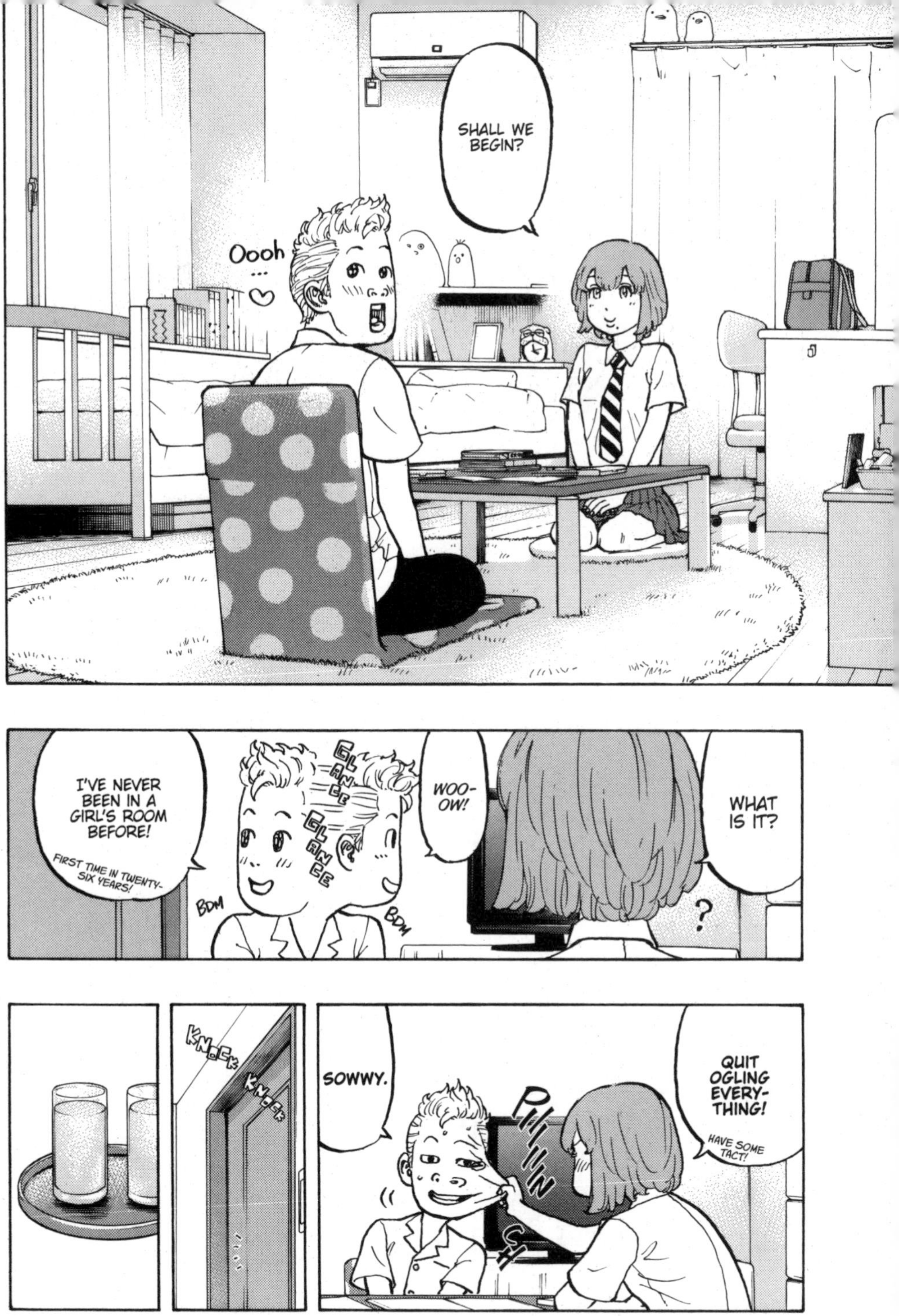
SHALL WE BEGIN?
Oooh ...
WHAT IS IT?
?
WOO-OW!
GLANCE GLANCE
BDM BDM
I'VE NEVER BEEN IN A GIRL'S ROOM BEFORE!
FIRST TIME IN TWENTY-SIX YEARS!
QUIT OGLING EVERYTHING!
HAVE SOME TACT!
PIIIINCH
SOWWY.
KNOCK KNOCK

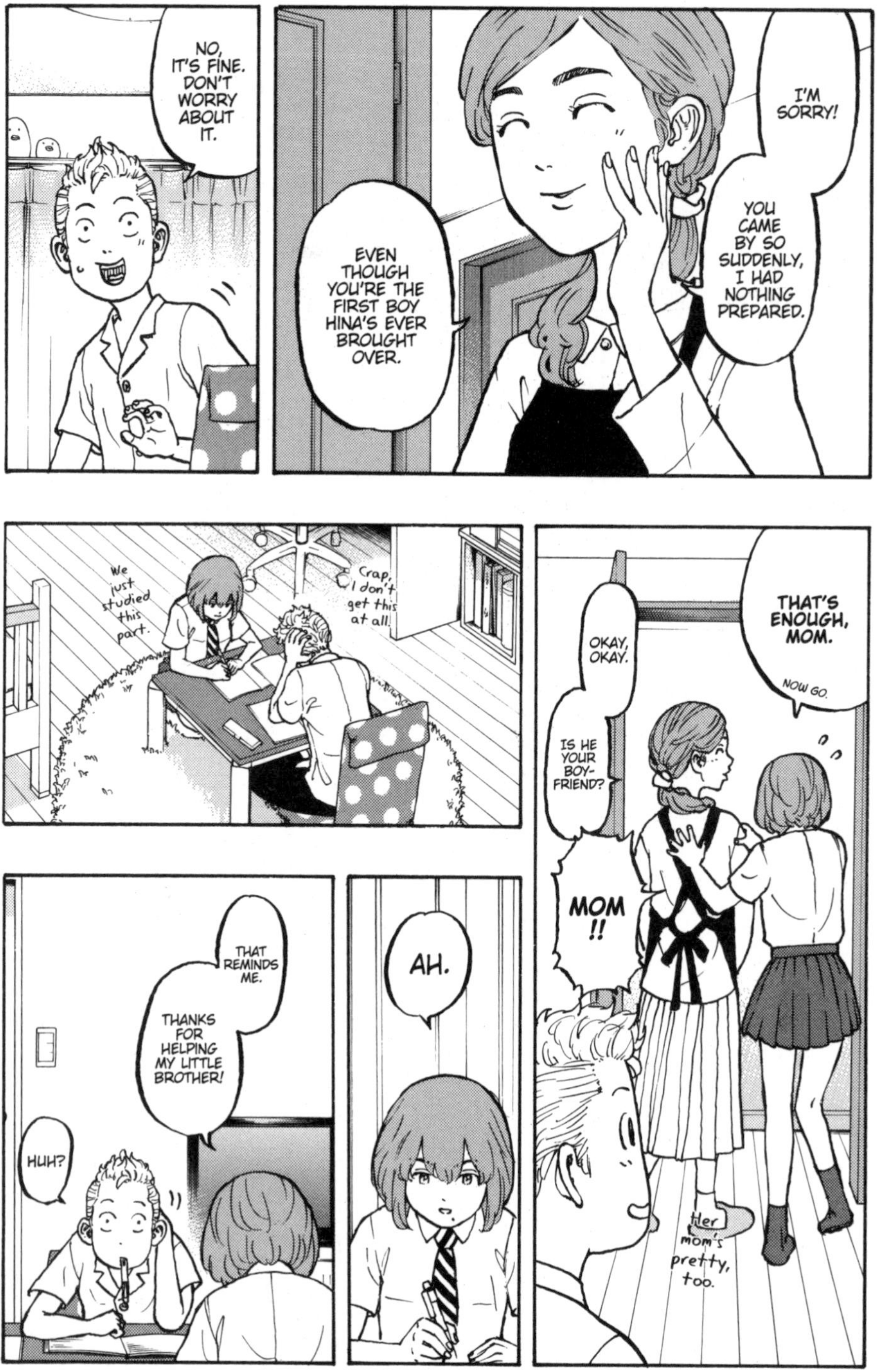
I'M SORRY!
YOU CAME BY SO SUDDENLY, I HAD NOTHING PREPARED.
EVEN THOUGH YOU'RE THE FIRST BOY HINA'S EVER BROUGHT OVER.
NO, IT'S FINE. DON'T WORRY ABOUT IT.
THAT'S ENOUGH, MOM.
NOW GO.
OKAY, OKAY.
IS HE YOUR BOY-FRIEND?
MOM!!
Her mom's pretty, too.
Crap, I don't get this at all.
We just studied this part.
AH.
THAT REMINDS ME.
THANKS FOR HELPING MY LITTLE BROTHER!
HUH?

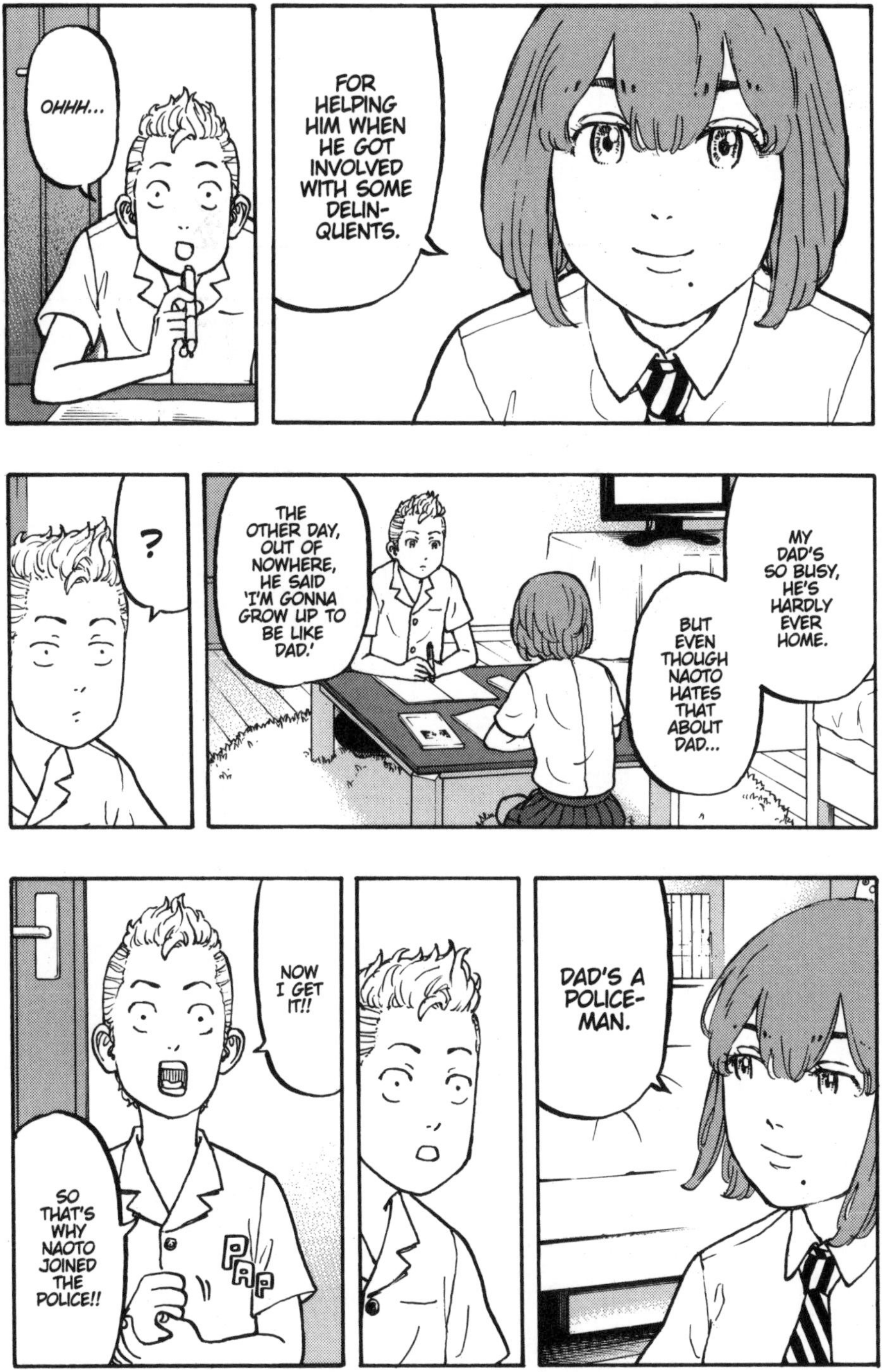
FOR HELPING HIM WHEN HE GOT INVOLVED WITH SOME DELIN-QUENTS.
OHHH...
MY DAD'S SO BUSY, HE'S HARDLY EVER HOME.
BUT EVEN THOUGH NAOTO HATES THAT ABOUT DAD...
THE OTHER DAY, OUT OF NOWHERE, HE SAID 'I'M GONNA GROW UP TO BE LIKE DAD.'
?
DAD'S A POLICE-MAN.
NOW I GET IT!!
SO THAT'S WHY NAOTO JOINED THE POLICE!!

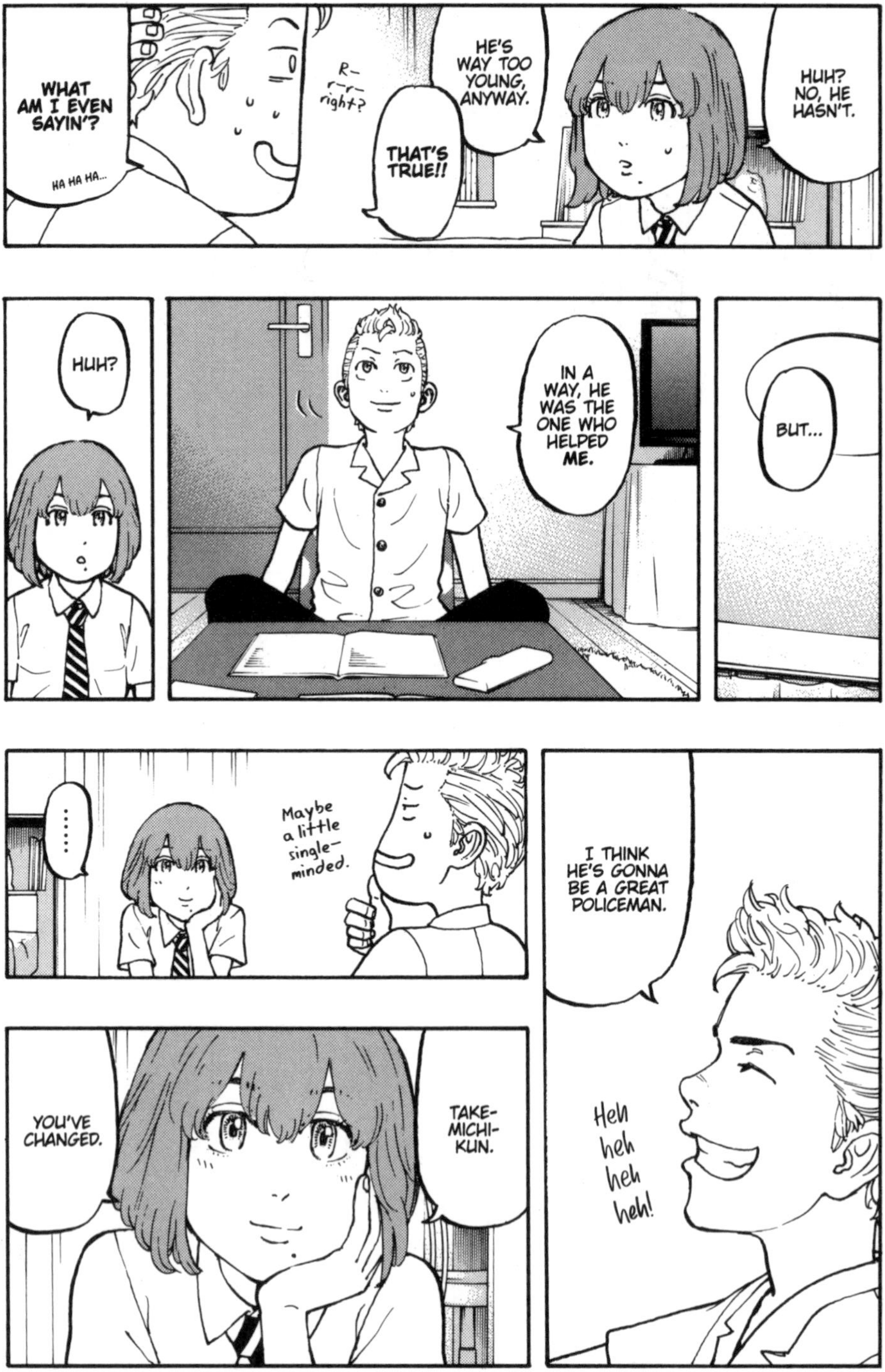
HUH? NO, HE HASN'T.
HE'S WAY TOO YOUNG, ANYWAY.
R-r-r-right?
THAT'S TRUE!!
WHAT AM I EVEN SAYIN'?
HA HA HA...
BUT...
IN A WAY, HE WAS THE ONE WHO HELPED ME.
HUH?
I THINK HE'S GONNA BE A GREAT POLICEMAN.
Heh heh heh heh!
Maybe a little single-minded.
......
TAKE-MICHI-KUN.
YOU'VE CHANGED.

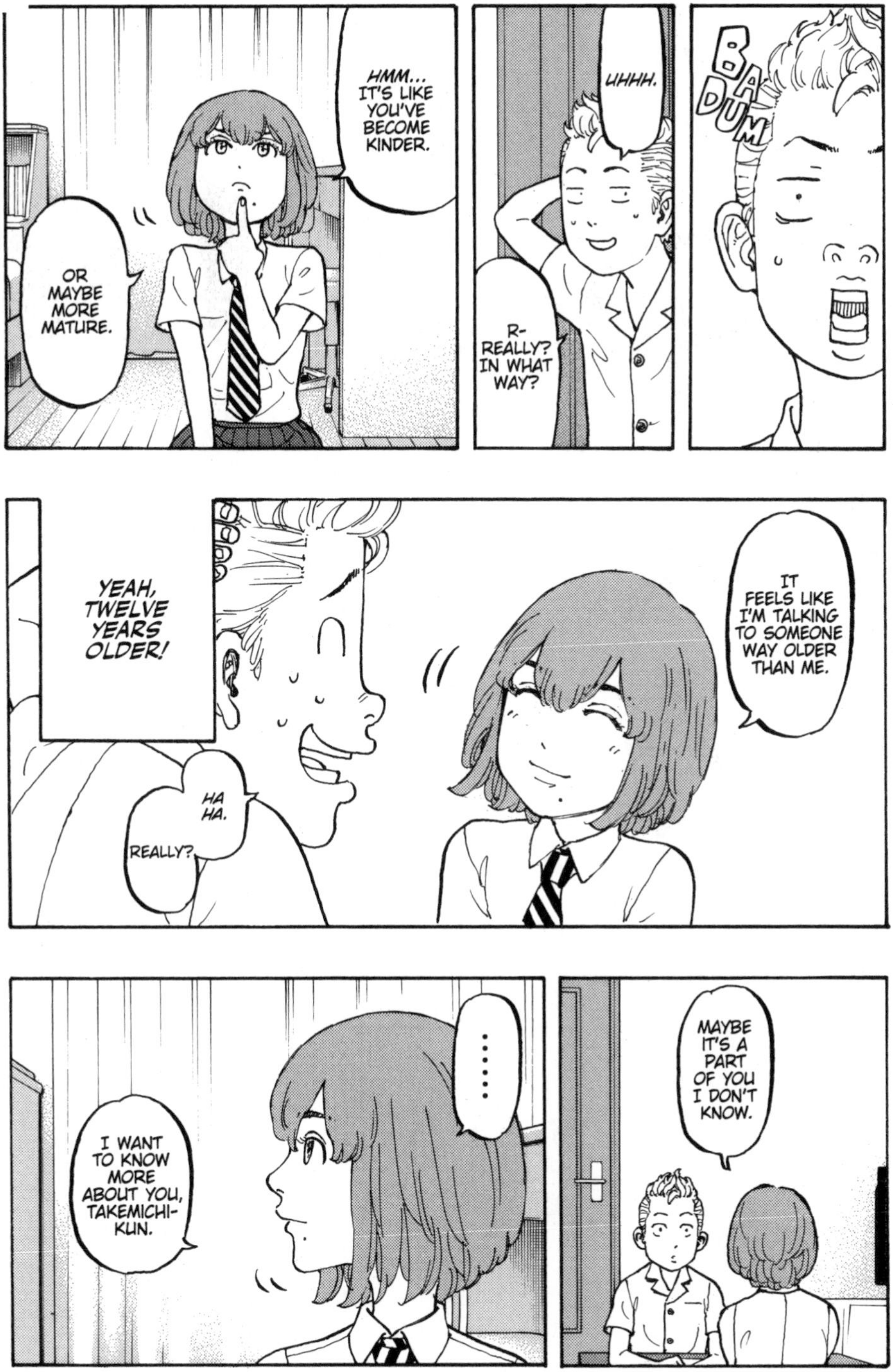
BADUM
UHHH.
R-REALLY? IN WHAT WAY?
HMM... IT'S LIKE YOU'VE BECOME KINDER.
OR MAYBE MORE MATURE.
IT FEELS LIKE I'M TALKING TO SOMEONE WAY OLDER THAN ME.
HA HA.
REALLY?
YEAH, TWELVE YEARS OLDER!
MAYBE IT'S A PART OF YOU I DON'T KNOW.
......
I WANT TO KNOW MORE ABOUT YOU, TAKEMICHI-KUN.

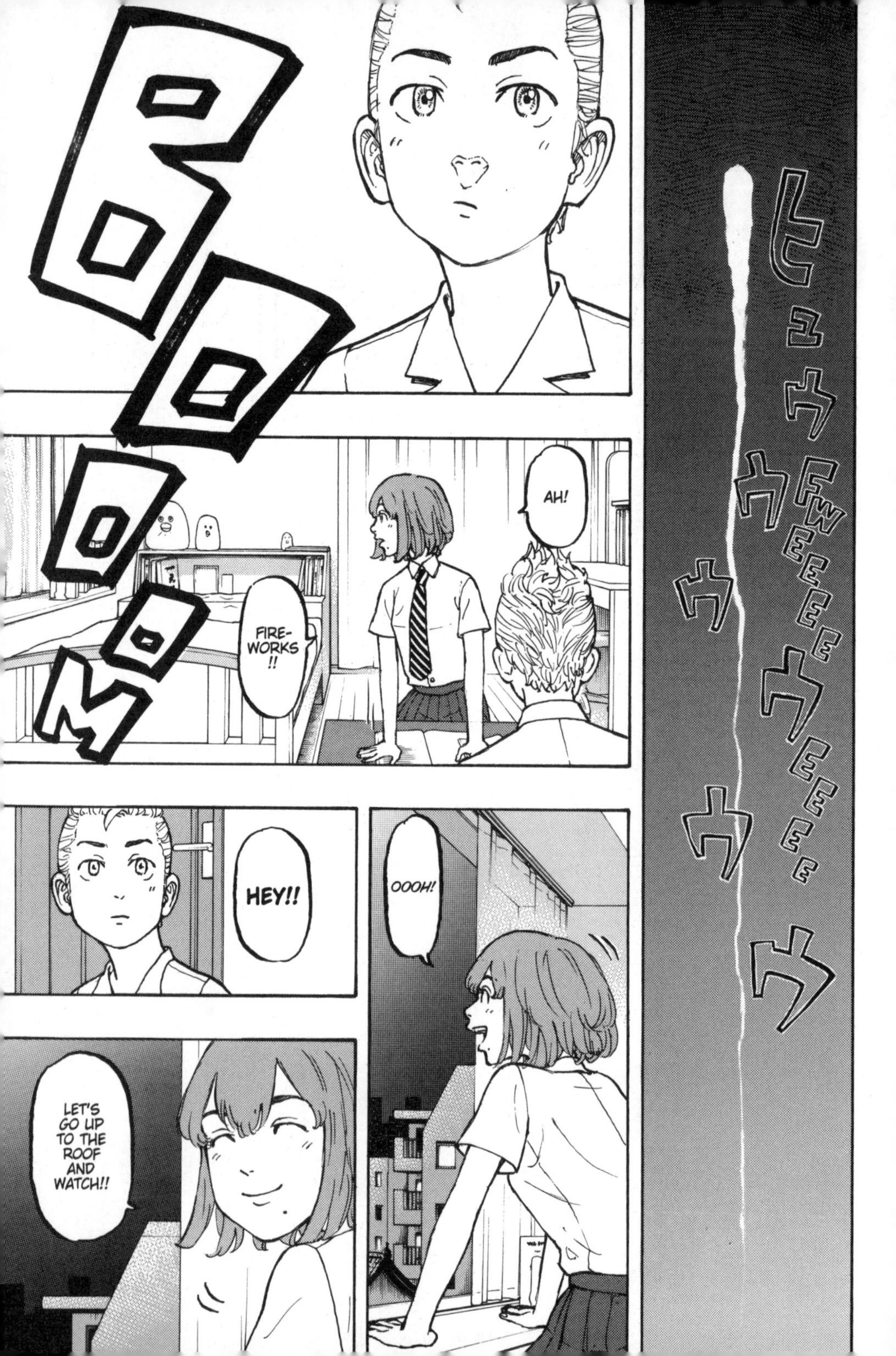
ヒュウウウウウウ
FWEEEEEEEEE
POOOOM
AH!
FIRE-WORKS!!
OOOH!
HEY!!
LET'S GO UP TO THE ROOF AND WATCH!!

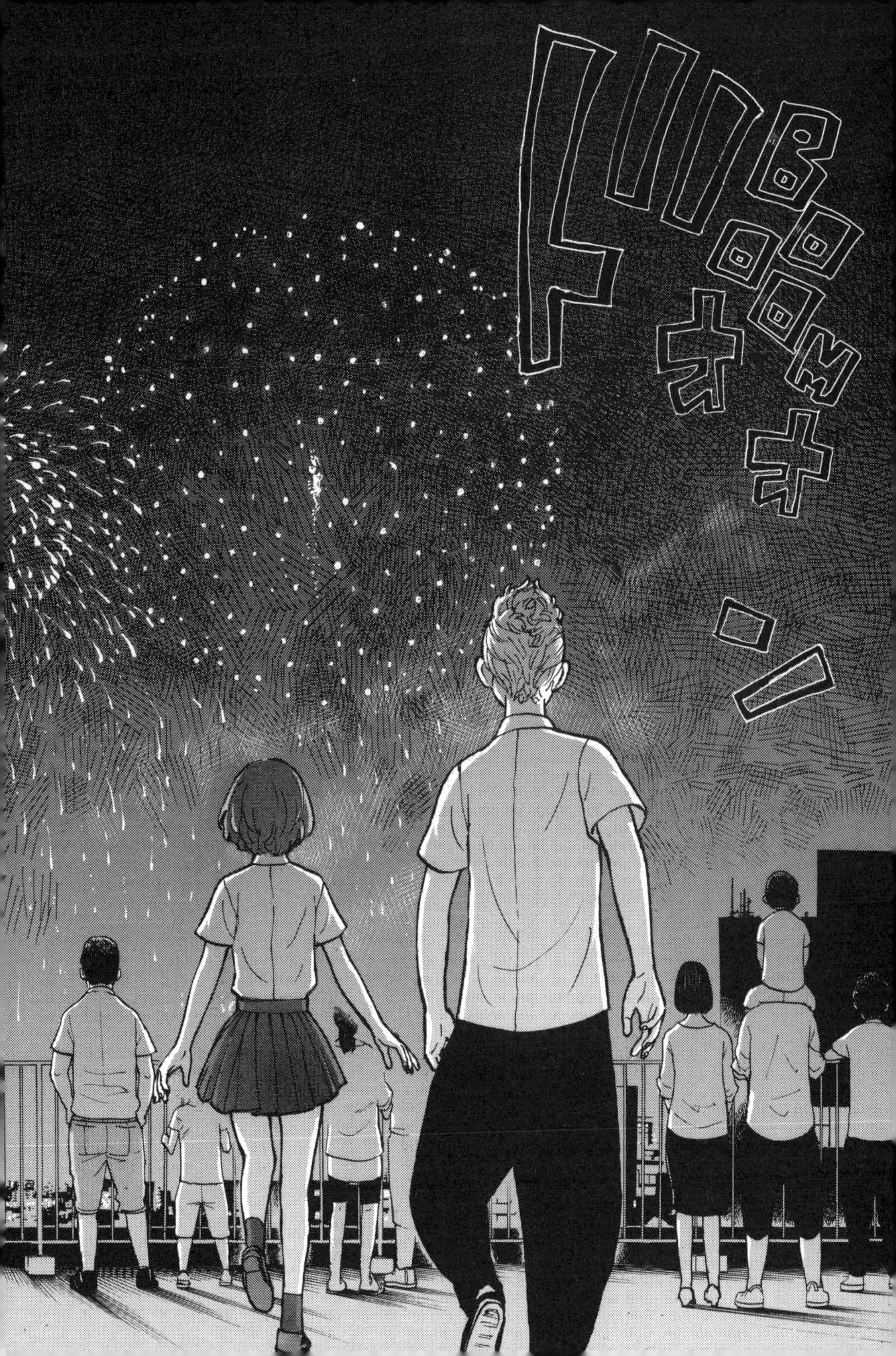
ドオオン!
BOOOM

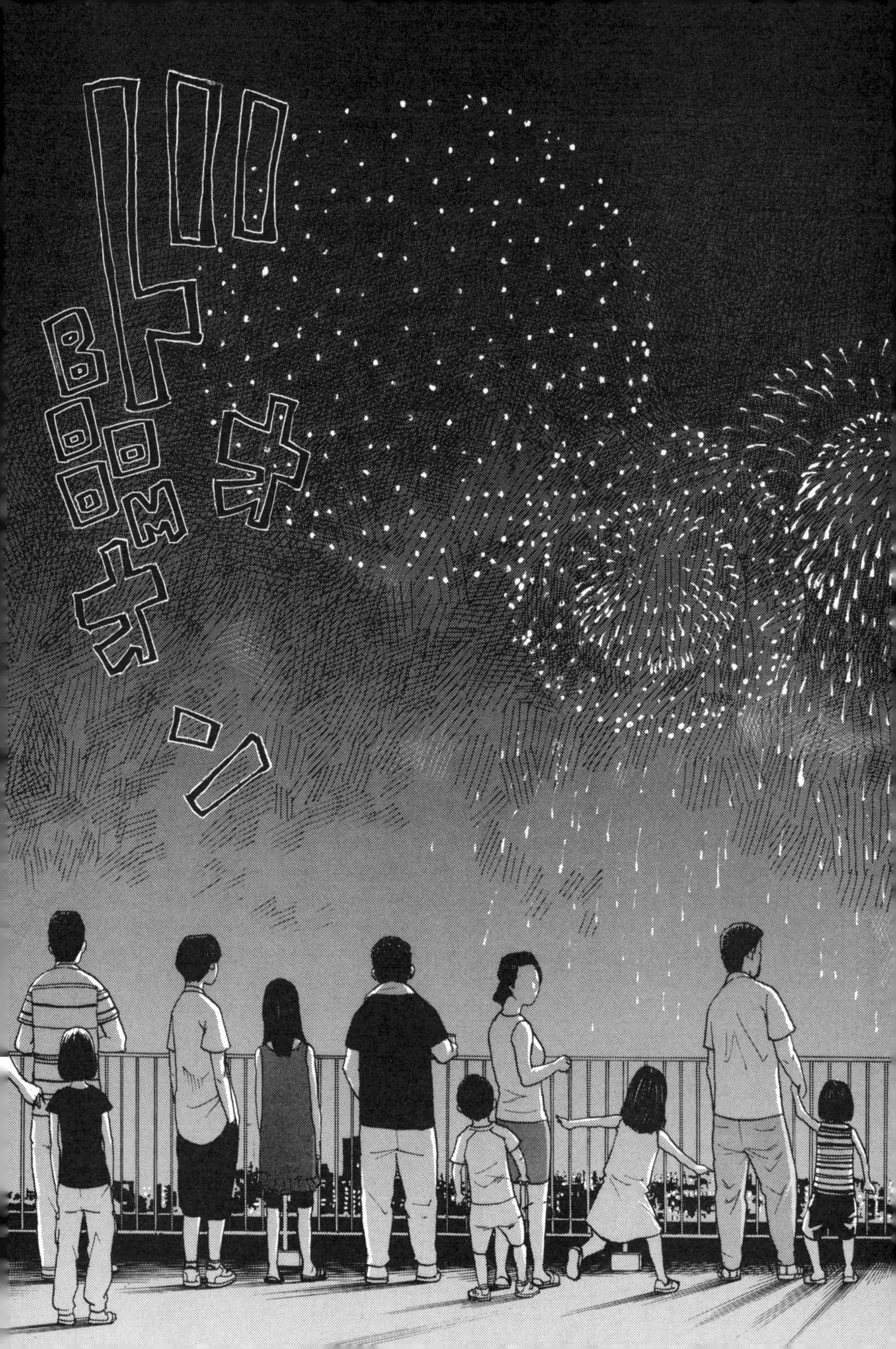
ドオオン
BOOOM

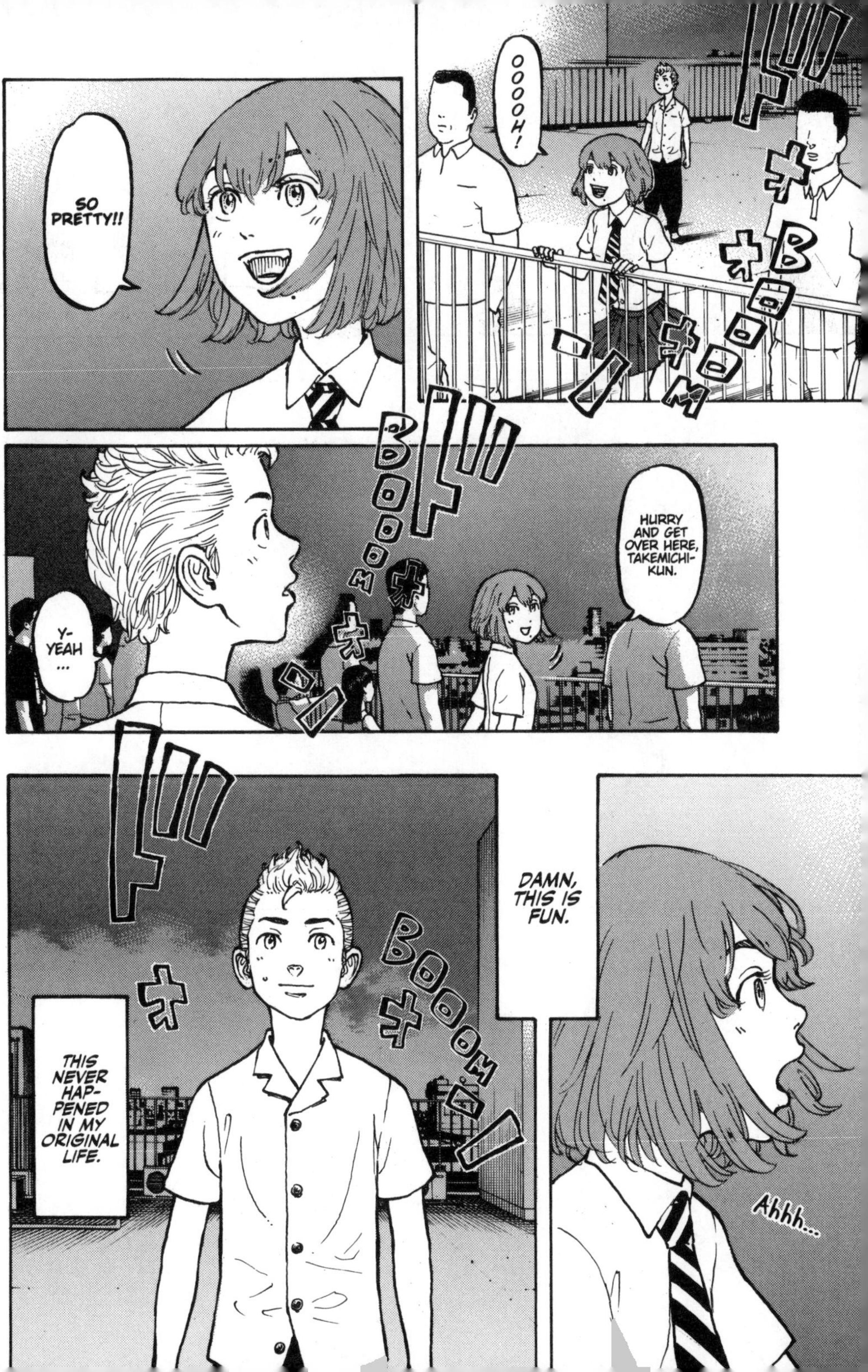
OOOOH!
BOOOOM
SO PRETTY!!
BOOOOOM
HURRY AND GET OVER HERE, TAKEMICHI-KUN.
Y-YEAH...
DAMN, THIS IS FUN.
Ahhh...
BOOOOM
THIS NEVER HAP-PENED IN MY ORIGINAL LIFE.

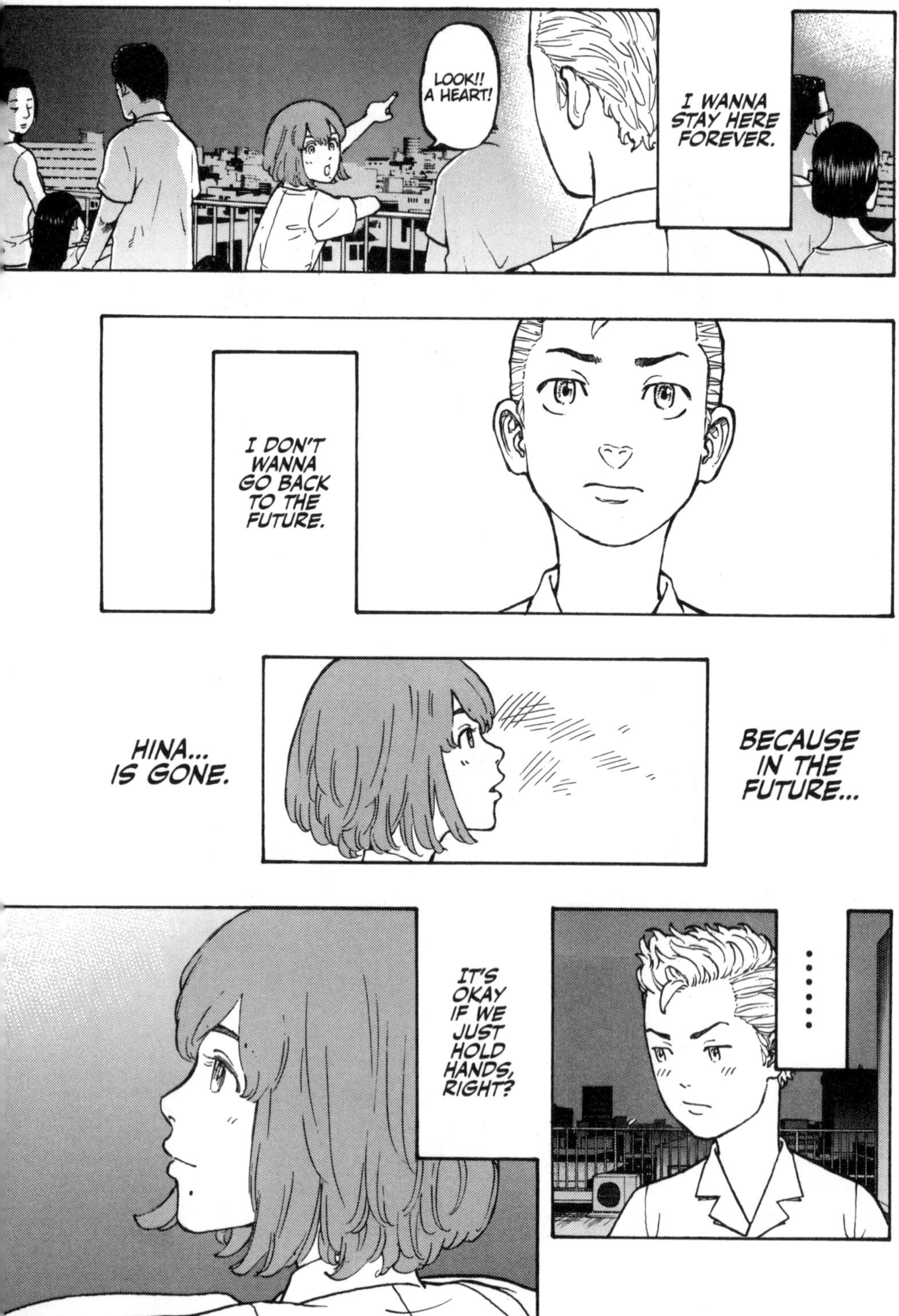
I WANNA STAY HERE FOREVER.
LOOK!! A HEART!
I DON'T WANNA GO BACK TO THE FUTURE.
BECAUSE IN THE FUTURE...
HINA... IS GONE.
......
IT'S OKAY IF WE JUST HOLD HANDS, RIGHT?

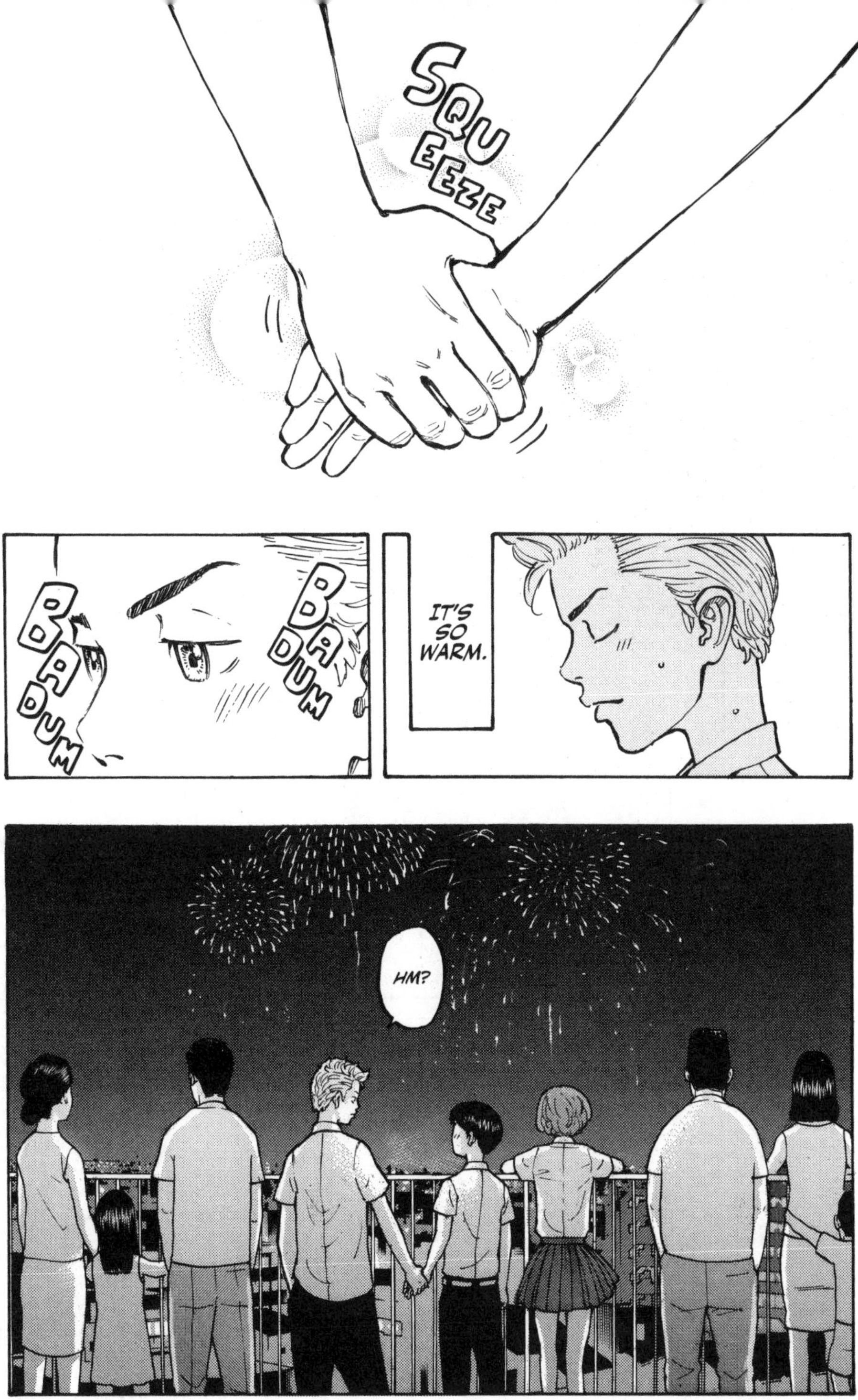
SQUEEZE
IT'S SO WARM.
BADUM
BADUM
HM?

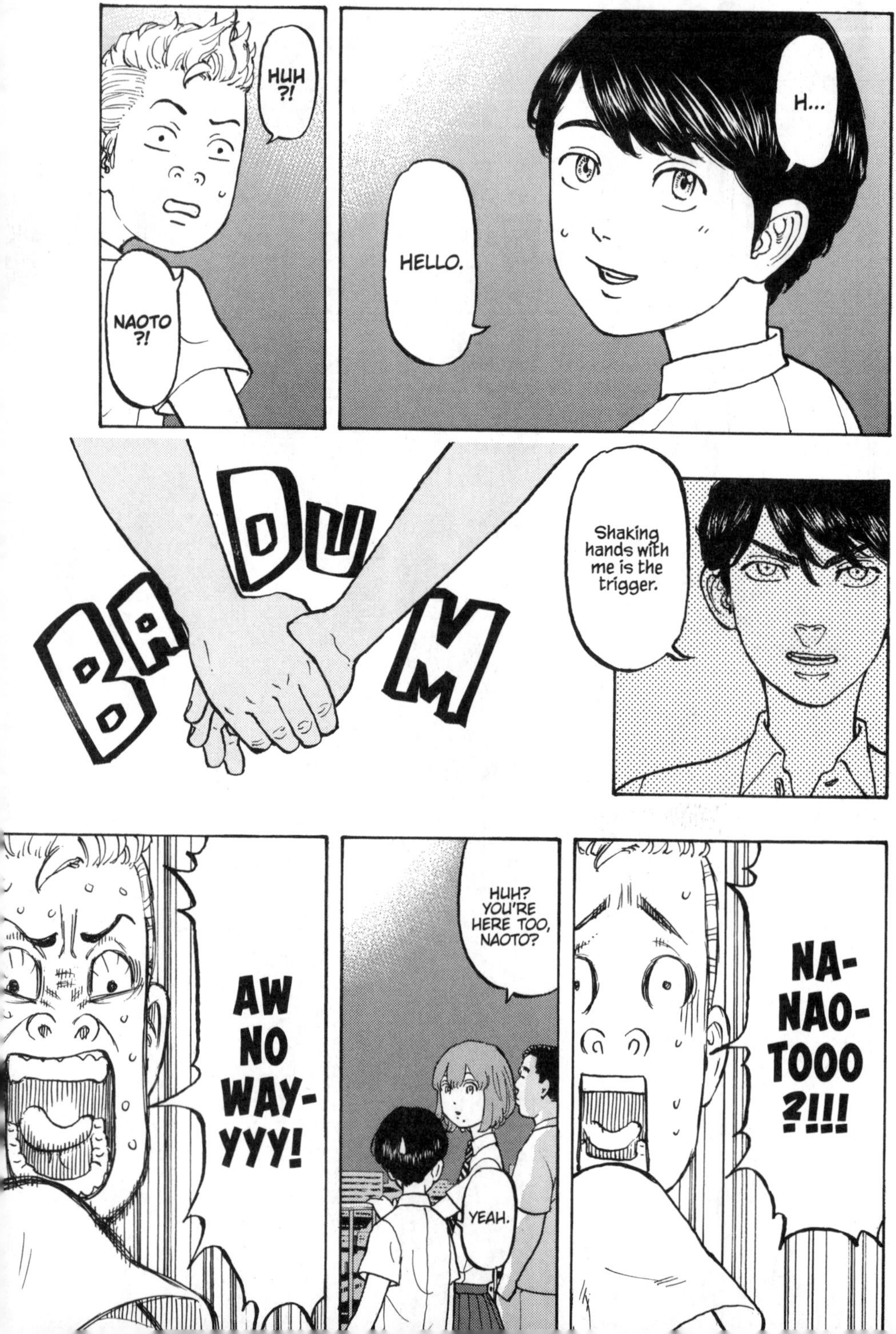
H...
HELLO.
HUH ?!
NAOTO ?!
Shaking hands with me is the trigger.
BADUM
NA-NAO-TOOO ?!!!
HUH? YOU'RE HERE TOO, NAOTO?
YEAH.
AW NO WAY-YYY!

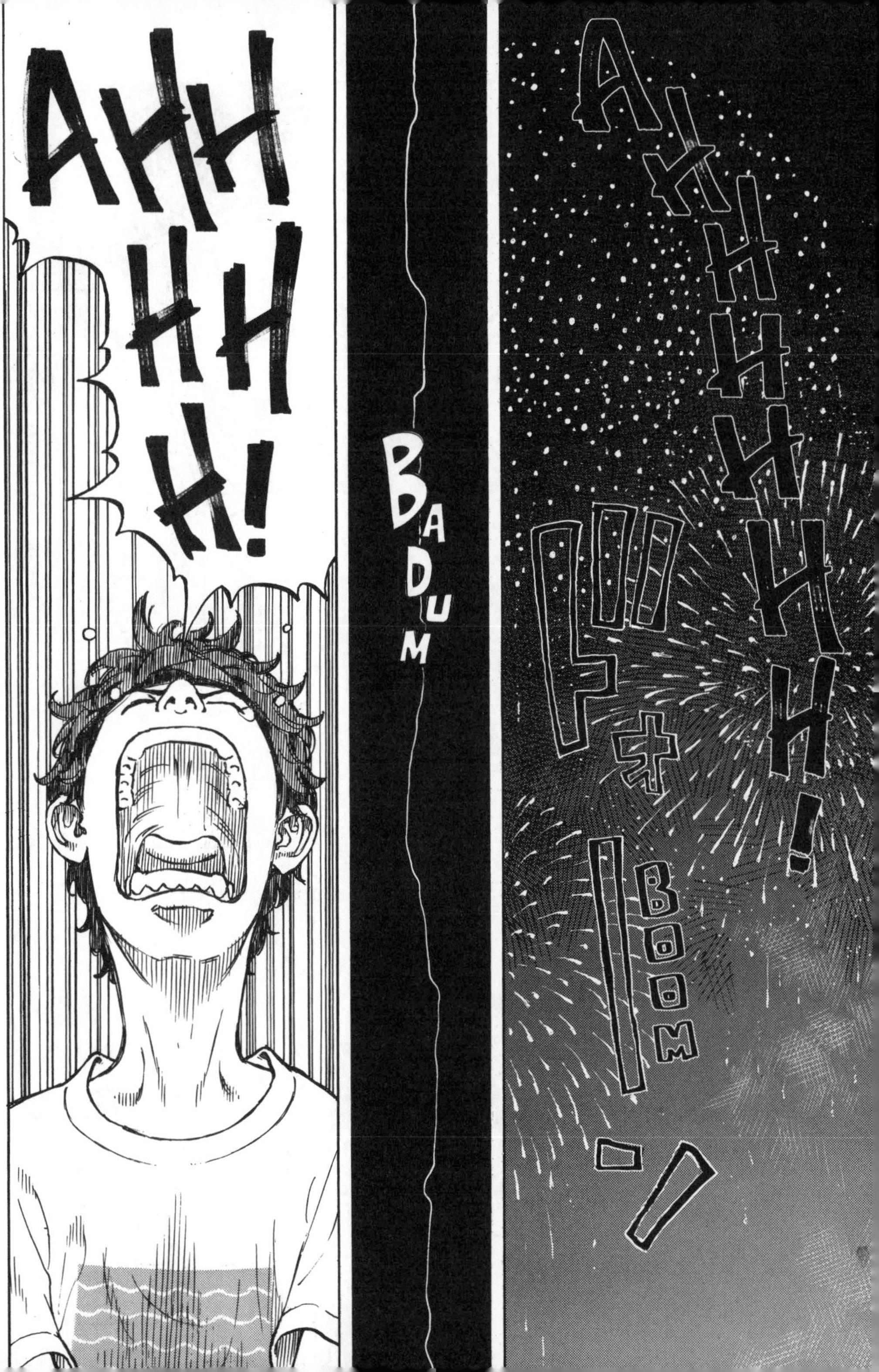

AHHHHHH!
BOOM
BADUM
AHHHHH!

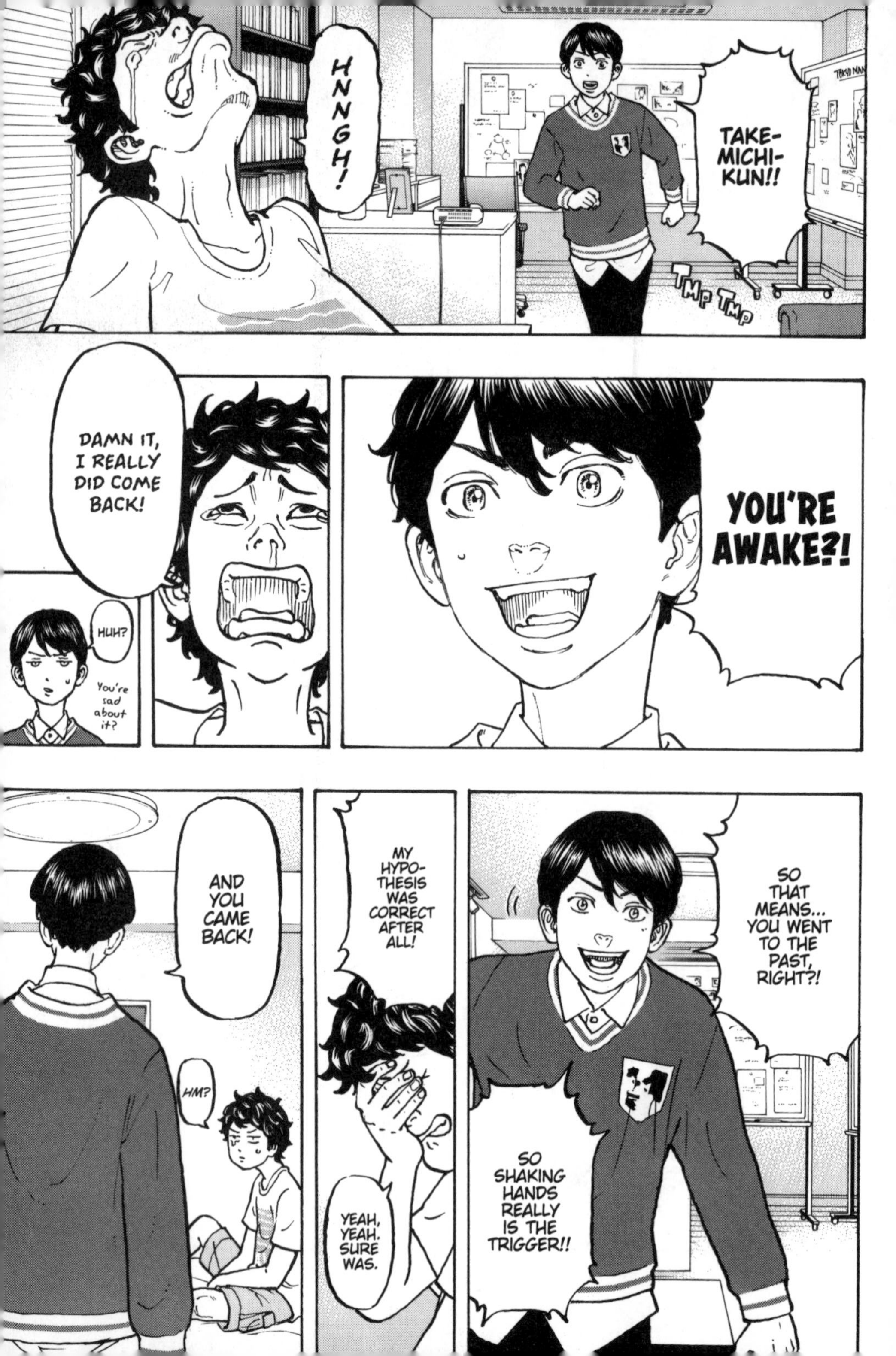
TAKE-MICHI-KUN!!
TMP TMP
HNNGH!
YOU'RE AWAKE?!
DAMN IT, I REALLY DID COME BACK!
HUH?
You're sad about it?
SO THAT MEANS... YOU WENT TO THE PAST, RIGHT?!
SO SHAKING HANDS REALLY IS THE TRIGGER!!
MY HYPO-THESIS WAS CORRECT AFTER ALL!
YEAH, YEAH. SURE WAS.
AND YOU CAME BACK!
HM?

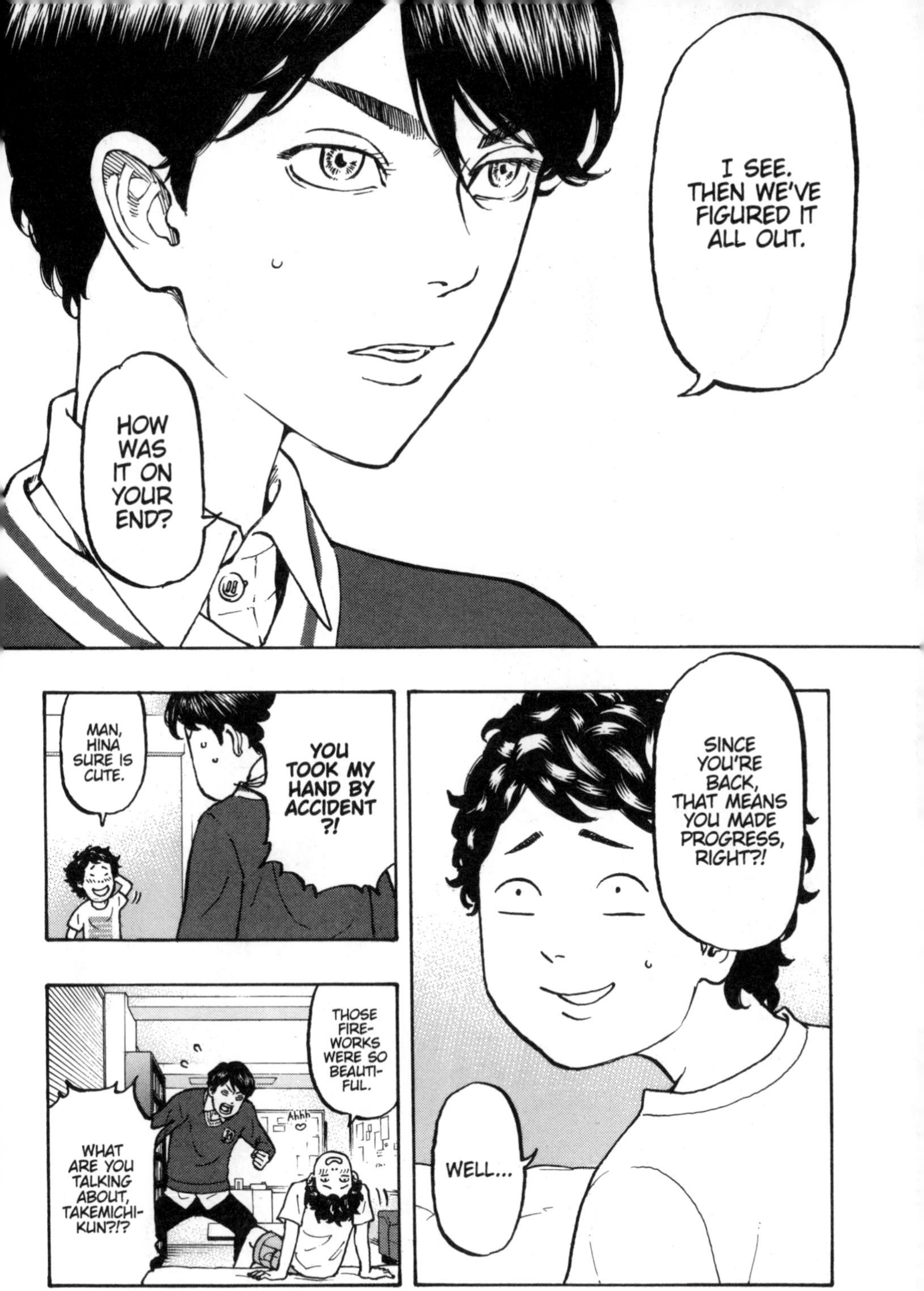
I SEE. THEN WE'VE FIGURED IT ALL OUT.
HOW WAS IT ON YOUR END?
SINCE YOU'RE BACK, THAT MEANS YOU MADE PROGRESS, RIGHT?!
WELL...
YOU TOOK MY HAND BY ACCIDENT ?!
MAN, HINA SURE IS CUTE.
THOSE FIRE-WORKS WERE SO BEAUTI-FUL.
Ahhh
WHAT ARE YOU TALKING ABOUT, TAKEMICHI-KUN?!?

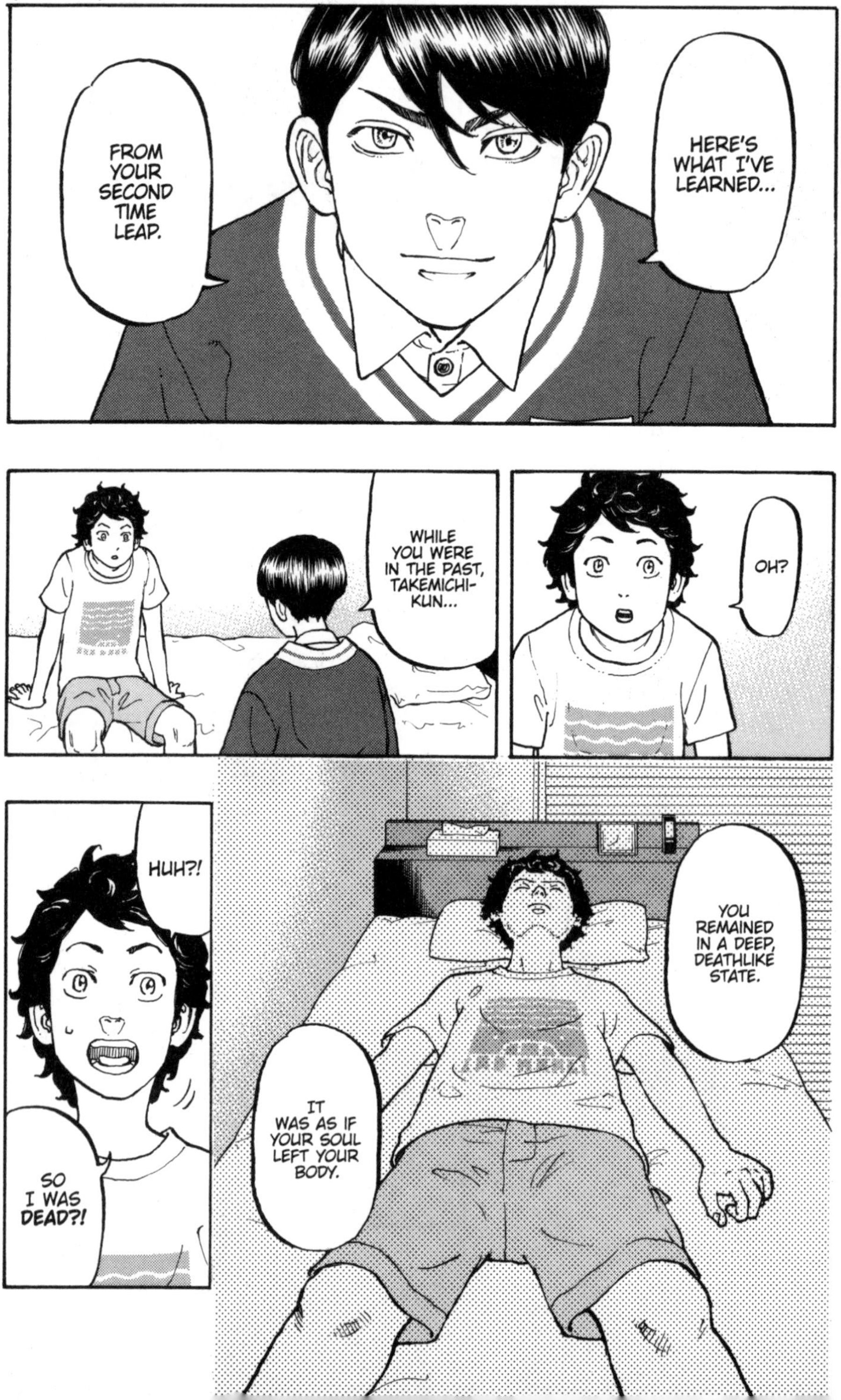
HERE'S WHAT I'VE LEARNED...
FROM YOUR SECOND TIME LEAP.
OH?
WHILE YOU WERE IN THE PAST, TAKEMICHI-KUN...
YOU REMAINED IN A DEEP, DEATHLIKE STATE.
IT WAS AS IF YOUR SOUL LEFT YOUR BODY.
HUH?!
SO I WAS DEAD?!

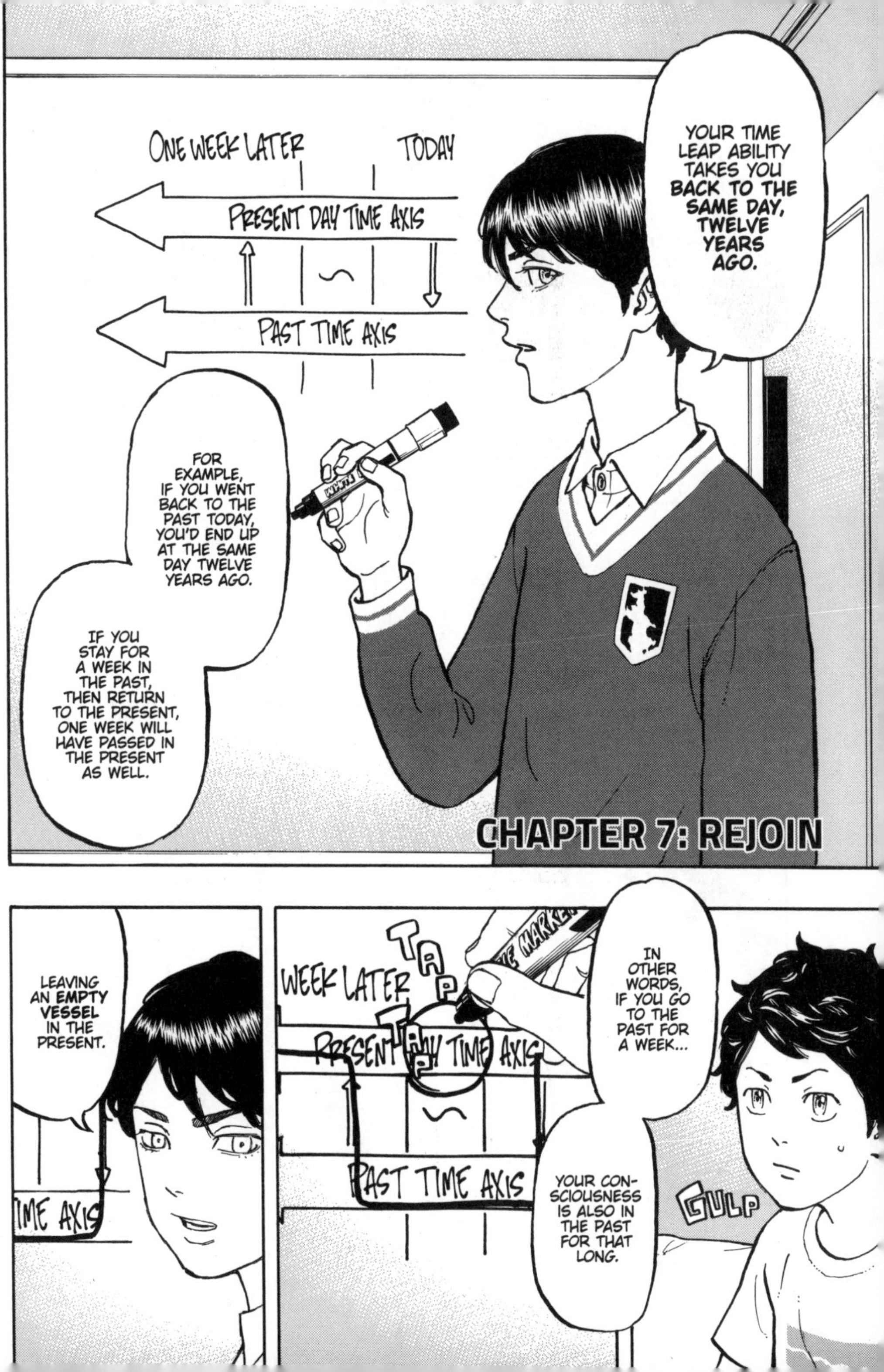
YOUR TIME LEAP ABILITY TAKES YOU BACK TO THE SAME DAY, TWELVE YEARS AGO.
ONE WEEK LATER
TODAY
PRESENT DAY TIME AXIS
PAST TIME AXIS
FOR EXAMPLE, IF YOU WENT BACK TO THE PAST TODAY, YOU'D END UP AT THE SAME DAY TWELVE YEARS AGO.
IF YOU STAY FOR A WEEK IN THE PAST, THEN RETURN TO THE PRESENT, ONE WEEK WILL HAVE PASSED IN THE PRESENT AS WELL.
CHAPTER 7: REJOIN
IN OTHER WORDS, IF YOU GO TO THE PAST FOR A WEEK...
TAP
TAP
WEEK LATER
PRESENT DAY TIME AXIS
PAST TIME AXIS
YOUR CON-SCIOUSNESS IS ALSO IN THE PAST FOR THAT LONG.
GULP
LEAVING AN EMPTY VESSEL IN THE PRESENT.
TIME AXIS

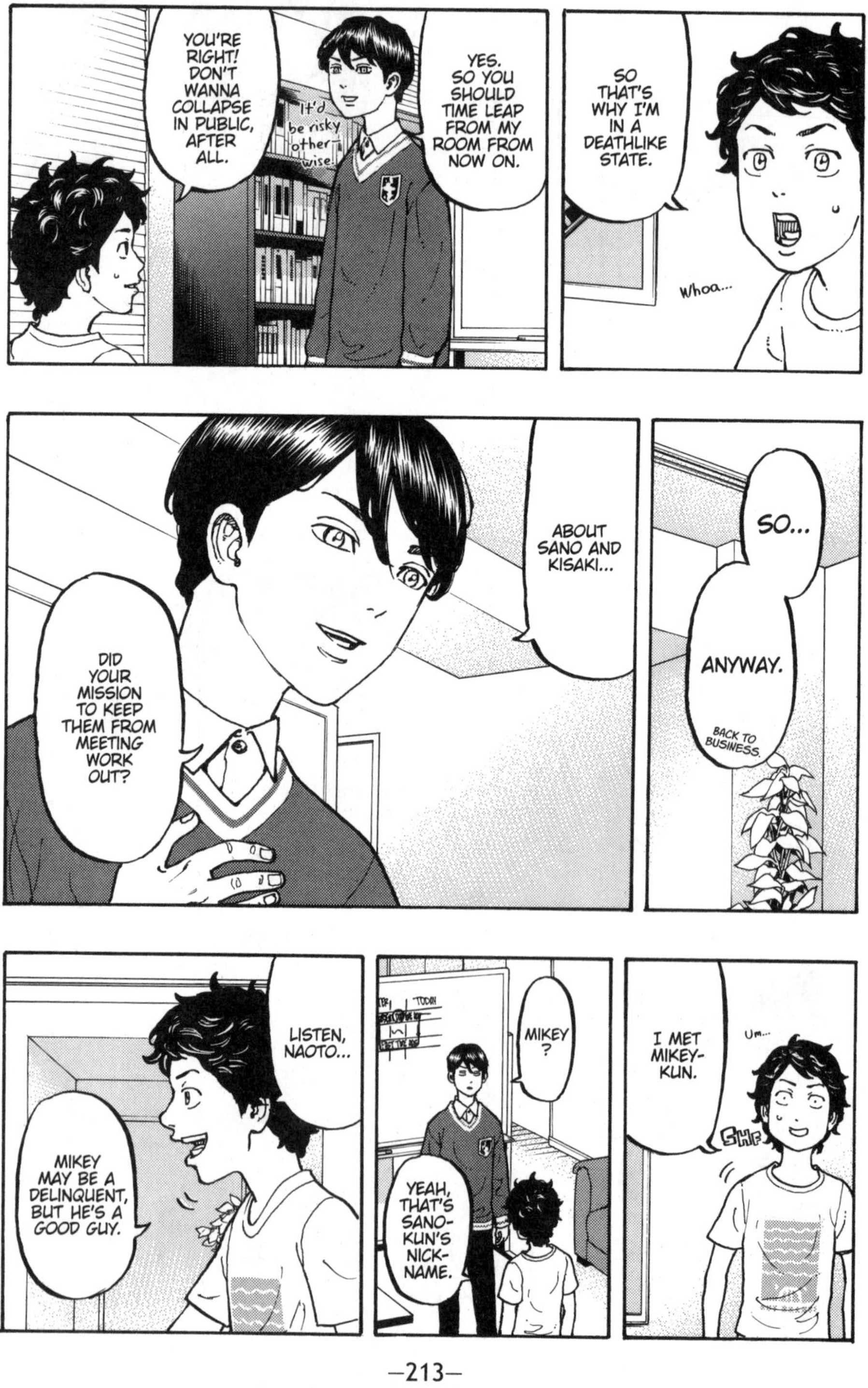
SO THAT'S WHY I'M IN A DEATHLIKE STATE.
Whoa...
YES. SO YOU SHOULD TIME LEAP FROM MY ROOM FROM NOW ON.
It'd be risky otherwise.
YOU'RE RIGHT! DON'T WANNA COLLAPSE IN PUBLIC, AFTER ALL.
SO...
ANYWAY.
BACK TO BUSINESS.
ABOUT SANO AND KISAKI...
DID YOUR MISSION TO KEEP THEM FROM MEETING WORK OUT?
Um...
I MET MIKEY-KUN.
SHF
MIKEY?
YEAH, THAT'S SANO-KUN'S NICKNAME.
LISTEN, NAOTO...
MIKEY MAY BE A DELINQUENT, BUT HE'S A GOOD GUY.

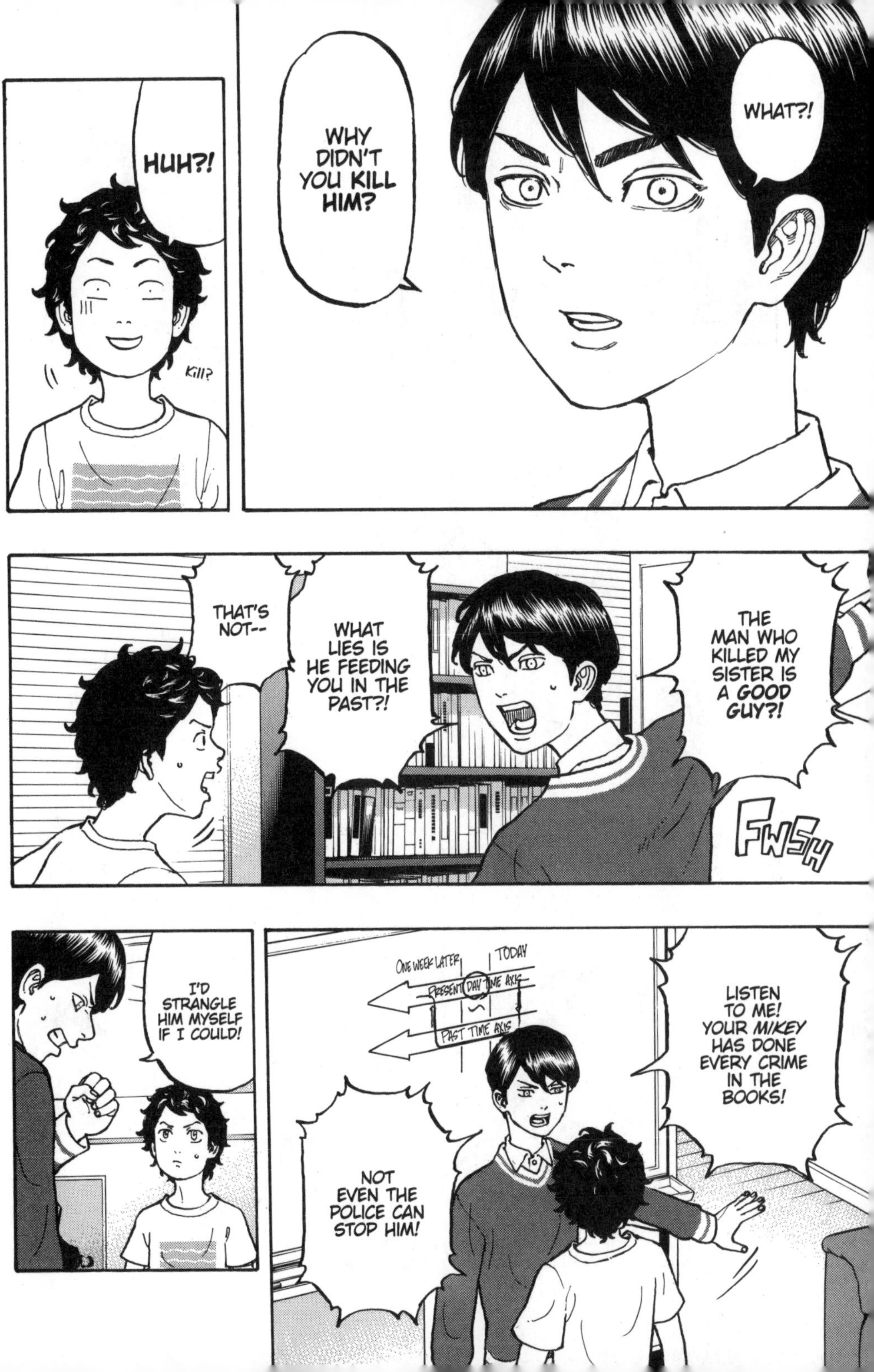
WHAT?!
WHY DIDN'T YOU KILL HIM?
HUH?!
Kill?
THE MAN WHO KILLED MY SISTER IS A GOOD GUY?!
FWSH
WHAT LIES IS HE FEEDING YOU IN THE PAST?!
THAT'S NOT--
LISTEN TO ME! YOUR MIKEY HAS DONE EVERY CRIME IN THE BOOKS!
TODAY
ONE WEEK LATER
PRESENT DAY TIME AXIS
PAST TIME AXIS
NOT EVEN THE POLICE CAN STOP HIM!
I'D STRANGLE HIM MYSELF IF I COULD!

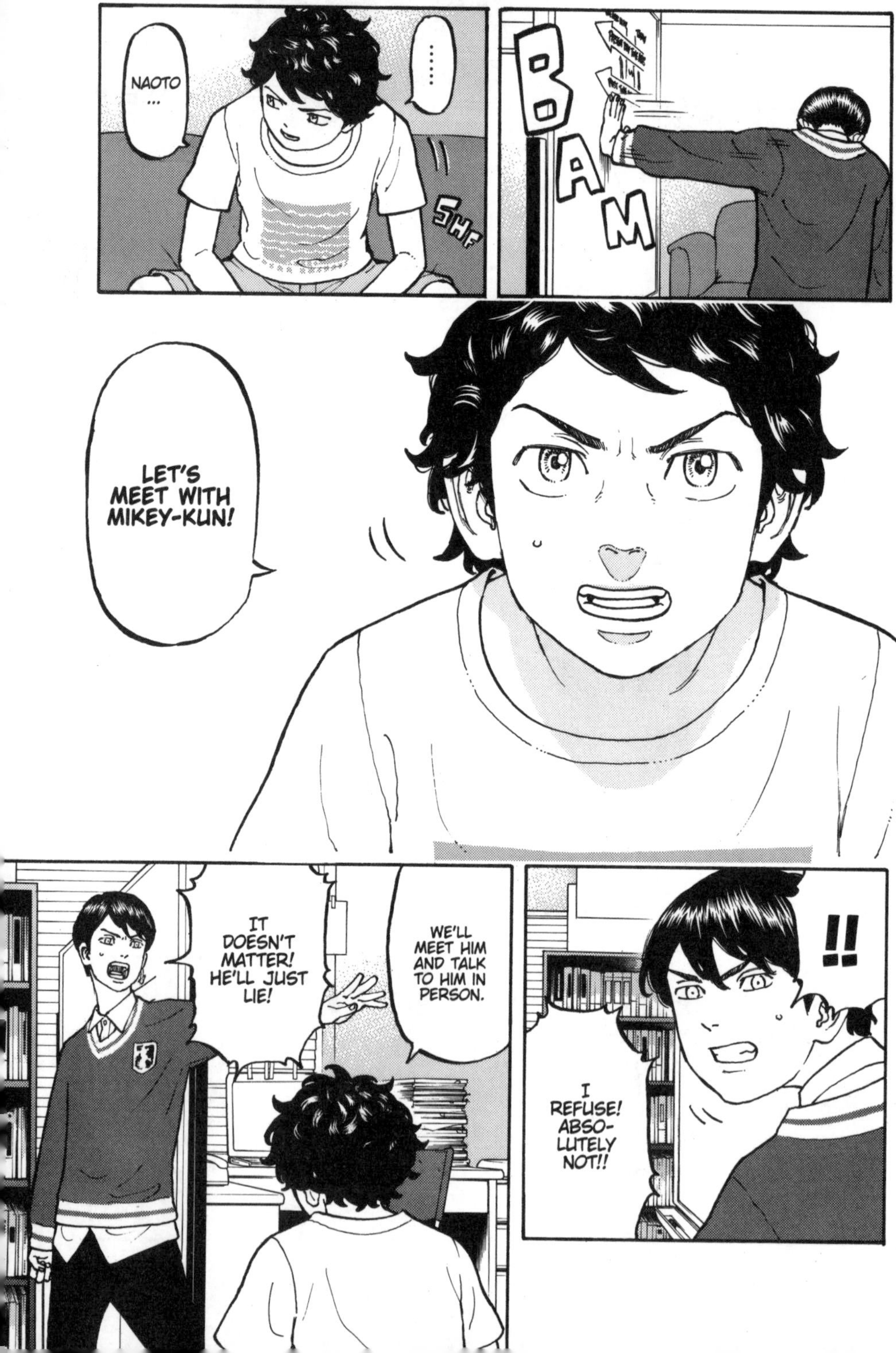
BAM
......
NAOTO ...
SHF
LET'S MEET WITH MIKEY-KUN!
!!
I REFUSE! ABSO-LUTELY NOT!!
WE'LL MEET HIM AND TALK TO HIM IN PERSON.
IT DOESN'T MATTER! HE'LL JUST LIE!

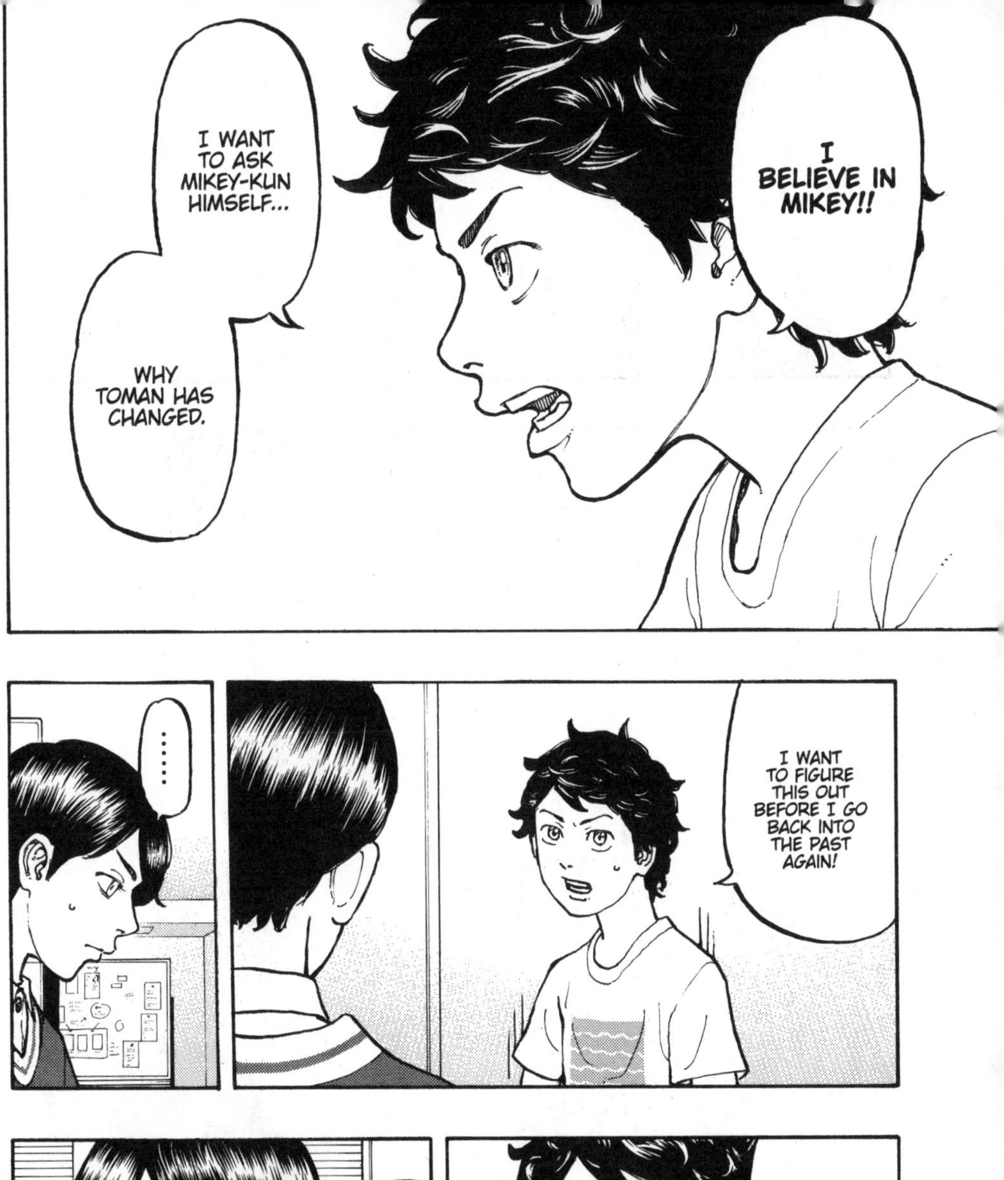
I BELIEVE IN MIKEY!!
I WANT TO ASK MIKEY-KUN HIMSELF...
WHY TOMAN HAS CHANGED.
I WANT TO FIGURE THIS OUT BEFORE I GO BACK INTO THE PAST AGAIN!
......
LET'S SEARCH FOR MIKEY-KUN TOGETHER!
PLEASE, NAOTO!

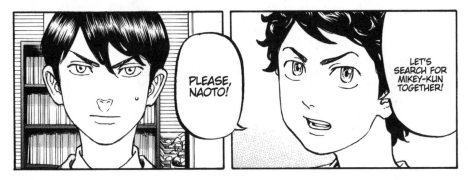

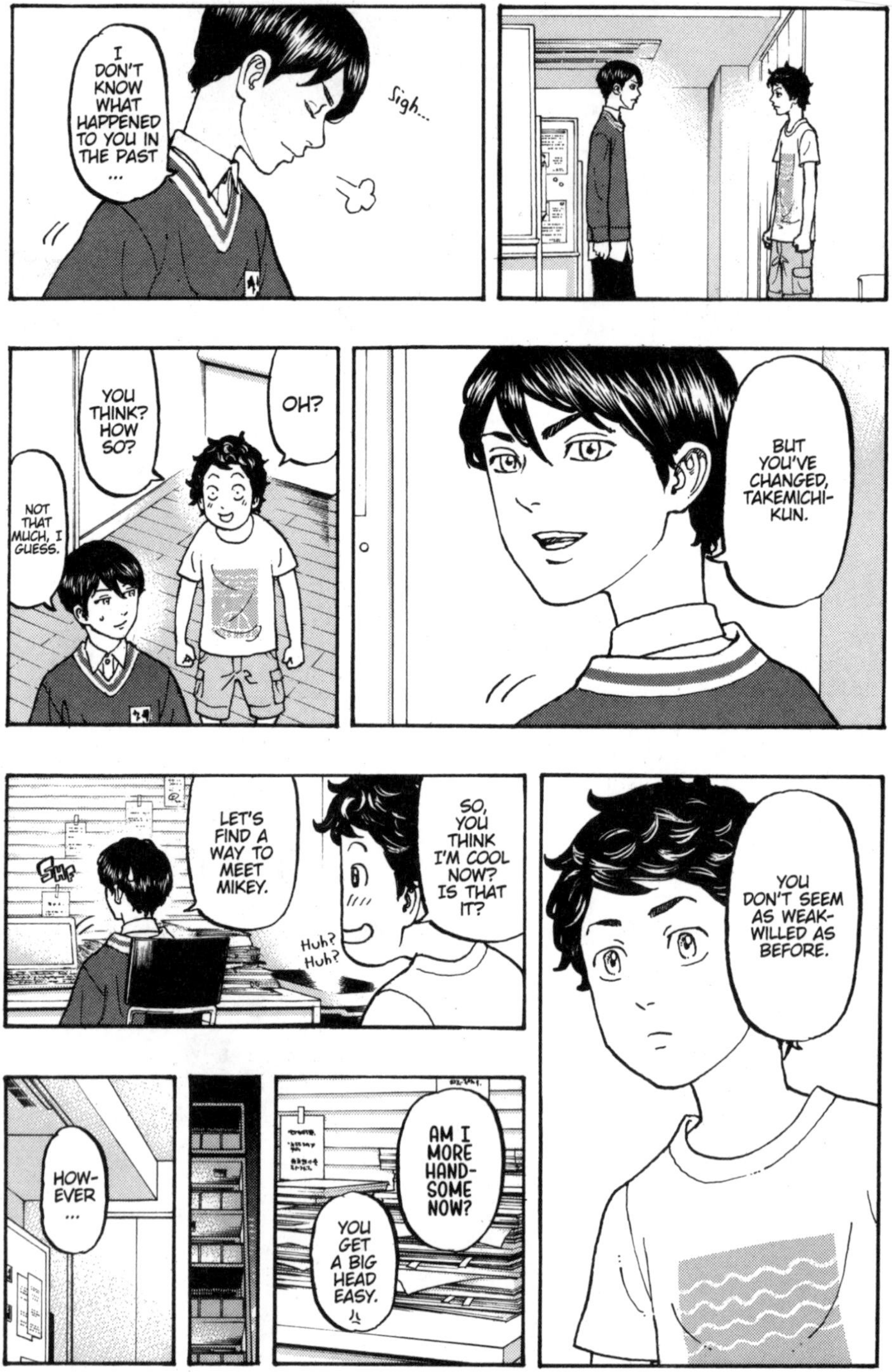
Sigh...
I DON'T KNOW WHAT HAPPENED TO YOU IN THE PAST ...
BUT YOU'VE CHANGED, TAKEMICHI-KUN.
OH?
YOU THINK? HOW SO?
NOT THAT MUCH, I GUESS.
YOU DON'T SEEM AS WEAK-WILLED AS BEFORE.
SO, YOU THINK I'M COOL NOW? IS THAT IT?
Huh? Huh?
LET'S FIND A WAY TO MEET MIKEY.
SHP
AM I MORE HAND-SOME NOW?
YOU GET A BIG HEAD EASY.
HOW-EVER ...

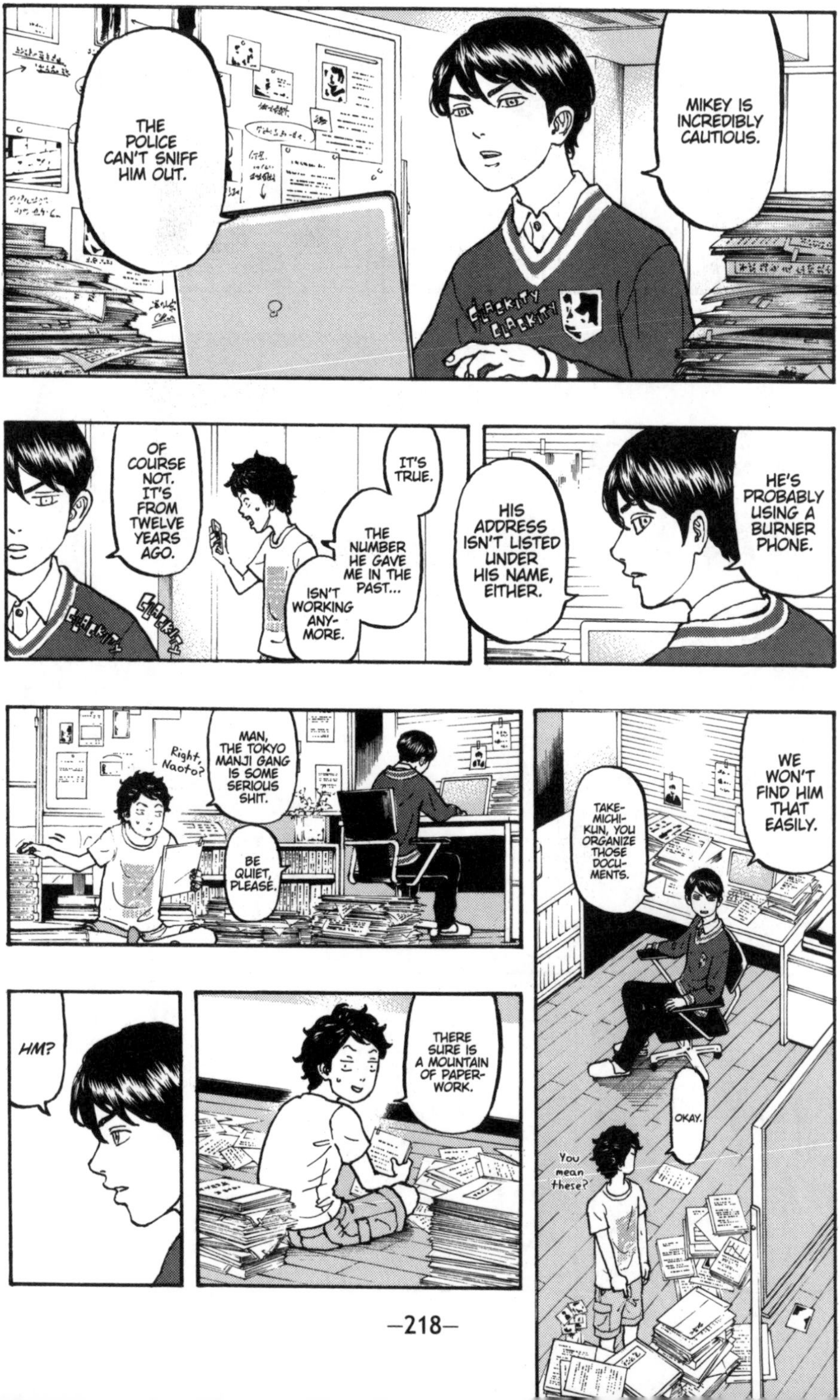
MIKEY IS INCREDIBLY CAUTIOUS.
THE POLICE CAN'T SNIFF HIM OUT.
CLACKITY CLACKITY
HE'S PROBABLY USING A BURNER PHONE.
HIS ADDRESS ISN'T LISTED UNDER HIS NAME, EITHER.
IT'S TRUE.
THE NUMBER HE GAVE ME IN THE PAST...
ISN'T WORKING ANYMORE.
OF COURSE NOT. IT'S FROM TWELVE YEARS AGO.
WE WON'T FIND HIM THAT EASILY.
TAKE-MICHI-KUN, YOU ORGANIZE THOSE DOCUMENTS.
OKAY.
You mean these?
MAN, THE TOKYO MANJI GANG IS SOME SERIOUS SHIT.
Right, Naoto?
BE QUIET, PLEASE.
THERE SURE IS A MOUNTAIN OF PAPERWORK.
HM?

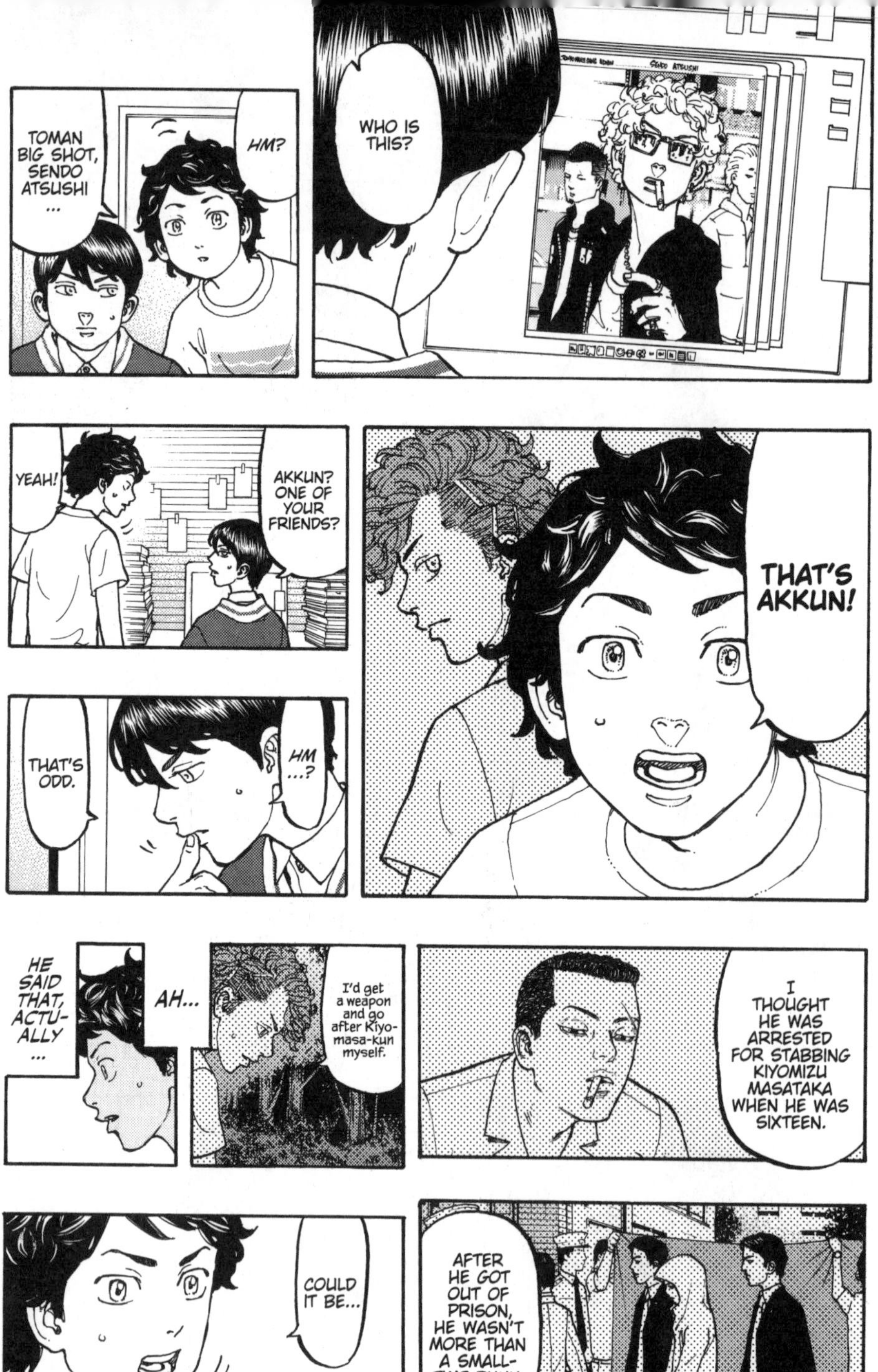

WHO IS THIS?
SENDO ATSUSHI
HM?
TOMAN BIG SHOT, SENDO ATSUSHI ...
THAT'S AKKUN!
AKKUN? ONE OF YOUR FRIENDS?
YEAH!
HM ...?
THAT'S ODD.
I THOUGHT HE WAS ARRESTED FOR STABBING KIYOMIZU MASATAKA WHEN HE WAS SIXTEEN.
I'd get a weapon and go after Kiyomasa-kun myself.
AH...
HE SAID THAT, ACTUALLY ...
AFTER HE GOT OUT OF PRISON, HE WASN'T MORE THAN A SMALL-TIME PUNK.
COULD IT BE...

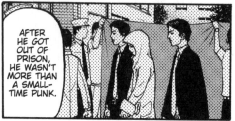

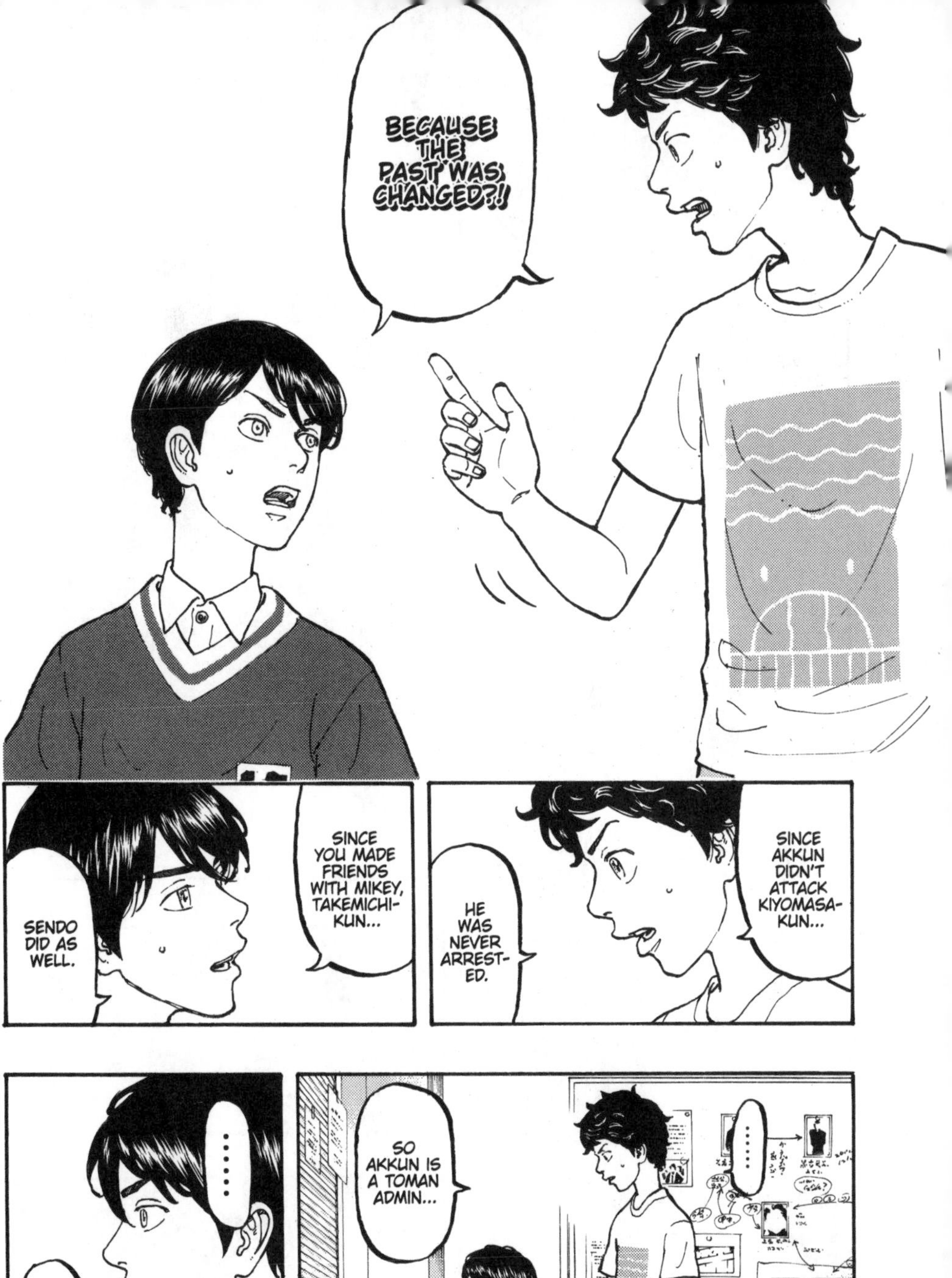

BECAUSE THE PAST WAS CHANGED?!
SINCE AKKUN DIDN'T ATTACK KIYOMASA-KUN...
HE WAS NEVER ARREST-ED.
SINCE YOU MADE FRIENDS WITH MIKEY, TAKEMICHI-KUN...
SENDO DID AS WELL.
......
SO AKKUN IS A TOMAN ADMIN...
......
!

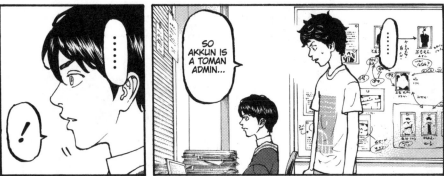

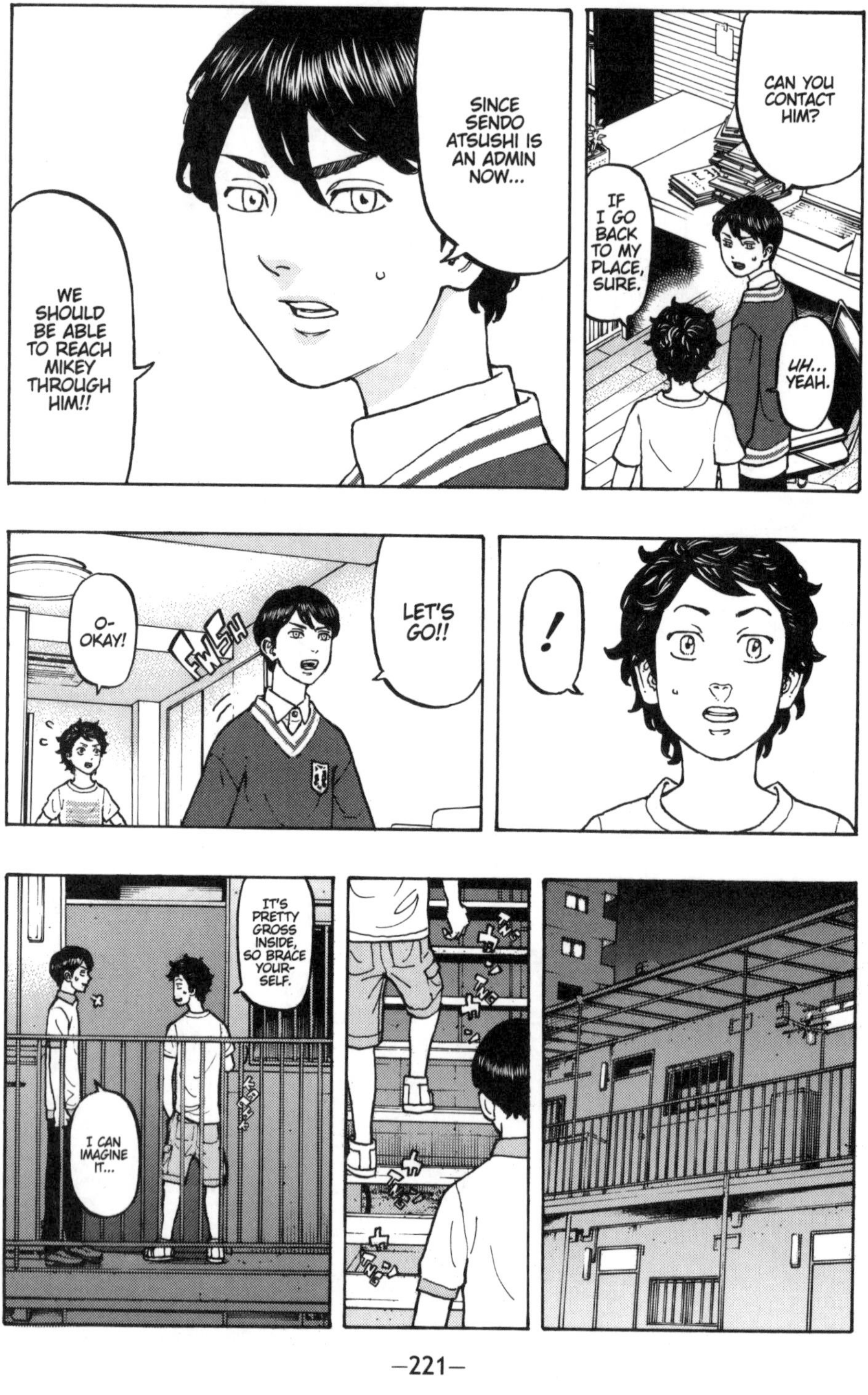
CAN YOU CONTACT HIM?
IF I GO BACK TO MY PLACE, SURE.
UH... YEAH.
SINCE SENDO ATSUSHI IS AN ADMIN NOW...
WE SHOULD BE ABLE TO REACH MIKEY THROUGH HIM!!
!
LET'S GO!!
FWSH
O-OKAY!
IT'S PRETTY GROSS INSIDE, SO BRACE YOURSELF.
I CAN IMAGINE IT...

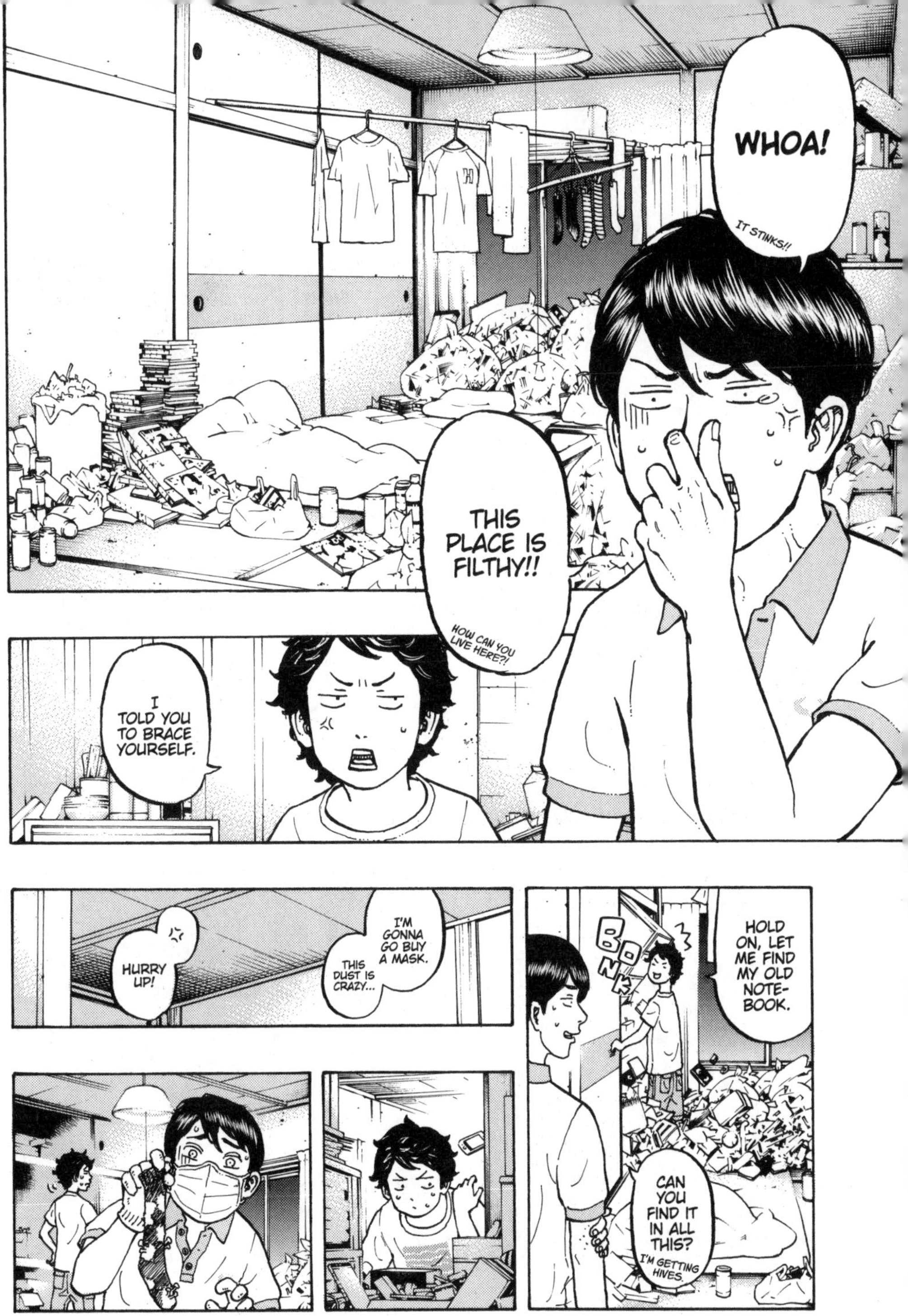
WHOA!
IT STINKS!!
THIS PLACE IS FILTHY!!
HOW CAN YOU LIVE HERE?!
I TOLD YOU TO BRACE YOURSELF.
HOLD ON, LET ME FIND MY OLD NOTE-BOOK.
BONK
CAN YOU FIND IT IN ALL THIS?
I'M GETTING HIVES.
I'M GONNA GO BUY A MASK.
THIS DUST IS CRAZY...
HURRY UP!

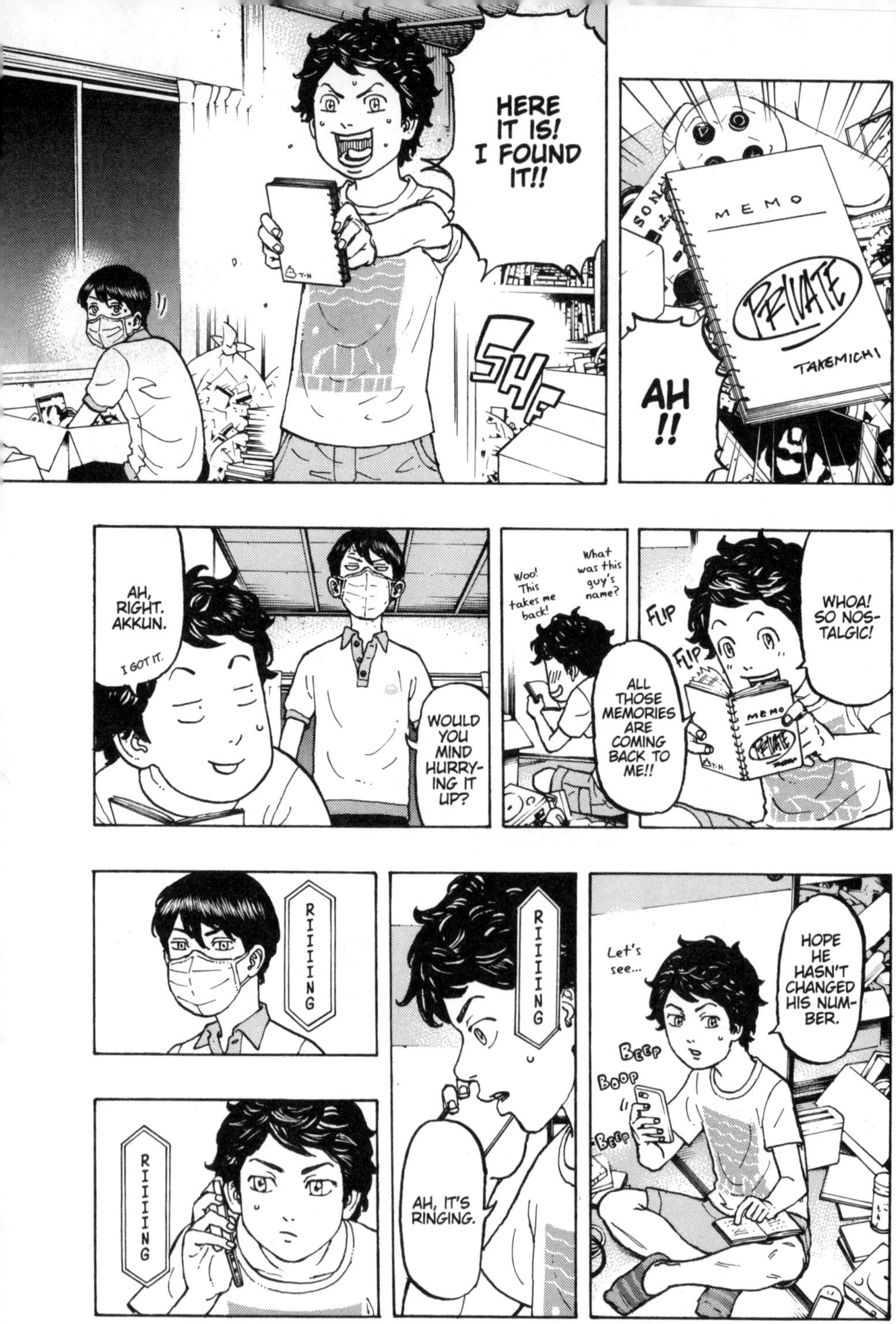
MEMO
PRIVATE
TAKEMICHI
AH!!
HERE IT IS! I FOUND IT!!
T·H
SHF
WHOA! SO NOSTALGIC!
FLIP
FLIP
ALL THOSE MEMORIES ARE COMING BACK TO ME!!
MEMO
PRIVATE
What was this guy's name?
Woo! This takes me back!
WOULD YOU MIND HURRYING IT UP?
AH, RIGHT. AKKUN.
I GOT IT.
HOPE HE HASN'T CHANGED HIS NUMBER.
Let's see...
BEEP
BOOP
BEEP
RIIIING
AH, IT'S RINGING.
RIIIING
RIIIING

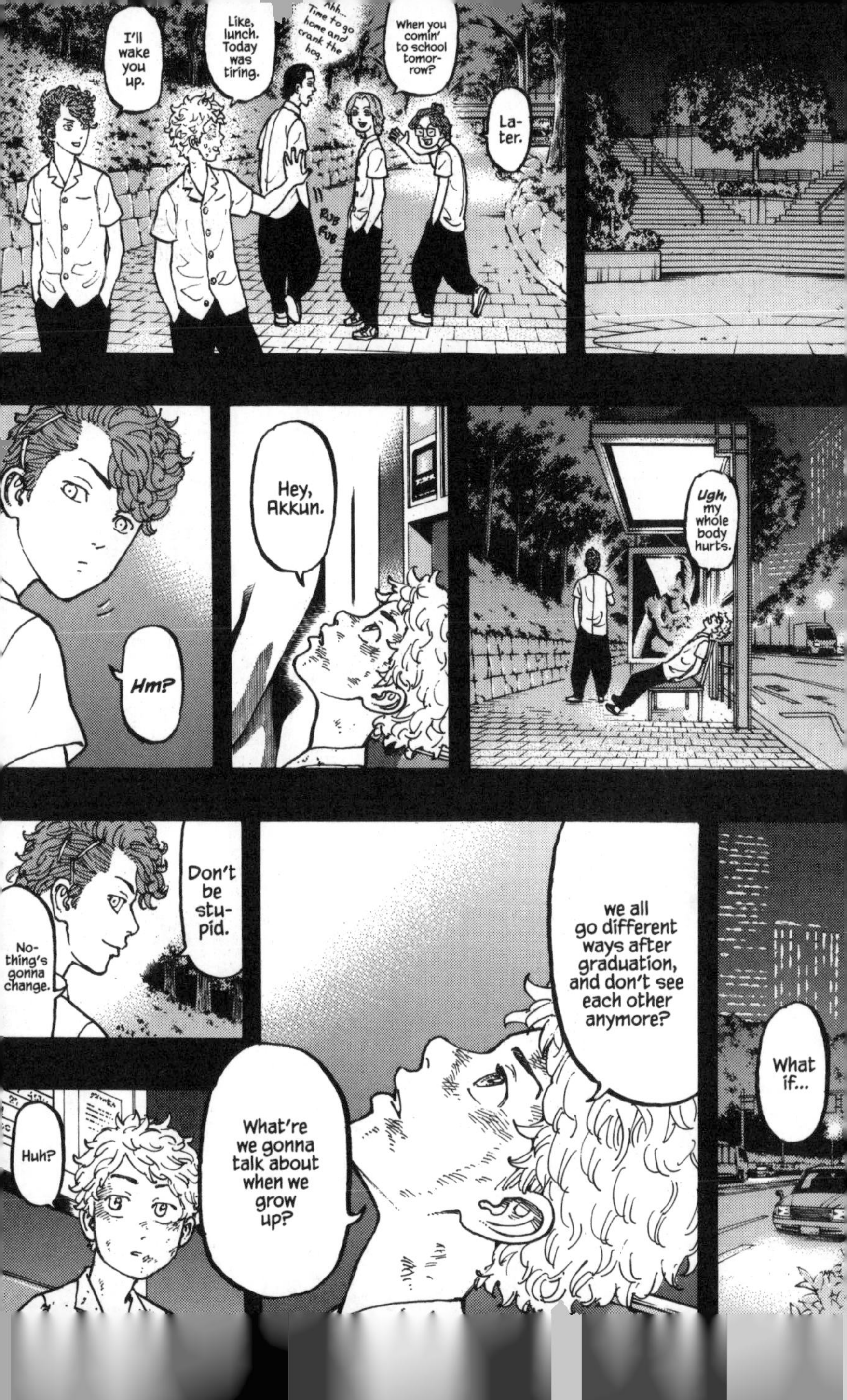
La-ter.
When you comin' to school tomor-row?
Ahh... Time to go home and crank the hog.
Like, lunch. Today was tiring.
RUB RUB
I'll wake you up.
Ugh, my whole body hurts.
Hey, Akkun.
Hm?
What if...
we all go different ways after graduation, and don't see each other anymore?
What're we gonna talk about when we grow up?
Don't be stu-pid.
No-thing's gonna change.
Huh?

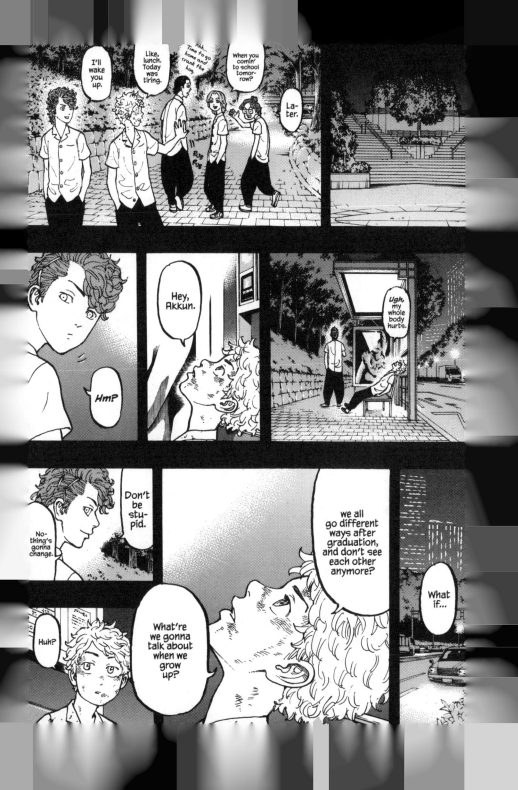

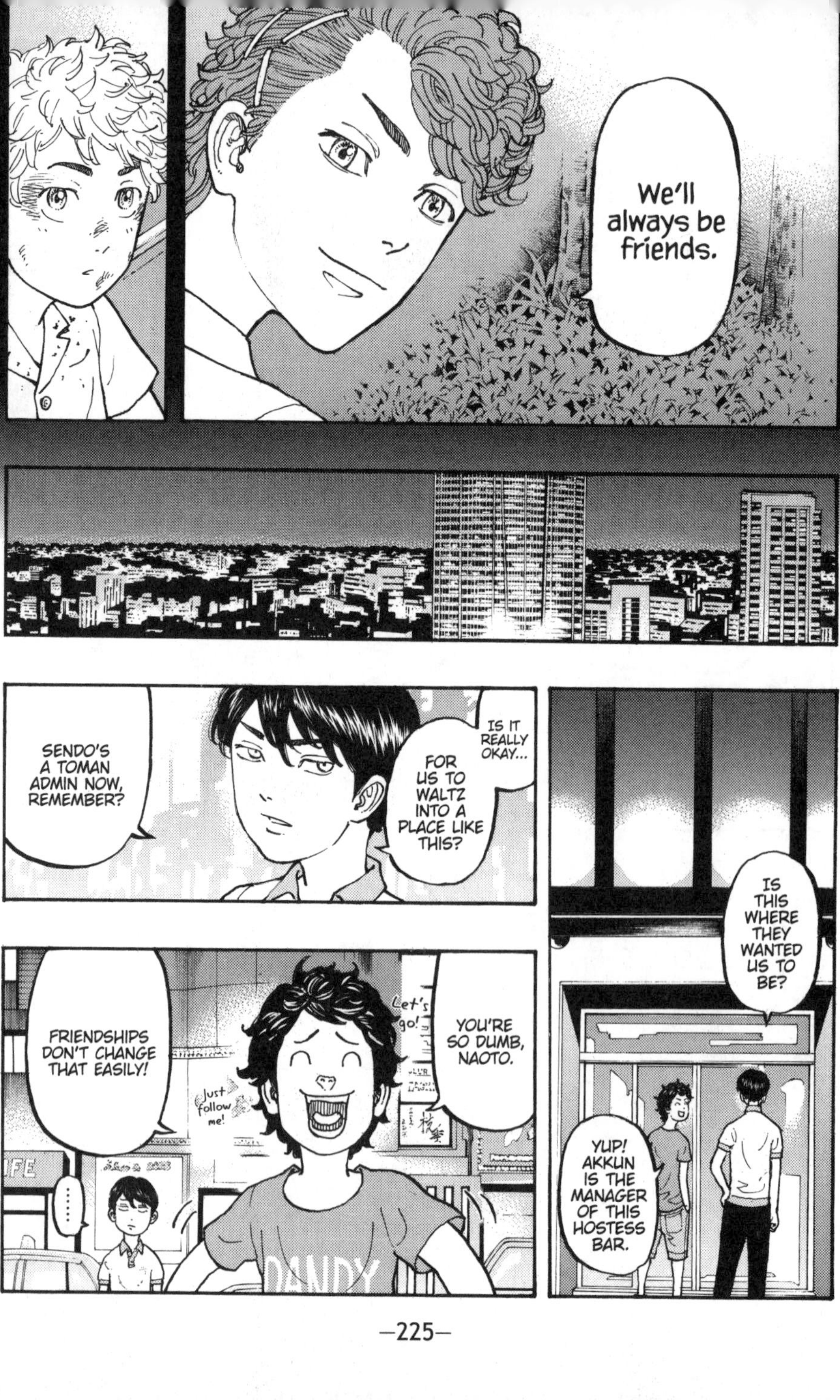
We'll always be friends.
IS THIS WHERE THEY WANTED US TO BE?
YUP! AKKUN IS THE MANAGER OF THIS HOSTESS BAR.
IS IT REALLY OKAY...
FOR US TO WALTZ INTO A PLACE LIKE THIS?
SENDO'S A TOMAN ADMIN NOW, REMEMBER?
YOU'RE SO DUMB, NAOTO.
Let's go!
Just follow me!
FRIENDSHIPS DON'T CHANGE THAT EASILY!
......
DANDY

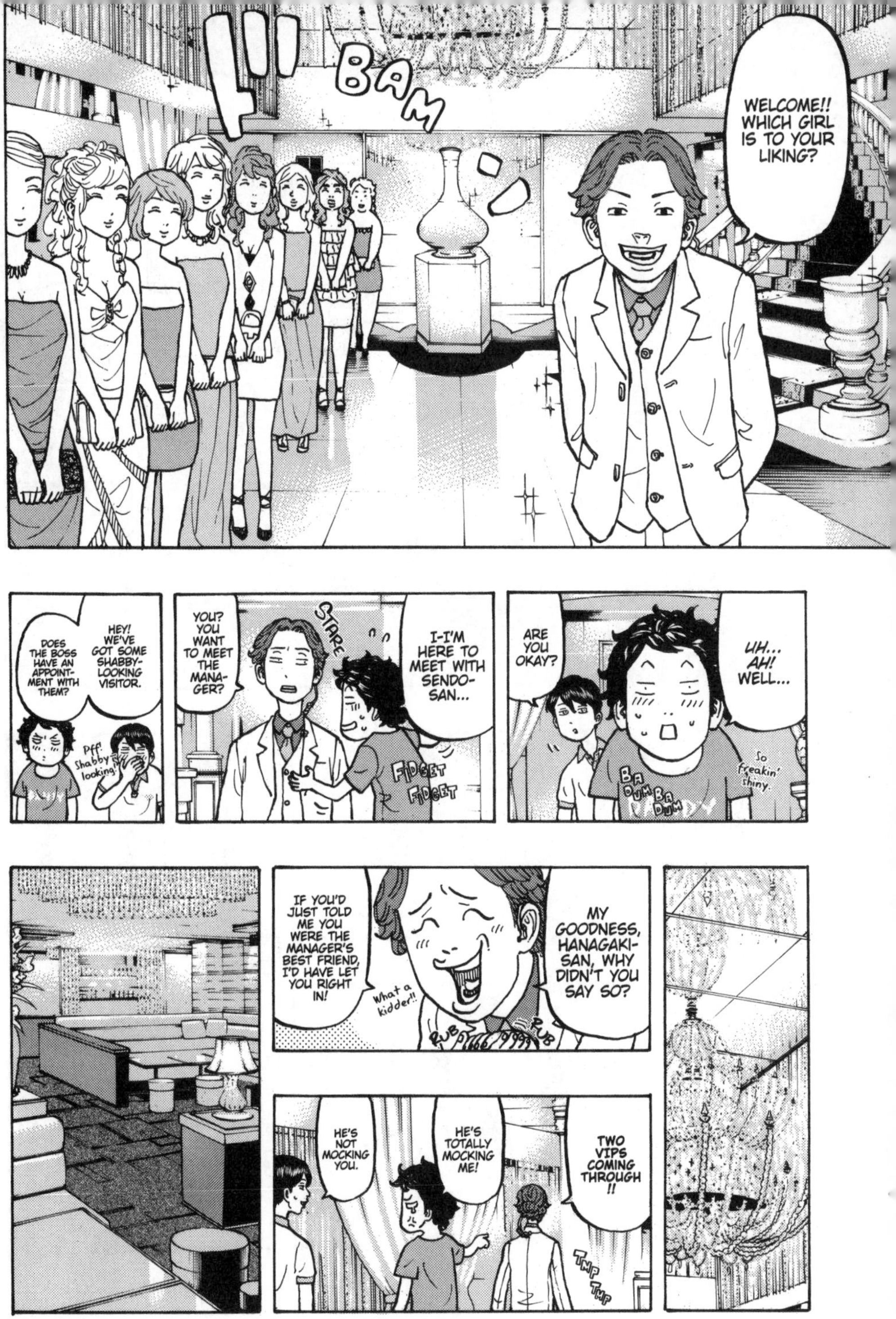
BAM
WELCOME!! WHICH GIRL IS TO YOUR LIKING?
UH... AH! WELL...
So freakin' shiny.
BA DUM BA DUM
ARE YOU OKAY?
I-I'M HERE TO MEET WITH SENDO-SAN...
STARE
YOU? YOU WANT TO MEET THE MANA-GER?
FIDGET FIDGET
HEY! WE'VE GOT SOME SHABBY-LOOKING VISITOR.
DOES THE BOSS HAVE AN APPOINT-MENT WITH THEM?
Pff! Shabby looking!
MY GOODNESS, HANAGAKI-SAN, WHY DIDN'T YOU SAY SO?
IF YOU'D JUST TOLD ME YOU WERE THE MANAGER'S BEST FRIEND, I'D HAVE LET YOU RIGHT IN!
What a kidder!!
RUB RUB
TWO VIPS COMING THROUGH!!
TMP TMP
HE'S TOTALLY MOCKING ME!
HE'S NOT MOCKING YOU.

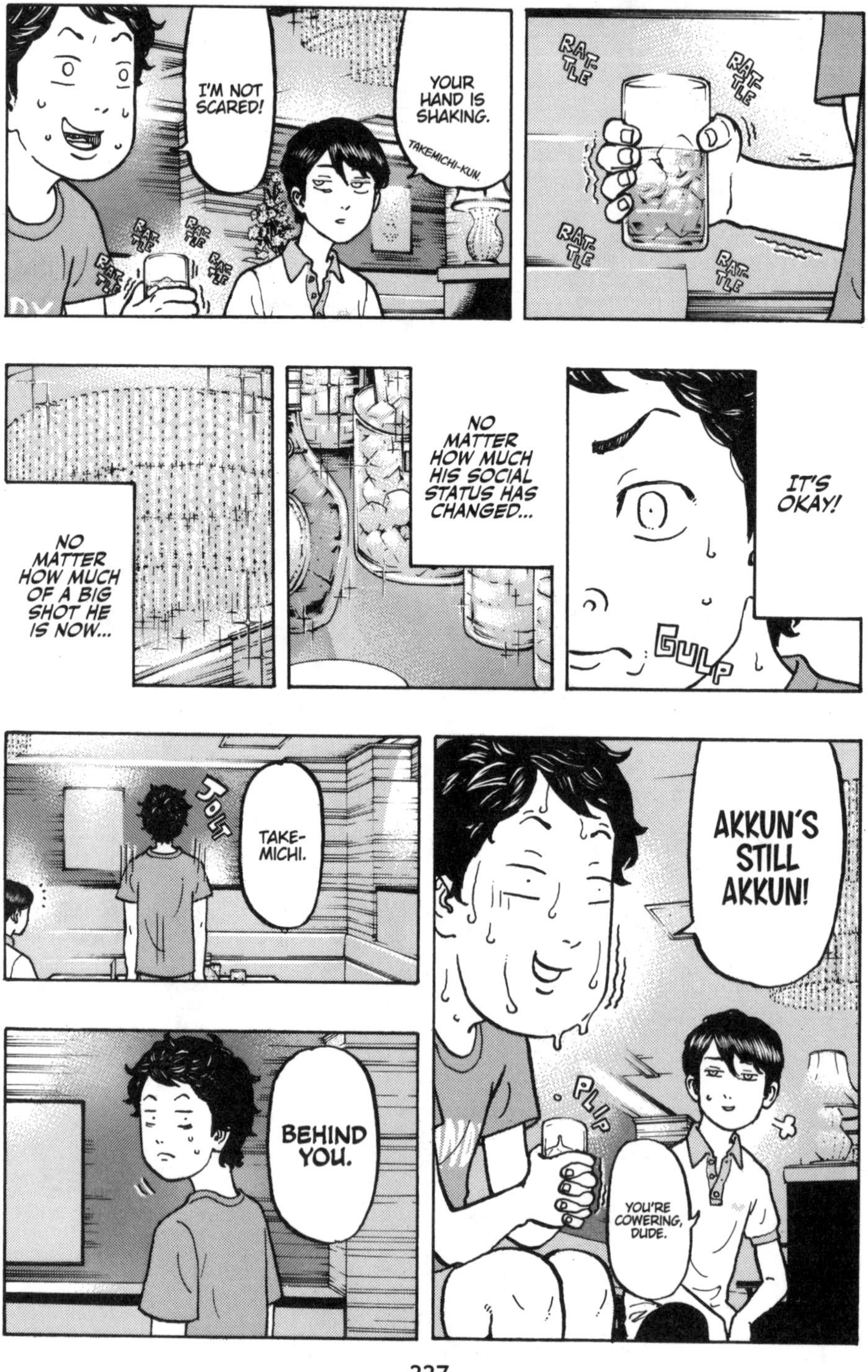
RATTLE
RATTLE
RATTLE
RATTLE
YOUR HAND IS SHAKING.
TAKEMICHI-KUN.
I'M NOT SCARED!
RATTLE
RATTLE
RATTLE
RATTLE
IT'S OKAY!
GULP
NO MATTER HOW MUCH HIS SOCIAL STATUS HAS CHANGED...
NO MATTER HOW MUCH OF A BIG SHOT HE IS NOW...
AKKUN'S STILL AKKUN!
PLIP
YOU'RE COWERING, DUDE.
TAKE-MICHI.
JOLT
BEHIND YOU.

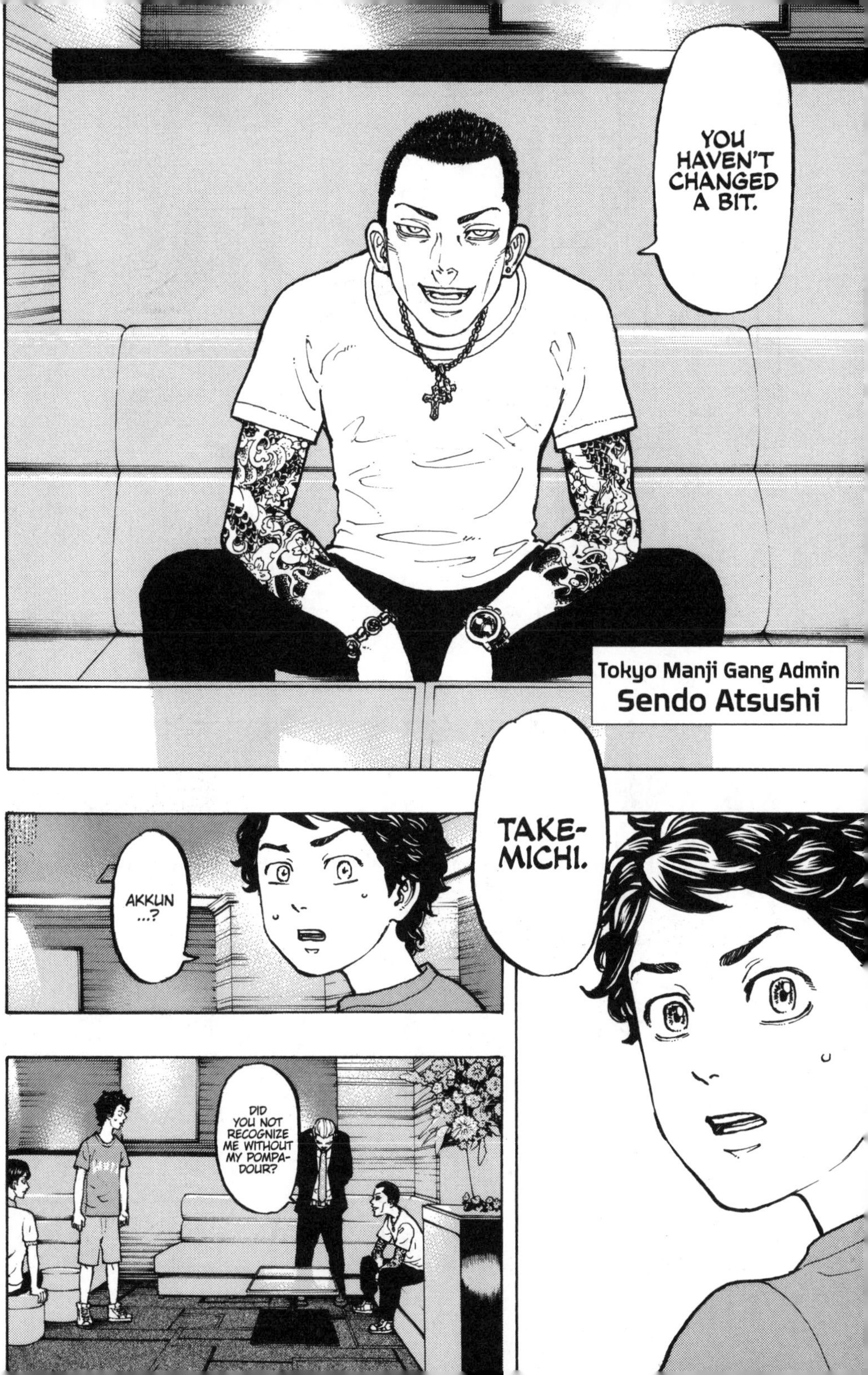
YOU HAVEN'T CHANGED A BIT.
Tokyo Manji Gang Admin
Sendo Atsushi
TAKE-MICHI.
AKKUN ...?
DID YOU NOT RECOGNIZE ME WITHOUT MY POMPA-DOUR?

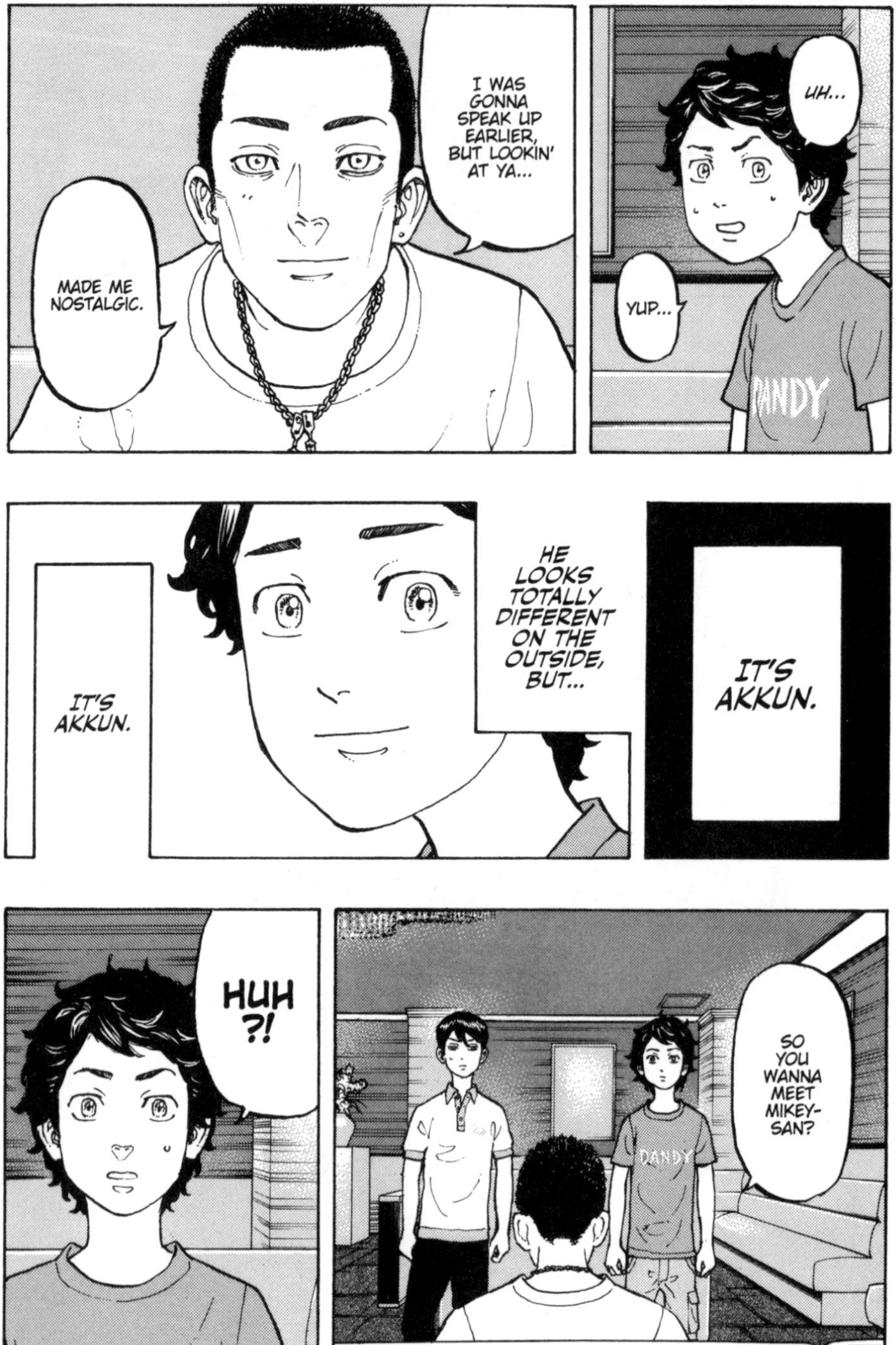
UH...
YUP...
DANDY
I WAS GONNA SPEAK UP EARLIER, BUT LOOKIN' AT YA...
MADE ME NOSTALGIC.
IT'S AKKUN.
HE LOOKS TOTALLY DIFFERENT ON THE OUTSIDE, BUT...
IT'S AKKUN.
SO YOU WANNA MEET MIKEY-SAN?
DANDY
HUH ?!

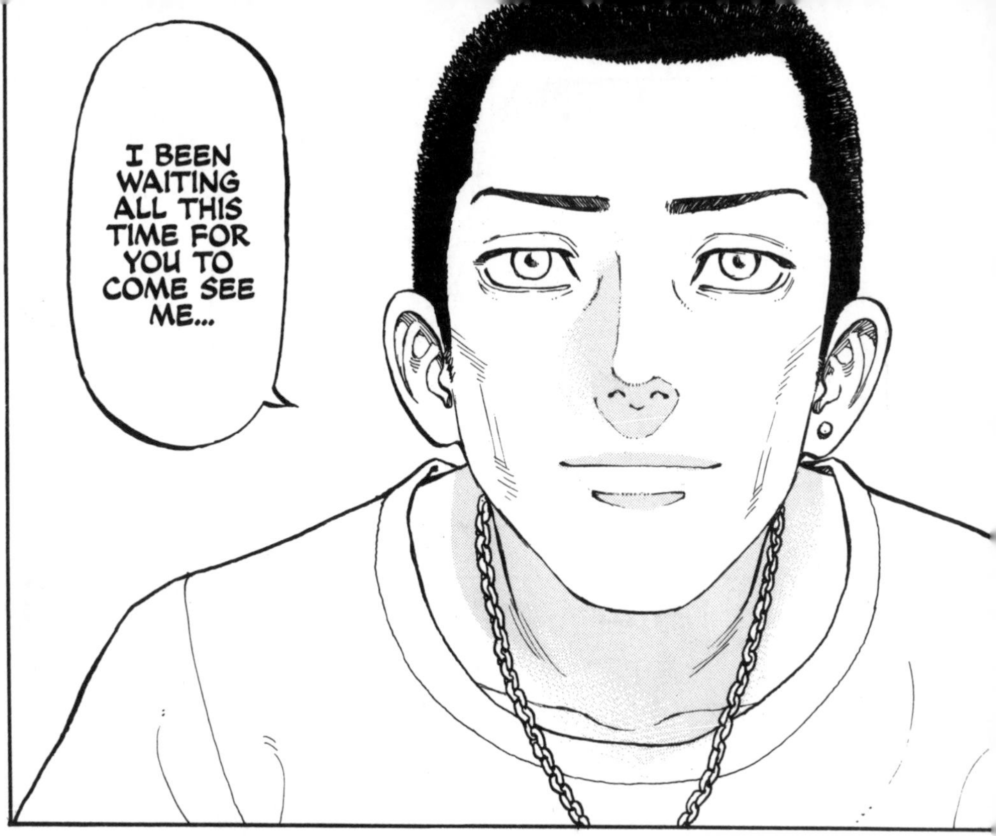
I BEEN WAITING ALL THIS TIME FOR YOU TO COME SEE ME...

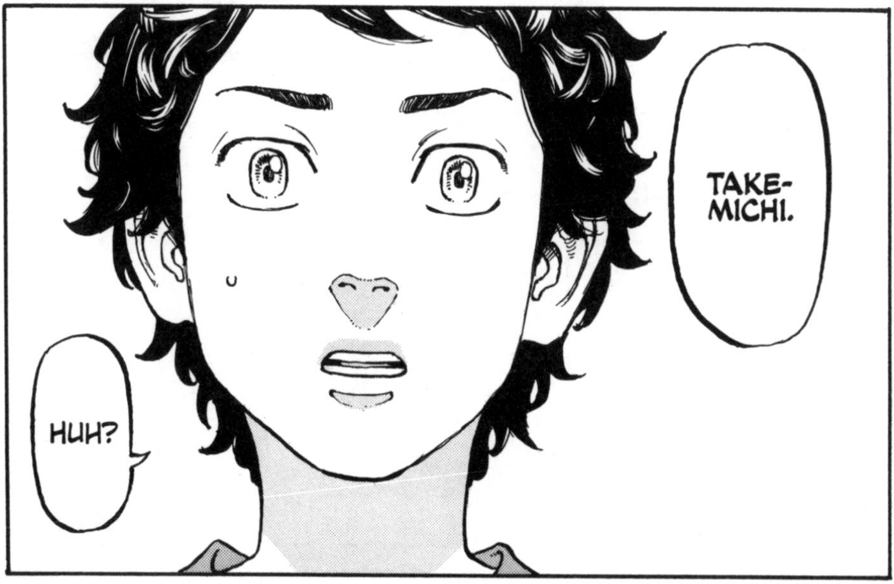
TAKE-MICHI.
HUH?

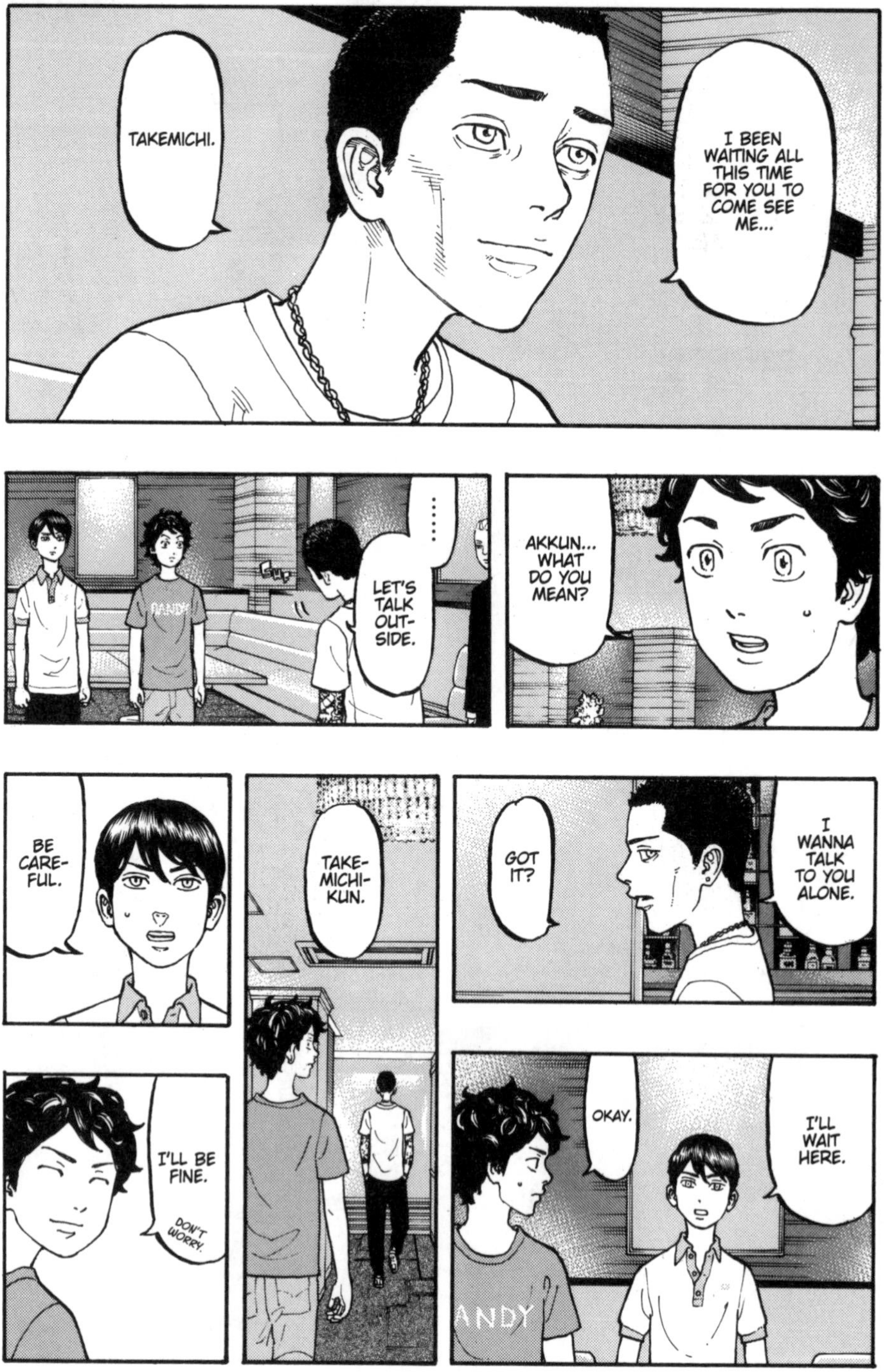
I BEEN WAITING ALL THIS TIME FOR YOU TO COME SEE ME...
TAKEMICHI.
AKKUN... WHAT DO YOU MEAN?
......
LET'S TALK OUT-SIDE.
I WANNA TALK TO YOU ALONE.
GOT IT?
I'LL WAIT HERE.
OKAY.
TAKE-MICHI-KUN.
BE CARE-FUL.
I'LL BE FINE.
DON'T WORRY.

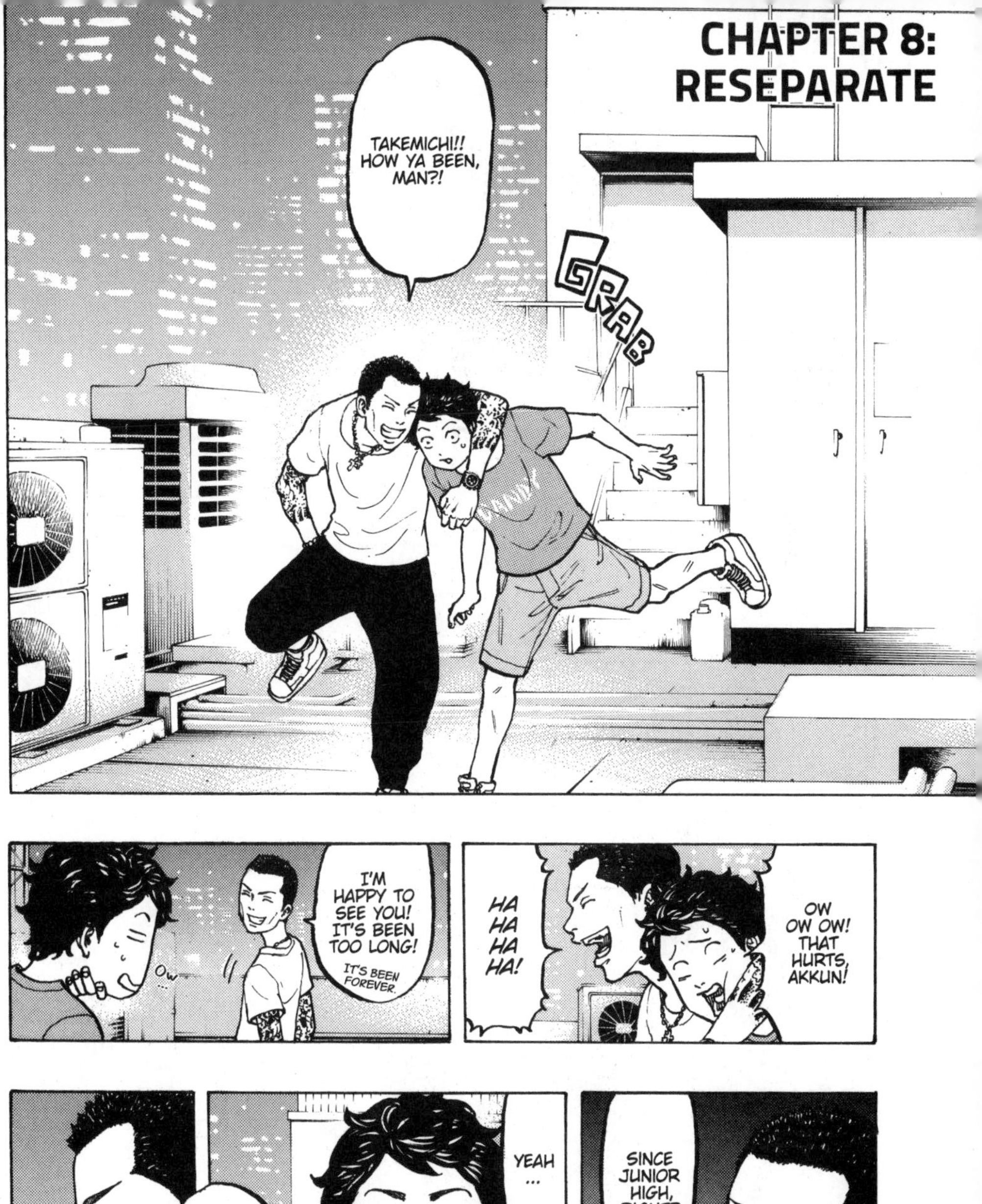
CHAPTER 8: RESEPARATE
TAKEMICHI!! HOW YA BEEN, MAN?!
GRAB
OW OW OW! THAT HURTS, AKKUN!
HA HA HA HA!
I'M HAPPY TO SEE YOU! IT'S BEEN TOO LONG!
IT'S BEEN FOREVER.
OW...
SINCE JUNIOR HIGH, RIGHT?
YEAH ...
IT'S BEEN LIKE TEN YEARS SINCE YOU'VE SEEN ME.
......

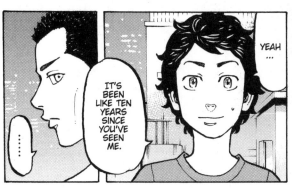

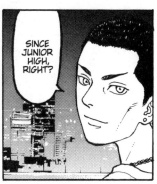

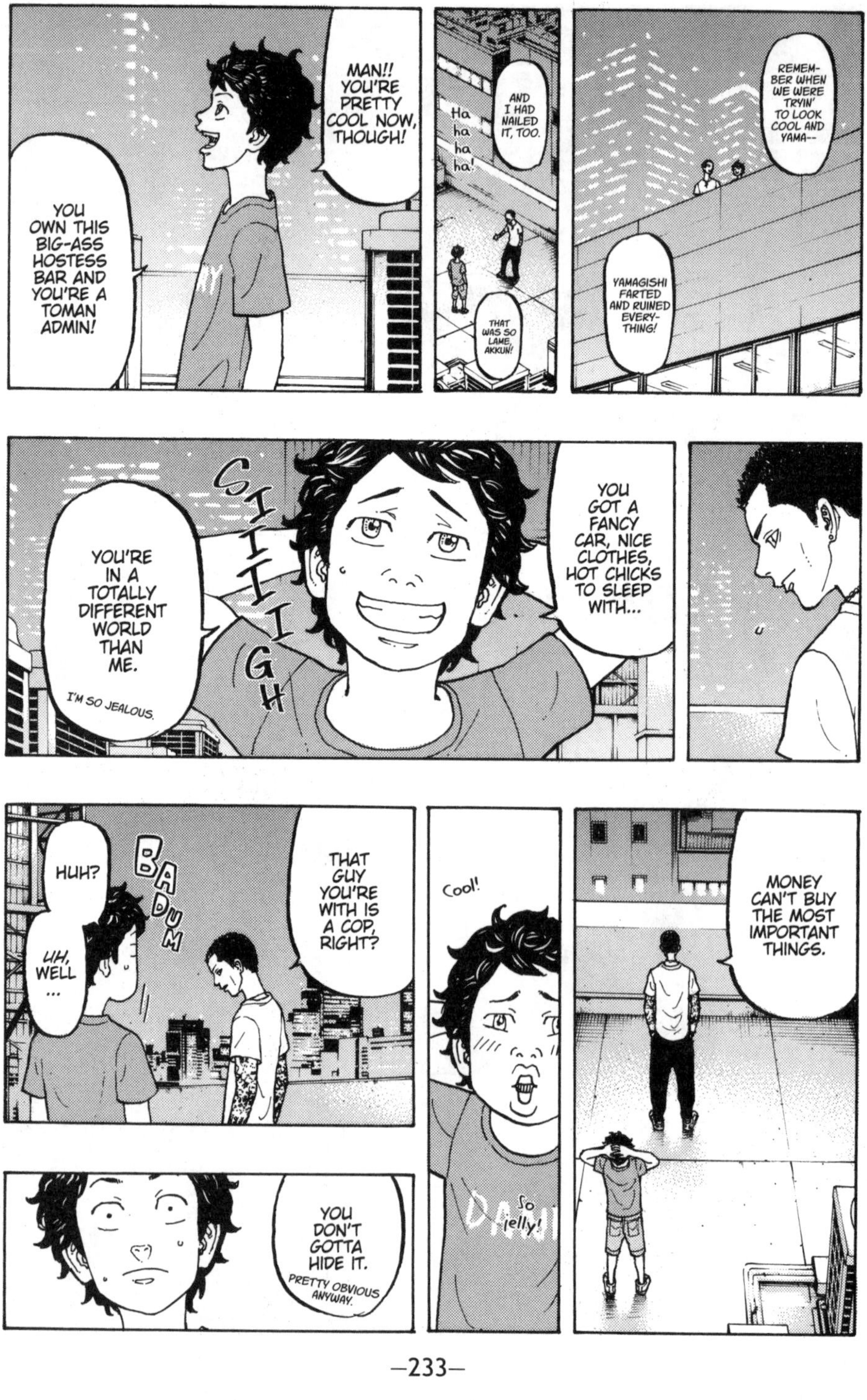
REMEMBER WHEN WE WERE TRYIN' TO LOOK COOL AND YAMA--
YAMAGISHI FARTED AND RUINED EVERYTHING!
AND I HAD NAILED IT, TOO.
Ha ha ha ha!
THAT WAS SO LAME, AKKUN!
MAN!! YOU'RE PRETTY COOL NOW, THOUGH!
YOU OWN THIS BIG-ASS HOSTESS BAR AND YOU'RE A TOMAN ADMIN!
YOU GOT A FANCY CAR, NICE CLOTHES, HOT CHICKS TO SLEEP WITH...
SIIIIGH
YOU'RE IN A TOTALLY DIFFERENT WORLD THAN ME.
I'M SO JEALOUS.
MONEY CAN'T BUY THE MOST IMPORTANT THINGS.
Cool!
So jelly!
THAT GUY YOU'RE WITH IS A COP, RIGHT?
BADUM
HUH?
UH, WELL ...
YOU DON'T GOTTA HIDE IT.
PRETTY OBVIOUS ANYWAY.

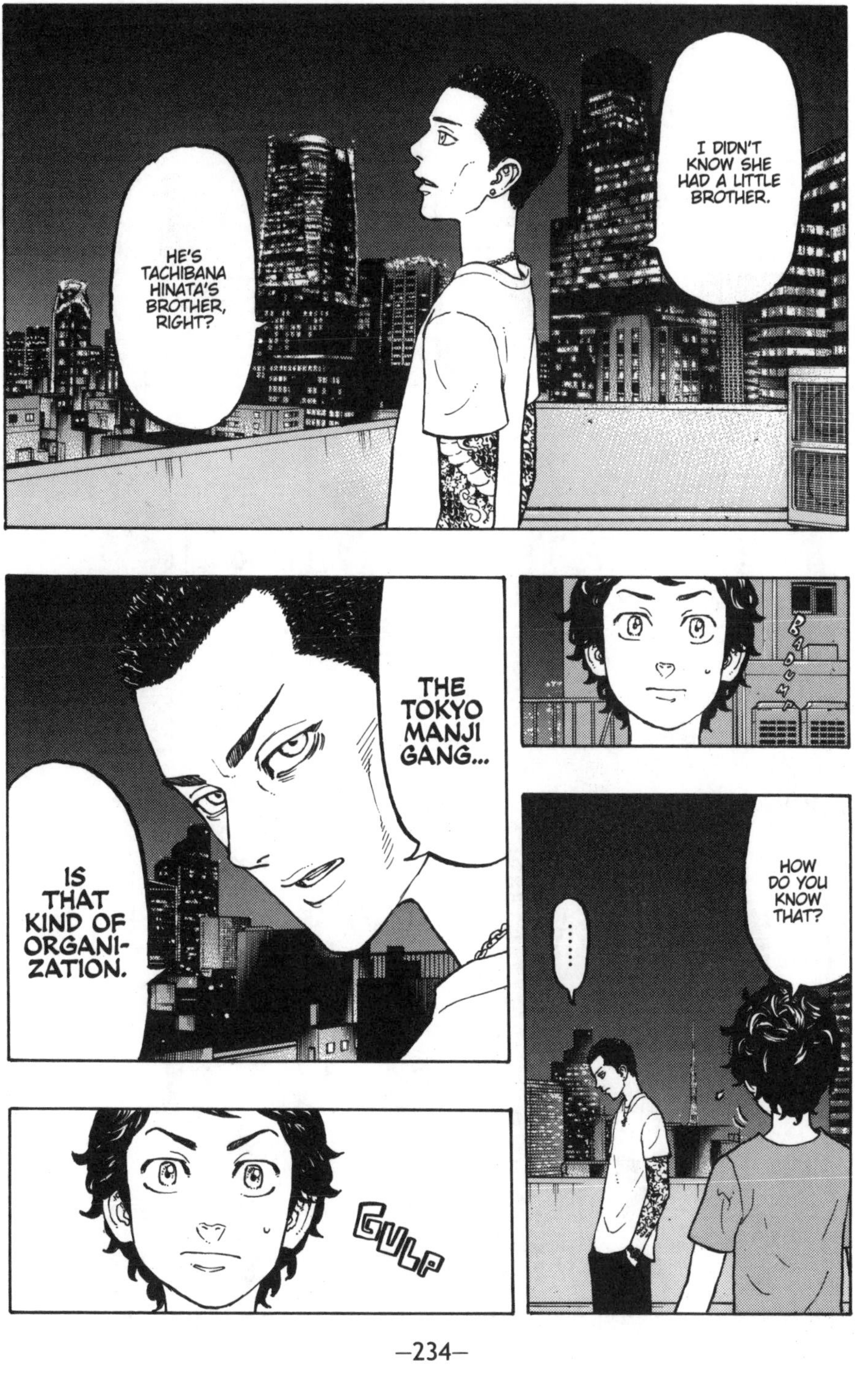
I DIDN'T KNOW SHE HAD A LITTLE BROTHER.
HE'S TACHIBANA HINATA'S BROTHER, RIGHT?
BADUMP
HOW DO YOU KNOW THAT?
......
THE TOKYO MANJI GANG...
IS THAT KIND OF ORGANIZATION.
GULP

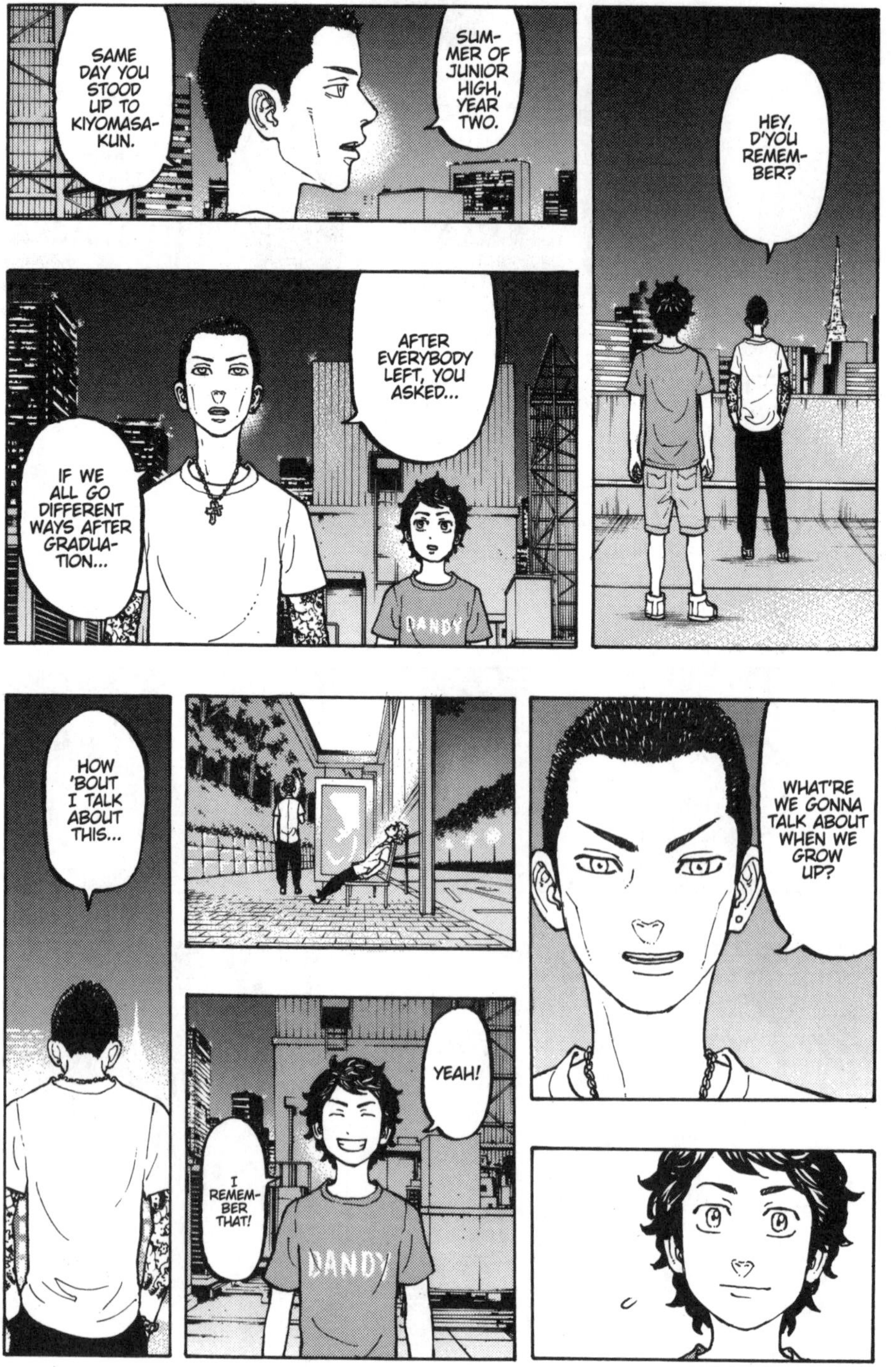
HEY, D'YOU REMEMBER?
SUMMER OF JUNIOR HIGH, YEAR TWO.
SAME DAY YOU STOOD UP TO KIYOMASA-KUN.
AFTER EVERYBODY LEFT, YOU ASKED...
IF WE ALL GO DIFFERENT WAYS AFTER GRADUATION...
DANDY
WHAT'RE WE GONNA TALK ABOUT WHEN WE GROW UP?
YEAH!
I REMEMBER THAT!
HOW 'BOUT I TALK ABOUT THIS...

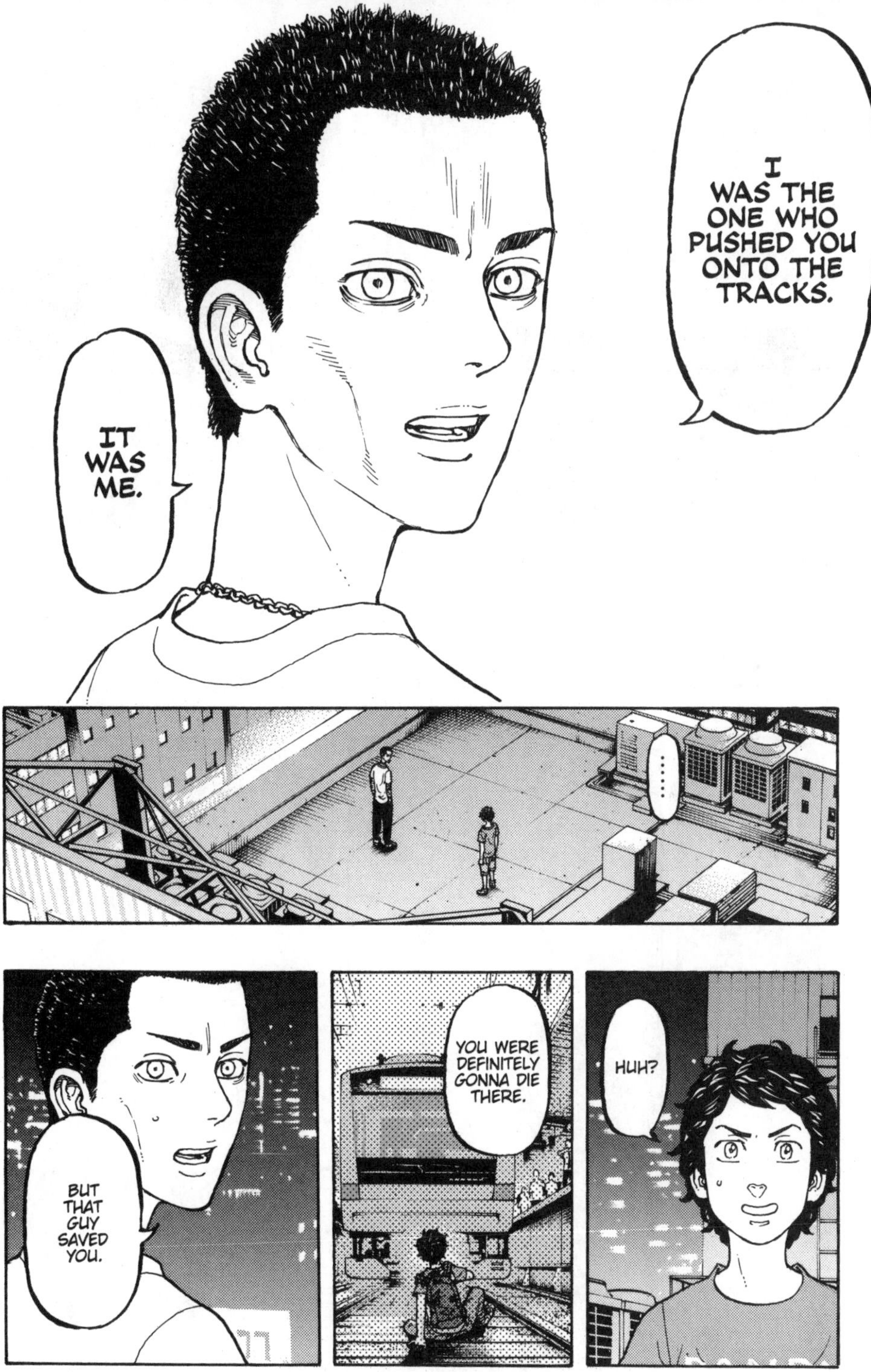
I WAS THE ONE WHO PUSHED YOU ONTO THE TRACKS.
IT WAS ME.
......
HUH?
YOU WERE DEFINITELY GONNA DIE THERE.
BUT THAT GUY SAVED YOU.

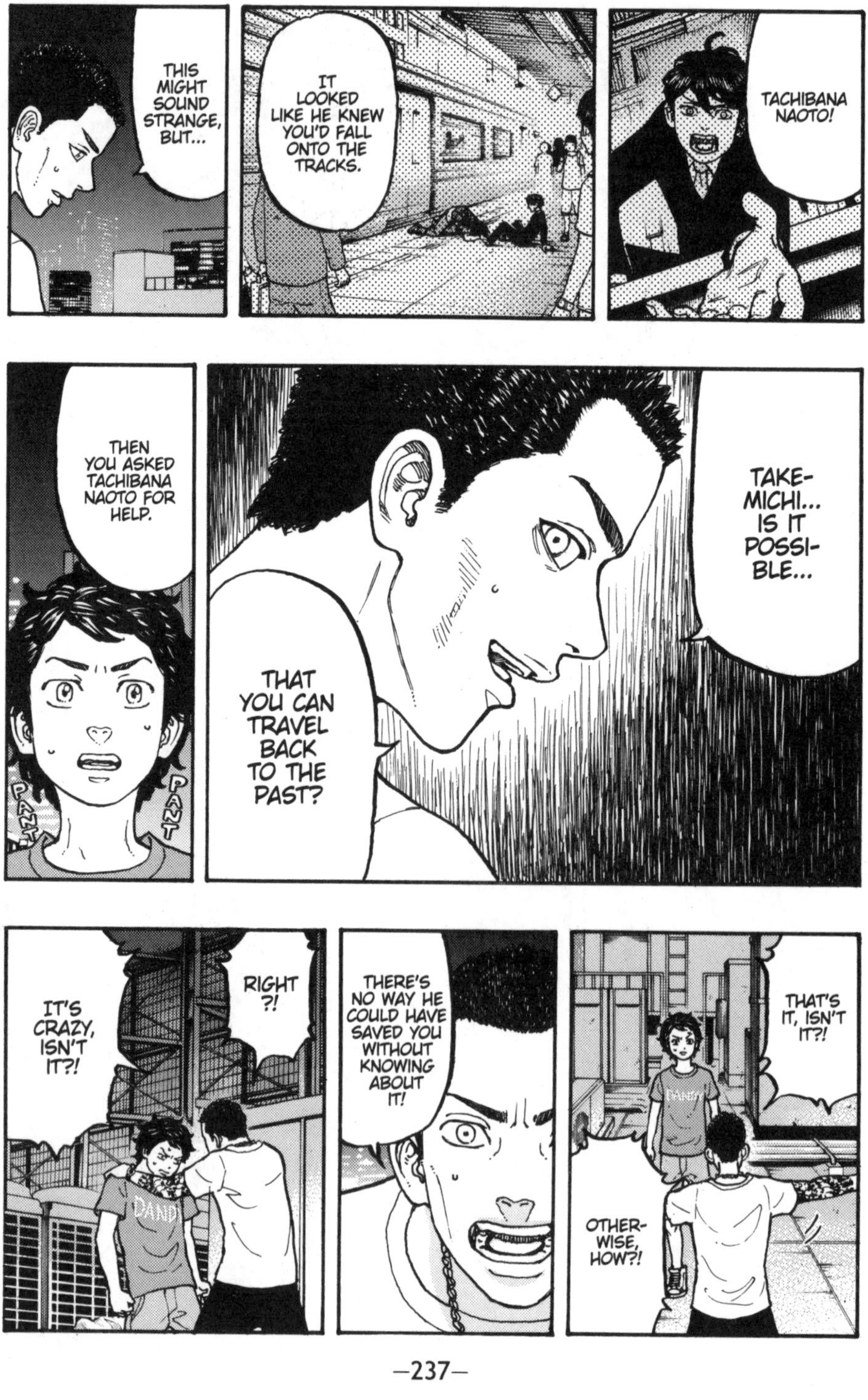
TACHIBANA NAOTO!
IT LOOKED LIKE HE KNEW YOU'D FALL ONTO THE TRACKS.
THIS MIGHT SOUND STRANGE, BUT...
TAKE-MICHI... IS IT POSSIBLE...
THAT YOU CAN TRAVEL BACK TO THE PAST?
THEN YOU ASKED TACHIBANA NAOTO FOR HELP.
PANT
PANT
THAT'S IT, ISN'T IT?!
OTHER-WISE, HOW?!
THERE'S NO WAY HE COULD HAVE SAVED YOU WITHOUT KNOWING ABOUT IT!
RIGHT?!
IT'S CRAZY, ISN'T IT?!

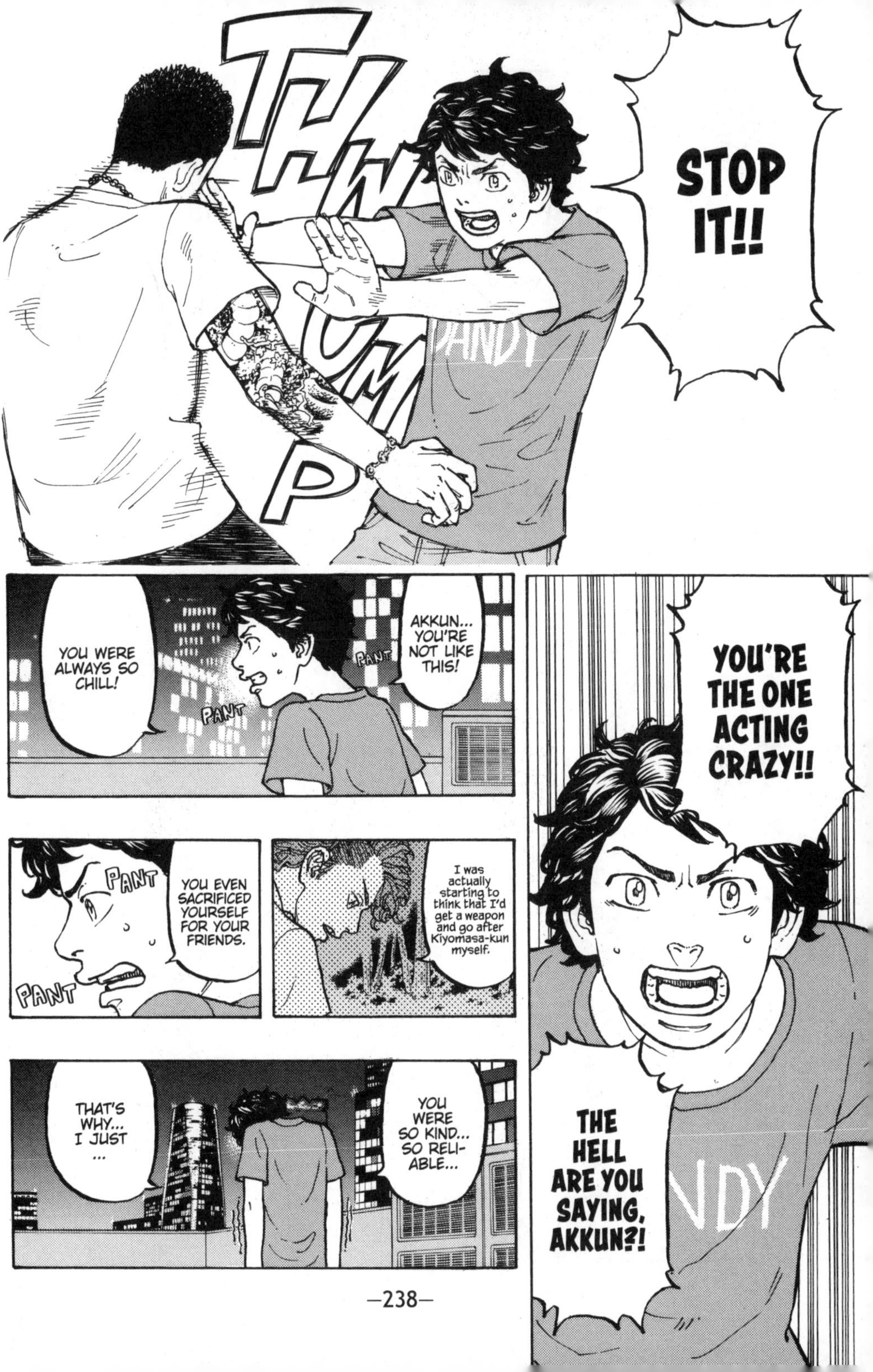
THWUMP
STOP IT!!
YOU'RE THE ONE ACTING CRAZY!!
THE HELL ARE YOU SAYING, AKKUN?!
AKKUN... YOU'RE NOT LIKE THIS!
PANT
YOU WERE ALWAYS SO CHILL!
PANT
I was actually starting to think that I'd get a weapon and go after Kiyomasa-kun myself.
PANT
YOU EVEN SACRIFICED YOURSELF FOR YOUR FRIENDS.
PANT
YOU WERE SO KIND... SO RELI-ABLE...
THAT'S WHY... I JUST ...

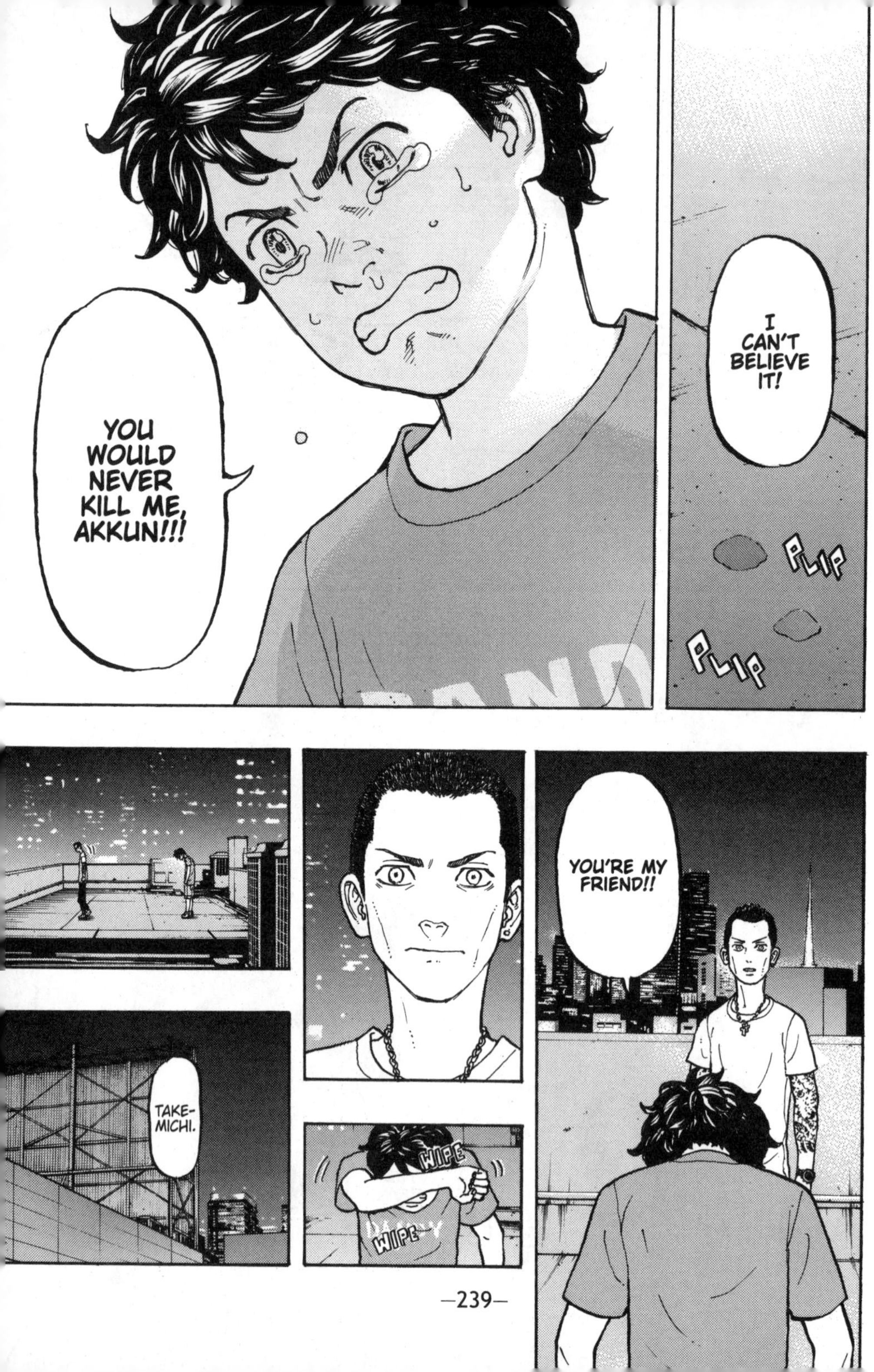
I CAN'T BELIEVE IT!
PLIP
PLIP
YOU WOULD NEVER KILL ME, AKKUN!!!
YOU'RE MY FRIEND!!
WIPE
WIPE
TAKE-MICHI.

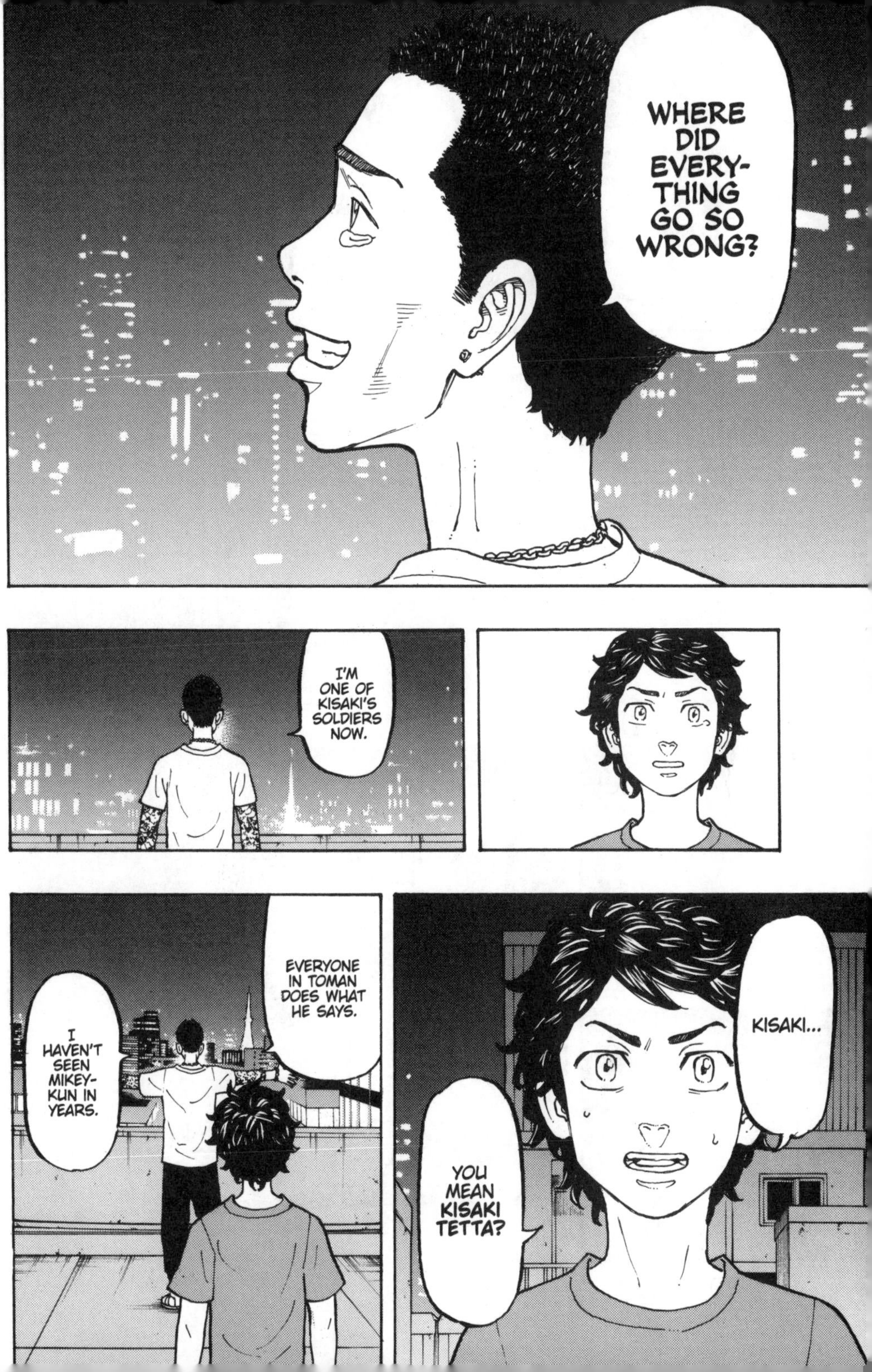
WHERE DID EVERY-THING GO SO WRONG?
I'M ONE OF KISAKI'S SOLDIERS NOW.
KISAKI...
YOU MEAN KISAKI TETTA?
EVERYONE IN TOMAN DOES WHAT HE SAYS.
I HAVEN'T SEEN MIKEY-KUN IN YEARS.

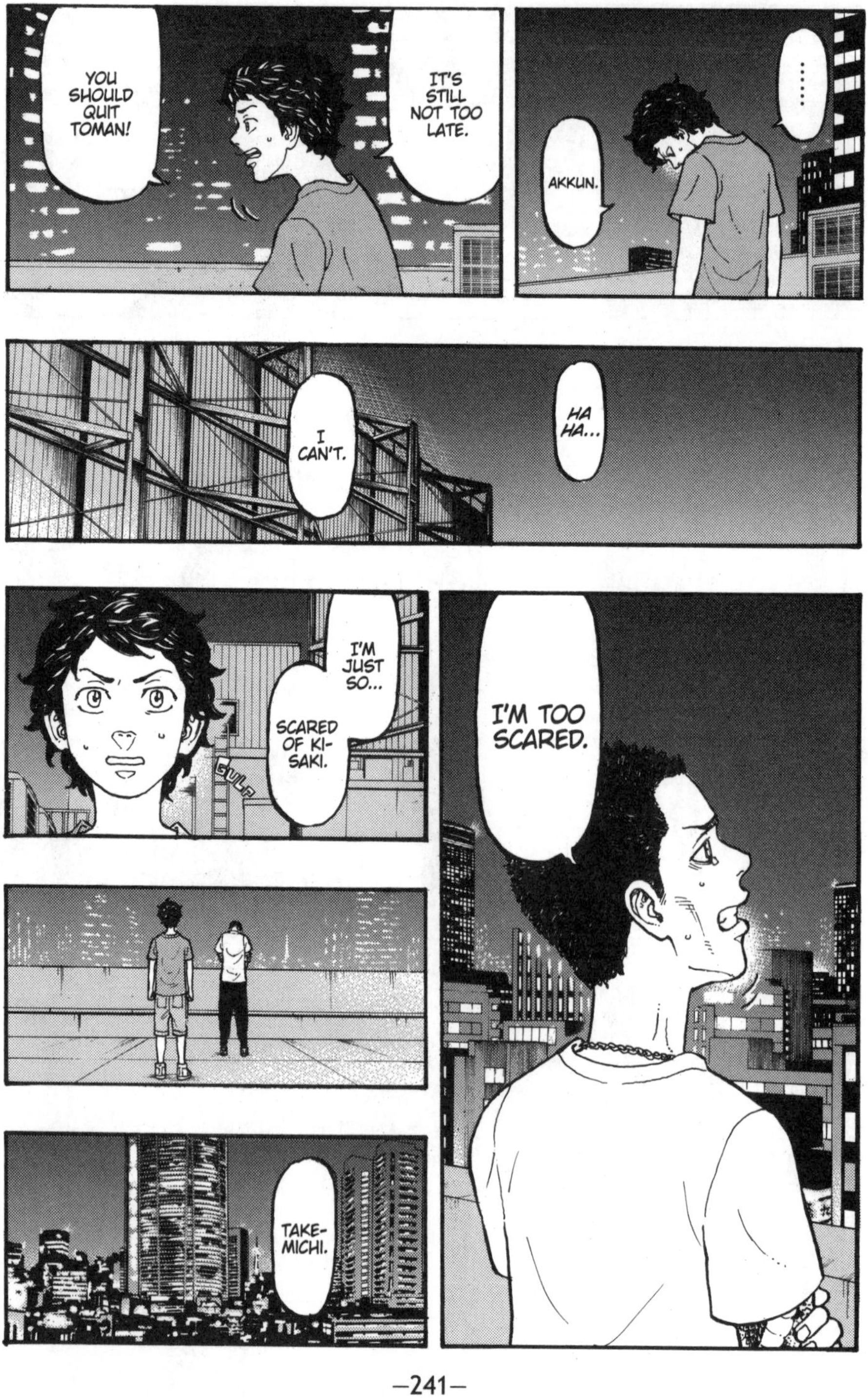
......
AKKUN.
IT'S STILL NOT TOO LATE.
YOU SHOULD QUIT TOMAN!
HA HA...
I CAN'T.
I'M TOO SCARED.
I'M JUST SO...
SCARED OF KI-SAKI.
GULP
TAKE-MICHI.

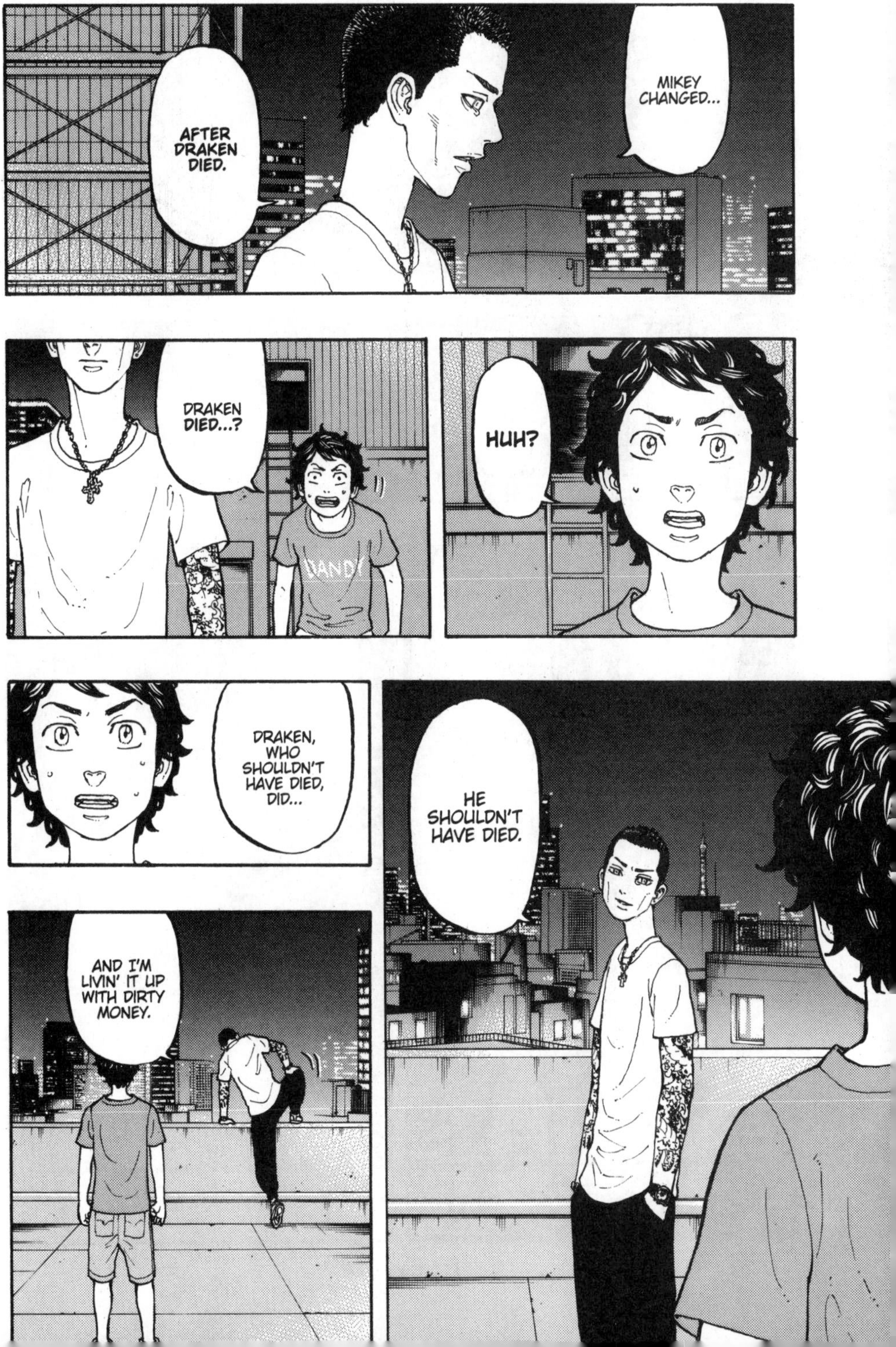
MIKEY CHANGED...
AFTER DRAKEN DIED.
HUH?
DRAKEN DIED...?
HE SHOULDN'T HAVE DIED.
DRAKEN, WHO SHOULDN'T HAVE DIED, DID...
AND I'M LIVIN' IT UP WITH DIRTY MONEY.

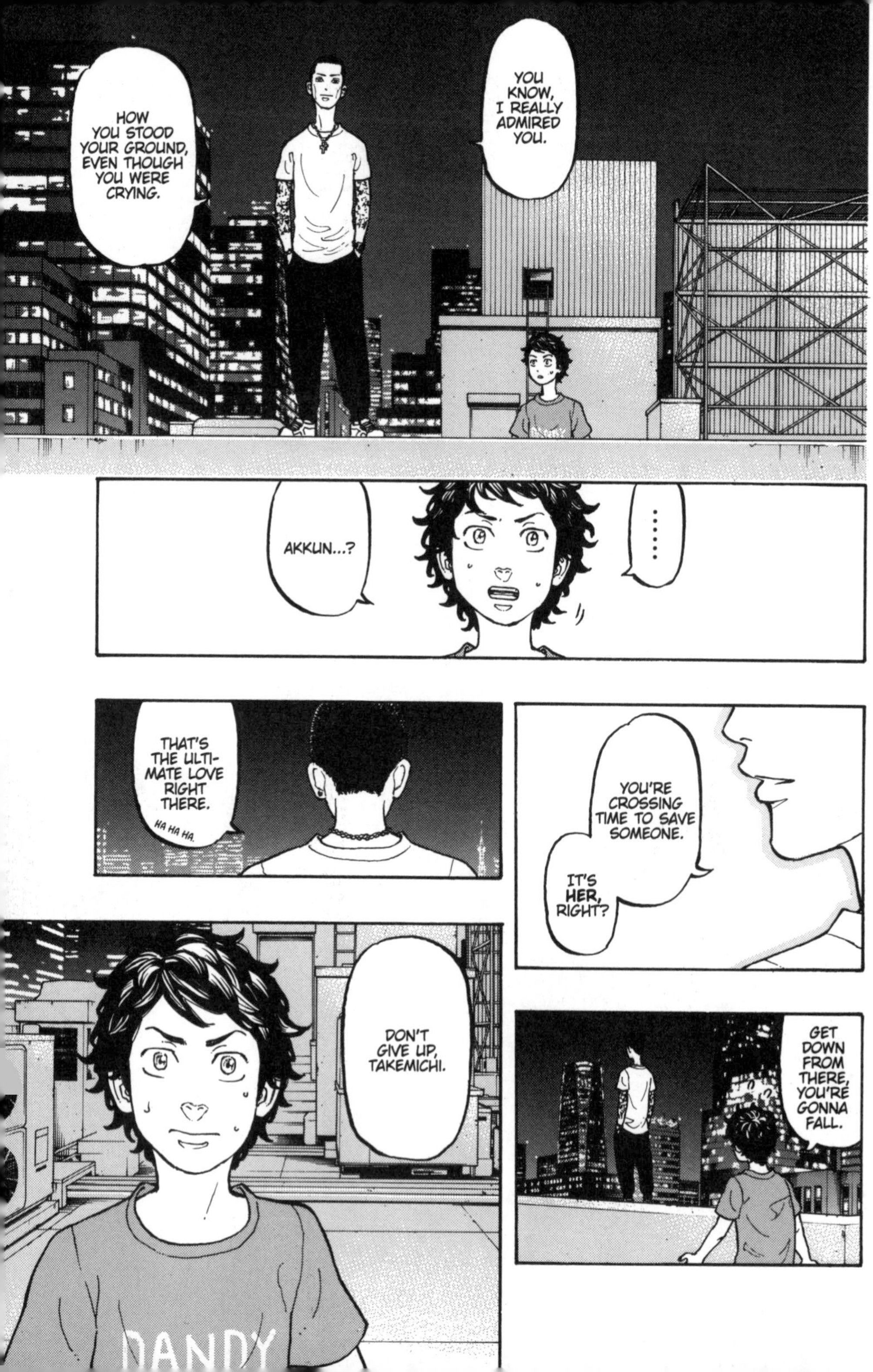
YOU KNOW, I REALLY ADMIRED YOU.
HOW YOU STOOD YOUR GROUND, EVEN THOUGH YOU WERE CRYING.
......
AKKUN...?
YOU'RE CROSSING TIME TO SAVE SOMEONE.
IT'S **HER**, RIGHT?
THAT'S THE ULTI-MATE LOVE RIGHT THERE.
HA HA HA.
GET DOWN FROM THERE, YOU'RE GONNA FALL.
DON'T GIVE UP, TAKEMICHI.
DANDY

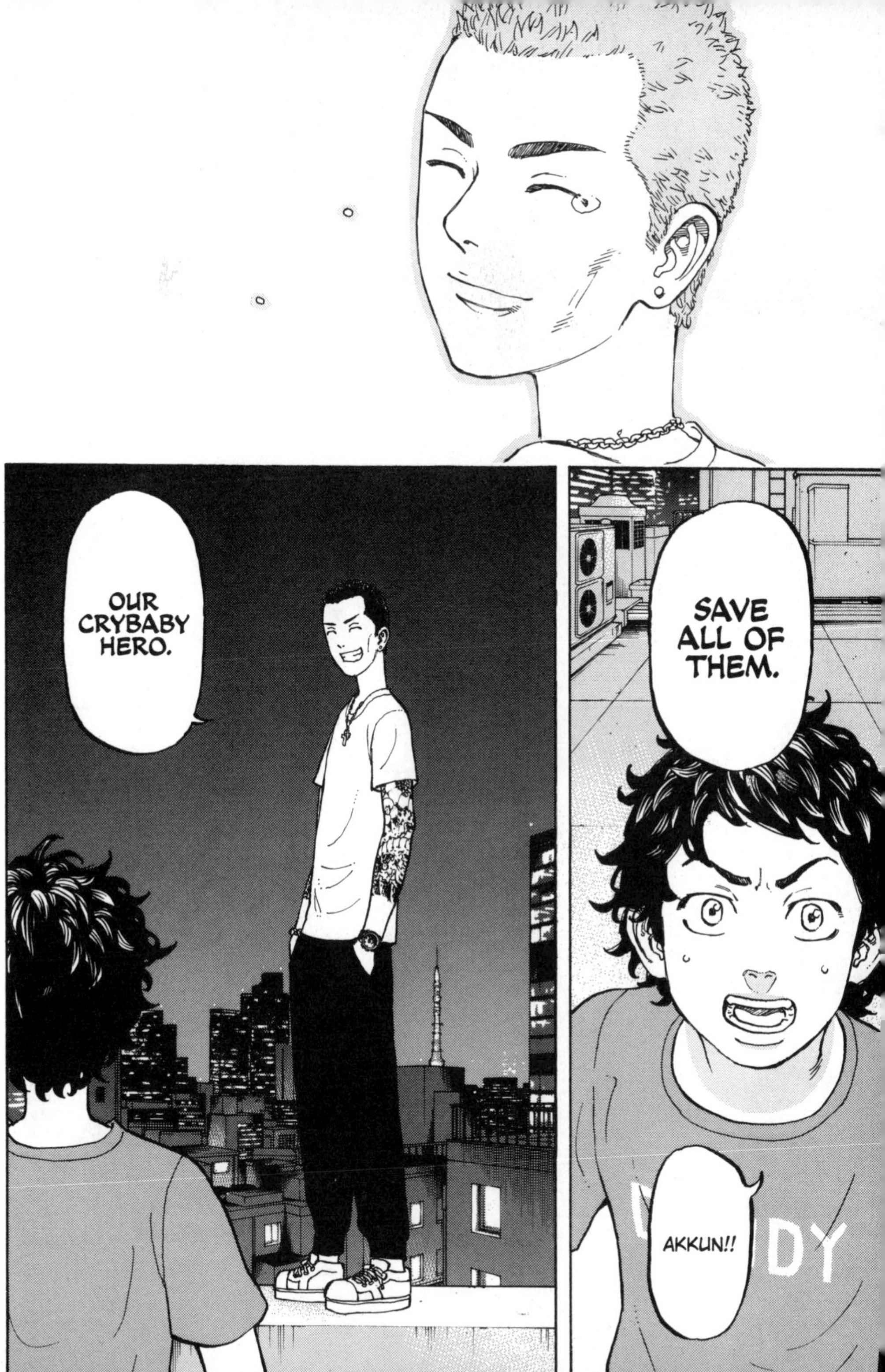
SAVE ALL OF THEM.
AKKUN!!
OUR CRYBABY HERO.

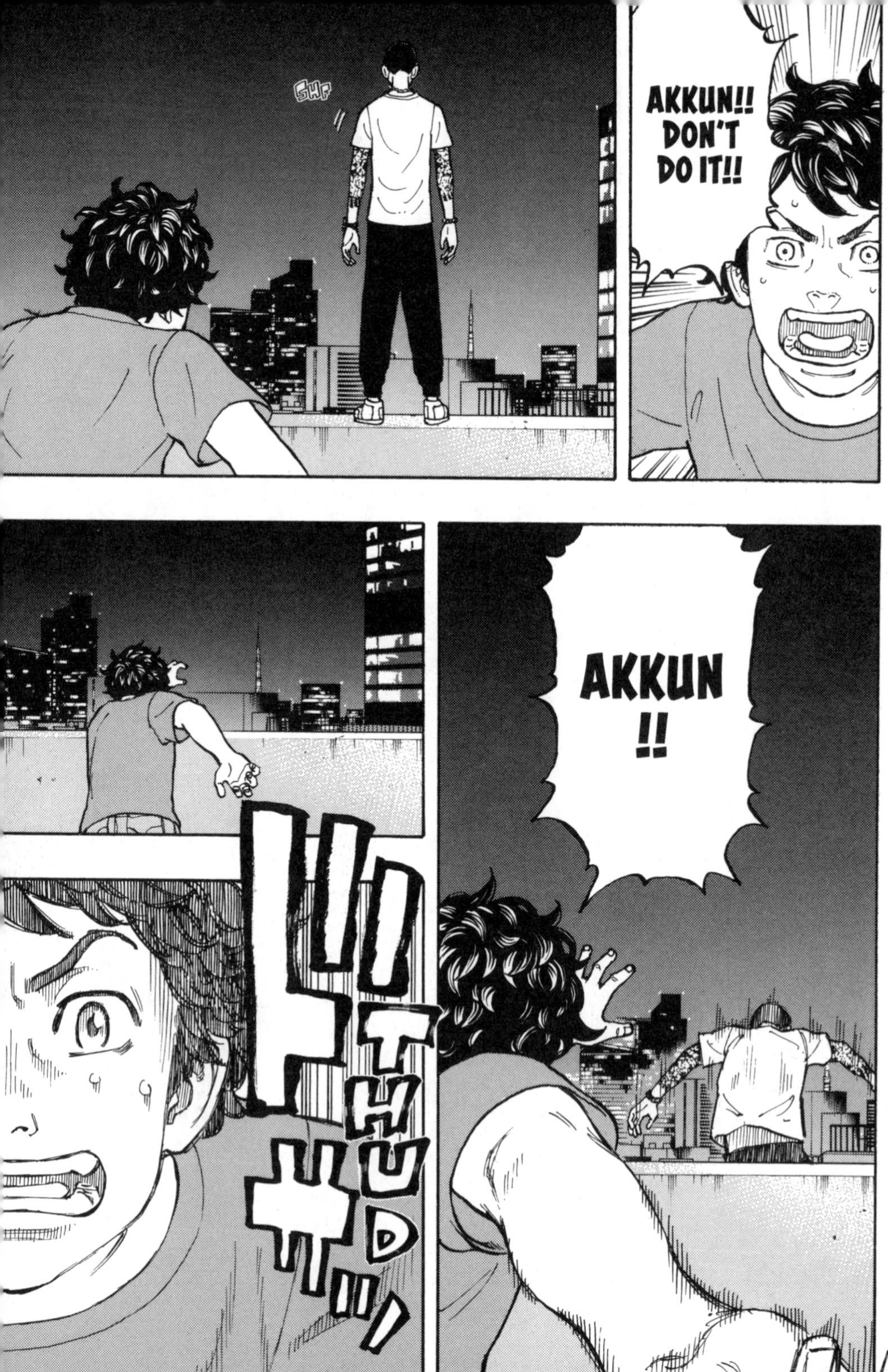
AKKUN!! DON'T DO IT!!
SHP
AKKUN !!
THUD

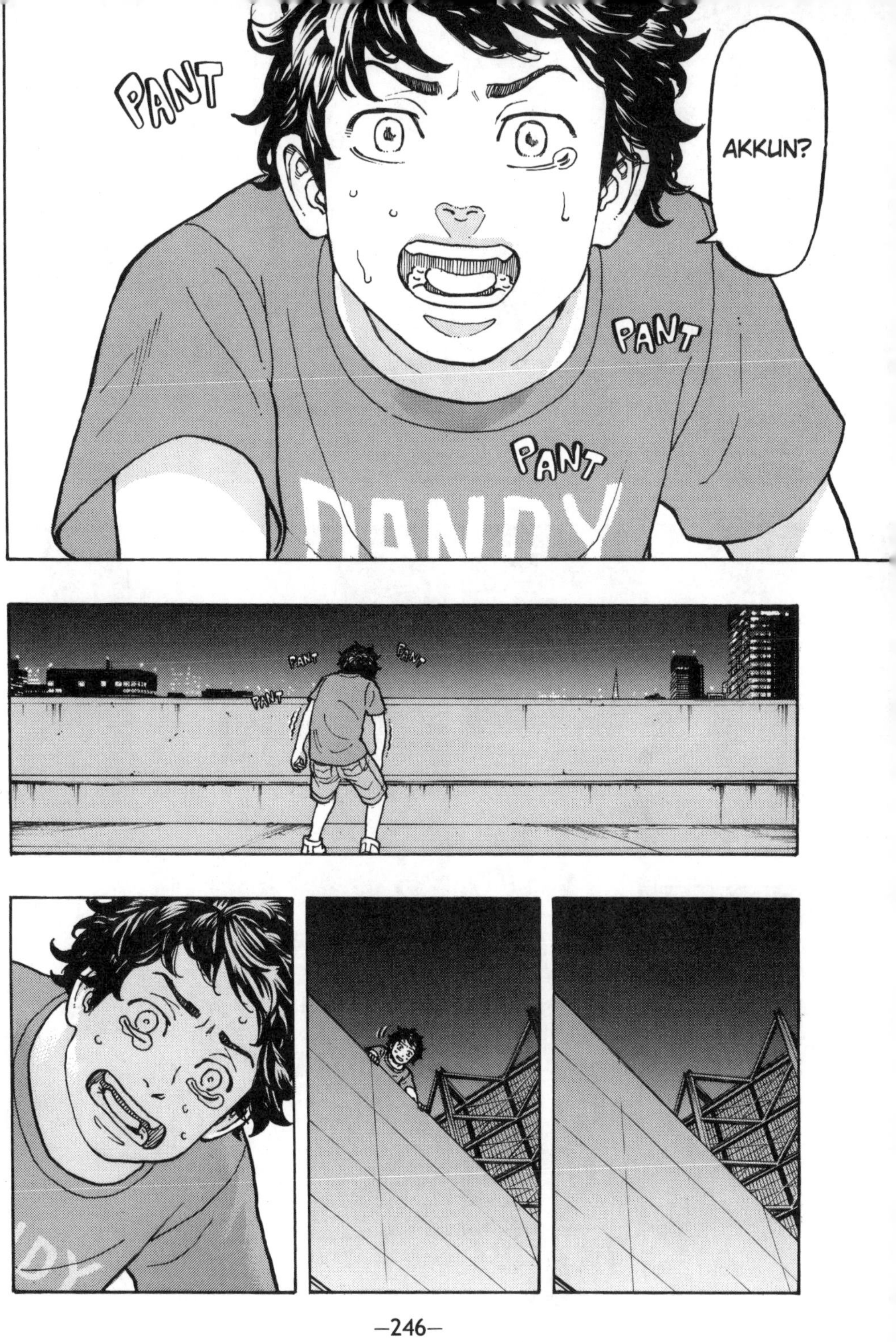

AKKUN?
PANT
PANT
PANT
PANT
PANT
PANT

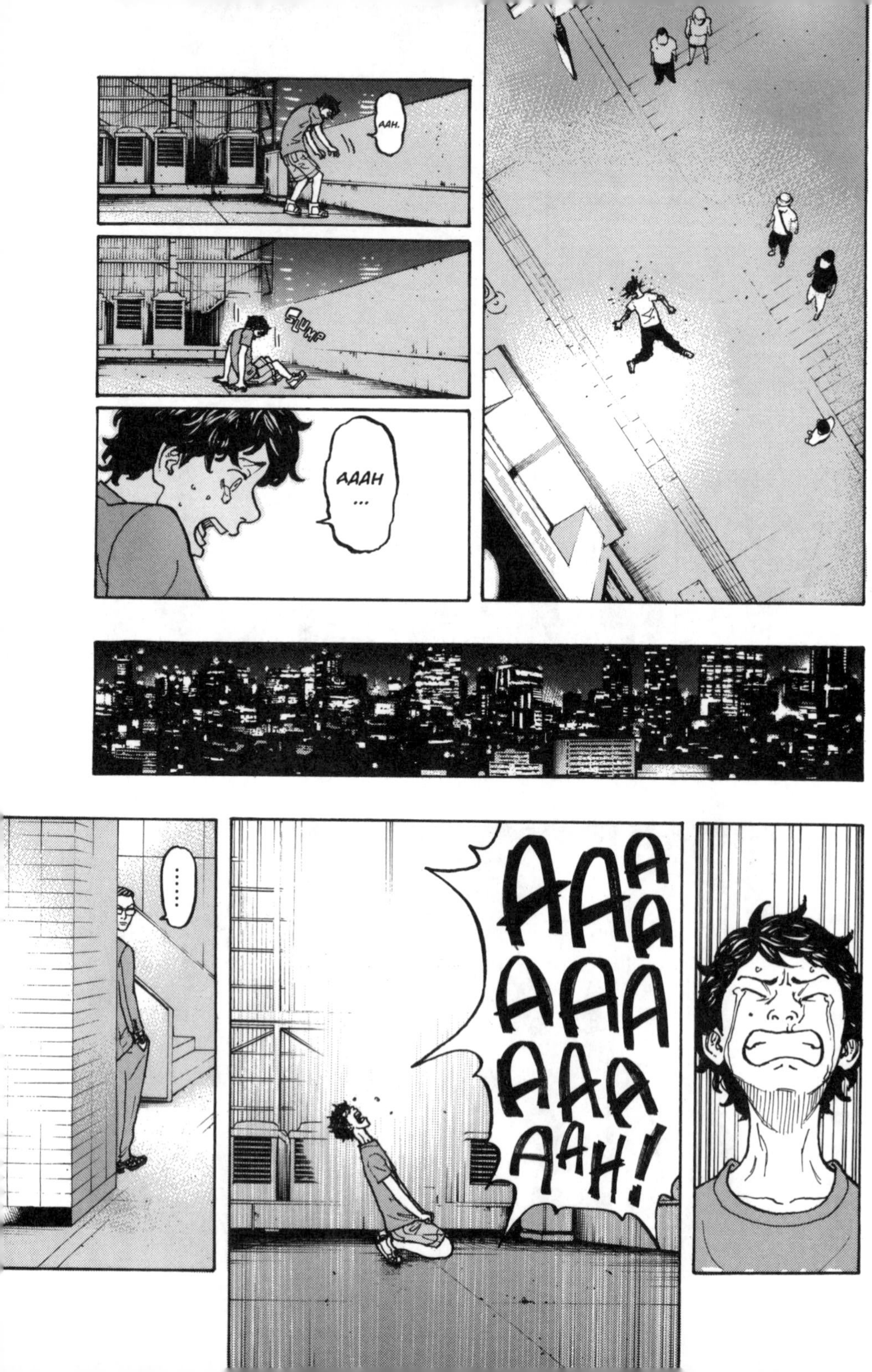
AAH.
SLUMP
AAAH ...
AAAAAAAAAAAAH!
......

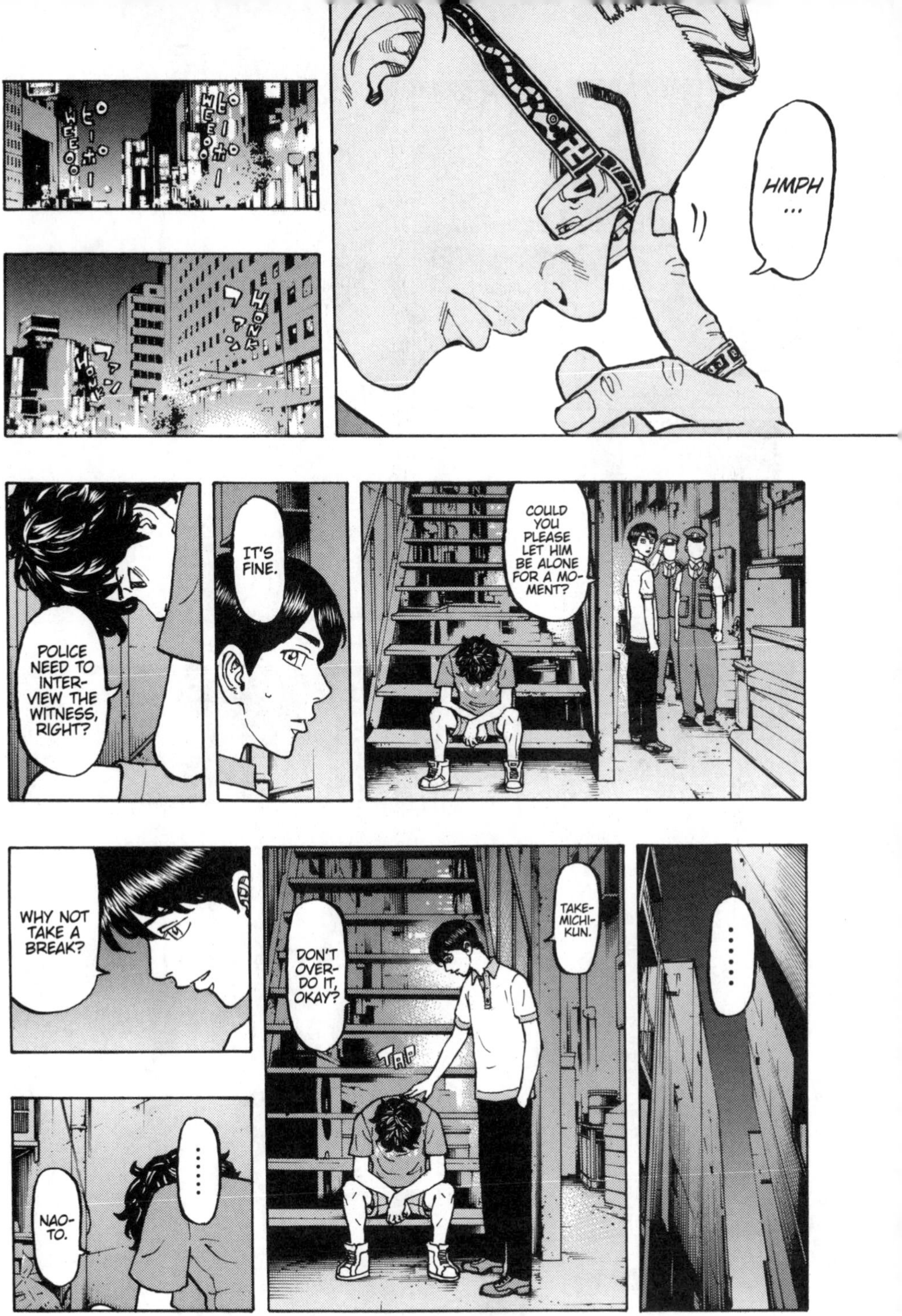
HMPH ...
WEEOO
WEEOO
HONK
HONK
COULD YOU PLEASE LET HIM BE ALONE FOR A MOMENT?
IT'S FINE.
POLICE NEED TO INTER-VIEW THE WITNESS, RIGHT?
......
TAKE-MICHI-KUN.
DON'T OVER-DO IT, OKAY?
TAP
WHY NOT TAKE A BREAK?
......
NAO-TO.

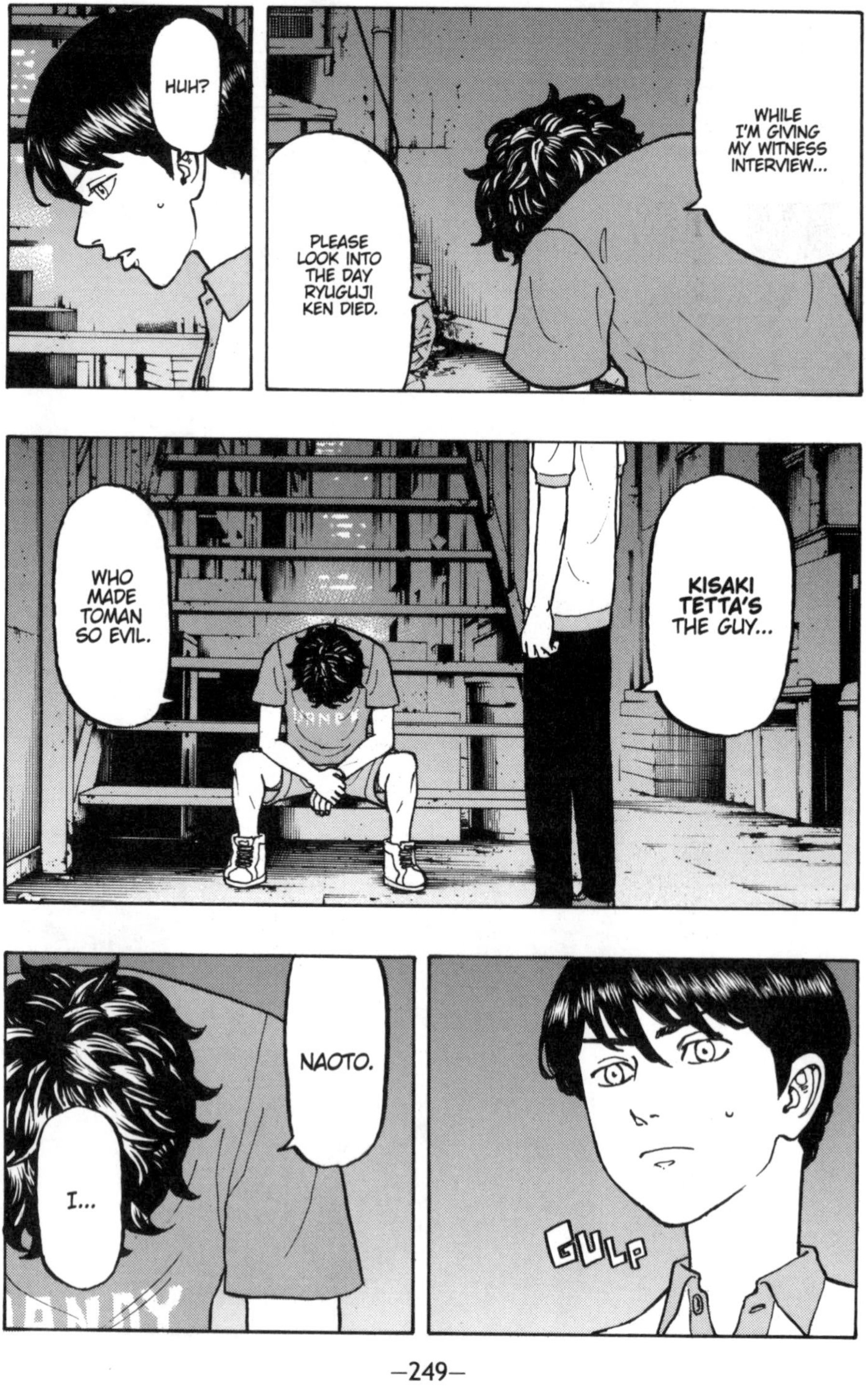
WHILE I'M GIVING MY WITNESS INTERVIEW...
PLEASE LOOK INTO THE DAY RYUGUJI KEN DIED.
HUH?
KISAKI TETTA'S THE GUY...
WHO MADE TOMAN SO EVIL.
GULP
NAOTO.
I...

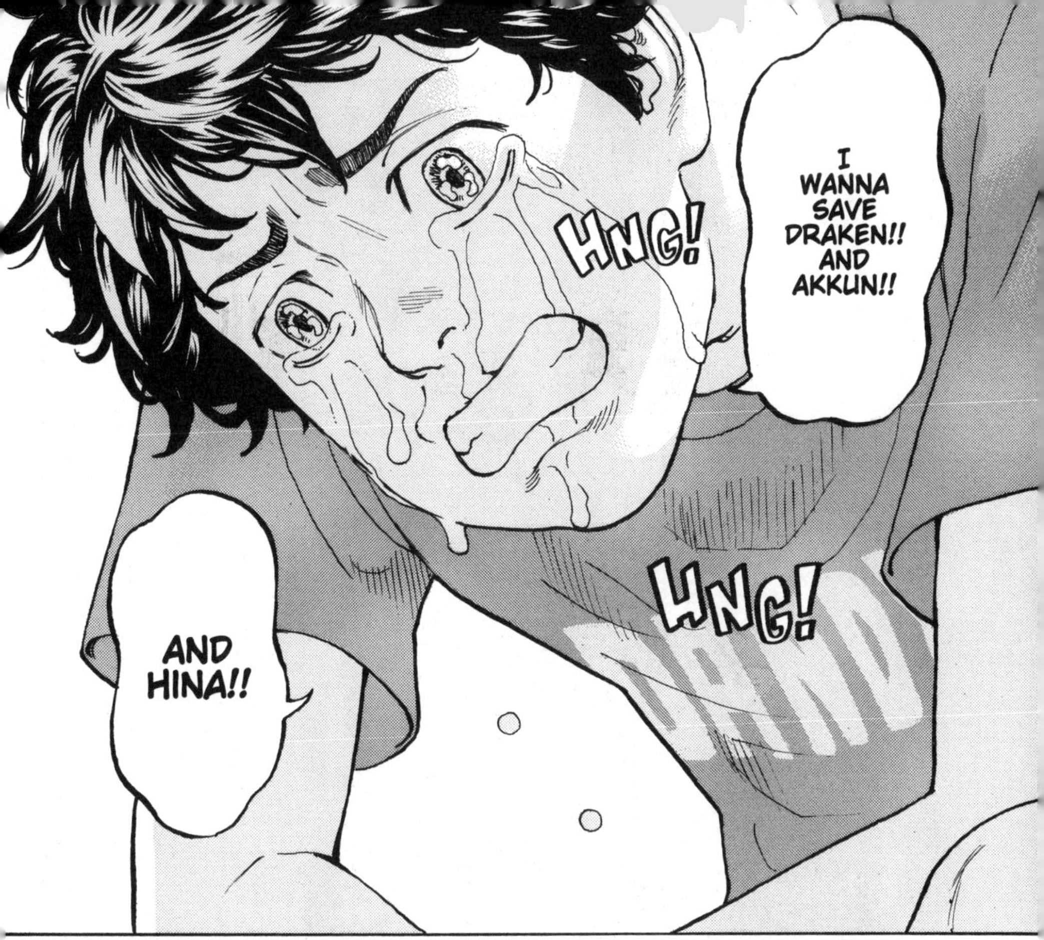
I WANNA SAVE DRAKEN!! AND AKKUN!!
HNG!
HNG!
AND HINA!!

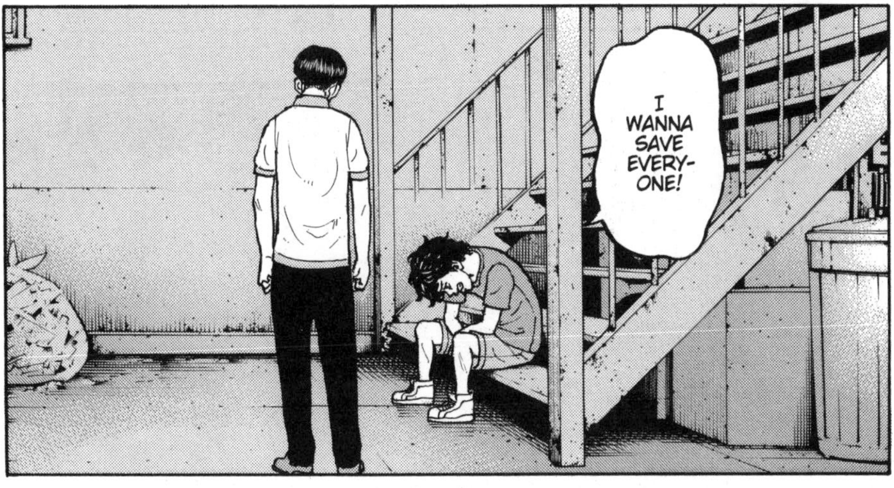
I WANNA SAVE EVERY-ONE!

CHAPTER 9: RELEAP

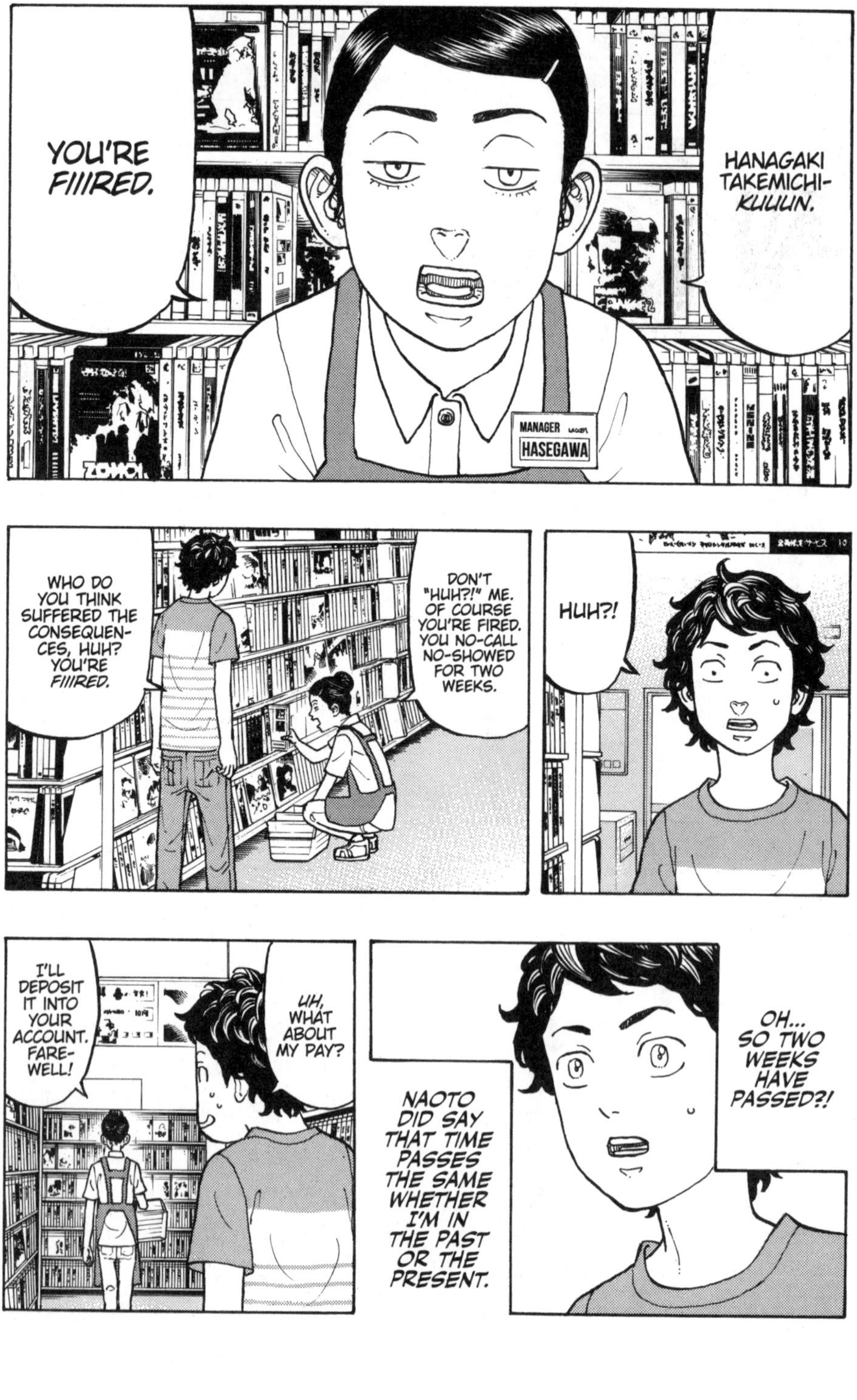
HANAGAKI TAKEMICHI-KUUUN.
YOU'RE FIIIRED.
MANAGER
HASEGAWA
HUH?!
DON'T "HUH?!" ME. OF COURSE YOU'RE FIRED. YOU NO-CALL NO-SHOWED FOR TWO WEEKS.
WHO DO YOU THINK SUFFERED THE CONSEQUENCES, HUH? YOU'RE FIIIRED.
OH... SO TWO WEEKS HAVE PASSED?!
NAOTO DID SAY THAT TIME PASSES THE SAME WHETHER I'M IN THE PAST OR THE PRESENT.
UH, WHAT ABOUT MY PAY?
I'LL DEPOSIT IT INTO YOUR ACCOUNT. FAREWELL!

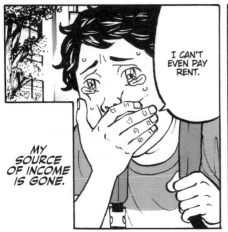

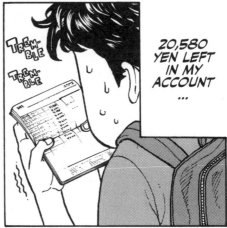

20,580 YEN LEFT IN MY ACCOUNT ...
TREMBLE
TREMBLE
I CAN'T EVEN PAY RENT.
MY SOURCE OF INCOME IS GONE.
HOW AM I SUPPOSED TO LIVE FROM NOW ON?
I've got no hope for the future.
HOW'S A LOSER LIKE ME GONNA SAVE HINA...?
AND AKKUN?
AND DRAKEN?
I CAN'T EVEN SAVE MYSELF.
HOW DEPRESSING...
Fired...

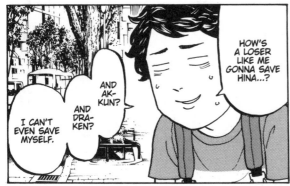

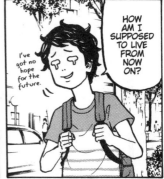

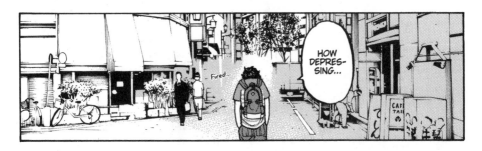

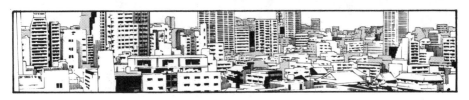

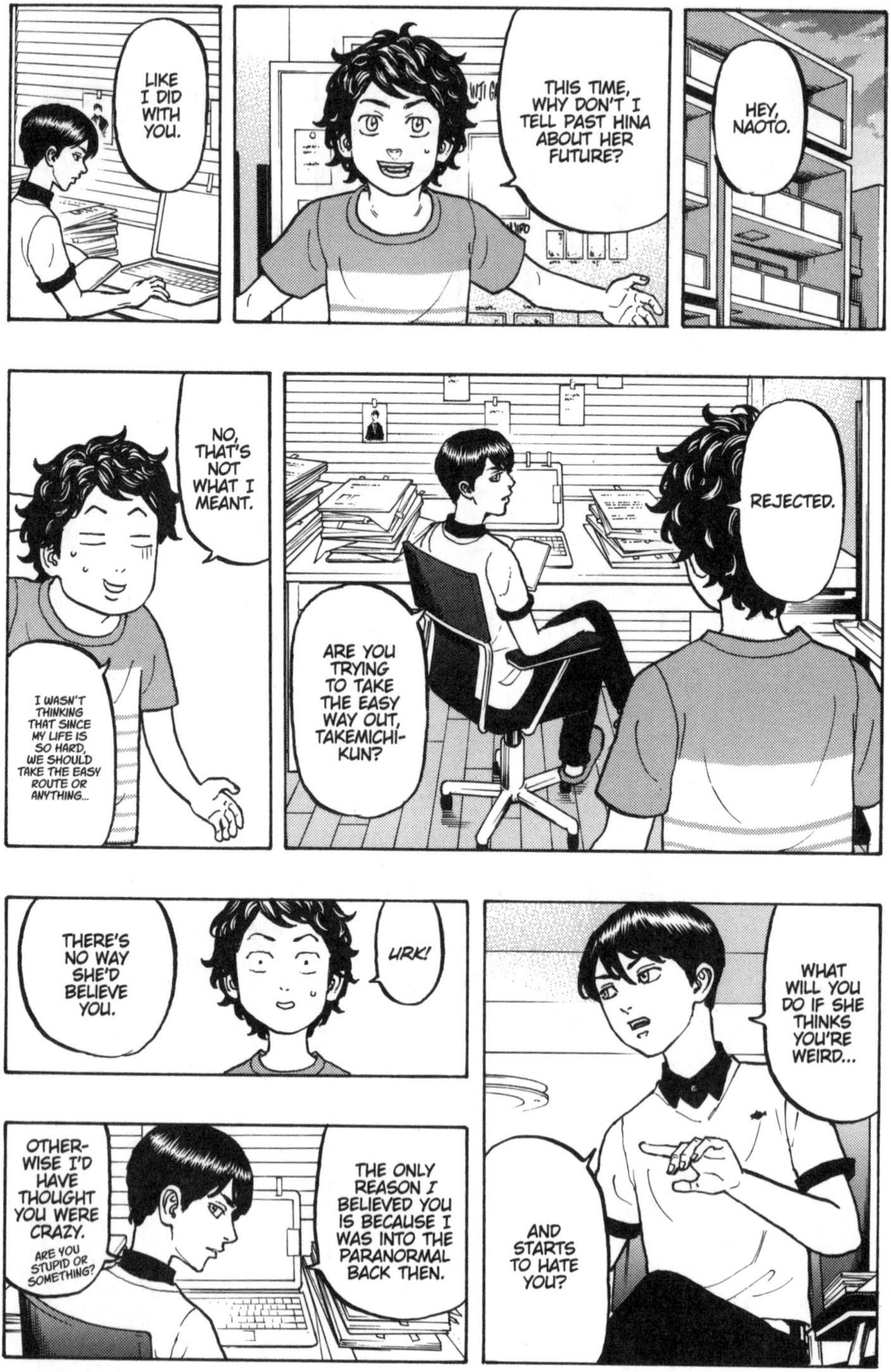
HEY, NAOTO.
THIS TIME, WHY DON'T I TELL PAST HINA ABOUT HER FUTURE?
LIKE I DID WITH YOU.
REJECTED.
ARE YOU TRYING TO TAKE THE EASY WAY OUT, TAKEMICHI-KUN?
NO, THAT'S NOT WHAT I MEANT.
I WASN'T THINKING THAT SINCE MY LIFE IS SO HARD, WE SHOULD TAKE THE EASY ROUTE OR ANYTHING...
WHAT WILL YOU DO IF SHE THINKS YOU'RE WEIRD...
AND STARTS TO HATE YOU?
URK!
THERE'S NO WAY SHE'D BELIEVE YOU.
THE ONLY REASON *I* BELIEVED YOU IS BECAUSE I WAS INTO THE PARANORMAL BACK THEN.
OTHER-WISE I'D HAVE THOUGHT YOU WERE CRAZY.
ARE YOU STUPID OR SOMETHING?

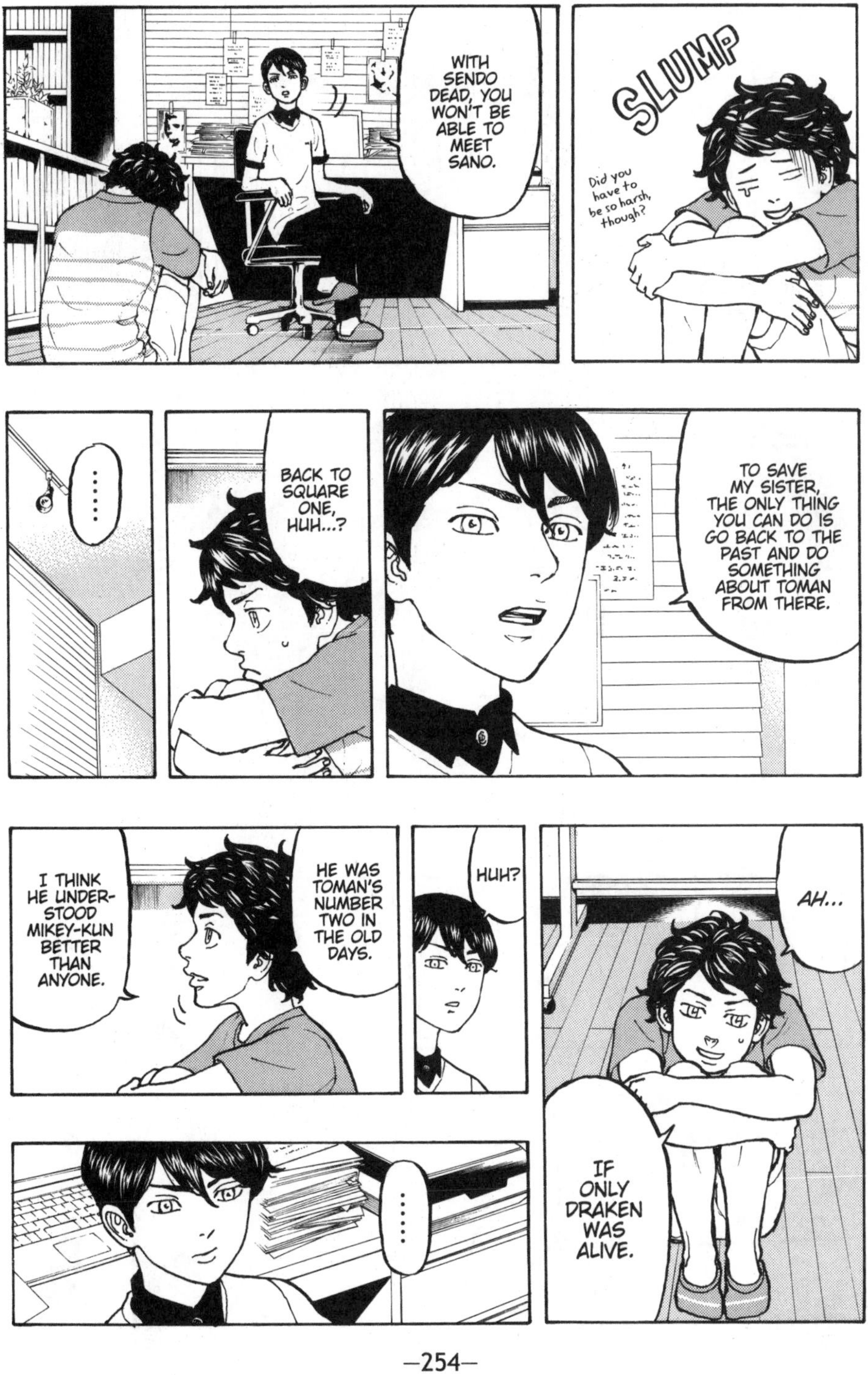
SLUMP
Did you have to be so harsh, though?
WITH SENDO DEAD, YOU WON'T BE ABLE TO MEET SANO.
TO SAVE MY SISTER, THE ONLY THING YOU CAN DO IS GO BACK TO THE PAST AND DO SOMETHING ABOUT TOMAN FROM THERE.
BACK TO SQUARE ONE, HUH...?
......
AH...
IF ONLY DRAKEN WAS ALIVE.
HUH?
HE WAS TOMAN'S NUMBER TWO IN THE OLD DAYS.
I THINK HE UNDER-STOOD MIKEY-KUN BETTER THAN ANYONE.
......

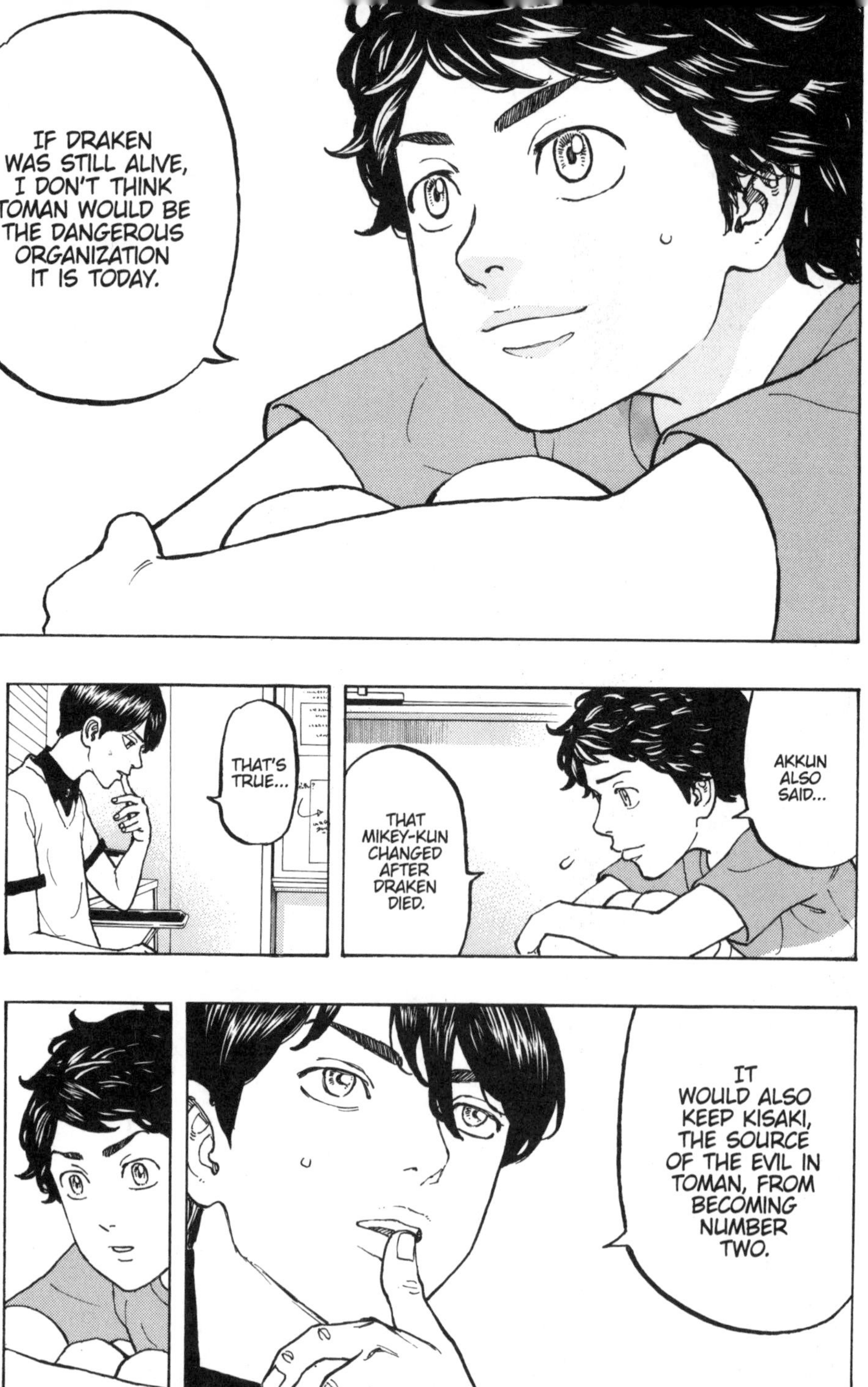
IF DRAKEN WAS STILL ALIVE, I DON'T THINK TOMAN WOULD BE THE DANGEROUS ORGANIZATION IT IS TODAY.
AKKUN ALSO SAID...
THAT MIKEY-KUN CHANGED AFTER DRAKEN DIED.
THAT'S TRUE...
IT WOULD ALSO KEEP KISAKI, THE SOURCE OF THE EVIL IN TOMAN, FROM BECOMING NUMBER TWO.

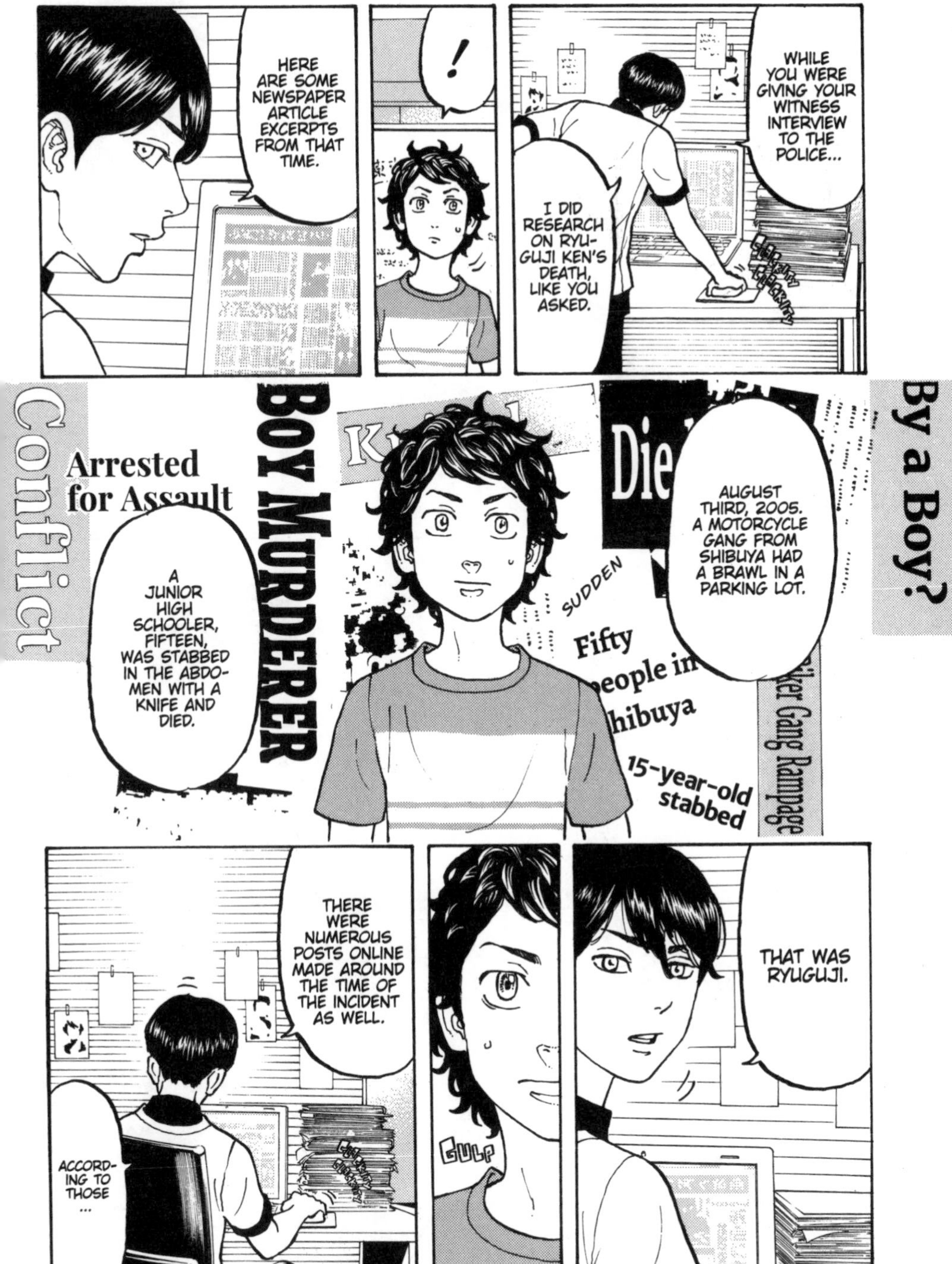
WHILE YOU WERE GIVING YOUR WITNESS INTERVIEW TO THE POLICE...
I DID RESEARCH ON RYUGUJI KEN'S DEATH, LIKE YOU ASKED.
!
HERE ARE SOME NEWSPAPER ARTICLE EXCERPTS FROM THAT TIME.
By a Boy?
AUGUST THIRD, 2005. A MOTORCYCLE GANG FROM SHIBUYA HAD A BRAWL IN A PARKING LOT.
Die
ker Gang Rampage
SUDDEN
Fifty
eople in
hibuya
15-year-old stabbed
BOY MURDERER
A JUNIOR HIGH SCHOOLER, FIFTEEN, WAS STABBED IN THE ABDOMEN WITH A KNIFE AND DIED.
Arrested for Assault
Conflict
THAT WAS RYUGUJI.
GULP
THERE WERE NUMEROUS POSTS ONLINE MADE AROUND THE TIME OF THE INCIDENT AS WELL.
ACCORDING TO THOSE...

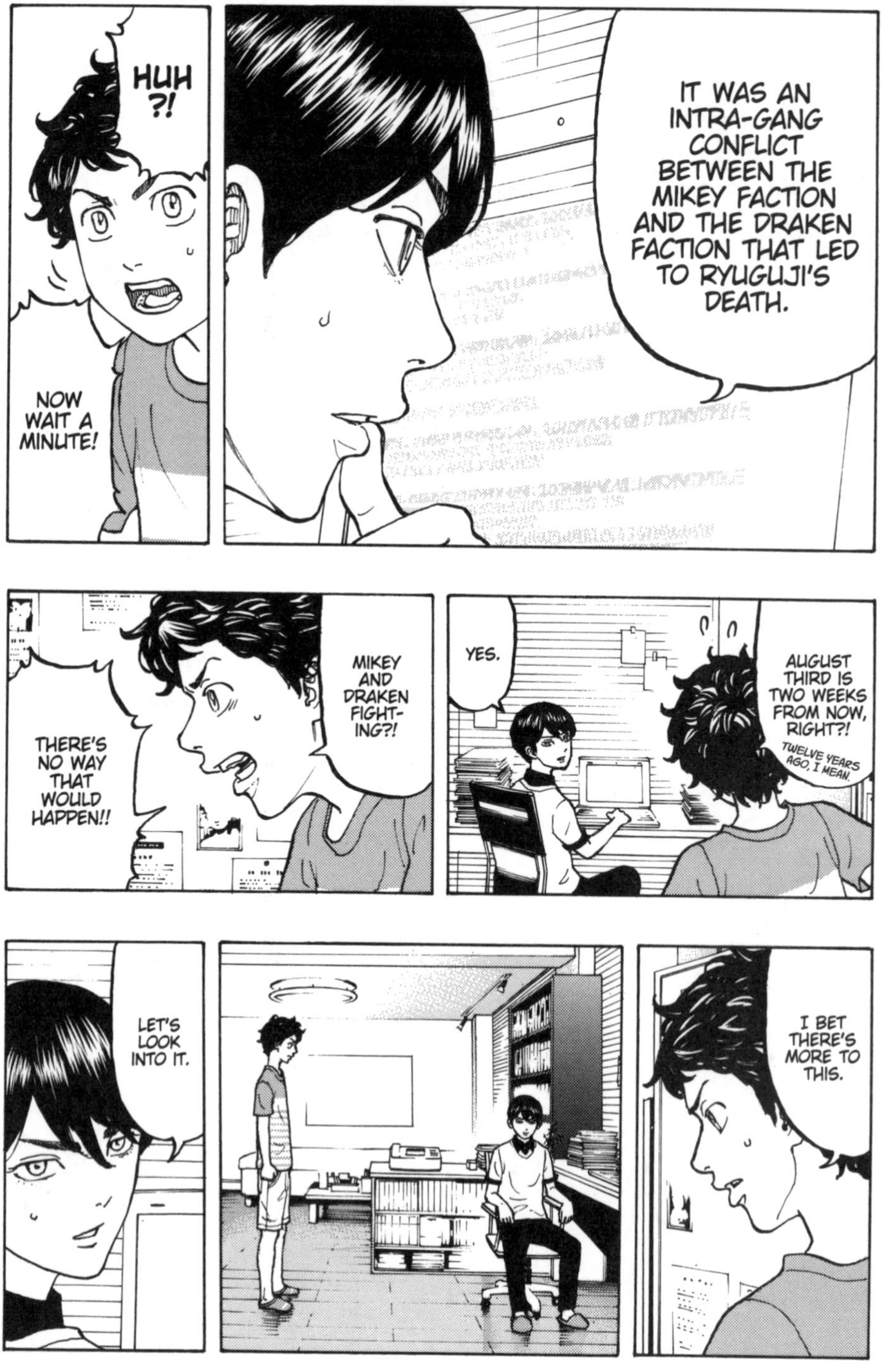
IT WAS AN INTRA-GANG CONFLICT BETWEEN THE MIKEY FACTION AND THE DRAKEN FACTION THAT LED TO RYUGUJI'S DEATH.
HUH ?!
NOW WAIT A MINUTE!
AUGUST THIRD IS TWO WEEKS FROM NOW, RIGHT?!
TWELVE YEARS AGO, I MEAN.
YES.
MIKEY AND DRAKEN FIGHT-ING?!
THERE'S NO WAY THAT WOULD HAPPEN!!
I BET THERE'S MORE TO THIS.
LET'S LOOK INTO IT.

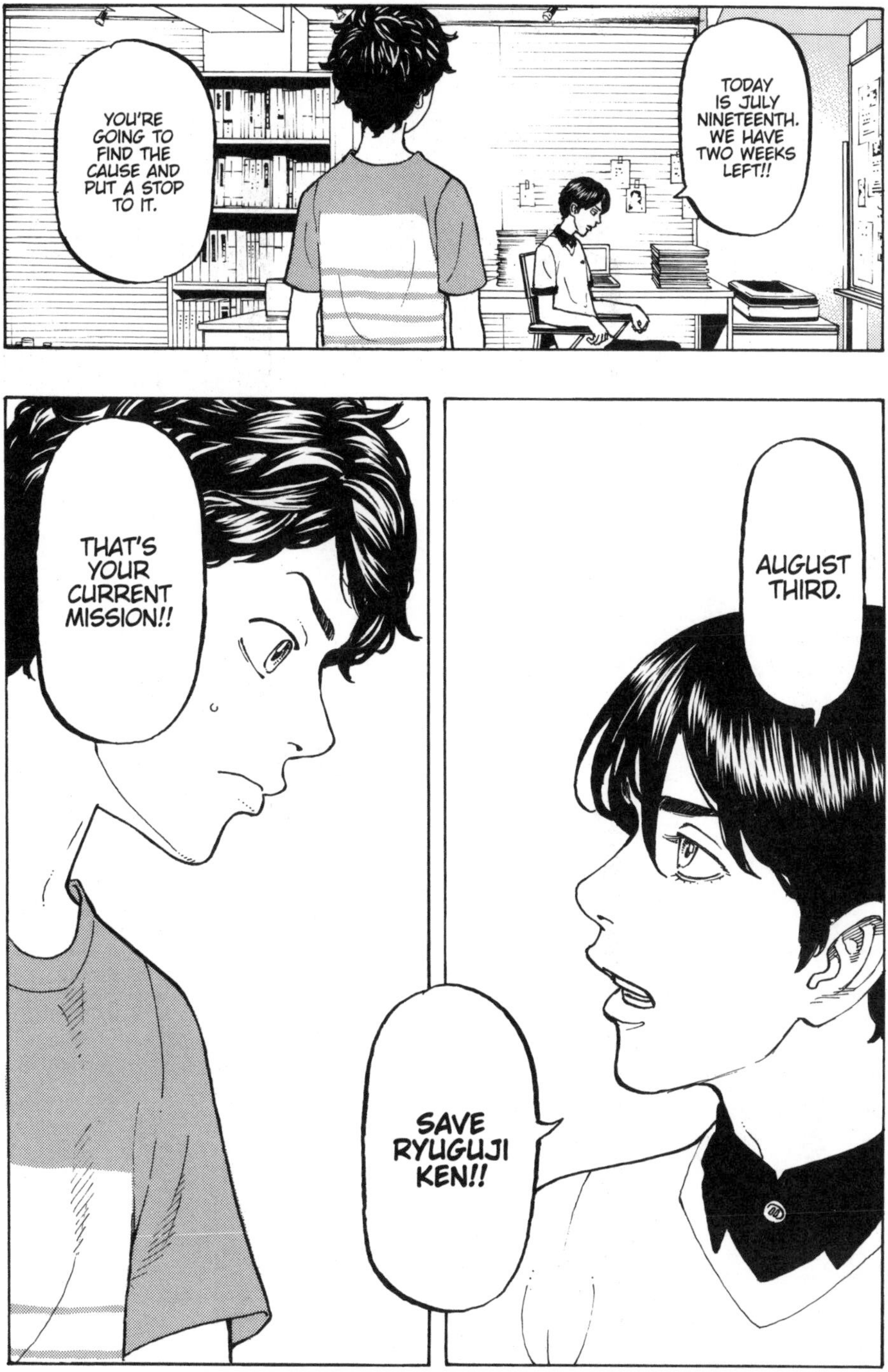
TODAY IS JULY NINETEENTH. WE HAVE TWO WEEKS LEFT!!
YOU'RE GOING TO FIND THE CAUSE AND PUT A STOP TO IT.
AUGUST THIRD.
SAVE RYUGUJI KEN!!
THAT'S YOUR CURRENT MISSION!!

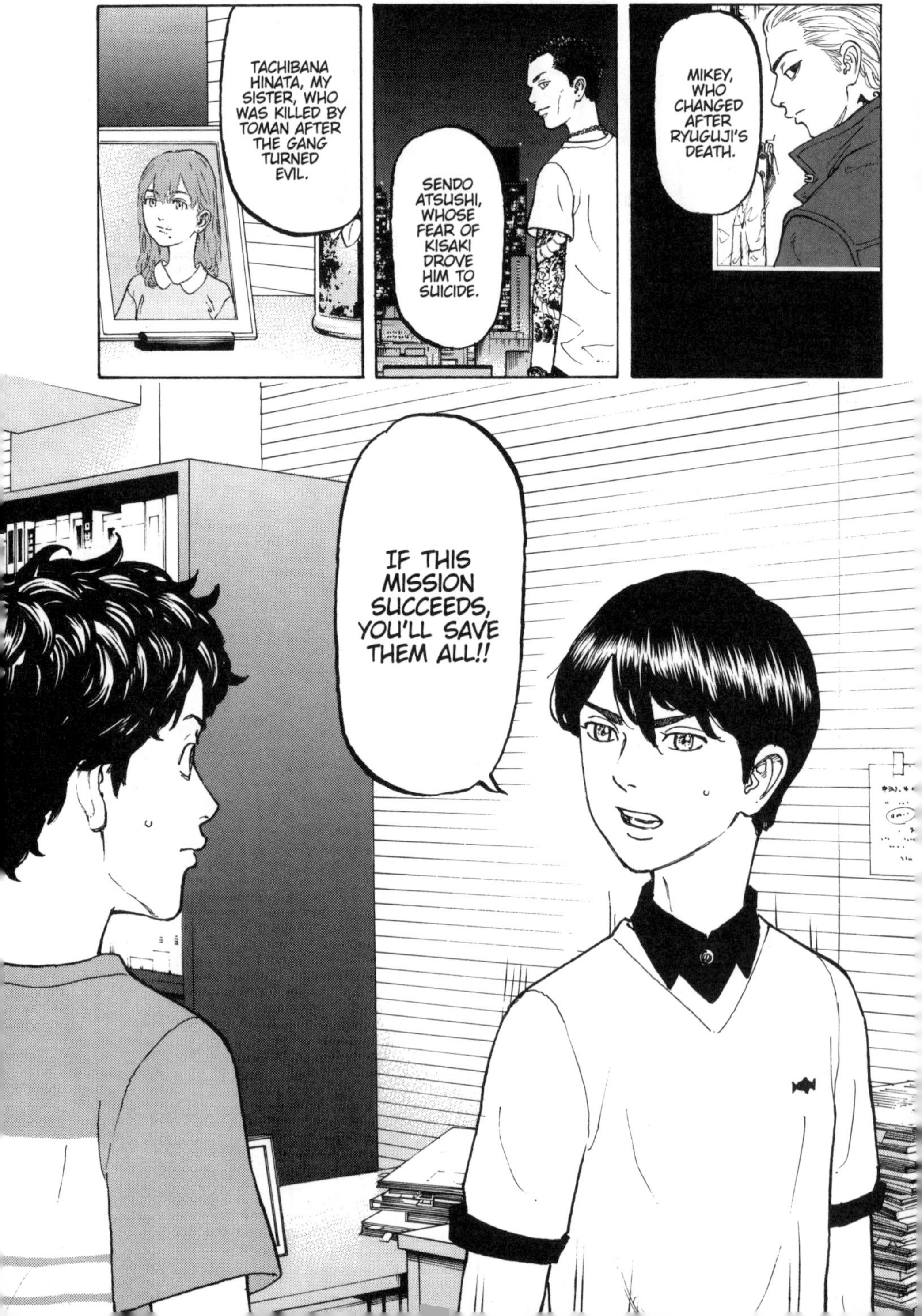
MIKEY, WHO CHANGED AFTER RYUGUJI'S DEATH.
SENDO ATSUSHI, WHOSE FEAR OF KISAKI DROVE HIM TO SUICIDE.
TACHIBANA HINATA, MY SISTER, WHO WAS KILLED BY TOMAN AFTER THE GANG TURNED EVIL.
IF THIS MISSION SUCCEEDS, YOU'LL SAVE THEM ALL!!

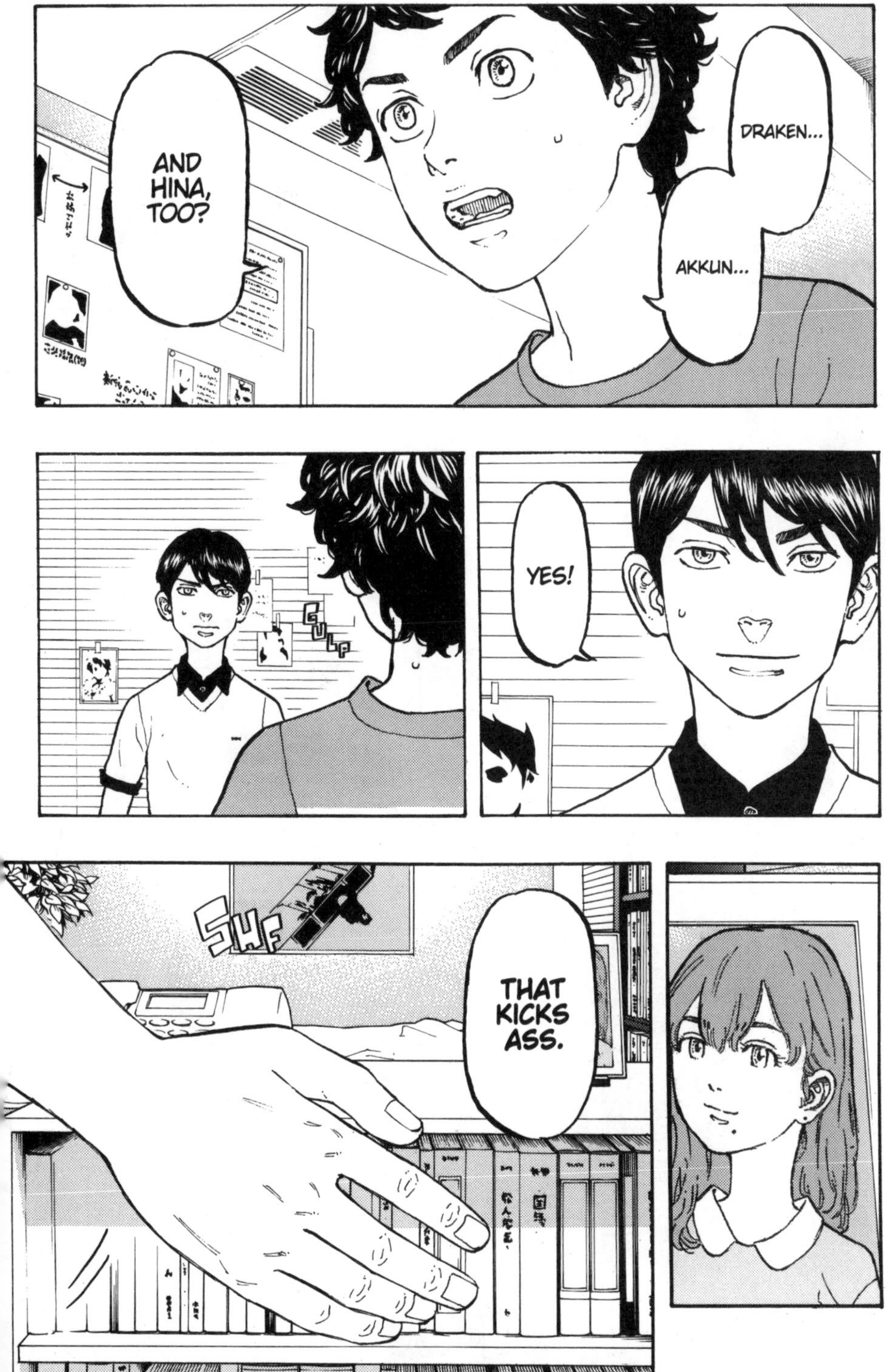
DRAKEN...
AKKUN...
AND HINA, TOO?
YES!
GULP
THAT KICKS ASS.
SHF

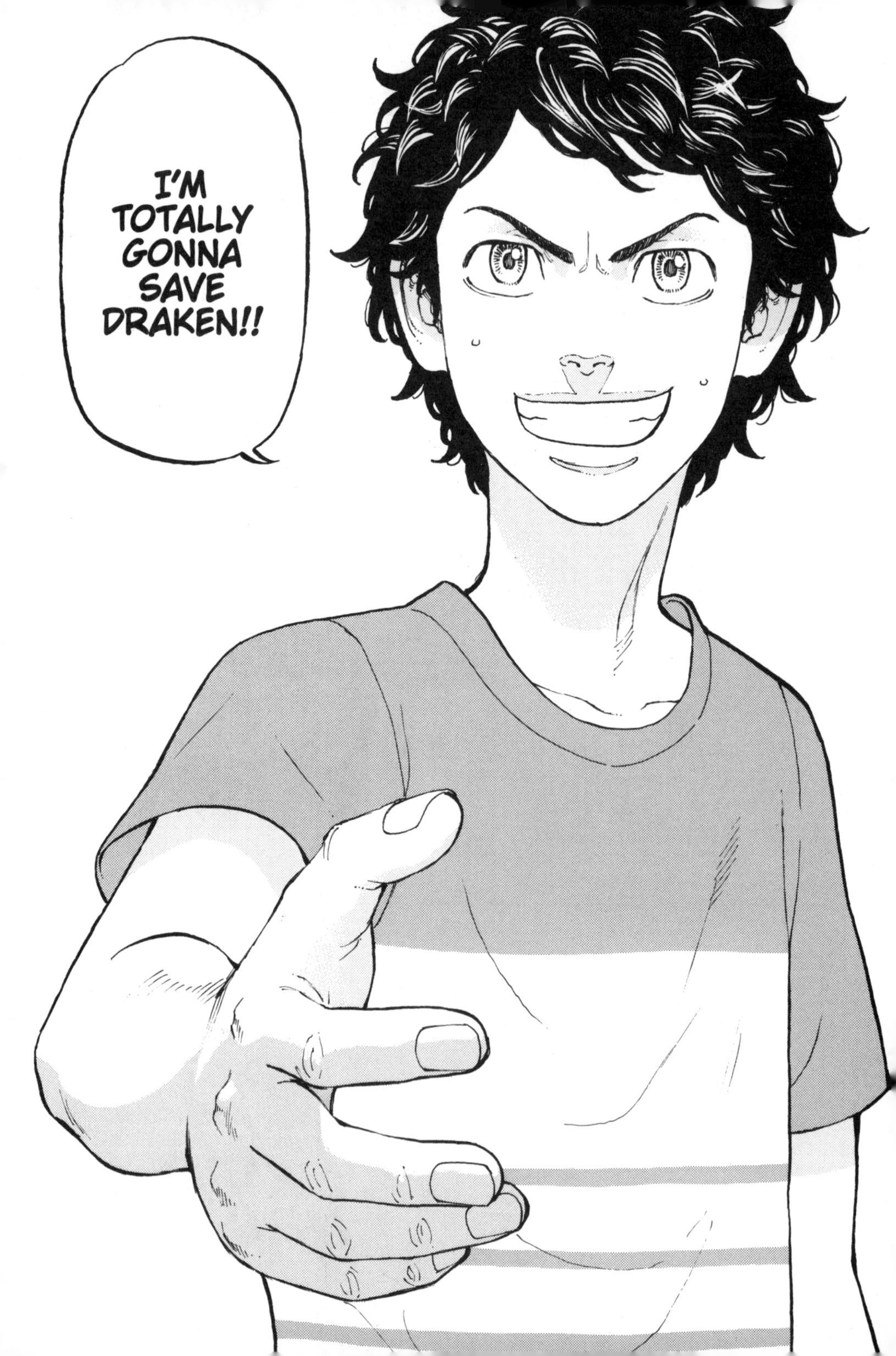
I'M TOTALLY GONNA SAVE DRAKEN!!

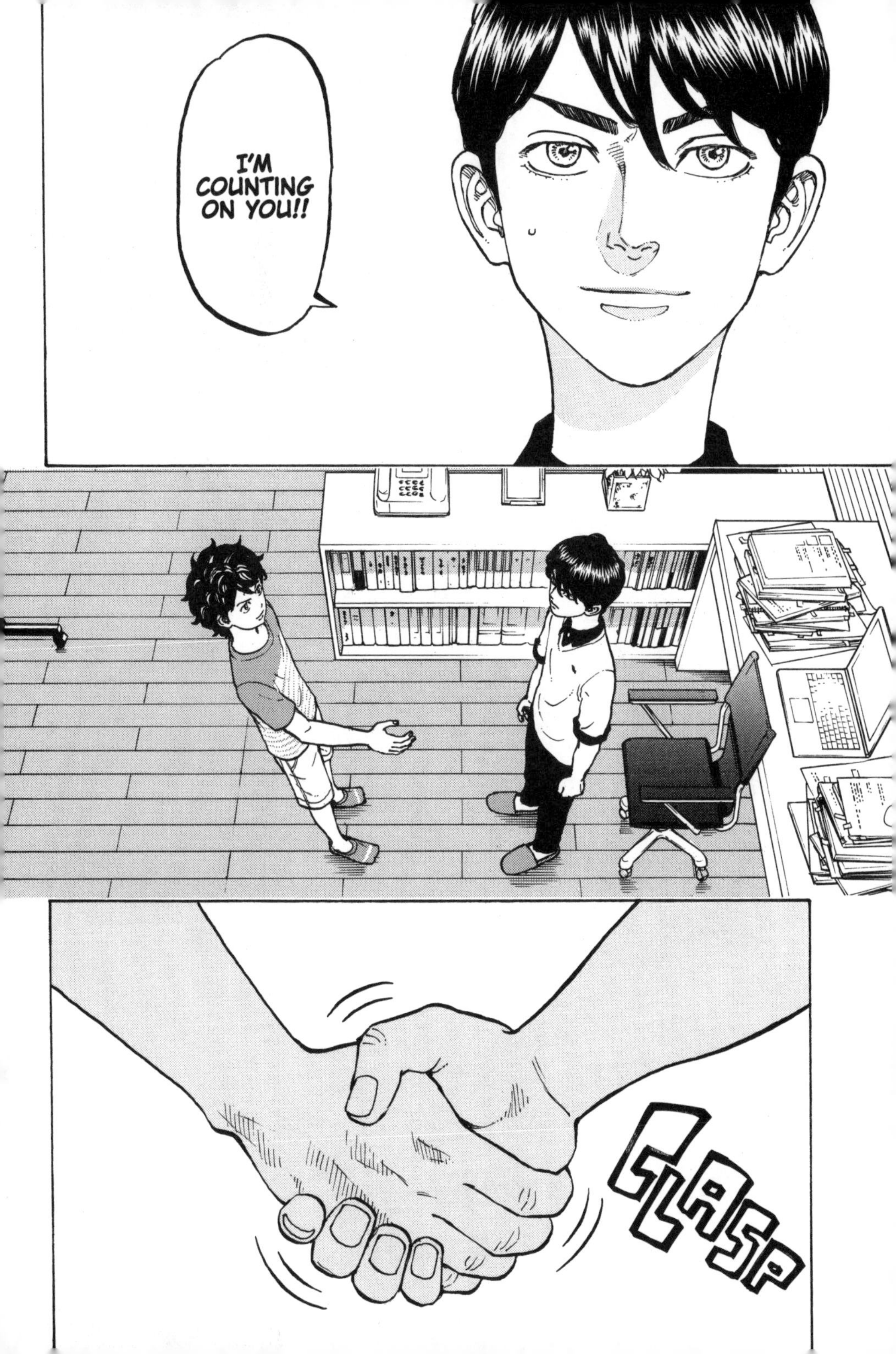
I'M COUNTING ON YOU!!
CLASP

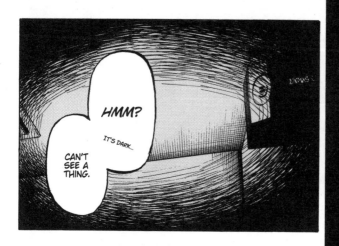

HMM?

IT'S DARK...

CAN'T SEE A THING.

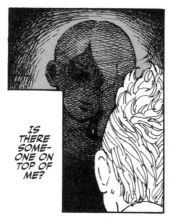

SOME-THING FEELS HEAVY.

IS THERE SOME-ONE ON TOP OF ME?

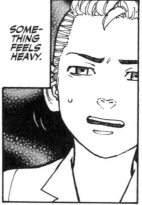

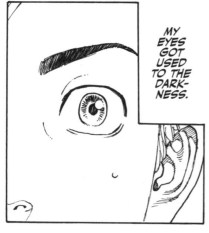

MY EYES GOT USED TO THE DARK-NESS.

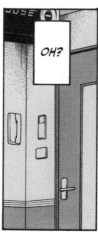

OH?

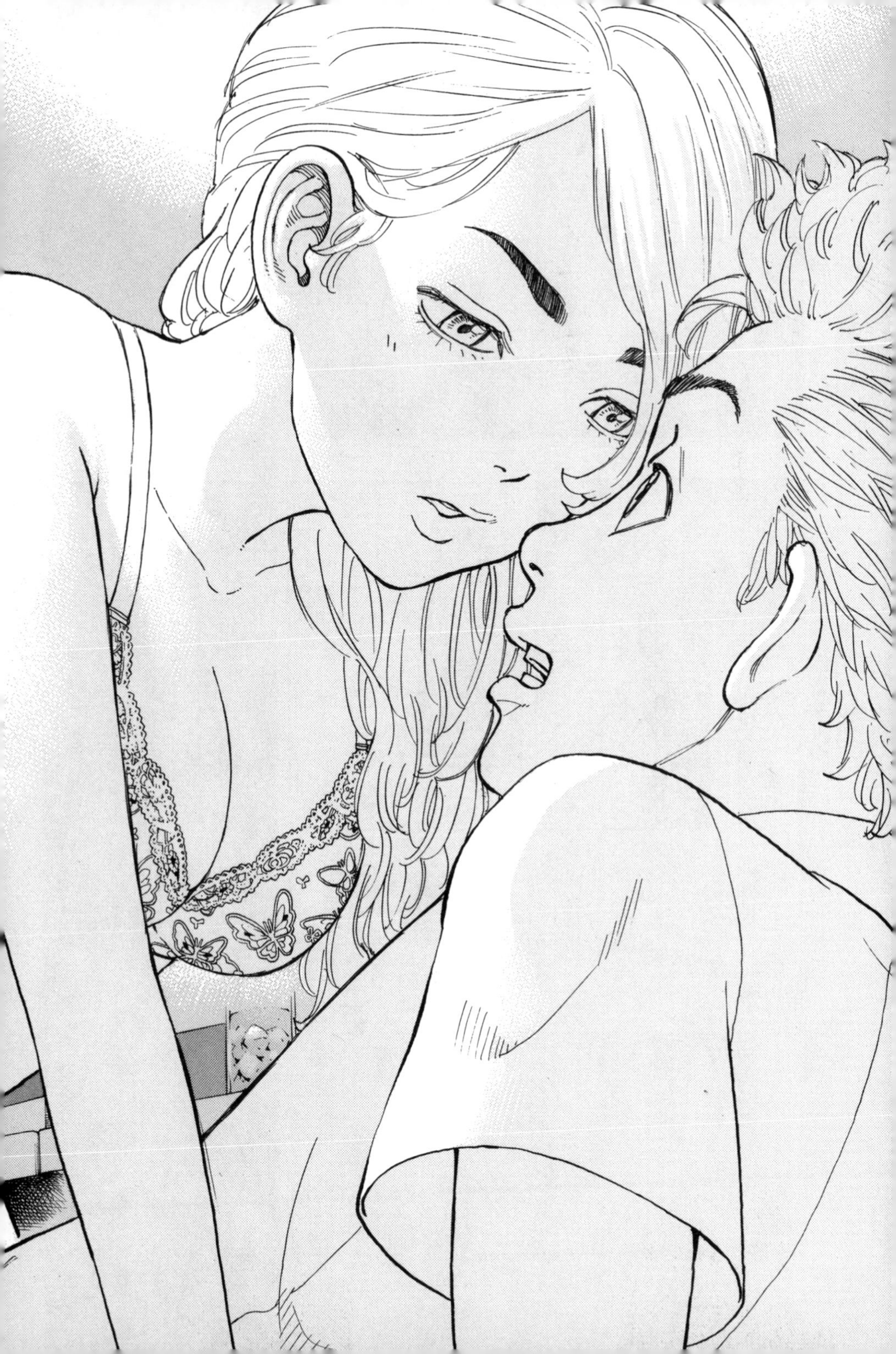

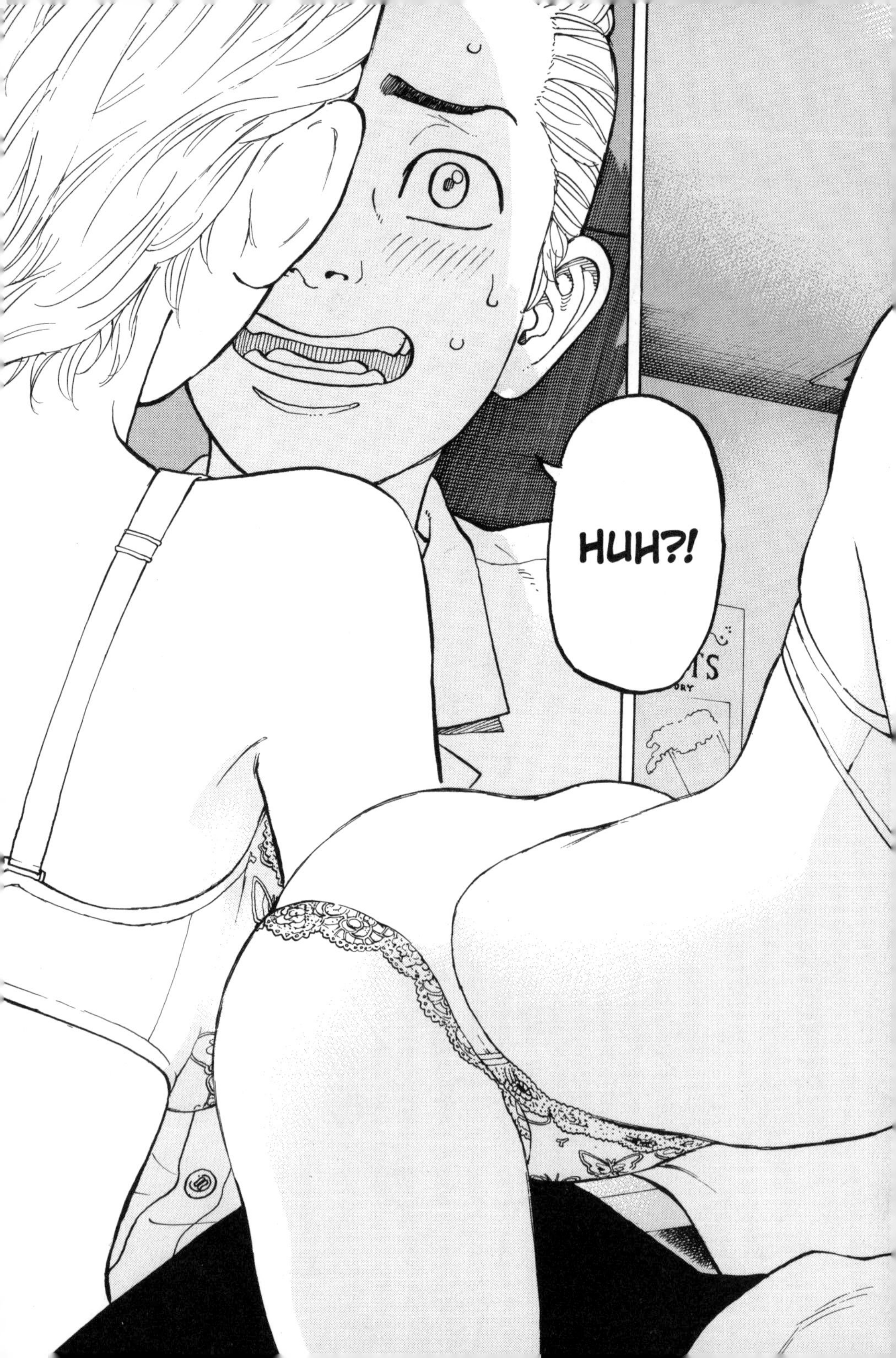
HUH?!

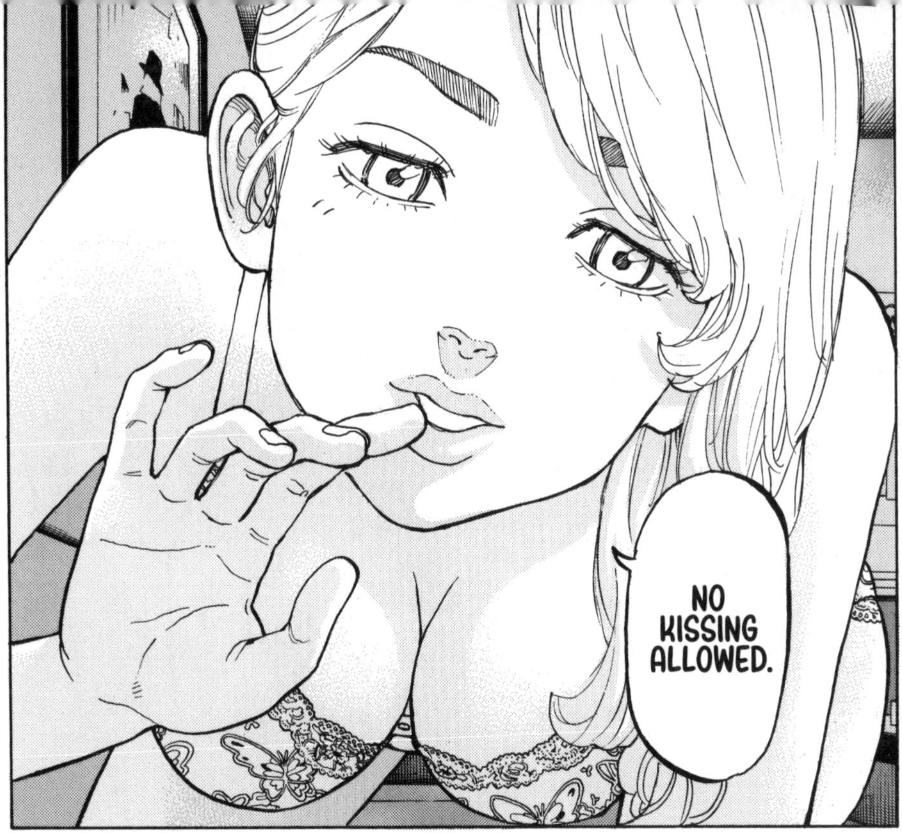
NO KISSING ALLOWED.
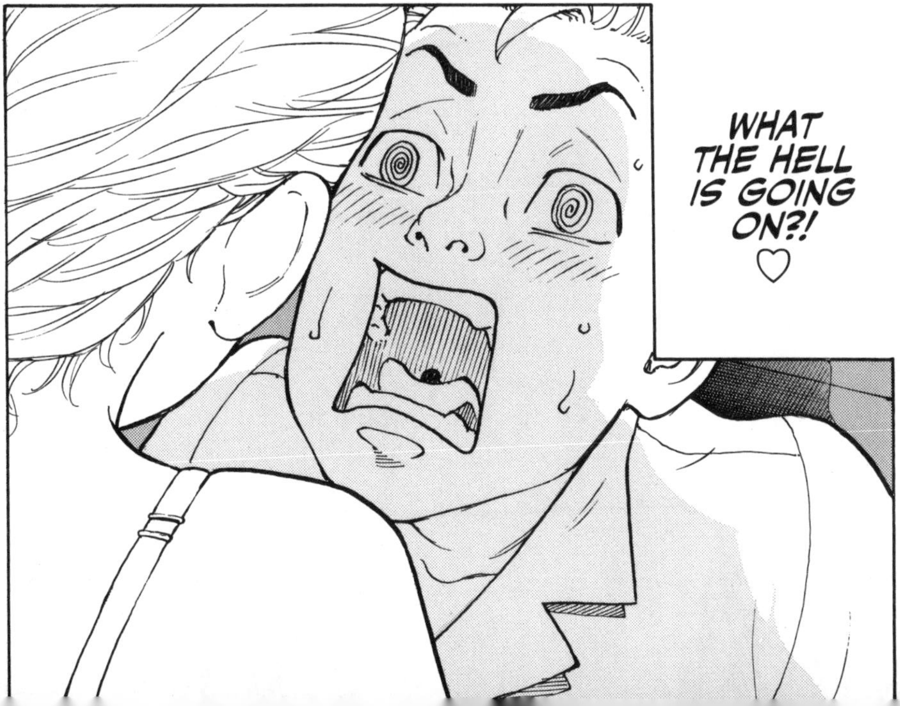
WHAT THE HELL IS GOING ON?! ♡

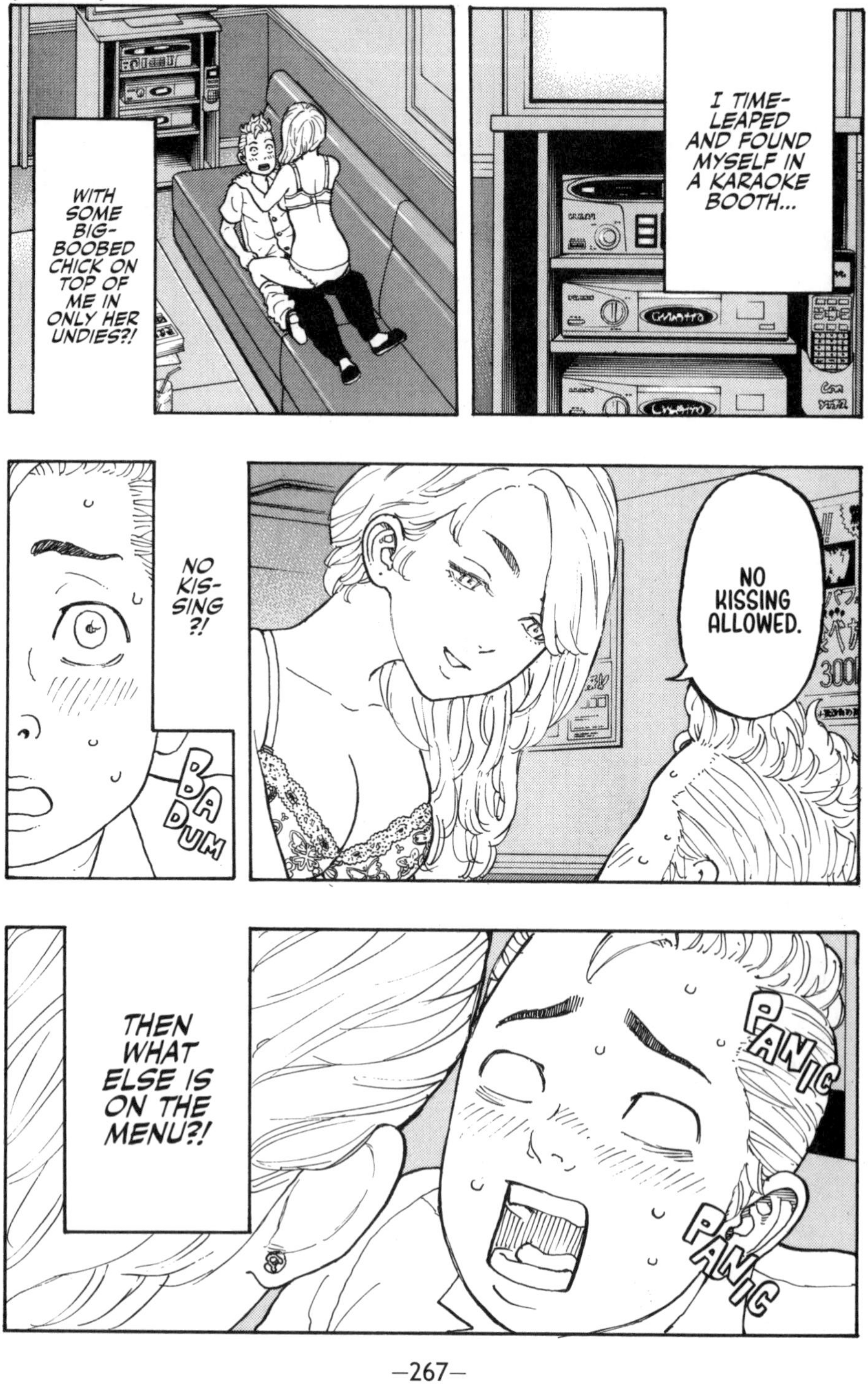
I TIME-LEAPED AND FOUND MYSELF IN A KARAOKE BOOTH...
WITH SOME BIG-BOOBED CHICK ON TOP OF ME IN ONLY HER UNDIES?!
NO KISSING ALLOWED.
NO KISSING?!
BA DUM
PANIC
PANIC
THEN WHAT ELSE IS ON THE MENU?!

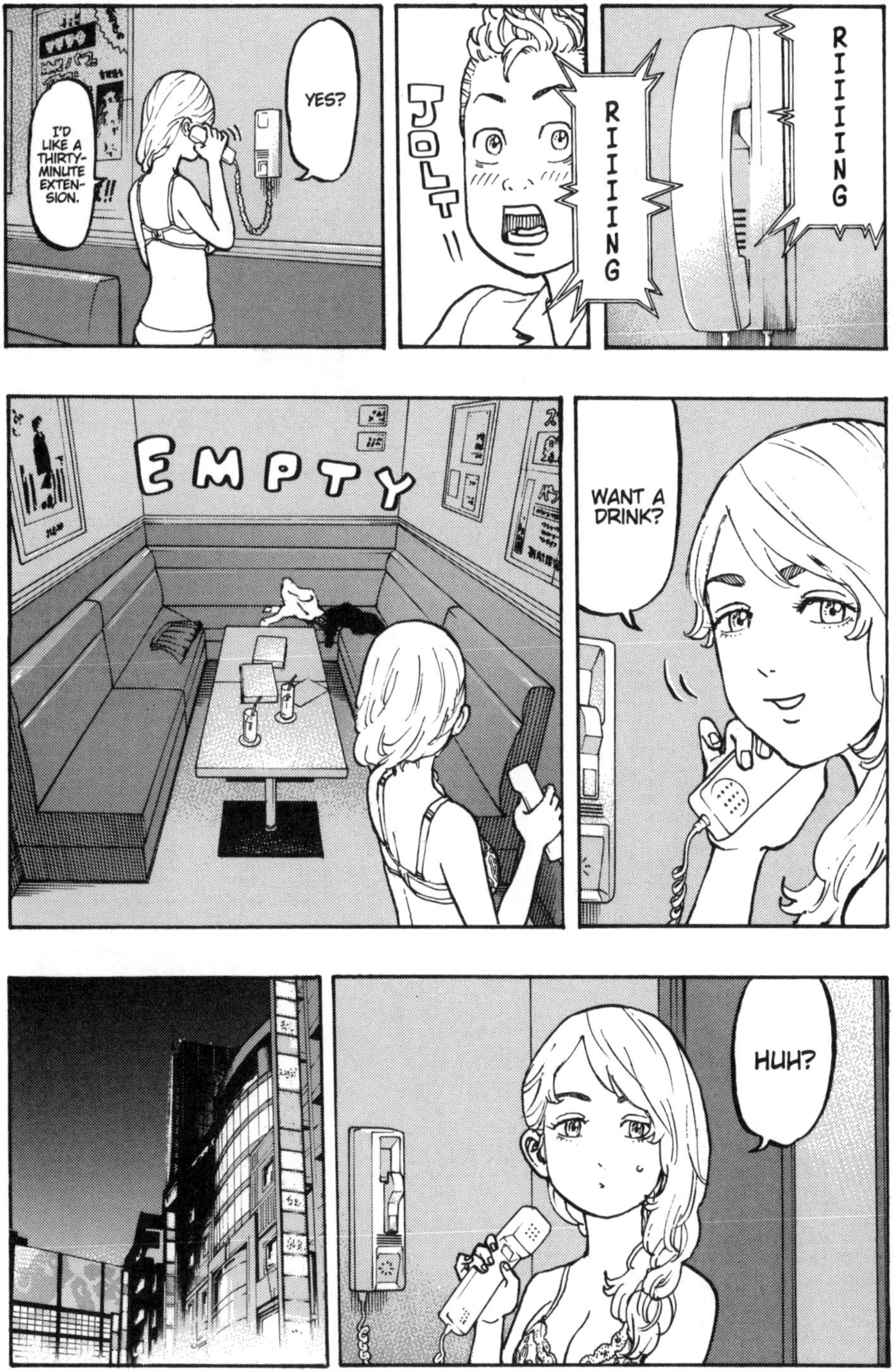
RIIIING
RIIIING
JOLT
YES?
I'D LIKE A THIRTY-MINUTE EXTENSION.
WANT A DRINK?
EMPTY
HUH?

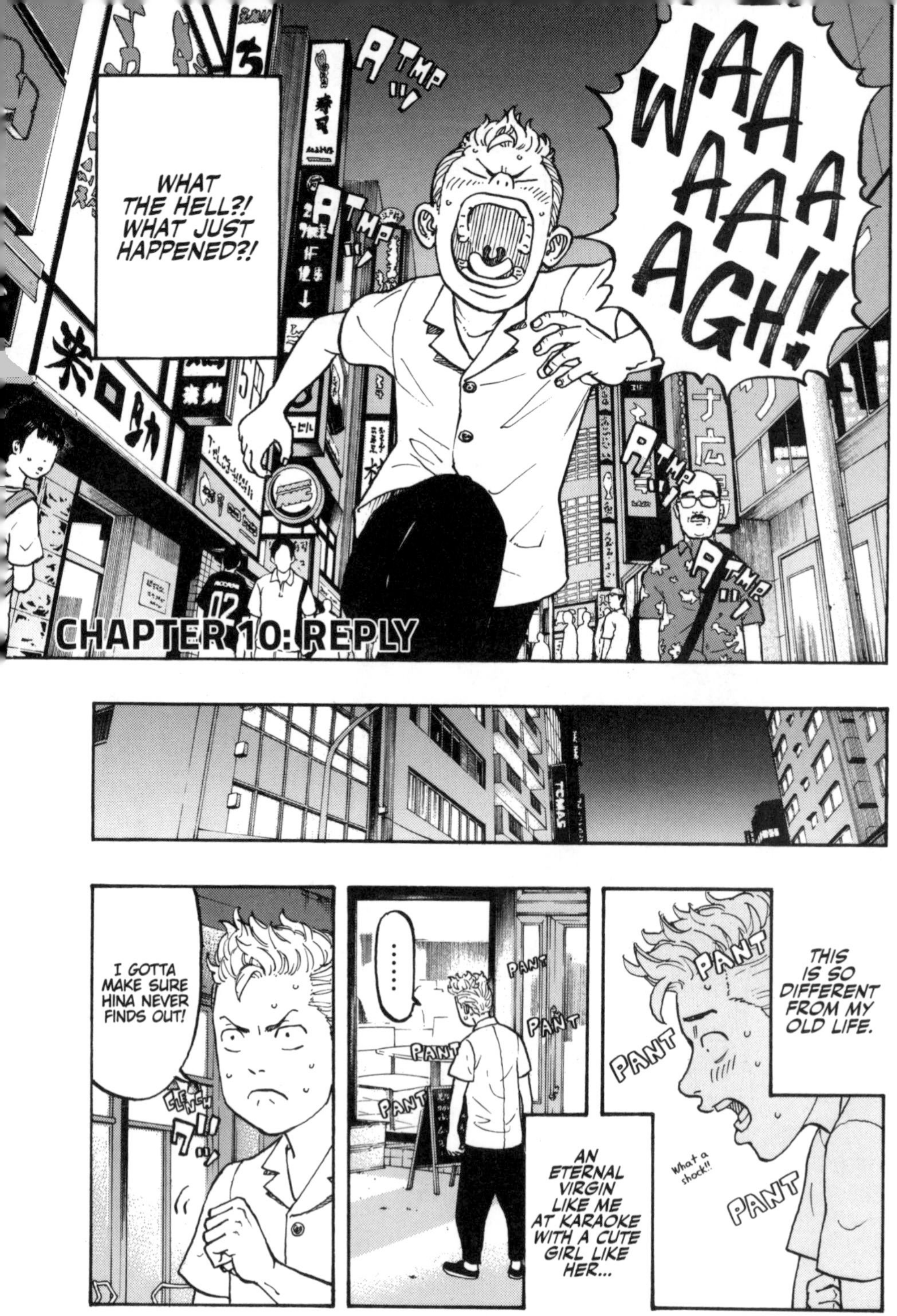
WAAAAAAAAGH!!
TMP
TMP
TMP
TMP
WHAT THE HELL?! WHAT JUST HAPPENED?!
CHAPTER 10: REPLY
THIS IS SO DIFFERENT FROM MY OLD LIFE.
PANT
PANT
What a shock!!
PANT
PANT
AN ETERNAL VIRGIN LIKE ME AT KARAOKE WITH A CUTE GIRL LIKE HER...
......
PANT
PANT
PANT
PANT
I GOTTA MAKE SURE HINA NEVER FINDS OUT!
CLENCH

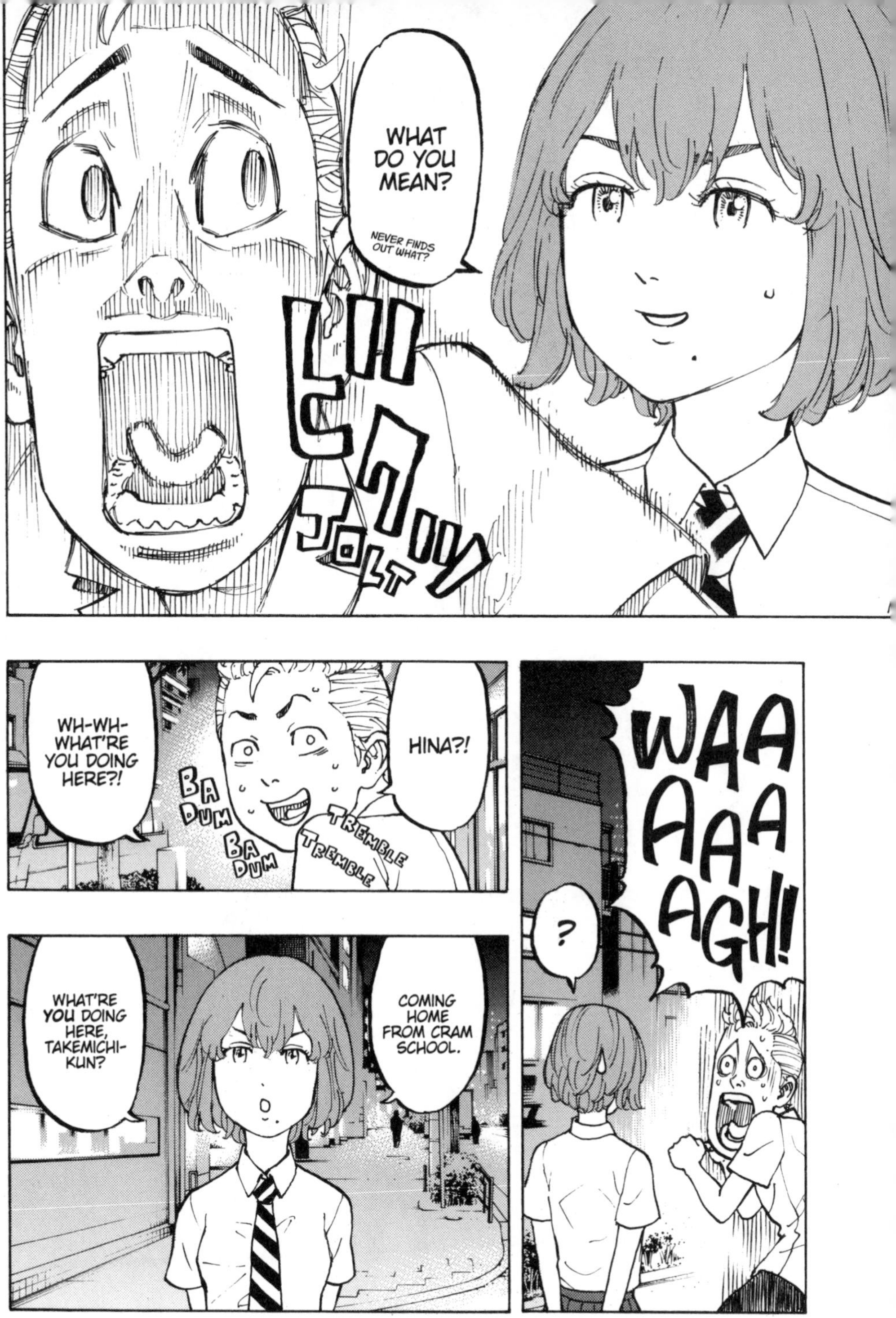
WHAT DO YOU MEAN?
NEVER FINDS OUT WHAT?
JOLT
WAAAAAAGH!
?
HINA?!
WH-WH-WHAT'RE YOU DOING HERE?!
BA DUM BA DUM
TREMBLE TREMBLE
COMING HOME FROM CRAM SCHOOL.
WHAT'RE YOU DOING HERE, TAKEMICHI-KUN?

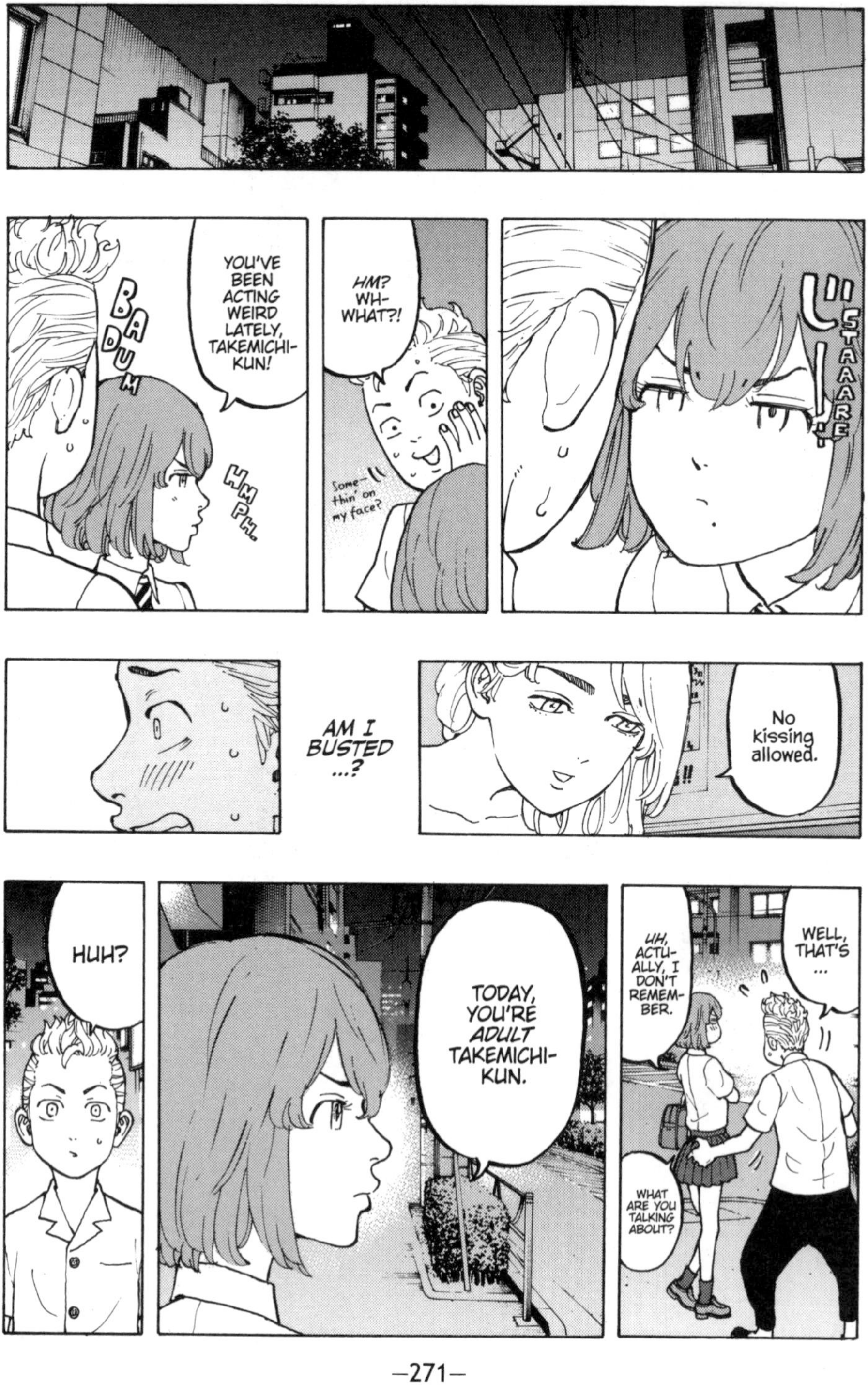

じー!!
STAAAARE
HM? WH-WHAT?!
Some-thin' on my face?
YOU'VE BEEN ACTING WEIRD LATELY, TAKEMICHI-KUN!
BADUM
HMPH.
No kissing allowed.
AM I BUSTED ...?
WELL, THAT'S ...
UH, ACTUALLY, I DON'T REMEMBER.
WHAT ARE YOU TALKING ABOUT?
TODAY, YOU'RE ADULT TAKEMICHI-KUN.
HUH?

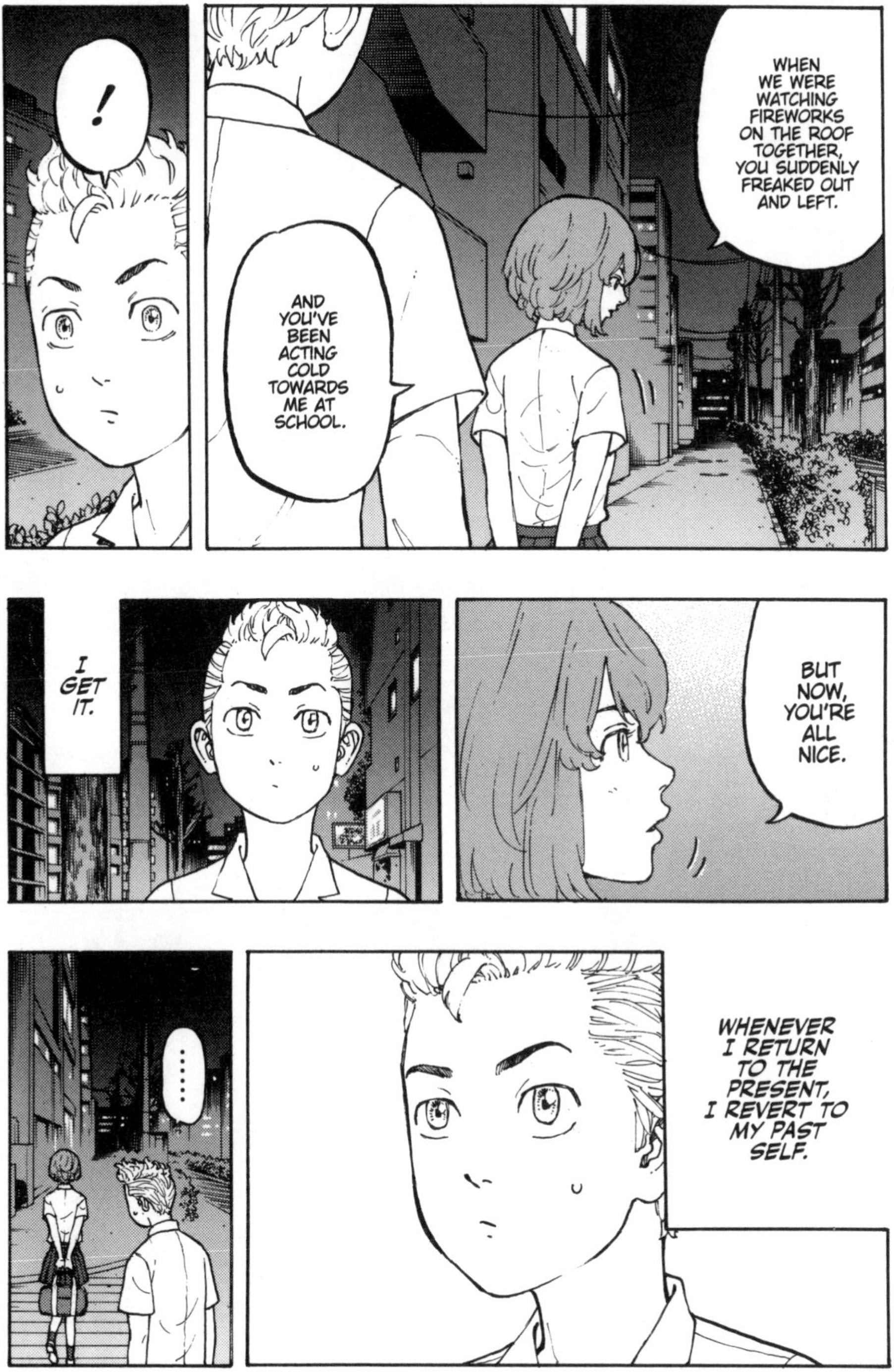
WHEN WE WERE WATCHING FIREWORKS ON THE ROOF TOGETHER, YOU SUDDENLY FREAKED OUT AND LEFT.
AND YOU'VE BEEN ACTING COLD TOWARDS ME AT SCHOOL.
!
BUT NOW, YOU'RE ALL NICE.
I GET IT.
WHENEVER I RETURN TO THE PRESENT, I REVERT TO MY PAST SELF.
......

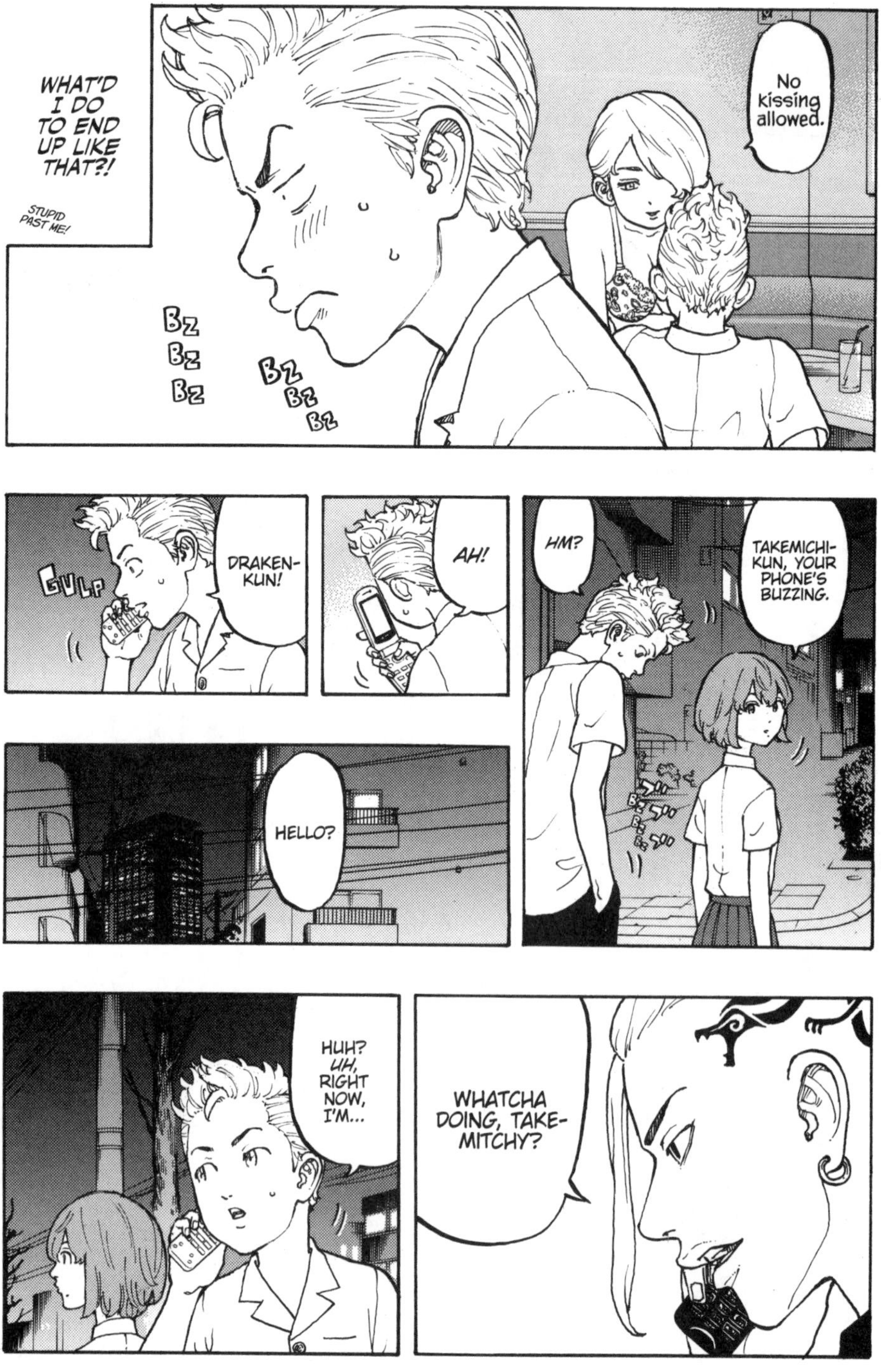
No kissing allowed.
WHAT'D I DO TO END UP LIKE THAT?!
STUPID PAST ME!
BZ BZ BZ
BZ BZ BZ
TAKEMICHI-KUN, YOUR PHONE'S BUZZING.
HM?
AH!
DRAKEN-KUN!
GULP
HELLO?
WHATCHA DOING, TAKE-MITCHY?
HUH? UH, RIGHT NOW, I'M...

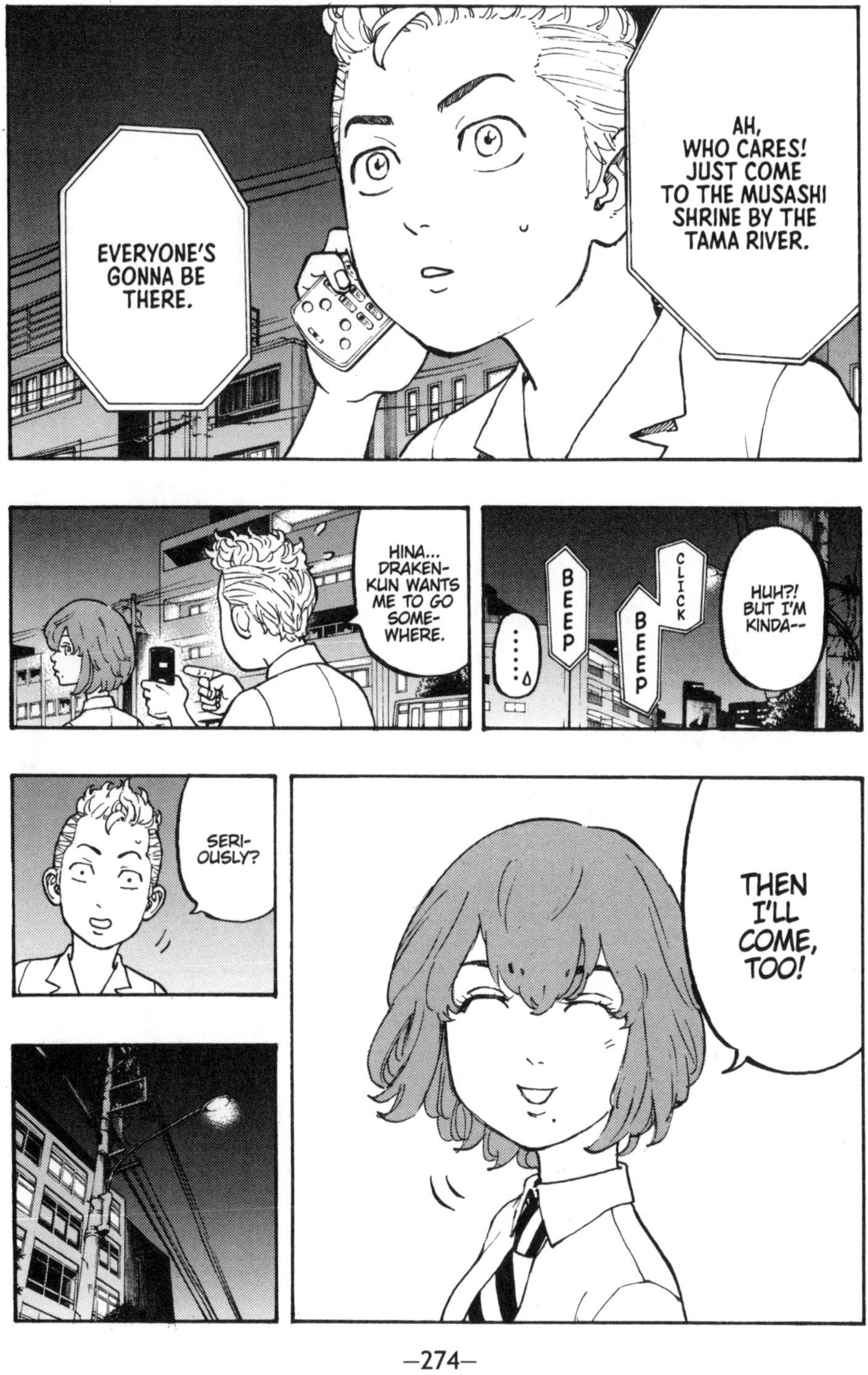
AH, WHO CARES! JUST COME TO THE MUSASHI SHRINE BY THE TAMA RIVER.
EVERYONE'S GONNA BE THERE.
HUH?! BUT I'M KINDA--
CLICK
BEEP
BEEP
......
HINA... DRAKEN-KUN WANTS ME TO GO SOME-WHERE.
THEN I'LL COME, TOO!
SERI-OUSLY?

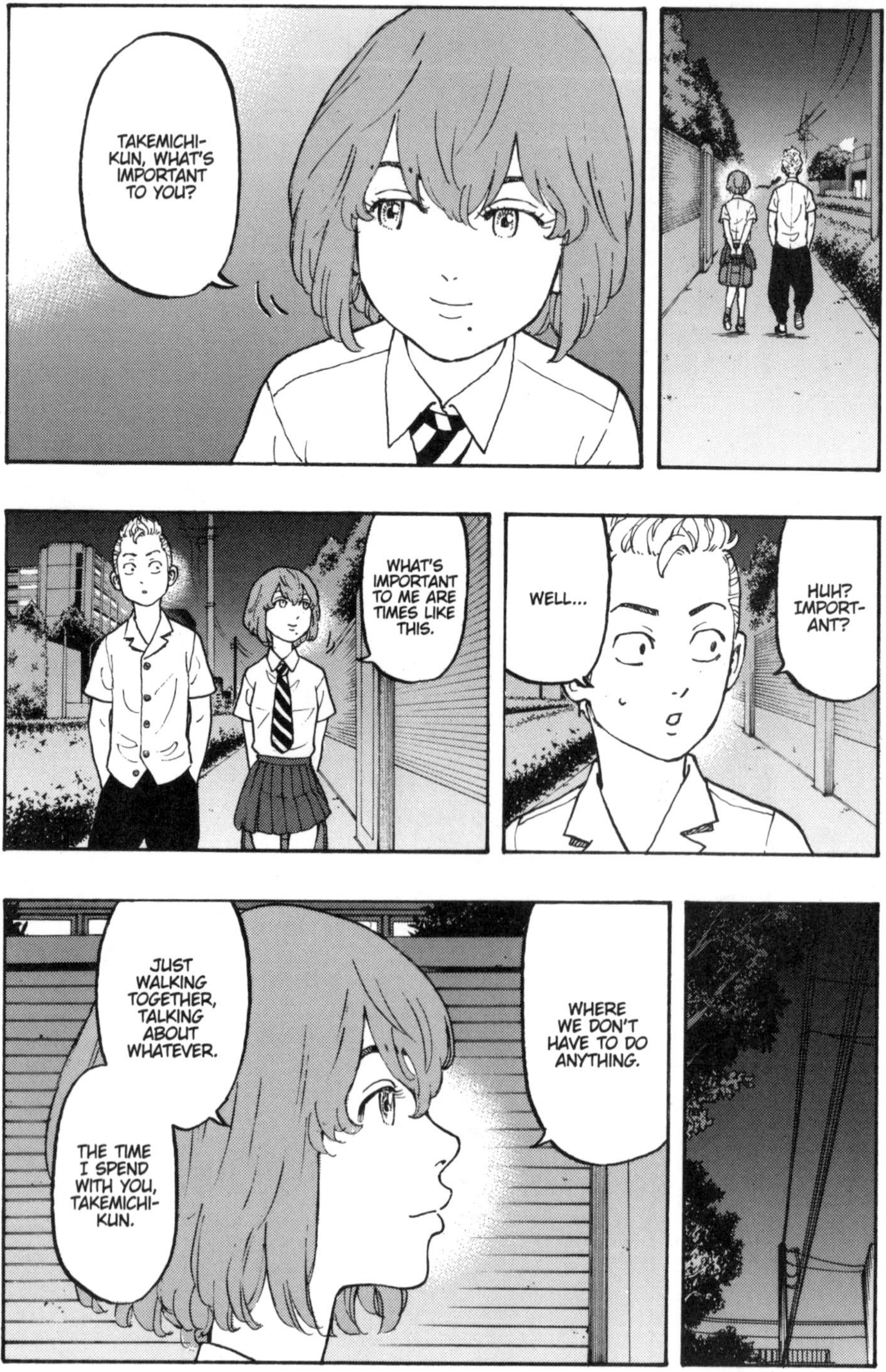

TAKEMICHI-KUN, WHAT'S IMPORTANT TO YOU?
HUH? IMPORTANT?
WELL...
WHAT'S IMPORTANT TO ME ARE TIMES LIKE THIS.
WHERE WE DON'T HAVE TO DO ANYTHING.
JUST WALKING TOGETHER, TALKING ABOUT WHATEVER.
THE TIME I SPEND WITH YOU, TAKEMICHI-KUN.

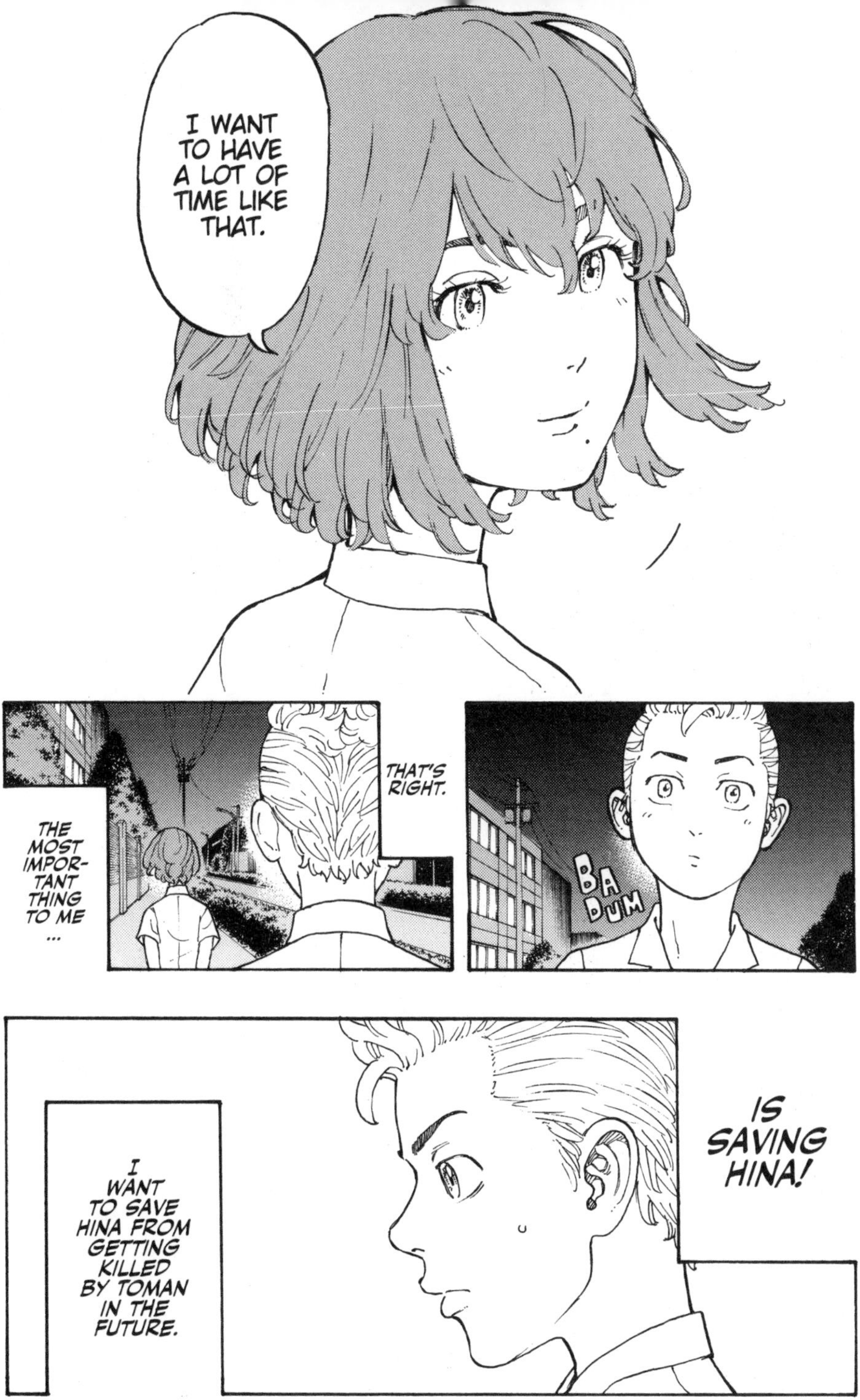
I WANT TO HAVE A LOT OF TIME LIKE THAT.
BA DUM
THAT'S RIGHT.
THE MOST IMPOR-TANT THING TO ME ...
IS SAVING HINA!
I WANT TO SAVE HINA FROM GETTING KILLED BY TOMAN IN THE FUTURE.

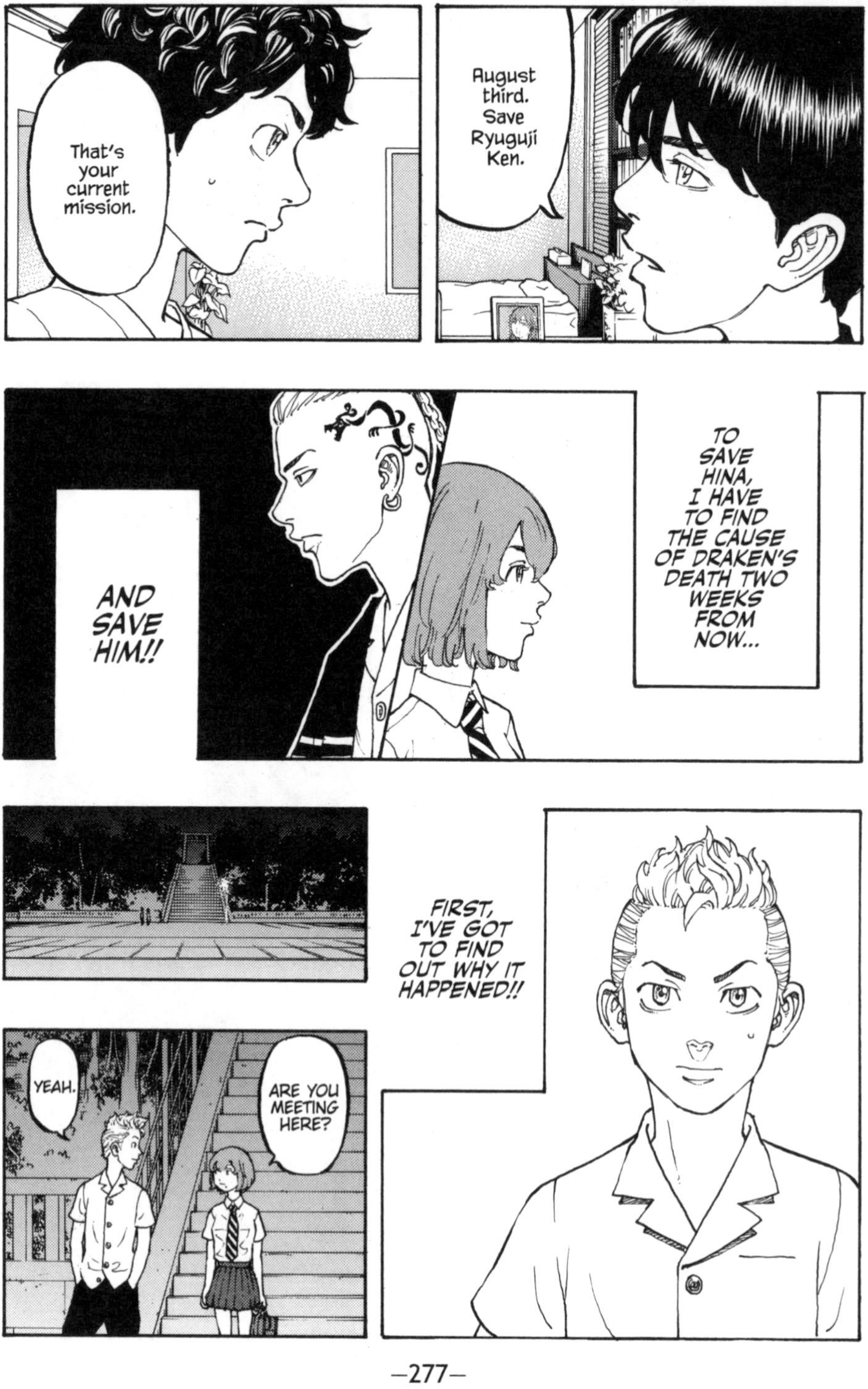
August third. Save Ryuguji Ken.
That's your current mission.
TO SAVE HINA, I HAVE TO FIND THE CAUSE OF DRAKEN'S DEATH TWO WEEKS FROM NOW...
AND SAVE HIM!!
FIRST, I'VE GOT TO FIND OUT WHY IT HAPPENED!!
ARE YOU MEETING HERE?
YEAH.

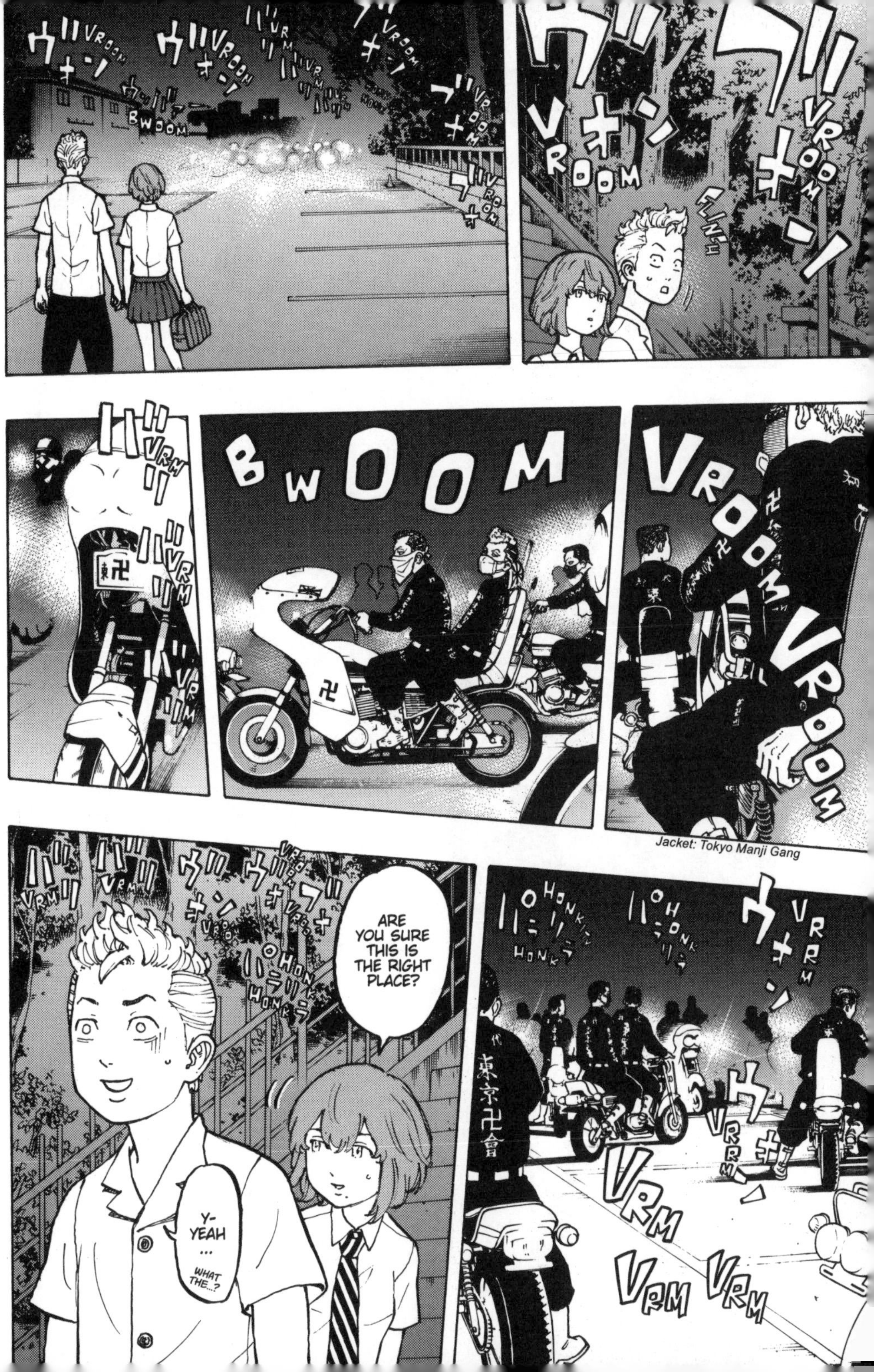
VROOM
VROOM
FLINCH
VROOM
VROOM
BWOOM
VRM
VROOM
VROOM
BWOOM
VRM
Jacket: Tokyo Manji Gang
HONK
HONK
VRRM
VRRM
VRM
VRM
VRM
東京卍會
ARE YOU SURE THIS IS THE RIGHT PLACE?
Y-YEAH... WHAT THE...?
VRM
VRM
HONK

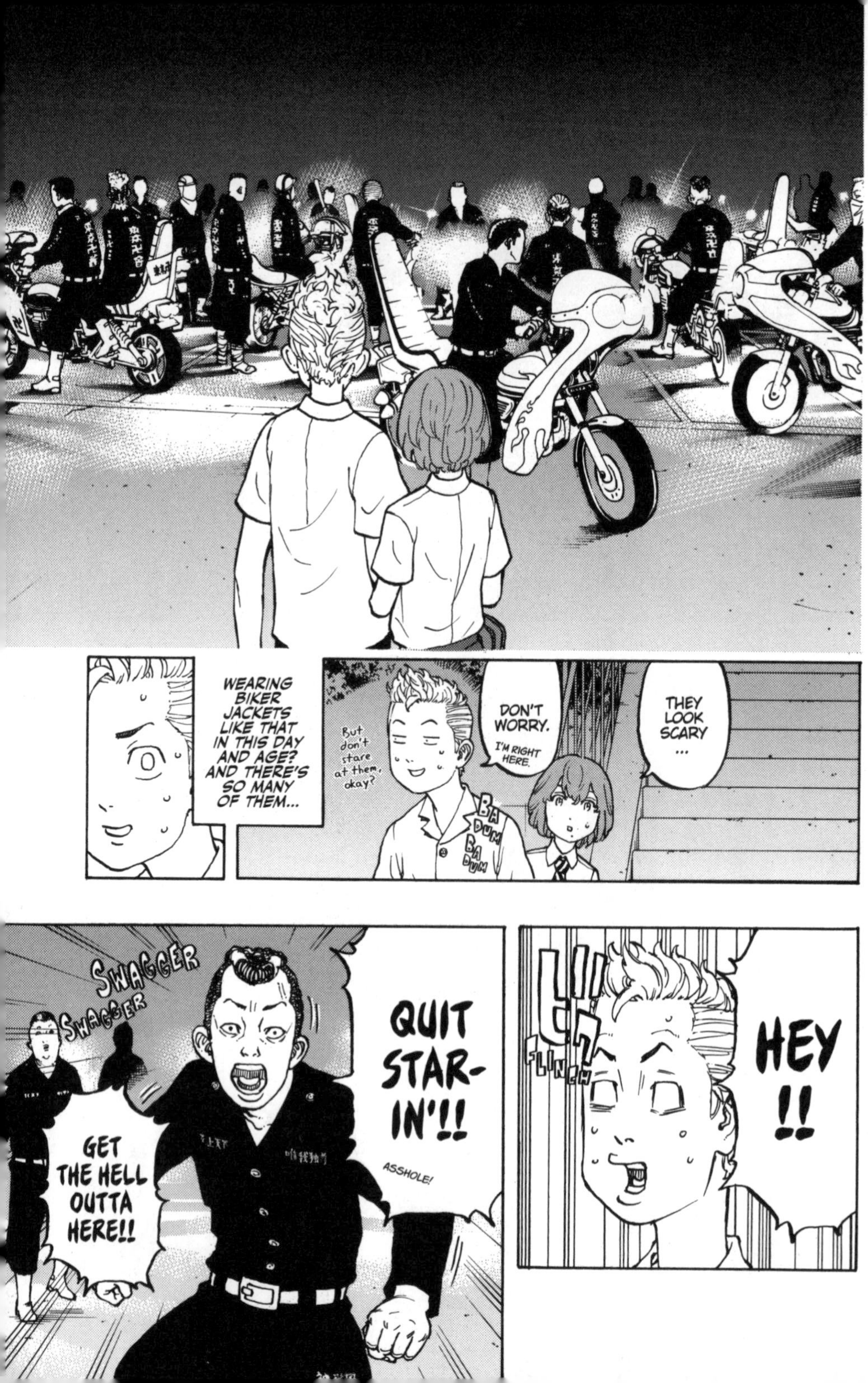
THEY LOOK SCARY ...
DON'T WORRY.
I'M RIGHT HERE.
But don't stare at them, okay?
BA DUM BA DUM
WEARING BIKER JACKETS LIKE THAT IN THIS DAY AND AGE? AND THERE'S SO MANY OF THEM...
HEY!!
FLINCH
QUIT STAR-IN'!!
ASSHOLE!
SWAGGER
SWAGGER
GET THE HELL OUTTA HERE!!

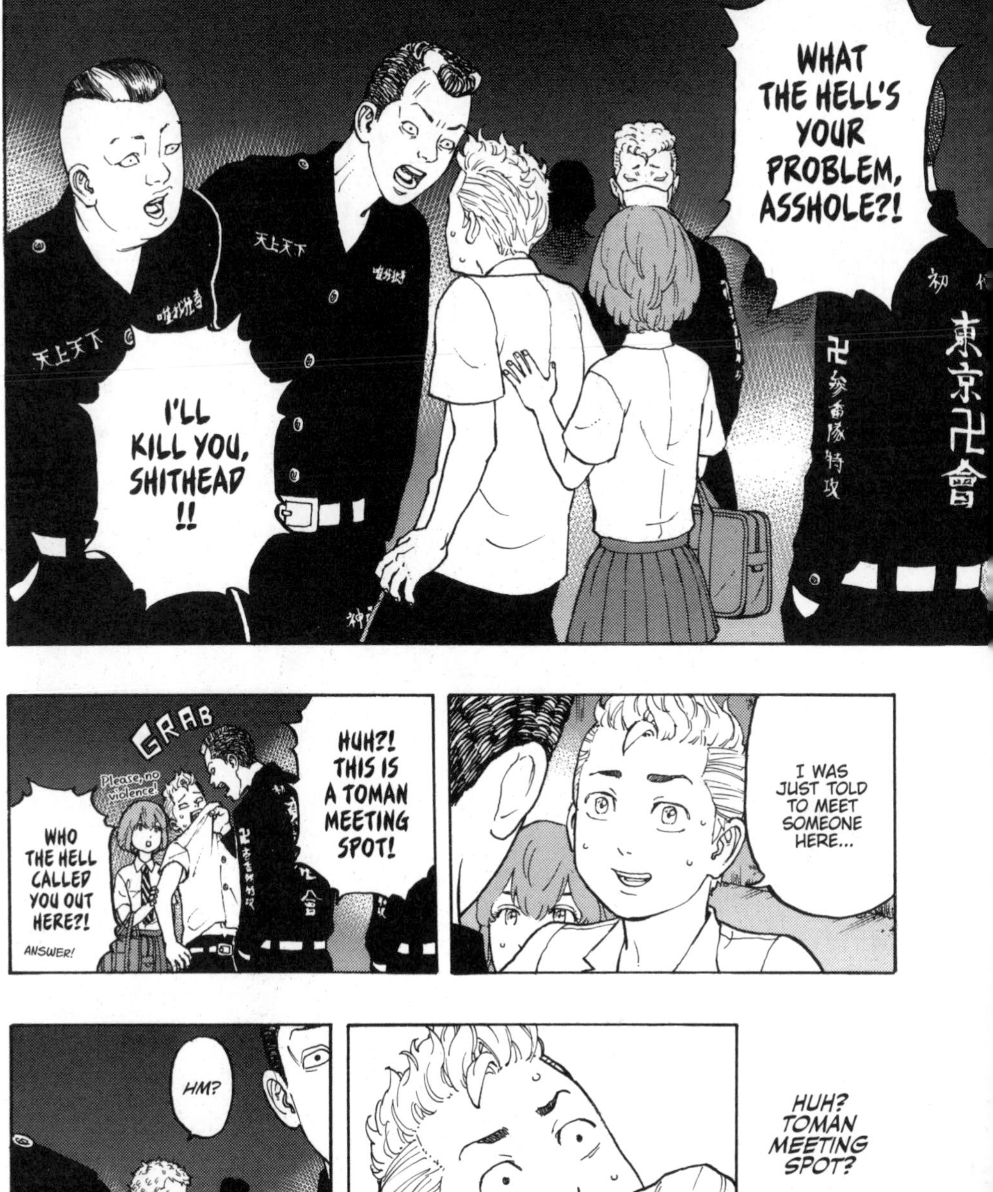
WHAT THE HELL'S YOUR PROBLEM, ASSHOLE?!
I'LL KILL YOU, SHITHEAD!!
東京卍會
天上天下
I WAS JUST TOLD TO MEET SOMEONE HERE...
HUH?! THIS IS A TOMAN MEETING SPOT!
GRAB
Please, no violence!
WHO THE HELL CALLED YOU OUT HERE?!
ANSWER!
HUH? TOMAN MEETING SPOT?
HM?

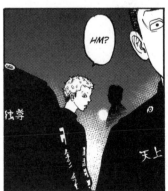

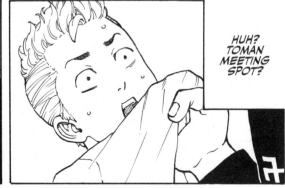

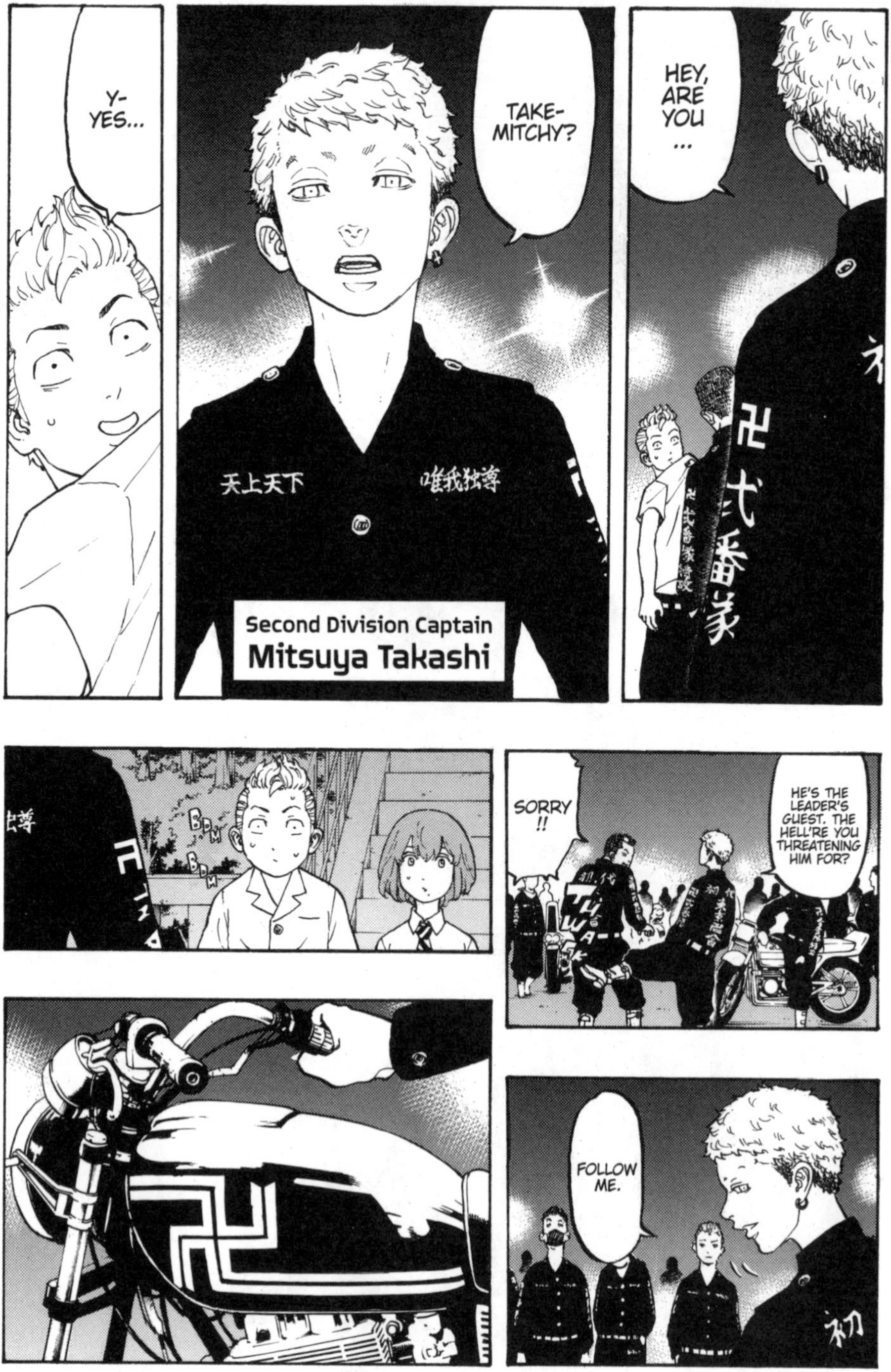
HEY, ARE YOU ...
TAKE-MITCHY?
唯我独尊
天上天下
Second Division Captain
Mitsuya Takashi
Y-YES...
HE'S THE LEADER'S GUEST. THE HELL'RE YOU THREATENING HIM FOR?
SORRY!!
THWAK
BDM
BDM
FOLLOW ME.

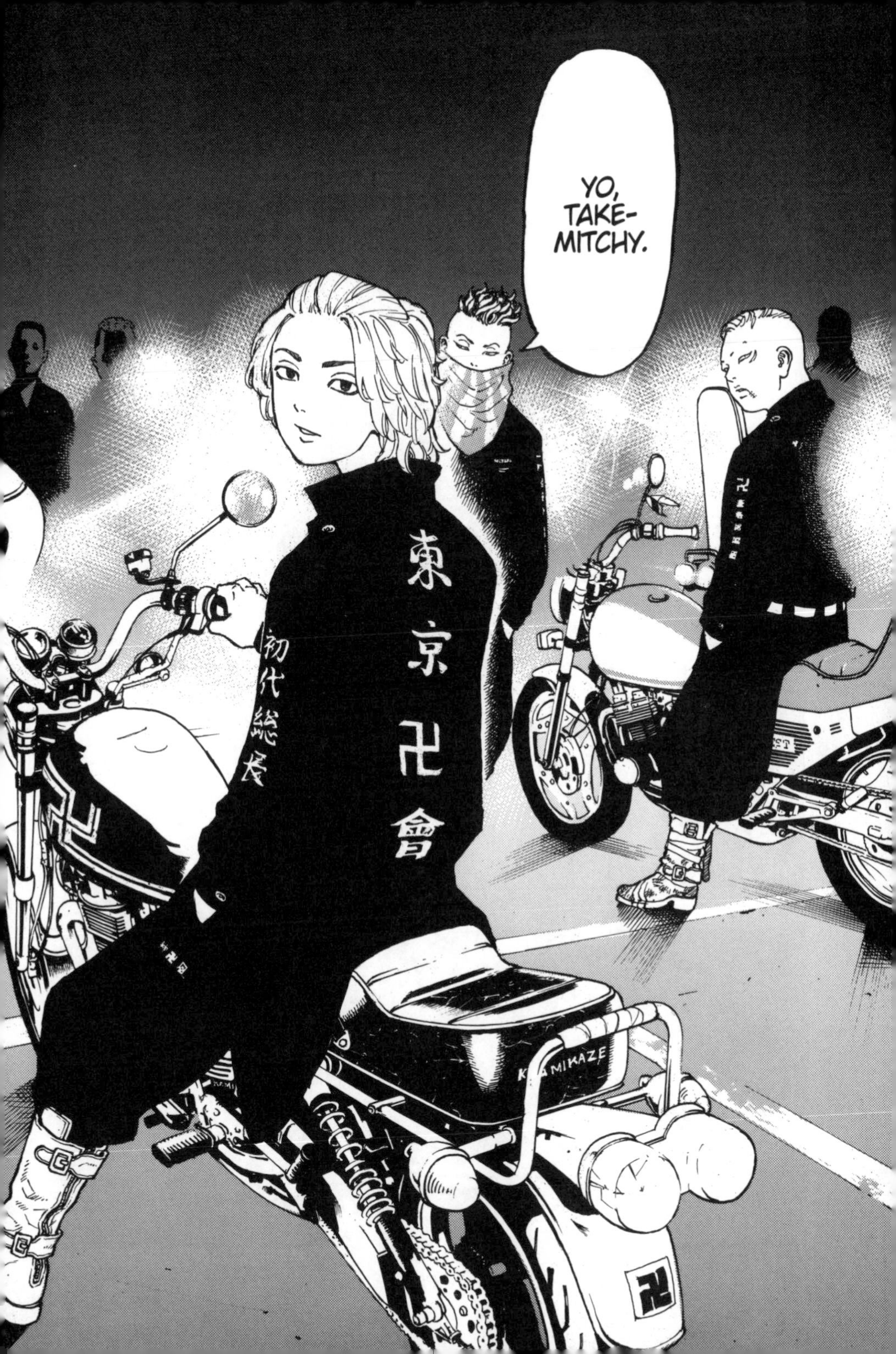
YO, TAKE-MITCHY.
東京卍會
初代総長
KAMIKAZE

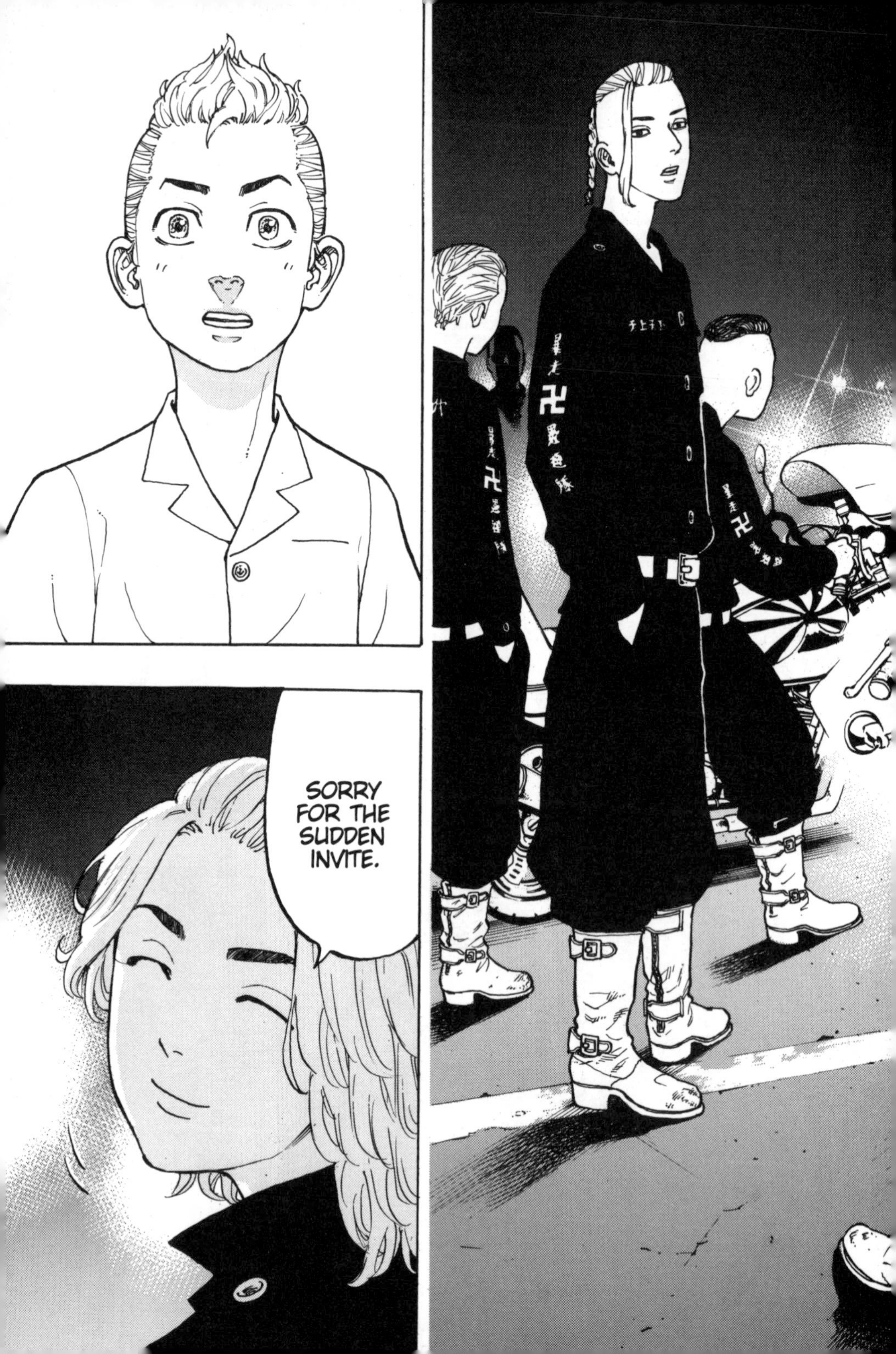
SORRY FOR THE SUDDEN INVITE.

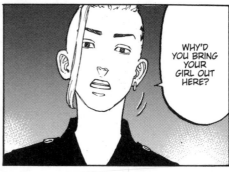

WHY'D YOU BRING YOUR GIRL OUT HERE?
SORRY.
I DIDN'T THINK IT WAS GONNA BE LIKE THIS.
AH! HINA-CHAN, SORRY ABOUT THE OTHER DAY.
I WAS JUST TESTING TAKEMITCHY. DIDN'T MEAN TO SCARE YOU.
OH! NO, IT'S TOTALLY OKAY!!
HEY! EMMA!!
HUH?
EMMA...?
HERE I AAAM!

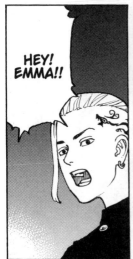

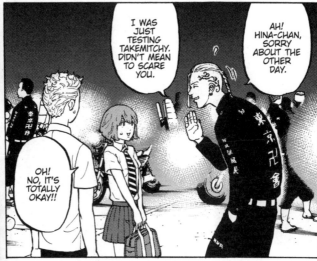

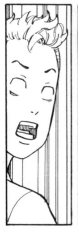

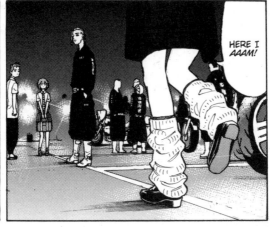

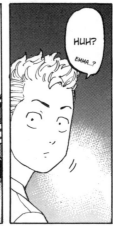

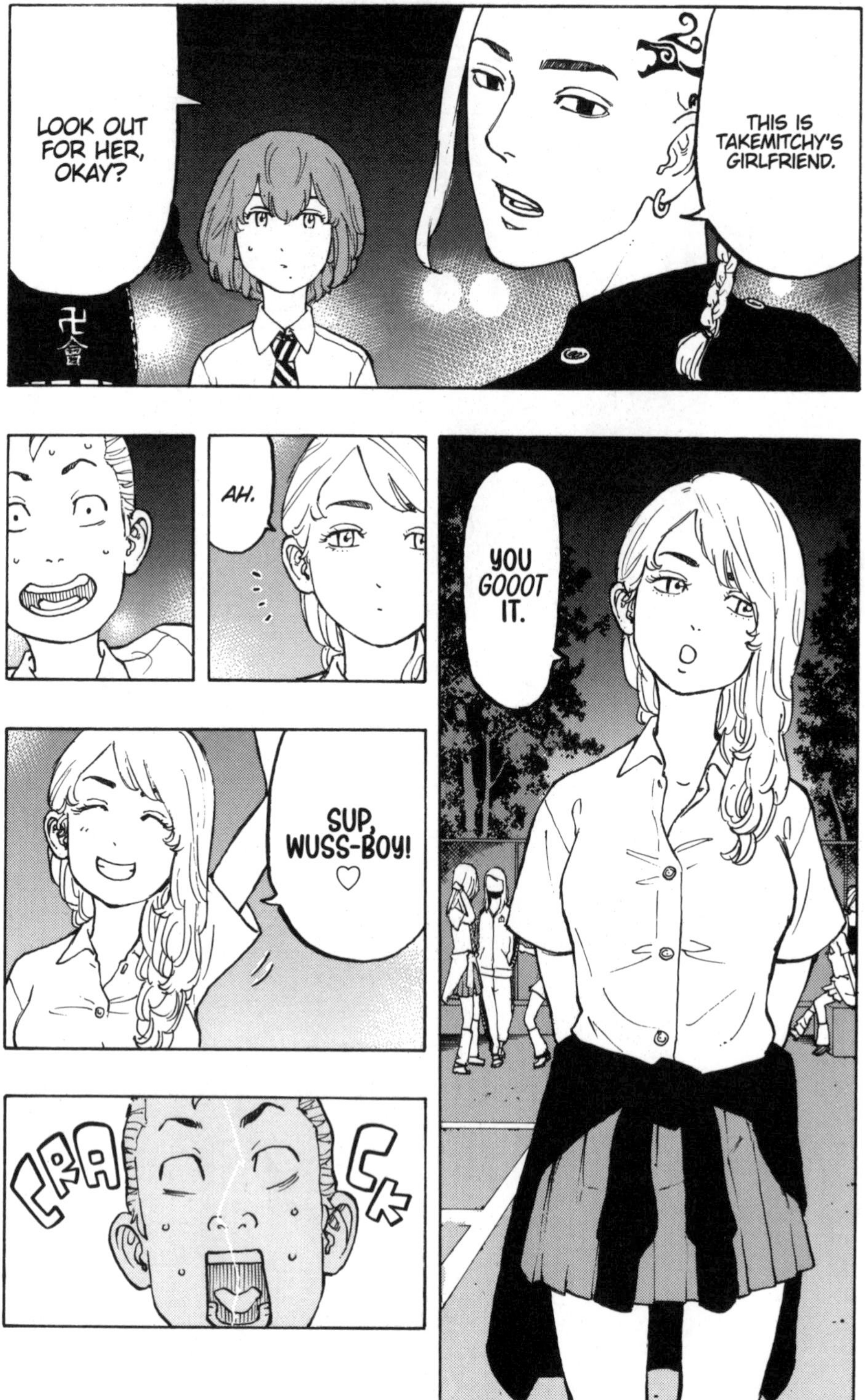
THIS IS TAKEMITCHY'S GIRLFRIEND.
LOOK OUT FOR HER, OKAY?
卍會
YOU GOOOT IT.
AH.
SUP, WUSS-BOY! ♡
CRACK

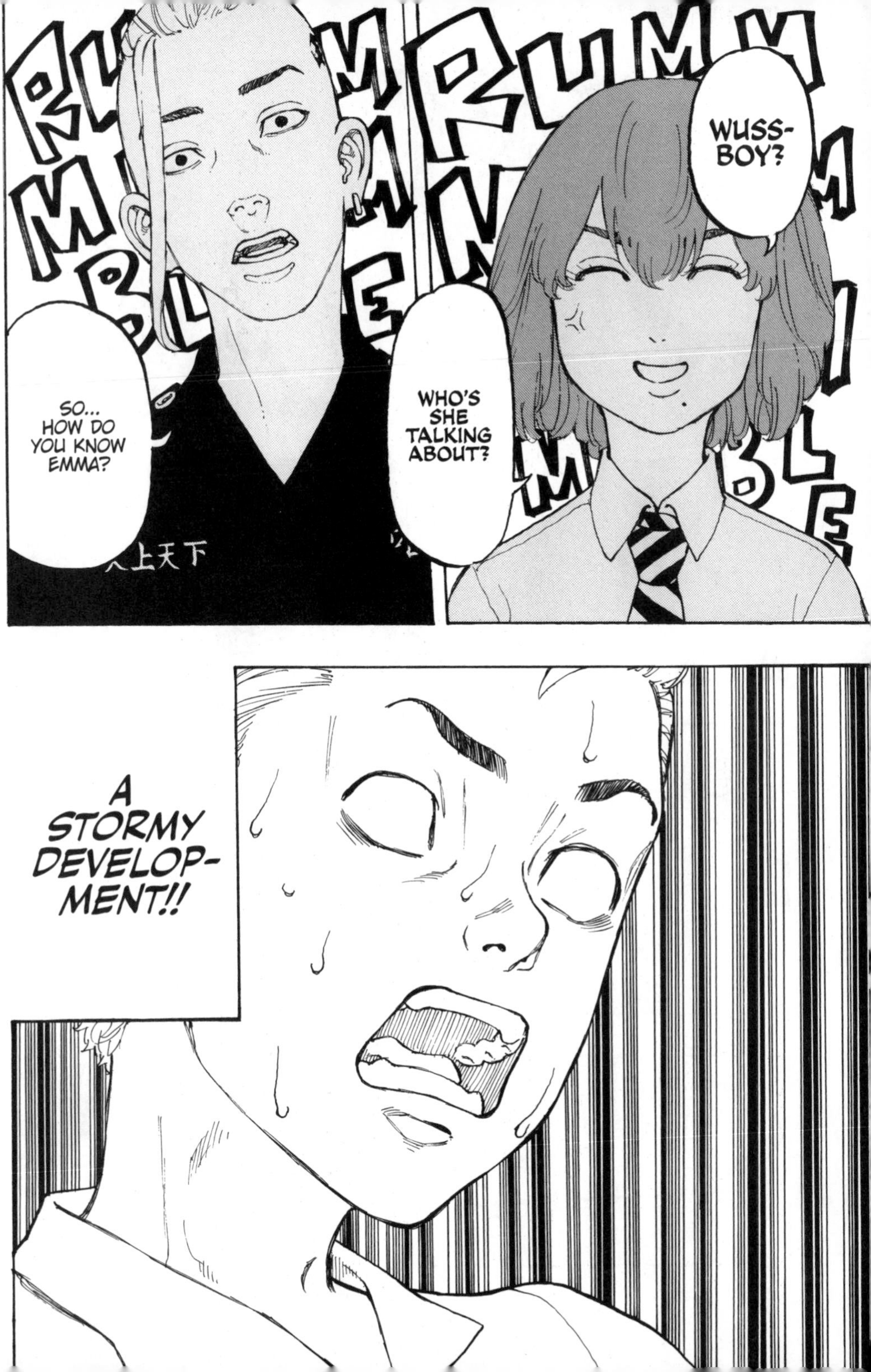
WUSS-BOY?
WHO'S SHE TALKING ABOUT?
SO... HOW DO YOU KNOW EMMA?
A STORMY DEVELOPMENT!!

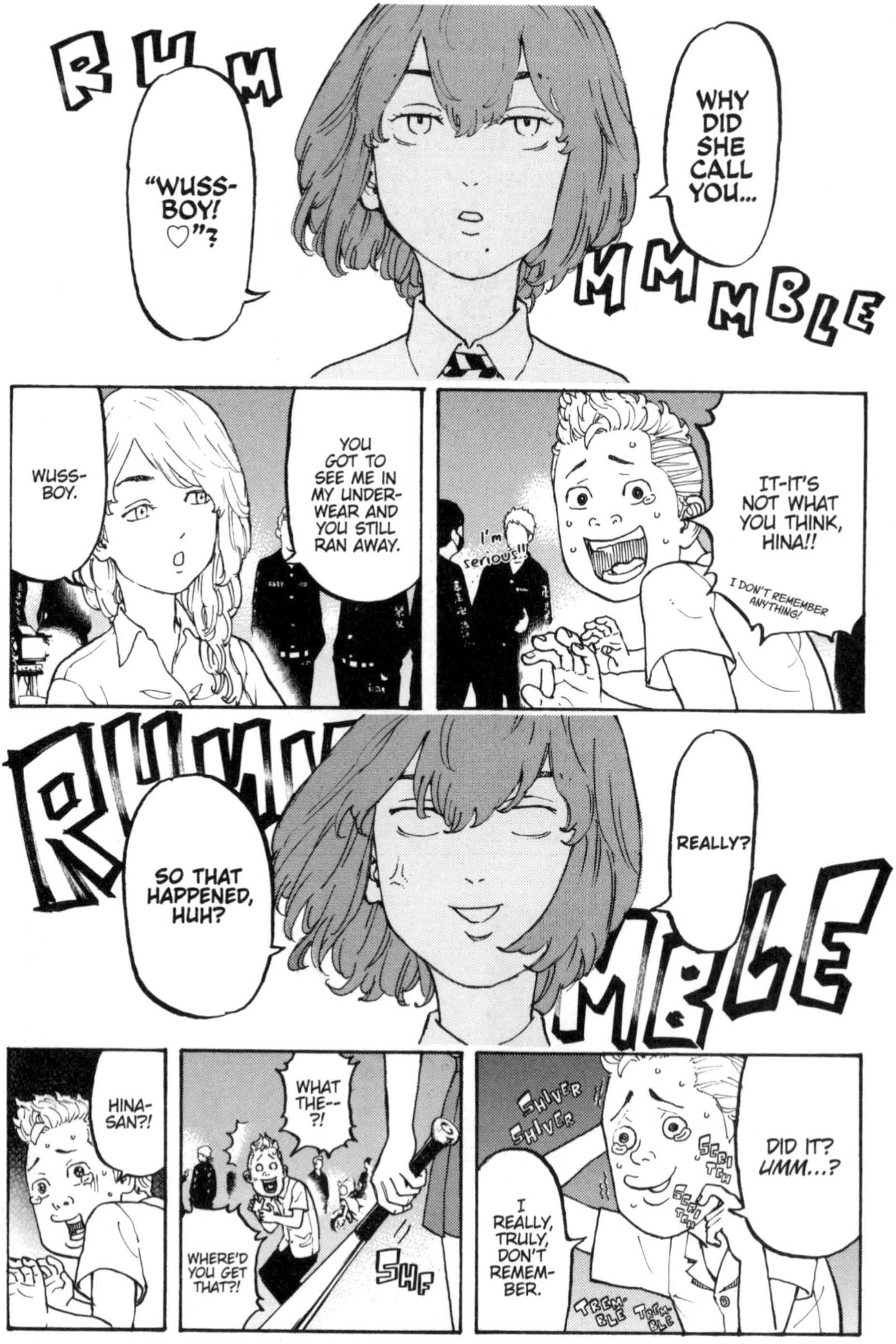
WHY DID SHE CALL YOU...
“WUSS-BOY! ♡”?
RUMMMMMBLE
IT-IT'S NOT WHAT YOU THINK, HINA!!
I DON'T REMEMBER ANYTHING!
I'm serious!!
YOU GOT TO SEE ME IN MY UNDER-WEAR AND YOU STILL RAN AWAY.
WUSS-BOY.
REALLY?
SO THAT HAPPENED, HUH?
DID IT? UMM...?
SHIVER SHIVER
SCRITCH SCRITCH
I REALLY, TRULY, DON'T REMEM-BER.
TREMBLE TREMBLE
WHAT THE--?!
WHERE'D YOU GET THAT?!
SHF
HINA-SAN?!

CHAPTER 11: REBURN

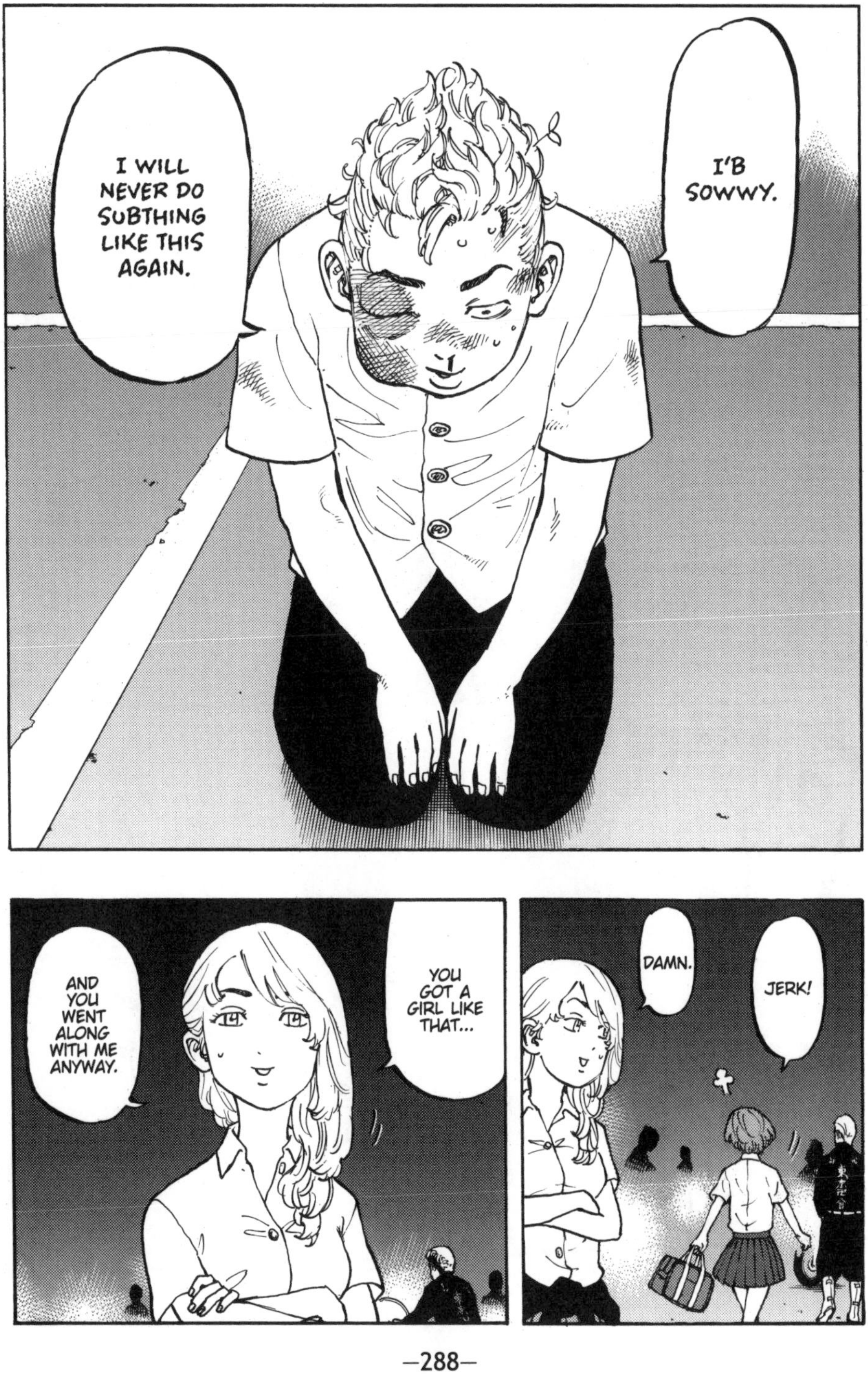
I'B SOWWY.
I WILL NEVER DO SUBTHING LIKE THIS AGAIN.
JERK!
DAMN.
YOU GOT A GIRL LIKE THAT...
AND YOU WENT ALONG WITH ME ANYWAY.

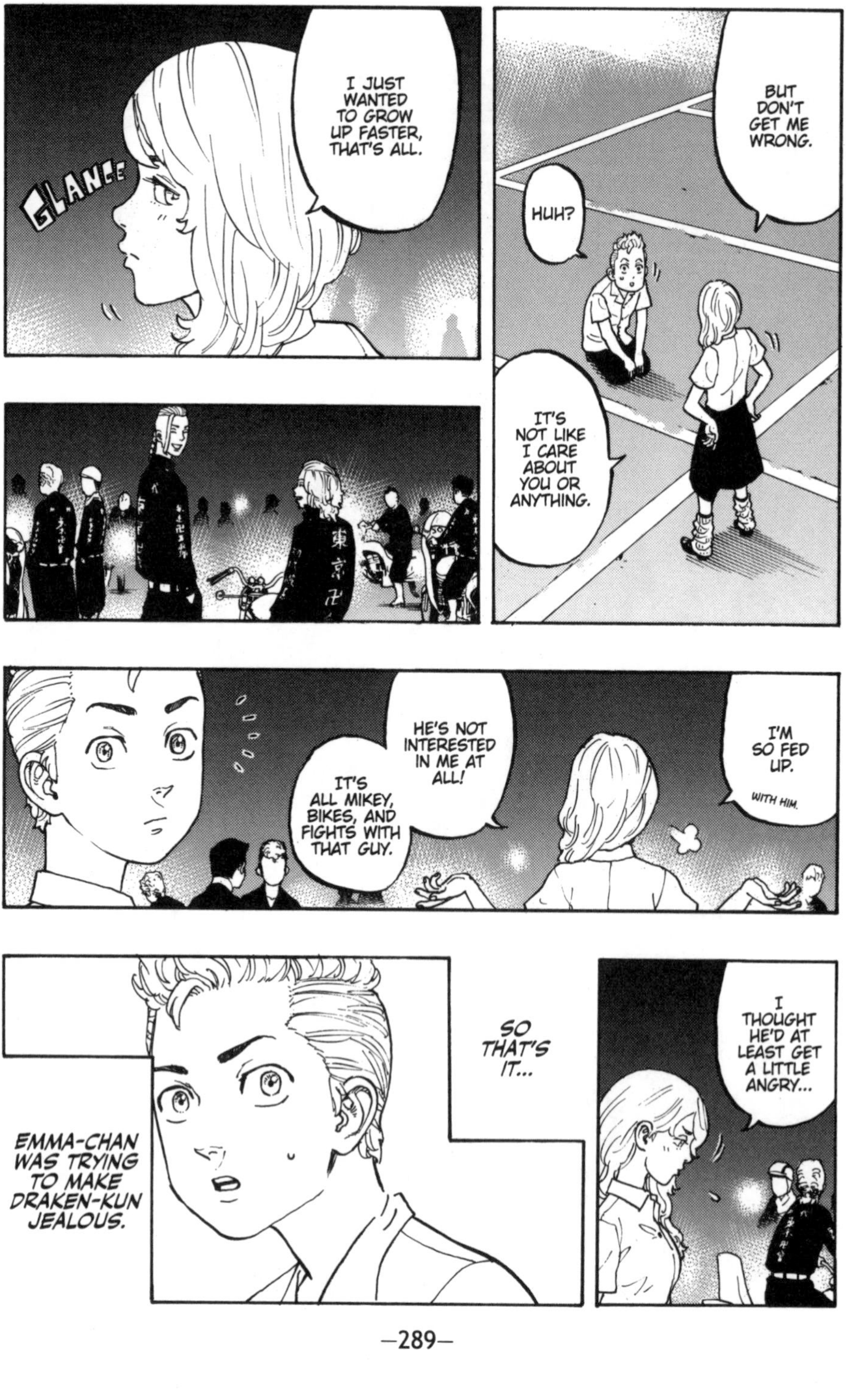
BUT DON'T GET ME WRONG.
HUH?
IT'S NOT LIKE I CARE ABOUT YOU OR ANYTHING.
I JUST WANTED TO GROW UP FASTER, THAT'S ALL.
GLANCE
I'M SO FED UP.
WITH HIM.
HE'S NOT INTERESTED IN ME AT ALL!
IT'S ALL MIKEY, BIKES, AND FIGHTS WITH THAT GUY.
I THOUGHT HE'D AT LEAST GET A LITTLE ANGRY...
SO THAT'S IT...
EMMA-CHAN WAS TRYING TO MAKE DRAKEN-KUN JEALOUS.

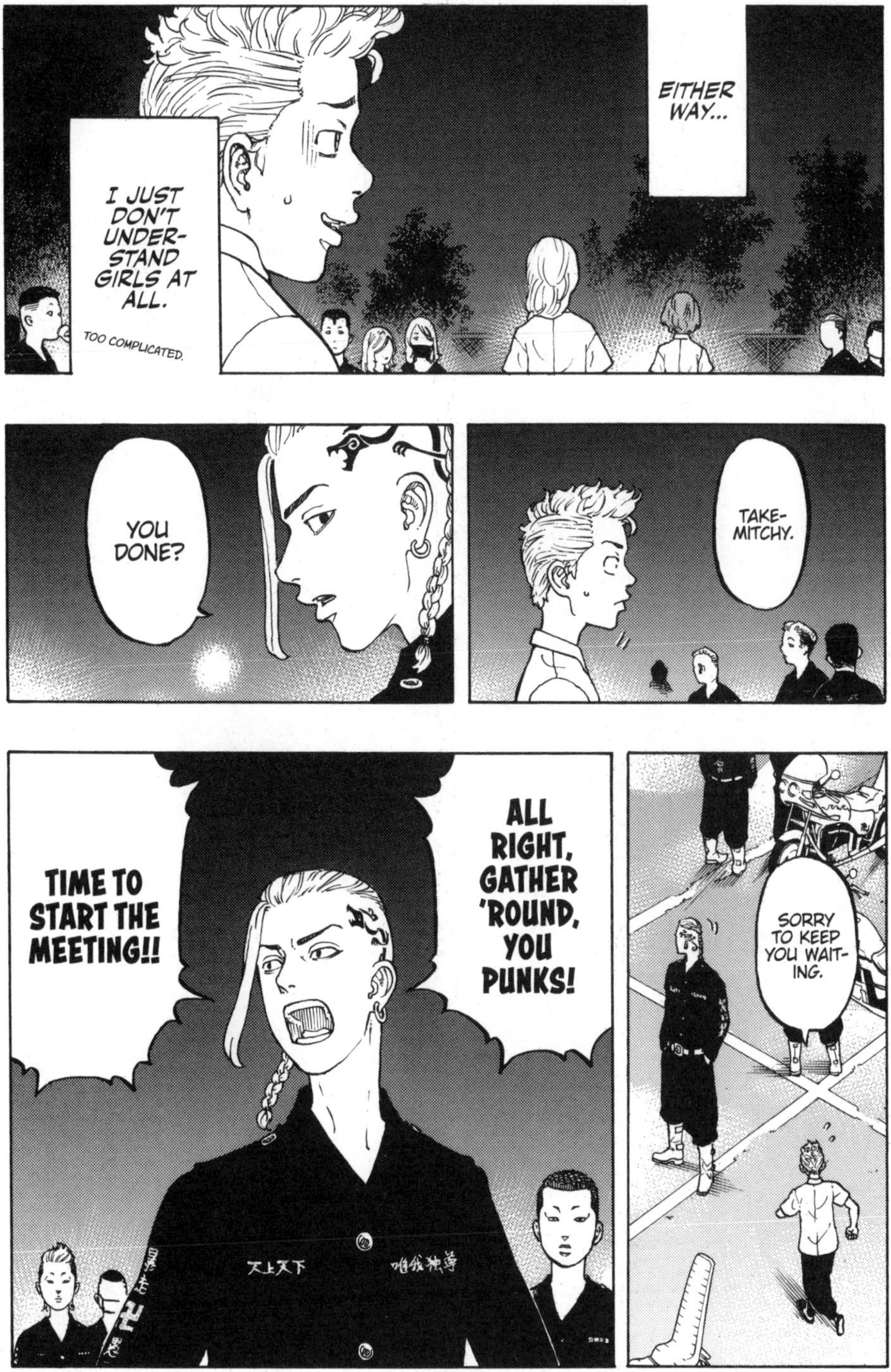
EITHER WAY...
I JUST DON'T UNDER-STAND GIRLS AT ALL.
TOO COMPLICATED.
TAKE-MITCHY.
YOU DONE?
SORRY TO KEEP YOU WAIT-ING.
ALL RIGHT, GATHER 'ROUND, YOU PUNKS!
TIME TO START THE MEETING!!
天上天下
唯我独尊

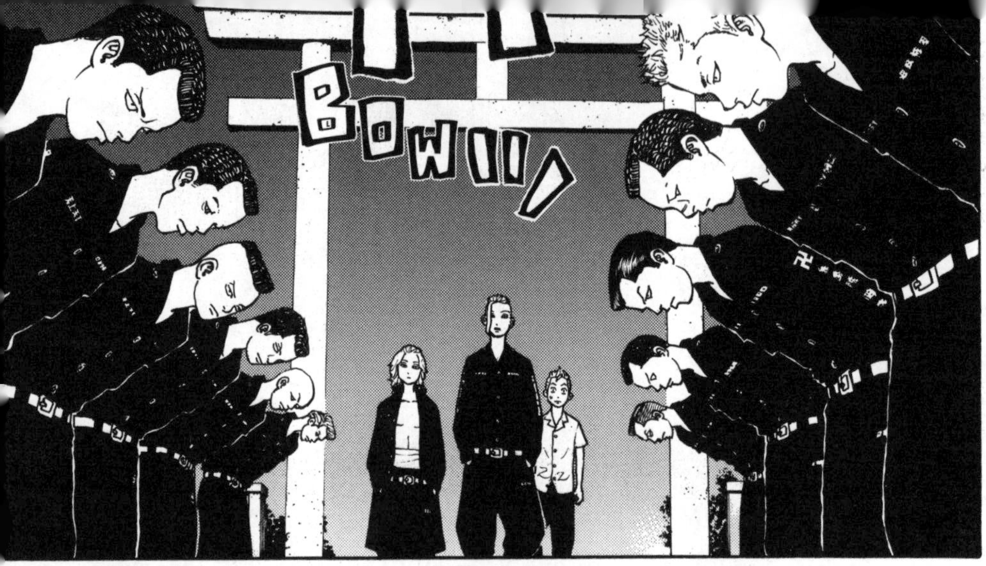
BOW

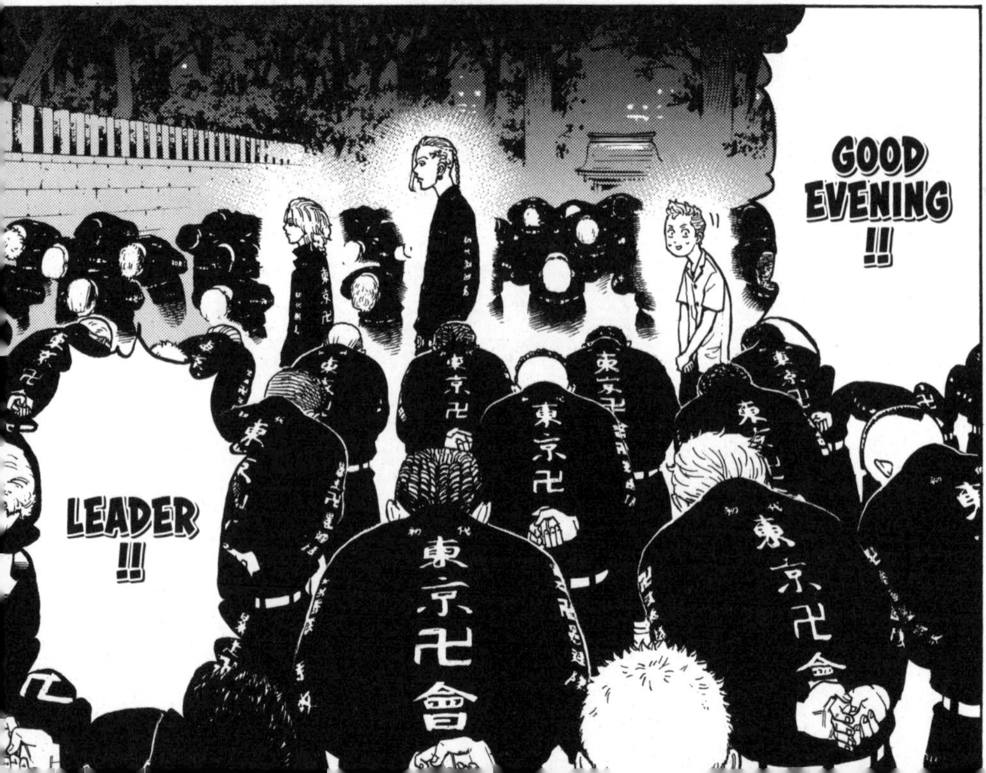
GOOD EVENING !!
LEADER !!
東京卍會

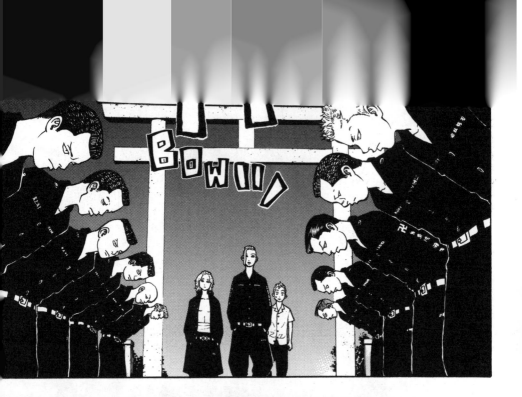

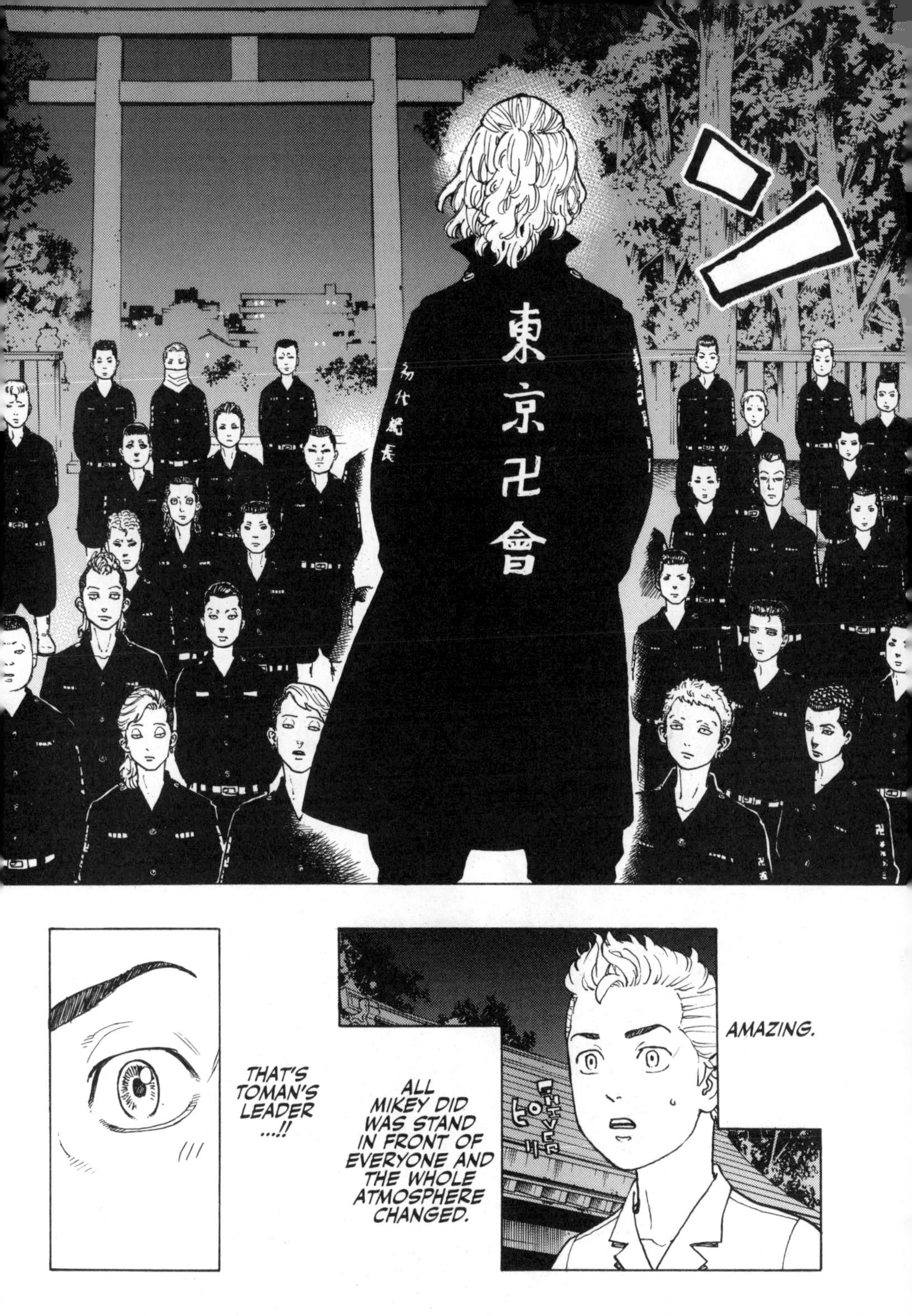
東京卍會
AMAZING.
ALL MIKEY DID WAS STAND IN FRONT OF EVERYONE AND THE WHOLE ATMOSPHERE CHANGED.
THAT'S TOMAN'S LEADER ...!!

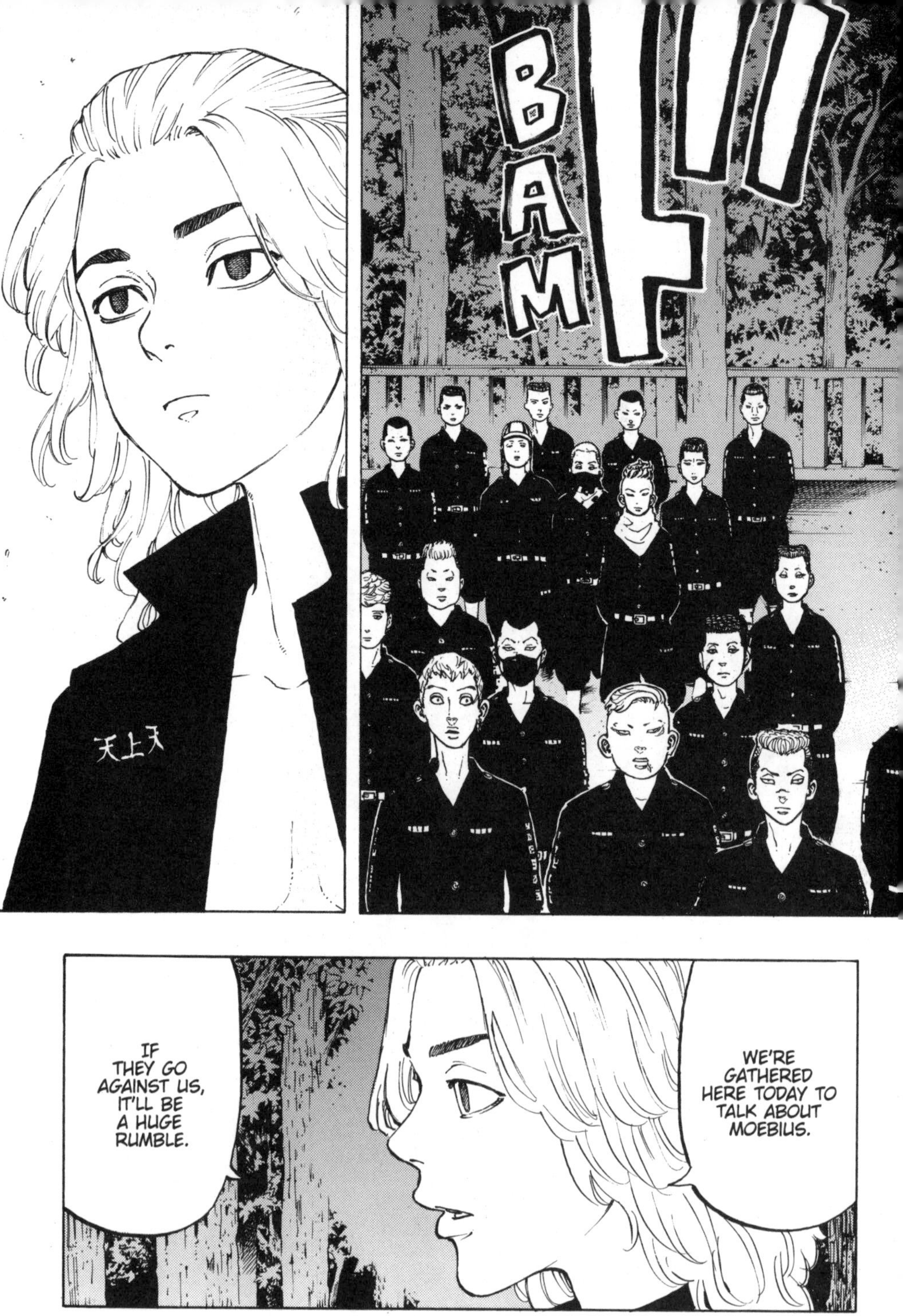
BAM!!
天上天
WE'RE GATHERED HERE TODAY TO TALK ABOUT MOEBIUS.
IF THEY GO AGAINST US, IT'LL BE A HUGE RUMBLE.

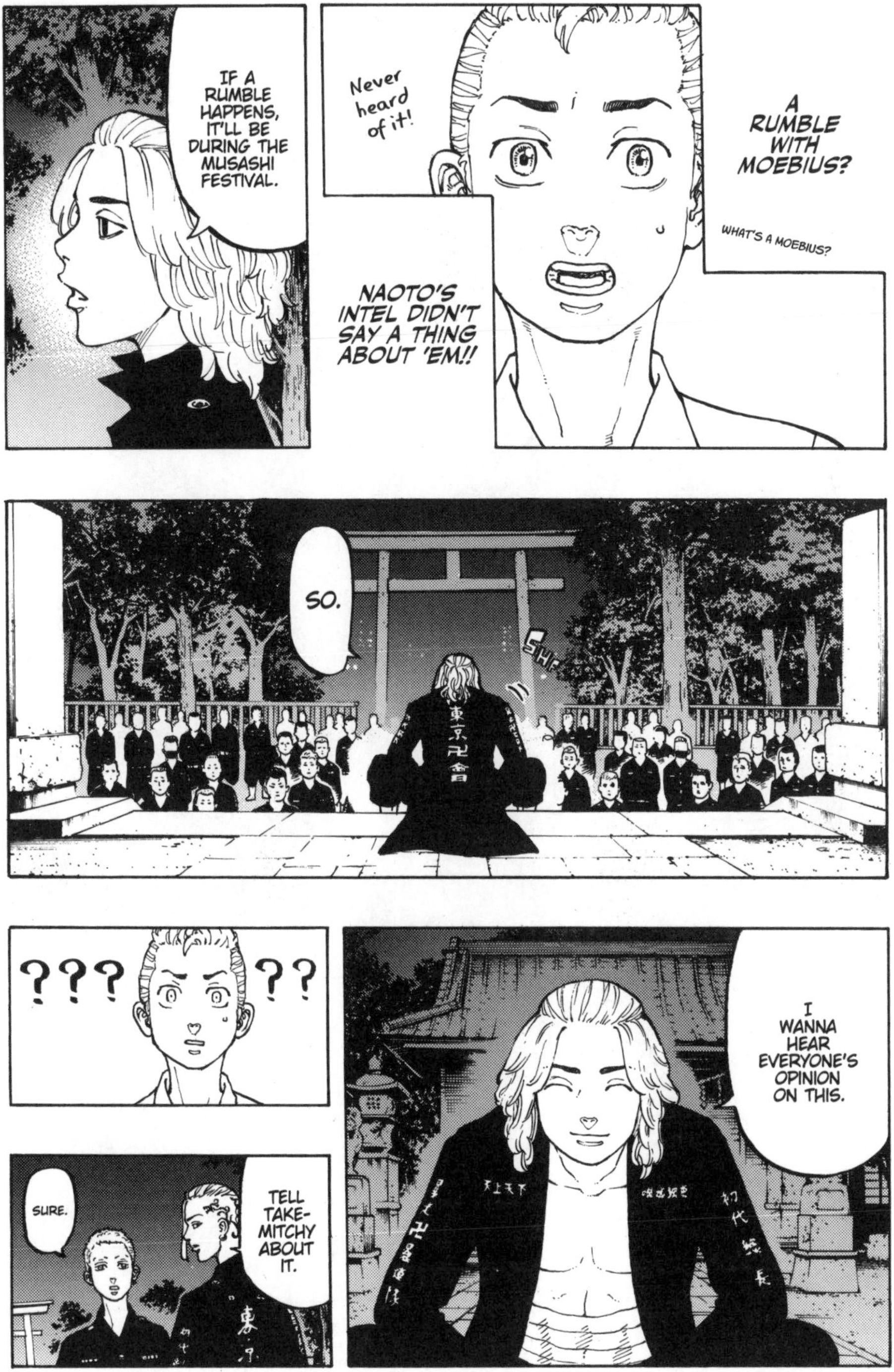
A RUMBLE WITH MOEBIUS?
Never heard of it!
WHAT'S A MOEBIUS?
NAOTO'S INTEL DIDN'T SAY A THING ABOUT 'EM!!
IF A RUMBLE HAPPENS, IT'LL BE DURING THE MUSASHI FESTIVAL.
SO.
SHF
東京卍會
I WANNA HEAR EVERYONE'S OPINION ON THIS.
??? ??
TELL TAKE-MITCHY ABOUT IT.
SURE.

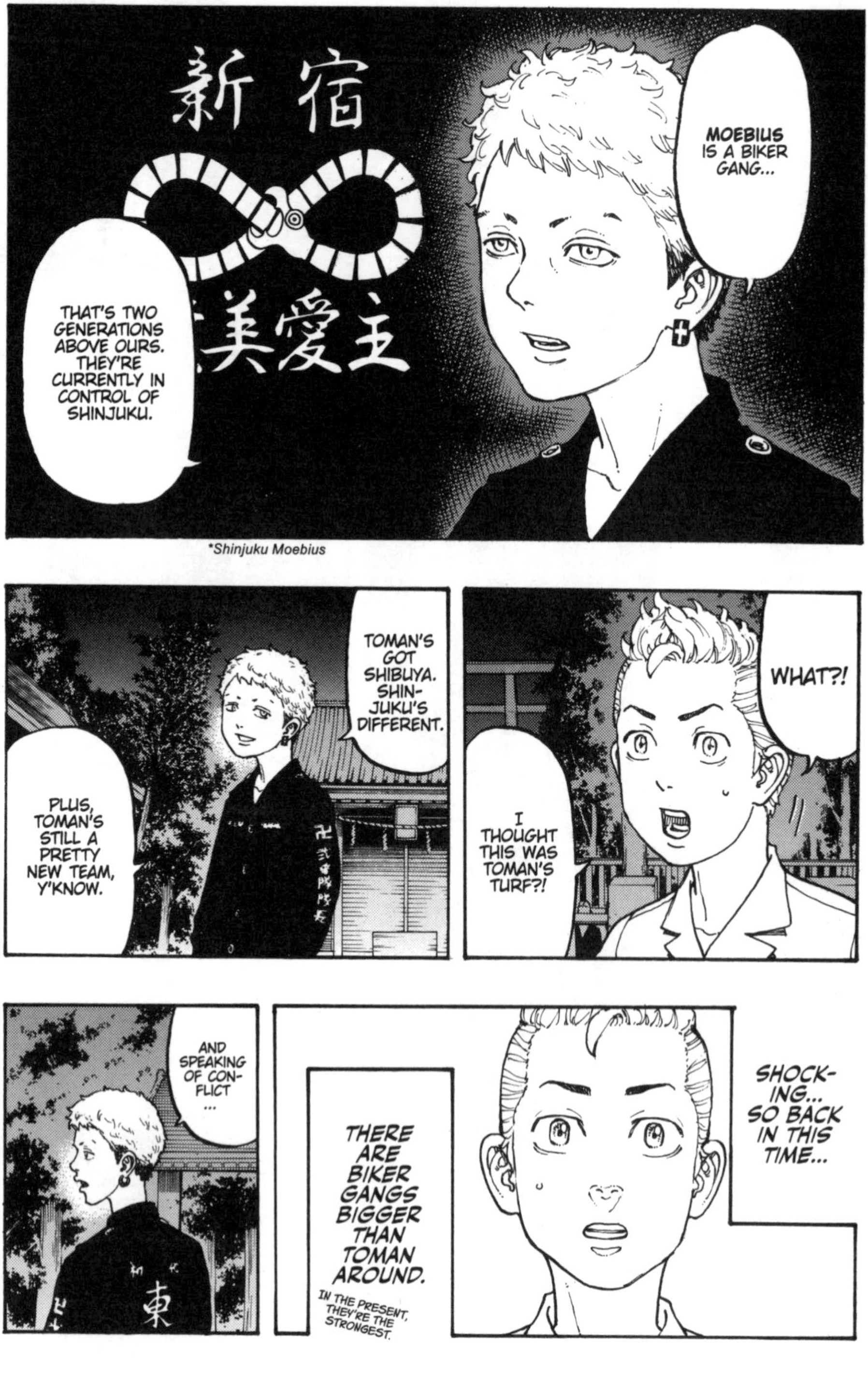
新宿
MOEBIUS IS A BIKER GANG...
THAT'S TWO GENERATIONS ABOVE OURS. THEY'RE CURRENTLY IN CONTROL OF SHINJUKU.
*Shinjuku Moebius
WHAT?!
I THOUGHT THIS WAS TOMAN'S TURF?!
TOMAN'S GOT SHIBUYA. SHIN-JUKU'S DIFFERENT.
PLUS, TOMAN'S STILL A PRETTY NEW TEAM, Y'KNOW.
SHOCK-ING... SO BACK IN THIS TIME...
THERE ARE BIKER GANGS BIGGER THAN TOMAN AROUND.
IN THE PRESENT, THEY'RE THE STRONGEST.
AND SPEAKING OF CON-FLICT...

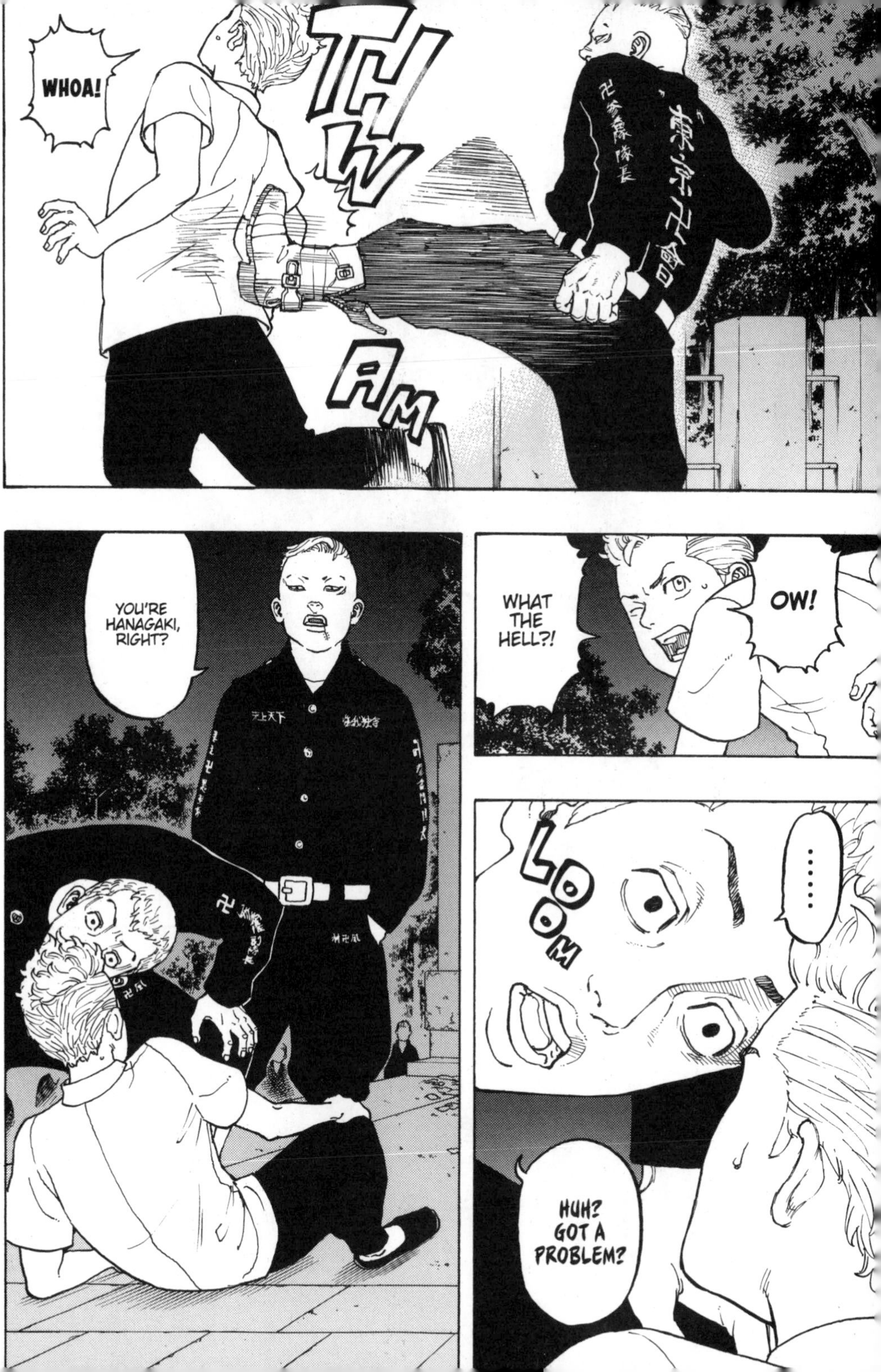
THWAM
WHOA!
OW!
WHAT THE HELL?!
......
LOOM
HUH? GOT A PROBLEM?
YOU'RE HANAGAKI, RIGHT?

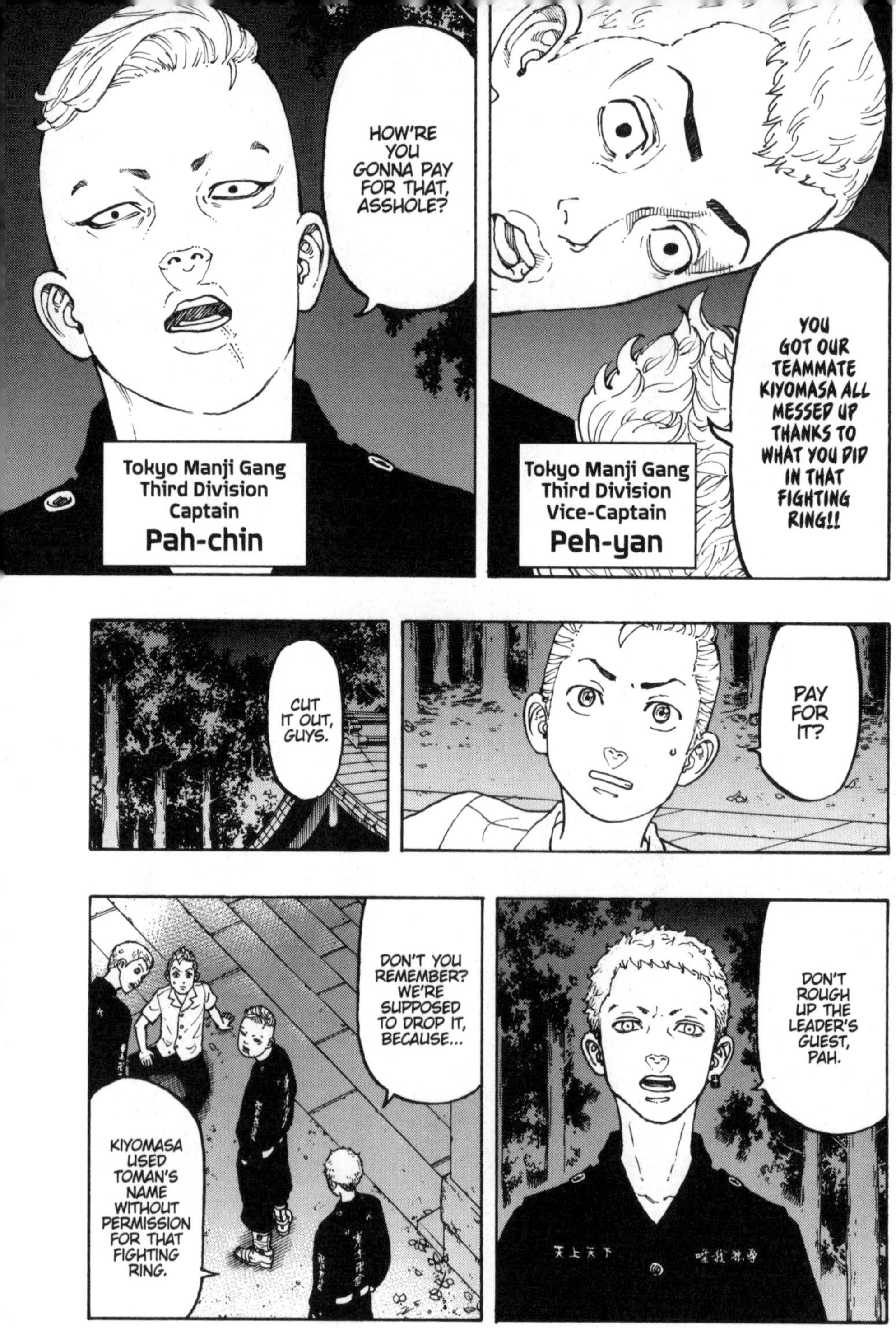
YOU GOT OUR TEAMMATE KIYOMASA ALL MESSED UP THANKS TO WHAT YOU DID IN THAT FIGHTING RING!!
Tokyo Manji Gang Third Division Vice-Captain Peh-yan
HOW'RE YOU GONNA PAY FOR THAT, ASSHOLE?
Tokyo Manji Gang Third Division Captain Pah-chin
PAY FOR IT?
CUT IT OUT, GUYS.
DON'T ROUGH UP THE LEADER'S GUEST, PAH.
天上天下
唯我独尊
DON'T YOU REMEMBER? WE'RE SUPPOSED TO DROP IT, BECAUSE...
KIYOMASA USED TOMAN'S NAME WITHOUT PERMISSION FOR THAT FIGHTING RING.

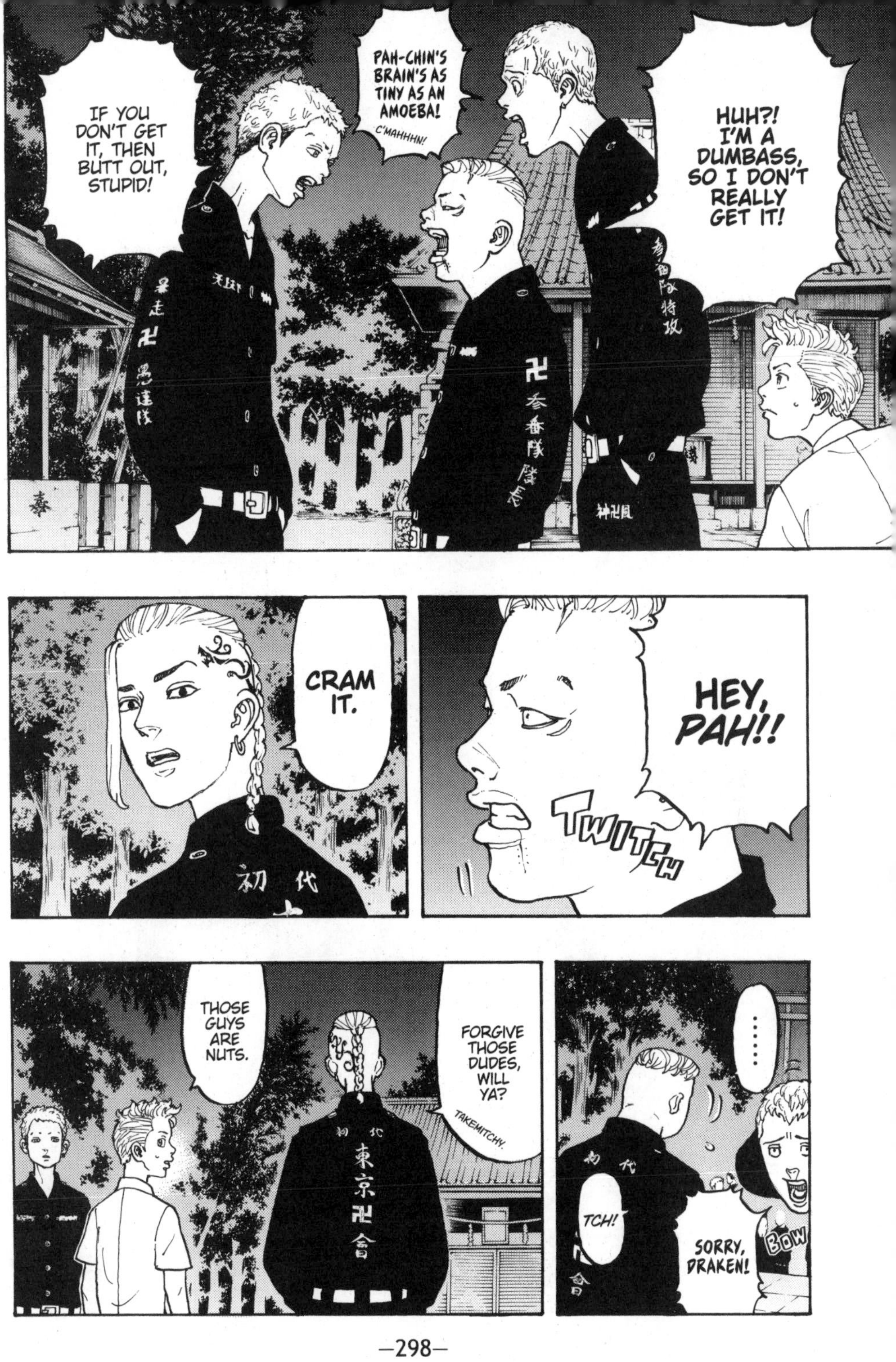
HUH?! I'M A DUMBASS, SO I DON'T REALLY GET IT!
PAH-CHIN'S BRAIN'S AS TINY AS AN AMOEBA!
C'MAHHHN!
IF YOU DON'T GET IT, THEN BUTT OUT, STUPID!
HEY, PAH!!
TWITCH
CRAM IT.
......
BOW
SORRY, DRAKEN!
TCH!
FORGIVE THOSE DUDES, WILL YA?
TAKEMITCHY.
THOSE GUYS ARE NUTS.

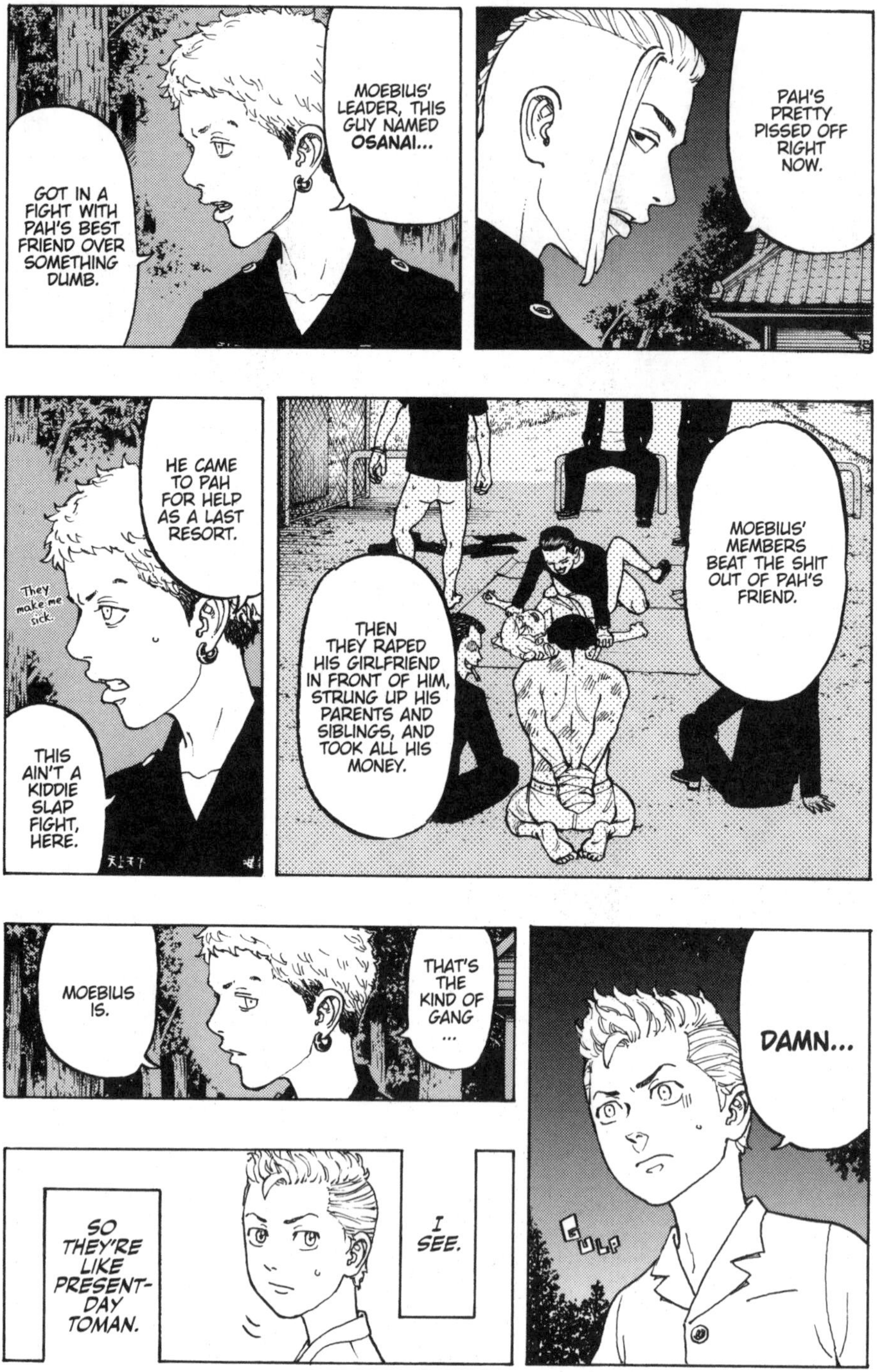
PAH'S PRETTY PISSED OFF RIGHT NOW.
MOEBIUS' LEADER, THIS GUY NAMED OSANAI...
GOT IN A FIGHT WITH PAH'S BEST FRIEND OVER SOMETHING DUMB.
MOEBIUS' MEMBERS BEAT THE SHIT OUT OF PAH'S FRIEND.
THEN THEY RAPED HIS GIRLFRIEND IN FRONT OF HIM, STRUNG UP HIS PARENTS AND SIBLINGS, AND TOOK ALL HIS MONEY.
HE CAME TO PAH FOR HELP AS A LAST RESORT.
They make me sick.
THIS AIN'T A KIDDIE SLAP FIGHT, HERE.
DAMN...
GULP
THAT'S THE KIND OF GANG ...
MOEBIUS IS.
I SEE.
SO THEY'RE LIKE PRESENT-DAY TOMAN.

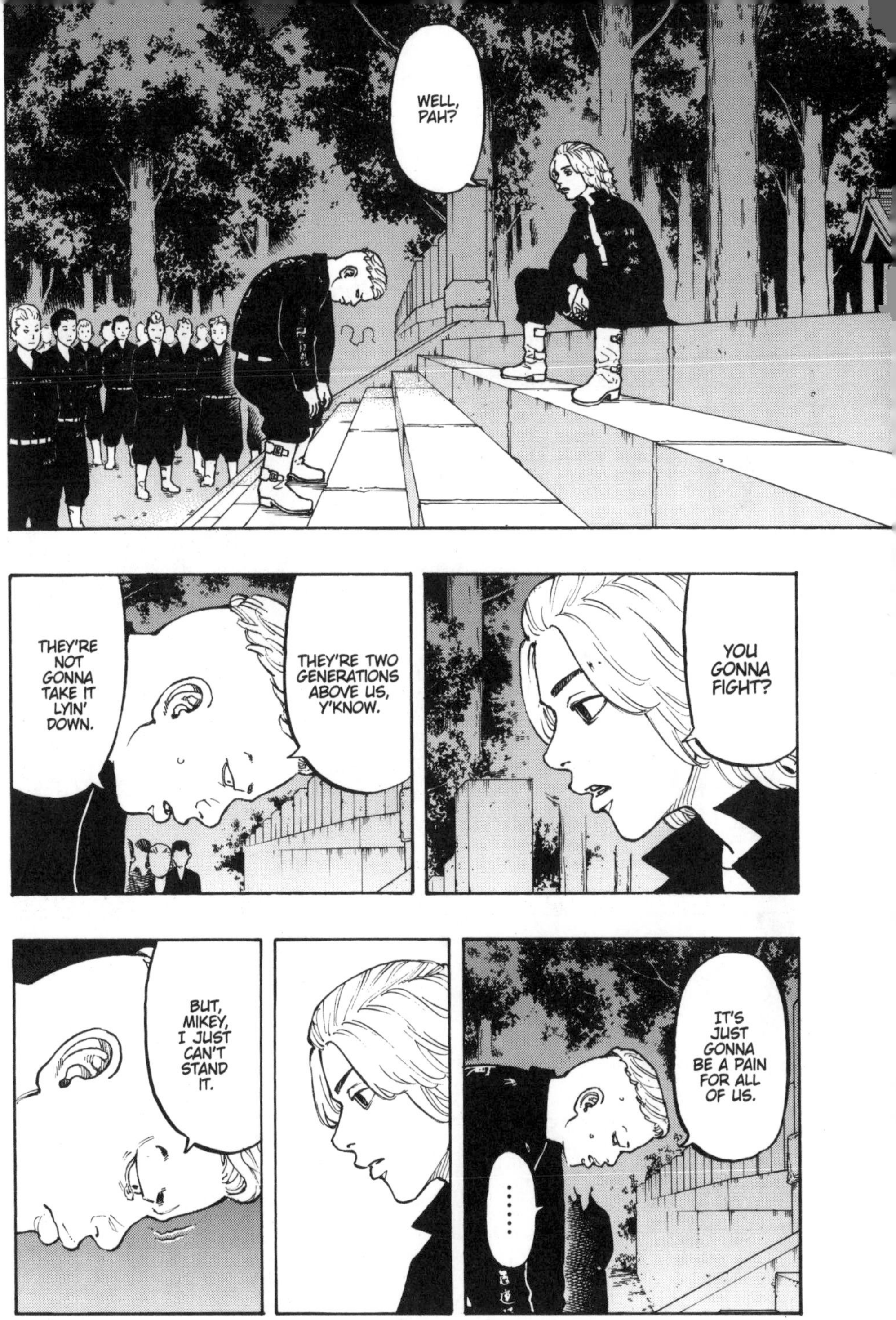
WELL, PAH?
YOU GONNA FIGHT?
THEY'RE TWO GENERATIONS ABOVE US, Y'KNOW.
THEY'RE NOT GONNA TAKE IT LYIN' DOWN.
IT'S JUST GONNA BE A PAIN FOR ALL OF US.
......
BUT, MIKEY, I JUST CAN'T STAND IT.

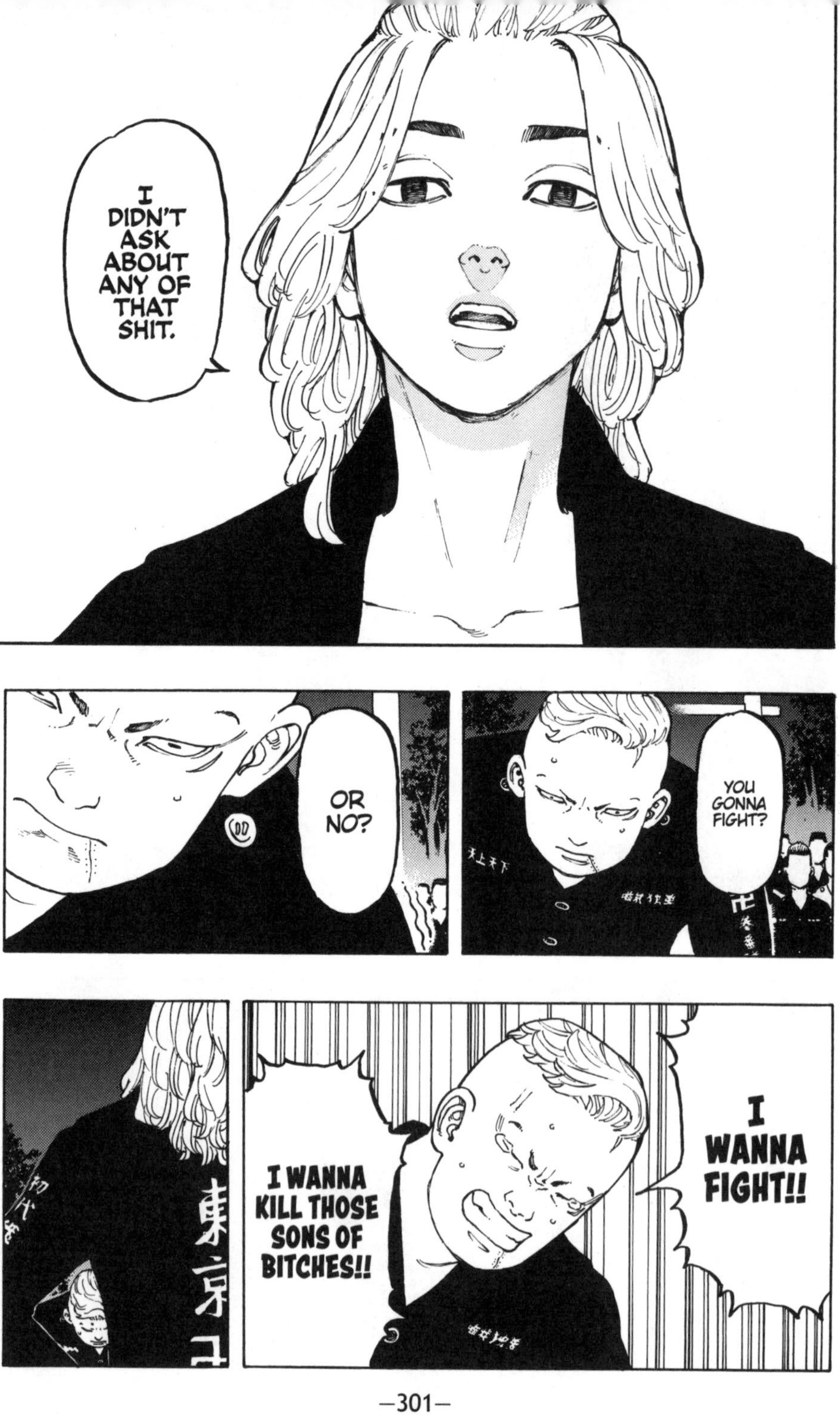
I DIDN'T ASK ABOUT ANY OF THAT SHIT.
YOU GONNA FIGHT?
OR NO?
I WANNA FIGHT!!
I WANNA KILL THOSE SONS OF BITCHES!!

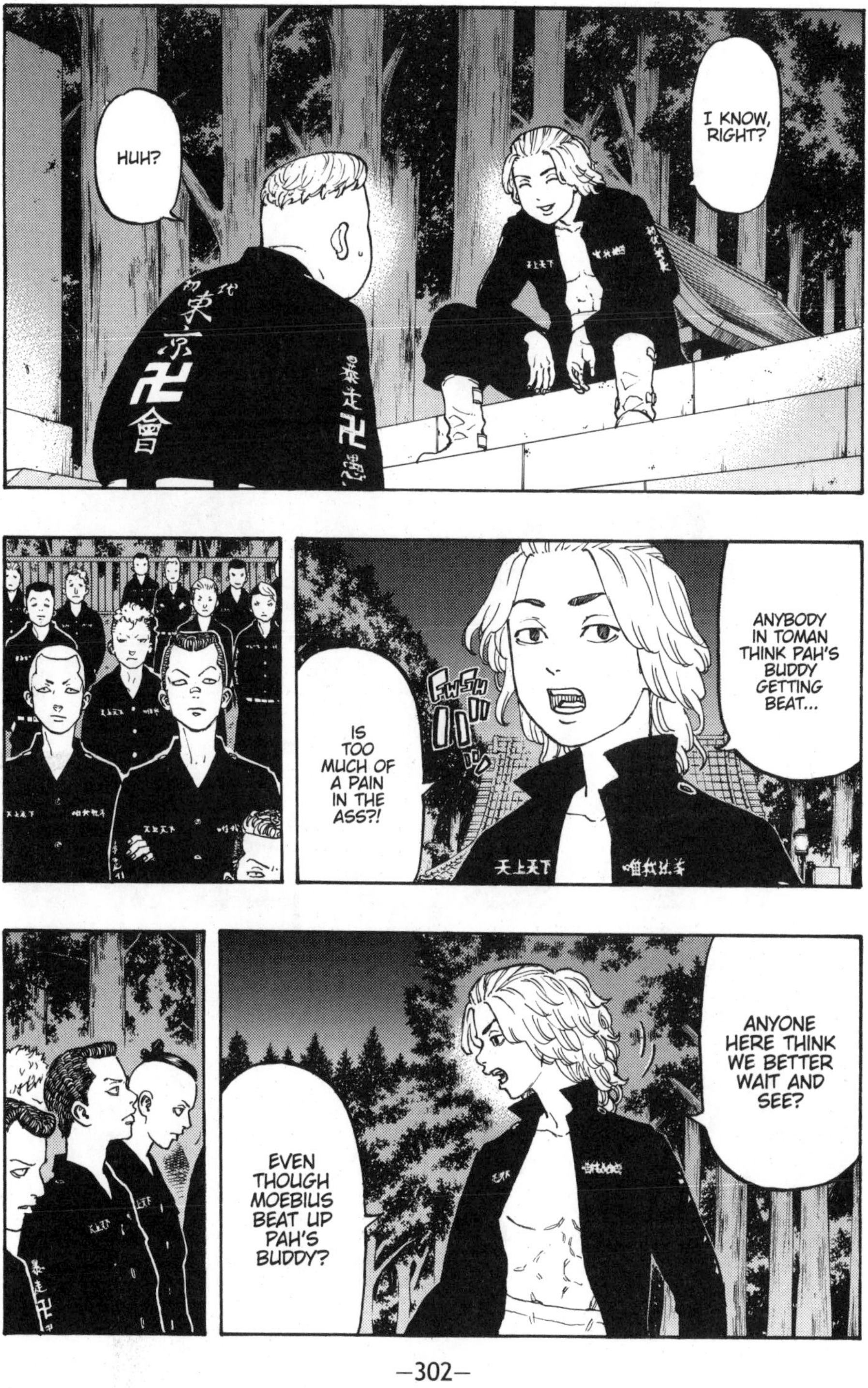
I KNOW, RIGHT?
HUH?
ANYBODY IN TOMAN THINK PAH'S BUDDY GETTING BEAT...
FWSH
IS TOO MUCH OF A PAIN IN THE ASS?!
ANYONE HERE THINK WE BETTER WAIT AND SEE?
EVEN THOUGH MOEBIUS BEAT UP PAH'S BUDDY?

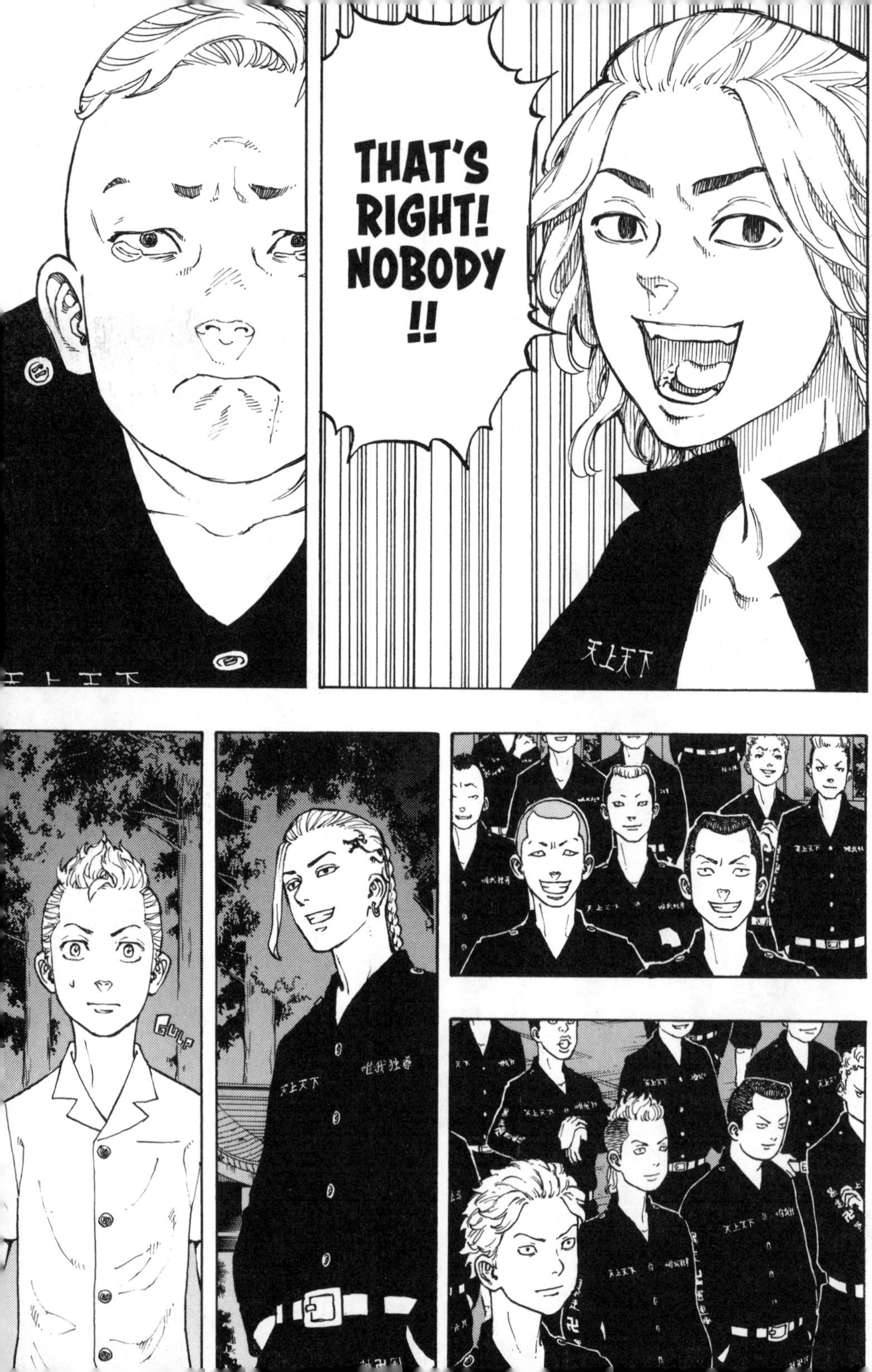
THAT'S RIGHT! NOBODY !!
天上天下
GULP

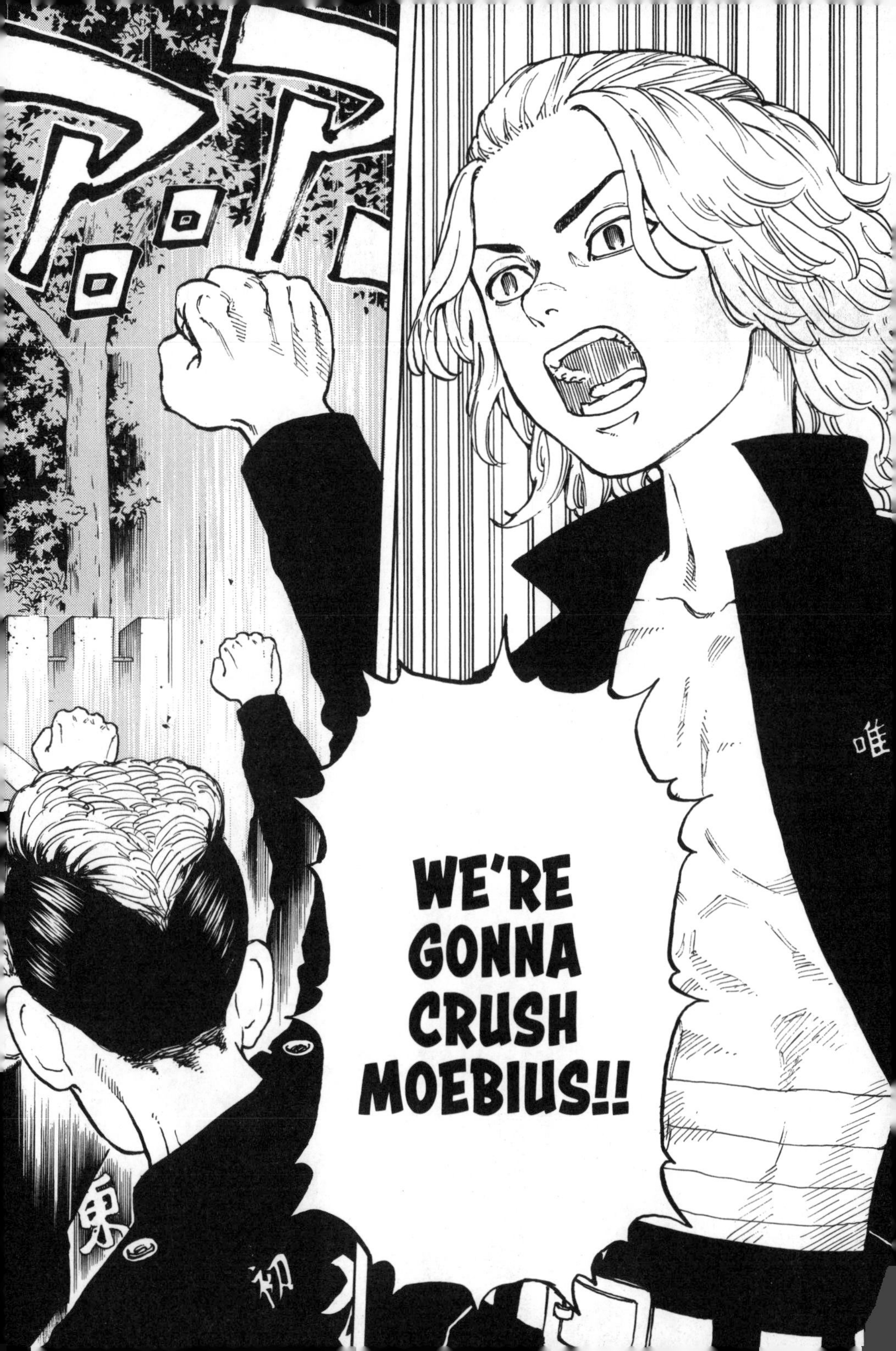
WE'RE GONNA CRUSH MOEBIUS!!

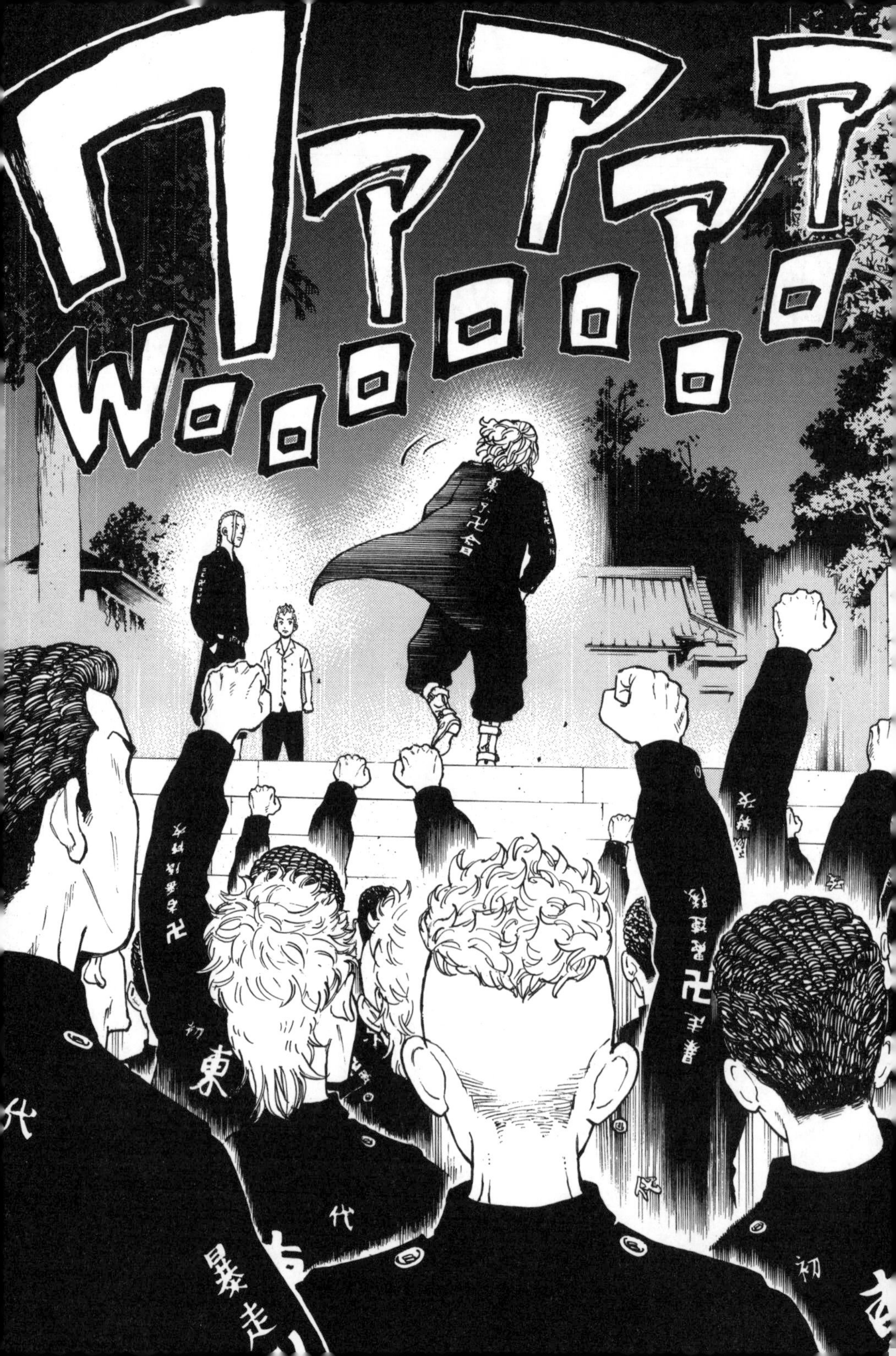
ワアアアア
WOOOOOOOO

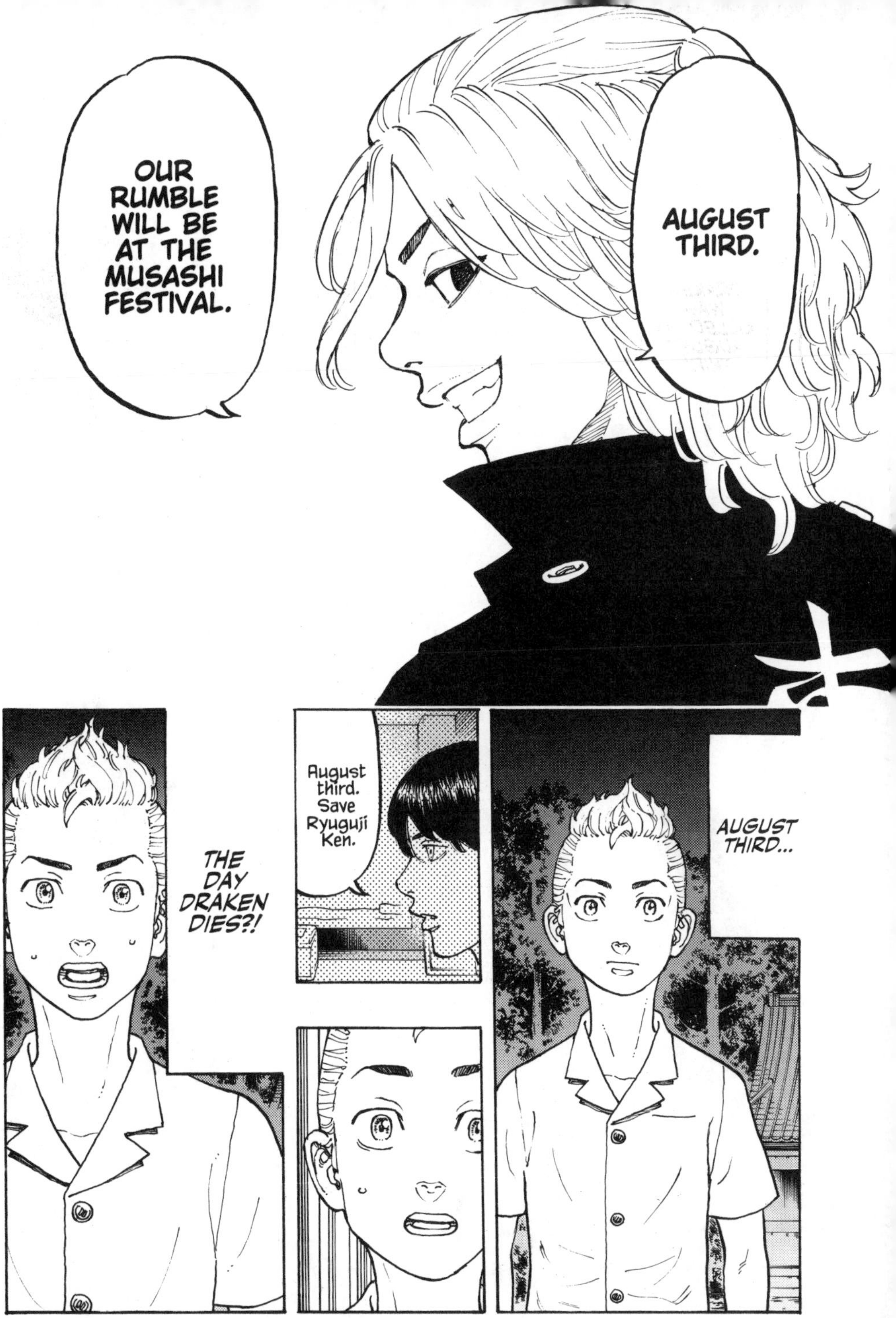
AUGUST THIRD.
OUR RUMBLE WILL BE AT THE MUSASHI FESTIVAL.
AUGUST THIRD...
August third. Save Ryuguji Ken.
THE DAY DRAKEN DIES?!

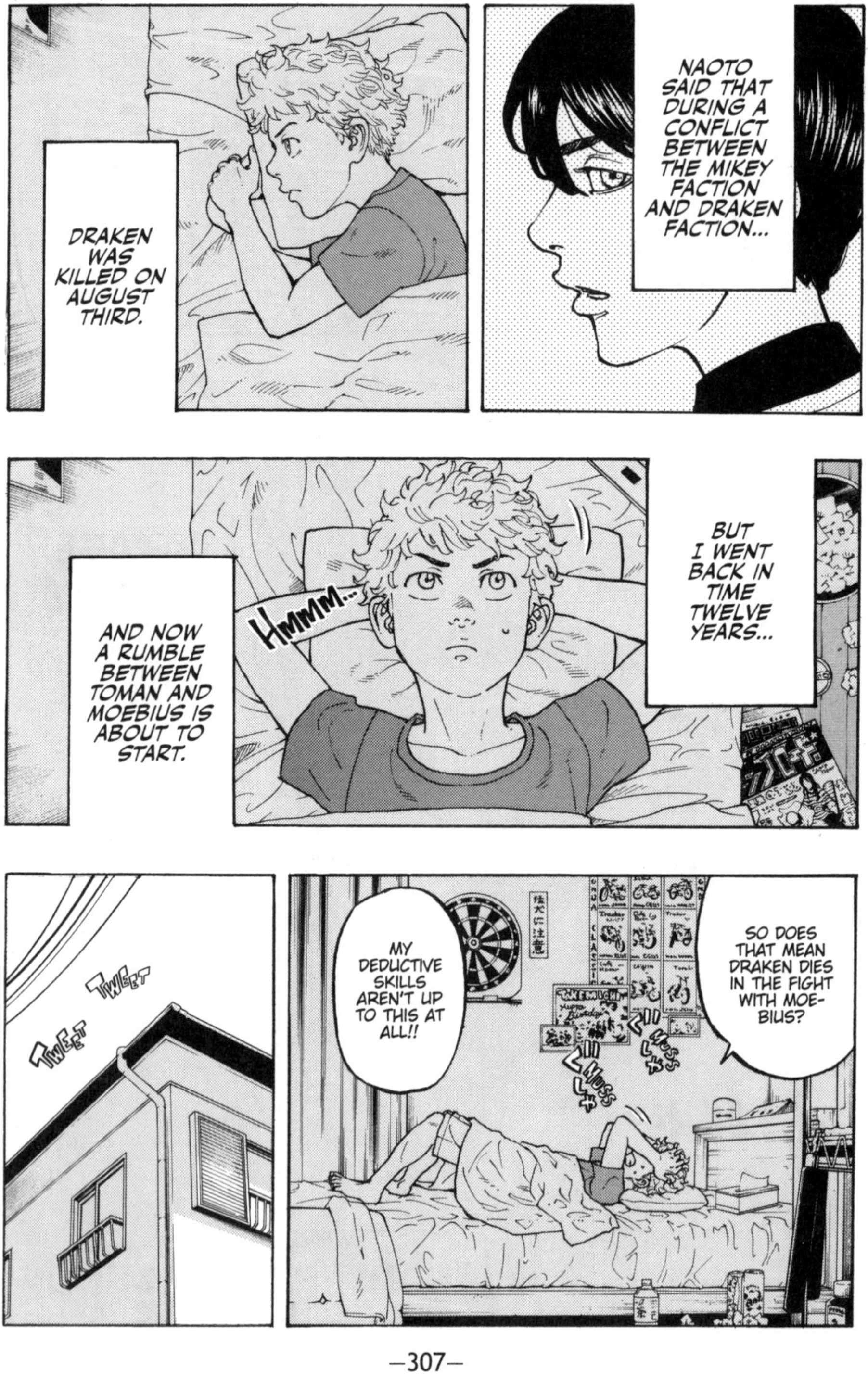
NAOTO SAID THAT DURING A CONFLICT BETWEEN THE MIKEY FACTION AND DRAKEN FACTION...
DRAKEN WAS KILLED ON AUGUST THIRD.
BUT I WENT BACK IN TIME TWELVE YEARS...
HMMM...
AND NOW A RUMBLE BETWEEN TOMAN AND MOEBIUS IS ABOUT TO START.
SO DOES THAT MEAN DRAKEN DIES IN THE FIGHT WITH MOE-BIUS?
MY DEDUCTIVE SKILLS AREN'T UP TO THIS AT ALL!!
MUSS
MUSS
TWEET
TWEET

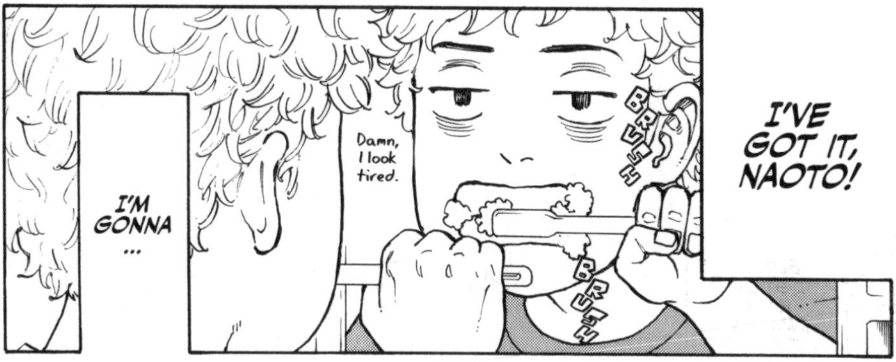
I'VE GOT IT, NAOTO!
BRUSH
BRUSH
Damn, I look tired.
I'M GONNA ...

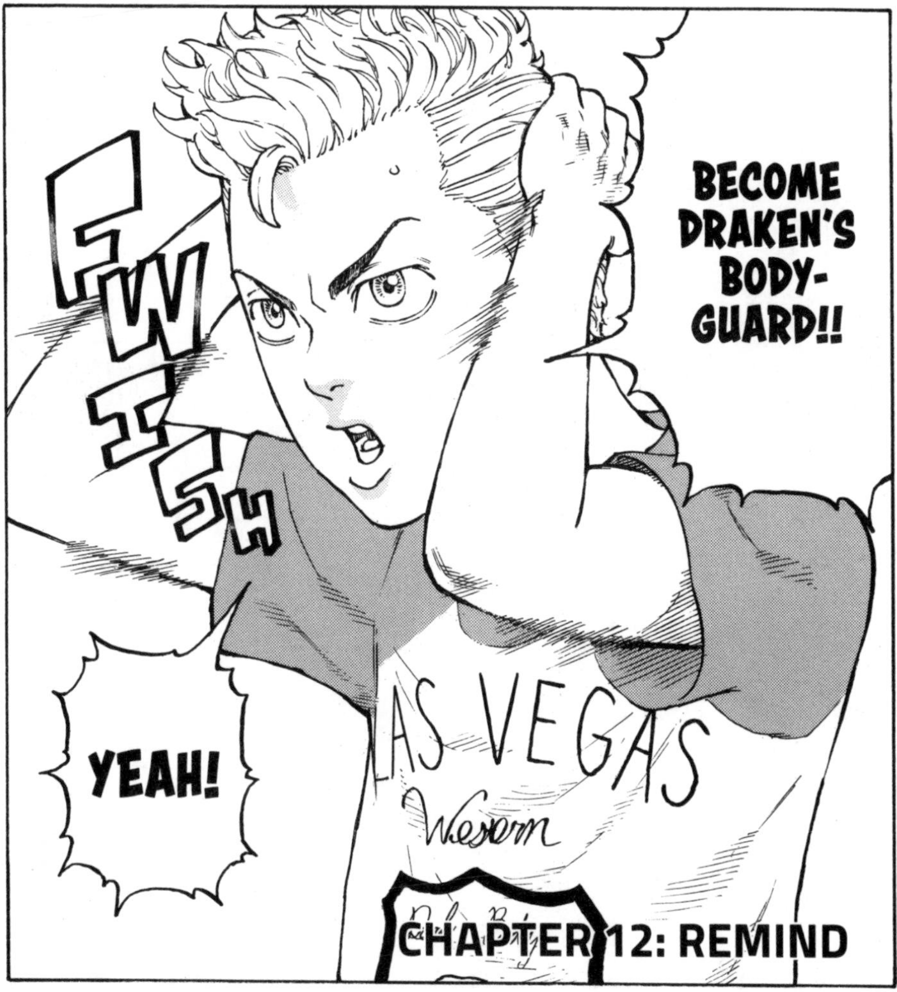
BECOME DRAKEN'S BODY-GUARD!!
FWISH
YEAH!

CHAPTER 12: REMIND

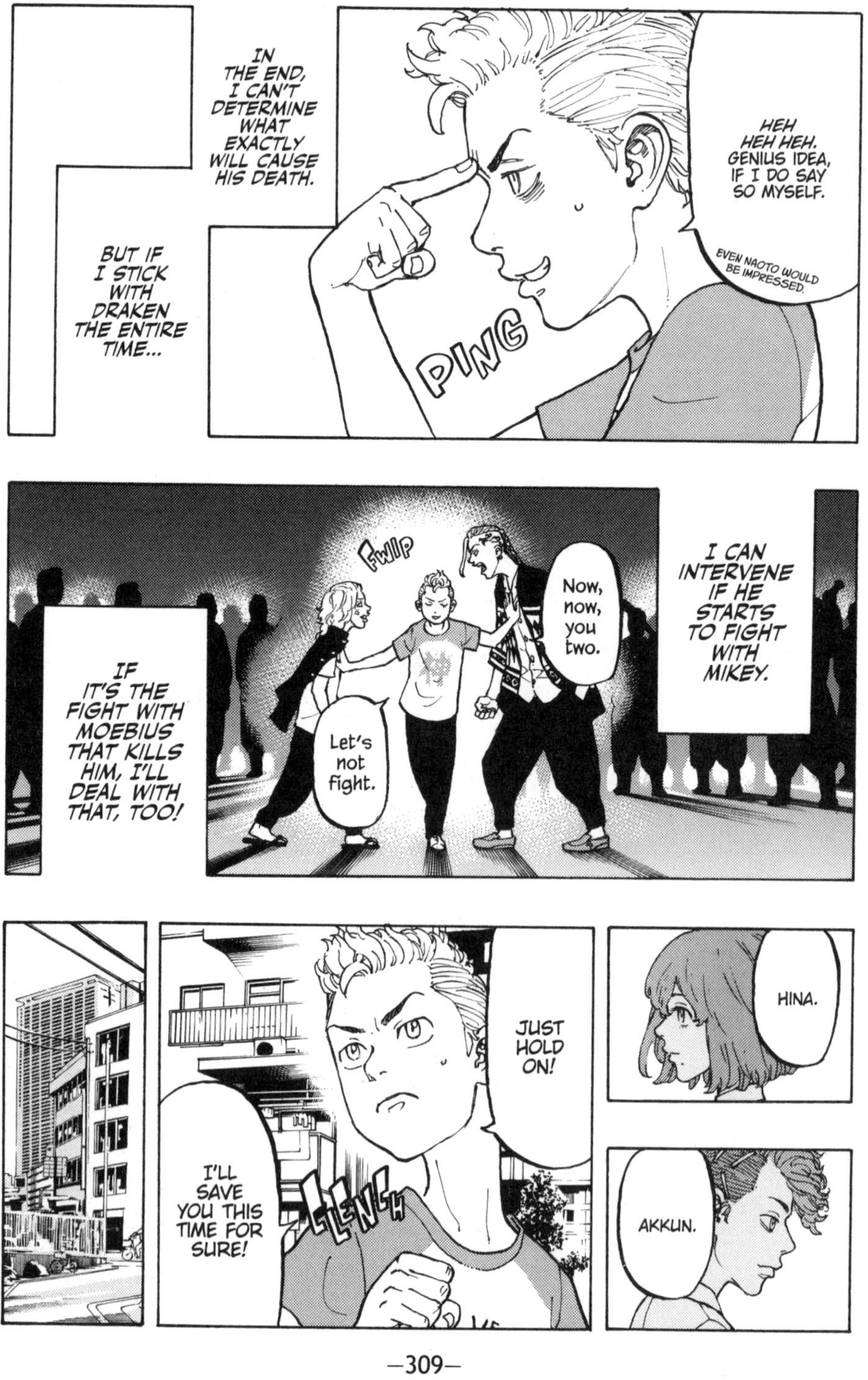
HEH HEH HEH. GENIUS IDEA, IF I DO SAY SO MYSELF.
EVEN NAOTO WOULD BE IMPRESSED.
IN THE END, I CAN'T DETERMINE WHAT EXACTLY WILL CAUSE HIS DEATH.
PING
BUT IF I STICK WITH DRAKEN THE ENTIRE TIME...
I CAN INTERVENE IF HE STARTS TO FIGHT WITH MIKEY.
Now, now, you two.
FWIP
Let's not fight.
IF IT'S THE FIGHT WITH MOEBIUS THAT KILLS HIM, I'LL DEAL WITH THAT, TOO!
HINA.
AKKUN.
JUST HOLD ON!
CLENCH
I'LL SAVE YOU THIS TIME FOR SURE!

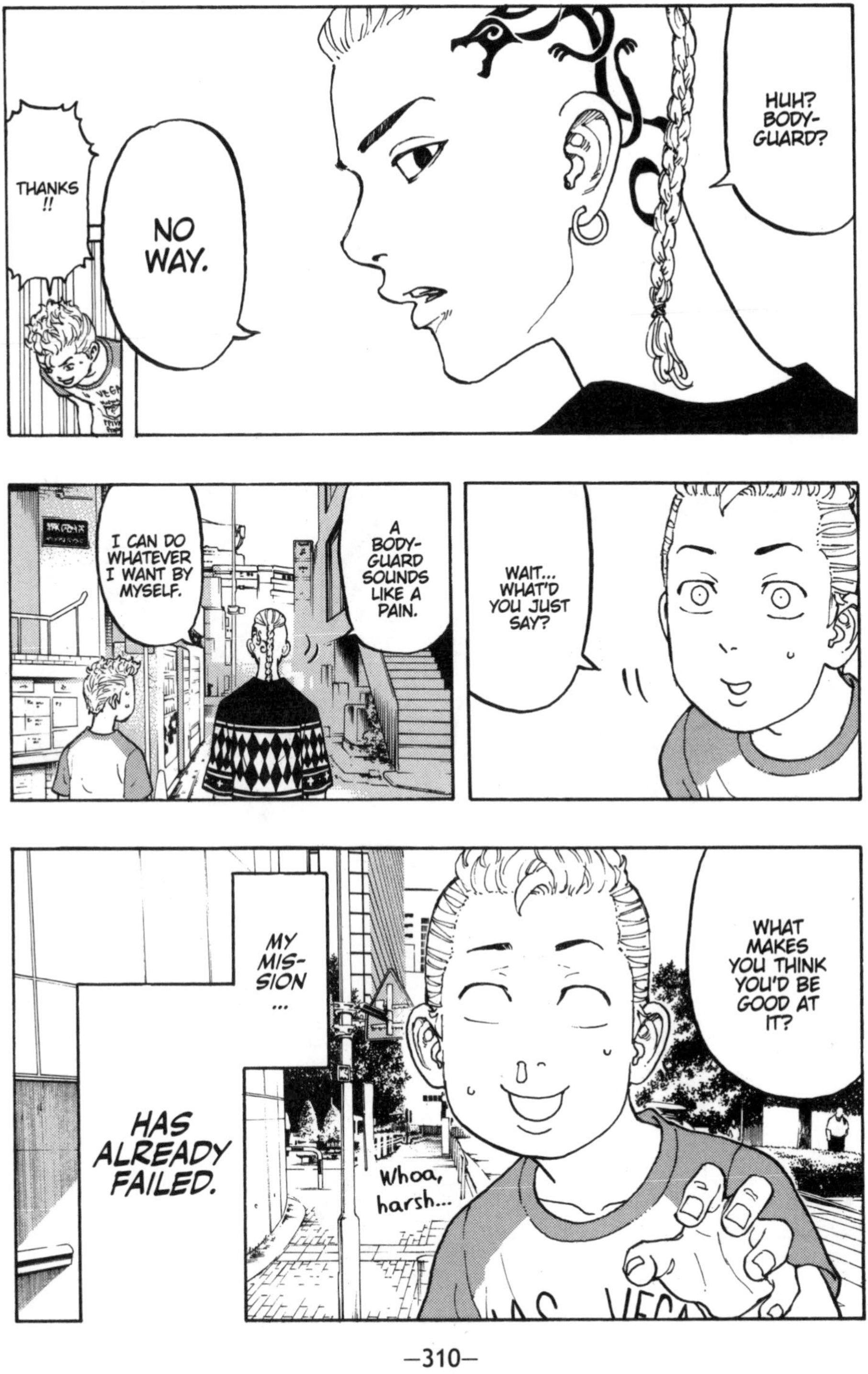
HUH? BODY-GUARD?
NO WAY.
THANKS!!
WAIT... WHAT'D YOU JUST SAY?
A BODY-GUARD SOUNDS LIKE A PAIN.
I CAN DO WHATEVER I WANT BY MYSELF.
WHAT MAKES YOU THINK YOU'D BE GOOD AT IT?
Whoa, harsh...
MY MIS-SION...
HAS ALREADY FAILED.

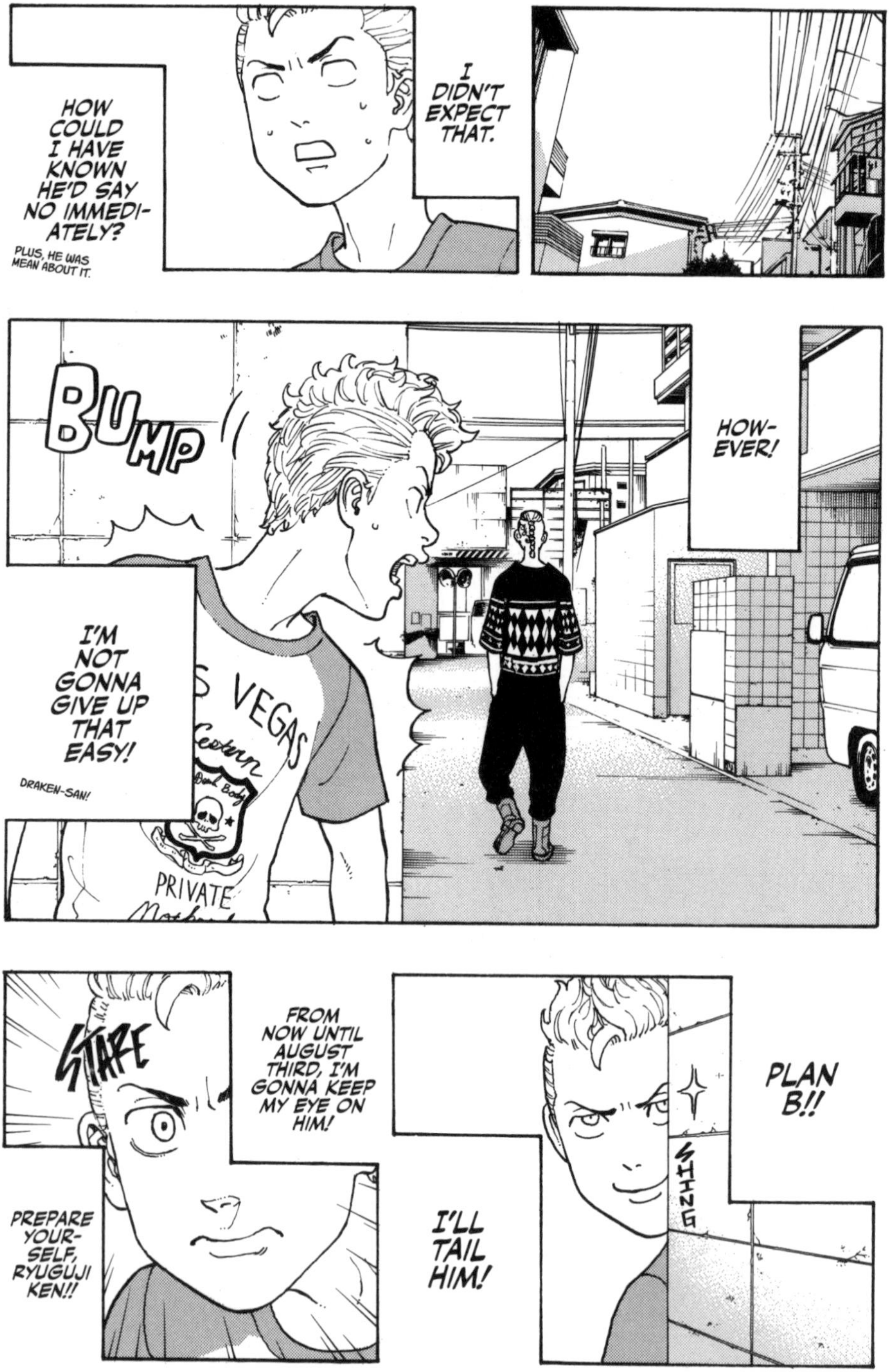
I DIDN'T EXPECT THAT.
HOW COULD I HAVE KNOWN HE'D SAY NO IMMEDIATELY?
PLUS, HE WAS MEAN ABOUT IT.
HOWEVER!
BUMP
I'M NOT GONNA GIVE UP THAT EASY!
DRAKEN-SAN!
PRIVATE
PLAN B!!
SHING
I'LL TAIL HIM!
STARE
FROM NOW UNTIL AUGUST THIRD, I'M GONNA KEEP MY EYE ON HIM!
PREPARE YOURSELF, RYUGUJI KEN!!

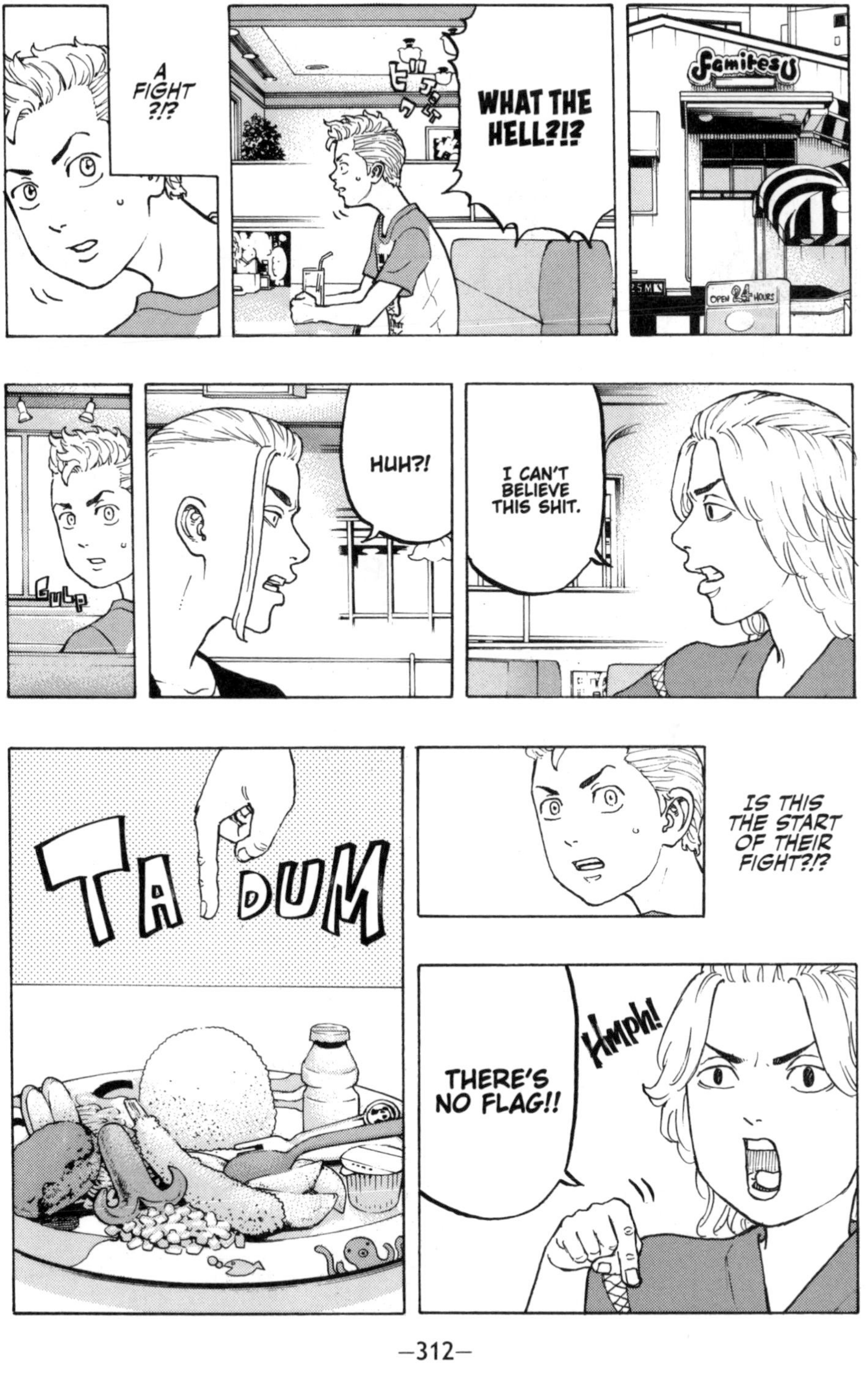
Famitesu
OPEN 24 HOURS
WHAT THE HELL?!?
A FIGHT ?!?
I CAN'T BELIEVE THIS SHIT.
HUH?!
Gulp
IS THIS THE START OF THEIR FIGHT?!?
Hmph!
THERE'S NO FLAG!!
TA DUM

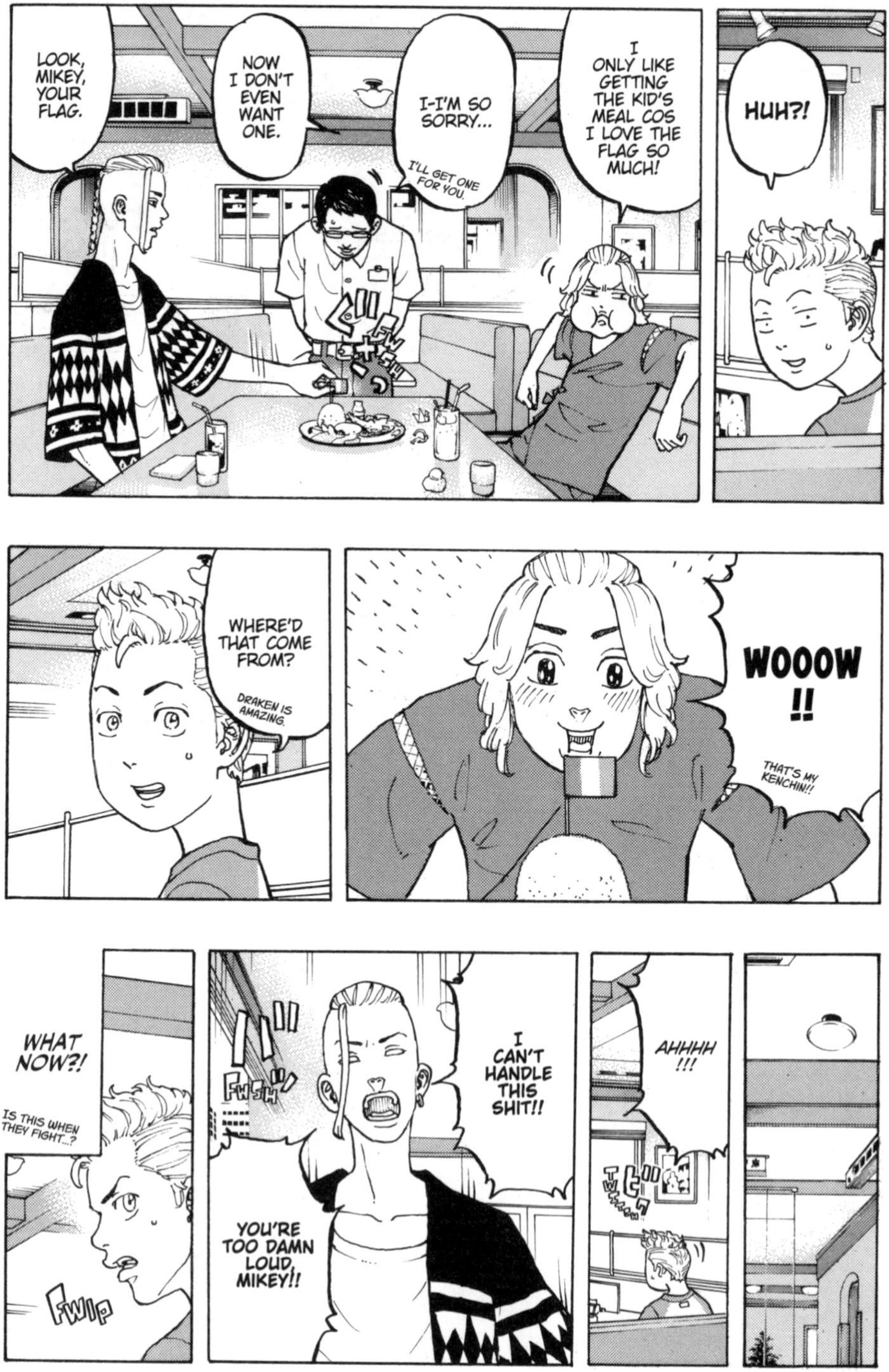
HUH?!
I ONLY LIKE GETTING THE KID'S MEAL COS I LOVE THE FLAG SO MUCH!
I-I'M SO SORRY...
I'LL GET ONE FOR YOU.
NOW I DON'T EVEN WANT ONE.
LOOK, MIKEY, YOUR FLAG.
WOOOW!!
THAT'S MY KENCHIN!!
WHERE'D THAT COME FROM?
DRAKEN IS AMAZING.
AHHHH!!!
TWITCH
I CAN'T HANDLE THIS SHIT!!
FWSH
YOU'RE TOO DAMN LOUD, MIKEY!!
WHAT NOW?!
IS THIS WHEN THEY FIGHT...?
FWIP

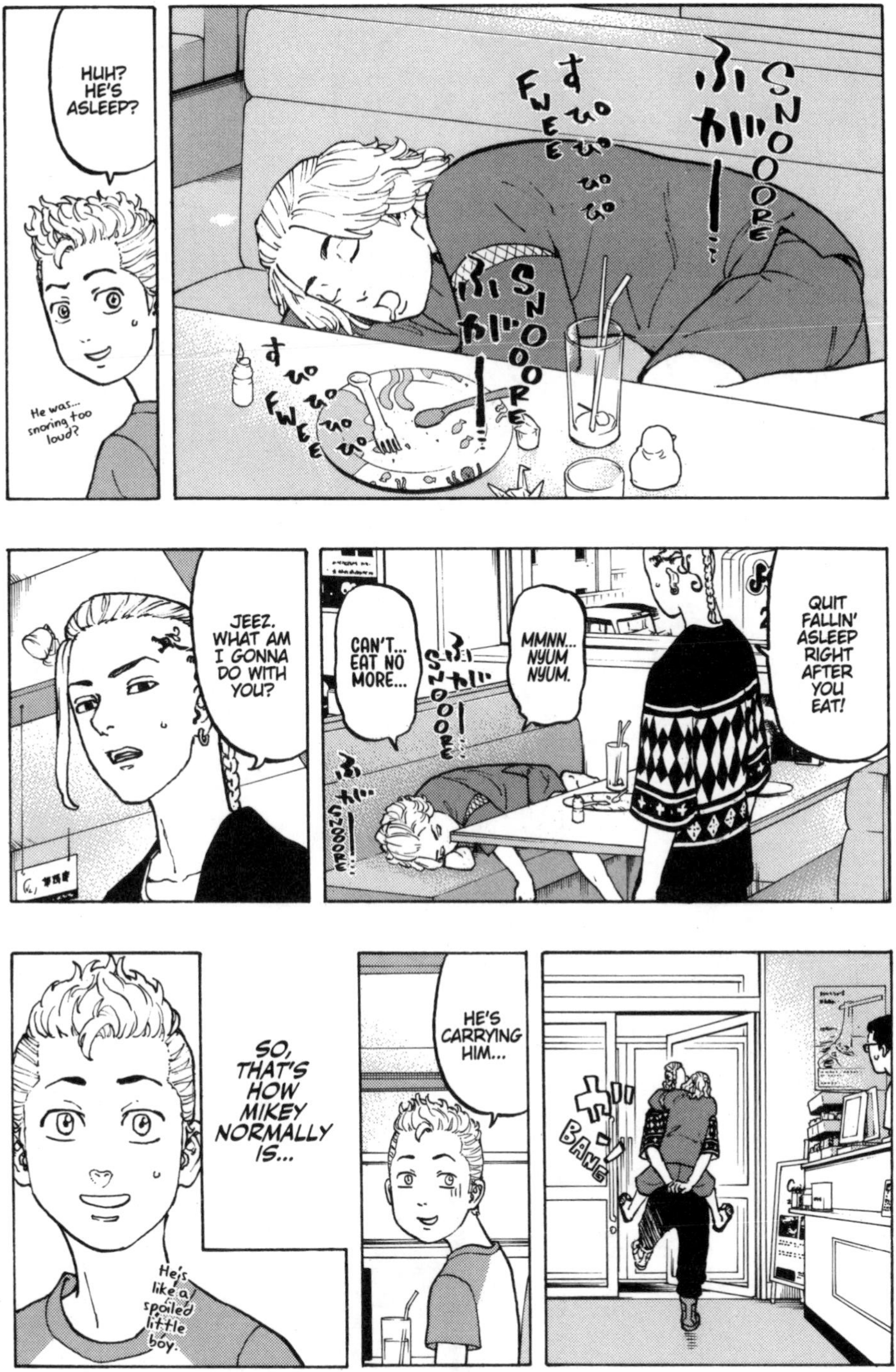

ふがー!!
SNOOORE
すぴぴぴぴ
FWEE
ふがー!!
SNOOOORE
すぴぴぴぴ
FWEE
HUH? HE'S ASLEEP?
He was... snoring too loud?
QUIT FALLIN' ASLEEP RIGHT AFTER YOU EAT!
MMNN... NYUM NYUM.
ふがー!!
SNOOOORE
CAN'T... EAT NO MORE...
ふがー!!
SNOOORE
JEEZ. WHAT AM I GONNA DO WITH YOU?
ガッ
BANG
HE'S CARRYING HIM...
SO, THAT'S HOW MIKEY NORMALLY IS...
He's like a spoiled little boy.

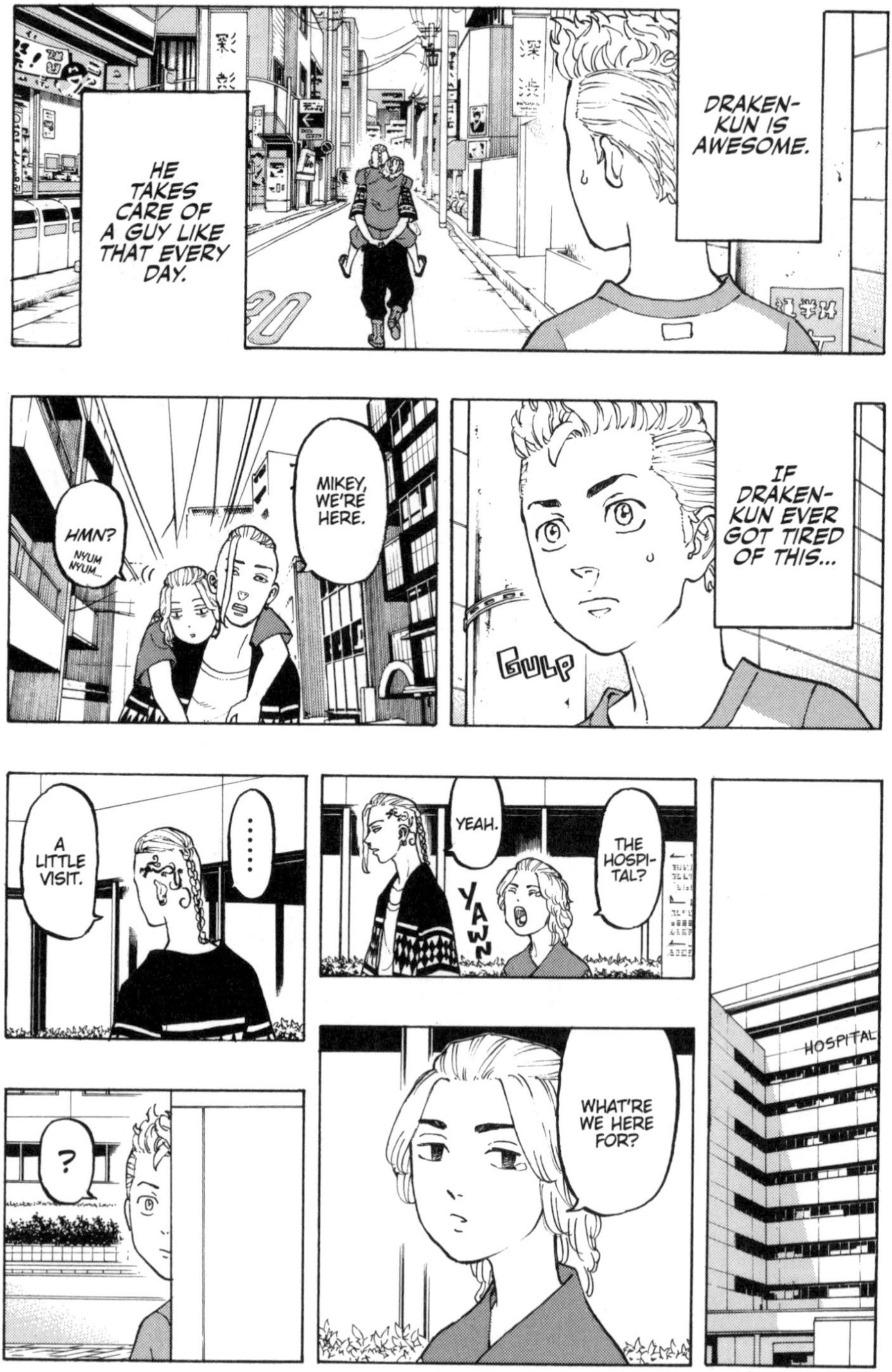
DRAKEN-KUN IS AWESOME.
HE TAKES CARE OF A GUY LIKE THAT EVERY DAY.
IF DRAKEN-KUN EVER GOT TIRED OF THIS...
GULP
MIKEY, WE'RE HERE.
HMN?
NYUM NYUM...
HOSPITAL
THE HOSPITAL?
YEAH.
YAWN
......
A LITTLE VISIT.
WHAT'RE WE HERE FOR?
?

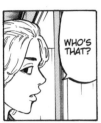

WHO'S THAT?
PAH'S FRIEND'S GIRL-FRIEND.
PAH FROM TOMAN ...
I just can't stand it.
Moebius' members beat the shit out of Pah's friend.
Then they raped his girlfriend in front of him.
THIS IS THE CAUSE OF THE FIGHT...
WITH MOE-BIUS.

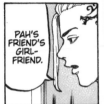

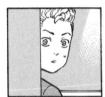

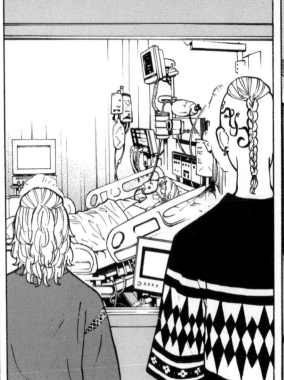

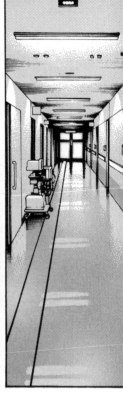

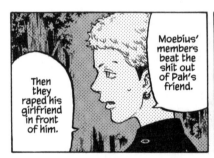

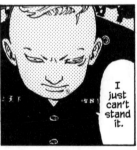

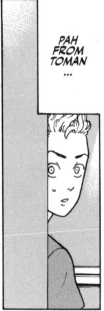

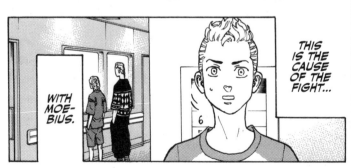

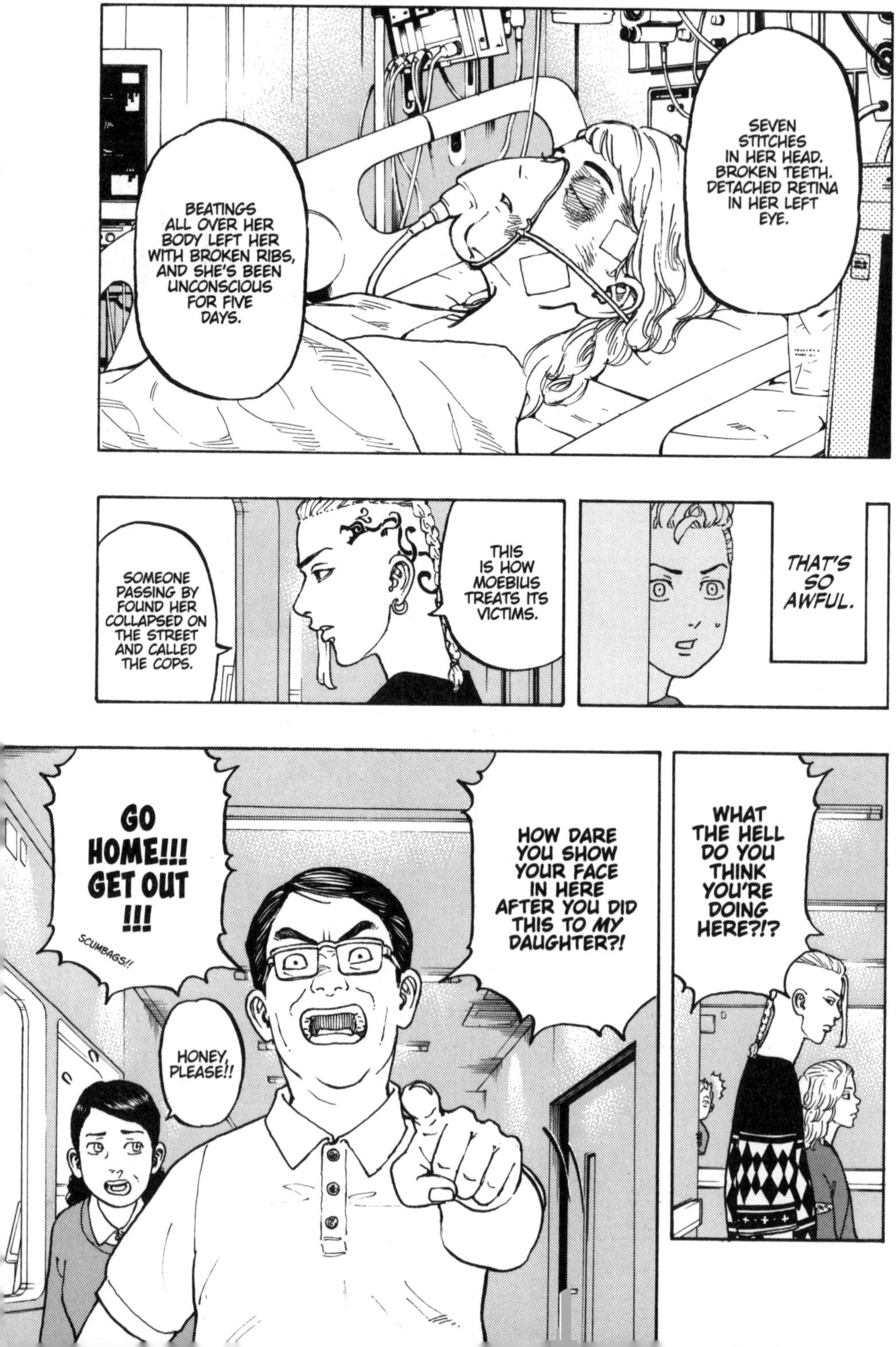
SEVEN STITCHES IN HER HEAD. BROKEN TEETH. DETACHED RETINA IN HER LEFT EYE.
BEATINGS ALL OVER HER BODY LEFT HER WITH BROKEN RIBS, AND SHE'S BEEN UNCONSCIOUS FOR FIVE DAYS.
THAT'S SO AWFUL.
THIS IS HOW MOEBIUS TREATS ITS VICTIMS.
SOMEONE PASSING BY FOUND HER COLLAPSED ON THE STREET AND CALLED THE COPS.
WHAT THE HELL DO YOU THINK YOU'RE DOING HERE?!?
HOW DARE YOU SHOW YOUR FACE IN HERE AFTER YOU DID THIS TO MY DAUGHTER?!
GO HOME!!! GET OUT!!!
SCUMBAGS!!
HONEY, PLEASE!!

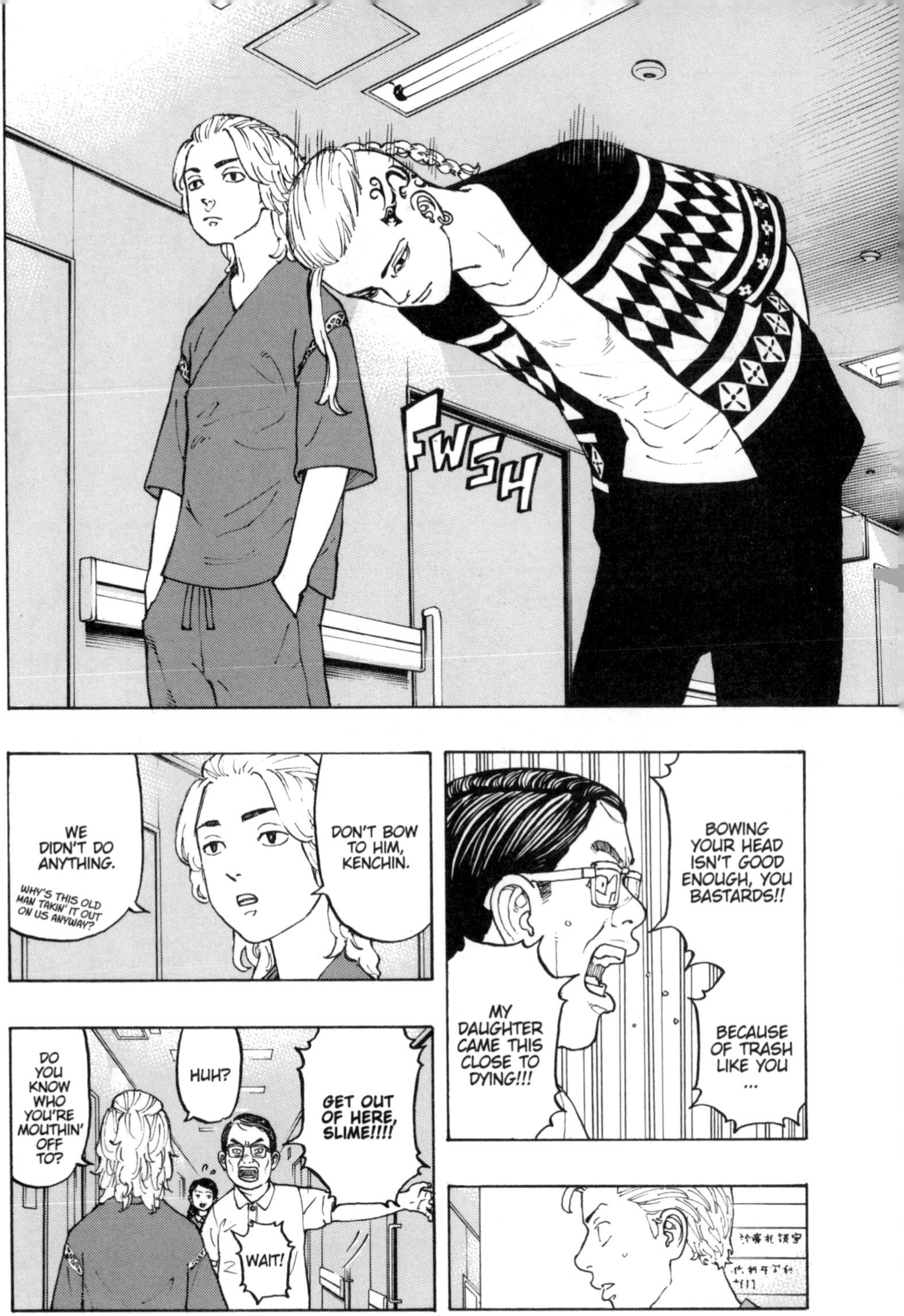
FWSH
BOWING YOUR HEAD ISN'T GOOD ENOUGH, YOU BASTARDS!!
BECAUSE OF TRASH LIKE YOU ...
MY DAUGHTER CAME THIS CLOSE TO DYING!!!
DON'T BOW TO HIM, KENCHIN.
WE DIDN'T DO ANYTHING.
WHY'S THIS OLD MAN TAKIN' IT OUT ON US ANYWAY?
GET OUT OF HERE, SLIME!!!!
HUH?
DO YOU KNOW WHO YOU'RE MOUTHIN' OFF TO?
WAIT!

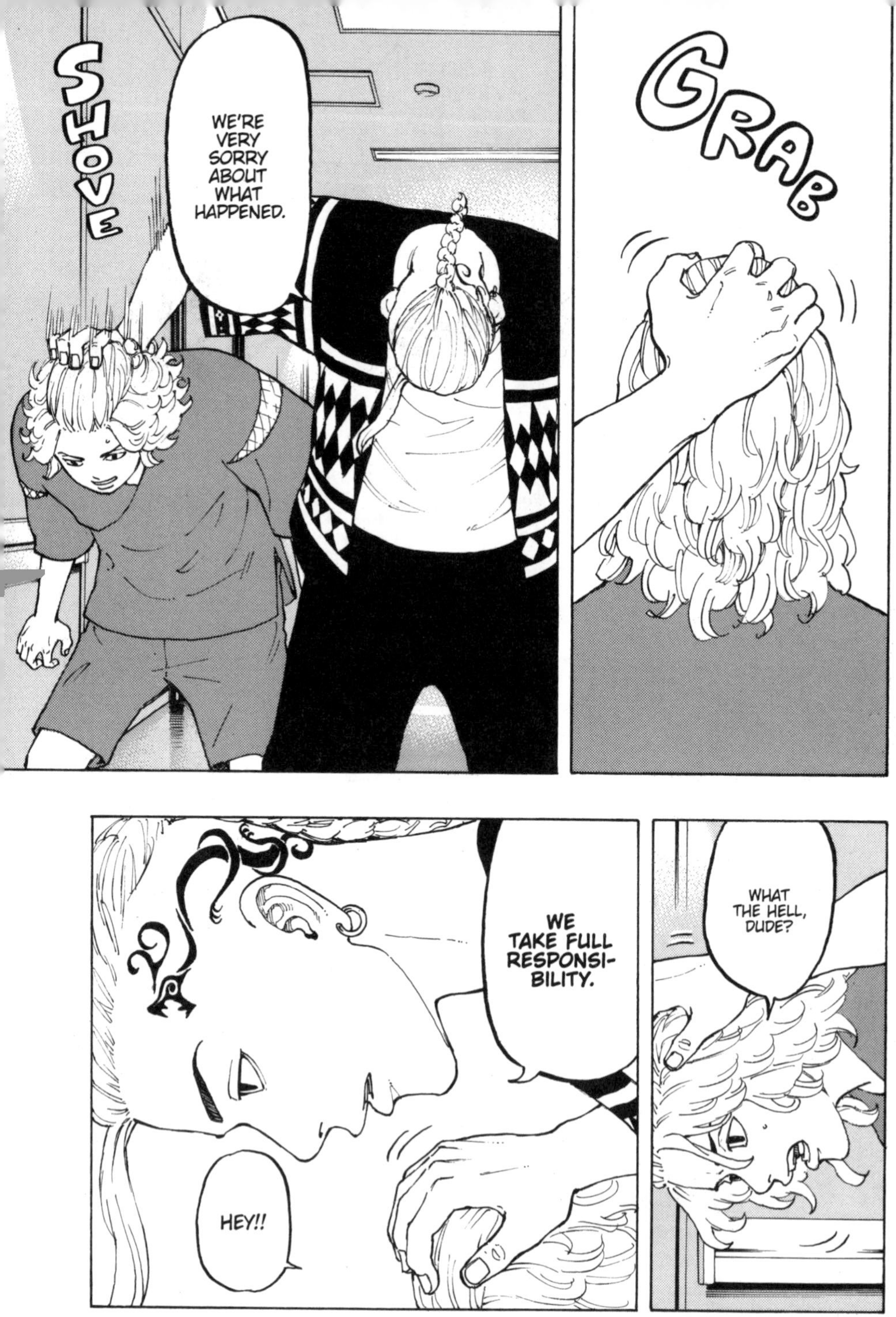
GRAB
SHOVE
WE'RE VERY SORRY ABOUT WHAT HAPPENED.
WHAT THE HELL, DUDE?
WE TAKE FULL RESPONSI-BILITY.
HEY!!

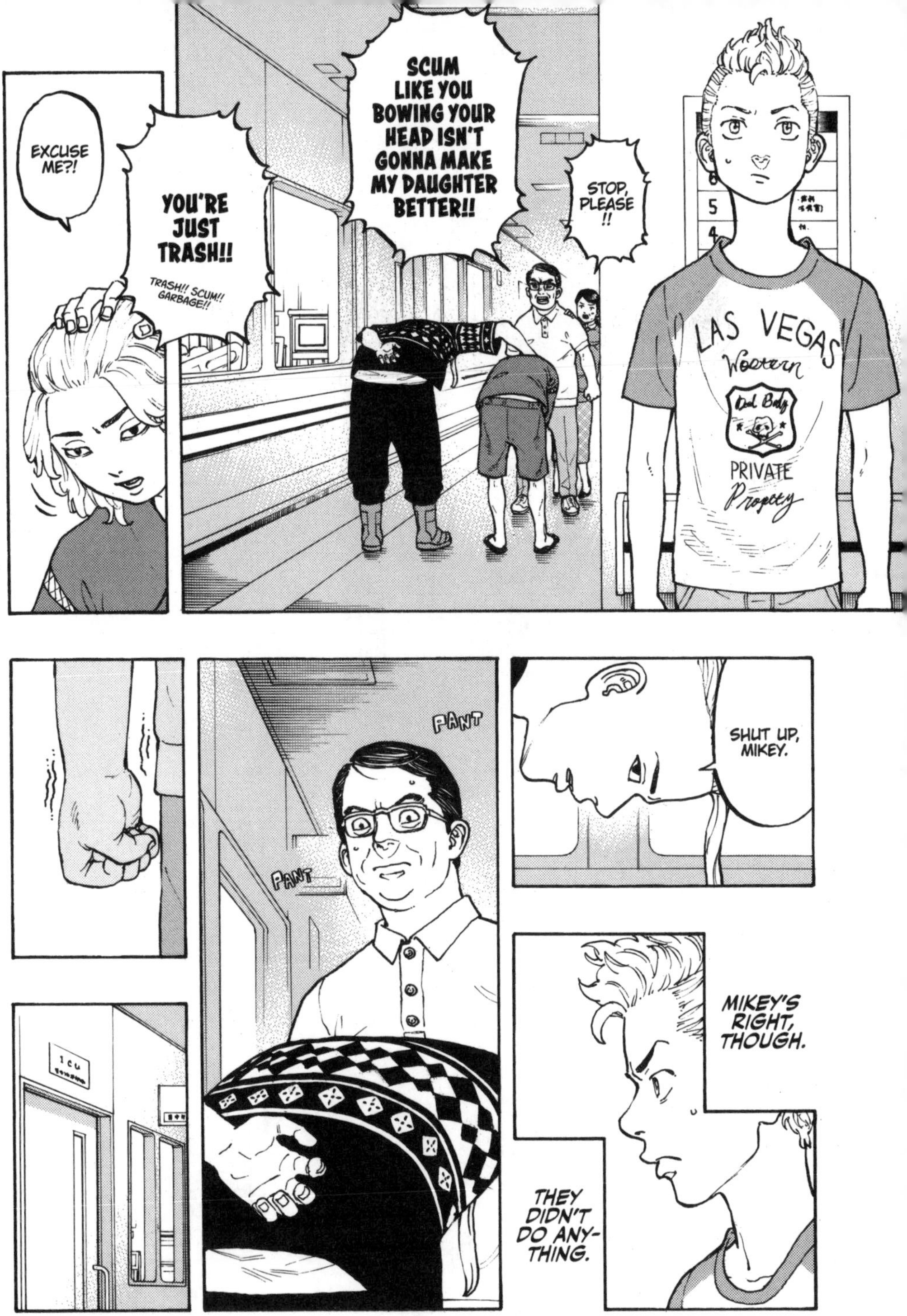
STOP, PLEASE!!
SCUM LIKE YOU BOWING YOUR HEAD ISN'T GONNA MAKE MY DAUGHTER BETTER!!
YOU'RE JUST TRASH!!
TRASH!! SCUM!! GARBAGE!!
EXCUSE ME?!
SHUT UP, MIKEY.
MIKEY'S RIGHT, THOUGH.
THEY DIDN'T DO ANY-THING.
PANT
PANT

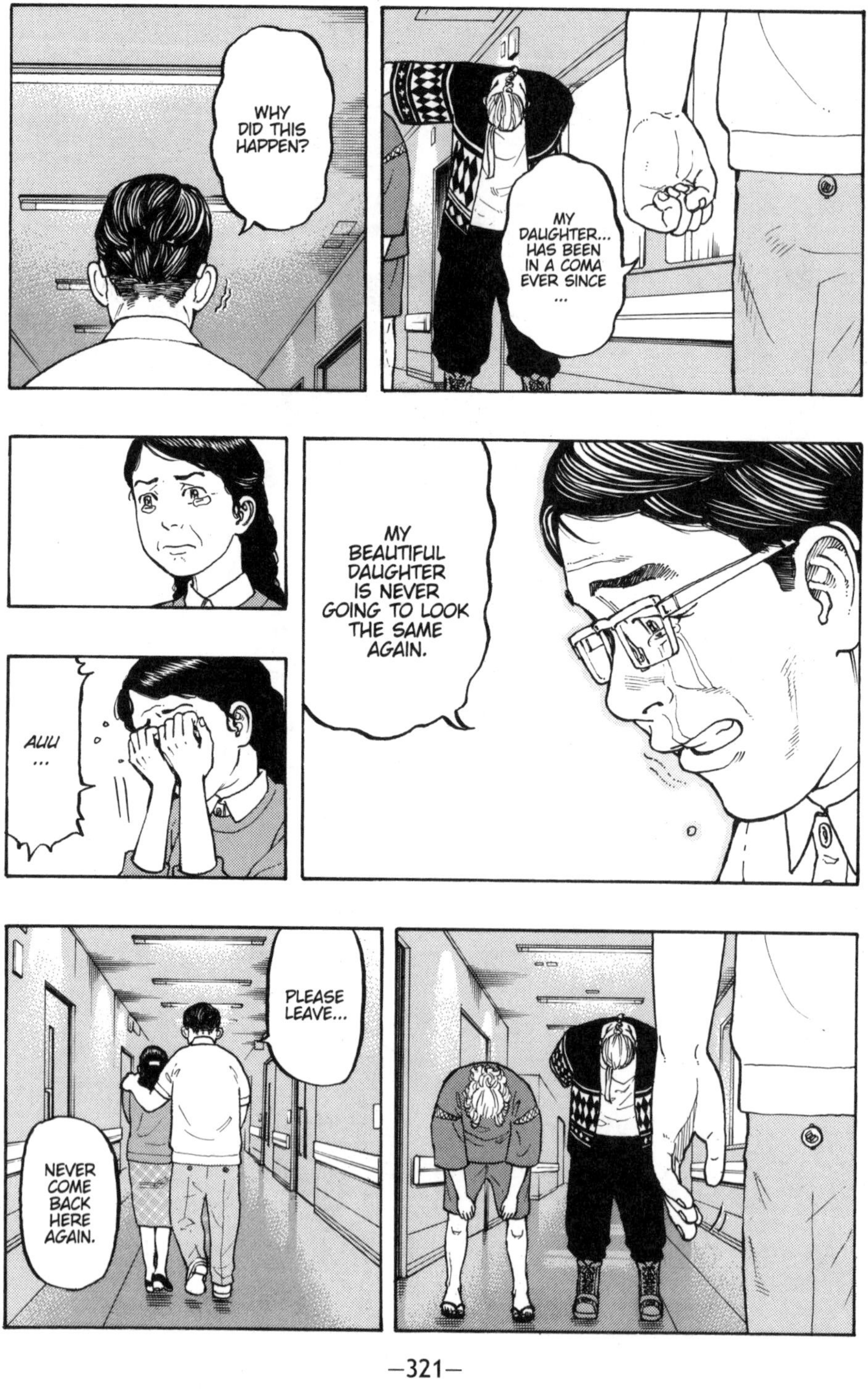
MY DAUGHTER... HAS BEEN IN A COMA EVER SINCE ...
WHY DID THIS HAPPEN?
MY BEAUTIFUL DAUGHTER IS NEVER GOING TO LOOK THE SAME AGAIN.
AUU ...
PLEASE LEAVE...
NEVER COME BACK HERE AGAIN.

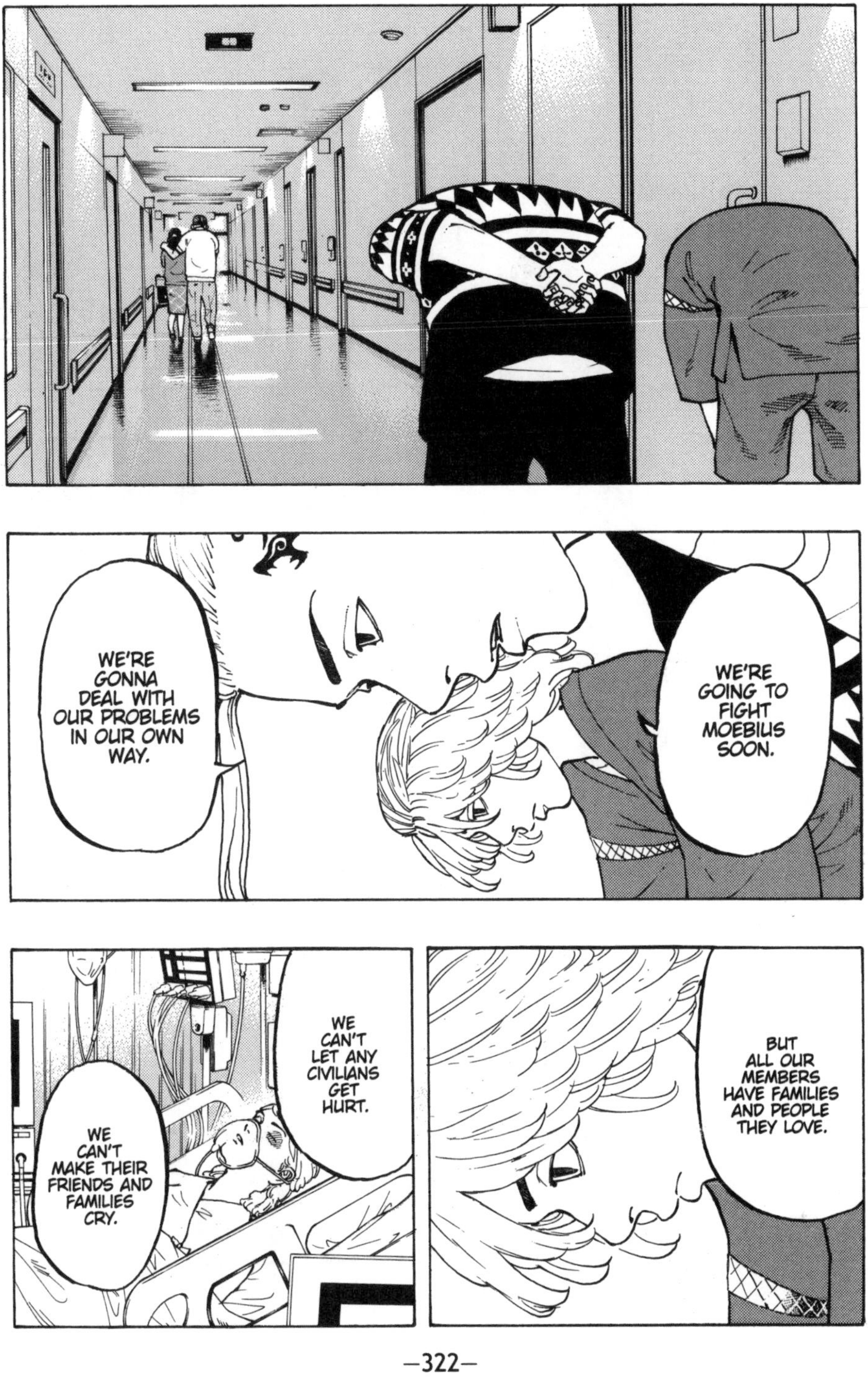
WE'RE GOING TO FIGHT MOEBIUS SOON.
WE'RE GONNA DEAL WITH OUR PROBLEMS IN OUR OWN WAY.
BUT ALL OUR MEMBERS HAVE FAMILIES AND PEOPLE THEY LOVE.
WE CAN'T LET ANY CIVILIANS GET HURT.
WE CAN'T MAKE THEIR FRIENDS AND FAMILIES CRY.

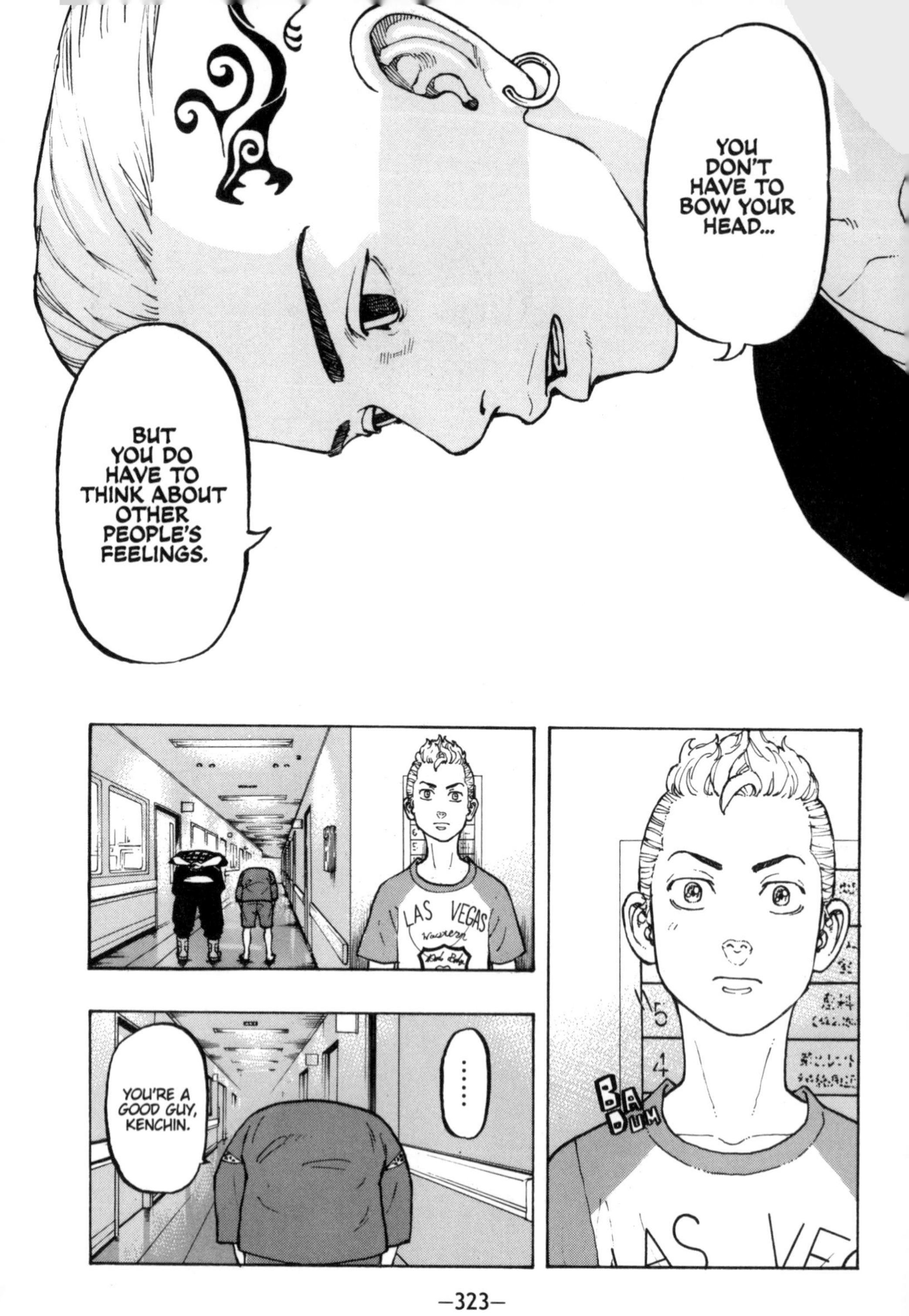
YOU DON'T HAVE TO BOW YOUR HEAD...
BUT YOU DO HAVE TO THINK ABOUT OTHER PEOPLE'S FEELINGS.
BA DUM
......
YOU'RE A GOOD GUY, KENCHIN.

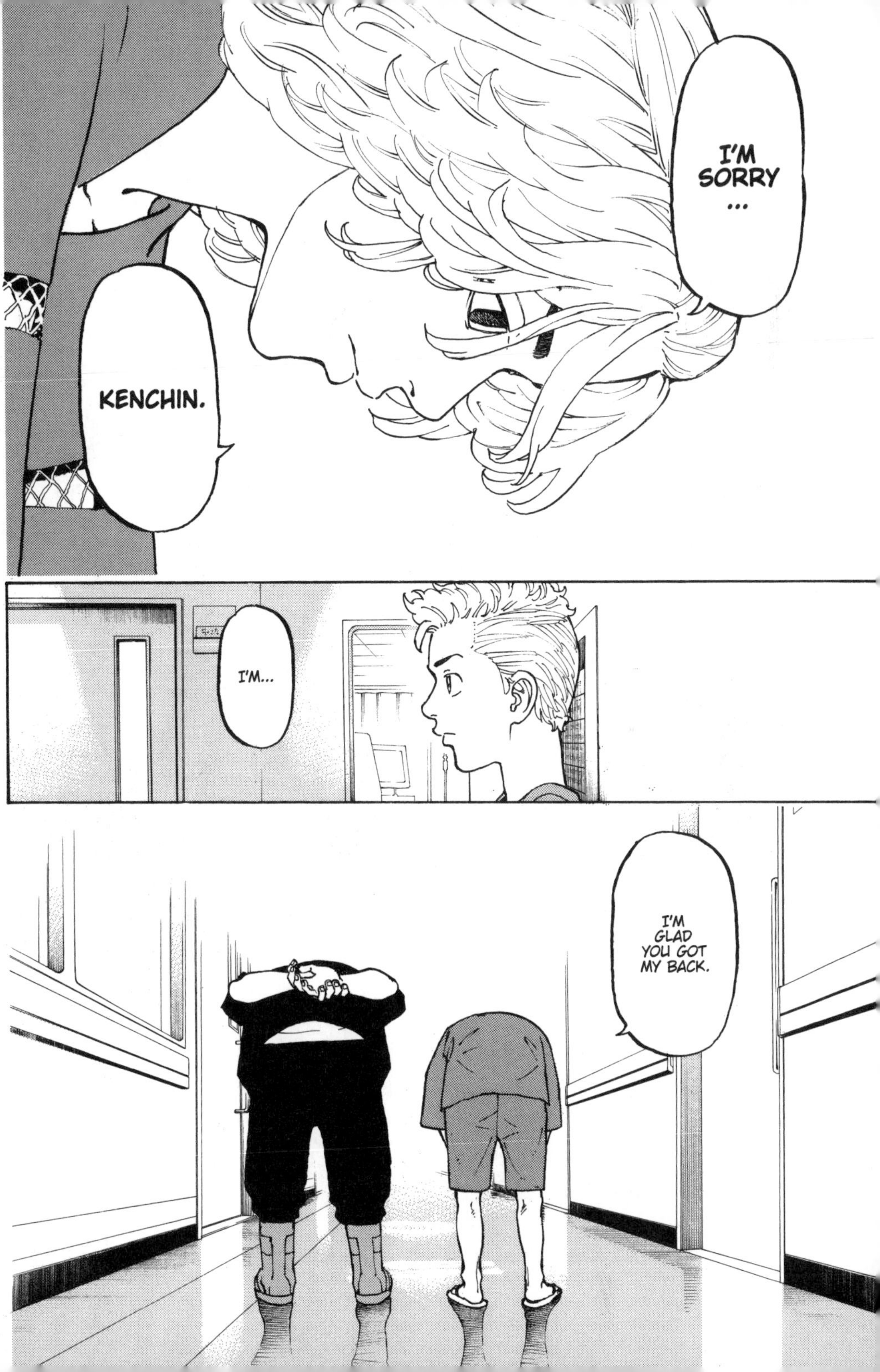
I'M SORRY ...
KENCHIN.
I'M...
I'M GLAD YOU GOT MY BACK.

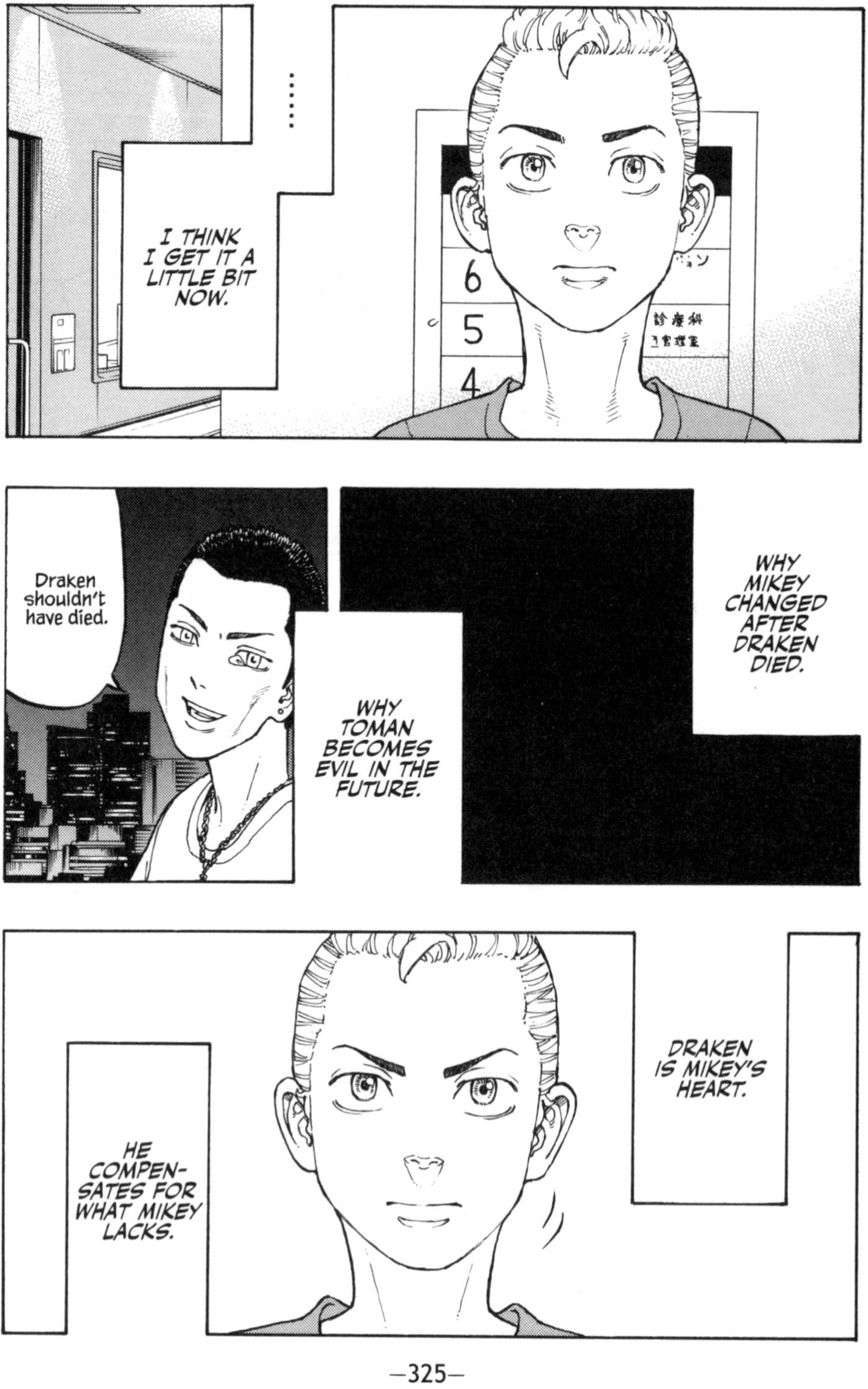

......
I THINK I GET IT A LITTLE BIT NOW.
WHY MIKEY CHANGED AFTER DRAKEN DIED.
WHY TOMAN BECOMES EVIL IN THE FUTURE.
Draken shouldn't have died.
DRAKEN IS MIKEY'S HEART.
HE COMPEN-SATES FOR WHAT MIKEY LACKS.

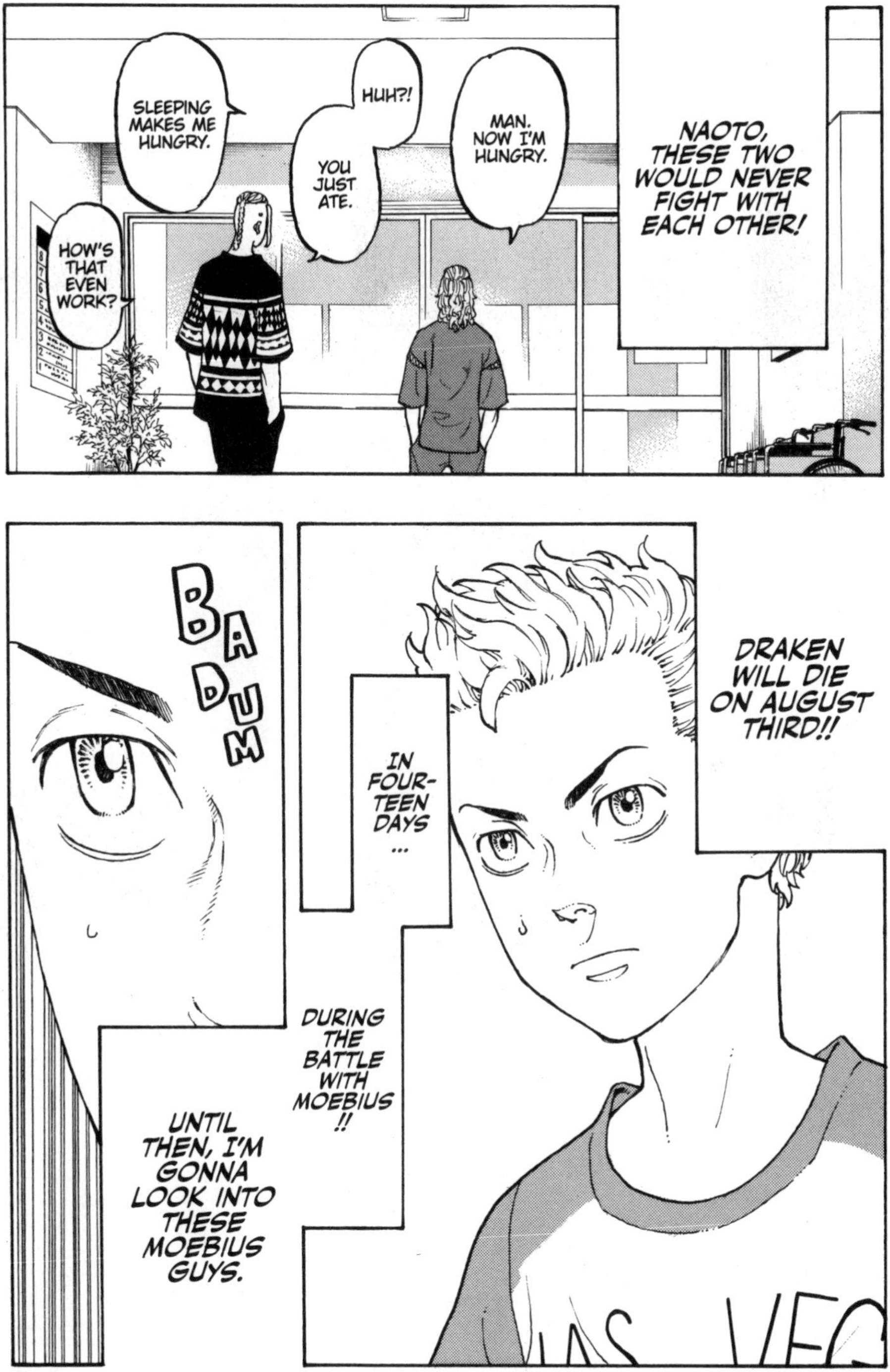
NAOTO, THESE TWO WOULD NEVER FIGHT WITH EACH OTHER!
MAN. NOW I'M HUNGRY.
HUH?!
YOU JUST ATE.
SLEEPING MAKES ME HUNGRY.
HOW'S THAT EVEN WORK?
DRAKEN WILL DIE ON AUGUST THIRD!!
IN FOURTEEN DAYS...
DURING THE BATTLE WITH MOEBIUS!!
BADUM
UNTIL THEN, I'M GONNA LOOK INTO THESE MOEBIUS GUYS.

TOKYO
Revengers

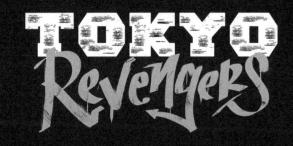

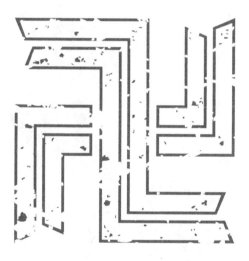

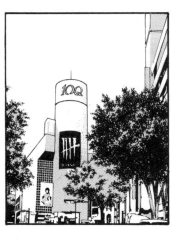

I WAS BORN IN SHIBUYA'S RED-LIGHT DISTRICT.

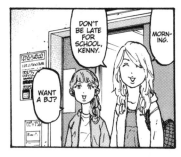

10Q

NEVER KNEW MY DAD, MY MOM WAS A PROSTITUTE. WHEN I WAS TWO YEARS OLD, SHE DISAPPEARED.

PLEASE SIGN HERE.
YOU'RE A TALL ONE, KENNY-BOY.
I DRINK MY MILK EVERY DAY.

I LIVED AT A MASSAGE PARLOR.

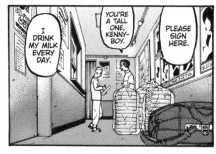

MORN-ING.
DON'T BE LATE FOR SCHOOL, KENNY.
WANT A BJ?

I WAS A FIFTH-YEAR IN ELEMENTARY SCHOOL.

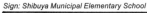

Sign: Shibuya Municipal Elementary School

GOOD MORN-ING!
GOOD MORN-ING!
KEN-KUN.

I GREW UP SUR-ROUNDED BY PINK TOWELS AND THE SMELL OF LOTION.

BOW
BOW
BOW

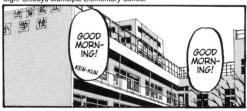

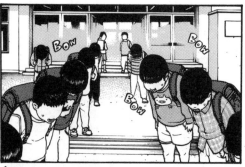

CHAPTER EXTRA: ZERO

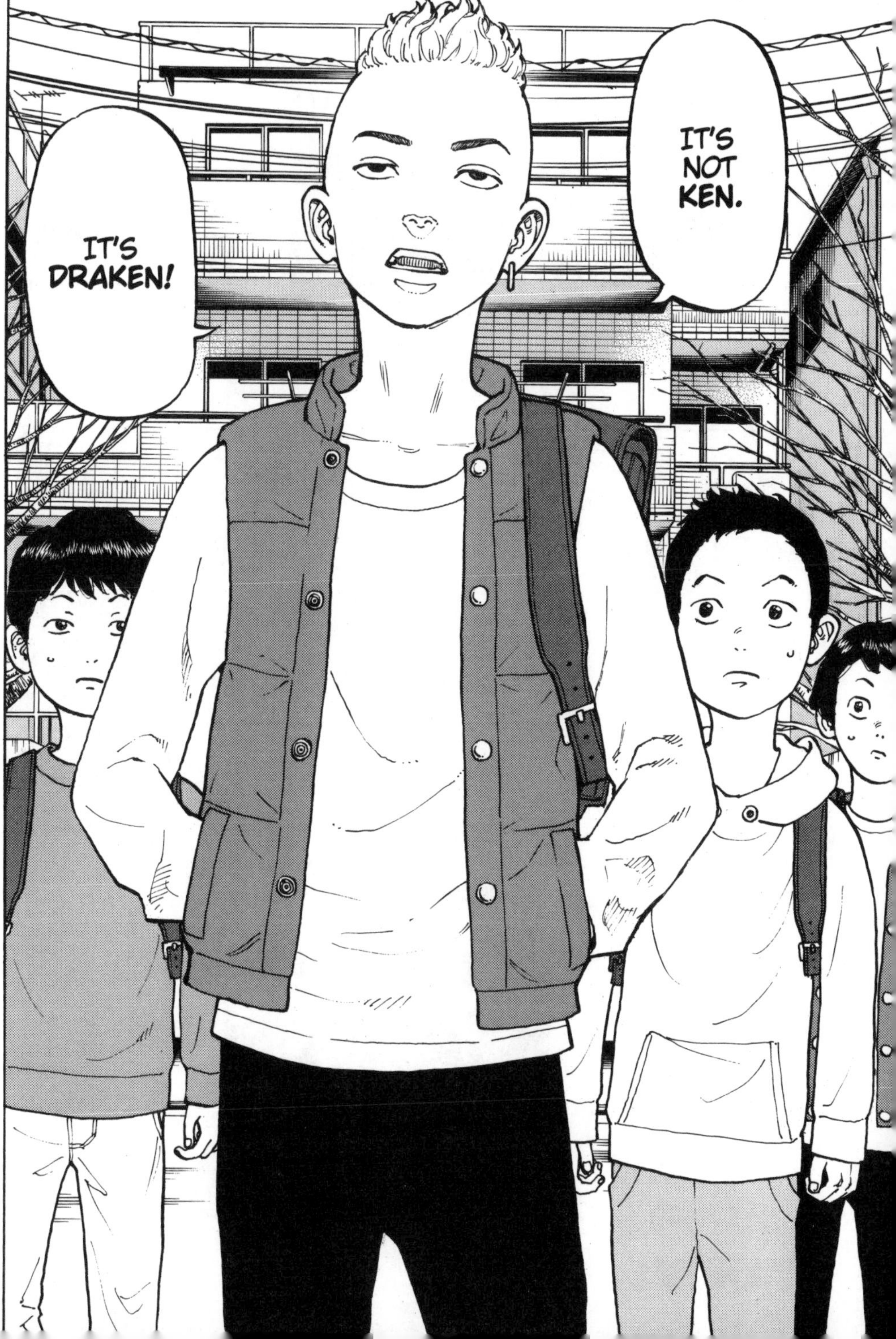
IT'S NOT KEN.
IT'S DRAKEN!

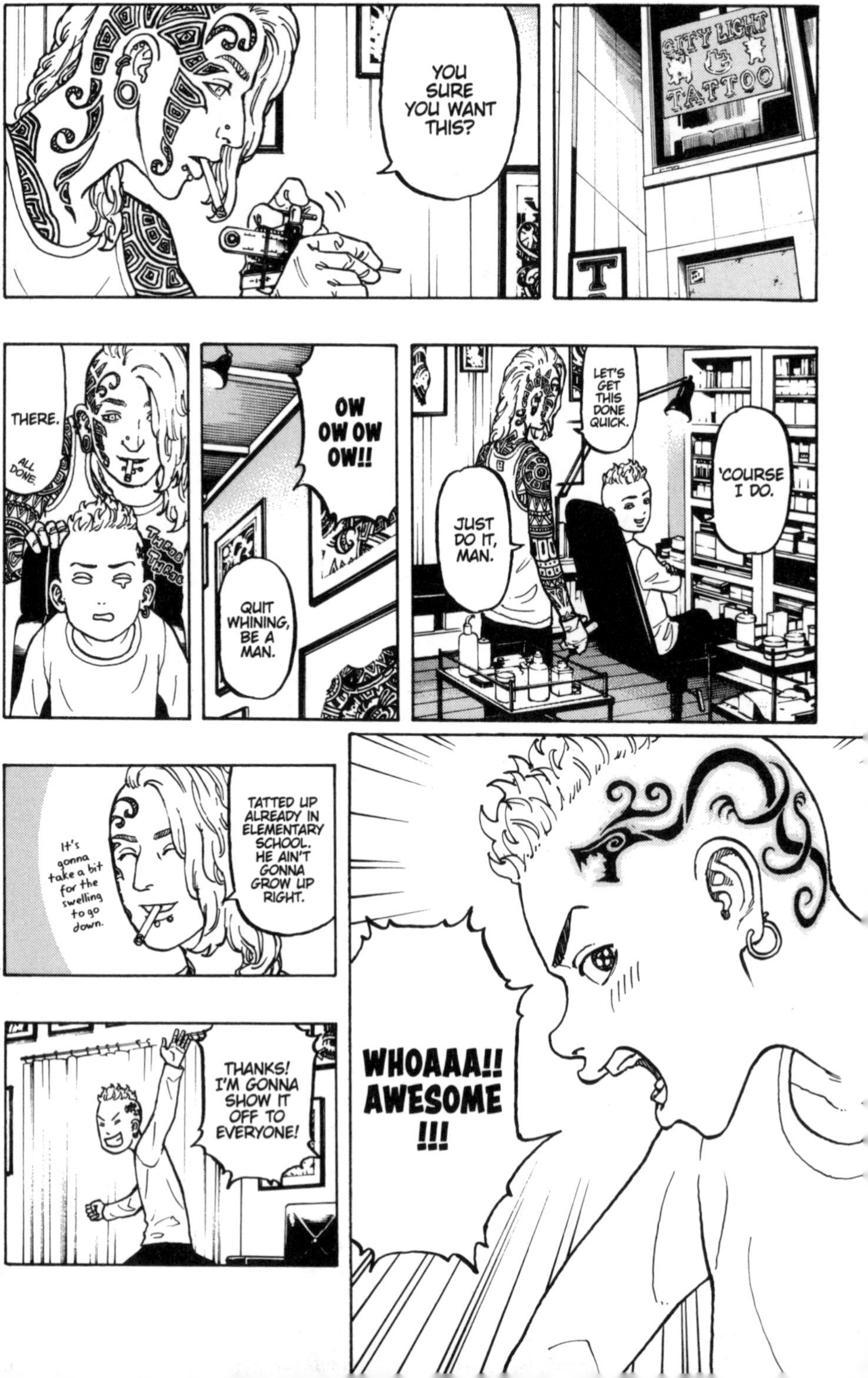
CITY LIGHT TATTOO
YOU SURE YOU WANT THIS?
'COURSE I DO.
LET'S GET THIS DONE QUICK.
JUST DO IT, MAN.
OW OW OW OW!!
QUIT WHINING, BE A MAN.
THERE.
ALL DONE.
THROB THROB
WHOAAA!! AWESOME!!!
TATTED UP ALREADY IN ELEMENTARY SCHOOL. HE AIN'T GONNA GROW UP RIGHT.
It's gonna take a bit for the swelling to go down.
THANKS! I'M GONNA SHOW IT OFF TO EVERYONE!

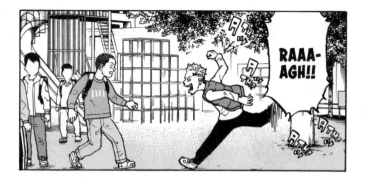

I WAS BIGGER THAN ALL THE NEARBY JUNIOR HIGH STUDENTS.
RAAA-AGH!!
TMP
TMP
TMP
TMP
THWUD!
I'M RYUGUJI KEN FROM FOURTH ELEMENTARY!
CALL ME DRAKEN!!
IF YOU SEE THIS DRAGON, YOU BETTER HIDE!
EVEN MOST JUNIOR HIGH SCHOOLERS WOULDN'T SCREW WITH A FIFTH GRADER WITH A DRAGON TATTOO.

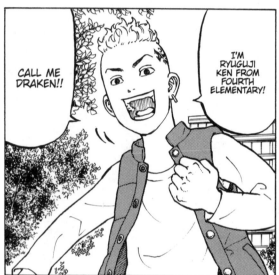

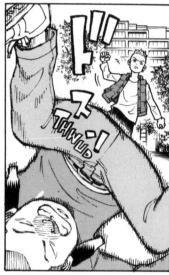

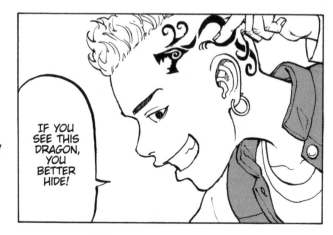

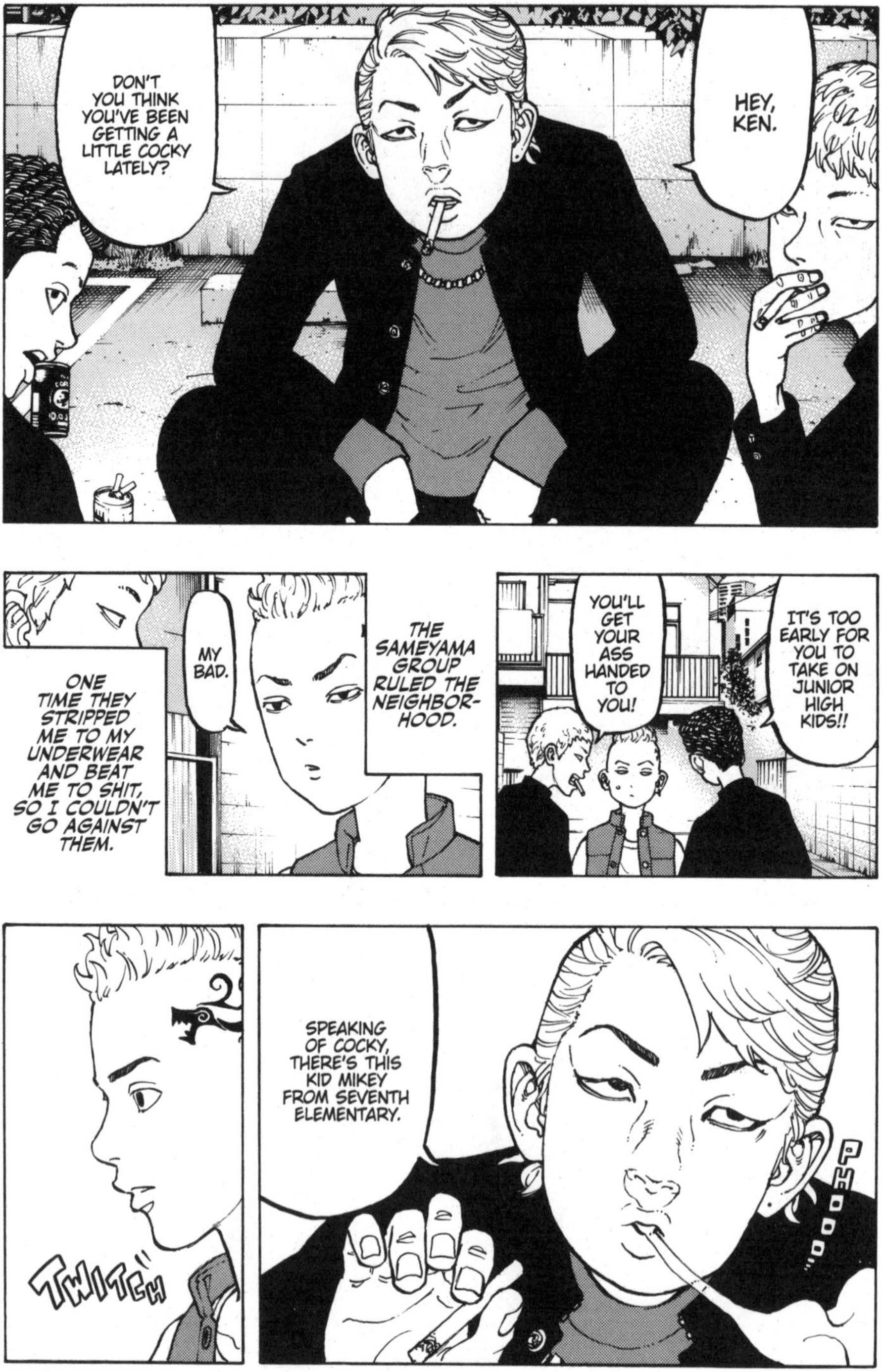

HEY, KEN.
DON'T YOU THINK YOU'VE BEEN GETTING A LITTLE COCKY LATELY?
IT'S TOO EARLY FOR YOU TO TAKE ON JUNIOR HIGH KIDS!!
YOU'LL GET YOUR ASS HANDED TO YOU!
THE SAMEYAMA GROUP RULED THE NEIGHBOR-HOOD.
MY BAD.
ONE TIME THEY STRIPPED ME TO MY UNDERWEAR AND BEAT ME TO SHIT, SO I COULDN'T GO AGAINST THEM.
SPEAKING OF COCKY, THERE'S THIS KID MIKEY FROM SEVENTH ELEMENTARY.
PHOOOO...
TWITCH

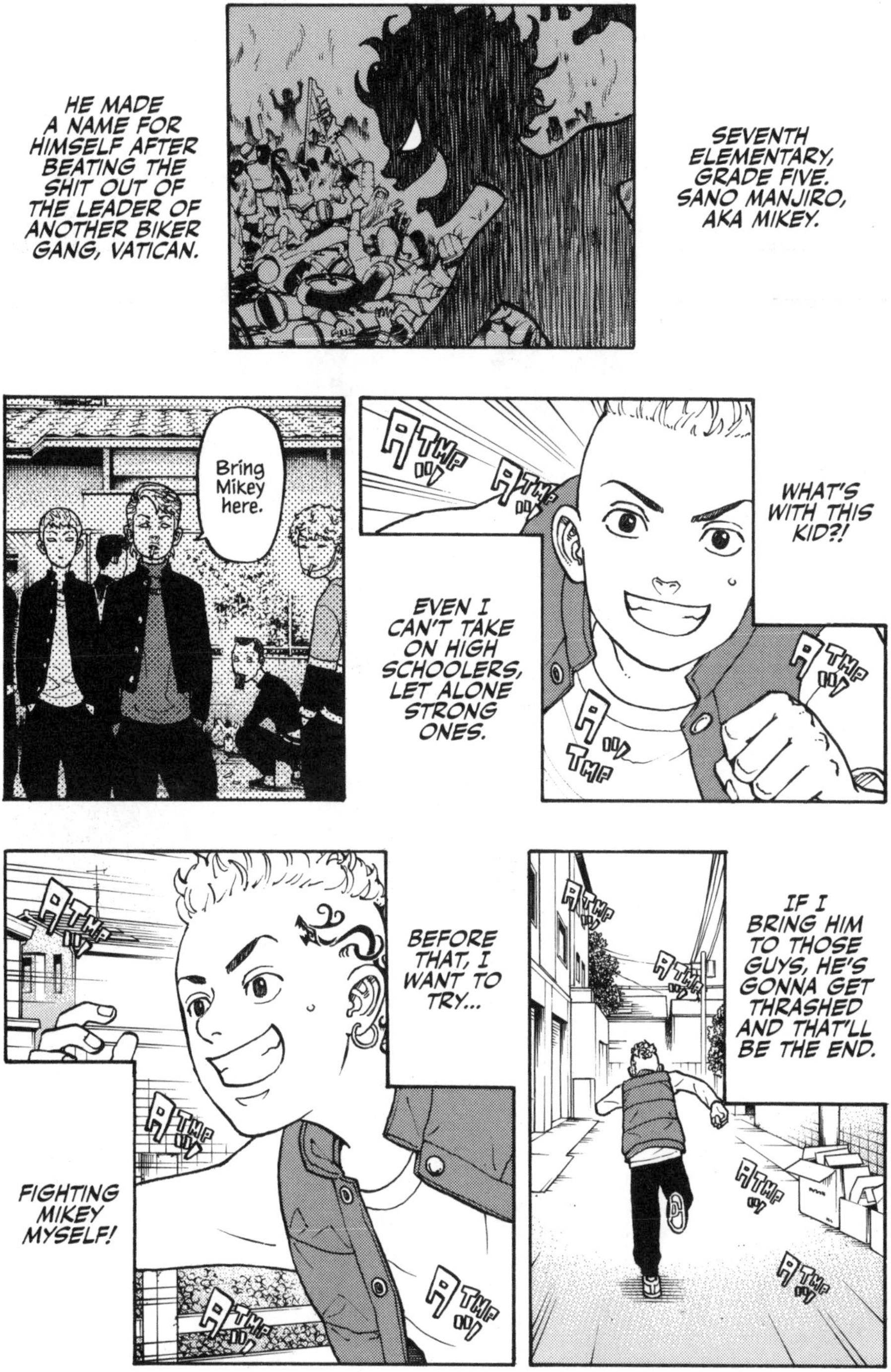
SEVENTH ELEMENTARY, GRADE FIVE. SANO MANJIRO, AKA MIKEY.
HE MADE A NAME FOR HIMSELF AFTER BEATING THE SHIT OUT OF THE LEADER OF ANOTHER BIKER GANG, VATICAN.
TMP
TMP
WHAT'S WITH THIS KID?!
TMP
EVEN I CAN'T TAKE ON HIGH SCHOOLERS, LET ALONE STRONG ONES.
TMP
Bring Mikey here.
IF I BRING HIM TO THOSE GUYS, HE'S GONNA GET THRASHED AND THAT'LL BE THE END.
TMP
TMP
TMP
TMP
BEFORE THAT, I WANT TO TRY...
TMP
TMP
FIGHTING MIKEY MYSELF!
TMP
TMP

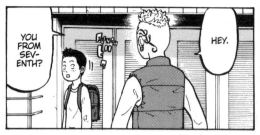

HEY.
YOU FROM SEV-ENTH?
I'M LOOKIN' FOR MIKEY. YOU SEEN HIM?
OH YEAH, MIKEY-KUN WAS JUST--
AH!
MIKEY-KUN.
HUH?
GULP

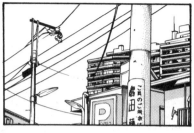

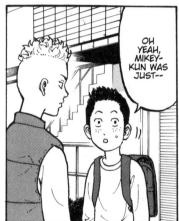

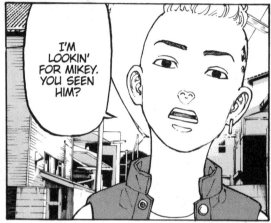

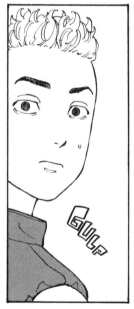

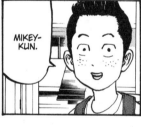

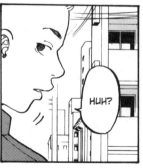

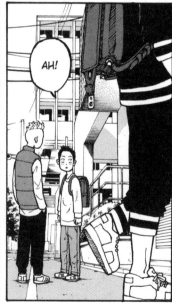

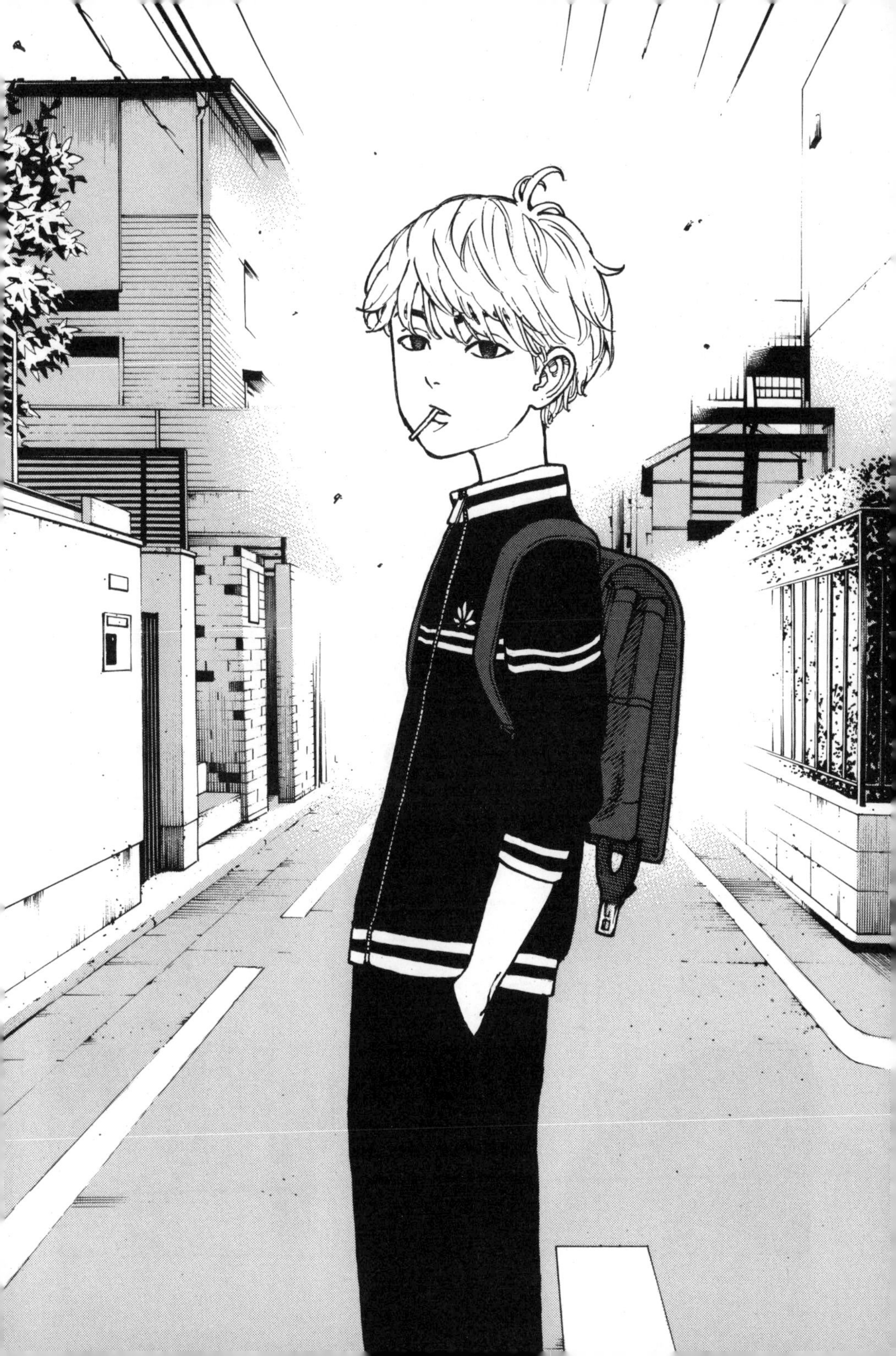

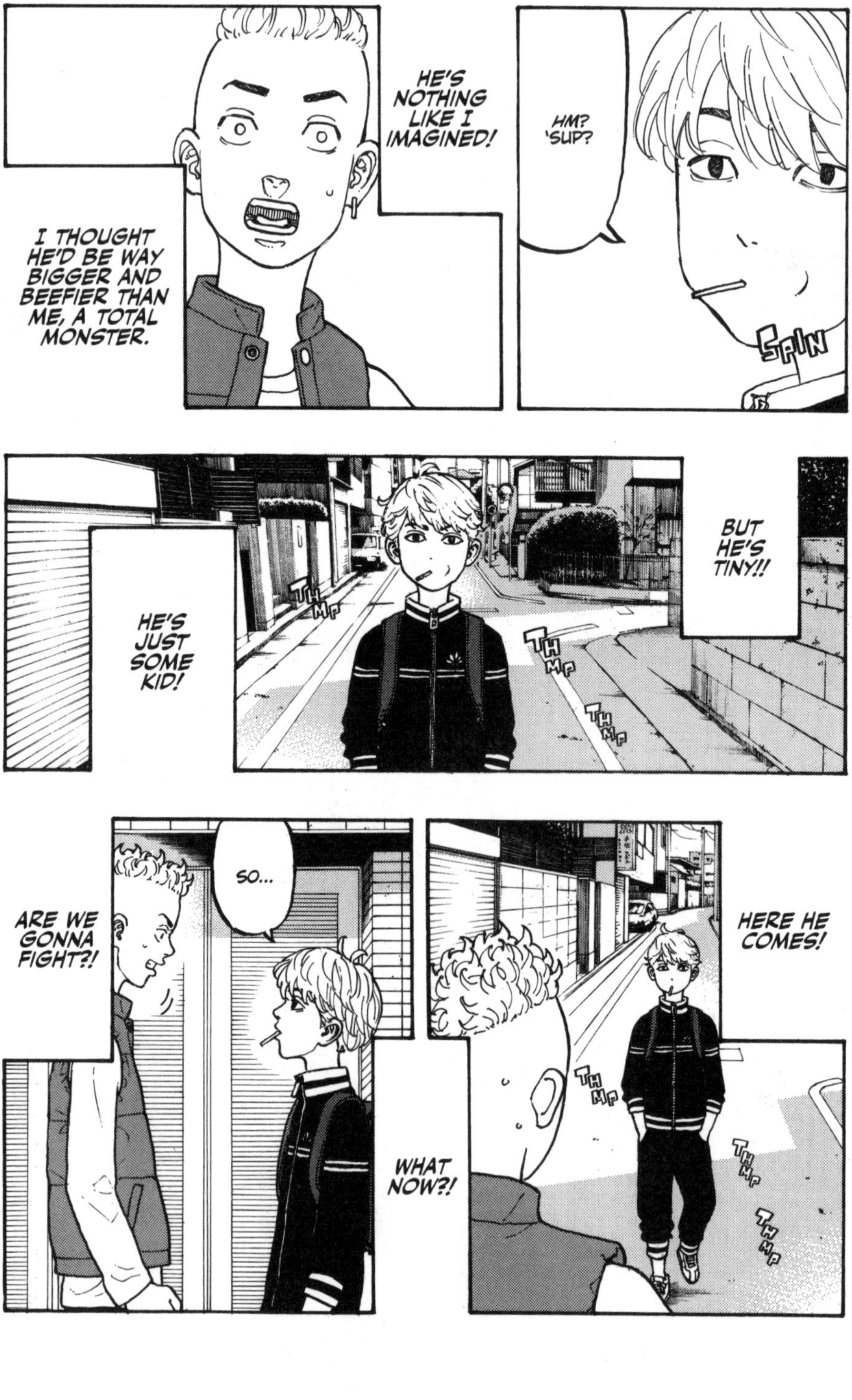
HM? 'SUP?
SPIN
HE'S NOTHING LIKE I IMAGINED!
I THOUGHT HE'D BE WAY BIGGER AND BEEFIER THAN ME, A TOTAL MONSTER.
BUT HE'S TINY!!
THMP
THMP
THMP
HE'S JUST SOME KID!
HERE HE COMES!
THMP
THMP
THMP
SO...
ARE WE GONNA FIGHT?!
WHAT NOW?!

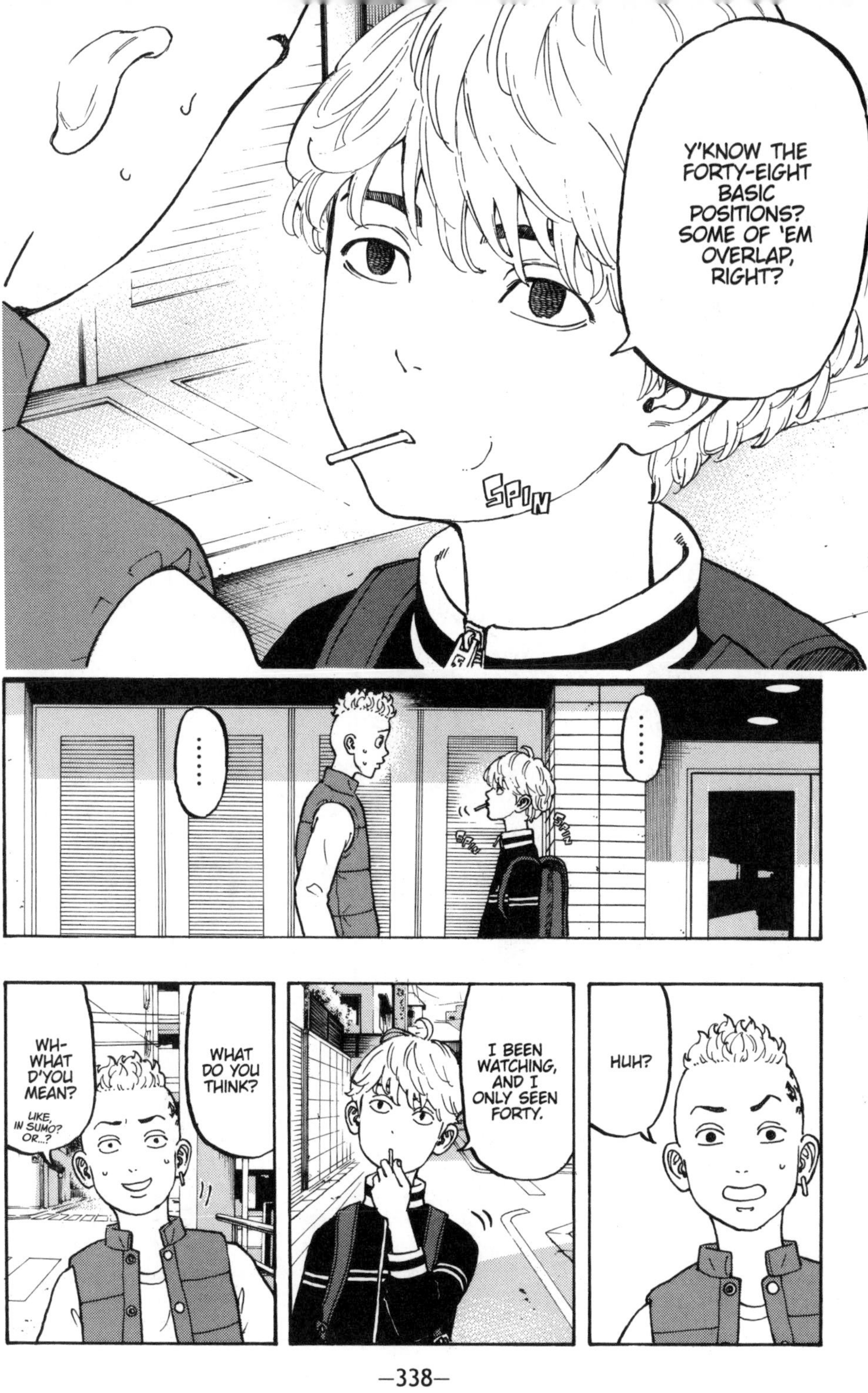
Y'KNOW THE FORTY-EIGHT BASIC POSITIONS? SOME OF 'EM OVERLAP, RIGHT?
SPIN
......
......
SPIN
SPIN
HUH?
I BEEN WATCHING, AND I ONLY SEEN FORTY.
WHAT DO YOU THINK?
WH- WHAT D'YOU MEAN?
LIKE, IN SUMO? OR...?

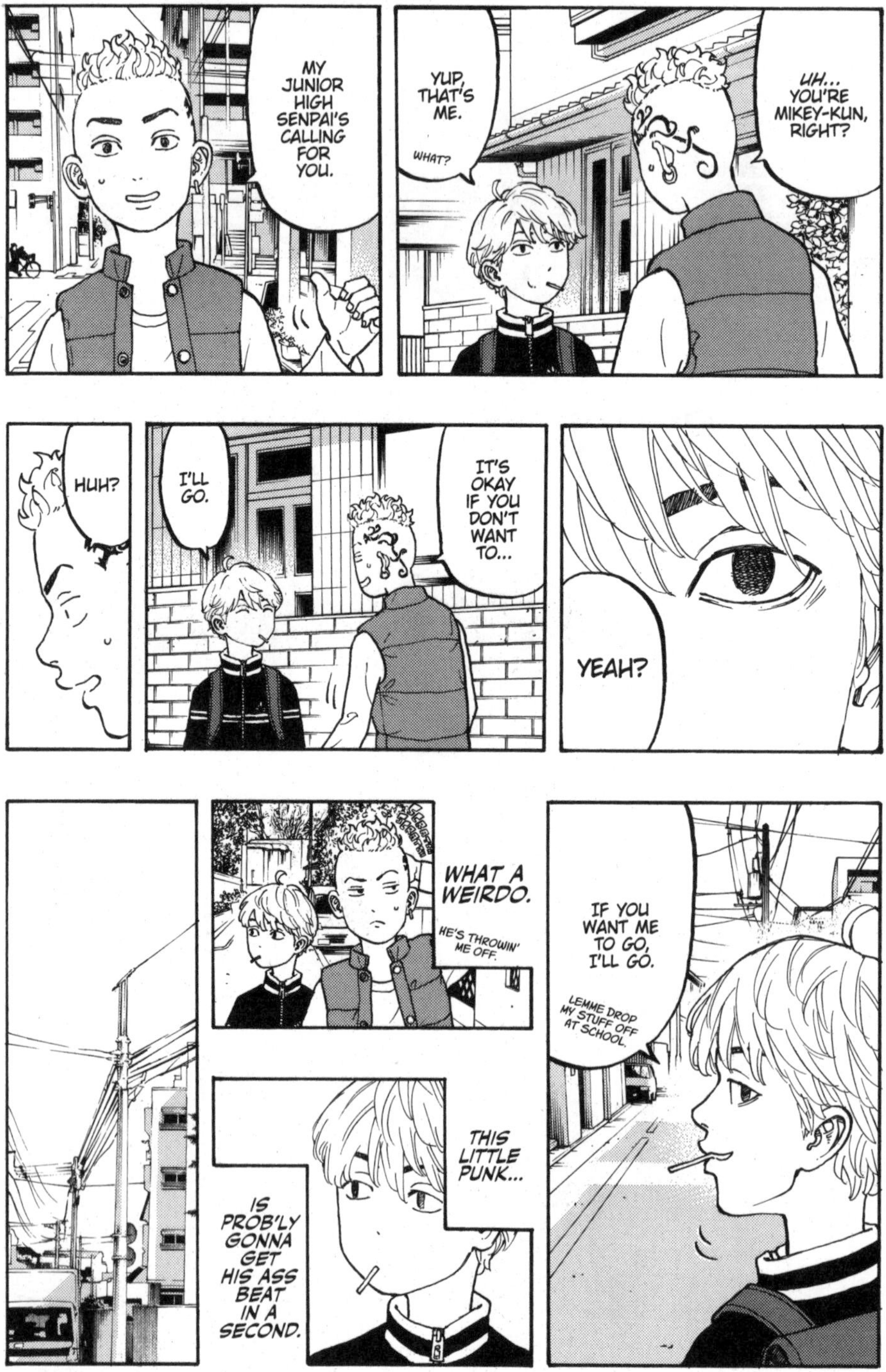
UH... YOU'RE MIKEY-KUN, RIGHT?
YUP, THAT'S ME.
WHAT?
MY JUNIOR HIGH SENPAI'S CALLING FOR YOU.
YEAH?
IT'S OKAY IF YOU DON'T WANT TO...
I'LL GO.
HUH?
IF YOU WANT ME TO GO, I'LL GO.
LEMME DROP MY STUFF OFF AT SCHOOL.
WHAT A WEIRDO.
HE'S THROWIN' ME OFF.
THIS LITTLE PUNK...
IS PROB'LY GONNA GET HIS ASS BEAT IN A SECOND.

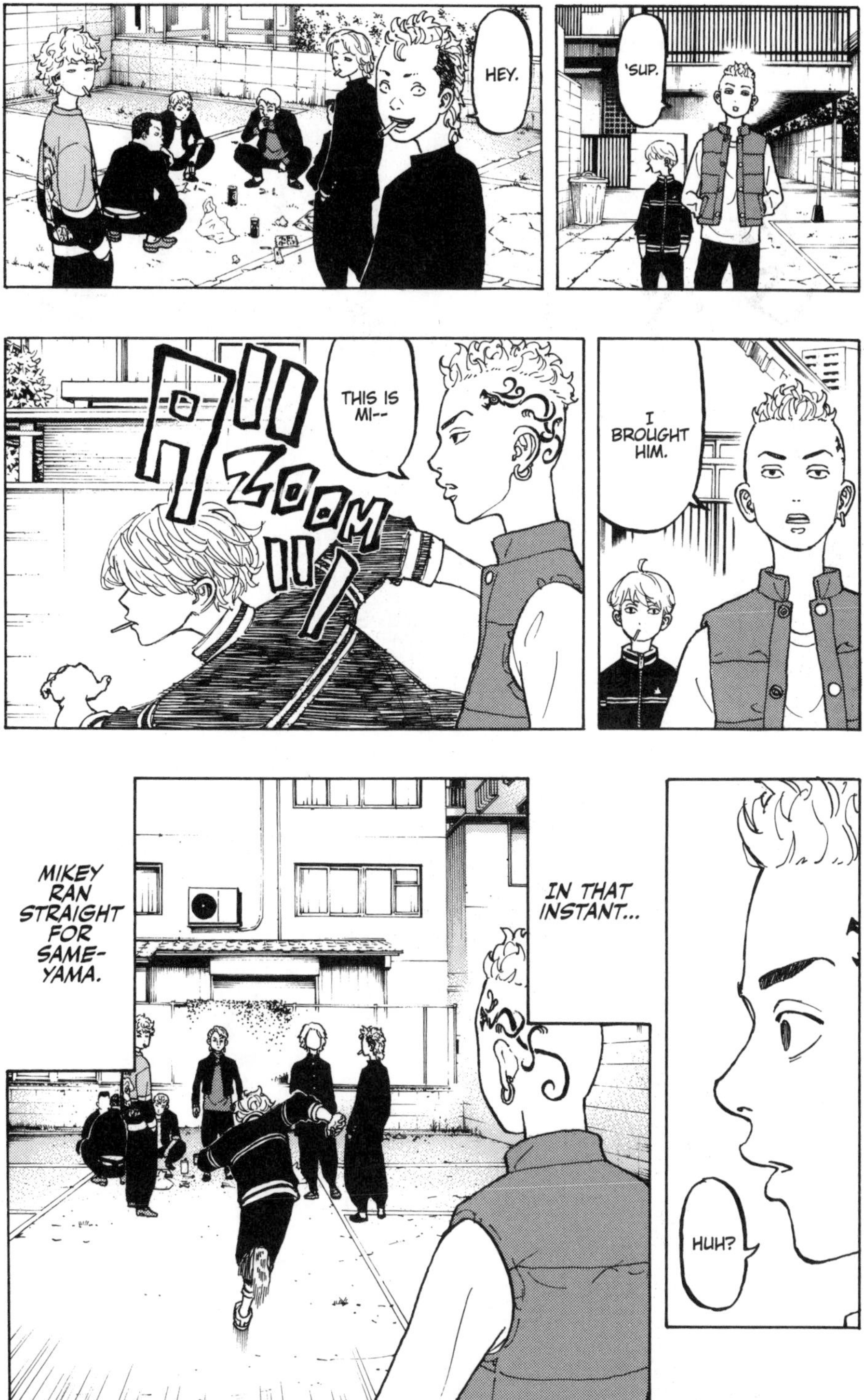
'SUP.
HEY.
I BROUGHT HIM.
THIS IS MI--
ZOOM
HUH?
IN THAT INSTANT...
MIKEY RAN STRAIGHT FOR SAME-YAMA.

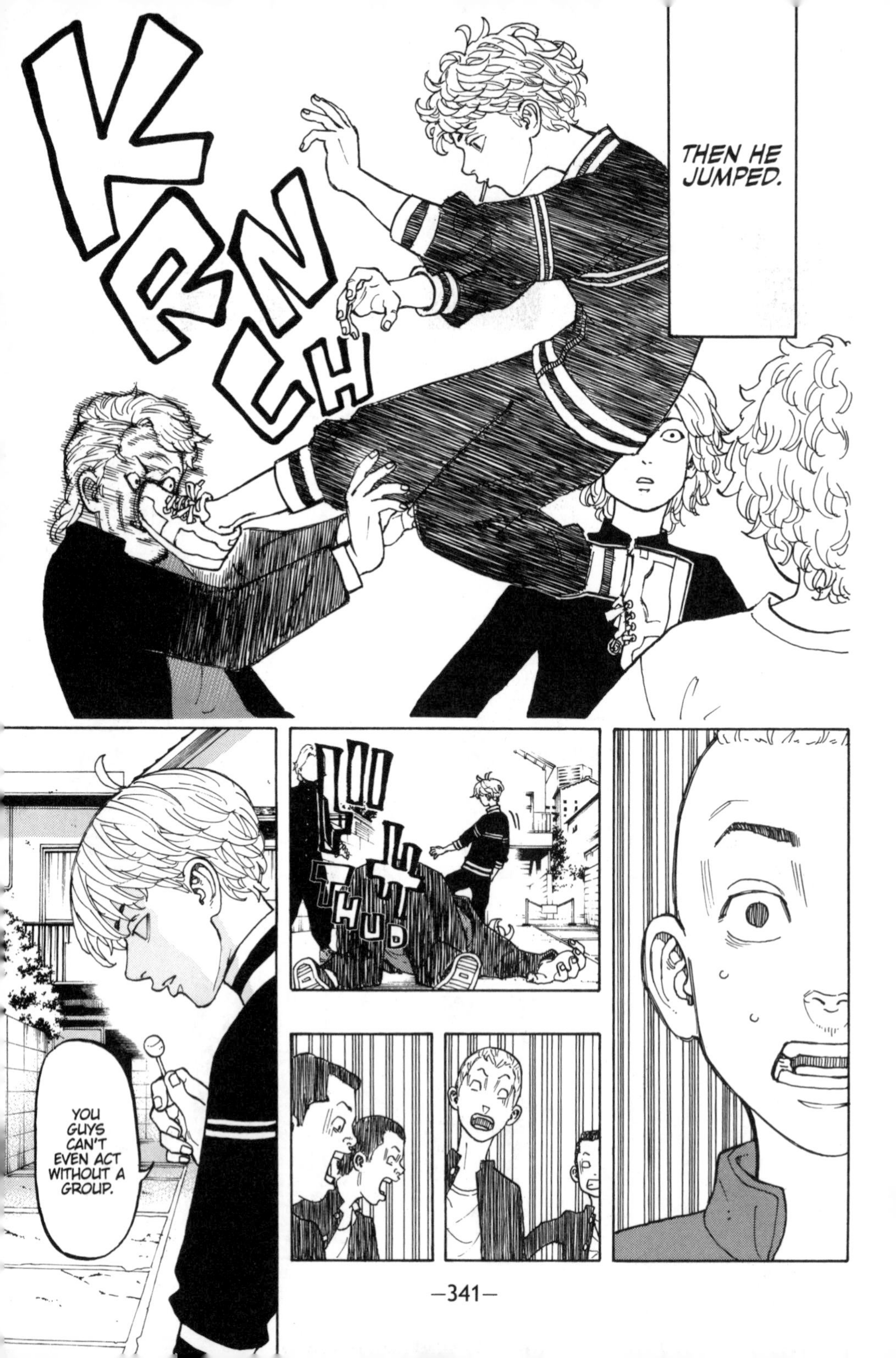
THEN HE JUMPED.
KRNCH
THUD
YOU GUYS CAN'T EVEN ACT WITHOUT A GROUP.

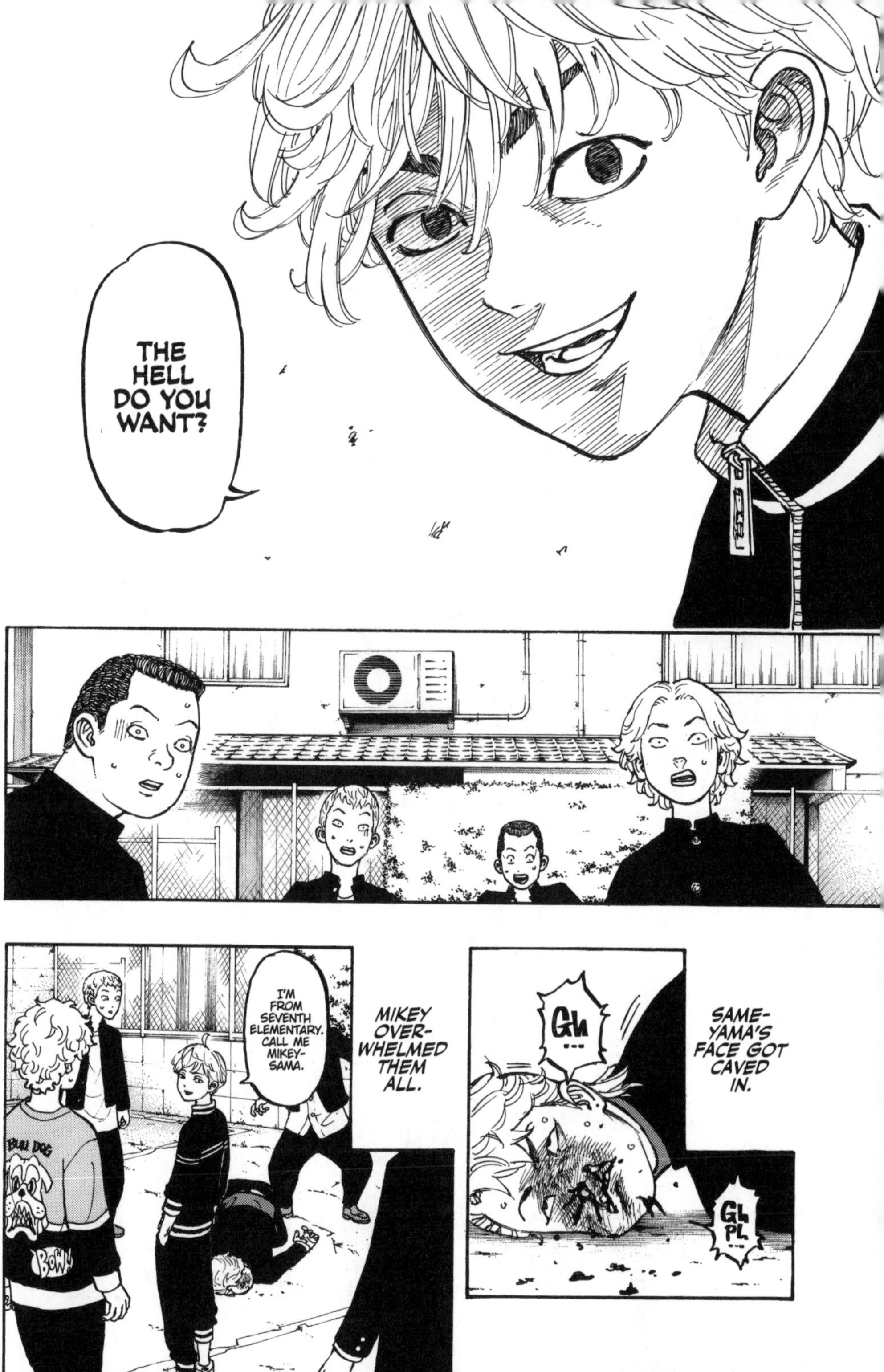
THE HELL DO YOU WANT?
Gh...
SAME-YAMA'S FACE GOT CAVED IN.
Gl Pl...
MIKEY OVER-WHELMED THEM ALL.
I'M FROM SEVENTH ELEMENTARY. CALL ME MIKEY-SAMA.
BULL DOG
BOW

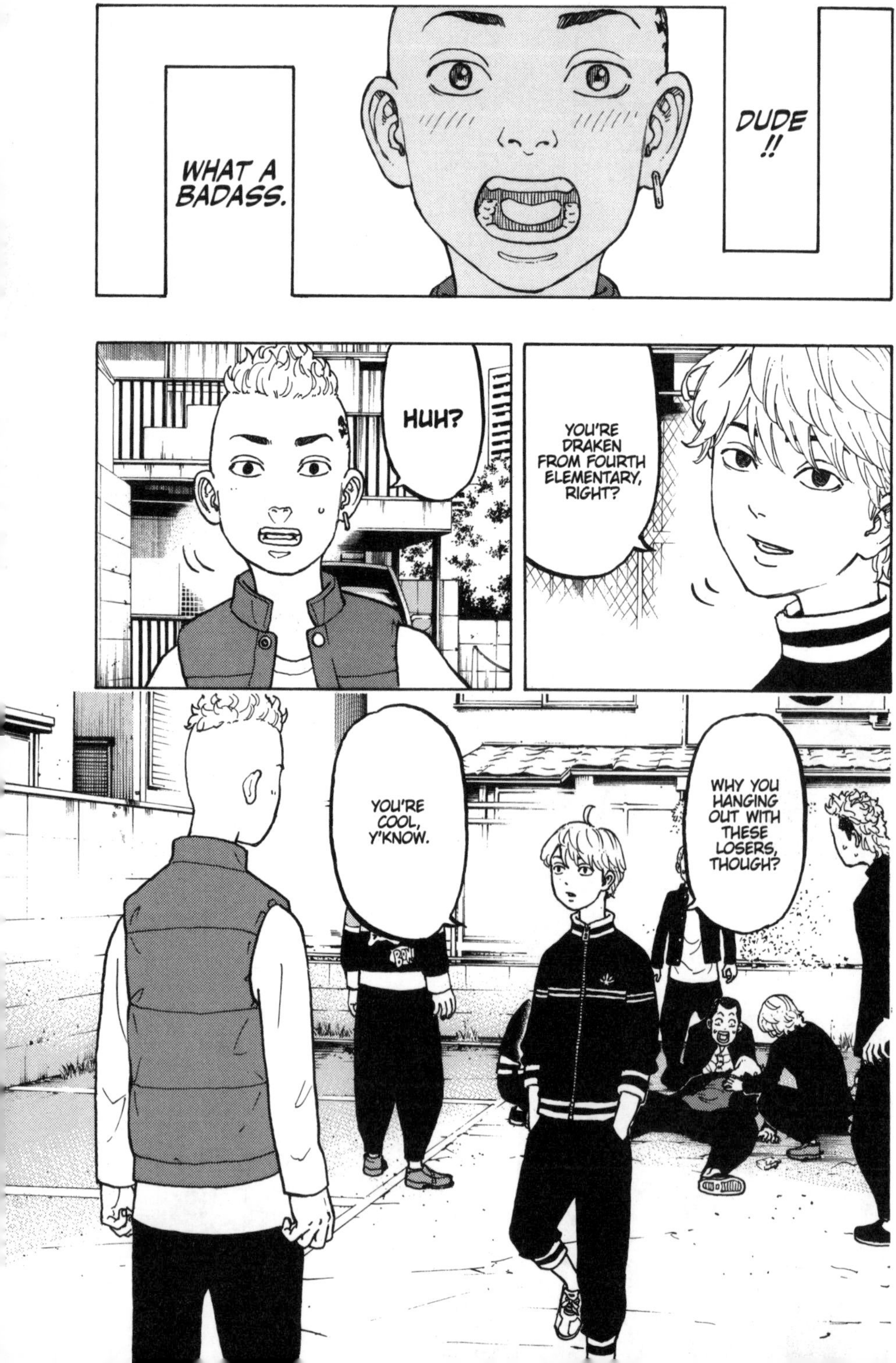
DUDE !!
WHAT A BADASS.
YOU'RE DRAKEN FROM FOURTH ELEMENTARY, RIGHT?
HUH?
WHY YOU HANGING OUT WITH THESE LOSERS, THOUGH?
YOU'RE COOL, Y'KNOW.

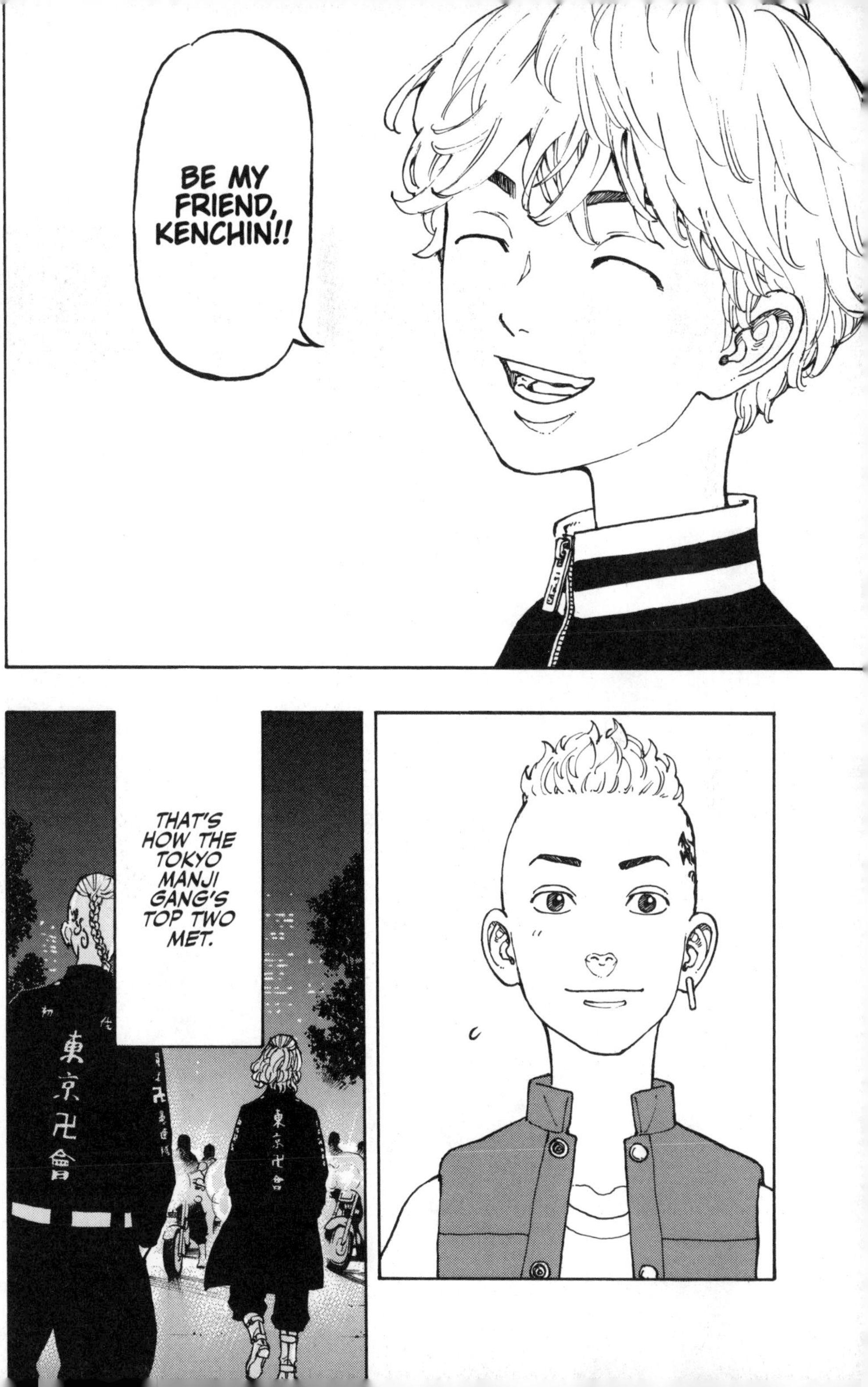
BE MY FRIEND, KENCHIN!!
THAT'S HOW THE TOKYO MANJI GANG'S TOP TWO MET.

TOKYO
Revengers

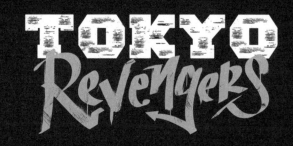

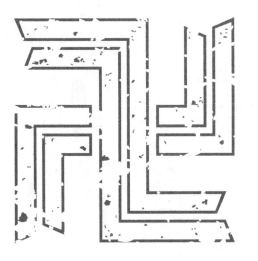

CHAPTER 13: REGRET

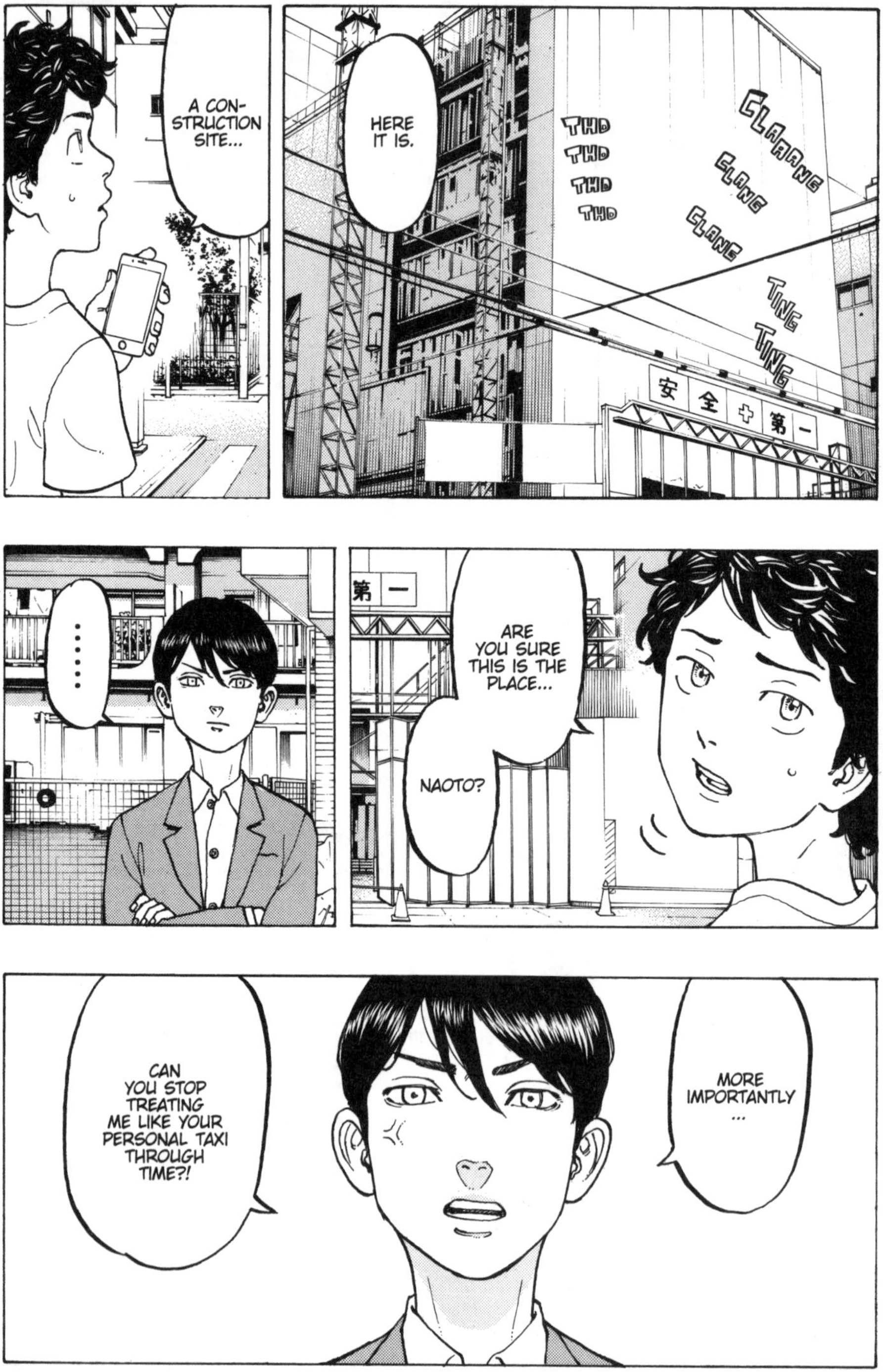
HERE IT IS.
THD THD THD THD
CLAAANG
CLANG
CLANG
TING
TING
安全第一
A CON-STRUCTION SITE...
ARE YOU SURE THIS IS THE PLACE...
NAOTO?
第一
......
MORE IMPORTANTLY ...
CAN YOU STOP TREATING ME LIKE YOUR PERSONAL TAXI THROUGH TIME?!

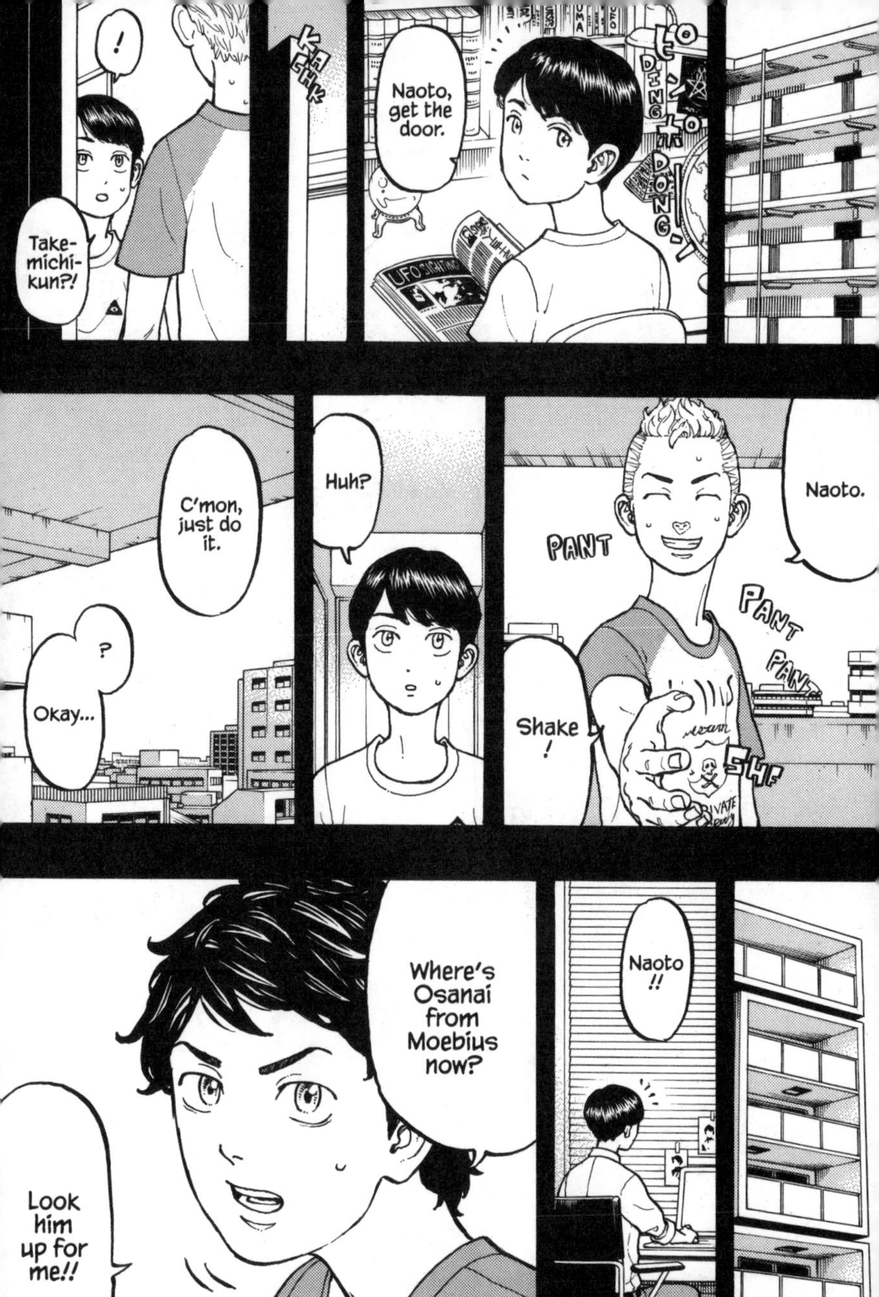

DING-DONG-
Naoto, get the door.
UFO SIGHTING
KACHK
!
Take-michi-kun?!
Naoto.
PANT
PANT
PANT
Shake!
SHF
Huh?
C'mon, just do it.
?
Okay...
Naoto!!
Where's Osanai from Moebius now?
Look him up for me!!

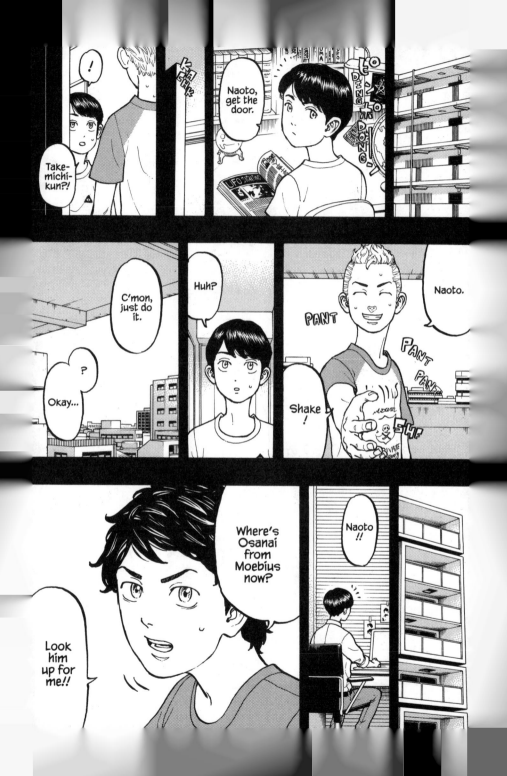

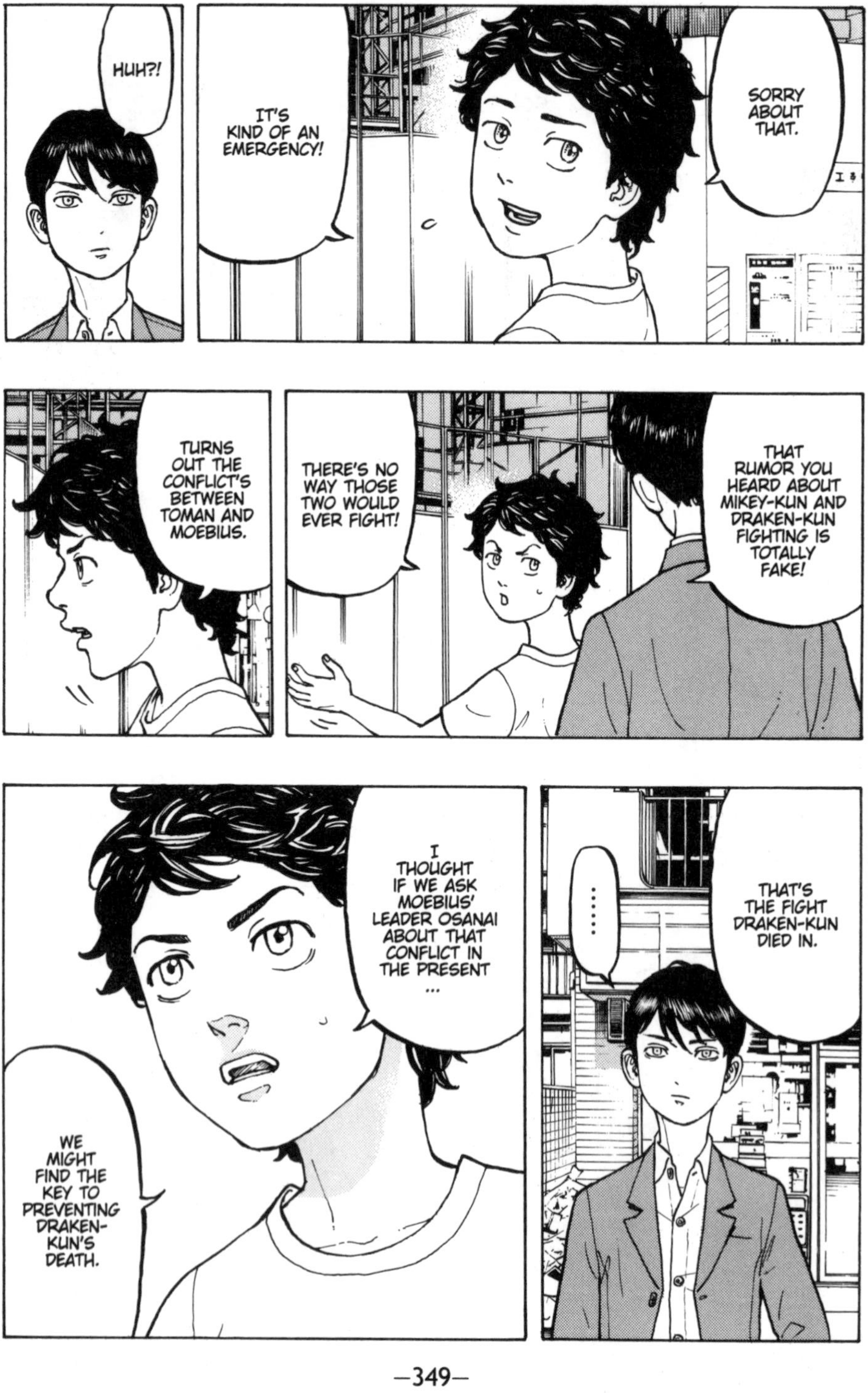
SORRY ABOUT THAT.
IT'S KIND OF AN EMERGENCY!
HUH?!
THAT RUMOR YOU HEARD ABOUT MIKEY-KUN AND DRAKEN-KUN FIGHTING IS TOTALLY FAKE!
THERE'S NO WAY THOSE TWO WOULD EVER FIGHT!
TURNS OUT THE CONFLICT'S BETWEEN TOMAN AND MOEBIUS.
THAT'S THE FIGHT DRAKEN-KUN DIED IN.
......
I THOUGHT IF WE ASK MOEBIUS' LEADER OSANAI ABOUT THAT CONFLICT IN THE PRESENT ...
WE MIGHT FIND THE KEY TO PREVENTING DRAKEN-KUN'S DEATH.

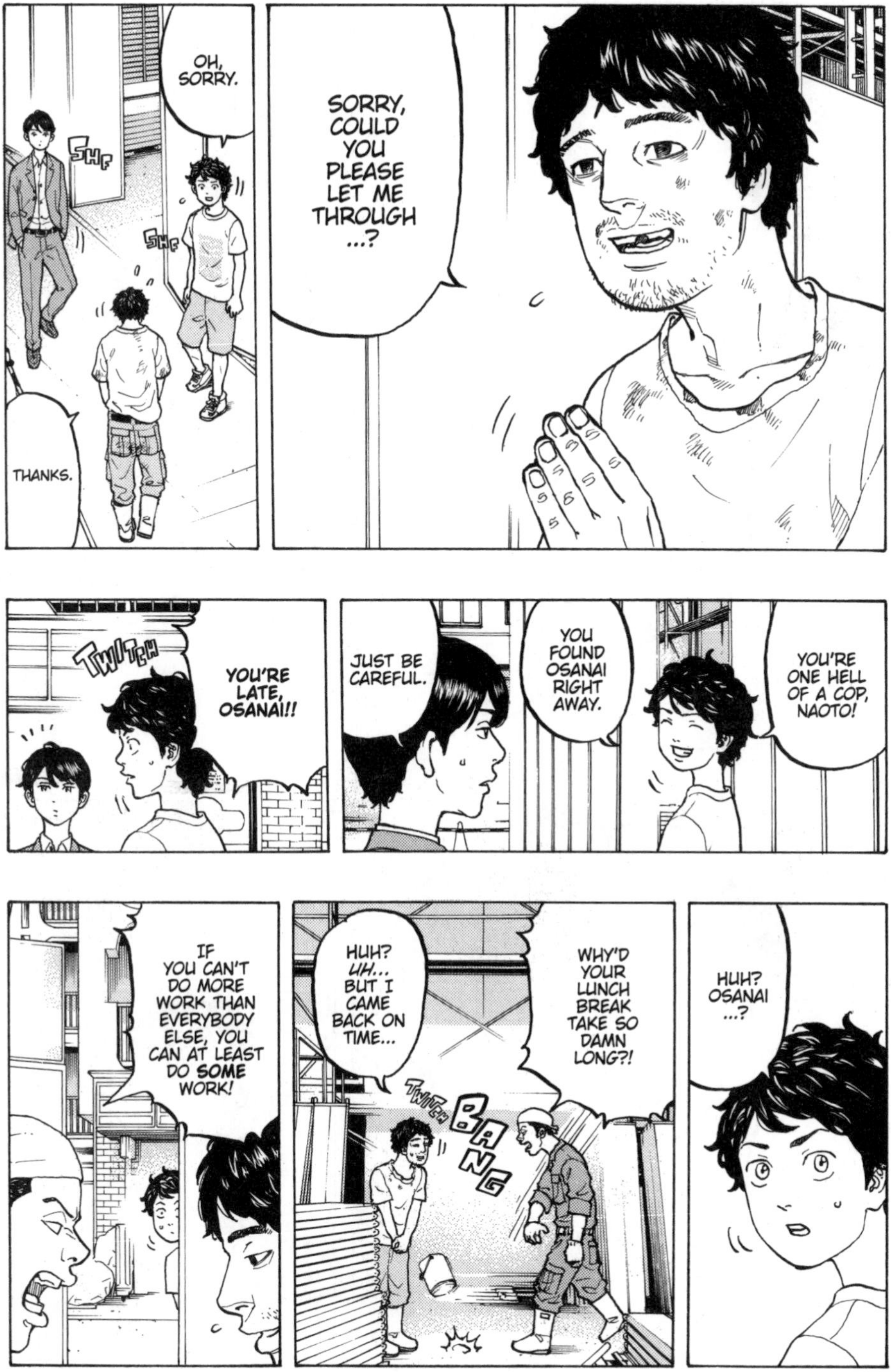
SORRY, COULD YOU PLEASE LET ME THROUGH...?
OH, SORRY.
SHF
SHF
THANKS.
YOU'RE ONE HELL OF A COP, NAOTO!
YOU FOUND OSANAI RIGHT AWAY.
JUST BE CAREFUL.
TWITCH
YOU'RE LATE, OSANAI!!
HUH? OSANAI...?
WHY'D YOUR LUNCH BREAK TAKE SO DAMN LONG?!
HUH? *UH...* BUT I CAME BACK ON TIME...
TWITCH
BANG
IF YOU CAN'T DO MORE WORK THAN EVERYBODY ELSE, YOU CAN AT LEAST DO **SOME** WORK!

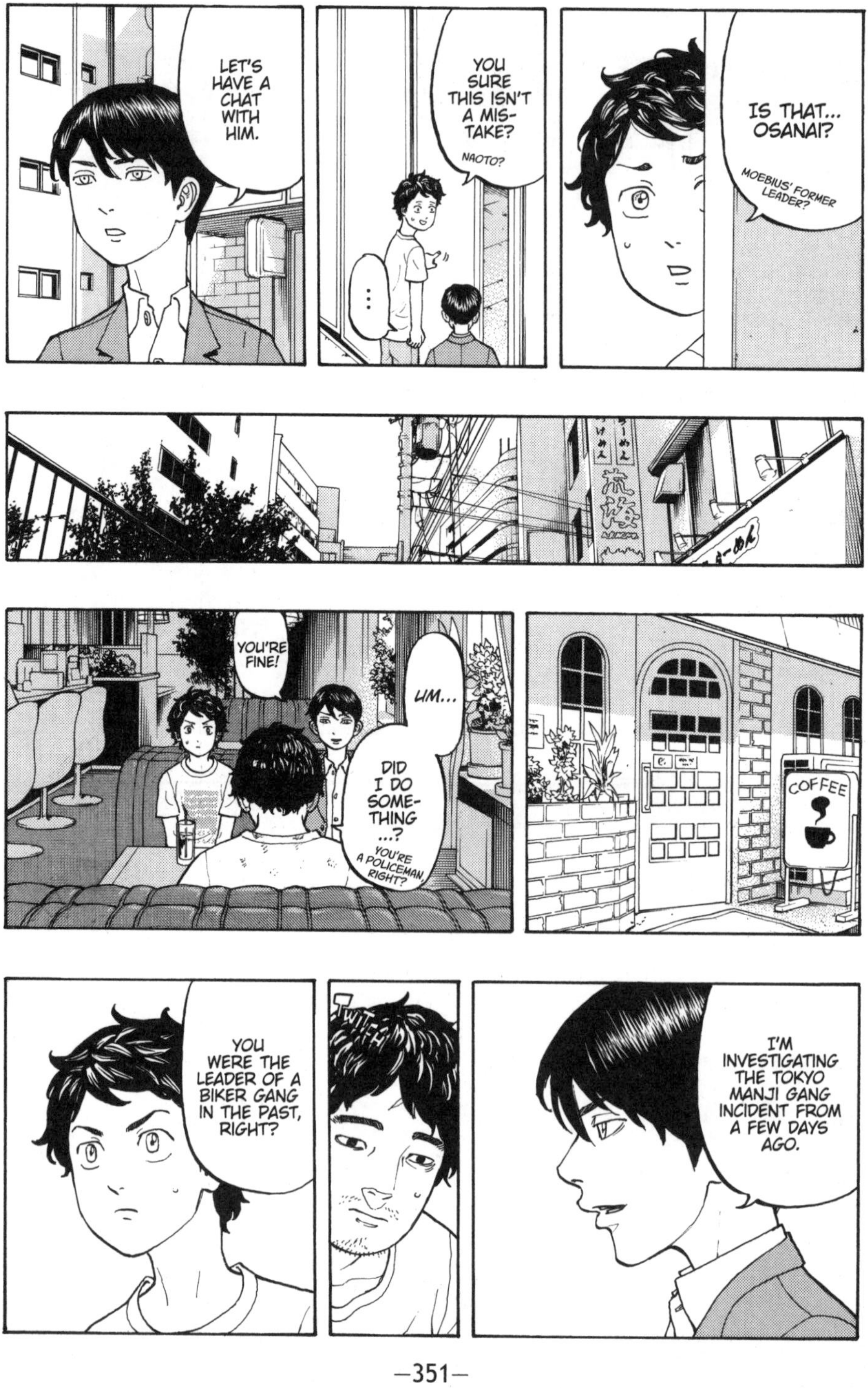
IS THAT... OSANAI?
MOEBIUS' FORMER LEADER?
YOU SURE THIS ISN'T A MIS-TAKE?
NAOTO?
...
LET'S HAVE A CHAT WITH HIM.
COFFEE
UM...
DID I DO SOMETHING ...?
YOU'RE A POLICEMAN, RIGHT?
YOU'RE FINE!
I'M INVESTIGATING THE TOKYO MANJI GANG INCIDENT FROM A FEW DAYS AGO.
TWITCH
YOU WERE THE LEADER OF A BIKER GANG IN THE PAST, RIGHT?

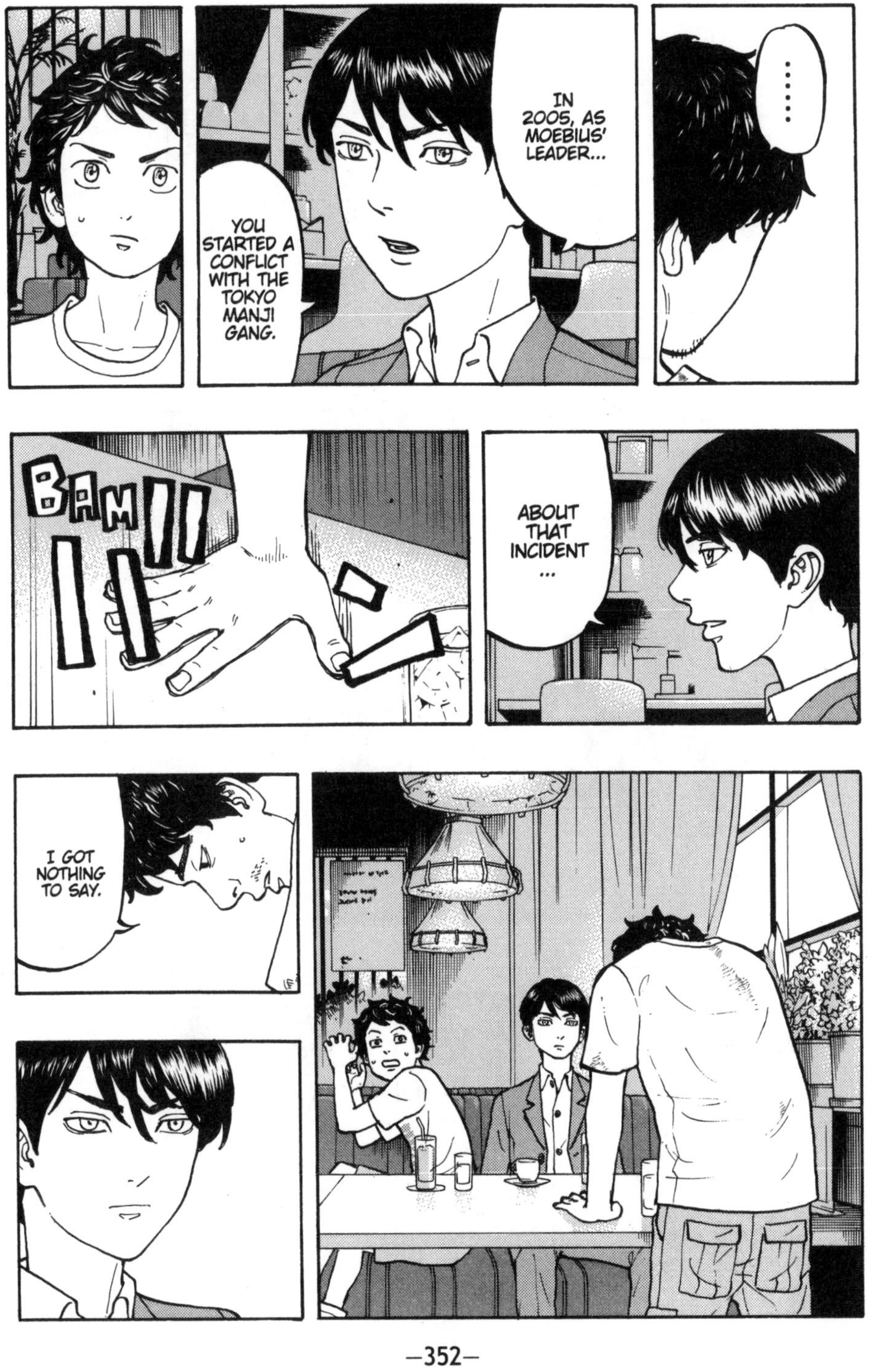
......
IN 2005, AS MOEBIUS' LEADER...
YOU STARTED A CONFLICT WITH THE TOKYO MANJI GANG.
ABOUT THAT INCIDENT ...
BAM!!
I GOT NOTHING TO SAY.

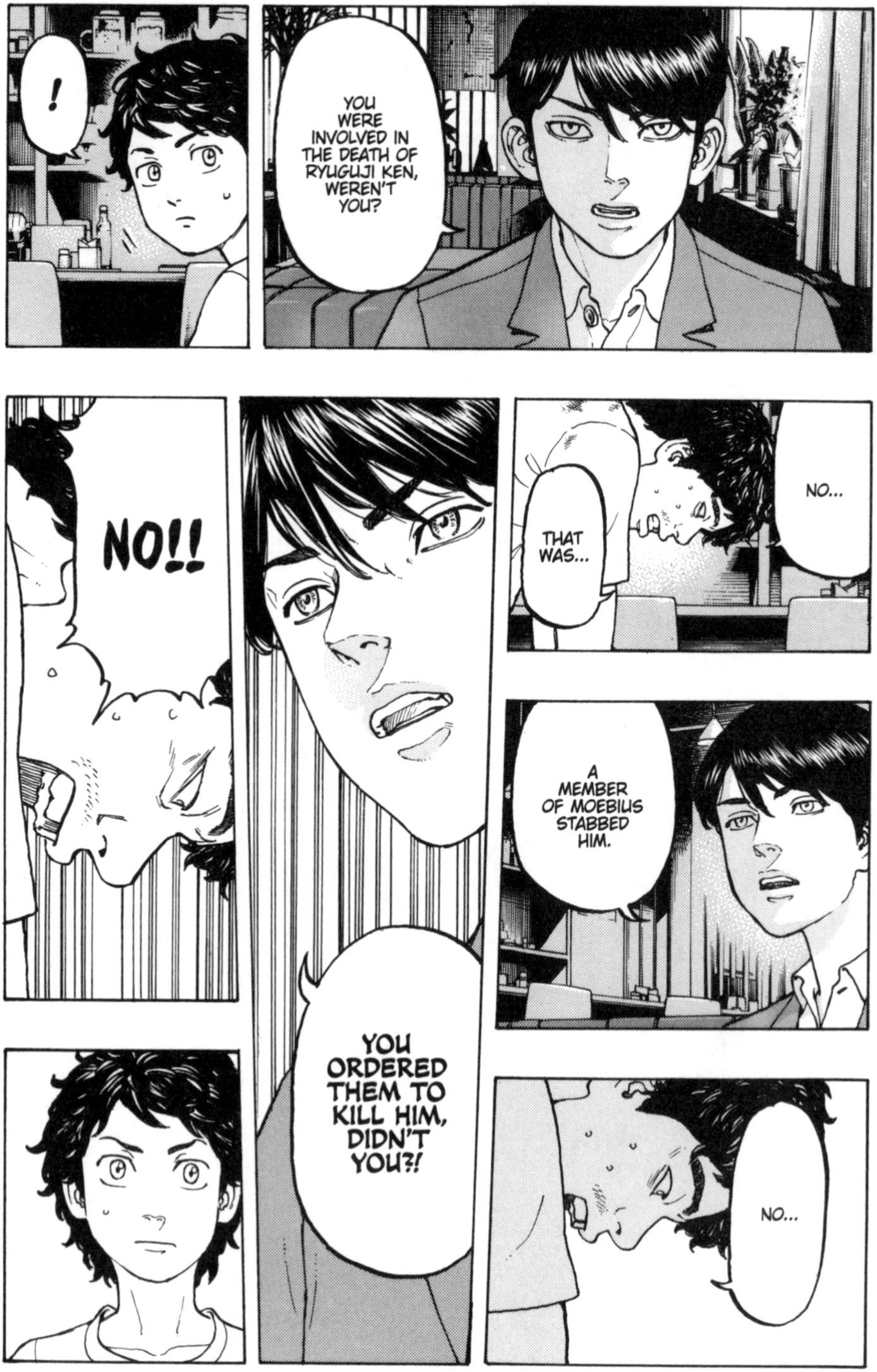
YOU WERE INVOLVED IN THE DEATH OF RYUGUJI KEN, WEREN'T YOU?
!
NO...
THAT WAS...
A MEMBER OF MOEBIUS STABBED HIM.
NO...
YOU ORDERED THEM TO KILL HIM, DIDN'T YOU?!
NO!!

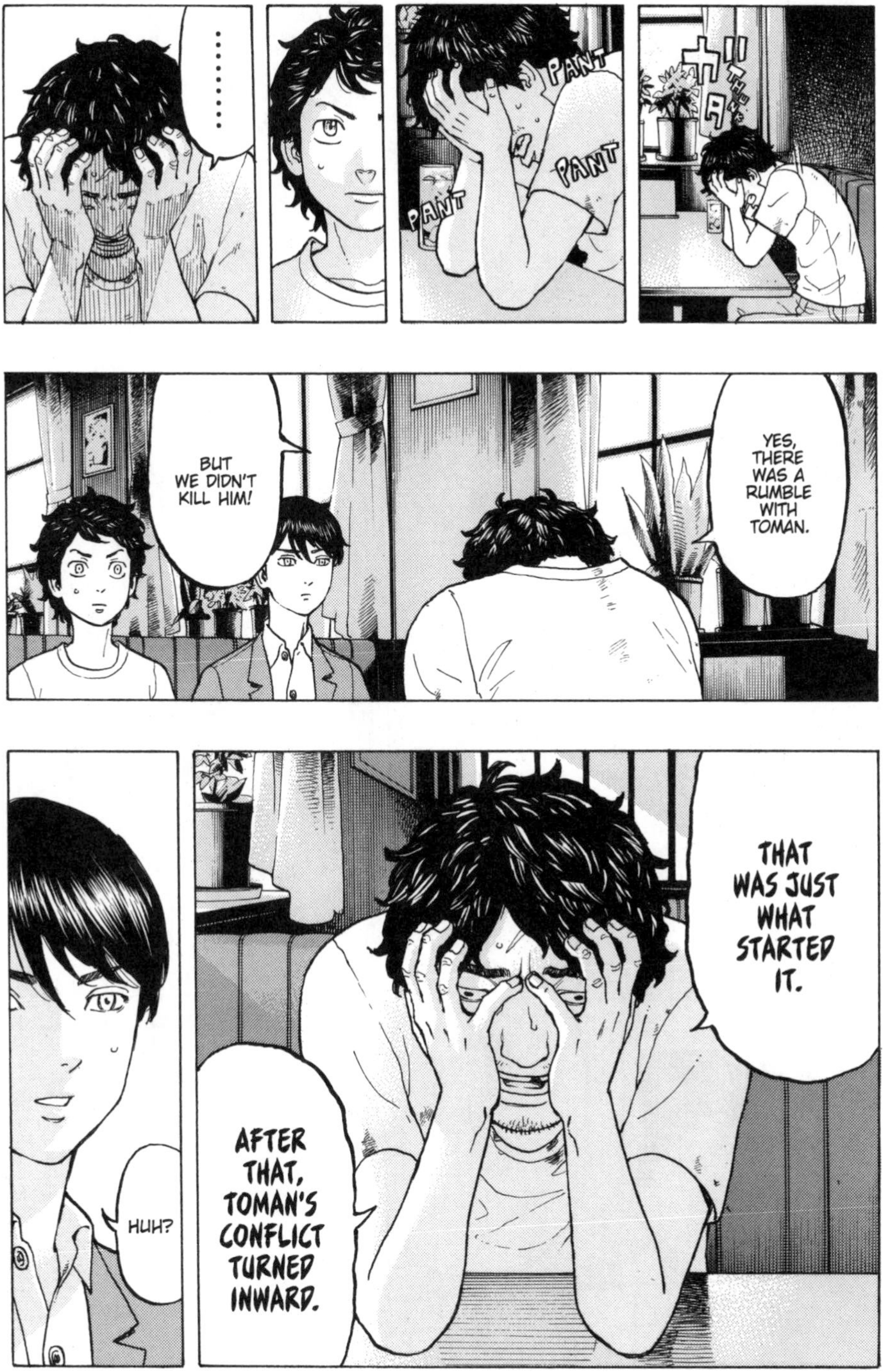
ガタ
THUNK
PANT
PANT
PANT
......
YES, THERE WAS A RUMBLE WITH TOMAN.
BUT WE DIDN'T KILL HIM!
THAT WAS JUST WHAT STARTED IT.
AFTER THAT, TOMAN'S CONFLICT TURNED INWARD.
HUH?

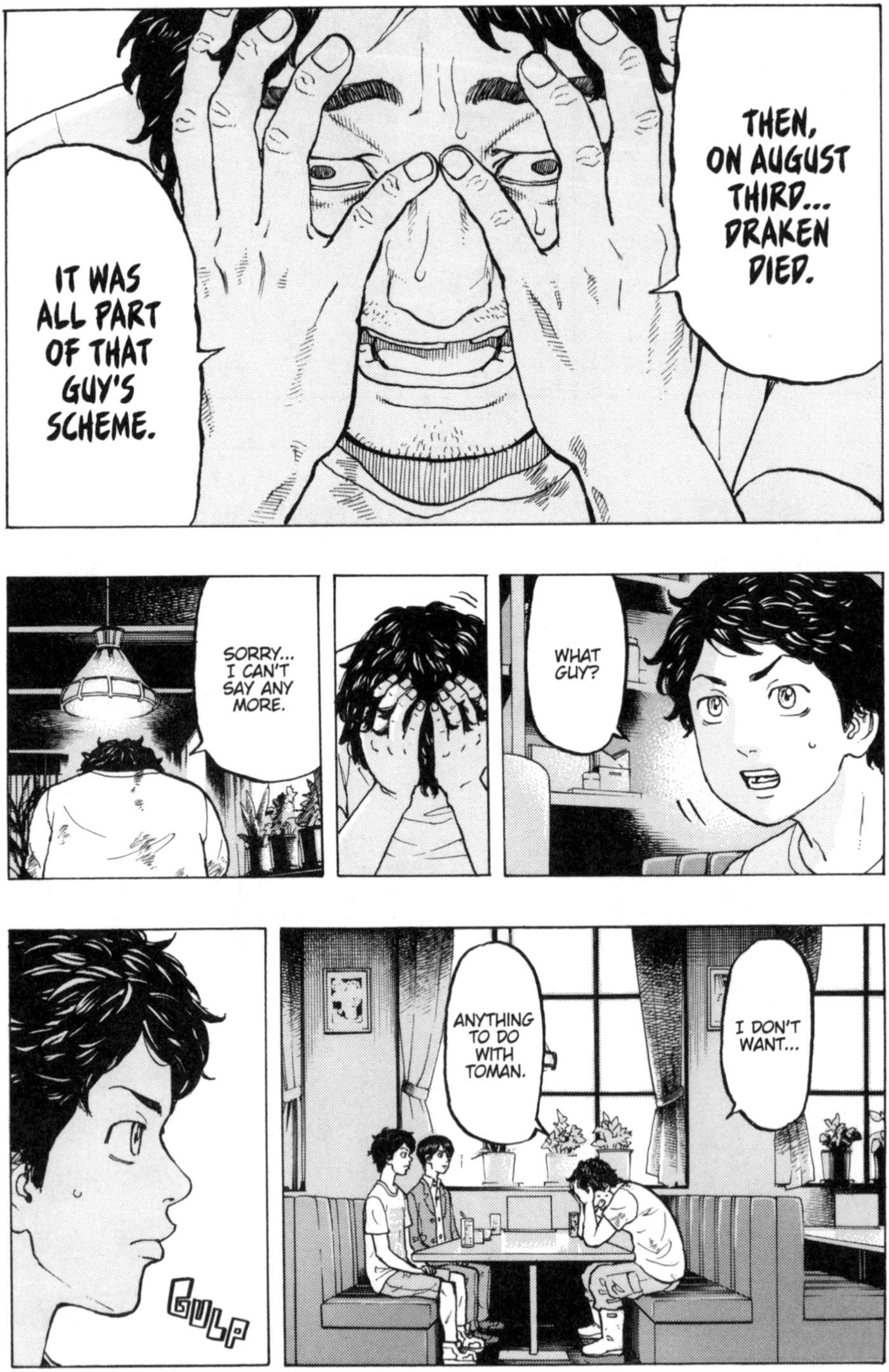
THEN, ON AUGUST THIRD... DRAKEN DIED.
IT WAS ALL PART OF THAT GUY'S SCHEME.
WHAT GUY?
SORRY... I CAN'T SAY ANY MORE.
I DON'T WANT...
ANYTHING TO DO WITH TOMAN.
GULP

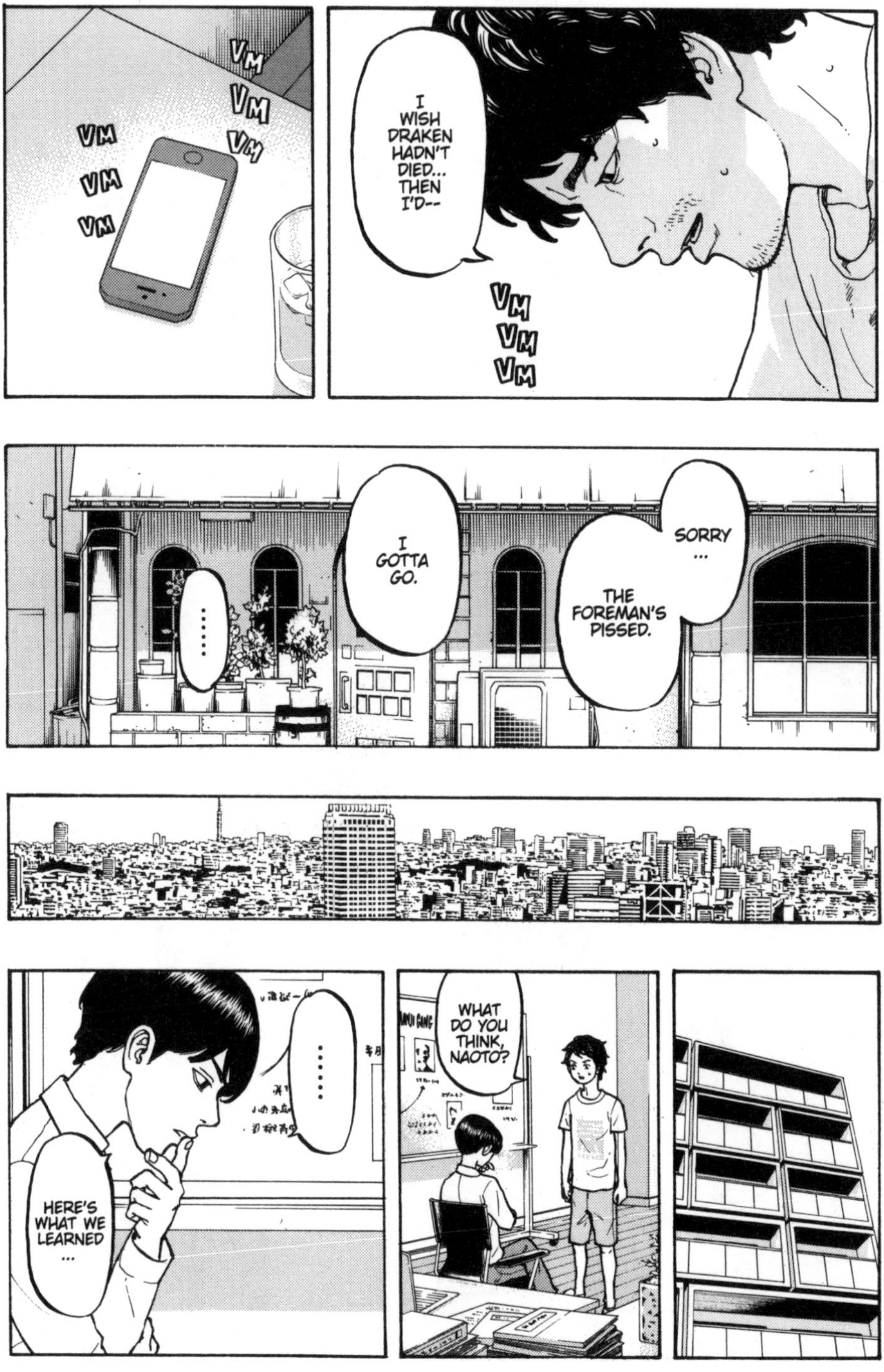
I WISH DRAKEN HADN'T DIED... THEN I'D--
VM VM VM
VM VM VM
VM VM VM
SORRY ...
THE FOREMAN'S PISSED.
I GOTTA GO.
......
WHAT DO YOU THINK, NAOTO?
......
HERE'S WHAT WE LEARNED ...

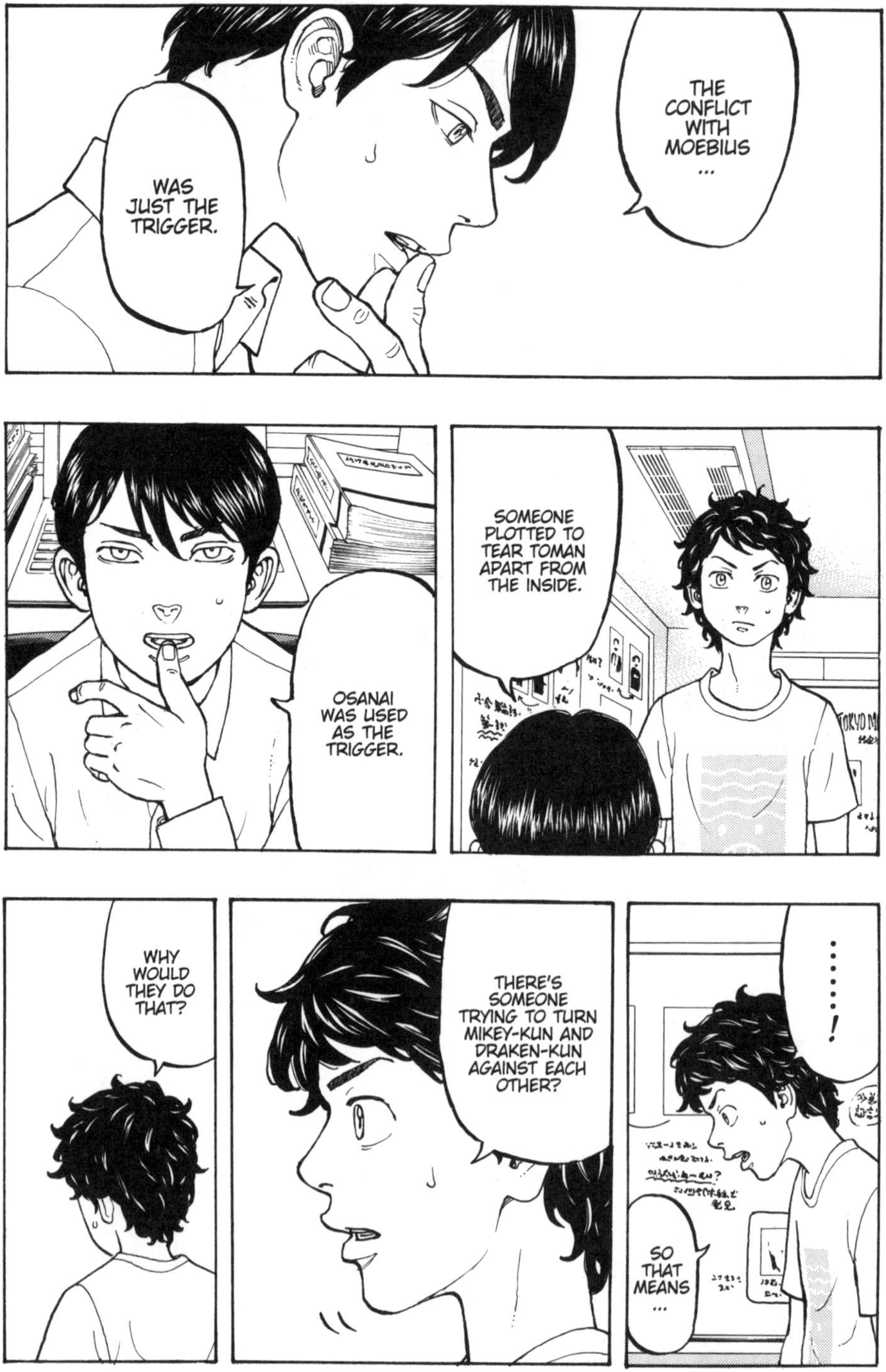
THE CONFLICT WITH MOEBIUS ...
WAS JUST THE TRIGGER.
SOMEONE PLOTTED TO TEAR TOMAN APART FROM THE INSIDE.
OSANAI WAS USED AS THE TRIGGER.
......!
SO THAT MEANS ...
THERE'S SOMEONE TRYING TO TURN MIKEY-KUN AND DRAKEN-KUN AGAINST EACH OTHER?
WHY WOULD THEY DO THAT?

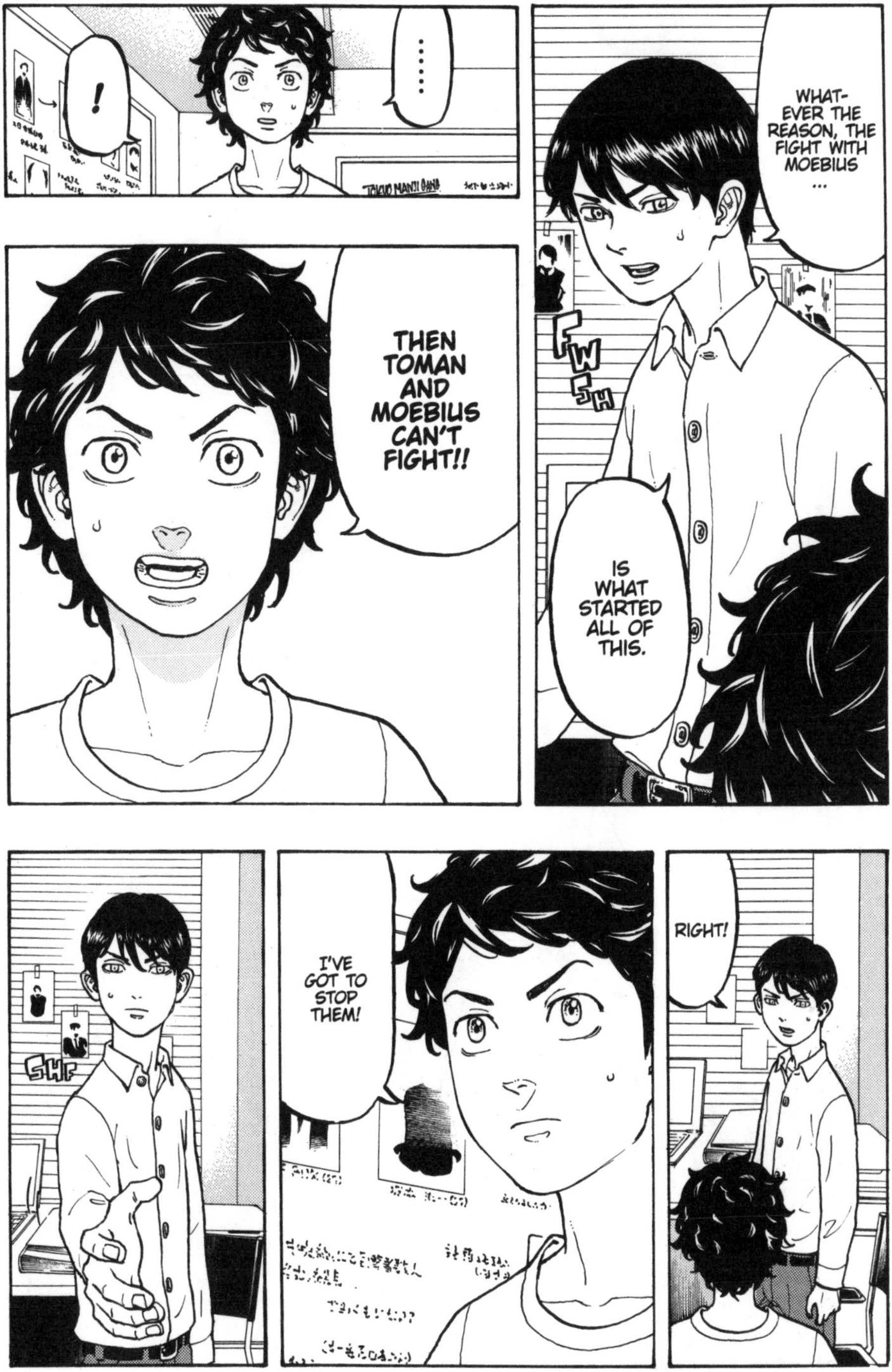
WHAT-EVER THE REASON, THE FIGHT WITH MOEBIUS ...
FWSH
IS WHAT STARTED ALL OF THIS.
......
!
TOKYO MANJI GANG
THEN TOMAN AND MOEBIUS CAN'T FIGHT!!
RIGHT!
I'VE GOT TO STOP THEM!
SHF

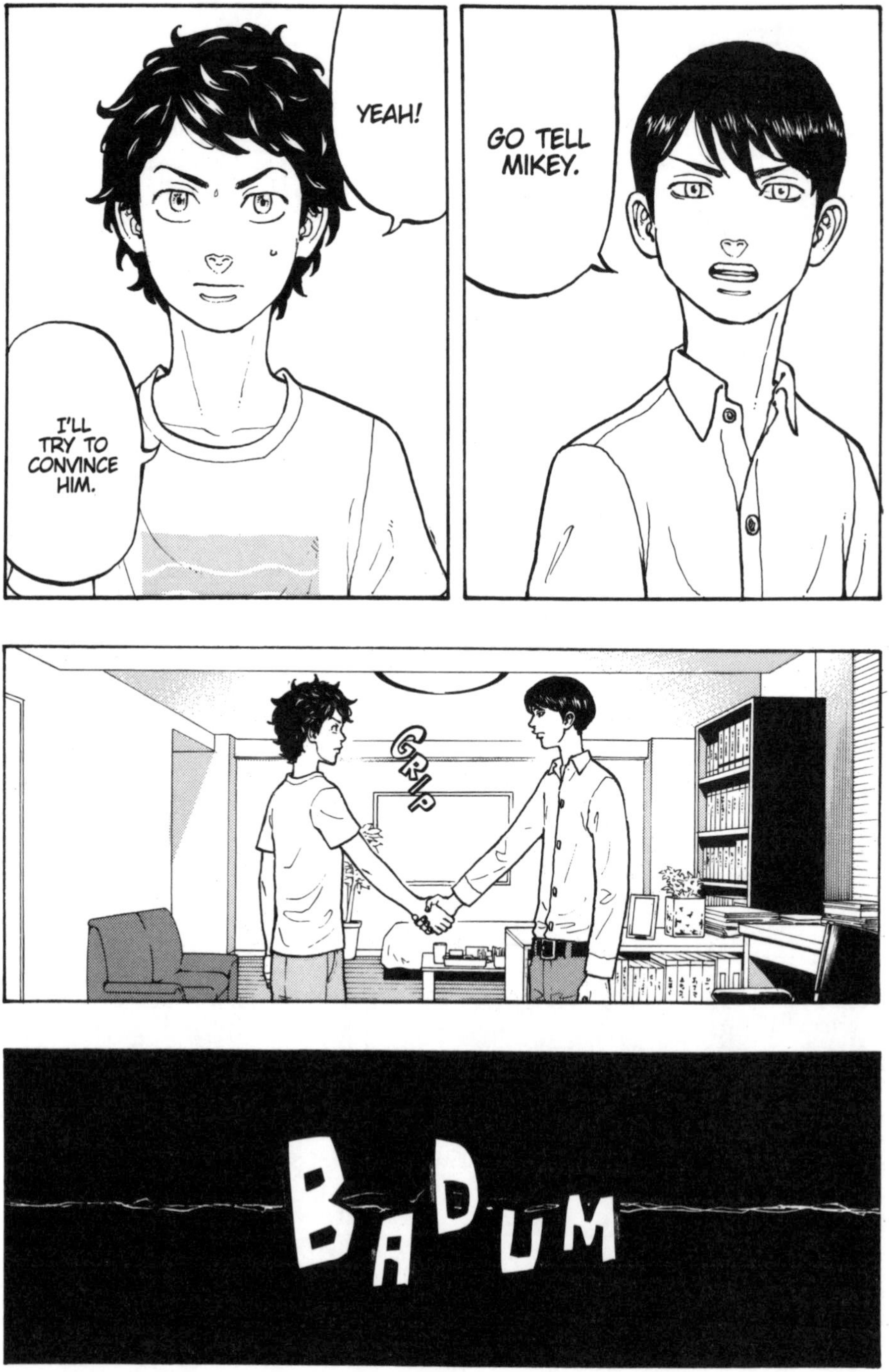
GO TELL MIKEY.
YEAH!
I'LL TRY TO CONVINCE HIM.
GRIP
BADUM

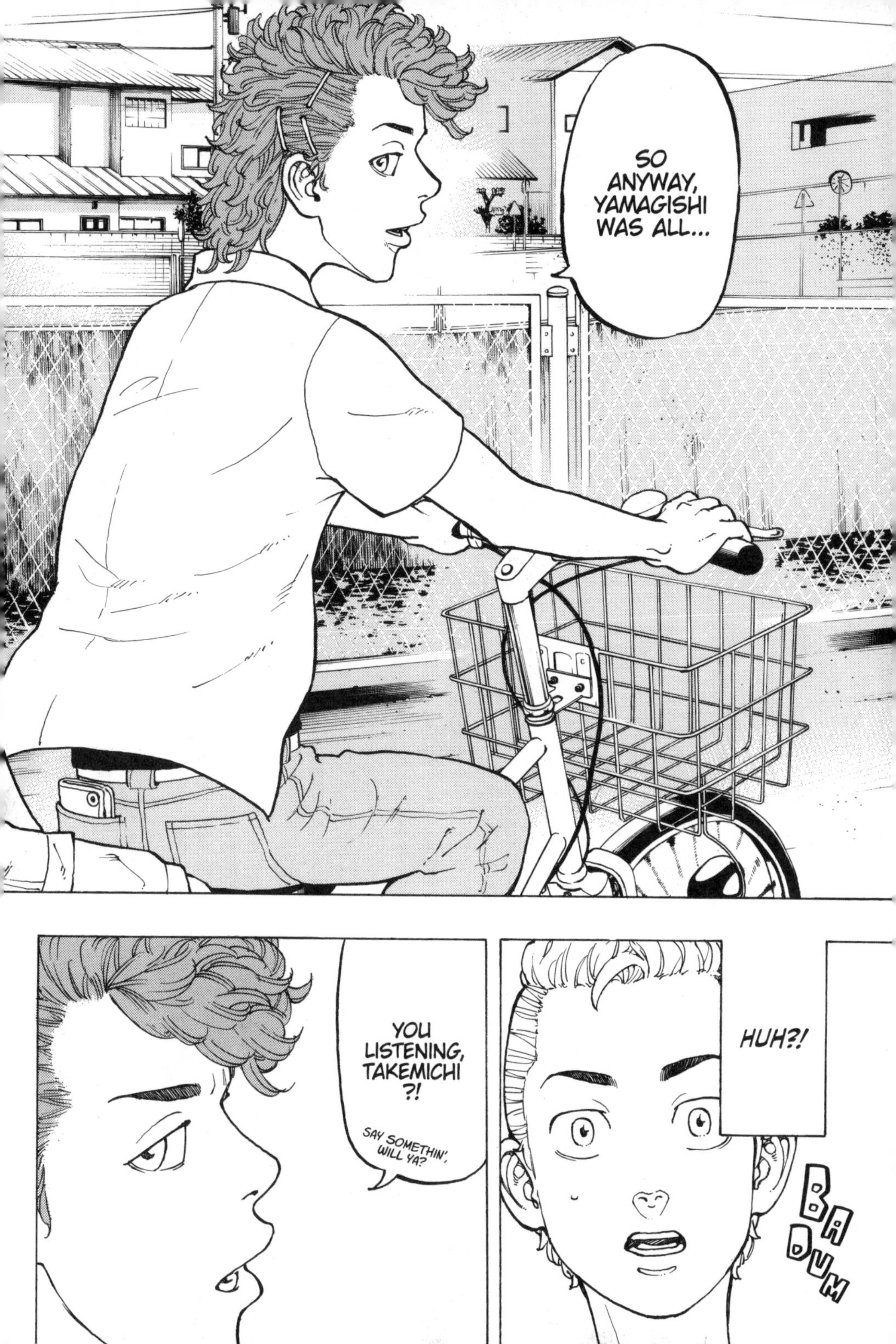
SO ANYWAY, YAMAGISHI WAS ALL...
HUH?!
BA DUM
YOU LISTENING, TAKEMICHI?!
SAY SOMETHIN', WILL YA?

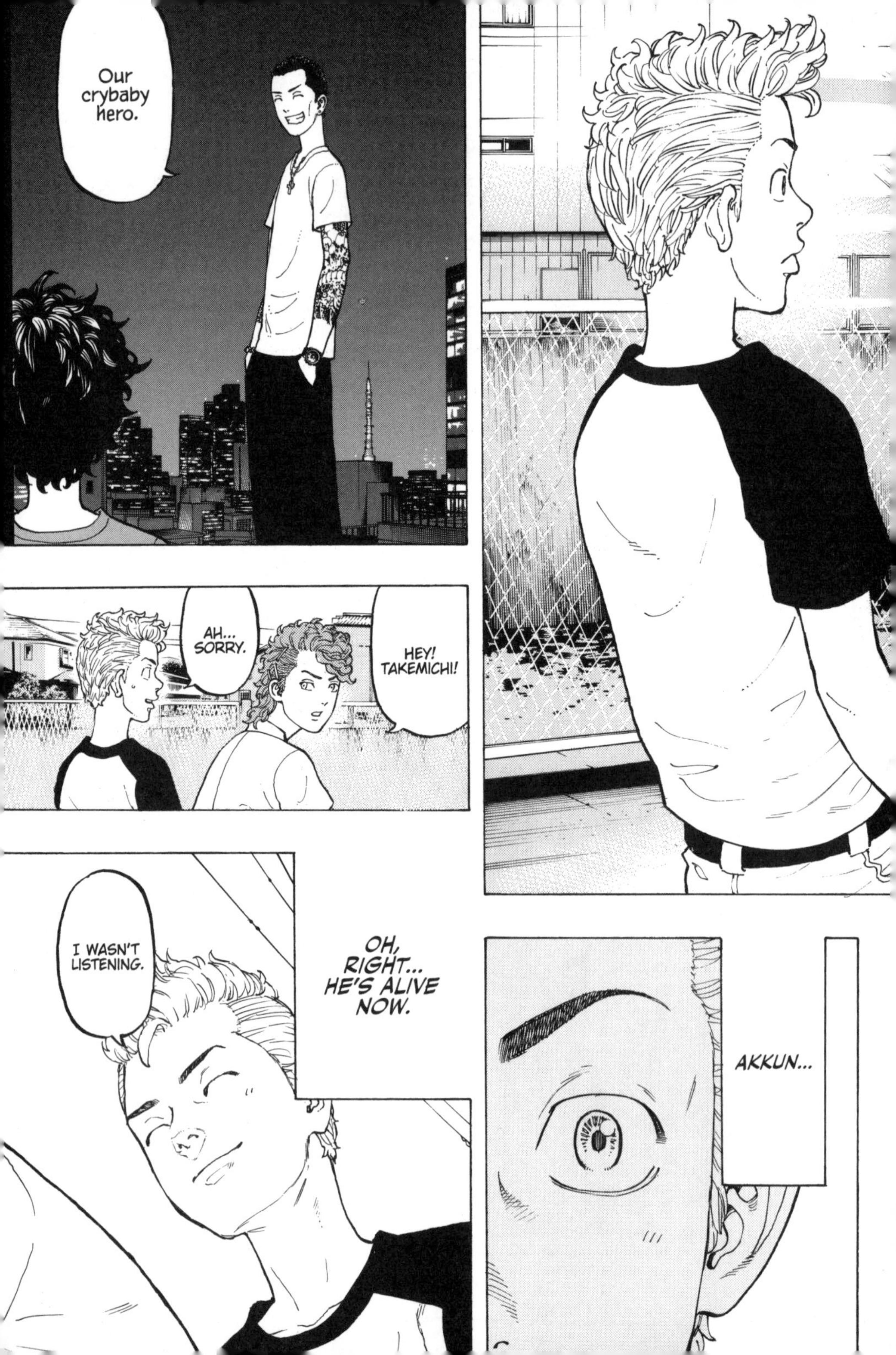
Our crybaby hero.
HEY! TAKEMICHI!
AH... SORRY.
AKKUN...
OH, RIGHT... HE'S ALIVE NOW.
I WASN'T LISTENING.

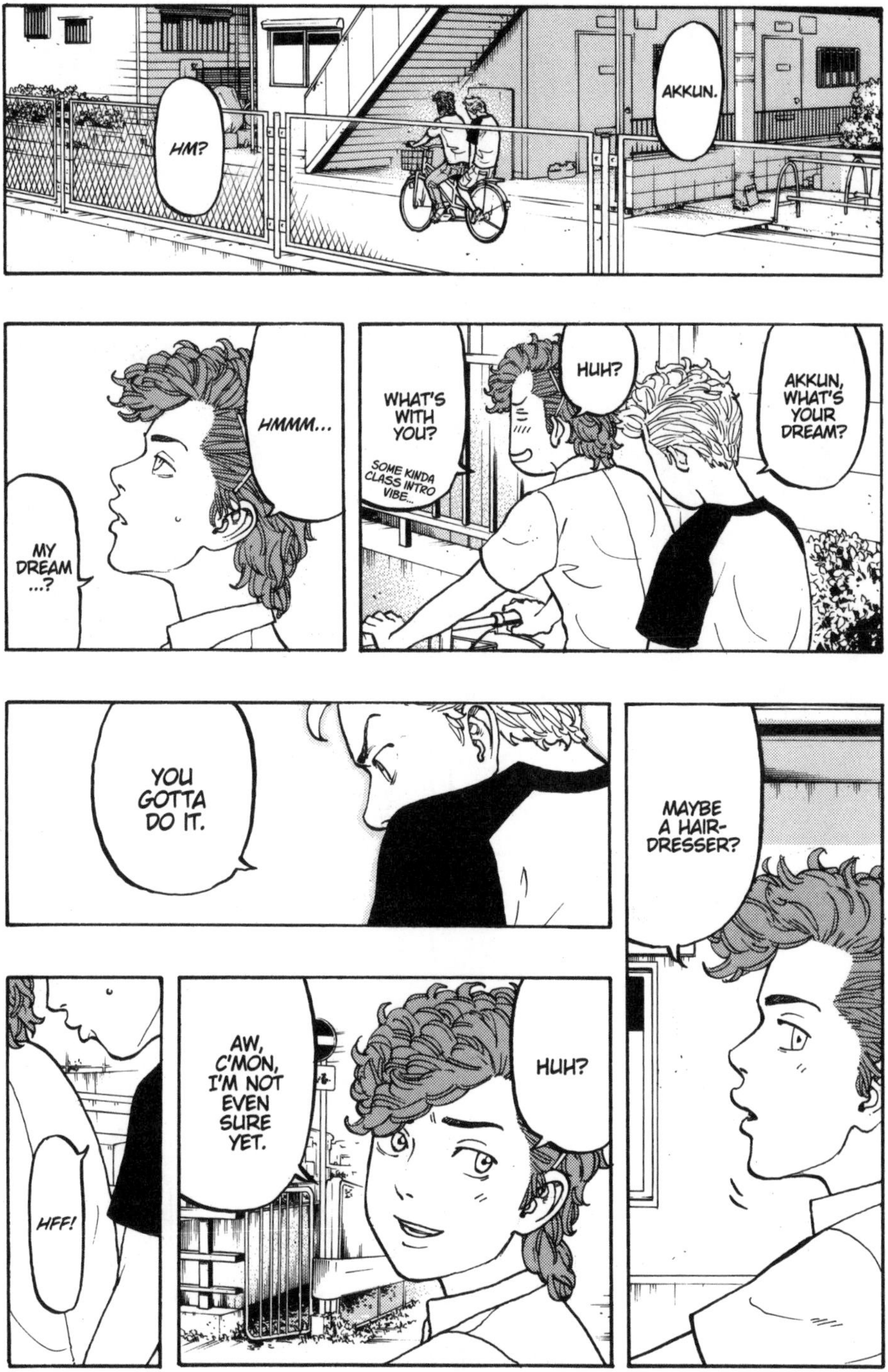
AKKUN.
HM?
AKKUN, WHAT'S YOUR DREAM?
HUH?
WHAT'S WITH YOU?
SOME KINDA CLASS INTRO VIBE...
HMMM...
MY DREAM ...?
MAYBE A HAIR-DRESSER?
YOU GOTTA DO IT.
HUH?
AW, C'MON, I'M NOT EVEN SURE YET.
HFF!

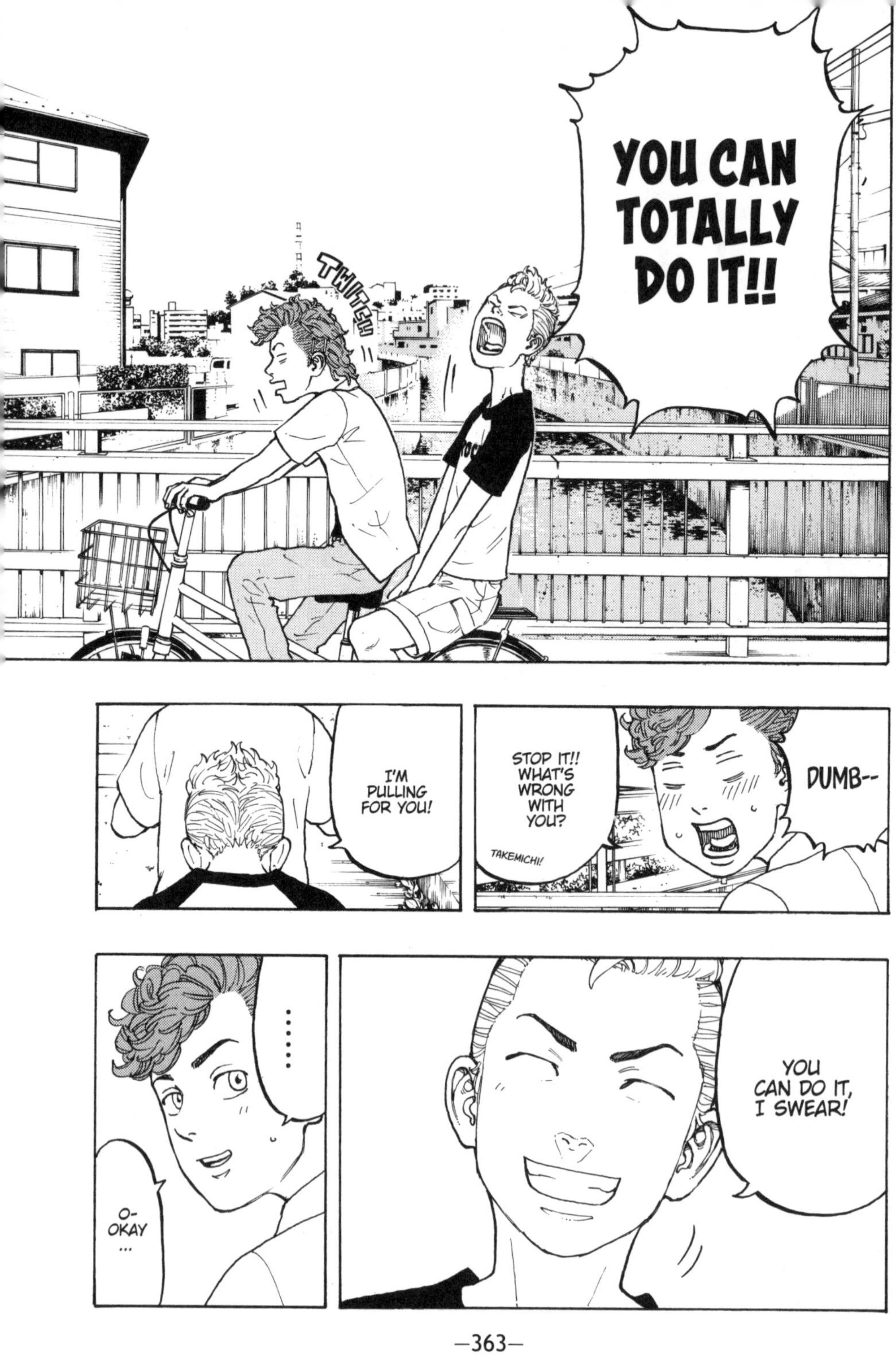
YOU CAN TOTALLY DO IT!!
TWITCH
DUMB--
STOP IT!! WHAT'S WRONG WITH YOU?
TAKEMICHI!
I'M PULLING FOR YOU!
YOU CAN DO IT, I SWEAR!
......
O-OKAY ...

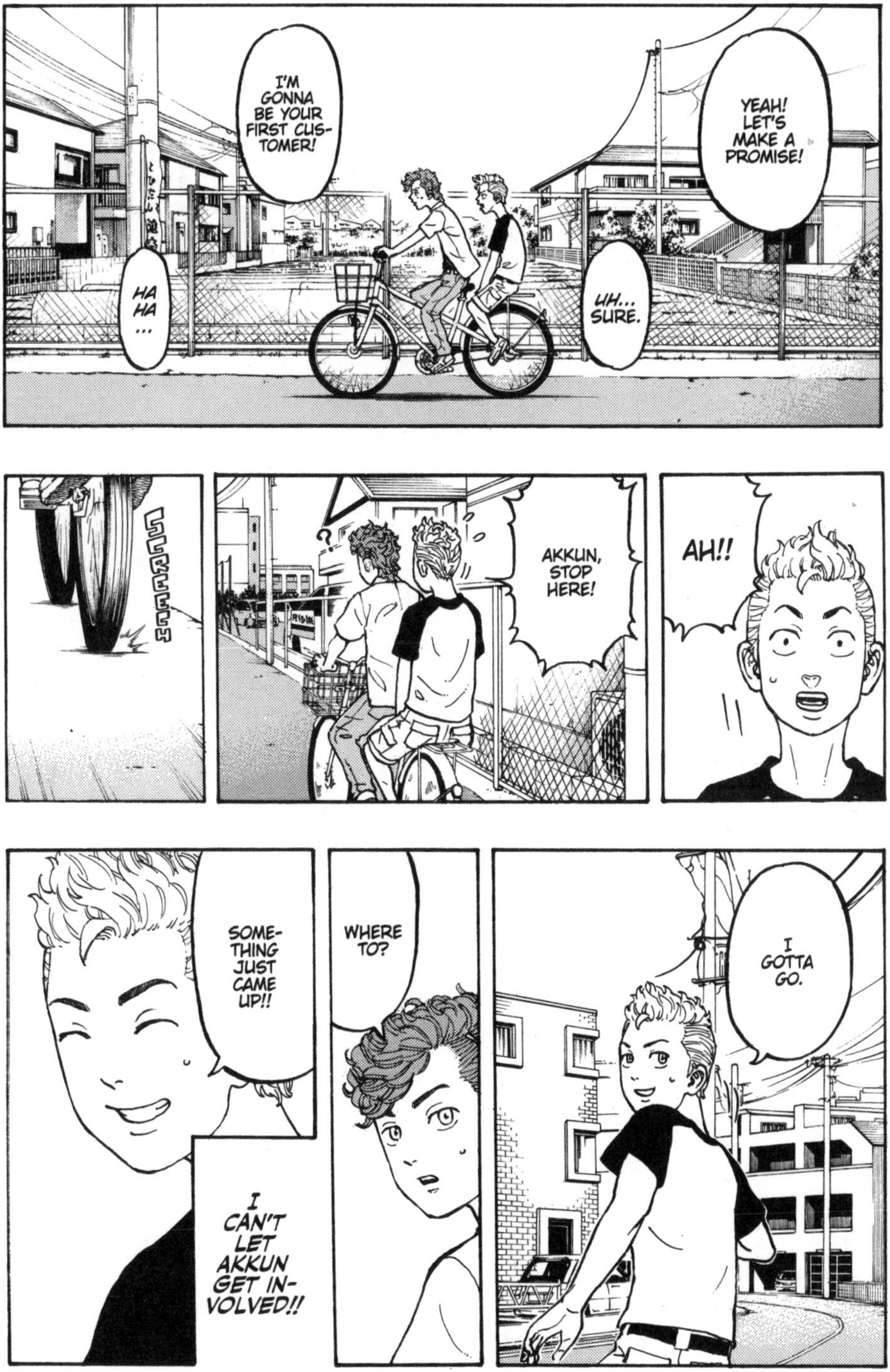
YEAH! LET'S MAKE A PROMISE!
I'M GONNA BE YOUR FIRST CUS-TOMER!
UH... SURE.
HA HA ...
AH!!
AKKUN, STOP HERE!
SCREECH
I GOTTA GO.
WHERE TO?
SOME-THING JUST CAME UP!!
I CAN'T LET AKKUN GET IN-VOLVED!!

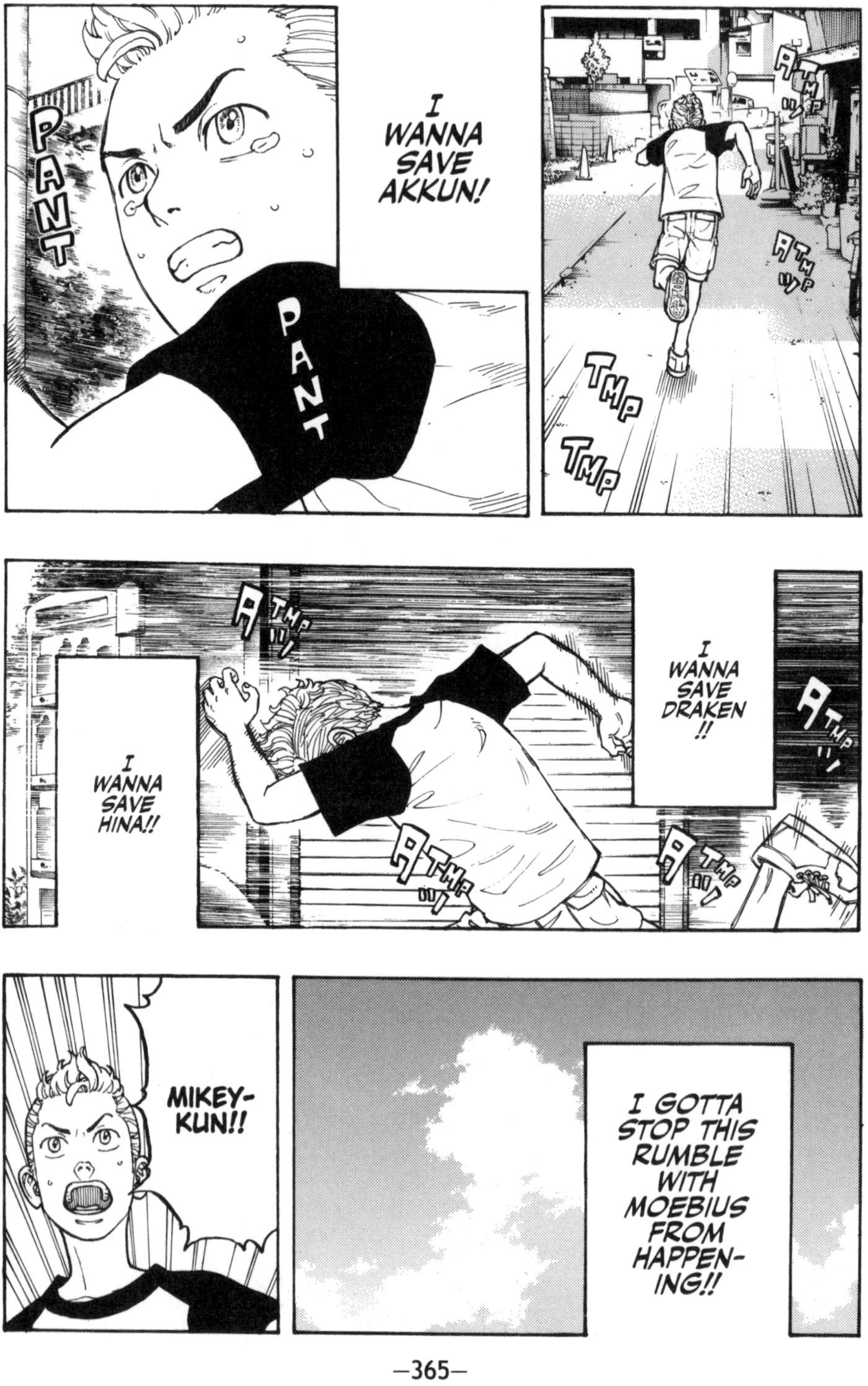

TMP
TMP
TMP
TMP
I WANNA SAVE AKKUN!
PANT
PANT
I WANNA SAVE DRAKEN!!
TMP
TMP
TMP
TMP
I WANNA SAVE HINA!!
I GOTTA STOP THIS RUMBLE WITH MOEBIUS FROM HAPPENING!!
MIKEY-KUN!!

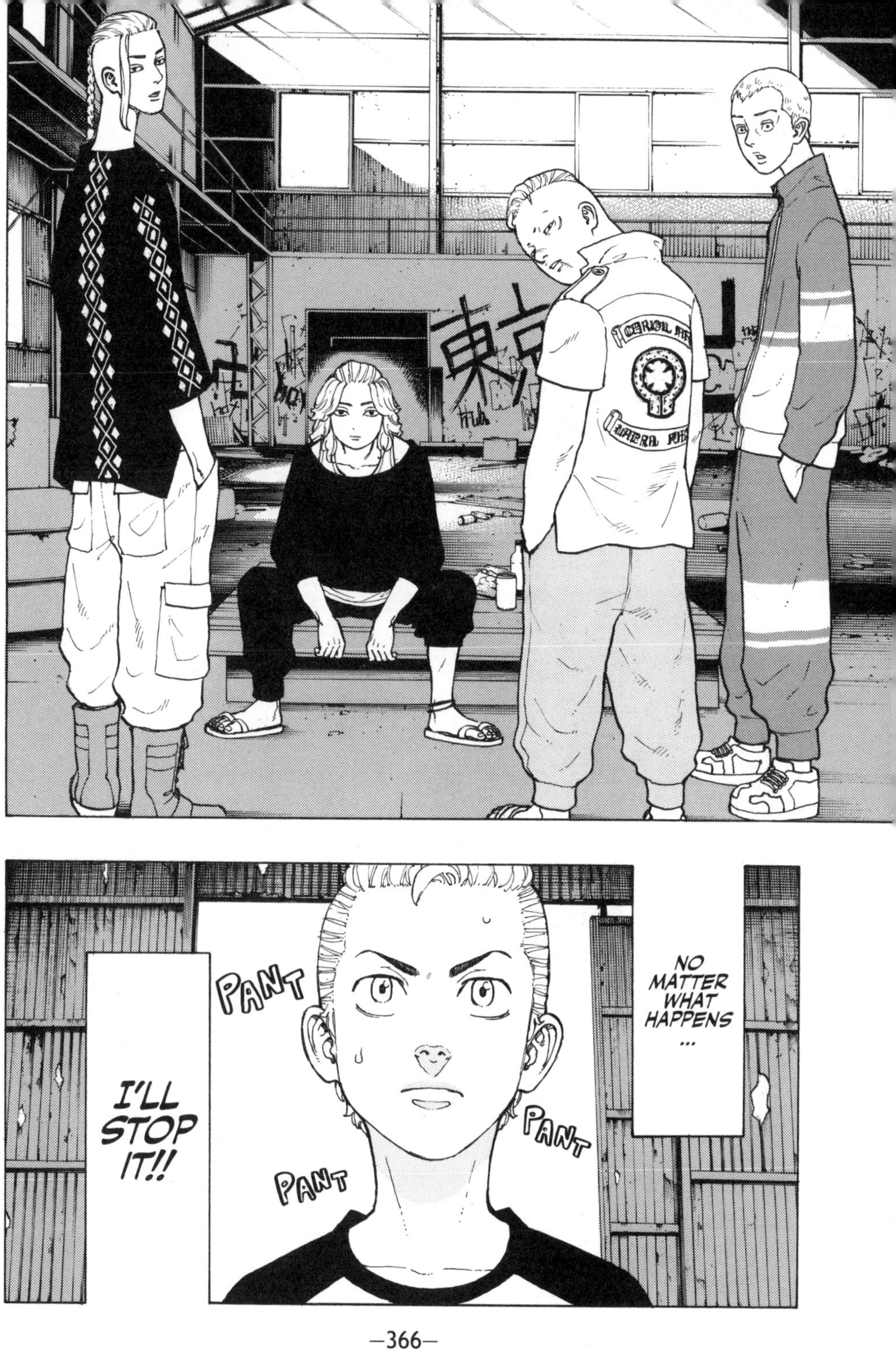
NO MATTER WHAT HAPPENS ...
PANT
PANT
PANT
I'LL STOP IT!!

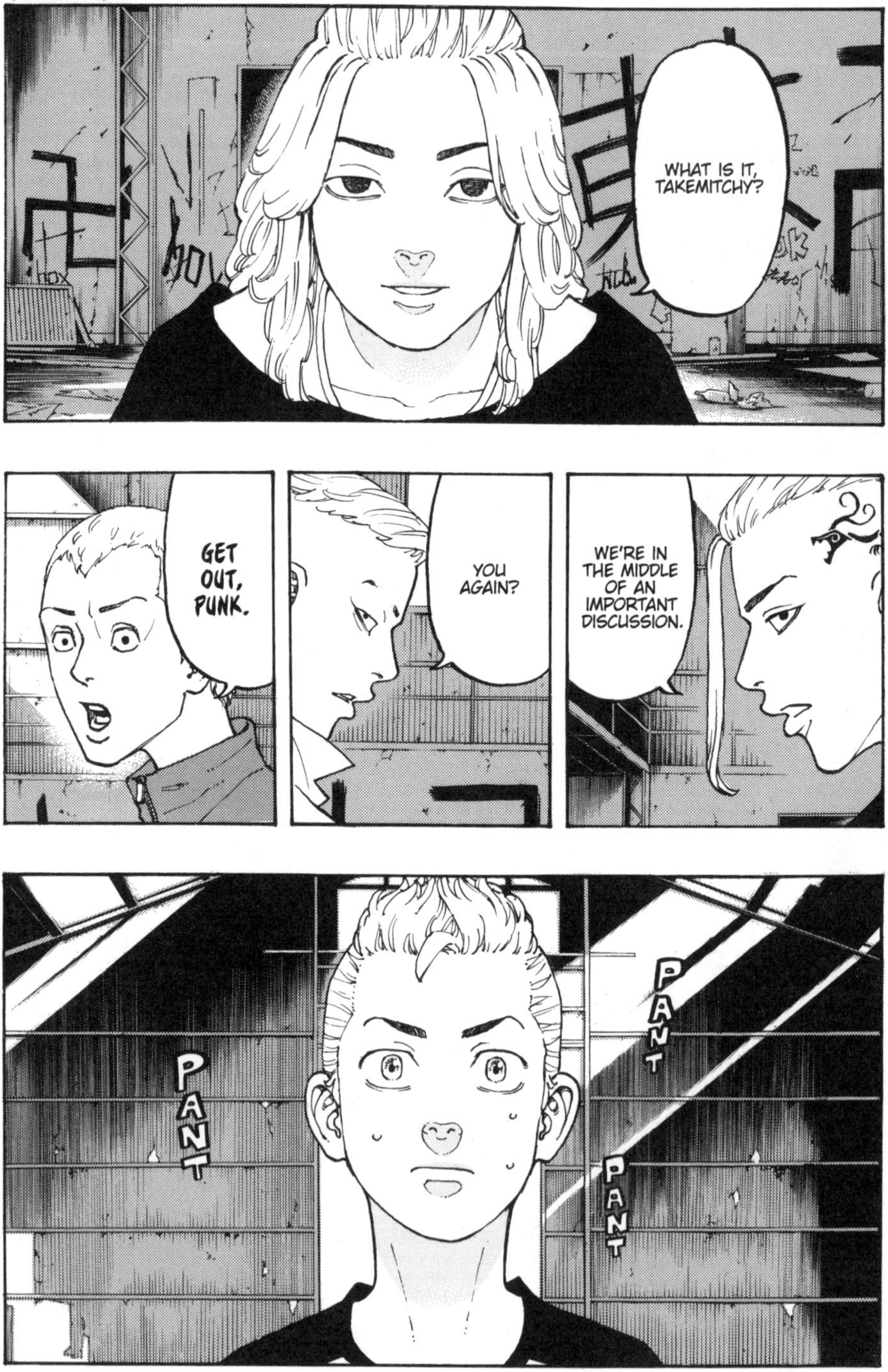
WHAT IS IT, TAKEMITCHY?
WE'RE IN THE MIDDLE OF AN IMPORTANT DISCUSSION.
YOU AGAIN?
GET OUT, PUNK.
PANT
PANT
PANT

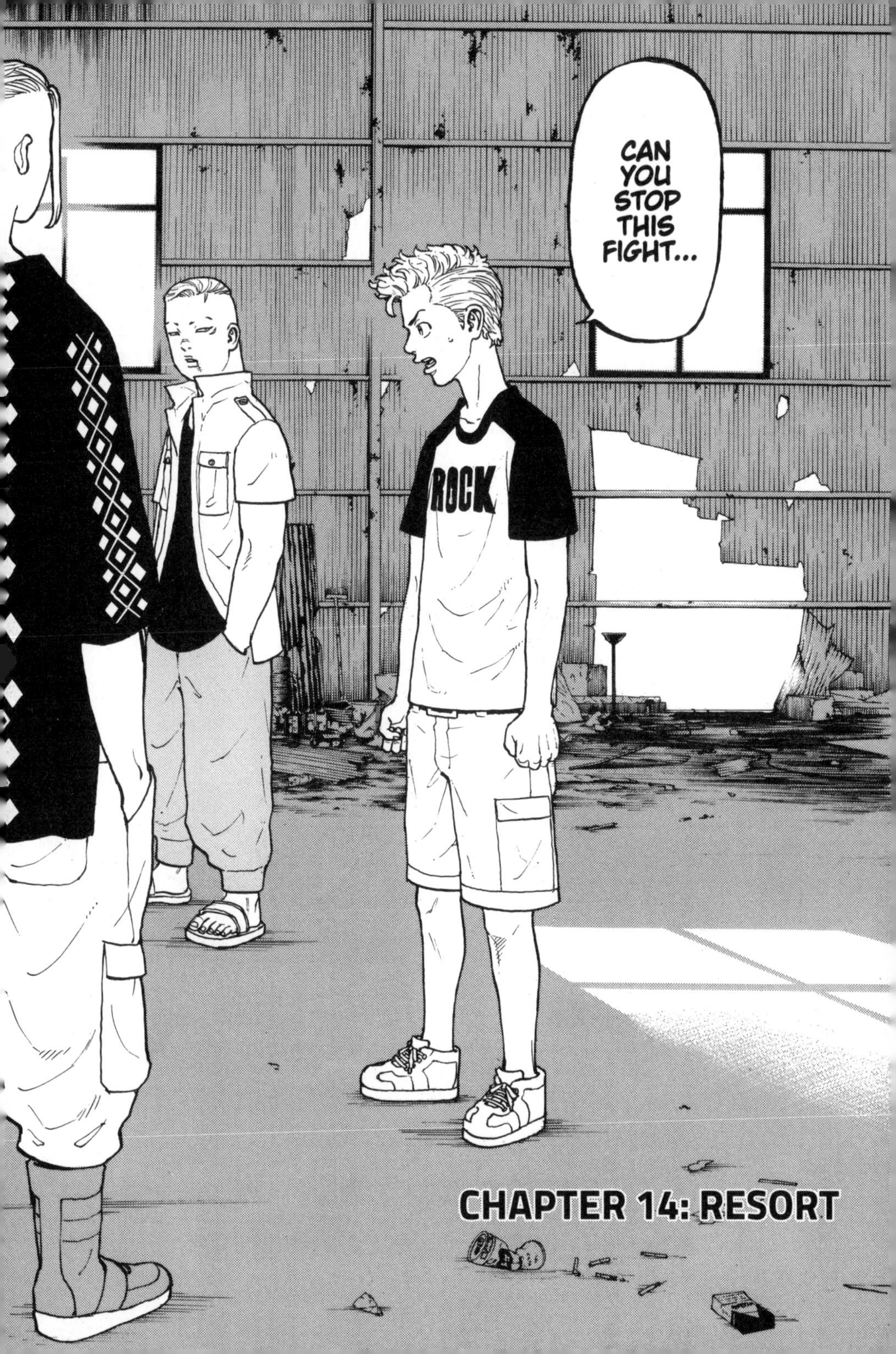
CAN YOU STOP THIS FIGHT...
ROCK
CHAPTER 14: RESORT

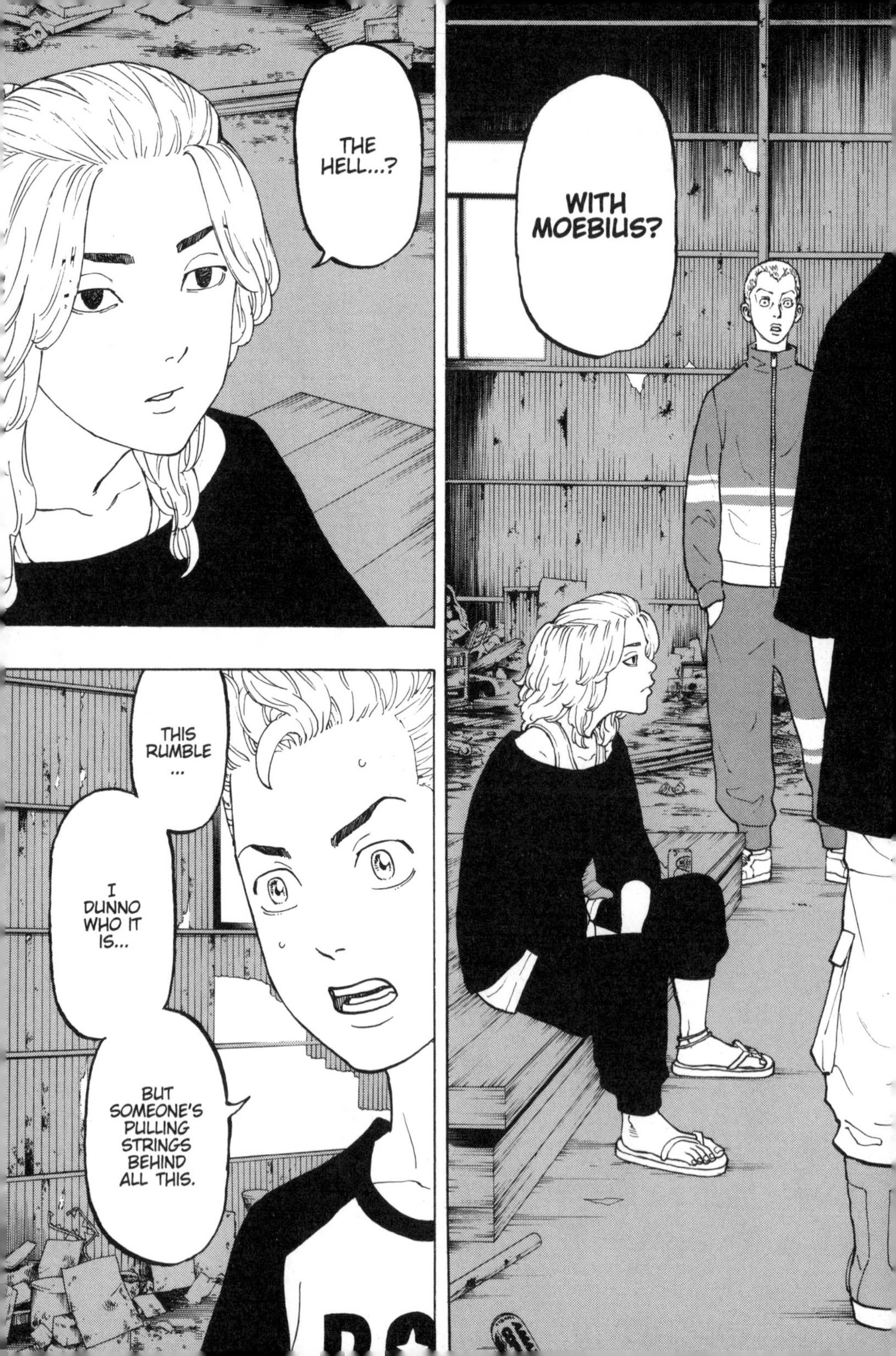
WITH MOEBIUS?
THE HELL...?
THIS RUMBLE ...
I DUNNO WHO IT IS...
BUT SOMEONE'S PULLING STRINGS BEHIND ALL THIS.

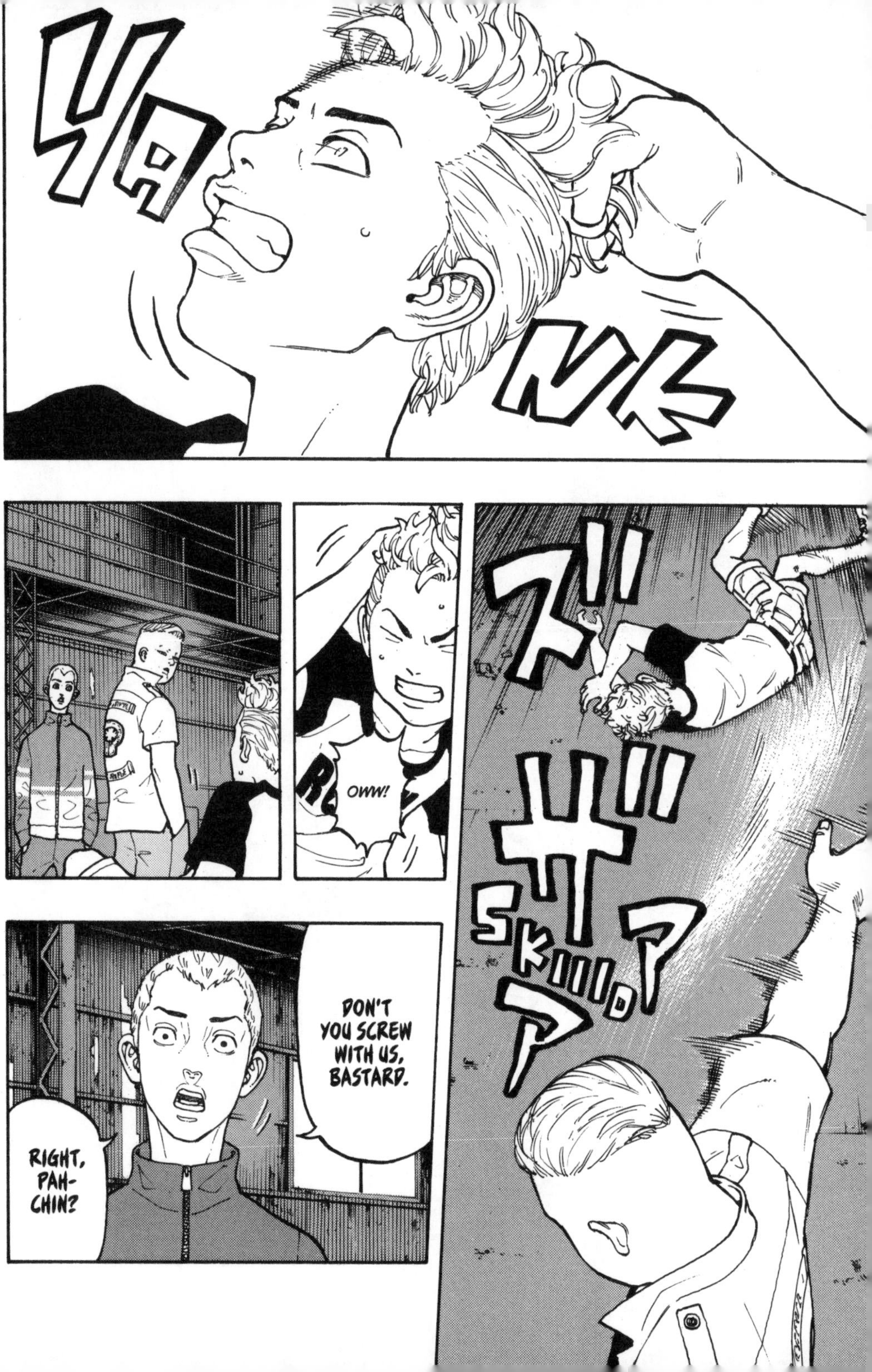
NK
SKIIID
OWW!
DON'T YOU SCREW WITH US, BASTARD.
RIGHT, PAH-CHIN?

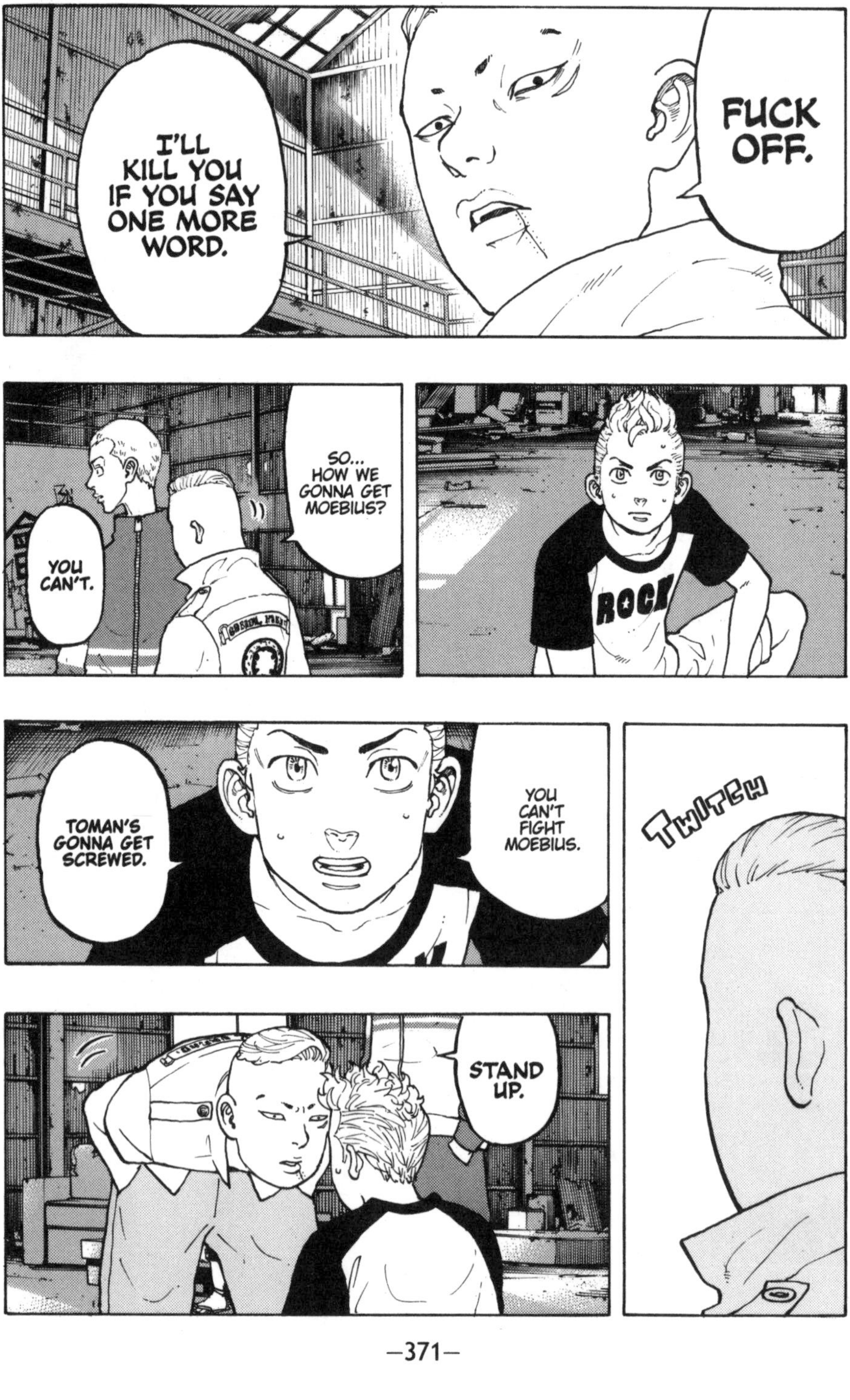
FUCK OFF.
I'LL KILL YOU IF YOU SAY ONE MORE WORD.
SO... HOW WE GONNA GET MOEBIUS?
YOU CAN'T.
TWITCH
YOU CAN'T FIGHT MOEBIUS.
TOMAN'S GONNA GET SCREWED.
STAND UP.

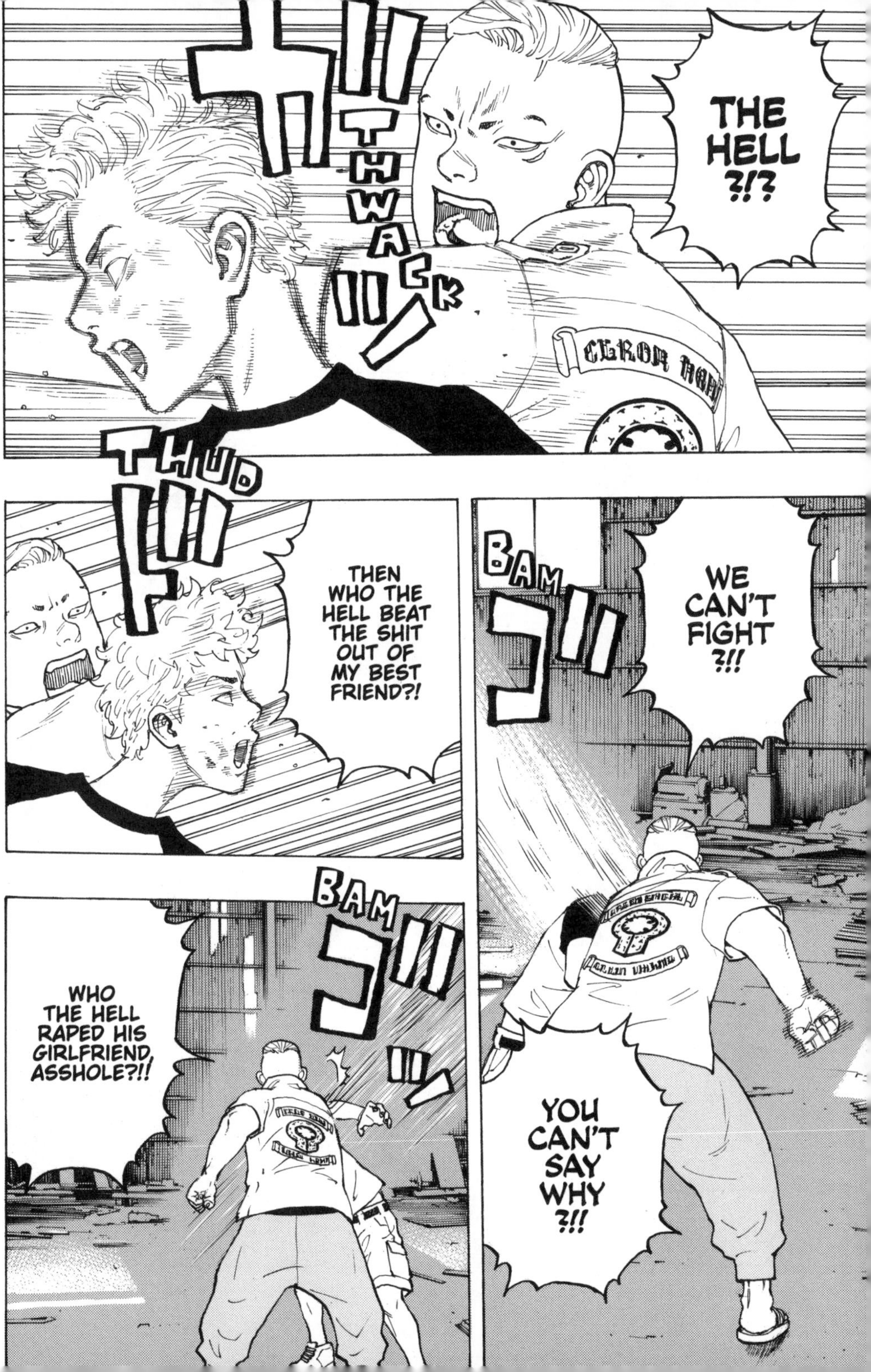
THWACK
THE HELL ?!?
BAM
WE CAN'T FIGHT ?!!
YOU CAN'T SAY WHY ?!!
THUD
THEN WHO THE HELL BEAT THE SHIT OUT OF MY BEST FRIEND?!
BAM
WHO THE HELL RAPED HIS GIRLFRIEND, ASSHOLE?!!

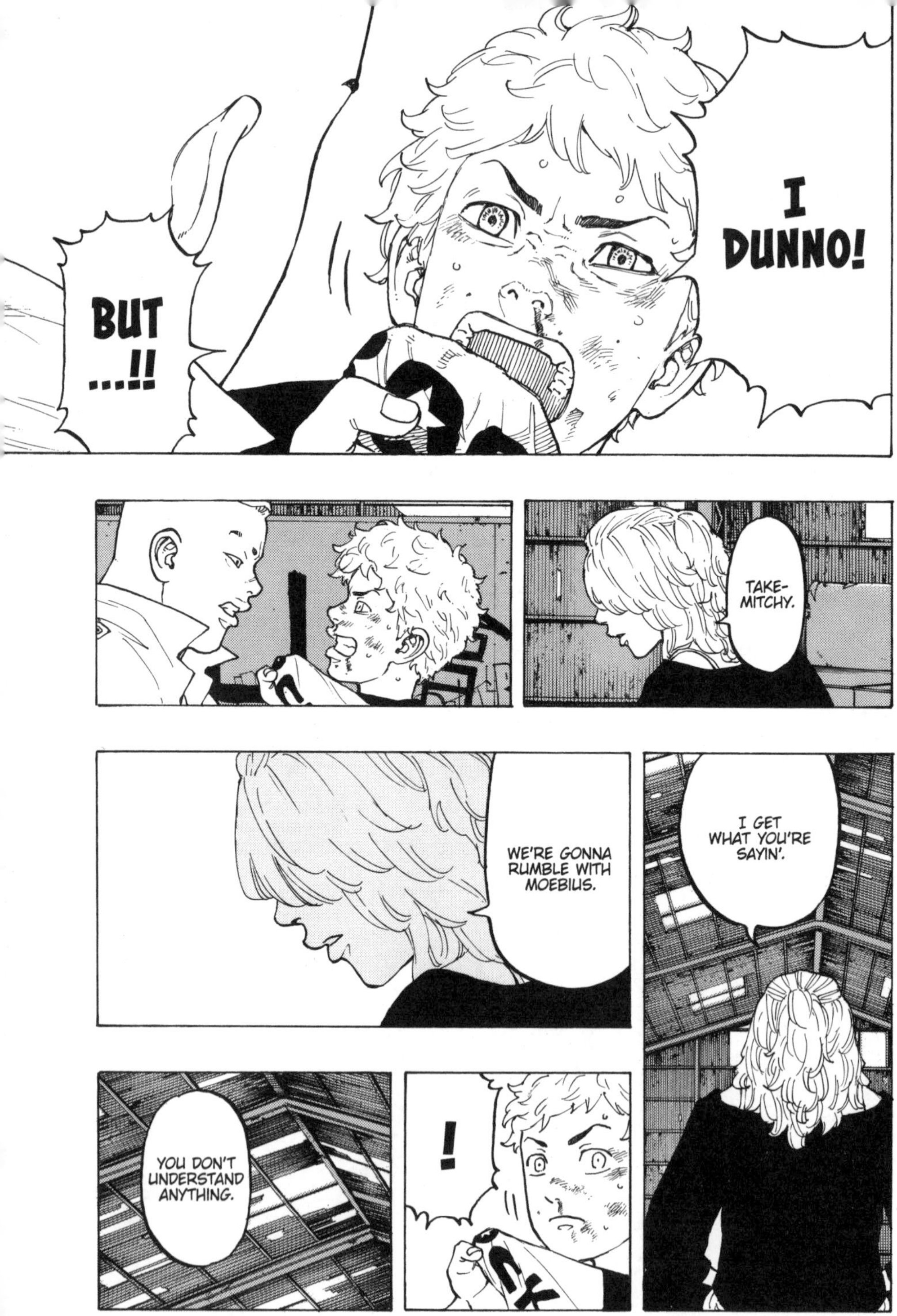
I DUNNO!
BUT ...!!
TAKE-MITCHY.
I GET WHAT YOU'RE SAYIN'.
WE'RE GONNA RUMBLE WITH MOEBIUS.
!
YOU DON'T UNDERSTAND ANYTHING.

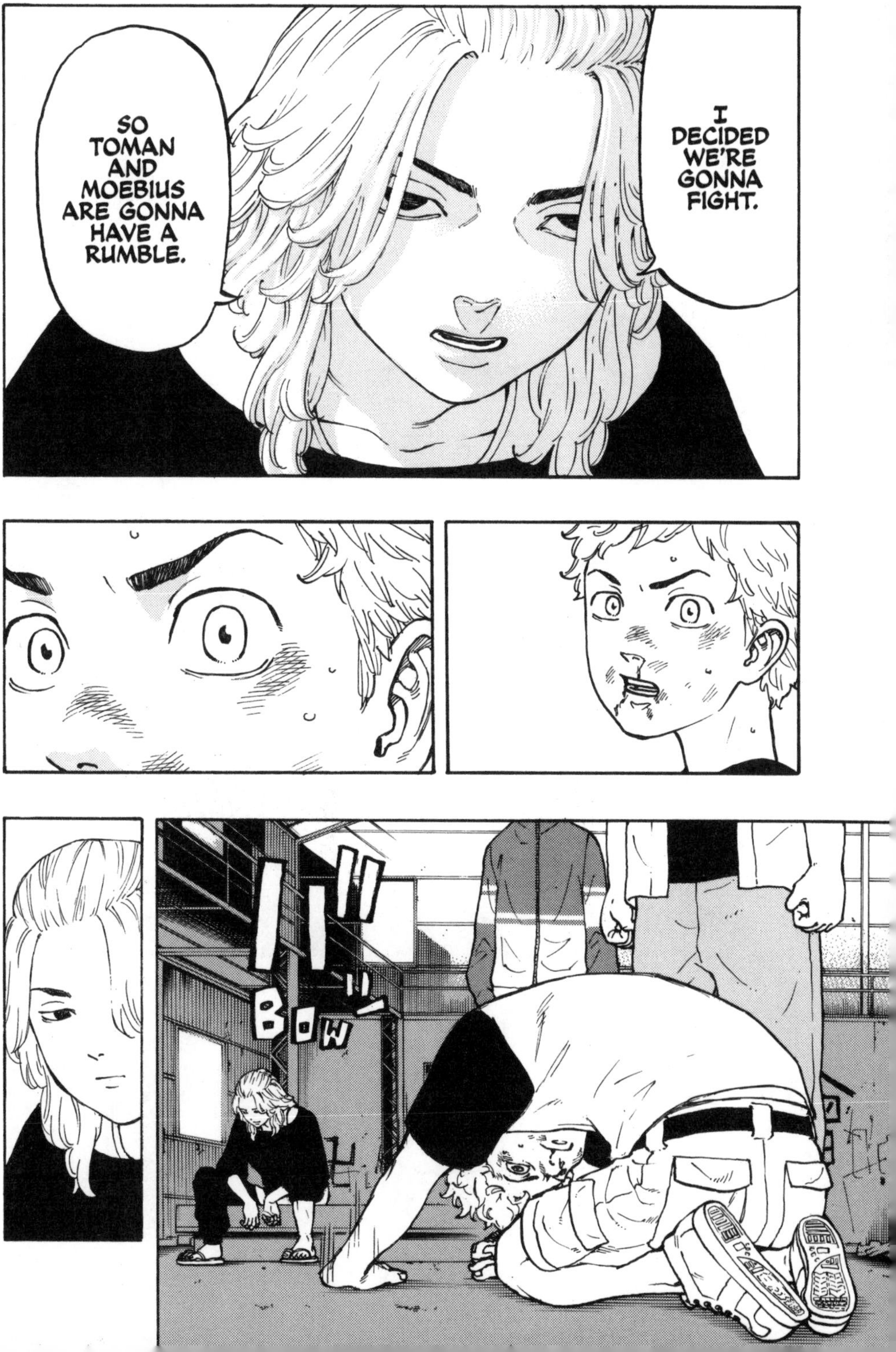
I DECIDED WE'RE GONNA FIGHT.
SO TOMAN AND MOEBIUS ARE GONNA HAVE A RUMBLE.
BOW

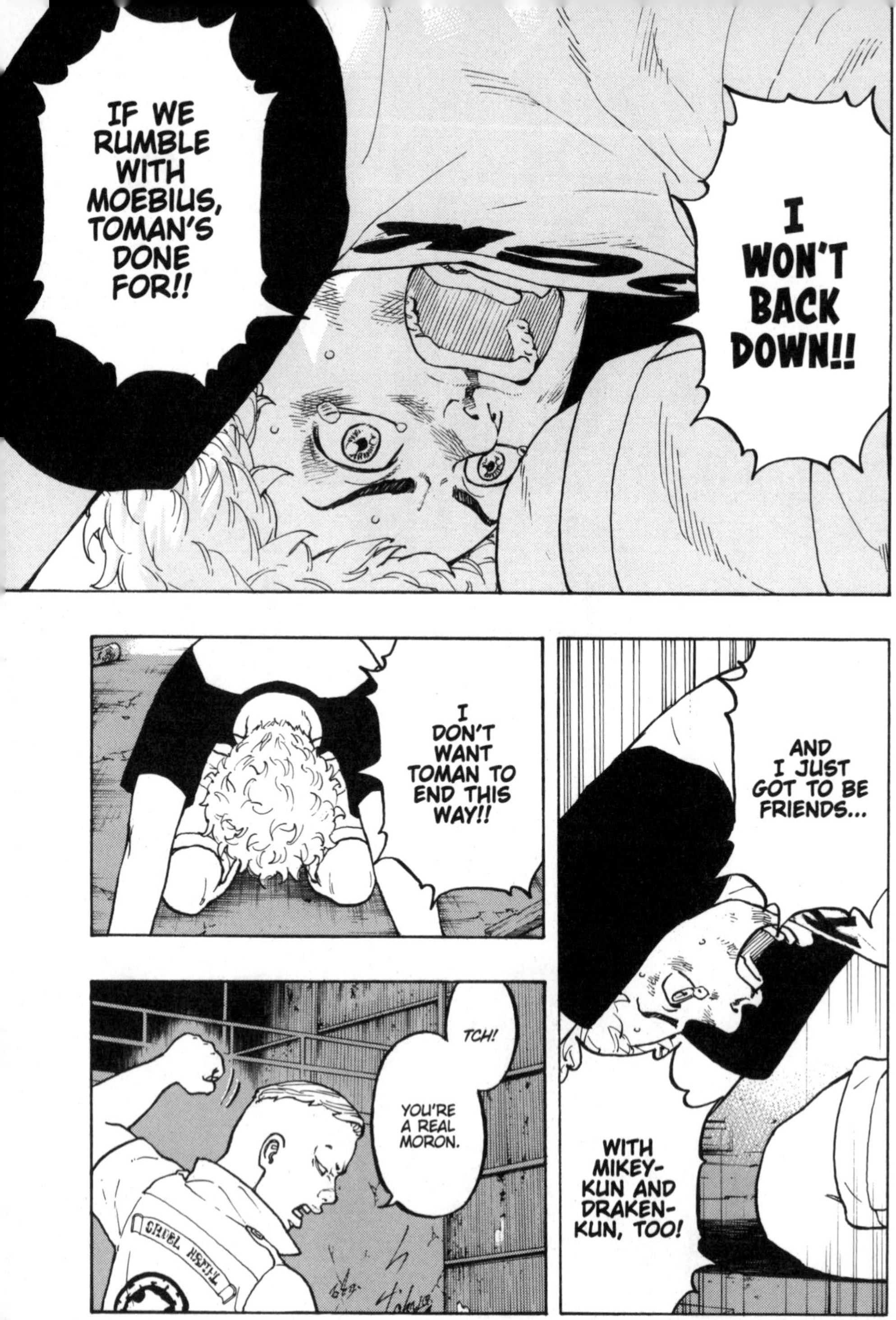
I WON'T BACK DOWN!!
IF WE RUMBLE WITH MOEBIUS, TOMAN'S DONE FOR!!
AND I JUST GOT TO BE FRIENDS...
WITH MIKEY-KUN AND DRAKEN-KUN, TOO!
I DON'T WANT TOMAN TO END THIS WAY!!
TCH!
YOU'RE A REAL MORON.

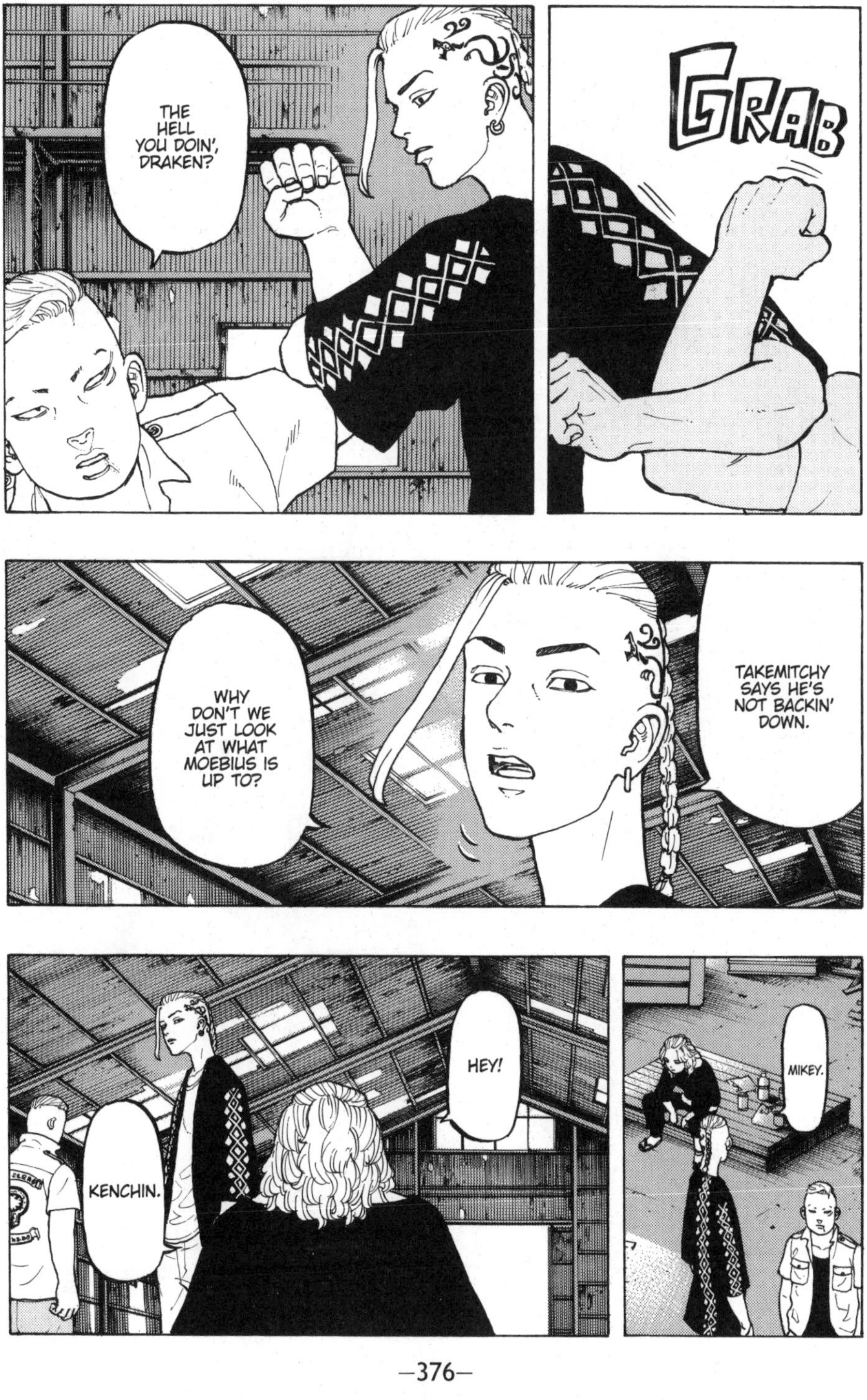
GRAB
THE HELL YOU DOIN', DRAKEN?
TAKEMITCHY SAYS HE'S NOT BACKIN' DOWN.
WHY DON'T WE JUST LOOK AT WHAT MOEBIUS IS UP TO?
MIKEY.
HEY!
KENCHIN.

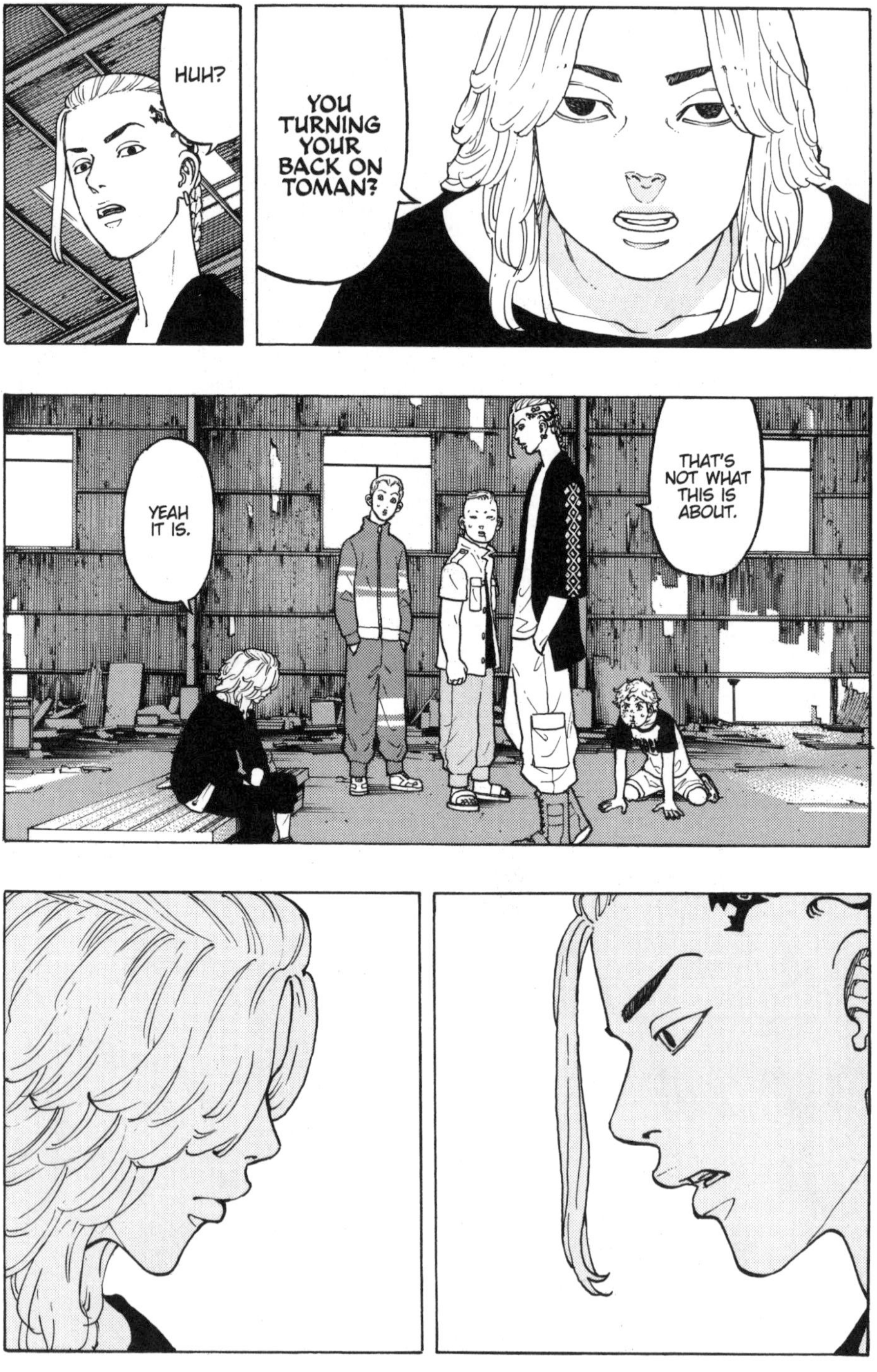
YOU TURNING YOUR BACK ON TOMAN?
HUH?
THAT'S NOT WHAT THIS IS ABOUT.
YEAH IT IS.

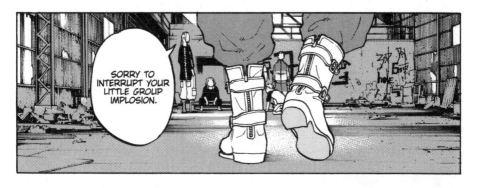

SORRY TO INTERRUPT YOUR LITTLE GROUP IMPLOSION.
BUT I KEEP HEARIN' *MOEBIUS, MOEBIUS.*
FWIP
SWIP
COULD YOU KEEP OUR NAME OUT OF YOUR DIRTY MOUTHS...
YOU JUNIOR HIGH BABIES?
?
IT'S YOU!

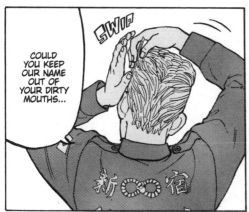

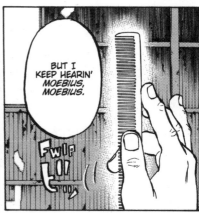

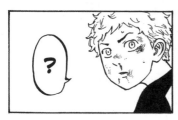

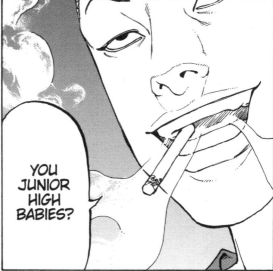

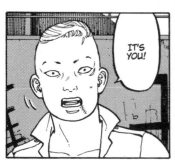

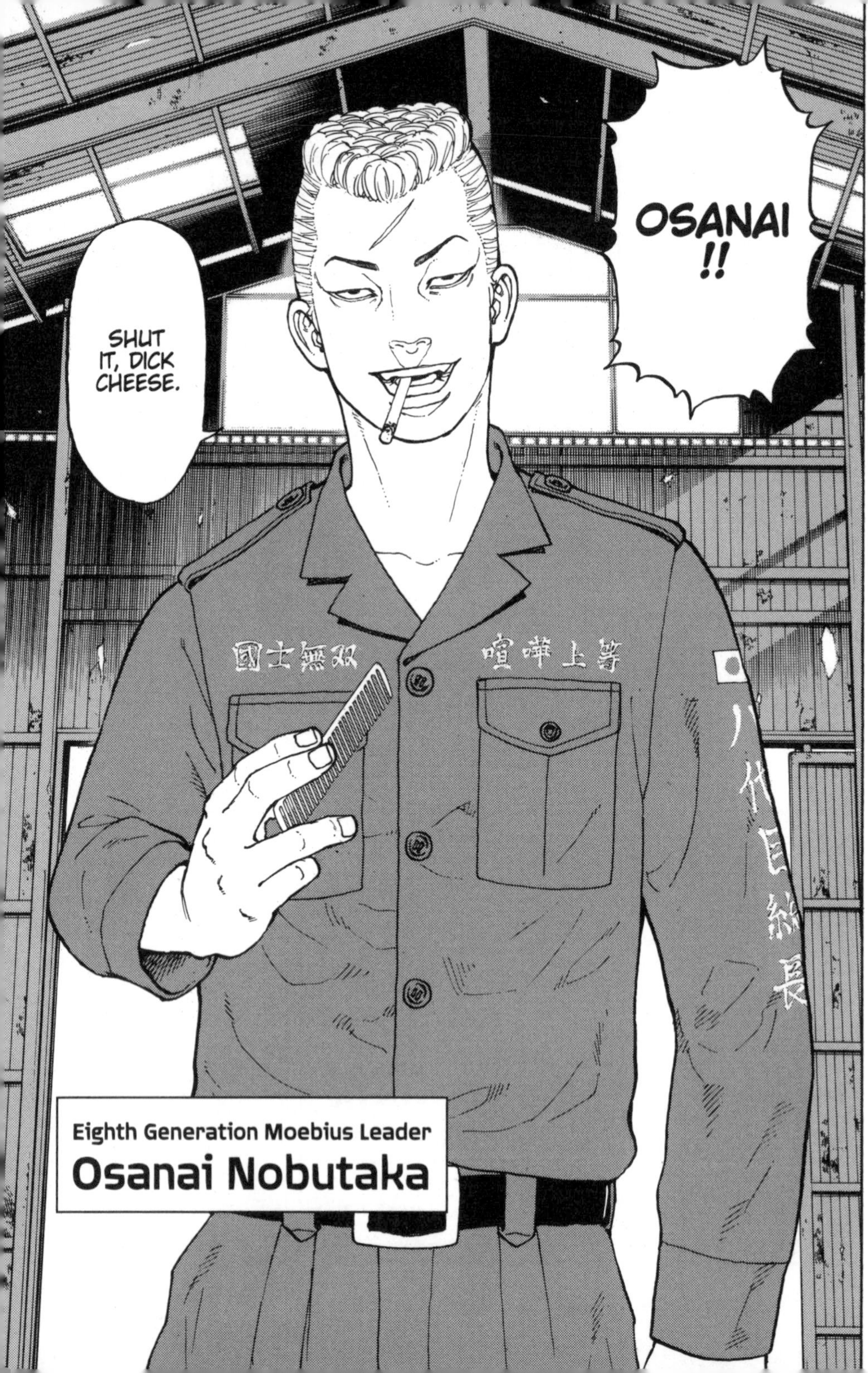
OSANAI !!
SHUT IT, DICK CHEESE.
國士無双
喧嘩上等
八代目総長
Eighth Generation Moebius Leader
Osanai Nobutaka

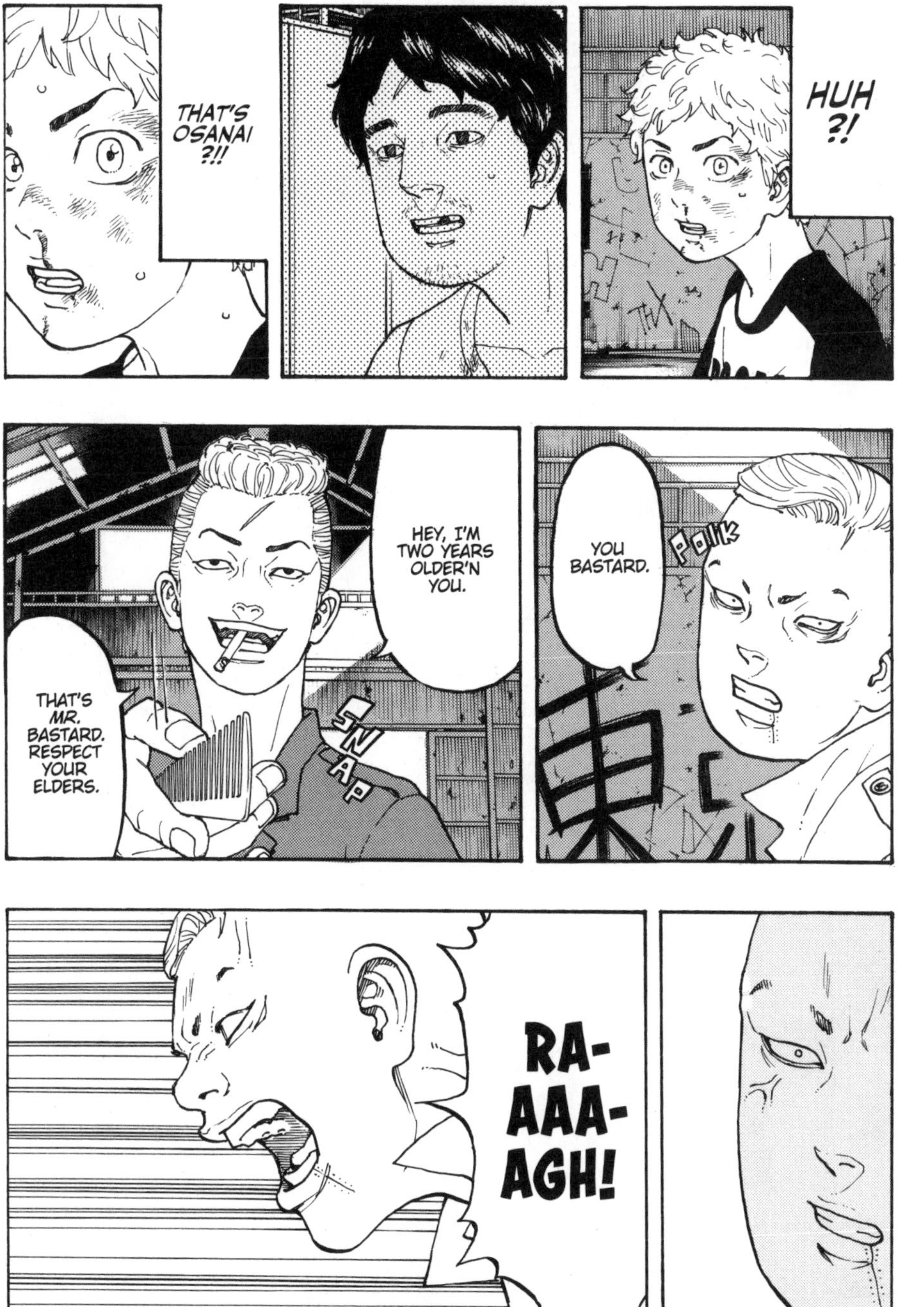
HUH ?!
THAT'S OSANAI ?!!
POIIK
YOU BASTARD.
HEY, I'M TWO YEARS OLDER'N YOU.
SNAP
THAT'S MR. BASTARD. RESPECT YOUR ELDERS.
RA-AAAA-AGH!

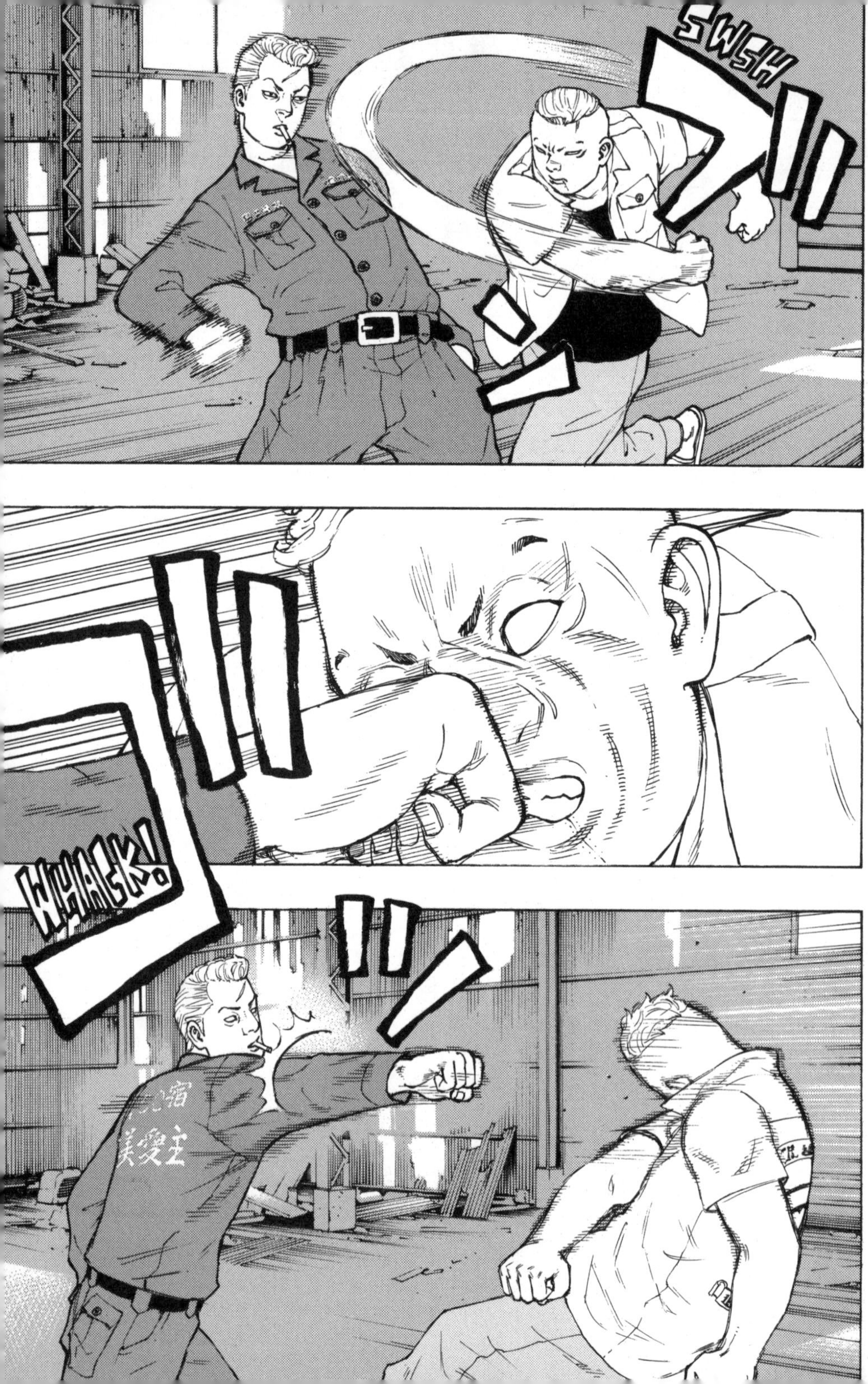

SWSH
WHACK!

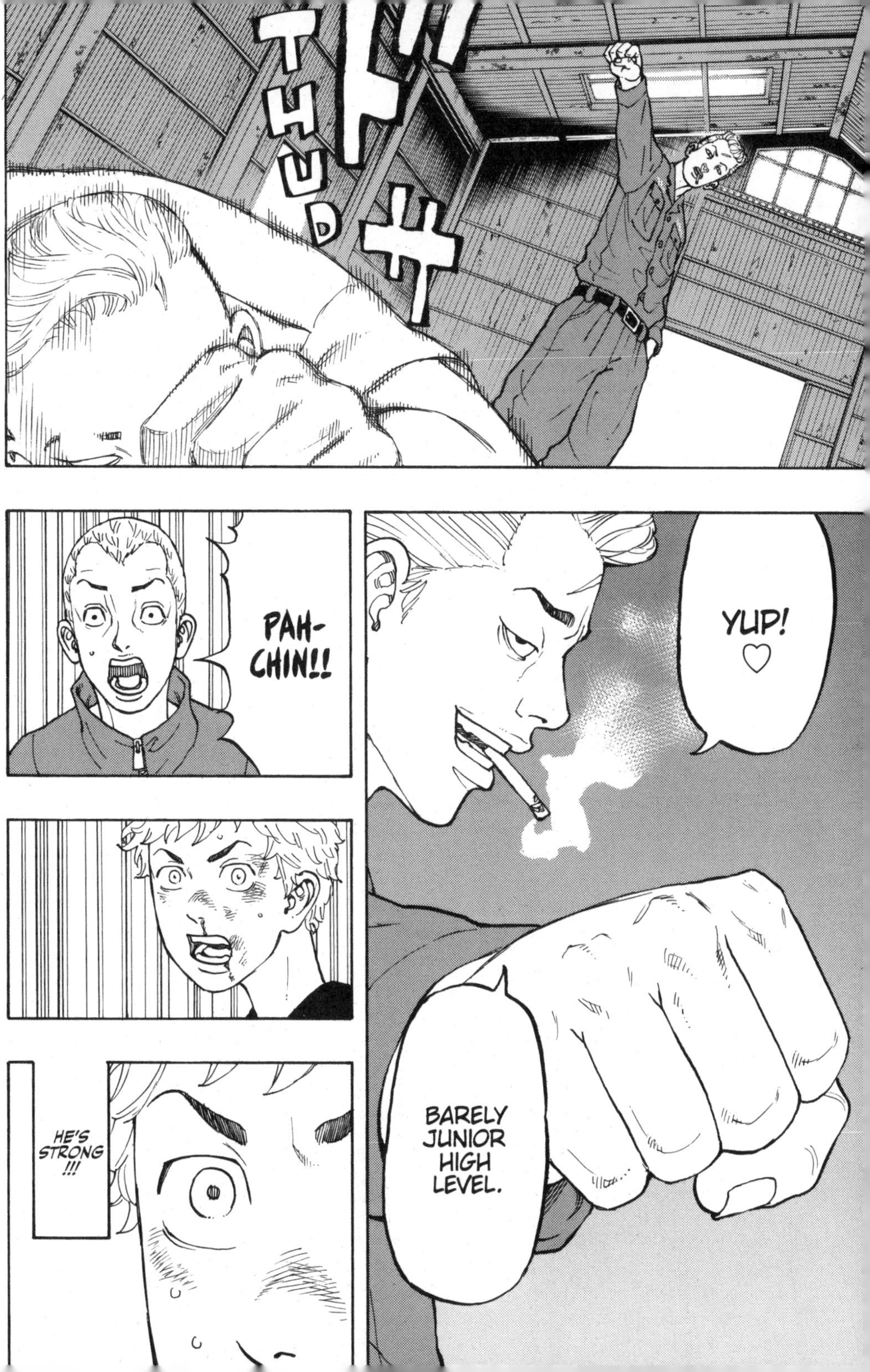
THUD
YUP! ♡
BARELY JUNIOR HIGH LEVEL.
PAH-CHIN!!
HE'S STRONG!!!

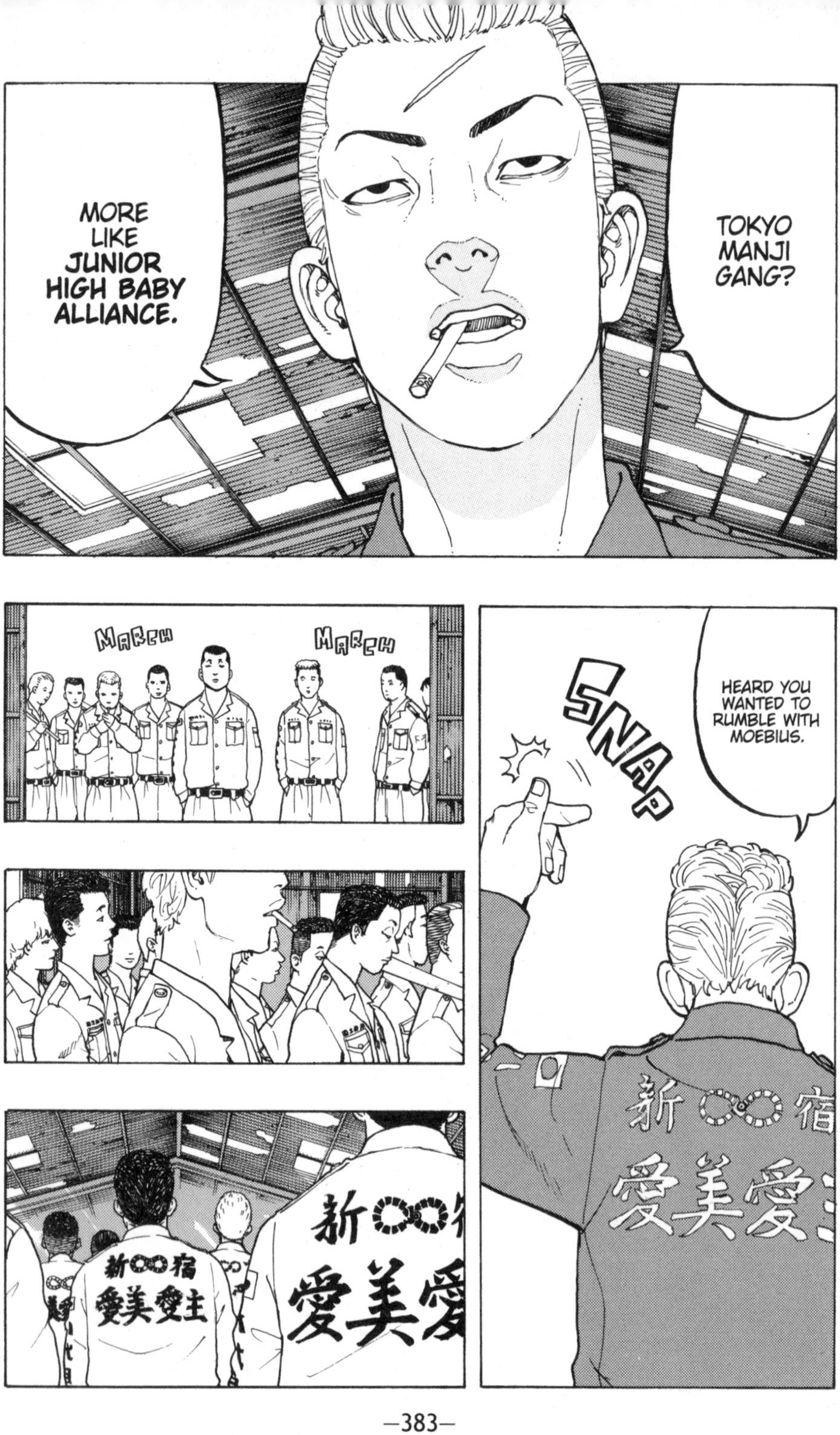
TOKYO MANJI GANG?
MORE LIKE JUNIOR HIGH BABY ALLIANCE.
HEARD YOU WANTED TO RUMBLE WITH MOEBIUS.
SNAP
MARCH
MARCH
新∞宿
愛美愛主

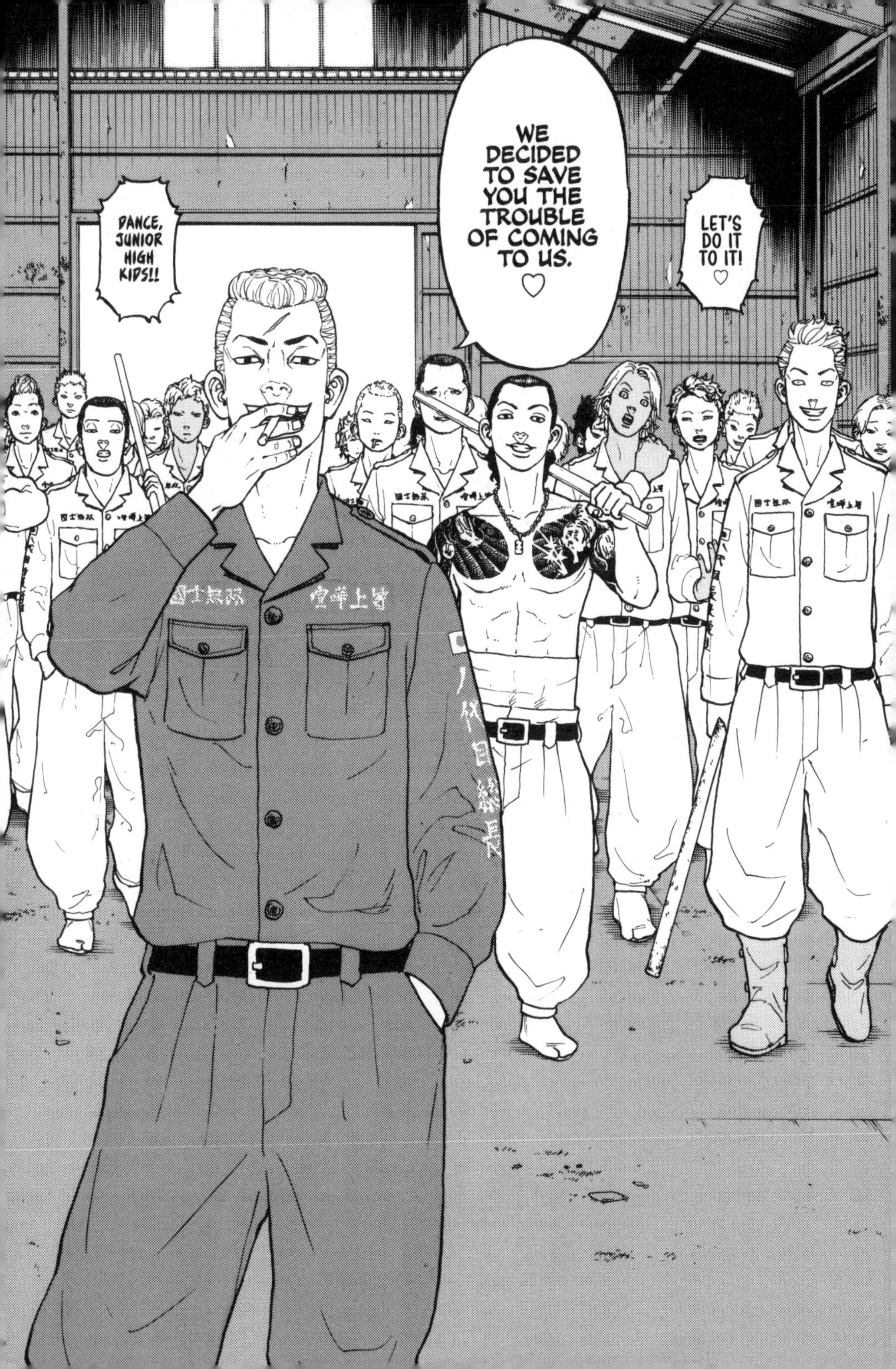
LET'S DO IT TO IT! ♡
WE DECIDED TO SAVE YOU THE TROUBLE OF COMING TO US. ♡
DANCE, JUNIOR HIGH KIDS!!

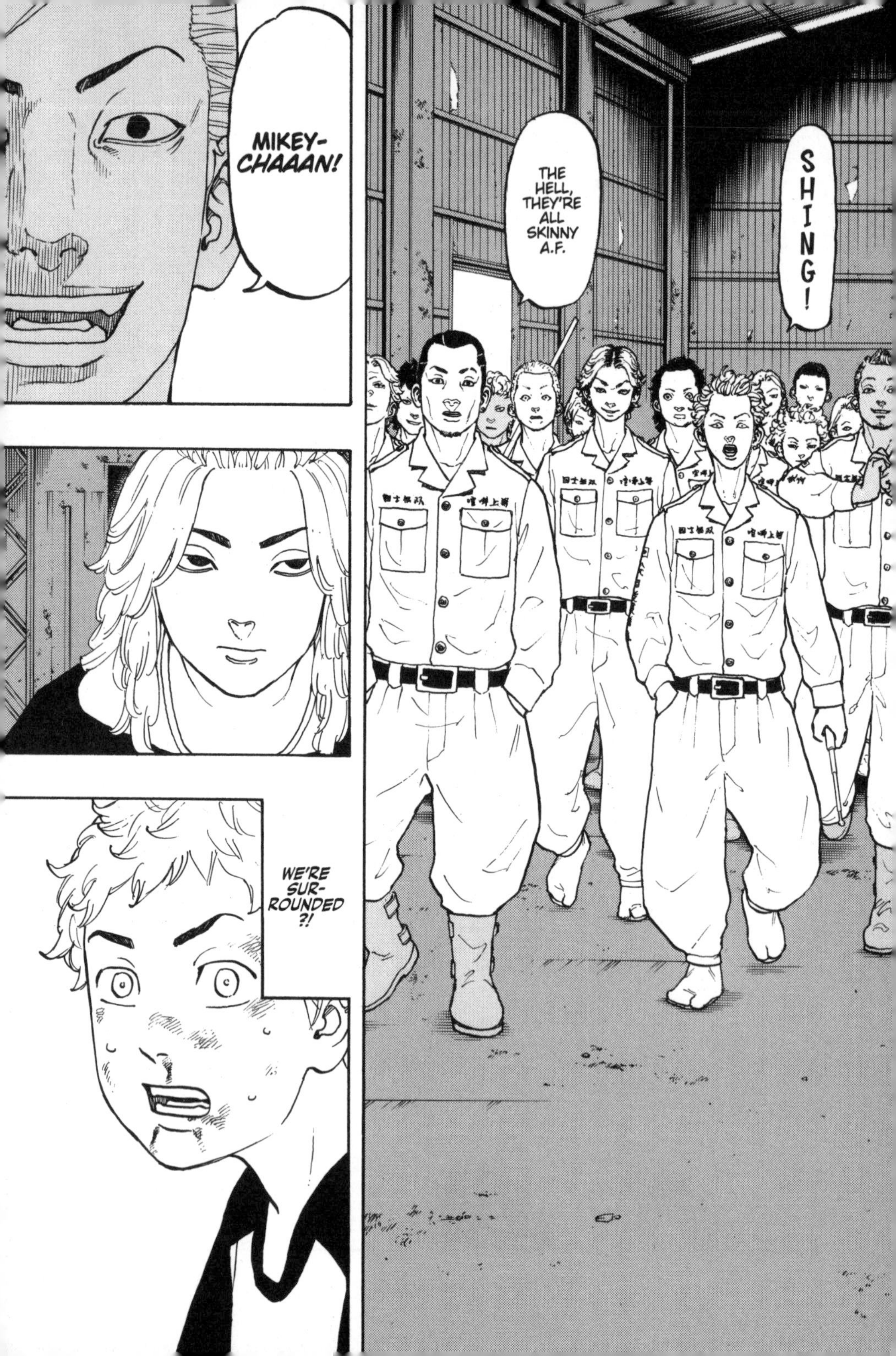
SHING!
THE HELL, THEY'RE ALL SKINNY A.F.
MIKEY-CHAAAN!
WE'RE SUR-ROUNDED?!

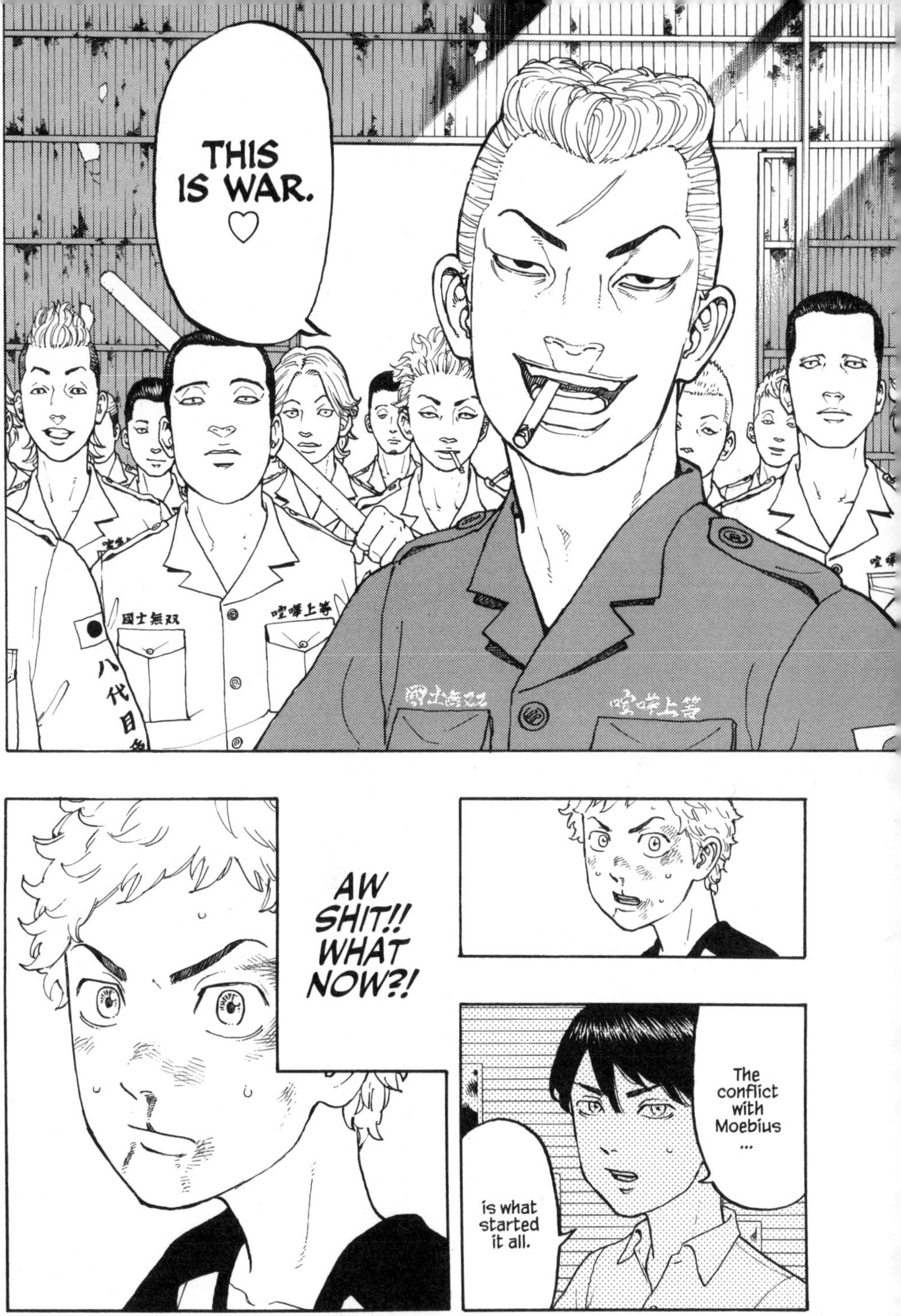
THIS IS WAR. ♡
国士無双
喧嘩上等
The conflict with Moebius ...
is what started it all.
AW SHIT!! WHAT NOW?!

TO BE CONTINUED

TOKYO Revengers

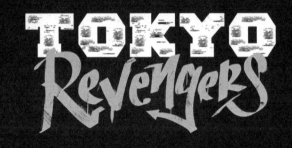

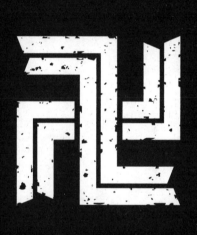

TOKKO-FUKU

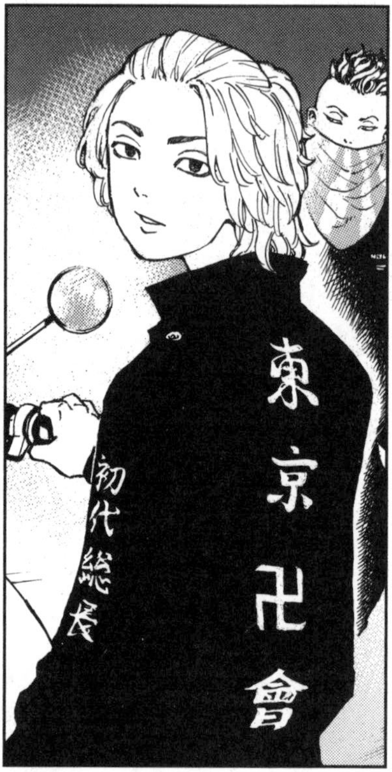
東京卍會
初代総長

Tokko-fuku means "special attack uniform." This is often depicted as the long *gakuran* jacket worn by gang members, along with loose, billowy pants and long boots. The outfit was inspired by military uniforms, as well as the clothes of the blue-collar working class.

Other members of Toman wear overalls with their specific gang embroidery. Each uniform is custom made, with embroidered accents reflecting its owner. The gang's name is typically on the back, and the left arm indicates their rank and platoon. It's common to use complicated kanji characters that look impressive for the embroidery, such as old-fashioned kanji for the numbers.

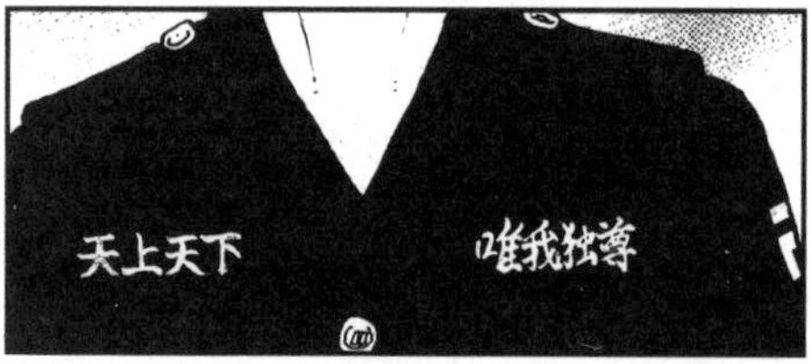
天上天下
唯我独尊

The chest embroidery (天上天下唯我独尊) is based on a Buddhist saying known in Japan. Siddhartha Gautama is said to have taken seven steps away from his mother after birth and said, "Throughout heaven and earth, I alone am the honored one."

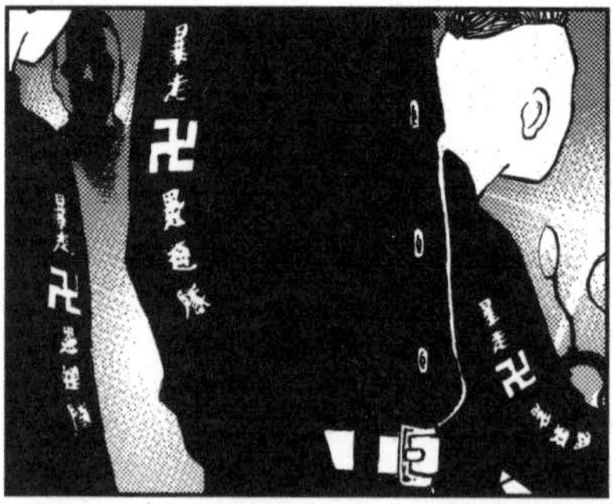

The embroidery on the right arm (暴走卍愚連隊) contains the root word *bousou* (暴走), "running wild," which also appears in the common name for biker gangs in Japan–*bousouzoku.*

Moebius' jackets have different characters, including (団士無双) "distinguished person," and (喧嘩上等) which can be read as either "good at fighting" or "bring it on," meaning they're wearing a challenge right on their breast.

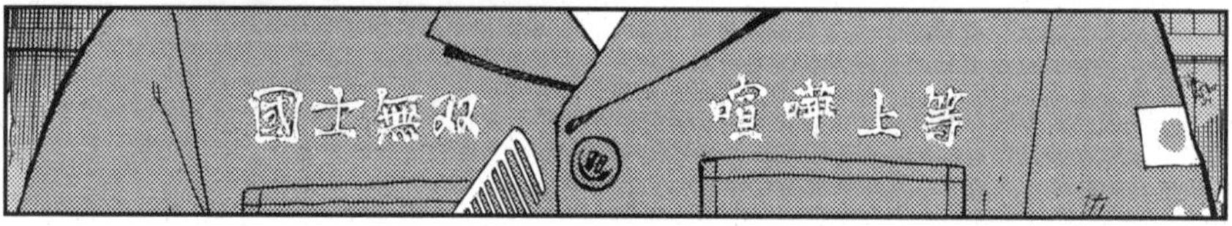
國士無双
喧嘩上等

GANG NAMES

Of the gang names that have appeared in *Tokyo Revengers* thus far, only Toman is a Japanese name. The gangs Vatican and Moebius have cool English names that have been assigned even cooler kanji. Moebius, typically written メビウス in Japanese, instead uses the characters 愛 (love), 美 (beauty), and 主 (master). The meanings aren't meant to be literal, but are noteworthy because these kanji can be read as "Moebius." This is also true for Vatican, which is written as 罰 (punishment) and 漢 (China/Chinese), and pronounced *bachikan*.

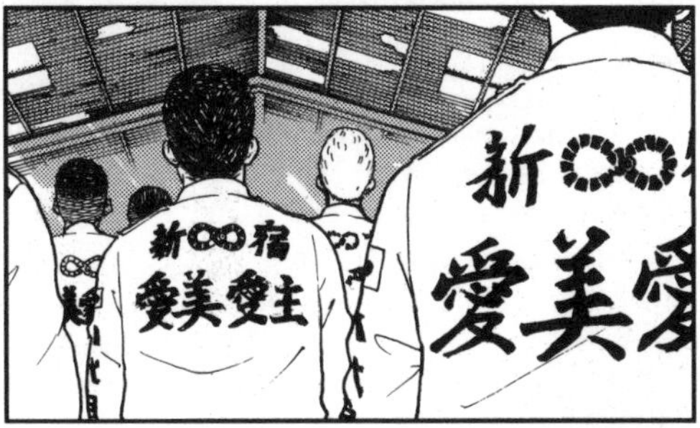
新∞宿
愛美愛主

TOKYO Revengers

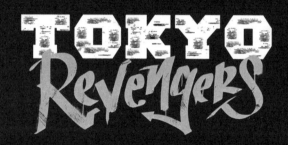

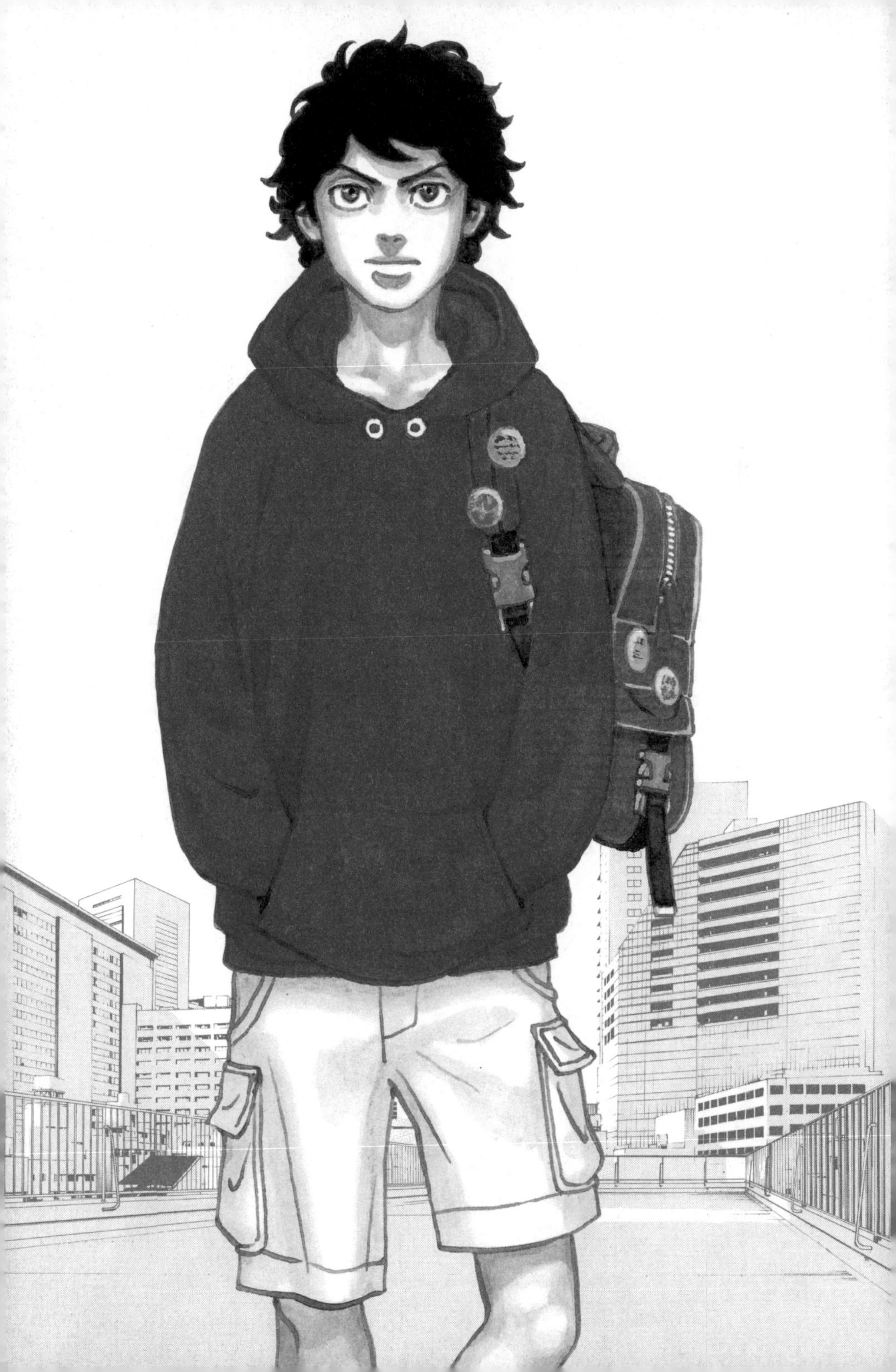

TOKYO Revengers

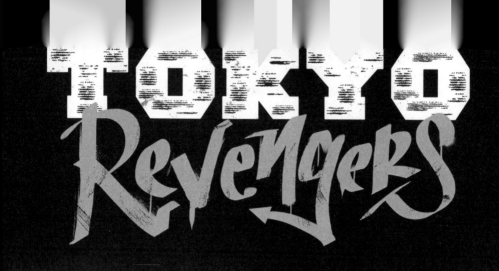

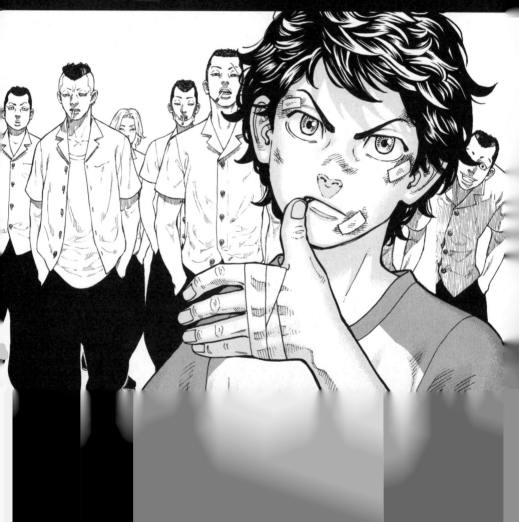

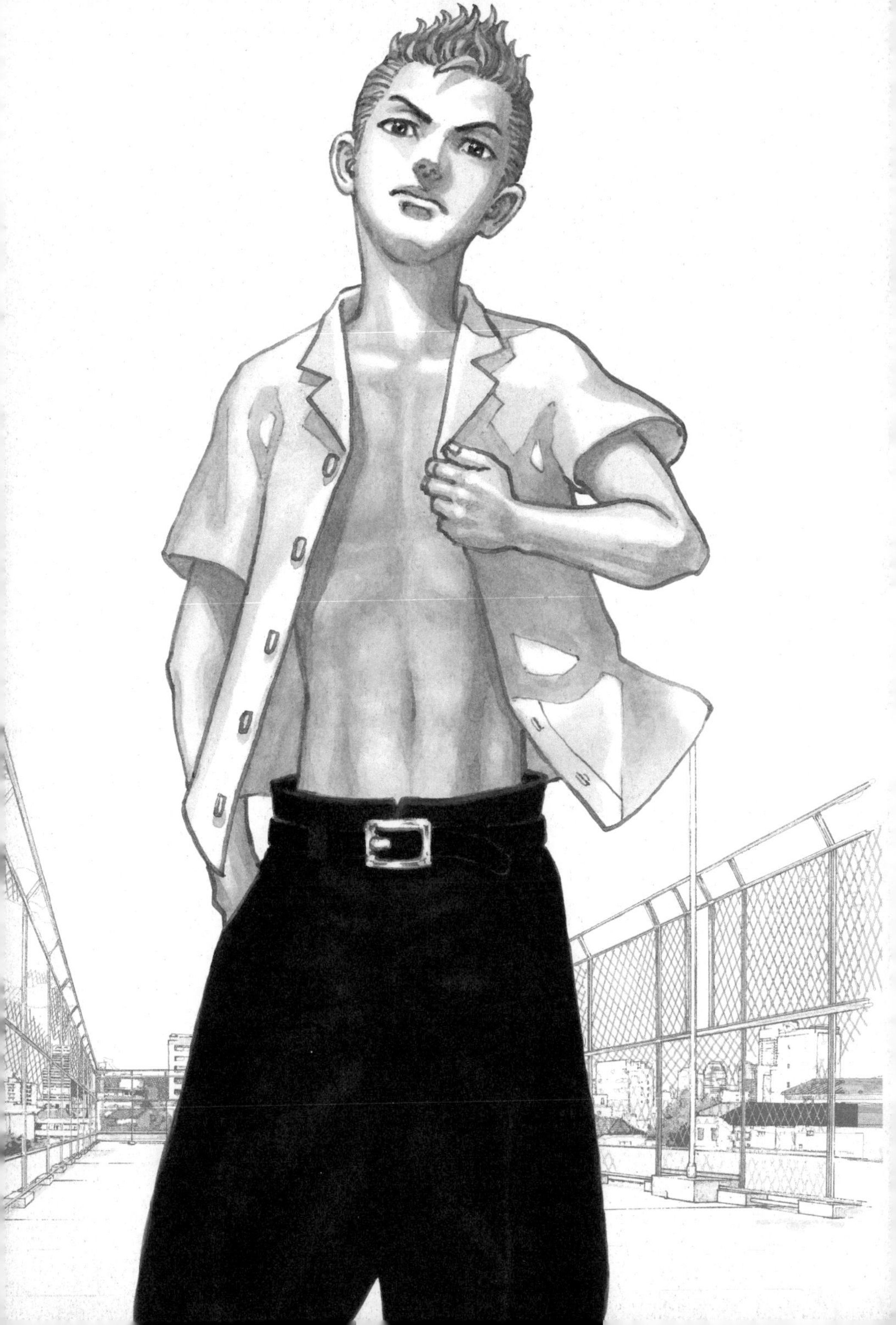

TOKYO Revengers

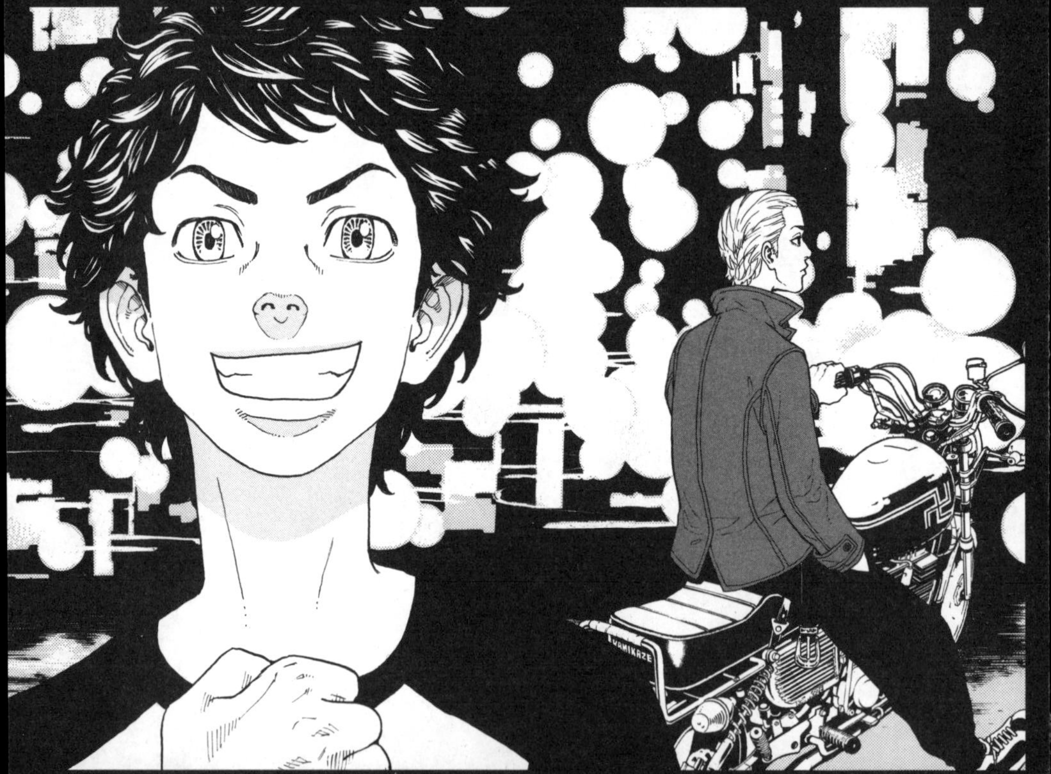

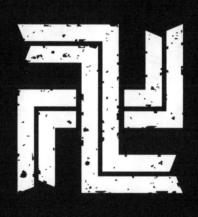

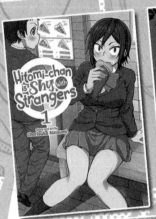
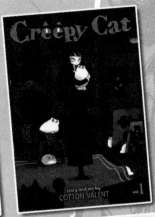
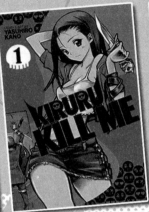
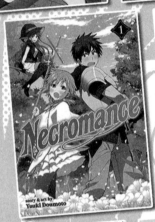
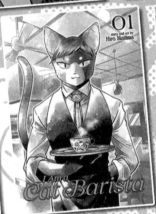
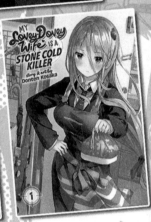
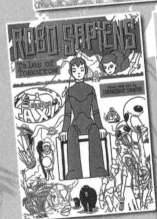
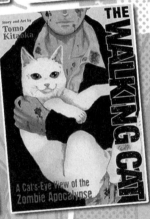
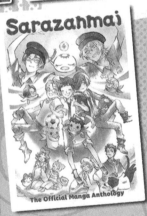

SEVEN SEAS ENTERTAINMENT PRESENTS

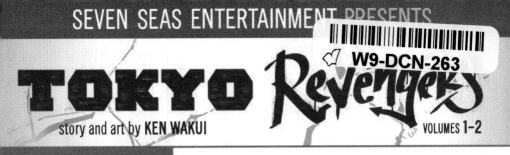

TOKYO Revengers

story and art by **KEN WAKUI**

VOLUMES 1–2

TRANSLATION
Project Ceres

LETTERING
Robert Harkins

COVER AND LOGO DESIGN
H. Qi

COPY EDITOR
Dawn Davis

EDITOR
Abby Lehrke

PRODUCTION DESIGNER
Christina McKenzie

PRODUCTION MANAGER
Lissa Pattillo

PREPRESS TECHNICIAN
Melanie Ujimori

PRINT MANAGER
Rhiannon Rasmussen-Silverstein

EDITOR-IN-CHIEF
Julie Davis

ASSOCIATE PUBLISHER
Adam Arnold

PUBLISHER
Jason DeAngelis

Tokyo Revengers Omnibus Vol. 1

First published in Japan in 2017 by Kodansha Ltd., Tokyo.
Publication rights for this English edition arranged through Kodansha Ltd., Tokyo.

Seven Seas press and purchase enquiries can be sent to Marketing Manager Lianne Sentar at press@gomanga.com. Information regarding the distribution and purchase of digital editions is available from Digital Manager CK Russell at digital@gomanga.com.

Standard Edition: 978-1-63858-571-8
Variant Edition: 978-1-68579-339-5
Printed in Canada
First Printing: May 2022
10 9 8 7 6 5 4 3 2 1

READING DIRECTIONS

This book reads from ***right to left***, Japanese style. If this is your first time reading manga, you start reading from the top right panel on each page and take it from there. If you get lost, just follow the numbered diagram here. It may seem backwards at first, but you'll get the hang of it! Have fun!!

1
2
3
4
5
6
7
8
9

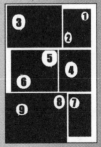

Follow us online: www.SevenSeasEntertainment.com